M000014050

Oxford
Mini
School
SPANISH
DICTIONARY

Editorial Manager: Valerie Grundy
New Edition: Nicholas Rollin
with the assistance of Carmen Fernández-Marsden

OXFORD
UNIVERSITY PRESS

OXFORD
UNIVERSITY PRESS

Great Clarendon Street, Oxford OX2 6DP

Oxford University Press is a department of the University of Oxford.
It furthers the University's objective of excellence in research,
scholarship, and education by publishing worldwide in

Oxford   New York

Auckland Cape Town Dar es Salaam Hong Kong Karachi
Kuala Lumpur Madrid Melbourne Mexico City Nairobi
New Delhi Shanghai Taipei Toronto

With offices in

Argentina Austria Brazil Chile Czech Republic France Greece
Guatemala Hungary Italy Japan Poland Portugal Singapore
South Korea Switzerland Thailand Turkey Ukraine Vietnam

Oxford is a registered trade mark of Oxford University Press
in the UK and in certain other countries

© Oxford University Press 2012

Database right Oxford University Press (maker)

First published 1998
Revised first edition 2002
Second edition 2004
Third edition 2007
This edition 2012

British Library Cataloguing in Publication Data
Data available

ISBN: 978 019 275709 8

10 9 8 7 6

Printed in India by Manipal Technologies Limited

Paper used in the production of this book is a natural, recyclable product
made from wood grown in sustainable forests. The manufacturing process
conforms to the environmental regulations of the country of origin.

INTRODUCTION

This dictionary has been specially written for students who are in their first years of learning Spanish all the way through to preparing for exams. We have paid particular attention to making the dictionary user-friendly. With the help of bold headwords, alphabet tabs, easy-to-follow signposts, and examples, the right translation can quickly be found. Spanish verbs on both sides of the dictionary are numbered to direct the student to the appropriate table in the centre pages.

Throughout the writing of this dictionary we have worked in close consultation with students, teachers, inspectors, and examining boards. We gratefully acknowledge the examining boards AQA (formerly NEAB and SEG), OCR, and EDEXCEL, who have read and commented on the dictionary text.

Since the first edition of this dictionary there have been many changes in Spanish life. Not least has been the introduction of the euro. This new edition takes full account of these changes and many new words and examples have been included in order to provide the best possible learner's dictionary of Spanish at this level.

HOW A BILINGUAL DICTIONARY WORKS

A bilingual dictionary contains two languages. When you look up a word in one of the languages, it gives the translation for that word in the other language. This dictionary is divided into two halves separated by a section of dark-edged pages. In the first half you look up Spanish words, which are in alphabetical order, to find out what they mean in English and in the second half you look up English words, also in alphabetical order, to find out how to say them in Spanish. The dark-edged pages are verb tables and you can see how to use them further on in this section.

At each entry you will find not only translations but also other information that will help you get the right translation and use the word correctly. Here is a guide to the different things you will find printed in an entry:

headword   a word you look up in the dictionary

translation   translations are the only things that are in 'ordinary' type in the dictionary. They are *always* typed like this, and something which is typed in a different way can *never* be a translation

noun   word class (part of speech): tells you whether the word you are looking up is a noun, a verb, an adjective, or some other part of speech. A headword can be more than one part of speech. For instance, book can be a noun *(she was reading a book)* or a verb *(I've booked the seats)*

(signpost)   helpful information: to guide you to the right translation, to show you how to use the translation, or to give you extra information

example   a phrase or sentence using the word you have looked up. You should read through them carefully to see if they are close to what you want to understand or say

Masc.   gender: after a Spanish noun, to tell you that it is masculine

Fem.   gender: after a Spanish noun, to tell you that it is feminine. *Fem.* also shows the feminine form of some adjectives

•   indicates a phrasal verb such as *to carry on*

★   shows an idiomatic expression such as *over the moon*

[27]   verb number – tells you which verb table to look up in the dark-edged centre pages of the dictionary

You can think of a dictionary entry as being made out of different sorts of building bricks. In the entries below you can see how they fit together to help you find what you need. The more you use your dictionary, the more confident you will feel about finding your way around it.

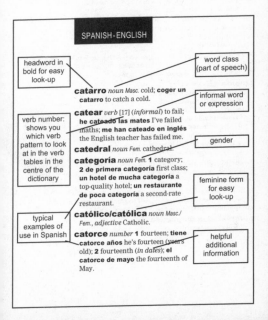

SPANISH-ENGLISH

headword in bold for easy look-up

word class (part of speech)

catarro *noun Masc.* cold; **coger un catarro** to catch a cold.

informal word or expression

catear *verb* [17] (*informal*) to fail; **he cateado las mates** I've failed maths; **me han cateado en inglés** the English teacher has failed me.

verb number: shows you which verb pattern to look at in the verb tables in the centre of the dictionary

gender

catedral *noun Fem.* cathedral.

categoría *noun Fem.* **1** category; **2 de primera categoría** first class; **un hotel de mucha categoría** a top-quality hotel; **un restaurante de poca categoría** a second-rate restaurant.

feminine form for easy look-up

typical examples of use in Spanish

católico/católica *noun Masc./ Fem., adjective* Catholic.

catorce *number* **1** fourteen; **tiene catorce años** he's fourteen (years old); **2** fourteenth (*in dates*); **el catorce de mayo** the fourteenth of May.

helpful additional information

USING THE DICTIONARY

To find out what a Spanish word means

Suppose you want to find out what the Spanish word **comida** means. You need to use the first half of the dictionary to find the Spanish word that you are looking for. To help you do this, the guide words at the top of each page show the alphabetical range of words on the pages you have open. Notice that hyphens and spaces between words in Spanish headwords make no difference to their alphabetical order.

When you find the entry for **comida** you will find the translation. But you will also see that **comida** is a noun and because all nouns are either masculine or feminine in Spanish, you are given the gender *Fem.* (*Fem.* = feminine, *Masc.* = masculine).

However, it often happens that a Spanish word has more than one translation in English. If you look at the entry for **comida** you can see that there are three different translations, each of which is numbered:

comida *noun* Fem. **1** food;
  tenemos suficiente comida we
  have enough food; **la comida
  rápida** fast food; **2** lunch; **a la hora
  de la comida** at lunch time;
  3 meal; **cuatro comidas al día**
  four meals a day; **mi comida
  fuerte es a mediodía** I have my
  main meal at midday.

So **comida** can mean *food*, *lunch*, or *meal*. You will need to look at all the translations and decide which one fits best in the sentence you are trying to understand.

Most adjectives in Spanish have a masculine form and a feminine form. Both of these are given as headwords, so if you are trying to find out what **complicada** means, you will be able to find it easily:

complicado/complicada
  adjective complicated.

To find an English word and how to say it in Spanish

You can see that it is quite easy, once you know how the dictionary works, to look up a Spanish word and find out what it means. Students usually find it harder to use the dictionary to find out how to say something in Spanish. This dictionary is written specially to help you do this and to make it easy to find the right way of saying things in Spanish.

Suppose you want to know how to say **garden** in Spanish. Look up the word in the second part of the dictionary. If you follow the same method of looking through the alphabetical order of the headwords as you did when you were looking up a Spanish word, you will find the entry **garden** on page 427.

garden *noun* jardín *Masc.*

Now you can see that the Spanish word for garden is *jardín*. But if you want to make a sentence using a noun such as jardín you need to know whether it is masculine or feminine. The *Masc.* after jardín tells you that it is masculine so *in the garden* is **en el jardín**.

It is not always easy to work out which Spanish word you need. When the dictionary gives you more than one translation, it is very important to take the time to read through the whole entry. If you look up **hall** the entry looks like this:

hall *noun* **1** (*in a house*) entrada
Fem.; **2** (*public*) salón *Masc.;* **the village hall** el salón de actos del pueblo; **3 a concert hall** una sala de conciertos.

You can see that **1** tells you that the Spanish word for a hall in your house is **entrada**, **2** that the word for a public place like a village hall or a school hall is **salón**, and **3** that the phrase for a concert hall is **sala de conciertos**.

Remember that the information which is in brackets and italics, or both, is there to guide you to the right translation but *will never be* the translation itself. Often it is not enough to find the translation of one single word. In the case of frequently used words, the dictionary also gives you a selection of common phrases you will want to use. In the entry **hair** you can see how the translation works in different expressions:

hair *noun* **1** pelo *Masc.;* **to have short hair** tener [9] el pelo corto; **to brush your hair** cepillarse [17] el pelo; **to wash your hair** lavarse [17] el pelo; **to have your hair cut** cortarse [17] el pelo; **she's had her hair cut** se ha cortado el pelo; **2 a hair** (*from the head*) un pelo; (*from the body*) un vello.

HOW TO USE THE VERB TABLES

On the Spanish side of the dictionary all the headwords which are verbs look like this: **cerrar** *verb* [29]. On the English side of the dictionary all the verbs given as translations of English verbs look like this: **frighten** *verb* asustar [17].

If you look at the pages edged in blue in the centre of the dictionary, you will find tables showing you how to use the different types of Spanish verbs.

The verb **cerrar** above has the number 29. If you look up number 29 in the verb tables you will find the tense patterns for this verb. The same is true for verb numbers after Spanish verbs in the English-Spanish side of the dictionary.

With practice you will soon be able to find your way easily around the dictionary and identify what you are looking for in each entry. Some entries may seem long and complicated at first glance. Reading carefully through the signposts and examples will lead you to the translation you need.

Aa

a *preposition* (note that 'a + el' becomes 'al') **1** to; **iremos a Italia** we'll go to Italy; **tuerce a la derecha** turn right; **voy a casa** I'm going home; **2 está a la izquierda** it's on the left; **sentados a la mesa** sitting at the table; **siéntate al sol** sit in the sun; **estaban a mi lado** they were by my side; **3** at; **a las diez** at ten o'clock; **a medianoche** at midnight; **se casó a los treinta años** she married at thirty; **¿a qué hora termina?** what time does it finish?; **4 hoy estamos a dos de enero** it's the second of January today; **5 está a diez kilómetros de aquí** it's ten kilometres from here; **la vi a lo lejos** I saw her in the distance; **6 dos veces al día** twice a day; **están a tres euros el kilo** they're three euros a kilo; **a ochenta kilómetros por hora** at eighty kilometres an hour; **7 ir a pie** to go on foot; **hecho a mano** handmade; **escrito a mano** handwritten; **a lápiz** in pencil; **8** to; **se lo di a Laura** I gave it to Laura; **le mandé un regalo a mi madre** I sent a present to my mother; **le da clases de piano a mi hermana** he gives my sister piano lessons; **9** (*not translated after certain verbs when followed by a person*) **no se lo dije a Mar** I didn't tell Mar; **vi a tu madre** I saw your mother; **10 voy a hacer los deberes** I'm going to do my homework; **nos fuimos a dormir** we went to sleep; **se han ido a nadar** they've gone swimming; **salimos a pasear** we went out for a walk; **11** (*in commands*) **¡a dormir!** go to sleep!; **¡a callar!** shut up!; **¡a comer!** food's ready!

abadía *noun Fem.* abbey.

abajo *adverb* **1 aquí abajo** down here; **allí abajo** down there; **2** downstairs; **hay otro piso abajo** there's another flat downstairs; **los vecinos de abajo** the downstairs neighbours; **3 el piso de abajo** the flat below, the bottom flat.

abalanzarse *reflexive verb* [22] **abalanzarse sobre alguien/algo** to leap on somebody/something; **se abalanzaron hacia la ventana** they rushed towards the window.

abandonado/abandonada *adjective* **1** deserted; **2** abandoned; **sentirse abandonado** to feel abandoned; **3** neglected.

abandonar *verb* [17] **1** to leave; **abandonó a su familia** he left his family; **2** to abandon; **abandonar el barco** to abandon ship.

abanico *noun Masc.* fan.

abarrotado/abarrotada *adjective* packed; **un bar abarrotado de gente** a bar packed with people.

abecedario *noun Masc.* alphabet.

abedul *noun Masc.* birch.

abeja *noun Fem.* bee.

abejón, abejorro *noun Masc.* bumble-bee.

abertura *noun Fem.* opening.

abeto *noun Masc.* fir.

a b c d e f g h i j k l m n ñ o p q r s t u v w x y z

abierto/abierta adjective
1 open; **la puerta está abierta** the door's open; **abierto al público** open to the public; **abierto de par en par** wide open; **siempre dejas el grifo abierto** you always leave the tap running; 2 open-minded; **mis padres son muy abiertos** my parents are very open-minded.

abochornado/abochornada adjective embarrassed.

abogado/abogada noun Masc./Fem. 1 lawyer; 2 solicitor.

abolir verb [19] to abolish.

abolladura noun Fem. dent.

abollar verb [17] to dent.
abollarse reflexive verb [17] to get dented.

abonar verb [17] 1 to pay (a bill); 2 to fertilize (a field or plant).
abonarse reflexive verb [17] 1 to subscribe; **abonarse a una revista** to subscribe to a magazine; 2 to buy a season ticket.

abono noun Masc. 1 fertilizer; 2 a season ticket.

abordar verb [17] 1 to tackle (a problem); 2 to raise (a subject).

aborrecer verb [35] to detest.

aborto noun Masc. 1 abortion; 2 miscarriage.

abotonarse reflexive verb [17] to do your buttons up; **me abotoné la chaqueta** I buttoned my jacket up.

abrasado/abrasada adjective
1 burnt; **murieron abrasados** they burned to death; 2 **estoy abrasada** I'm boiling.

abrasador/abrasadora adjective burning.

abrasar verb [17] to burn.

abrazar verb [22] to hug.
abrazarse reflexive verb [22] to hug each other.

abrazo noun Masc. hug.

abrebotellas noun Masc. (does not change in the plural) bottle opener.

abrelatas noun Masc. (does not change in the plural) tin opener.

abreviatura noun Fem. abbreviation.

abridor noun Masc. 1 bottle opener; 2 tin opener.

abrigar verb [28] to be warm (a jumper or coat).
abrigarse reflexive verb [28] to wrap up warmly.

abrigo noun Masc. 1 coat; 2 **ropa de abrigo** warm clothes.

abril noun Masc. April.

abrir verb [46] 1 to open; **abre la ventana** open the window; **abrió la boca para hablar** he opened his mouth to speak; **no abrió la boca en toda la tarde** she didn't say a word all afternoon; **abrir algo de par en par** to open something wide; 2 to turn on (a tap); **abrir el agua** to turn the water on; 3 **¡abran paso!** make way!
abrirse reflexive verb [46] to open; **la puerta se abrió** the door opened.

abrocharse reflexive verb [17]
1 to do up your buttons; **abróchate la chaqueta** do your jacket up; 2 to

fasten (a seat belt); **abróchense los cinturones** fasten your seat belts.

absoluto/absoluta adjective
1 absolute; **2 en absoluto** not at all; **'¿te importa?' – 'en absoluto'** 'do you mind?' – 'not at all'.

absorbente adjective absorbent.

absorber verb [18] to absorb.

abstracto/abstracta adjective abstract.

absurdo/absurda adjective absurd.

abuchear verb [17] to boo; **the crowd booed the referee** el público abucheó al árbitro.

abuelo/abuela noun Masc./Fem.
1 grandfather/grandmother;
2 mis abuelos my grandparents.

aburrido/aburrida adjective
1 boring; **ser aburrido/aburrida** to be boring; **2** bored; **estar aburrido/aburrida** to be bored.

aburrimiento noun Masc.
boredom; **¡qué aburrimiento!** how boring!

aburrirse reflexive verb [19] to get bored.

abusar verb [17] **1 abusar (de)** to take too much/many (alcohol or pills, for example); **2 abusar de** to take advantage of; **están abusando de tu amabilidad** they are taking advantage of your kindness.

abusiva/abusiva adjective
1 excessive (price); **2** unfair (a law or rule, for example).

abuso noun Masc. **1** abuse; **el abuso del alcohol** alcohol abuse;
2 outrage; **¡esto es un verdadero abuso!** this is really outrageous!

aC abbreviation (short for: antes de Cristo) BC, before Christ.

acá adverb here; **¡ven acá!** come here!

acabado/acabada adjective
finished.

acabar verb [17] **1** to finish; **aún no he acabado de leer el libro** I haven't finished reading the book yet; **¿has acabado con el lápiz?** have you finished with the pencil?;
2 to be over; **cuando acabó la fiesta** when the party was over;
3 to end; **la palabra acaba en 'r'** the word ends in 'r'; **la historia acaba bien** the story has a happy ending; **4 acabar de hacer** to have just done; **acabo de hablar con él** I've just spoken to him; **acaban de llegar** they've just arrived; **acabábamos** we had just finished.

acabarse reflexive verb [17] **1** to be over (a party or film, for example); **cuando se acabó la clase** when the class was over; **2** to run out (money or food, for example); **se ha acabado el pan** we've run out of bread; **se me acabó el dinero** I ran out of money.

academia noun Fem. school; **academia de idiomas** language school.

académico/académica adjective academic.

acampada noun Fem. camping; **ir de acampada** to go camping.

acampar verb [17] to camp.

a
b
c
d
e
f
g
h
i
j
k
l
m
n
ñ
o
p
q
r
s
t
u
v
w
x
y
z

acantilado noun Masc. cliff.

acariciar verb [17] **1** to caress (a person); **2** to stroke (a cat or dog).

acaso adverb por si acaso just in case.

acatarrado/acatarrada adjective estar acatarrado/acatarrada to have a cold.

acatarrarse reflexive verb [17] to catch a cold.

acceder verb [18] **1** acceder a algo to agree to something; **2** to access (information or a file).

accesible adjective **1** accessible (a place, for example); **2** affordable.

accesorios plural noun Masc. accessories.

accidental adjective accidental.

accidente noun Masc. accident; tener un accidente/sufrir un accidente to have an accident; un accidente de circulación a road accident.

acción noun Fem. **1** act; una buena acción a good deed; **2** share (in a company).

acebo noun holly.

aceite noun Masc. oil; aceite de oliva olive oil.

aceitoso/aceitosa adjective oily.

aceituna noun Fem. olive.

acelerador noun Masc. accelerator; pisar el acelerador to put your foot down (accelerate).

acelerar verb [17] to accelerate.

acento noun Masc. **1** accent; tener acento andaluz to have an Andalusian accent; casi no tienes acento you have hardly any accent; **2** accent (on a letter in written Spanish); un acento agudo an acute accent.

acentuarse reflexive verb [20] to have an accent; se acentúa en la última sílaba it has an accent on the last syllable.

aceptable adjective acceptable.

aceptar verb [17] **1** to accept (an invitation or apology, for example); **2** aceptar hacer to agree to do; aceptaron dejármelo they agreed to lend it to me.

acera noun Fem. pavement.

acerca de preposition about.

acercar verb [31] **1** acerqué la silla a la ventana I moved the chair nearer the window; acércame un poco la lámpara bring the lamp closer to me; **2** to pass; acércame ese libro pass me that book; **3** acercar a alguien a to give somebody a lift to; me acercó a la oficina she gave me a lift to the office.

acercarse reflexive verb [31] to come/go nearer; acércate más come/get closer; se acercó a la ventana she went over to the window.

acero noun Masc. steel.

acertado/acertada adjective right (decision or answer).

acertar verb [29] **1** to be right; ¡has acertado! you've got it right!; **2** acertar algo to get something right; **3** acertar en el blanco to hit the target.

ácido noun Masc. acid.

acierto noun Masc. **1** correct answer; **2** good decision; **ese regalo ha sido un acierto** that present was a good idea.

aclaración noun Fem. explanation.

aclarar verb [17] to make clear. **aclararse** reflexive verb [17] (informal) to understand; **aún no me aclaro** I still don't understand.

acné noun Masc. acne.

acoger verb [3] **1** to receive (news or a proposal); **2** to take in (refuge).

acompañar verb [17] **1** to go with; **la acompañé al dentista** I went with her to the dentist's; **te acompaño a tu casa** I'll see you home; **2** to keep company; **el perro me acompaña mucho** the dog keeps me company.

aconsejar verb [17] to advise.

acordarse reflexive verb [24] to remember; **no me acuerdo** I don't remember; **acordarse de algo** to remember something.

acorde noun Masc. chord.

acordeón noun Masc. accordion.

acortar verb [17] to shorten.

acostarse reflexive verb [24] **1** to go to bed; **¿a qué hora te acuestas?** what time do you go to bed?; **2 acostarse con alguien** to sleep with somebody.

acostumbrado/ acostumbrada adjective **estar acostumbrado/acostumbrada a algo** to be used to something; **está acostumbrada a tener muchos deberes** she's used to having lots of homework.

acostumbrarse reflexive verb [17] **acostumbrarse a algo** to get used to something.

acróbata noun Masc./Fem. acrobat.

actitud noun Fem. attitude.

actividad noun Fem. activity.

activo/activa adjective active.

acto noun Masc. **1** act; **2 en el acto** immediately.

actor noun Masc. actor.

actriz noun Fem. actress; **quiere ser actriz** she wants to be an actress.

actuación noun Fem. performance (in a play or film).

actual adjective present, current; **la situación actual** the present situation; **el actual presidente** the current president.

actualidad noun Fem. **1 en la actualidad** at present, at the moment; **en la actualidad viven en Madrid** at present they're living in Madrid; **2** nowadays; **en la actualidad es más fácil viajar** nowadays it's easier to travel.

actualmente adverb **1** at present; **actualmente trabaja en un banco** at present he's working in a bank; **2** nowadays; **actualmente se fabrica con máquinas** nowadays it's made by machine.

actuar verb [20] to act.

acuarela noun Fem. watercolour.

acuario[1] noun Masc. aquarium.

a b c d e f g h i j k l m n ñ o p q r s t u v w x y z

acuario² noun Masc./Fem. Aquarius; **soy acuario** I'm an Aquarius.

Acuario noun Masc. Aquarius.

acudir verb [19] **acudir a** to attend.

acuerdo noun Masc. **1** agreement; **llegaron a un acuerdo** they reached an agreement; **2 estar de acuerdo (en algo)** to agree (on something); **están de acuerdo en la fecha** they agree on the date; **no estoy de acuerdo** I don't agree; **ponerse de acuerdo** to come to an agreement; **3 ¡de acuerdo!** okay!

acusación noun Fem. accusation.

acusar verb [17] to accuse; **acusar a alguien de algo** to accuse somebody of something; **me acusó de mentir** he accused me of lying.

acústica noun Fem. acoustics.

adaptador noun Masc. adaptor (electrical).

adaptar verb [17] to adapt.

adaptarse reflexive verb [17] **adaptarse a** to adapt to.

a. de C. abbreviation (short for: antes de Cristo) BC, before Christ.

adecuado/adecuada adjective **1 adecuado/adecuada para** suitable for; **2 el momento adecuado** the right moment.

adelantado/adelantada adjective **1** advanced; **2** fast (a clock or watch); **tu reloj va adelantado** your watch is fast; **3 pagar por adelantado** to pay in advance.

adelantamiento noun Masc. overtaking.

adelantar verb [17] **1** to bring forward (a date or trip); **2** to overtake (when driving); **3 adelantar el reloj** to put the clock forward.

adelante adverb **1** forward; **ir hacia adelante** to go forward; **2 seguir adelante** to go on; **3 más adelante** further on; **4** later; **5 ¡adelante!** come in!

adelgazar verb [22] to lose weight; **he adelgazado tres kilos** I've lost three kilos.

además adverb **1** besides; **además, no es mi problema** besides, it's not my problem; **no ayuda y además se queja** he doesn't help and on top of that he complains; **2 además de** apart from; **además de eso, no sabes conducir** apart from that, you can't drive; **además de estos tres, tengo cinco más** besides these three, I've got five more; **son tres, además de la madre** there are three, not counting the mother.

adentro adverb inside, in; **vete adentro** go inside.

adicto/adicta adjective **adicto/ adicta a** addicted to.

adiós exclamation **1** bye!; **2** hello! (when passing somebody in the street).

aditivo noun Masc. additive.

adivinanza noun Fem. riddle.

adivinar verb [17] to guess.

adivino/adivina noun Masc./Fem. fortune-teller.

adjetivo noun Masc. adjective.

adjuntar verb [17] **1** to enclose; **2** to attach.

adjunto/adjunta adjective enclosed.

administración noun Fem. administration; **la administración pública** the civil service.

admirable adjective admirable.

admiración noun Fem. **1** admiration; **sentir admiración por alguien** to admire someone; **2** signo de admiración exclamation mark.

admirador/admiradora noun Masc./Fem. admirer.

admirar verb [17] to admire.

admitir verb [19] **1** to admit; **admitió su responsabilidad** she admitted her responsibility; **2** 'no se admiten perros' 'no dogs'; 'no se admiten devoluciones' 'goods cannot be returned'.

adolescente noun Masc./Fem. adolescent.

adónde adverb where; **¡adónde vas?** where are you going?

adonde adverb where; **la ciudad adonde iban** the city where they were going.

adoptar verb [17] to adopt.

adoptivo/adoptiva adjective **1** adoptive (parents); **2** adopted (child).

adorar verb [17] to adore.

adorno noun Masc. ornament; **los adornos de Navidad** Christmas decorations.

adquirir verb [47] to acquire.

adrede adverb on purpose.

aduana noun Fem. customs; **libre de derechos de aduana** duty-free.

adulto/adulta noun Masc./Fem., **adulto** adjective adult.

adverbio noun Masc. adverb.

advertencia noun Fem. warning.

advertir verb [14] to warn; **quedas/estás advertido** you've been warned; **le advertí que no llegase tarde otra vez** I warned him not to be late again.

aéreo/aérea adjective air (traffic); **el puente aéreo** the shuttle.

aerobic noun (plural **aerobics**) Masc. aerobics.

aeropuerto noun Masc. airport.

aerosol noun Masc. aerosol.

afán noun Masc. eagerness; **tienen afán de aprender** they are eager to learn.

afectar verb [17] to affect.

afecto noun Masc. affection; **tenerle afecto a alguien/sentir afecto por alguien** to be fond of somebody.

afectuoso/afectuosa adjective affectionate (person); **recibe un afectuoso saludo** kind regards (in a letter).

afeitarse reflexive verb [17] **1** to shave; **hoy no me he afeitado** I haven't shaved today; **2** to shave off (a beard or moustache).

afición noun Fem. interest, hobby; **¿qué aficiones tienes?** what are your interests?; **por afición** as a hobby.

aficionado/aficionada *adjective* ser aficionado/ aficionada a algo to be fond of something.

aficionado/aficionada *noun Masc./Fem.* **1** fan; un aficionado al jazz a jazz fan; un aficionado al rugby a rugby fan; para los aficionados a la cocina for those who like cooking; **2** amateur; un grupo de aficionados a group of amateurs.

aficionarse *reflexive verb* [17] aficionarse a algo to become fond of something.

afilar *verb* [17] to sharpen.

afinar *verb* [17] to tune (*an instrument*).

afirmación *noun Fem.* **1** statement; **2** yes answer.

afirmar *verb* [17] **1** to state; afirmó que era de su familia he stated that it belonged to his family; **2** afirmar con la cabeza to nod.

afirmativo/afirmativa *adjective* affirmative.

aflojar *verb* [17] **1** to loosen; **2** aflojar la marcha to slow down.

afónico/afónica *adjective* estar afónico/afónica to have lost your voice.

afortunadamente *adverb* fortunately.

afortunado/afortunada *adjective* fortunate.

África *noun Fem.* Africa.

africano/africana *noun Masc./ Fem., adjective* African.

afuera *adverb* outside, out; salimos afuera we went outside.

afueras *plural noun Fem.* las afueras the outskirts.

agachar *verb* [17] agachar la cabeza to lower your head.

agacharse *reflexive verb* [17] **1** to bend down; **2** to duck.

agarrar *verb* [17] to grab.

agarrarse *reflexive verb* [17] to hold on; se agarró a la barandilla she held on to the handrail.

agencia *noun Fem.* agency; agencia inmobiliaria estate agent's office; agencia de viajes travel agency.

agenda *noun Fem.* diary.

agente *noun Masc./Fem.* **1** agent; agente inmobiliario estate agent; **2** agente de policía police officer.

agitar *verb* [17] to shake.

agosto *noun Masc.* August.

agotado/agotada *adjective* **1** worn out; estoy agotado I'm worn out; **2** sold out; **3** flat (*a battery*).

agotador/agotadora *adjective* exhausting.

agotarse *reflexive verb* [17] **1** to wear yourself out; **2** to sell out (*goods*); **3** to go flat (*a battery*); **4** to run out (*reserves or supplies*); **5** se me está agotando la paciencia my patience is running out.

agradable *adjective* pleasant.

agradecer *verb* [35] **1** agradecerle algo a alguien to be grateful to somebody for something; te agradezco tu

ayuda I'm grateful for your help; **2** to thank; **te lo agradezco** thank you; **¡y así nos lo agradeceis!** and that's all the thanks we get from you!

agradecido/agradecida ·*adjective* grateful; **le estoy muy agradecido** I'm very grateful to you.

agradecimiento *noun Masc.* gratitude.

agresión *noun Fem.* aggression.

agresivo/agresiva *adjective* aggressive.

agricultor/agricultora *noun Masc./Fem.* farmer.

agricultura *noun Fem.* **1** agriculture; **2** farming; **agricultura biológica** organic farming.

agrio/agria *adjective* sour.

agua *noun Fem.* water (*even though 'agua' is feminine, it is takes 'el' or 'un' in the singular*) **el agua está fría** the water is cold; **agua mineral con gas** sparkling mineral water; **agua mineral sin gas** still mineral water; **agua potable** drinking water; **agua corriente** running water; **agua de colonia** eau de cologne; **★ estar más claro que el agua** to be crystal clear (*literally: to be clearer than water*).

aguacate *noun Masc.* avocado.

aguacero *noun Masc.* downpour.

aguafiestas *noun Masc./Fem.* (*does not change in the plural*) spoilsport.

aguanieve *noun Fem.* sleet.

aguantar *verb* [17] **1** to bear (*pain or heat*); **no aguanto este calor** I can't bear this heat; **2** to take; **no aguanto más** I can't take any more; **3 aguantar la respiración** to hold your breath; **aguantar la risa** to stop yourself laughing; **4** to hold (*an object*) **aguanta esta caja un momento** hold this box for a minute.

aguantarse *reflexive verb* [17] **tendrás que aguantarte** you'll have to put up with it.

agudo/aguda *adjective* **1** acute (*pain*); **2** acute (*an accent*); **3** high-pitched (*a voice or sound*); **4** stressed on the last syllable (*a word*).

aguijón *noun Masc.* sting.

águila *noun Fem.* eagle (*even though 'águila' is feminine, it takes 'el' or 'un' in the singular*) **vimos un águila** we saw an eagle.

aguja *noun Fem.* **1** needle (*for sewing or knitting*); **2** hand (*of a watch or clock*).

agujero *noun Masc.* hole.

agujetas *plural noun Fem.* stiffness; **tengo muchas agujetas** I'm really stiff.

ahí *adverb* **1** there; **ahí están** there they are; **ponlo ahí** put it there; **2 tenemos que ir por ahí** we have to go that way; **dejó las llaves por ahí** she left the keys somewhere.

ahijado/ahijada *noun Masc./Fem.* **1** godson/goddaughter; **2 mis ahijados** my godchildren.

ahogado/ahogada adjective
1 morir ahogado to drown;
2 morir ahogado to suffocate.

ahogarse reflexive verb [28] 1 to
drown; **se ahogó en el río** he
drowned in the river; 2 to
suffocate.

ahora adverb 1 now; **¿qué vas a
hacer ahora?** what are you going
to do now?; **de ahora en adelante**
from now on; **ahora mismo** right
now; 2 nowadays; 3 in a moment;
ahora vuelvo I'll be back in a
moment; **ahora lo hago** I'll do it in
a moment; **ahora viene** he's
coming; 4 **por ahora** for the time
being.

ahorcar verb [31] to hang
(execute).

ahorcarse reflexive verb [31] to
hang yourself.

ahorrar verb [17] to save.

ahorros plural noun Masc.
savings; **todos mis ahorros** all my
savings.

ahumado/ahumada adjective
smoked.

aire noun Masc. 1 air; **al aire libre**
in the open air; **teatro al aire libre**
open-air theatre; **mis hijos
disfrutan jugando al aire libre** my
children enjoy playing outdoors;
aire acondicionado air
conditioning; **salir a tomar el aire**
to go out for some fresh air; 2 wind;
hace mucho aire it's very windy;
3 **tiene un aire interesante** he
looks interesting; **llegó con aire
preocupado** she arrived looking
worried.

aislado/aislada adjective
isolated.

ajedrez noun Masc. chess; **jugar al
ajedrez** to play chess.

ajillo noun Masc. **al ajillo** with
garlic; **gambas al ajillo** garlic
prawns.

ajo noun Masc. garlic; **un diente de
ajo** a clove of garlic; **una cabeza
de ajo** a head of garlic.

ajustar verb [17] 1 to adjust (a seat
or safety belt); 2 to fit.

al (formed by 'a + el'; look under 'a'
for more examples) 1 **fuimos al
colegio** we went to school; **se lo di
al camarero** I gave it to the waiter;
2 (with infinitive) when; **al salir
nos encontramos con Marta**
when we were leaving we met
Marta; **tengan cuidado al bajar
del autobús** be careful when
leaving the bus.

ala¹ noun Fem. (even though 'ala' is
feminine, it takes 'el' or 'un' in the
singular) 1 wing; **el ala del avión**
the wing of the plane; **el pájaro
batió las alas** the bird beat its
wings; **el hospital tiene dos alas**
the hospital has two wings; 2 brim
(of a hat).

ala² noun Masc./Fem. winger.

alabanza noun Fem. praise.

alabar verb [17] to praise.

alambre noun Masc. wire;
alambre de púas barbed wire.

alargador noun Masc. extension
lead.

alargar verb [28] 1 to lengthen; **voy
a alargar esta falda un poco** I'm
going to lengthen this skirt a bit;

2 to extend (*a visit or holiday, for example*); **el presidente ha alargado su visita** the president has extended his visit; **3** to stretch out (*an arm*); **alargué el brazo para alcanzarlo** I stretched out my arm to reach it.

alargarse *reflexive verb* [28] **1** to get longer; **los días se van alargando** the days are getting longer; **2** to go on; **la conferencia se alargó mucho** the conference went on for a long time.

alarma *noun Fem.* alarm; **alarma contra incendios** fire alarm.

alarmante *adjective* alarming.

albañil *noun Masc.* **1** builder; **2** bricklayer.

albaricoque *noun Masc.* apricot.

albergue *noun Masc.* **1** hostel; **albergue juvenil** youth hostel; **2** refuge (*in the mountains*).

albóndiga *noun Fem.* meatball.

albornoz *noun Masc.* bathrobe.

alborotar *verb* [17] **alborotar a los niños** to get the children excited.
alborotarse *reflexive verb* [17] to get excited.

alboroto *noun Masc.* racket; **¡qué alboroto!** what a racket!

álbum *noun Masc.* album; **un álbum de fotografías** a photograph album; **el mejor álbum del grupo** the group's best album.

alcachofa *noun Fem.* artichoke.

alcalde *noun Masc.* mayor.

alcaldesa *noun Fem.* mayoress, mayor (*woman*).

alcanzar *verb* [22] **1** to reach; **la temperatura alcanzó los cuarenta grados** the temperature reached forty; **no alcanzo a la ventana** I can't reach the window; **2** to catch up with; **no pude alcanzar al resto del grupo** I couldn't catch up with the rest of the group; **3** **alcanzarle algo a alguien** to pass somebody something; **¿me alcanzas las tijeras?** can you pass me the scissors?

alcohol *noun Masc.* alcohol.

alcohólico/alcohólica *noun Masc./Fem., adjective* alcoholic.

alcoholismo *noun Masc.* alcoholism.

aldaba *noun Fem.* knocker.

aldea *noun Fem.* village.

aldeano/aldeana *noun Masc./Fem.* villager.

alegrar *verb* [17] to cheer up; **verla les alegró un poco** seeing her cheered them up a bit; **me alegra saberlo** I'm glad to hear it.
alegrarse *reflexive verb* [17] to be happy; **me alegro mucho por ellos** I'm very happy for them; **¡cuánto me alegro!** I'm so happy!; **se alegró de venir** he was glad to come; **me alegro de haberte llamado** I'm glad I phoned you; **me alegro de verte** it's nice to see you.

alegre *adjective* **1** happy; **una cara alegre** a happy face; **2** cheerful; **soy una persona muy alegre** I'm a

a b c d e f g h i j k l m n ñ o p q r s t u v w x y z

a **b** **c** **d** **e** **f** **g** **h** **i** **j** **k** **l** **m** **n** **ñ** **o** **p** **q** **r** **s** **t** **u** **v** **w** **x** **y** **z**

cheerful kind of person; **3** bright (*a colour*).

alegría *noun Fem.* happiness; **¡qué alegría veros!** it's great to see you!; **¡qué alegría me das!** that makes me really happy!; **saltar de alegría** to jump for joy.

alejar *verb* [17] **alejar algo de alguien** to move something away from somebody.

alejarse *reflexive verb* [17] to move away; **¡aléjate del fuego!** move away from the fire!.

alemán[1] *noun Masc.* German (*the language*).

alemán[2]**/alemana** *noun Masc./ Fem., adjective* German.

Alemania *noun Fem.* Germany.

alergia *noun Fem.* allergy; **tener alergia a algo** to be allergic to something; **alergia al polen** hayfever.

alerta *adjective* **1** alert.

alerta *noun Fem.* **estar alerta por algo** to be on the alert for something; **hay que estar al alerta por los carteristas** be on the alert for pickpockets.

alfabético/alfabética *adjective* alphabetical; **por orden alfabético** in alphabetical order.

alfabeto *noun Masc.* alphabet.

alfarería *noun Fem.* pottery.

alféizar *noun Masc.* sill; **el alféizar de la ventana** the windowsill.

alfiler *noun Masc.* pin.

alfombra *noun Fem.* **1** rug; **2** carpet.

alfombrilla *noun Fem.* mat; **alfombrilla de baño** bath mat.

alga *noun Fem.* seaweed.

algo *pronoun* **1** something; **algo así** something like that; **¿te pasa algo?** is there something wrong?; **2** anything; **¿has cogido algo de aquí?** have you taken anything from here?; **3** some; **algo de leche** some milk; **4** any; **¿tienes algo de leche?** do you have any milk?

algo *adverb* a bit; **estoy algo cansado** I'm a bit tired.

algodón *noun Masc.* cotton; **una camisa de algodón** a cotton shirt.

alguien *pronoun* **1** somebody, someone; **vino alguien preguntando por ti** somebody came asking for you; **2** anybody, anyone; **¿has hablado con alguien?** have you talked to anybody?

algún SEE **alguno/alguna**.

alguno/alguna *pronoun*
1 alguno/alguna one; **alguno de vosotros** one of you; **tiene que haber alguno aquí** there must be one here; **para alguna de sus hijas** for one of her daughters; **2** algunos/algunas some; **faltan algunos** there are some missing; **3** (*in questions*) any; **tengo demasiadas plantas, ¿quieres alguna?** I've got too many plants, do you want any?

alguno *adjective* ('*alguno*' becomes '*algún*' before a masculine singular noun) **1** some; **compré algunos libros** I bought some books; **algún día iré** I'll go some day; **2** (*in questions*) any; **¿tienes alguna razón para no ir?** do you have any reason for not going?; **¿tienes**

algún problema? do you have any problems?; **3 en algún lugar** somewhere; **en algún momento** sometime; **4 alguna vez lo he pensado** I've thought about it sometimes; **¿has estado alguna vez en España?** have you ever been to Spain?

aliado/aliada noun Masc./Fem. ally.

aliado adjective allied.

alianza noun Fem. alliance.

aliarse reflexive verb [32] **aliarse con alguien** to form an alliance with somebody.

alicates plural noun Masc. **1** pliers; **unos alicates** a pair of pliers; **2** nail clippers.

aliento noun Masc. breath; **mal aliento** bad breath; **estar sin aliento** to be breathless; **recuperar el aliento** to get your breath back.

alimentar verb [17] **1** to feed; **2** to be nutritious; **las lentejas alimentan mucho** lentils are very nutritious.

alimentarse reflexive verb [17] to feed; **se alimentan de insectos** they feed on insects.

alimenticio/alimenticia adjective **productos alimenticios** foodstuffs; **valor alimenticio** nutritional value.

alimento noun Masc. **1** food; **el arroz es su alimento básico** rice is their staple food; **buenos alimentos** good food; **2 tiene mucho alimento** it's very nutritious.

aliñar verb [17] **1** to dress (salad); **2** to season.

aliño noun Masc. **1** salad dressing; **2** seasoning.

alioli noun Masc. garlic mayonnaise.

alistarse reflexive verb [17] to join up; **alistarse en el ejército** to join the army.

aliviar verb [17] to relieve (pain).

allá adverb **1** there; **allá abajo** down there; **¡allá voy!** here I come/go!; **ahora vamos para allá** we're on our way; **2 más allá** further away; **no lo pongas muy allá** don't put it too far away; **3 allá tú** that's your lookout.

allí adverb there; **allí arriba** up there; **lo puso por allí** she put it somewhere around there; **se fueron por allí** they went that way.

alma noun Fem. (even though 'alma' is feminine, it takes 'el' or 'un' in the singular) soul.

almacén noun Masc. warehouse.

almacenar verb [17] to store (goods).

almacenes plural noun Masc. **unos (grandes) almacenes** a department store.

almeja noun Fem. clam (shellfish).

almendra noun Fem. almond.

almíbar noun Masc. syrup; **peras en almíbar** pears in syrup.

almidón noun Masc. starch.

almohada noun Fem. pillow; **una almohada de plumas** a feather pillow; **una funda de almohada** a pillowcase; ★ **consultarlo con la**

almohada to sleep on it (*a decision*).

almohadón *noun Masc.* cushion.

almorzar *verb* [26] **1** to have a mid-morning snack; **2** to have lunch (*in some areas of Spain*).

almuerzo *noun Masc.* **1** mid-morning snack; **2** lunch (*in some areas of Spain*).

alojamiento *noun Masc.* accommodation, lodgings.

alojarse *reflexive verb* [17] to stay; **se alojaron en un hotel** they stayed in a hotel.

alondra *noun Fem.* lark (*bird*).

Alpes *plural noun Masc.* **los Alpes** the Alps.

alpinismo *noun Masc.* mountaineering.

alpinista *noun Masc./Fem.* mountaineer.

alquilar *verb* [17] **1** to rent; **hemos alquilado un apartamento en la playa** we've rented an apartment at the seaside; **2** to hire (*a car or equipment, for example*); **alquilar una bicicleta** to hire a bike; **3** to let (*a house, flat, or room*); **se aquila esa casa** that house is to let; **4** to hire out (*equipment*); **allí alquilan botas de esquiar** they hire out ski boots there.

alquilarse *reflexive verb* [17] **se aquila local** premises to let; **se alquilan coches** cars for hire.

alquiler *noun Masc.* **1** rent (*for a flat or premises*); **2** hire charge (*for cars or equipment*); **3 una casa de alquiler** a rented house; **una casa**

en alquiler a house to let; **coches de alquiler** hire cars.

alquitrán *noun Masc.* tar.

alrededor *adverb* **1** around; **a nuestro alrededor** around us; **mirar alrededor** to look around; **2 alrededor de algo** around something; **se sentaron alrededor de la mesa** they sat around the table; **3 de alrededor** surrounding; **los campos de alrededor** the surrounding fields.

alrededores *plural noun Masc.* **1** outskirts (*of a town or city*); **2** surrounding area (*of an airport or building*).

altavoz *noun Masc.* **1** loudspeaker; **2** megaphone.

alternar *verb* [17] to alternate.

alternarse *reflexive verb* [17] to take turns; **nos alternábamos para hacer la comida** we took turns to cook.

alternativa[1] *noun Fem.* alternative; **no tenemos otra alternativa** we have no alternative.

alternativo/alternativa[2] *adjective* alternative.

altitud *noun Fem.* altitude.

altivo/altiva *adjective* arrogant.

alto[1]/alta *adjective* **1** high; **la montaña más alta de España** the highest mountain in Spain; **habitaciones de techo alto** rooms with high ceilings; **los precios están muy altos** prices are very high; **en lo alto de la torre** at the top of the tower; **tiene la tensión alta** he has high blood pressure; **2** tall; **todos sus hijos son muy**

altos all their children are very tall; **¡qué alta está!** hasn't she grown!; **3** loud; **en voz alta** in a loud voice; **no pongas la radio tan alta** don't have the radio on so loud.

alto[2] *noun Masc.* de alto high; **un muro de dos metros de alto** a two-metre high wall.

alto *adverb* **1** loud; **habla un poco más alto, por favor** speak a little louder, please; **2** high; **volar alto** to fly high.

altura *noun Fem.* **1** height; **a la misma altura** at the same height; **¿qué altura tiene?** how high is it?; **2** altitude; **volar a una altura de 10.000m** to fly at an altitude of 10,000 metres; **3 a estas alturas** at this stage; **a estas alturas no importa** it doesn't matter at this stage.

alubia *noun Fem.* haricot bean.

alucinación *noun Fem.* hallucination.

alucinado/alucinada *adjective* (*informal*) **estar alucinado/ alucinada** to be stunned; **nos quedamos alucinados** we were stunned.

alucinante *adjective* (*informal*) amazing; **es un espectáculo alucinante** it's an amazing spectacle.

alucinar *verb* [17] (*informal*) **1** to amaze; **me alucina** it amazes me; **2** to be amazed; **con este disco es que alucinas** this record's amazing.

alud *noun Masc.* **1** avalanche; **2** landslide.

aluminio *noun Masc.* aluminium.

alumno/alumna *noun Masc./Fem.* pupil, student.

alusión *noun Fem.* allusion.

ama de casa *noun Fem.* (*even though 'ama de casa' is feminine, it takes 'el' or 'un' in the singular*) housewife; **un ama de casa** a housewife.

amabilidad *noun Fem.* kindness; **tuvieron la amabilidad de ayudarme** they were kind enough to help me.

amable *adjective* kind; **¿sería tan amable de sujetar esto?** would you be so kind as to hold this?

amado/amada *adjective* beloved; **mi amado** my beloved.

amaestrar *verb* [17] to train (*an animal*).

amanecer *noun Masc.* dawn; **al amanecer** at dawn.

amanecer *verb* [35] to get light; **¿a qué hora amanece?** what time does it get light?

amante *noun Masc./Fem.* lover.

amante *adjective* **ser amante de algo** to be fond of something; **son grandes amantes del cine** they're great film-lovers.

amapola *noun Fem.* poppy.

amar *verb* [17] to love.

amargo/amarga *adjective* bitter.

amarillo[1] *noun Masc.* yellow.

amarillo[2]**/amarilla** *adjective* yellow.

amasar *verb* [17] to knead (*dough*).

a
b
c
d
e
f
g
h
i
j
k
l
m
n
ñ
o
p
q
r
s
t
u
v
w
x
y
z

a
b
c
d
e
f
g
h
i
j
k
l
m
n
ñ
o
p
q
r
s
t
u
v
w
x
y
z

Amazonas *noun Masc.* **el Amazonas** the Amazon.

ambición *noun Fem.* ambition.

ambicioso/ambiciosa *adjective* ambitious.

ambientador *noun Masc.* air freshener.

ambiental *adjective* environmental.

ambiente *noun Masc.* **1** environment; **la contaminación del ambiente** the pollution of the environment; **2** atmosphere (*at a party, for example*); **había muy buen ambiente** there was a good atmosphere.

ambiguo/ambigua *adjective* ambiguous.

ambos/ambas *plural pronoun, plural adjective* both; **se lo dije a ambos** I told both of them; **ambas ciudades** both cities.

ambulancia *noun Fem.* ambulance.

ambulante *adjective* travelling; **un grupo de teatro ambulante** a travelling theatre group; **una biblioteca ambulante** a mobile library.

ambulatorio *noun Masc.* outpatients department.

amén *noun Masc.* amen.

amenaza *noun Fem.* threat.

amenazador/amenazadora *adjective* threatening.

amenazar *verb* [22] to threaten; **amenazó con despedirme** he threatened to fire me; **amenazar**

de muerte a alguien to threaten to kill somebody.

América *noun Fem.* America; **América Central** Central America; **América del Sur** South America; **América Latina** Latin America.

americana *noun Fem.* jacket.

americano/americana *noun Masc./Fem., adjective* American.

ametralladora *noun Fem.* machine gun.

amigo/amiga *noun Masc./Fem.* friend; **amigo/amiga por correspondencia** penfriend; **un amigo nuestro** a friend of ours; **un amigo de Carmen** a friend of Carmen's; **son amigos íntimos** they are very close friends; **mi amigo del alma** my best friend.

amigo *adjective* **son muy amigos** they are very good friends; **hacerse amigos** to become friends.

amistad *noun Fem.* friendship.

amistades *plural noun Fem.* friends; **mis amistades** my friends.

amistoso/amistosa *adjective* friendly.

amo/ama *noun Fem.* (*even though 'ama' is feminine, it takes 'el' or 'un' in the singular*) owner (*of an animal*); **el ama del perro** the owner of the dog.

amontonar *verb* [17] to pile up. **amontonarse** *reflexive verb* [17] to pile up.

amor *noun Masc.* **1** love; **amor mío** my love; **amor a primera vista** love at first sight; **2** amor propio self esteem; ★ por amor al arte for the sake of it.

amoroso/amorosa *adjective* las relaciones amorosas love relationships.

ampliar *verb* [32] **1** to enlarge (*a photograph*); **2** to extend (*a road or building*); **3** to increase (*vocabulary or knowledge*).

amplificador *noun Masc.* amplifier.

amplio/amplia *adjective* **1** wide (*a road*); **2** spacious (*a room*); **3** loose-fitting (*a garment*).

amplitud *noun Fem.* **1** width (*of a road*); **2** spaciousness (*of a room*).

ampolla *noun Fem.* blister; **me han salido ampollas en las manos** I've got blisters on my hands.

amueblar *verb* [17] to furnish (*a house or room*).

analfabeto/analfabeta *adjective* illiterate.

analgésico *noun Masc.* painkiller.

análisis *noun Masc.* analysis.

analizar *verb* [22] to analyse.

anatomía *noun Fem.* anatomy.

ancho[1] *noun Masc.* width; **¿cuánto tiene de ancho?/¿qué ancho tiene?** how wide is it?; **mide/tiene dos metros de ancho** it's two metres wide.

ancho[2]**/ancha** *adjective* **1** wide; **una carretera muy ancha** a very wide road; **2** broad; **ser ancho de espaldas** to have broad shoulders;

3 loose-fitting (*a garment*); **te está muy ancho** it's too loose for you.

anchoa *noun Fem.* anchovy.

anchura *noun Fem.* width; **tiene una anchura de cinco metros** it's five metres wide; **¿qué anchura tiene?** how wide is it?

anciano/anciana *noun* old man/old woman.

anciano *adjective* elderly; **un hombre muy anciano** a very elderly man.

ancla *noun Fem.* (*even though 'ancla' is feminine noun, it takes 'el' or 'un' in the singular*) anchor; **el ancla** the anchor; **echar (las) anclas** to drop anchor.

Andalucía *noun Fem.* Andalusia.

andamio *noun Masc.* scaffolding.

andar *verb* [21] **1** to walk; **¿has venido andando?** did you walk here?; **casi no podía andar** I could hardly walk; **2 ¿cómo andas?** how are you?; **¿cómo andas de dinero?** how are you doing for money?; **3** to work; **mi coche no anda** my car's not working; **4** (*expressing surprise*) **¡anda! si es Pedro** well, if it isn't Pedro!; **5** (*urging somebody to do something*) **anda, date prisa** come on, hurry up.

andén *noun Masc.* platform.

Andes *plural noun Masc.* **los Andes** the Andes.

Andorra *noun Fem.* Andorra.

andrajo *noun Masc.* rag; **iba vestido de andrajos** he was dressed in rags.

anécdota *noun Fem.* anecdote.

a b c d e f g h i j k l m n ñ o p q r s t u v w x y z

a
b
c
d
e
f
g
h
i
j
k
l
m
n
ñ
o
p
q
r
s
t
u
v
w
x
y
z

anestesía noun Fem.
1 anaesthesia; 2 anaesthetic.

anfitrión noun Masc. host.

anfitriona noun Fem. hostess.

ángel noun Masc. angel; **no es ningún angelito** he's no angel;
★ **que sueñes con los angelitos** sweet dreams (literally: dream with the angels).

angelical adjective angelic.

anginas plural noun Fem. throat infection; **tener anginas** to have a throat infection.

anglicano/anglicana noun Masc./Fem. Anglican.

anguila noun Fem. eel.

angustiado/angustiada adjective worried; **sus padres están angustiados porque no saben nada de él** his parents are really worried because they haven't heard from him.

angustiarse reflexive verb [17] to get worried; **no hay por qué angustiarse** there's no reason to get worried.

angustioso/angustiosa adjective worrying.

anillo noun Masc. ring; **anillo de boda** wedding ring.

animado/animada adjective
1 lively (a bar or party, for example); 2 in good spirits; **muy animada** she was in high spirits.

animal¹ noun Masc. animal; **animal doméstico** pet, domestic animal.

animal² noun Masc./Fem. brute; **es un animal** he's a brute.

animal adjective stupid; **¡qué animal eres!** you're so stupid!

animar verb [17] 1 to liven up (a party, for example); 2 to cheer up (a person); 3 to cheer on.

animarse reflexive verb [17] to cheer up; **¡anímate!** cheer up!

ánimo noun Masc. 1 **no tengo ánimo para nada** I don't feel in the mood for anything; **se la ve con mucho ánimo** she's in high spirits; **con el ánimo por los suelos** feeling really low; 2 **¡ánimo!** cheer up!

anís noun Masc. anisette.

aniversario noun Masc. anniversary.

anoche adverb last night; **anoche no dormí bien** I didn't sleep well last night; **antes de anoche** the night before last.

anochecer noun Masc. nightfall; **al anochecer** at nightfall.

anochecer verb [35] to get dark; **está anocheciendo** it's getting dark.

anónimo¹/**anónima** adjective anonymous.

anónimo² noun Masc. anonymous letter.

anormal adjective abnormal.

anotar verb [17] to write down.

ansiedad noun Fem. anxiety.

ante¹ noun Masc. suede.

ante² preposition before; **ante el juez** before the judge.

anteanoche adverb the night before last.

anteayer adverb the day before yesterday.

antemano *in phrase* **de antemano** in advance.

antena *noun Fem.* **1** aerial; **2** antenna.

antepasados *plural noun Masc.* ancestors.

anterior *adjective* previous; **la noche anterior** the previous night; **anterior a algo** prior to something.

antes *adverb* **1** before; **la noche antes** the night before; **deberías haberlo dicho antes** you should have said it before; **2** antes de before; **antes del viernes** before Friday; **piénsalo antes de comprarlo** think about it before you buy it; **3** earlier; **este año la primavera ha llegado antes** this year spring has come earlier; **a las cinco está bien, no hace falta que vengas antes** five is fine, you don't need to come any earlier; **4** first; **ésta va antes** this goes first; **5** lo antes posible as soon as possible.

antibiótico *noun Masc.* antibiotic.

anticipación *noun Fem.* **con mucha anticipación** well in advance; **con dos días de anticipación** two days in advance.

anticipo *noun Masc.* advance.

anticoncepción *noun* contraception.

anticonceptivo *noun Masc.* contraceptive.

anticuado/anticuada *adjective* old-fashioned.

antídoto *noun Masc.* antidote.

antigüedad *noun Fem.* **1** antique; **tienda de antigüedades** antique shop; **2** seniority (*at work*); **3** en la antigüedad in the old days.

antiguamente *adverb* in the old days.

antiguo/antigua *adjective* **1** old; **una costumbre muy antigua** a very old tradition; **2** former; **el antiguo presidente** the former president; **3** ancient; **una civilización antigua** an ancient civilization.

Antillas *plural noun Fem.* **las Antillas** the West Indies.

antipático/antipática *adjective* unpleasant; **es muy antipático** he's very unpleasant; **¡qué mujer más antipática!** what a horrible woman!

antojarse *reflexive verb* [17] **se le antojó un helado** he fancied an ice-cream; **se me antojó comprar el jarrón** I felt like buying the vase.

antropología *noun Fem.* anthropology.

anual *adjective* annual.

anualmente *adverb* yearly.

anunciar *verb* [17] **1** to announce (*news or a decision*); **2** to advertise (*a product, for example*).

anuncio *noun Masc.* **1** announcement; **2** advertisement.

anzuelo *noun Masc.* hook.

añadidura *in phrase* **por añadidura** in addition.

añadir *verb* [19] to add.

a b c d e f g h i j k l m n ñ o p q r s t u v w x y z

a b c d e f g h i j k l m n ñ o p q r s t u v w x y z

año noun Masc. **1** year; **el año pasado** last year; **los años cincuenta** the 50s; **el Año Nuevo** the New Year; **año bisiesto** leap year; **2** (*talking about age*) **mi madre tiene cincuenta años** my mother is fifty; **¿cuántos años tienes?** how old are you?

apagado/apagada *adjective* **1** off; **con la luz apagada** with the light off; **¿está la televisión apagada?** is the television off?; **2** out; **el fuego estaba casi apagado** the fire was almost out.

apagar verb [28] **1** to switch off (*the television or a light*); **2** to put out (*a fire or cigarette*).

apagón noun Masc. power cut.

aparato noun Masc. **1** appliance; **aparatos eléctricos** electrical appliances; **2** los aparatos de laboratorio laboratory equipment; **3** piece of apparatus (*in the gym*).

aparcamiento noun Masc. car park.

aparcar verb [31] to park.

aparecer verb [35] **1** to appear (*a person or symptom*); **2** to turn up (*a lost object*).

aparente *adjective* apparent.

apariencia noun Fem. **1** appearance; **a juzgar por las apariencias** judging by appearances; **en apariencia no estaba roto** it appeared not to be broken; **2** un niño de apariencia delicada a delicate-looking child.

apartado/apartada *adjective* isolated.

apartamento noun Masc. flat, apartment.

apartar verb [17] **1** to move away; **aparta la manta del fuego** move the blanket away from the fire; **2** to move out of the way; **aparta la planta para que pueda ver** move the plant out of the way so that I can see.

apartarse *reflexive verb* [17] to move away; **se apartó de la ventana** she moved away from the window.

aparte *adverb* **1** aside; **poner algo aparte** to put something aside; **llamar a alguien aparte** to call somebody aside; **2** separately; **esto lo pago aparte** I'll pay for this separately; **3** aparte de eso apart from that.

apasionado/apasionada *adjective* passionate.

apasionar verb [17] **el deporte me apasiona** I have a passion for sports; **la ópera no me apasiona** I'm not wild about opera.

apearse *reflexive verb* [17] **apearse de** to get off (*a bus or train*), to get out of (*a car*), to dismount from (*a horse*).

apellidarse *reflexive verb* [17] me apellido Alejos my surname is Alejos.

apellido noun Masc. surname; **¿qué apellido tienes?/¿cuál es tu apellido?** what's your surname?; **apellido de soltera** maiden name.

apenas *adverb* **1** hardly; **apenas hay suficiente** there's hardly enough; **2** hardly ever; **ahora**

apenas nos vemos we hardly ever see each other now; **3** scarcely; **hace apenas tres horas que se fueron** it's scarcely three hours since they went; **apenas lo veo** I can scarcely see it; **4 apenas me había sentado, cuando sonó el teléfono** no sooner had I sat down than the telephone rang.

apéndice noun Masc. appendix.

apendicitis noun Fem. appendicitis.

aperitivo noun Masc. **1** aperitif (before a meal); **2** nibbles (food).

apetecer verb [35] **no me apetece** I don't feel like it; **¿te apetece ir a cenar fuera?** do you fancy going out for dinner?; **haz lo que te apetezca** do whatever you feel like.

apetito noun Masc. appetite; **no tengo apetito** I don't feel hungry; **para abrir el apetito** to give you an appetite.

apio noun Masc. celery.

aplastar verb [17] to squash.

aplaudir verb [19] to applaud.

aplauso noun Masc. round of applause; **los aplausos del público** the applause of the audience.

aplazamiento noun Masc. postponement.

aplazar verb [22] to postpone.

aplicado/aplicada adjective hard-working.

aplicar verb [31] to apply.

apodo noun Masc. nickname.

apostar verb [24] to bet; **te apuesto cincuenta euros** I bet you fifty euros; **te apuesto a que no viene** I bet she won't come; **apostar a las carreras** to bet on horses; **apostaron por el favorito** they bet on the favourite.

apóstrofo noun Masc. apostrophe.

apoyar verb [17] **1** to support (a candidate or plan, for instance); **2** to lean; **apoyé la bicicleta en la pared** I leaned the bicycle against the wall; **3** to rest; **apoya la cabeza en este cojín** rest your head on this cushion.

apoyarse reflexive verb [17] **apoyarse en** to lean on; **me apoyé en la puerta** I leaned against the door.

apoyo noun Masc. support.

apreciar verb [17] **1** to appreciate; **2 apreciar a alguien** to be fond of somebody; **la aprecio mucho** I'm very fond of her.

aprecio noun Masc. **sentir aprecio por alguien** to be fond of somebody.

aprender verb [18] to learn; **aprender español** to learn Spanish; **aprender a conducir** to learn to drive; **aprender algo de memoria** to learn something by heart.

aprendiz/aprendiza noun Masc./Fem. apprentice.

aprendizaje noun Masc. apprenticeship.

apretado/apretada adjective tight.

a b c d e f g h i j k l m n ñ o p q r s t u v w x y z

a

apretar verb [29] **1** to press (a button); **2** to tighten (a bolt or knot); **3** apretar el acelerador to put your foot on the accelerator; **4** to be too tight (shoes); **5** to squeeze; me apretó el brazo she squeezed my arm.

apretón noun Masc. un apretón de manos a handshake.

aprieto noun Masc. predicament; meterse en un aprieto to get into a predicament; poner a alguien en un aprieto to put somebody in an awkward situation.

aprisa adverb quickly.

aprobar verb [24] **1** to approve (a plan or decision, for example); **2** to approve of (behaviour or an idea); **3** to pass; aprobar un examen to pass an exam.

aprovechado/aprovechada adjective es un aprovechado he takes advantage of people.

aprovechar verb [17] **1** to use; podemos aprovechar estos trozos de madera we can use these pieces of wood; **2** to make the most of (time or resources); **3** to take advantage of (an opportunity or offer); **4** aprovecé para decírselo I took the chance to tell him; quiero aprovechar esta oportunidad para ... I want to take this opportunity to ...; **5** ¡que aproveche! enjoy your meal!

aproximadamente adverb approximately, roughly.

aproximado/aproximada adjective approximate, rough.

aproximar verb [17] to bring nearer.

aproximarse reflexive verb [17] **1** to go/come up to; se aproximó a la ventana she went/came up to the window; **2** to approach; se aproximaba el momento the moment was approaching; se me aproximó un hombre a man approached me.

apto/apta adjective apto para algo suitable for something.

apuesta noun Fem. bet; hacerle una apuesta a alguien to make a bet with somebody; me hicieron una apuesta they made a bet with me.

apuntar verb [17] **1** to write down (telephone number or address, for example); **2** to point out; apuntó con el dedo hacia la torre she pointed out the tower; **3** to aim; me apuntó con la pistola he aimed the gun at me; **4** me apuntaron las respuestas they whispered the answers to me.

apuntarse reflexive verb [17] apuntarse a algo to enrol on something, to put your name down for something.

apuntes plural noun Masc. notes; tomar apuntes to take notes.

apuro noun Masc. estar en un apuro to be in a tight spot; pasar apuros to go through a lot.

aquel/aquella adjective **1** that; en aquel momento at that moment; **2** aquellos/aquellas those.

aquel/aquella pronoun **1** that one; quiero aquel I want that one;

2 aquellos/aquellas those; **estas no, dame aquellas** not these, give me those.

aquél/aquélla pronoun SEE aquel/aquella.

aquello pronoun that; **¿qué es aquello?** what's that?; **aquello que vimos** what we saw.

aquí adverb here; **lo puse aquí abajo** I put it down here; **aquí llegan** here they are; **debe estar por aquí** it must be around here; **el vino es de aquí** the wine is from here.

árabe[1] noun Masc. Arabic (the language).

árabe[2] noun Masc./Fem., adjective Arab.

Aragón noun Masc. Aragon.

aragonés/aragonesa noun Masc./Fem., adjective Aragonese.

araña noun Fem. spider.

arañar verb [17] to scratch.

arañazo noun Masc. scratch.

árbitro/árbitra noun Masc./Fem. **1** referee; **2** umpire.

árbol noun Masc. tree; **un árbol de Navidad** a Christmas tree.

arbusto noun Masc. shrub.

arcén noun Masc. hard shoulder (on the motorway).

archivador noun Masc. **1** filing cabinet; **2** ring binder.

archivar verb [17] to file.

archivo noun Masc. **1** archive; **2** file (on a computer).

arcilla noun Fem. clay.

arco noun Masc. **1** arch; **2** bow (for firing arrows or playing the violin); **3** arco iris rainbow.

arder verb [18] to burn; **el bosque estaba ardiendo** the forest was burning.

ardiente adjective burning.

ardilla noun Fem. squirrel.

área noun Fem. area (even though 'área' is feminine, it takes 'el' or 'un' in the singular) **el área de penalty** the penalty area; **las áreas más peligrosas** the most dangerous areas.

arena noun Fem. sand.

Argentina noun Fem. Argentina.

argentino/argentina noun Masc./Fem., adjective Argentinian.

argot noun Masc. slang; **el argot juvenil** youth slang.

argumento noun Masc. **1** argument; **2** plot (of a film, for example).

aries noun Masc./Fem. Aries; **soy aries** I'm Aries.

Aries noun Masc. Aries.

aritmética noun Fem. arithmetic.

arma noun Fem. weapon (even though 'arma' is a feminine noun, it takes 'el' or 'un' in the singular) **un arma de fuego** a fire arm; **armas nucleares** nuclear weapons; **un arma blanca** a knife (as a weapon).

armado/armada adjective armed.

armar verb [17] **1** to arm; **2** to assemble (a piece of furniture); **3** to pitch (a tent); **4** (informal) **armar ruido** to make a noise; **armar jaleo**

a b c d e f g h i j k l m n ñ o p q r s t u v w x y z

a
b
c
d
e
f
g
h
i
j
k
l
m
n
ñ
o
p
q
r
s
t
u
v
w
x
y
z

to make a racket; **armar un escándalo** to cause a scene.

armarse *reflexive verb* [17]
1 armarse un lío to get confused; **me armé un lío con las fechas** I got confused with the dates; **2 armarse de paciencia** to be patient.

armario *noun Masc.* wardrobe.

armonía *noun Fem.* harmony.

armónica *noun Fem.* harmonica.

armonioso/armoniosa *adjective* harmonious.

aro *noun Masc.* **1** hoop; **2** hoop earring.

aroma *noun Masc.* **1** scent; **2** aroma.

aromático/aromática *adjective* aromatic.

arpa *noun Fem.* harp (*even though 'arpa' is feminine, it takes 'el' or 'un' in the singular*).

arqueología *noun Fem.* archaeology.

arqueólogo/arqueóloga *noun Masc./Fem.* archaeologist.

arquitecto/arquitecta *noun Masc./Fem.* architect.

arquitectura *noun Fem.* architecture.

arrancar *verb* [31] **1** to tear out; **arrancar una hoja del cuaderno** to tear out a sheet from the notebook; **2** to tear off; **arrancar una etiqueta** to tear off a label; **3** to pull up (*a plant*); **4** to pull off (*a button*); **5** to snatch; **me arrancó el libro de las manos** she snached

the book from my hands; **6** to start (*a car or engine*).

arrastrar *verb* [17] to drag (*an object*).

arrastrarse *reflexive verb* [17] to crawl.

arrebatar *verb* [17] to snatch.

arreglado/arreglada *adjective*
1 tidy; **deja tu habitación arreglada** leave your room tidy; **2** well dressed; **siempre va muy arreglado** he's always very well dressed.

arreglar *verb* [17] **1** to fix; **2** to mend; **3** to tidy (*a room or house*); **4** to sort out (*a problem, for example*); **no te preocupes, yo lo arreglaré** don't worry, I'll sort it out.

arreglarse *reflexive verb* [17]
1 to get ready; **me arreglo enseguida y salimos** I'll get ready straight away and we can go out; **2** to dress up; **mi hermana siempre se arregla mucho** my sister always dresses up a lot; **3 arreglárselas** to manage; **se las arregla muy bien sola** she manages very well on her own.

arrepentirse *reflexive verb* [14] **arrepentirse de algo** to regret something; **no me arrepiento** I don't regret it.

arrestar *verb* [17] to arrest; **queda usted arrestado** you're under arrest.

arresto *noun Masc.* arrest.

arriba *adverb* **1** up; **aquí arriba** up here; **lo puse más arriba** I put it a bit higher up; **2 de arriba** (*next up*) above, *(highest)* top; **el cajón de arriba** *(the next up)* the drawer, above, *(highest)* the top drawer; **3** upstairs; **ha ido arriba** he's gone upstairs; **viven en el piso de arriba** they live upstairs; **4 arriba de todo** at the very top; **de arriba abajo** from top to bottom.

arriesgado/arriesgada *adjective* risky.

arriesgar *verb* [28] to risk.

arriesgarse *reflexive verb* [28] to take a risk.

arroba *noun Fem.* **1** @, at *(in email addresses; punto = dot)*; **juanrobledoARROBAeasycomPUNTOcom** juanrobledo@easycomDOTcom; **2** *(former measurement of weight)*

arrodillarse *reflexive verb* [17] to kneel down; **estaba arrodillado** he was on his knees.

arrogante *adjective* arrogant.

arrojar *verb* [17] to throw.

arropar *verb* [17] **1** to wrap up *(a child or sick person)*; **2** to tuck in *(in bed)*.

arroparse *reflexive verb* [17] to wrap up; **arrópate bien** wrap up well.

arroyo *noun Masc.* stream.

arroz *noun Masc.* rice.

arruga *noun Fem.* wrinkle.

arrugar *verb* [28] **1** to wrinkle; **2** to crease; **3** to crumple up.

arruinar *verb* [17] to ruin.

arruinarse *reflexive verb* [17] to go bankrupt.

arte *noun Masc.* art *('arte' is masculine in the singular and feminine in the plural)* **el arte moderno** modern art; **las artes gráficas** graphic arts; **★ por arte de magia** as if by magic.

artesanía *noun Fem.* crafts; **objetos de artesanía** handicrafts.

artesanía *noun Masc.* **1** craftsmanship; **2** craftwork.

artesano/artesana *noun Masc./ Fem.* craftsman/craftswoman.

ártico/ártica *adjective* Arctic.

Ártico *noun Masc.* **el Ártico** the Arctic.

articulación *noun Fem.* joint *(in arm, etc.)*.

artículo *noun Masc.* article; **el artículo definido** the definite article; **artículos de papelería** stationery.

artificial *adjective* artificial.

artista *noun Masc./Fem.* artist.

artístico/artística *adjective* artistic.

arzobispo *noun Masc.* archbishop.

asa *noun Fem.* handle *(even though 'asa' is feminine, it takes 'el' or 'un' in the singular)* **cógelo por el asa** take it by the handle.

asado *noun Masc.* roast.

asamblea *noun Fem.* meeting.

asar *verb* [17] **1** to roast *(meat)*; **2** to bake *(vegetables)*.

ascender *verb* [36] **1** to be promoted; **ha ascendido** he's been promoted; **2** to promote; **3** to rise *(temperature, prices or a balloon)*; **ascender a** to amount to; **la**

a b c d e f g h i j k l m n ñ o p q r s t u v w x y z

cuenta asciende a quinientos euros the bill amounts to five hundred euros.

ascenso noun Masc. promotion.

ascensor noun Masc. lift.

asco noun Masc. **le dio asco** it made him feel sick; **¡qué asco!** how disgusting!

asegurar verb [17] **1** to insure; **2** to secure; **3** to assure; **te aseguro que** ... I can assure you that ....

asegurarse reflexive verb [17] to make sure; **asegúrate de que cierras el grifo** make sure you turn the tap off.

asentir verb [14] **asentir con la cabeza** to nod (in agreement).

aseo noun Masc. toilet; **los aseos de señoras** the Ladies.

asesinar verb [17] to murder.

asesinato noun Masc. murder.

asesino/asesina noun Masc./ Fem. murderer.

asesor/asesora noun Masc./Fem. adviser.

asfixia noun Fem. **1** asphyxia; **2** suffocation; **tenía sensación de asfixia** I felt I was suffocating.

asfixiante adjective **1** asphyxiating (air or fumes); **2** suffocating (heat).

asfixiarse reflexive verb [17] **1** to suffocate; **2** to choke to death.

así adverb **1** like this; **hazlo así** do it like this; **2** like that; **el pueblo se llama Robellón, o algo así** the village is called Robellón, or something like that; **3** that way;

me llevaré el coche, así podremos volver pronto I'll tak[e] the car, that way we can come bac[k] early; **4** así que** so; **así que te va[s] de vacaciones** so you're going o[n] holiday; **5** así es** that's right; **6** as[í] así so, so; **'¿te gusta?' – 'así, as[í]** 'do you like it?' – 'so-so'; **7** ¡así m[e] gusta!** that's what I like to see!; **¡a[sí] se hace!** well done!

Asia noun Fem. Asia.

asiático/asiática noun Masc./ Fem., adjective Asian.

asiento noun Masc. seat; **asient[o] delantero** front seat; **asiento trasero** back seat.

asignatura noun Fem. subject.

asilo político noun Masc. political asylum.

asistenta noun Fem. cleaning lady; **¿hay servicio de asistent[a]** is there a maid service?

asistente social noun Masc./ Fem. social worker.

asistente noun Masc./Fem. assistant.

asma noun Fem. asthma (even though 'asma' is feminine, it take[s] 'el' or 'un' in the singular).

asmático/asmática adjective asthmatic.

asociación noun Fem. association.

asociar verb [17] to associate (tw[o] ideas or words, for example). **asociarse** reflexive verb [17] t[o] go into partnership (in business).

asomar verb [17] **asomar la cabeza** to stick your head out/i[n]

'no asomar la cabeza por la ventana' 'do not lean out of the window'.

asomarse *reflexive verb* [17] **se asomó a la ventana** he had a look out of the window; **'prohibido asomarse por la ventana'** 'do not lean out of the window'.

asombrar *verb* [17] to amaze; **me asombra su actitud** I'm amazed by her attitude.

asombrarse *reflexive verb* [17] to be amazed; **ya no me asombro con/de nada** nothing amazes me any more.

asombro *noun Masc.* surprise; **con cara de asombro** with a look of surprise on her face.

asombroso/asombrosa *adjective* amazing.

aspecto *noun Masc.* look; **tiene aspecto de policía** he looks like an policeman; **una mujer de aspecto elegante** an elegant-looking woman; **¿qué aspecto tenían?** what did they look like?; **tienes muy buen aspecto** you look very well.

áspero/áspera *adjective* rough.

aspirador *noun Masc.* SEE **aspiradora**.

aspiradora *noun Fem.* vacuum cleaner; **pasar la aspiradora por el salón** to vacuum the living room.

aspirina *noun Fem.* aspirin.

asterisco *noun Masc.* asterisk.

astilla *noun Fem.* splinter.

astrología *noun Fem.* astrology.

astrólogo/astróloga *noun Masc./Fem.* astrologer.

astronauta *noun Masc./Fem.* astronaut.

astronomía *noun Fem.* astronomy.

astrónomo/astrónoma *noun* astronomer.

astuto/astuta *adjective*
1 shrewd; **2** crafty; **eso fue muy astuto por su parte** that was very crafty of her.

asunto *noun Masc.* **1** matter; **asuntos de negocios** business matters; **un asunto complicado** a complicated matter; **2** business; **no quiero saber nada de este asunto** I don't want to know anything about this business; **no es asunto tuyo** mind your own business.

asustar *verb* [17] to frighten.

asustarse *reflexive verb* [17] to get frightened; **me asusté al oír un ruido** I got frightened when I heard a noise.

atacar *verb* [31] to attack.

atajo *noun Masc.* shortcut.

ataque *noun Masc.* **1** attack; **un ataque cardíaco/un ataque al corazón** a heart attack; **2** fit; **un ataque de celos** a fit of jealousy; **me dio un ataque de risa** I got a fit of the giggles.

atar *verb* [17] to tie (up).

atardecer *noun Masc.* dusk; **al atardecer** at dusk.

atardecer *verb* [35] to get dark; **estaba atardeciendo** it was getting dark.

a b c d e f g h i j k l m n ñ o p q r s t u v w x y z

a b c d e f g h i j k l m n ñ o p q r s t u v w x y z

atascar verb [31] to block (a pipe).
atascarse reflexive verb [31] to get blocked.

atasco noun Masc. **1** traffic jam; **2** blockage.

ataúd noun Masc. coffin.

atención noun Fem. attention; **presta atención** pay attention; **no pones atención en lo que haces** you don't concentrate on what you are doing; **¡atención, por favor!** your attention, please!

atender verb [36] **1** to pay attention; **atiende a la profesora** pay attention to your teacher; **2 ¿la atiende alguien?** are you being served?

atentado noun Masc. **un atentado terrorista** a terrorist attack.

atentado noun Masc. attack; **un atentado terrorista** a terrorist attack; **un atentado contra el presidente** an attempted assasination of the president.

atentamente adverb **1** attentively; **2 le saluda atentamente** yours faithfully, yours sincerely.

atento/atenta adjective attentive.

ateo/atea noun Masc./Fem. atheist.

aterrizaje noun Masc. landing (of a plane).

aterrizar verb [22] to land (a plane).

aterrorizar verb [22] to terrify.

ático noun Masc. **1** top-floor apartment; **2** loft.

atizador noun Masc. poker (for fire).

atlántico/atlántica adjective Atlantic.

Atlántico noun Masc. **el Atlántico** the Atlantic.

atlas noun Masc. atlas.

atleta noun Masc./Fem. athlete.

atlético/atlética adjective **1** athletic (person); **2 competición atlética** athletics competition.

atletismo noun Masc. athletics.

atómico/atómica adjective atomic.

átomo noun Masc. atom.

atracador/atracadora noun Masc./Fem. **1** robber; **2** mugger.

atracar verb [31] **1** to hold up (a bank or shop); **2** to mug (a person).

atracción noun Fem. attraction.

atraco noun Masc. **1** hold-up (of a bank or shop); **2** mugging.

atractivo/atractiva adjective attractive.

atraer verb [42] to attract.

atragantarse reflexive verb [17] **atragantarse con algo** to choke on something.

atrapar verb [17] to catch.

atrás adverb **1** back; **nos sentamos demasiado atrás** we sat too far back; **hacia atrás** backwards; **la parte de atrás** the back; **2** at the back; **esto va atrás** this goes at the back; **3 quedarse atrás** to be left behind.

atrasado/atrasada adjective **1** slow (a watch or clock); **llevo el reloj atrasado** my watch is slow;

2 backward (*a country*); **3** old-fashioned (*ideas or a person*); **4** behind; **voy atrasado en los estudios** I'm behind at school; **van muy atrasados con los ensayos** they're very behind with the rehearsals; **5 pagos atrasados** outstanding payments.

atrasar *verb* [17] **1** to put back (*a watch or clock*); **hay que atrasar los relojes una hora** we have to put the clocks back an hour; **2** to lose time (*a watch or clock*); **este reloj atrasa** this watch loses time; **3** to postpone.

atrasarse *reflexive verb* [17] to lose time (*a watch or clock*).

atravesar *verb* [29] to cross.

atrayente *adjective* appealing.

atreverse *reflexive verb* [18] to dare; **no me atrevo a preguntarle** I don't dare ask him.

atrevido/atrevida *adjective* **1** daring; **2** cheeky; **¡qué niño más atrevido!** what a cheeky child!

atropellar *verb* [17] to run over, to knock down; **lo atropelló un coche** he was run over by a car.

atún *noun Masc.* tuna.

au pair (*plural* **au pairs**) *noun Masc./Fem.* au pair.

audífono *noun Masc.* hearing aid.

aula *noun Fem.* (*even though 'aula' is feminine, it takes 'el' or 'un' in the singular*) **1** classroom; **2** lecture theatre.

aullido *noun Masc.* howl.

aumentar *verb* [17] **1** to increase; **aumentare! suelo** to give/get a

rise; **2** to rise (*temperature or pressure*).

aumento *noun Masc.* **1** increase; **2** rise.

aún *adverb* **1** still; **aún estoy esperando** I'm still waiting; **2** yet; **aún no se lo he dicho a ellos** I haven't told them yet; **3** even; **este es aún mejor** this one is even better.

aun *adverb* even; **aun así** even so; **ni aun con tu ayuda** not even with your help.

aunque *conjunction* **1** although; **aunque estaba cansada, la ayudé** although I was tired, I helped her; **2** even though; **3** even if; **aunque llegues tarde, llámame** even if you arrive late, give me a ring; **aunque no lo parezca** even if it doesn't look like it.

auricular *noun Masc.* **1** receiver (*of a phone*); **2 auriculares** headphones.

ausente *adjective* **estar ausente** to be absent, to be away.

Australia *noun Fem.* Australia.

australiano/australiana *noun Masc./Fem.*, *adjective* Australian.

Austria *noun Fem.* Austria.

austriaco/austriaca *noun Masc./Fem.*, *adjective* Austrian.

auténtico/auténtica *adjective* authentic.

auto *noun Masc.* car.

autoadhesivo *adjective* self-adhesive.

autobiografía *noun Fem.* autobiography.

a
b
c
d
e
f
g
h
i
j
k
l
m
n
ñ
o
p
q
r
s
t
u
v
w
x
y
z

autobús noun bus; **coger el autobús** to take the bus; **perder el autobús** to miss the bus.

autocar noun Masc. coach.

autoescuela noun Fem. driving school.

autógrafo noun Masc. autograph.

automático/automática adjective automatic.

automóvil noun Masc. car.

automovilismo noun Masc. motor racing.

automovilista noun Masc./Fem. motorist.

autonomía noun Fem.
1 autonomy; 2 autonomous region (of Spain).

autonómico/autonómica adjective regional (elections or a candidate).

autopista noun Fem. motorway.

autor/autora noun Masc./Fem. author.

autoridad noun Fem. authority.

autoritario/autoritaria adjective authoritarian.

autorización noun Fem. authorization.

autorizar verb [22] to authorize.

autoservicio noun Masc. 1 self-service restaurant; 2 supermarket.

autostop noun Masc. hitch-hiking; **hacer autostop** to hitch-hike.

autostop noun Masc. hitchhiking; **hacer autostop** to hitchhike.

autostopista noun Masc./Fem. hitch-hiker.

autovía noun Fem. dual carriageway.

auxiliar noun Masc./Fem. assistant; **auxiliar de vuelo** flight attendant.

auxilio noun Masc. aid; **acudir en auxilio de alguien** to go to the aid of somebody; **primeros auxilios** first aid.

avalancha noun Fem. avalanche.

avanzar verb [22] 1 to move forward (traffic or a person); 2 to make progress (a student or researcher); 3 to wind on (a tape).

avaricia noun Fem. greed.

avaricioso/avariciosa adjective greedy.

Avda. abbreviation (short for: avenida) Ave., Avenue.

ave noun Fem. bird (even though 'ave' is feminine, it takes 'el' or 'un' in the singular) **un ave** a bird; **las aves** the birds.

avellana noun Fem. hazelnut.

avenida noun Fem. avenue.

aventura noun Fem. adventure.

aventurero/aventurera adjective adventurous.

avergonzado/avergonzada adjective 1 ashamed; 2 embarrassed.

avería noun Fem. breakdown (of a car, for example); **sufrir una avería** to break down.

averiado/averiada adjective 1 broken down; 2 out of order.

avestruz noun Masc. ostrich.

avión noun Masc. aeroplane; **avión a reacción** jet (plane).

avisar verb [17] **1** avisar a alguien de algo to let somebody know about something; **le avisé del problema** I let him know about the problem; **me avisaron que llegarían tarde** they told me they would be late; **2** to warn; avisar a alguien del peligro to warn somebody about the danger; **3** avisar al médico to call the doctor.

aviso noun Masc. **1** warning; **el profesor ya le ha dado tres avisos** the teacher has already given him three warnings; **sin previo aviso** without prior warning; **2** notice; **hasta nuevo aviso** until further notice; **3** último aviso para los pasajeros del vuelo ... last call for passengers on flight ....

avispa noun Fem. wasp.

axila noun Fem. armpit.

ayer adverb yesterday; **antes de ayer** the day before yesterday.

ayuda noun Fem. **1** help; **ir en ayuda de alguien** to go to somebody's assistance; **2** aid.

ayudante noun Masc./Fem. helper, assistant.

ayudar verb [17] to help; **¿en qué puedo ayudarle?** how can I help you?

ayuntamiento noun Masc. **1** town council, city council; **2** town hall.

azafata noun Fem. **1** flight attendant; **2** trade fair attendant.

azar noun Masc. **1** chance; **por azar** by chance; **2** al azar at random.

azote noun Masc. smack.

azotea noun Fem. (flat) roof.

azúcar noun Masc. or Fem. sugar ('azúcar' always takes 'el', but it can take an adjective in the feminine form) **el azúcar blanca/blanco** white sugar; **el azúcar de caña** cane sugar; **azúcar glas/glaseado** icing; **el azúcar morena/moreno** brown sugar; **un terrón de azúcar** a sugar lump.

azucarero noun Masc. sugar bowl.

azul noun Masc. blue; **azul claro** light blue; **azul marino** navy blue; **azul celeste** sky blue.

azul adjective blue; **ojos azules** blue eyes.

azulejo noun Masc. tile.

Bb

baca noun Fem. luggage-rack.

bacalao noun Masc. cod.

bachillerato noun Masc. **1** secondary education; **2** Bachillerato (the two-year course leading to university entrance in Spain).

baguette noun Fem. baguette, French stick.

Bahamas noun Fem. (plural) **las Bahamas** the Bahamas; **las islas Bahamas** the Bahama Islands.

bahameño/bahameña adjective, noun Bahamian.

bahía noun Fem. bay.

bailar verb [17] to dance.

a
b
c
d
e
f
g
h
i
j
k
l
m
n
ñ
o
p
q
r
s
t
u
v
w
x
y
z

bailarín/bailarina noun Masc./ Fem. dancer.

baile noun Masc. **1** dance; **2** dancing; **una clase de baile** a dancing class.

bajar verb [17] **1** to bring down; **¿puedes bajarme el abrigo?** could you bring down my coat?; **2** to take down; **baja las maletas a recepción** take the suitcases down to reception; **3** to go down; **el ascensor está bajando** the lift's going down; **bajamos por las escaleras** we went down the stairs; **bajar la calle** to go down the street; **4** to come down; **¡ya bajo!** I'm coming down!; **creo que ya bajan** I think they're coming down now; **5** to fall (the temperature or prices); **6** to turn down (volume); **baja un poco la tele** turn the television down a bit; **7** to lower (a blind or prices).

bajarse reflexive verb [17] **bajarse de un coche** to get out of a car; **se bajó de la bicicleta** he got off the bike.

bajo[1] noun Masc. ground floor.

bajo preposition **1** under; **bajo los árboles** under the trees; **2** bajo cero below zero.

bajo adverb **1** low; **volar bajo** to fly low; **2** quietly; **hablar bajo** to speak quietly.

bajo[2]/**baja** adjective **1** short (a person); **soy bastante baja** I'm quite short; **2** low; **pon la música baja** put the music on low; **los precios están bajos** prices are low.

bala noun Fem. bullet.

balancín noun Masc. **1** swing seat; **2** seesaw; **3** rocking chair.

balanza noun Fem. scales.

balbucear, **balbucir** verb [17] to stammer.

balcón noun Masc. balcony.

baldosa noun Fem. tile.

Baleares plural noun Fem. **las islas Baleares** the Balearic Islands.

ballena noun Fem. whale.

ballet noun Masc. ballet.

balón noun Masc. ball; **un balón de fútbol** a football.

baloncesto noun Masc. basketball.

balonmano noun Masc. handball.

balonvolea noun Fem. volleyball.

balsa noun Fem. **1** raft; **2** pond.

banca noun banking Fem.

banco noun Masc. **1** bench (in a park); **2** pew (in church); **3** bank; **trabaja en un banco** she works in a bank.

banda noun Fem. **1** band (of musicians); **2** gang (of criminals); **3** banda sonora soundtrack.

bandeja noun Fem. tray.

bandera noun Fem. flag.

banderilla noun Fem. banderilla (a decorated dart used in bullfighting).

bandido/bandida noun Masc./ Fem. bandit.

banqueta noun Fem. stool.

banquete noun Masc. banquet; **un banquete de bodas** a wedding banquet.

bañador noun Masc. **1** swimming trunks; **2** swimming costume.

bañar verb [17] **bañar a** to bath (a baby).

bañarse reflexive verb [17] **1** to have a bath; **voy a bañarme esta noche** I'm going to have a bath tonight; **2** to have a swim; **¿te apetece bañarte?** do you fancy going for a swim?

bañera noun Fem. bath (bathtub).

baño noun Masc. **1** bath; **darse un baño** to have a bath; **voy a darme un baño** I'm going to have a bath; **2** swim; **darse un baño** to go for a swim; **¿te apetece darte un baño?** do you fancy going for a swim?; **3** bathroom; **¿dónde está el baño?** where's the bathroom?

bar noun Masc. bar.

baraja noun Fem. pack of cards.

barajar verb [17] to shuffle (cards).

barandilla noun Fem. rail.

baratija noun Fem. knick-knack.

barato/barata adjective cheap.

barba noun Fem. beard; **afeitarse la barba** to shave off your beard; **dejarse barba** to grow a beard; **voy a dejarme barba** I'm going to grow a beard.

barbacoa noun Fem. barbecue.

barbadense adjective, noun Barbadian.

Barbados noun Masc. Barbados.

barbaridad noun Fem. **1** fortune; **nos cobraron una barbaridad** they charged us a fortune; **2 eso es una barbaridad** that's far too much; **3** deja de decir

barbaridades stop talking nonsense; **4 ¡qué barbaridad!** my God!

barbero noun Masc. barber.

barbilla noun Fem. chin.

barca noun Fem. boat; **una barca de pesca** a fishing boat; **una barca de remos** a rowing boat.

Barcelona noun Fem. Barcelona.

barco noun Masc. **1** boat; **viajar en barco** to travel by boat; **un barco de pesca** a fishing boat; **2** ship; **un barco de guerra** a warship.

barniz noun Masc. **1** varnish; **2 barniz de uñas** nail varnish.

barómetro noun Masc. barometer.

barra noun Fem. **1** rail (for clothes); **2** bar; **una barra de jabón** a bar of soap; **nos sirvieron en la barra** they served us at the bar; **3 una barra de pan** a baguette; **4 una barra de labios** a lipstick.

barrer verb [18] to sweep.

barrera noun Fem. barrier.

barriga noun Fem. stomach, tummy; **tener dolor de barriga** to have a stomachache.

barril noun Masc. barrel.

barrio noun Masc. area (of a town); **los barrios bajos** the slums.

barro noun Masc. **1** mud; **lleno de barro** covered in mud; **2** clay (for making pots).

bártulos plural noun Masc. (informal) stuff, things; **coge todos tus bártulos** take all your stuff.

a

b

c

d

e

f

g

h

i

j

k

l

m

n

ñ

o

p

q

r

s

t

u

v

w

x

y

z

basar *verb* [17] to base; **basar algo en algo** to base something on something.

basarse *reflexive verb* [17] **¿en qué te basas para decir eso?** what basis do you have for saying that?

base *noun Fem.* **1** base; **2 base de datos** database; **3 base de maquillaje** foundation (*make-up*); **4 a base de** by; **lo aprendió a base de repetirlo** he learnt it by repeating it; ★ **a base de bien** (*informal*) a lot; **nos divertimos a base de bien** we enjoyed ourselves a lot.

básico/básica *adjective* basic.

bastante *adjective* **1** enough; **no tenemos bastante pan** we don't have enough bread; **ya tenemos bastantes sillas** we've got enough chairs now; **2** quite a lot of; **bastante gente** quite a lot of people; **bebimos bastante café** we drank quite a lot of coffee.

bastante *pronoun* enough; **con esto ya hay bastante** there's enough with this.

bastante *adverb* **1** enough; **¿has comido bastante?** have you eaten enough?; **2** (*before an adjective or adverb*) quite; **se puso bastante contenta** she was quite happy; **3** quite a lot; **ha mejorado bastante** he's improved quite a lot.

bastar *verb* [17] **1** to be enough; **con esto basta** this is enough; **¡ya basta!** that's enough!; **2 basta con preguntarle** you just need to ask him.

bastón *noun Masc.* walking stick.

bastoncillo *noun Masc.* cotton bud.

basura *noun Fem.* **1** rubbish; **hay que sacar la basura** we have to put the rubbish out; **2** dustbin, bin; **tirar algo a la basura** to throw something in the bin.

basurero[1] *noun Masc.* rubbish tip.

basurero[2]**/basurera** *noun Masc./Fem.* refuse collector.

bata *noun Fem.* **1** dressing gown; **2 una bata de médico** a white coat (*doctor's*).

batalla *noun Fem.* battle.

bate *noun Masc.* bat.

batería[1] *noun Fem.* **1** battery (*for a car*); **2** drum kit; **tocar la batería** to play the drums.

batería[2] *noun Masc./Fem.* drummer.

batido *noun Masc.* milkshake; **un batido de fresa** a strawberry milkshake.

batidora *noun Fem.* food mixer.

batir *verb* [19] **1** to beat; **batir las claras a punto de nieve** beat the egg whites until stiff; **2** to whip (*cream*); **3 batir un récord** to break a record.

baúl *noun Masc.* trunk (*for clothes*).

bautismo *noun Masc.* christening.

bautizar *verb* [22] to christen.

baya *noun Fem.* berry.

bayeta *noun Fem.* cloth (*for wiping*).

bebé *noun Masc.* baby.

beber *verb* [18] to drink; **¿quieres beber algo?** do you want something to drink?

bebida noun Fem. drink; **una bebida caliente** a hot drink.

beca noun Fem. **1** grant; **2** scholarship.

béisbol noun Masc. baseball.

belén noun Masc. nativity scene, crib.

belga noun Masc./Fem., adjective Belgian.

Bélgica noun Fem. Belgium.

belleza noun Fem. beauty.

bello/bella adjective beautiful.

bendito/bendita adjective **1** blessed; **2** holy (water or bread).

beneficiar verb [17] to benefit.

beneficio noun Masc. benefit.

benéfico/benéfica adjective charity; **una organización benéfica** a charity.

berenjena noun Fem. aubergine.

berro noun Masc. watercress.

besamel noun Fem. white sauce.

besar verb [17] to kiss.

beso noun Masc. kiss; **dame un beso** give me a kiss; **me dio un beso en la mejilla** he gave me a kiss on the cheek.

bestia noun Fem. **1** beast (animal); **2** ignorant person; **es un bestia, no sabe nada** he's so ignorant, he doesn't know a thing; **3** brute.

bestia adjective **1** ignorant; **2** **no seas bestia y habla mejor** don't be so rude, mind your language.

betún noun Masc. shoe polish.

Biblia noun Fem. Bible.

biblioteca noun Fem. library.

bibliotecario/bibliotecaria noun Masc./Fem. librarian.

bicho noun Masc. creepy-crawly.

bici noun Fem. (informal) bike; **montar en bici** to ride a bike.

bicicleta noun Fem. bicycle; **montar en bicicleta** to ride a bicycle; **¿sabes montar en bicicleta?** can you ride a bicycle?.

bien noun Masc. good; **la diferencia entre el bien y el mal** the difference between good and evil.

bien adverb, adjective **1** well; **lo has hecho muy bien** you've done it very well; **no me siento bien** I don't feel well; **'¿cómo están tus padres?' - 'muy bien, gracias'** 'how are your parents?' -'very well, thank you'; **¡bien hecho!** well done!; **¡muy bien!** (expressing approval) well done!; **2** all right; **¿estás bien en esa silla?** are you all right in that chair?; **así está bien** it's all right like this; **¡está bien!** (expressing agreement) all right!, okay!; **3** **huele bien** it smells nice; **sabe bien** it tastes nice; **4** **hablas muy bien español** you speak very good Spanish; **5** properly; **no funciona bien** it doesn't work properly; **6** **¡bien!** hoorray!

bienestar noun Masc. welfare.

bienvenida[1] noun Fem. welcome; **dar la bienvenida a alguien** to welcome somebody.

bienvenido/bienvenida[2] adjective welcome; **¡bienvenido!** welcome!; **aquí siempre sois**

a
b
c
d
e
f
g
h
i
j
k
l
m
n
ñ
o
p
q
r
s
t
u
v
w
x
y
z

bienvenidos you're always welcome here.

bigote *noun Masc.* moustache.

bikini *noun Masc.* bikini.

bilingüe *adjective* bilingual.

billar *noun Masc.* **1** billiards; **2** pool; **3** snooker.

billares *plural noun Masc.* amusement arcade.

billete *noun Masc.* **1** note (*money*); **un billete de cincuenta euros** a fifty euro note; **2** ticket; **un billete de tren** a train ticket; **un billete sencillo/un billete de ida** a single ticket; **un billete de ida y vuelta** a return ticket.

billetera *noun Masc./Fem.* wallet.

billetero *noun Masc.* SEE **billetera.**

biografía *noun Fem.* biography.

biología *noun Fem.* biology.

biólogo/bióloga *noun Masc./Fem.* biologist.

biquini *noun Masc.* bikini.

bisabuela *noun Fem.* great-grandmother.

bisabuelo *noun Masc.* **1** great-grandfather; **2 mis bisabuelos** my great-grandparents.

bisnieta *noun Fem.* great-granddaughter.

bisnieto *noun Masc.* **1** great-grandson; **2 mis bisnietos** my great-grandchildren.

bistec *noun Masc.* steak.

bizcocho *noun Masc.* sponge cake.

blanco[1] *noun Masc.* **1** white; **2** target; **dar en el blanco** to hit the target.

blanco[2]**/blanca** *adjective* white.

blando/blanda *adjective* **1** soft; **un colchón blando** a soft mattress; **la mantequilla se ha puesto blanda** the butter's gone soft; **2** tender (*meat*); **3** soft (*person*).

bloc *noun Masc.* writing pad.

bloque *noun Masc.* block; **un bloque de pisos** a block of flats.

bloquear *verb* [17] to block; **una muchedumbre nos bloqueaba el camino** a crowd was blocking our way.

blusa *noun Fem.* blouse.

bobo/boba *adjective* (*informal*) silly; **eres bobo** you are silly.

boca *noun Fem.* **1** mouth; **no abrió la boca en toda la tarde** he didn't say a word all afternoon; **2 una boca de metro** an entrance to the underground; **una boca de incendios** a fire hydrant; **una boca de riego** an irrigation hydrant; **3 boca arriba** face up (*card or photograph*); **pon el vaso boca arriba** put the glass the right way up; **túmbate boca arriba** lie on your back; **4 boca abajo** (*card or photograph*) face down; upside down; **estaba tumbado boca abajo** he was lying face down; **★ quedarse con la boca abierta** to be flabbergasted.

bocacalle *noun Fem.* side street; **es la segunda bocacalle a la derecha** it's the second turning on the right.

bocadillo *noun Masc.* **1** baguette sandwich; **un bocadillo de queso** a cheese baguette; **2** speech bubble.

bocado noun Masc. **1** mouthful (of food); **2** bite to eat.

bocata noun Fem. sandwich.

bocatería noun Fem. sandwich bar.

bochorno noun Masc. **1** hoy hace bochorno it's really muggy today; **2** embarrassment; ¡qué bochorno pasamos! we were so embarrassed!; fue un bochorno it was really embarrassing.

bocina noun Fem. horn (of a car).

boda noun Fem. wedding; bodas de plata silver wedding; bodas de oro golden wedding.

bodega noun Fem. **1** wine merchant's; **2** cellar; **3** wine bar.

bofetada noun Fem. slap.

bofetón noun Masc. slap.

boina noun Fem. beret.

bola noun Fem. **1** ball; una bola de nieve a snowball; una bola de billar a billiard ball; **2** scoop (of ice cream); **3** (informal) fib; contar bolas to tell fibs.

bolera noun Fem. bowling alley.

boletín noun Masc. **1** bulletin; boletín informativo news bulletin; boletín meteorológico weather report; **2** school report.

boleto noun Masc. **1** ticket (for a raffle or lottery); **2** coupon (football pools).

boli noun Masc. (informal) (ballpoint) pen.

bolígrafo noun Masc. ballpoint pen.

Bolivia noun Fem. Bolivia.

boliviano/boliviana noun Masc., Fem., adjective Bolivian.

bollo noun Masc. bun.

bolsa noun Fem. **1** bag; una bolsa de palomitas a bag of popcorn; una bolsa de plástico a plastic bag; una bolsa de viaje a travel bag; una bolsa de la basura a bin liner; mi bolsa de la compra my shopping bag; **2** la Bolsa (de valores) the stock exchange.

bolsillo noun Masc. pocket; un diccionario de bolsillo a pocket dictionary; libro de bolsillo paperback book.

bolso noun Masc. handbag; me robaron el bolso they stole my handbag; bolso de mano/bolso de viaje overnight bag.

bomba noun Fem. **1** bomb; pusieron una bomba en un restaurante they planted a bomb in a restaurant; lanzar una bomba to drop a bomb; la bomba atómica the atomic bomb; ★ pasarlo bomba to have a terrific time; **2** pump; una bomba de bicicleta a bicycle pump; una bomba de agua a water pump.

bombero/bombera noun Masc./ Fem. firefighter.

bombilla noun Fem. light bulb; se ha fundido la bombilla the bulb's gone.

bombón noun Masc. chocolate; una caja de bombones a box of chocolates.

bonachón/bonachona adjective (informal) kind.

bondad noun Fem. kindness.

bonito/bonita adjective **1** pretty; es una chica muy bonita she's a very pretty girl; un pueblo muy bonito a very pretty village; **2** nice; ropa bonita nice clothes.

bono noun Masc. voucher.

boquiabierto/boquiabierta adjective astonished; me quedé boquiabierto I was astonished.

bordado noun Masc. embroidery.

bordar verb [17] to embroider.

borde noun Masc. **1** edge; me di con el borde de la mesa I bumped myself on the edge of the table; se acercó al borde del andén he went up to the edge of the platform; **2** rim (of a glass or cup); **3** llenar algo hasta el borde to fill something to the brim; **4** el borde del río the river bank; **5** al borde de la guerra on the brink of war; al borde de las lágrimas on the verge of tears.

borde adjective (informal) stroppy; se puso muy borde conmigo he got very stoppy with me.

bordear verb [17] to go round (the edge of something); bordeamos el lago we went round the lake.

bordillo noun Masc. kerb.

bordo noun Masc. a bordo on board; subimos a bordo we went on board.

borrachera noun Fem. cogerse una borrachera to get drunk.

borracho/borracha noun Masc./Fem. drunk.

borracho adjective drunk; estaban borrachos they were drunk.

borrador noun Masc. **1** rough draft; hacedlo primero en borrador do it in rough first; papel de borrador rough paper; **2** board rubber (eraser).

borrar verb [17] **1** to rub out (a pencil mark or word); **2** to erase (a track or tape); **3** to clean (the blackboard).

borrarse reflexive verb [17] to fade; se ha borrado el nombre the name has faded.

borrasca noun Fem. **1** area of low pressure; **2** storm.

borrón noun blot.

borroso/borrosa adjective **1** blurred (image or photograph); **2** vague (memory).

bosque noun Masc. **1** wood; **2** forest; el bosque ecuatorial the tropical rainforest.

bostezar verb [22] to yawn.

bota noun Fem. boot; botas de esquiar ski boots; botas de agua wellingtons.

botadura noun Fem. launch (of ship).

botánica[1] noun Fem. botany.

botánico/botánica[2] adjective Masc./Fem. botanical.

botar verb [17] to launch (a ship).

botavara noun Fem. (of boat) boom.

bote noun Masc. **1** boat; un bote de pesca a fishing boat; un bote de remos a rowing boat; un bote salvavidas a lifeboat; **2** jar; un bote de aceitunas a jar of olives; **3** can; un bote de barniz a can of varnish; **4** jump; **pegar un bote** to jump; **pegué un bote de alegría** I jumped for joy.

botella *noun Fem.* bottle.

botijo *noun Masc.* drinking jug (*with a long spout: with practice you can drink the water as it spurts out in an arc*).

botiquín *noun Masc.* medicine cabinet; **botiquín de primeros auxilios** first aid kit.

botón *noun Masc.* button (*on a garment or a machine*); **se me ha caído un botón** I've lost a button; **coser un botón** to sew on a button; **para encender la tele tienes que apretar este botón** to switch on the television you have to press this button; **el botón de grabar** the record button.

boxeador/boxeadora *noun Masc./Fem.* boxer.

boxear *verb* [17] to box.

boxeo *noun Masc.* boxing; **un combate de boxeo** a boxing match.

bragas *plural noun Fem.* knickers, panties; **un par de bragas** a pair of knickers.

bragueta *noun Fem.* flies (*in trousers*).

brasileño/brasileña *noun Masc./Fem.*, *adjective* Brazilian.

bravo/brava *adjective* fierce (*animal*).

bravo *exclamation* ¡bravo! well done!, bravo!

brazo *noun Masc.* arm; **me cogió del brazo** he took me by the arm; **iban del brazo** they were arm in

arm; **cruza**... your arm... **brazos** he... his arms; **yo**... **brazos** I was ca... my arms; **el brazo**... arm of the sofa; ★ **co**... **abiertos** with open arm... **brazo derecho de alguien**... somebody's right-hand man/ woman.

brécol *noun Masc.* broccoli.

breve *adjective* short; **una pausa breve** a short pause.

brevemente *adective* briefly.

brezo *noun Masc.* heather.

bribón/bribona *noun Masc./Fem.* rascal.

bricolaje *noun Masc.* DIY.

brillante *noun Masc.* diamond.

brillante *adjective* **1** shiny; **2** bright (*light or colour*).

brillar *verb* [17] **1** to shine; **2** to sparkle.

brindar *verb* [17] to toast.

brindis *noun Masc.* toast; **hacer un brindis por alguien** to drink a toast to somebody.

brisa *noun Fem.* breeze.

británico/británica *noun Masc./ Fem.* British man/woman; **los británicos** the British.

británico *adjective* British.

brocha *noun Fem.* **1** paintbrush; **2 brocha de afeitar** shaving brush.

broche *noun Masc.* brooch.

broma *noun Fem.* joke; **hacerle/ gastarle una broma a alguien** to play a joke on somebody; **lo he**

brome...

a
b
c
d
e
f

i
j
k
l
m
n
ñ
o
p
q
r
s
t
u
v
w
x
y
z

...**ar**

...**o en broma** I was joking; ...**mas aparte** joking apart; **¡ni en ...oma!** no way!

...omear verb [17] to joke.

...romista noun Masc./Fem.,

...romista adjective **es un bromista/es muy bromista** he's always joking.

bronca noun Fem. (informal)
1 **armar una bronca** to kick up a fuss; **si no me devuelven el dinero, voy a armar una bronca** if they don't give me the money back I'm going to kick up a fuss;
2 telling-off; **echar una bronca a alguien** to tell somebody off; **tu madre te va a echar una buena bronca** your mum's going to give you a good telling-off.

bronceado/bronceada adjective suntanned.

bronceador noun Masc. suntan lotion.

broncearse reflexive verb [17] to get a suntan.

bronquitis noun Fem. bronchitis.

brote noun bud Masc..

bruja noun Fem. witch.

brujo noun Masc. wizard.

brújula noun Fem. compass.

bruma noun Fem. mist.

bruto/bruta adjective 1 ignorant;
2 rude; **es muy bruto, ¡dice unas cosas!** he's very rude, he says such things!; 3 **¡qué bruto! ¡cómo trata a su hijo!** what a brute! what a way to treat his child!.

buceador/buceadora noun Masc./Fem. diver.

bucear verb [17] to dive.

buen adjective SEE **bueno/buena**.

bueno[1] adverb 1 okay; **'¿quieres venir?' – 'bueno'** 'do you want to come?' – 'okay'; 2 **bueno, no importa** well, it doesn't matter; **bueno, no estoy segura** well, I'm not sure; **bueno, ya basta** right, that's enough.

bueno[2]**/buena** adjective ('bueno' becomes 'buen' before a masculine singular noun) 1 good; **es muy buena persona** she's a very good person; **de buena calidad** good quality; **ser bueno para algo** to be good at something; **es muy buena para las matemáticas** she's very good at maths; **es muy buen amigo mío** he's a very good friend of mine; **¡buen viaje!** have a good journey!; 2 **buenos días** good morning; **buenas tardes** good afternoon, good evening; **buenas noches** good evening, goodnight; 3 nice; **hace buen tiempo** the weather is nice; **el pastel estaba muy bueno** the cake was very nice; **¡está buenísimo!** it's delicious!

bufanda noun Fem. scarf.

bufar verb [17] to snort.

bufet noun Masc. buffet.

bufón noun Masc. clown (silly person).

buhardilla noun Fem. attic.

búho noun Masc. owl.

bujía noun Fem. spark plug.

bulto noun Masc. 1 shape; **vi un bulto en la oscuridad** I saw a shape in the darkness; 2 piece of luggage; **¿cuántos bultos llevas?**

how many pieces of luggage do you have?; **3** bag; **yo te llevos los bultos** I'll carry your bags for you; **iba cargada de bultos** she was carrying lots of bags; **4** bulk; **5** lump, swelling (*on the body*).

bungalow noun Masc. cabin, chalet (*in holiday resorts*).

buñuelo noun Masc. fritter.

buque noun Masc. ship; **buque de guerra** warship.

burbuja noun Fem. **1** bubble; **2 una bebida sin burbujas** a still drink; **una bebida con burbujas** a fizzy drink.

burdo/burda adjective coarse.

burlarse reflexive verb [17] **burlarse de alguien** to make fun of somebody; **¡deja de burlarte de mí!** stop making fun of me!

burocracia noun Fem. bureaucracy.

burrada noun Fem. **¡vaya burrada has dicho!** what a stupid thing to say; **¡no hagas esa burrada!** don't do such a stupid thing; **sólo dijo burradas** he just talked rubbish.

burro[1] noun Masc. **1** donkey; **2 es un burro** he's really stupid.
burro[2]**/burra** noun Masc./Fem. **es un burro** he's really stupid.
burro adjective stupid.

bus noun Masc. (*informal*) bus.

busca noun Fem. search; **ir en busca de algo** to go in search of something.

buscar verb [31] **1** to look for; **¿qué buscas?** what are you looking for?; **mi hermana está buscando trabajo** my sister's looking for a

job; **estoy buscando un ayudante** I'm looking for an assistant; **2** to look; **si no lo encuentras aquí busca en la oficina** if you don't find it here look in the office; **3 ir a buscar algo** to go to pick up something; **mañana iré a buscar mis cosas** I'll go and pick up my things tomorrow; **4 ir a buscar a alguien** to pick somebody up; **yo te iré a buscar al aeropuerto** I'll pick you up at the airport; **5 ir a buscar a alguien** to go to get someone (*the police or a doctor, for example*); **fueron a buscar a un médico enseguida** they went to get a doctor straight away.

búsqueda noun Fem. search.

butaca noun Fem. **1** armchair; **2** seat (*in a cinema or theatre*); **una butaca de patio** a seat in the stalls.

butano noun Masc. butane gas; **una bombona de butano** a bottle of butane gas.

buzo noun Masc. diver.

buzón noun Masc. **1** letterbox; **2** postbox.

Cc

caballa noun Fem. mackerel.

caballero noun Masc.
1 gentleman; **es un verdadero caballero** he's a real gentleman; **2** sir; **caballero, ¿me deja pasar?** could you let me through, sir?; **3 caballeros** Gents (*toilets*), men's department (*in a store*).

a b **caballo** noun Masc. **1** horse;
montar a caballo to ride a horse;
un caballo de carreras a
racehorse; **2** knight (in chess);
3 horse (in Spanish cards:
equivalent to the queen).

cabaña noun Fem. cabin.

cabecear verb [17] to head (a
ball).

cabecera noun Fem. **1** headboard;
2 head (of table); se sentó a la
cabecera de la mesa he sat at the
head of the table.

cabello noun Masc. hair; tener el
cabello rubio to have blond hair;
cabello rizado curly hair; cabello
liso straight hair.

caber verb [33] **1** caber en to fit
into; es demasiado grande, no
cabe en la caja it's too big, it
doesn't fit into the box; no vamos a
caber en el coche we won't all fit
in the car; **2** aquí ya no cabe nada
más there's no room for anything
else in here; ¿caben estos libros
en la maleta? is there room for
these books in the suitcase?;
3 caber por algo to fit through
something; no cabía por la puerta
it wouldn't fit through the door.

cabeza rapada noun Masc./Fem.
skinhead.

cabeza noun Fem. **1** head; me
duele la cabeza I've got a
headache; asentir con la cabeza
to nod; **2** lavarse la cabeza to
wash your hair; tengo que
lavarme la cabeza I've got to wash
my hair; **3** una cabeza de ajo a
bulb of garlic; **4** tirarse al agua de

cabeza to dive; **5** cabeza abajo
upside down; el cuadro está
cabeza abajo the picture's upside
down; **6** a la cabeza de at the head
of; iban a la cabeza de la
manifestación they were at the
head of the demonstration; ★ está
mal de la cabeza he's not right in
the head.

cabina noun Fem. **1** cab (of a lorry);
2 cockpit (of a plane); **3** cabin (on a
plane or boat); **4** booth (in a
language lab); **5** cabina de
teléfonos telephone box.

cabo noun Masc. **1** corporal;
2 cape; cabo de Buena Esperanza
Cape of Good Hope; **3** al cabo de
after; al cabo de tres semanas
after three weeks; **4** end (of a
length of rope or piece of string);
★ atar cabos to put two and two
together.

cabra noun Fem. goat.

cabré, **cabría**, etc. verb SEE
caber.

cacahuete noun Masc. peanut.

cacao noun Masc. **1** cocoa (drink);
2 lipsalve.

cacerola noun Fem. saucepan.

cachete noun Masc. slap.

cachorro/cachorra noun Masc./
Fem. puppy.

cada adjective **1** each; un alumno
de cada clase a pupil from each
class; hay diez para cada uno
there are ten each; **2** every; me
llaman cada día they phone me
every day; cada tres días every
three days; **3** cada vez más more
and more; se parecen cada vez

43

más they look more and more alike; **cada vez menos** less and less; **cada vez mejor** better and better; **lo hace cada vez mejor** she's getting better and better all the time; **cada vez peor** worse and worse.

cadena noun Fem. **1** chain; **una cadena de hierro** an iron chain; **una cadena antirrobo** a bicycle lock; **una cadena de supermercados** a supermarket chain; **2** channel (on the TV); **lo ponen en la segunda cadena** they're showing it on Channel Two; **3** station (on the radio); **4 cadena musical** hi-fi system; **5 cadenas** snow chains; **6 tirar de la cadena** to flush the toilet; **7 condenar a alguien a cadena perpetua** sentence somebody to life imprisonment.

cadera noun Fem. hip.

caer verb [34] **1** to fall; **el jarrón cayó al suelo** the vase fell to the ground; **2 dejar caer algo** to drop something (on purpose); **dejé caer la bandeja** I dropped the tray; **3 se dejó caer en el sofá** he flopped into the sofa; **4** (informal) **tu hermano me cae bien** I like your brother; **Ana me cae fatal** I can't stand Ana.

caerse reflexive verb [34] **1** to fall over; **tropecé y me caí** I tripped and fell over; **2** to fall; **casi se cayó del tejado** he almost fell from the roof; **me caí por las escaleras** I fell down the stairs; **se cayó de la bici** he fell off his bike; **3 se me cayó el plato** I dropped the plate

(accidentally); **4 se le ha caído un diente** he's lost a tooth; **se me está cayendo el pelo** I'm losing my hair.

café noun Masc. **1** coffee; **¿quieres un café?** do you want a cup of coffee?; **un café solo** a black coffee; **un café con leche** a white coffee; **un café cortado** a coffee with a dash of milk; **café descafeinado** decaffeinated coffee; **2** (place) cafe.

cafetera noun Fem. coffee maker.

cafetería noun Fem. café.

caído/caída adjective fallen.

caiga, caigo, etc. verb SEE **caer.**

caimán noun Masc. alligator Masc..

caja noun Fem. **1** box; **una caja de cartón** a cardboard box; **caja de las herramientas** toolbox; **caja de cambios** gearbox; **2** crate; **una caja de naranjas** a crate of oranges; **3** checkout (in a supermarket); **pague en caja** pay at the checkout; **4** till (in a shop); **5 una caja fuerte** a safe; **6 caja de ahorros** savings bank.

cajero/cajera noun Masc./Fem. **1** cashier; **2** checkout operator; **3 cajero automático** cash dispenser.

cajón noun Masc. drawer.

calabacín noun Masc. courgette.

calamar noun Masc. squid; **calamares a la romana** squid rings in batter.

calambre noun Masc. **1** cramp; **me dio un calambre** I got cramp; **2** electric shock; **la lámpara me ha**

a
b
c
d
e
f
g
h
i
j
k
l
m
n
ñ
o
p
q
r
s
t
u
v
w
x
y
z

a b c d e f g h i j k l m n ñ o p q r s t u v w x y z

dado calambre the lamp gave me an electric shock.

calamidad noun Fem. disaster.

calavera noun Fem. skull.

calcetín noun Masc. sock; **unos calcetines** a pair of socks.

calcomanía noun Fem. transfer (*sticker*).

calculadora noun Fem. calculator.

calcular verb [17] to calculate, to work out.

caldo noun Masc. **1** stock; **caldo de verdura** vegetable stock; **2** broth.

calefacción noun Fem. heating; **calefacción central** central heating; **calefacción de gas** gas heating.

calendario noun Masc. calendar.

calentador noun Masc. **1** boiler; **2** water heater.

calentar verb [29] **1** to heat (up); **voy a calentar la sopa** I'm going to heat up the soup; **2** to give off heat; **esta estufa calienta mucho** this heater gives off a lot of heat; **3** calentar los músculos to warm up (*before sport or dancing*).

calentarse reflexive verb [29] to heat up.

calidad noun Fem. quality; **materiales de calidad** high quality materials; **productos de mala calidad** poor quality products.

calienta, caliento, etc. verb SEE **calentar**.

caliente adjective **1** hot; **los platos están muy calientes** the

plates are very hot; **2** warm; **un baño caliente** a hot bath; **en el salón se está más caliente** it's warmer in the living-room.

calificación noun Fem. mark; **obtuvo buenas calificaciónes** he got good marks.

callado/callada adjective quiet; **¡estate callado!** be quiet!

callar verb [17] to be quiet; **calla, no oigo** be quiet, I can't hear; **¡calla ya!** shut up!

callarse reflexive verb [17] to go quiet; **al verla todos se callaron** everybody went quiet when they saw her; **¡cállate!** shut up!

calle noun Fem. street; **una calle cortada** a cul-de-sac; **una calle de sentido único** a one way street (*when writing an address, the word 'calle' is abbreviated to 'C/'*).

callejón noun Masc. alley; **un callejón sin salida** a blind alley.

calma noun Fem. calm; **hazlo con calma** do it calmly; **mantener la calma** to keep calm; **la ciudad está en calma** the city is calm.

calmar verb [17] to calm down.

calmarse reflexive verb [17] to calm down; **después de un rato me calmé** I calmed down after a while.

calor noun Masc. **1** heat; **el calor de la estufa** the heat of the stove; **2** hoy hace mucho calor it's very hot today; **¡qué calor hace!** it's so hot!; **3** tener calor to be hot; **tengo mucho calor** I'm very hot.

caluroso/calurosa adjective hot (*a day or place*).

calvo/calva *adjective* bald; **quedarse calvo** to go bald.

calzado *noun Masc.* footwear.

calzar *verb* [22] **¿qué número calzas?** what shoe size do you take?

calzoncillos *plural noun Masc.* underpants; **unos calzoncillos** a pair of underpants.

cama *noun Fem.* bed; **una cama individual** a single bed; **una cama doble/una cama de matrimonio** a double bed; **camas gemelas** twin beds; **una cama elástica** a trampoline; **hacer la cama** to make the bed; **¡a la cama!** off to bed!

cámara *noun Fem.* camera; **una cámara de fotos** a camera; **una cámara de vídeo** a video camera.

camarera *noun Fem.* 1 waitress; 2 **camarera de habitación** chambermaid.

camarero *noun Masc.* waiter.

camarón *noun Masc.* shrimp.

cambiar *verb* [17] 1 to change; **no has cambiado** you haven't changed; **cambiar libras a euros** to change pounds into euros; 2 **cambiar de** to change; **ha cambiado de trabajo** he's changed his job; **cambiar de idea** to change your mind; **cambiar de canal** to change channels; 3 to exchange; **quiero cambiar estos zapatos** I want to exchange these shoes; 4 **cambiar de casa** to move house; 5 to swap; **te cambio mi pluma por esa cinta** I'll swap my pen for that tape.

cambiarse *reflexive verb* [17] 1 to get changed; **voy a cambiarme y ahora vuelvo** I'm going to get changed, I'll be back in a minute; **voy a cambiarme de ropa** I'm going to change my clothes; 2 **cambiarse de sitio** to change places.

cambio *noun Masc.* 1 change; **un cambio a mejor** a change for the better; **ha habido un cambio de planes** there's been a change of plan; 2 exchange; **no se admiten cambios** goods will not be exchanged; 3 change; **¿tienes cambio?** do you have any change?; **me dieron mal el cambio** they gave me the wrong change; **'cambio'** 'bureau de change'; 4 **a cambio de** in return for; **a cambio de información** in return for information.

camello *noun Masc.* camel.

caminar *verb* [17] to walk; **me gusta caminar** I like walking.

caminata *noun Fem.* long walk.

camino *noun Masc.* 1 road; **todos los caminos están cortados** all the roads are closed; **el camino al éxito** the road to success; 2 path; **un camino por el bosque** a path through the forest; 3 way; **¿puede indicarme el camino a la estación?** could you tell me the way to the station?; **yo sé el camino** I know the way.

camión *noun Masc.* lorry; **el camión de la mudanza** the removal van; **un camión cisterna** a petrol tanker.

a
b
c
d
e
f
g
h
i
j
k
l
m
n
ñ
o
p
q
r
s
t
u
v
w
x
y
z

a

camionero/camionera noun Masc./Fem. lorry driver.

camioneta noun Fem. van.

camisa noun Fem. shirt.

camiseta noun Fem. **1** T-shirt; **2** vest.

camisón noun Masc. nightdress.

campamento noun Masc. camp; **se han ido de campamento** they've gone camping.

campana noun Fem. bell; **tocar la campana** to ring the bell.

campaña noun Fem. campaign; **campaña electoral** electoral campaign.

campeón/campeona noun Masc./Fem. champion.

campeonato noun Masc. championship.

campesino/campesina noun Masc./Fem. **1** country person; **2** peasant.

camping noun Masc. campsite; **ir de camping** to go camping.

campista noun Masc./Fem. camper.

campo noun Masc. **1** country; **una casa en el campo** a house in the country; **2** countryside; **el campo está muy bonito** the countryside looks very beautiful; **3** field; **un campo de trigo** a field of wheat; **4 un campo de fútbol** a football pitch.

cana noun Fem. white hair; **le están saliendo canas** he's going grey.

Canadá noun Masc. Canada.

canadiense noun Masc./Fem., adjective Canadian.

canal noun Masc. **1** channel (on the TV); **no cambies de canal** don't change channels; **2** channel (water); **el canal de la Mancha** the English Channel; **3** canal; **el canal de Panamá** the Panama Canal.

canario[1] noun Masc. canary.

canario[3]**/canaria** adjective of/ from the Canary Islands.

canario noun Masc./Fem. Canary Islander.

canasta noun Fem. basket.

canasto noun Masc. basket (usually with a lid).

cancelar verb [17] to cancel.

cáncer[1] noun Masc. cancer; **tiene cáncer** he's got cancer; **cáncer de mama** breast cancer; **cáncer de piel** skin cancer.

cáncer[2] noun Masc./Fem. Cancer; **soy Cáncer** I'm Cancer.

Cáncer noun Masc. Cancer.

cancha noun Fem. court; **una cancha de baloncesto** a basketball court.

canción noun Fem. song; **canción de cuna** lullaby.

candelabro noun Masc. candlestick; **un candelabro dorado** a brass candlestick.

candidato/candidata noun Masc./Fem. candidate.

canela noun Fem. cinnamon; **canela en rama** stick cinnamon; **canela en polvo** ground cinnamon.

cangrejo noun Masc. **1** crab; **2** crayfish.

canguro[1] noun Masc. kangaroo.

canguro[2] noun Masc./Fem. babysitter.

canica noun Fem. marble; **jugar a las canicas** to play marbles.

canoa noun Fem. canoe.

cansado/cansada adjective **1** tired; **estoy muy cansado** I'm very tired; **2** tiring; **esperar es muy cansado** waiting's very tiring.

cansar verb [17] **1** to make tired; **le cansa andar** walking makes him tired; **2** to be tiring; **es un trabajo que cansa mucho** it's a very tiring job; **3** to be boring; **esta música cansa un poco** this music's a bit boring.

cansarse reflexive verb [17] **1** to get tired; **se cansa muy fácilmente** he gets tired very easily; **se me cansa la vista** my eyes get tired; **2** to get bored; **me canso de repetir siempre lo mismo** I get bored always repeating the same thing.

Cantábrico noun Masc. **el mar Cantábrico** the Bay of Biscay.

cantante noun Masc./Fem. singer.

cantar verb [17] to sing.

cantera noun Fem. quarry.

cantidad noun Fem. **1** amount; **una enorme cantidad de nieve** a huge amount of snow; **¿qué cantidad de vasos necesitamos?** how many glasses do we need?; **es increíble la cantidad de aceite gastas** it's incredible how much

oil you use; **3** tanta cantidad so much; **no pongas tanta cantidad de leche** don't put so much milk in; **4** cantidad de/cantidades de lots of; **había cantidad de gente** there were lots of people; **con grandes cantidades de flores** with lots of flowers; **5** sum; **una cantidad importante de dinero** a considerable sum of money.

cantina noun Fem. **1** cafeteria; **2** canteen.

caña noun Fem. **1** cane; **caña de azúcar** sugar cane; **2** caña de pescar** fishing rod.

cañería noun Fem. pipe.

cañón noun Masc. cannon.

capa noun Fem. **1** layer; **la capa de ozono** the ozone layer; **2** cape, cloak.

capacidad noun Fem. capacity.

capaz adjective **1** capable; **es capaz de cualquier cosa** he's capable of anything; **soy capaz de no ir** I'm quite capable of not going; **2** able; **no fueron capaces de darme una respuesta** they weren't able to give me an answer.

capital noun Fem. **1** capital; **la capital de España** the capital of Spain; **2** Valencia capital** the city of Valencia (as opposed to the province).

capitán/capitana noun Masc./Fem. captain (in sports).

capítulo noun Masc. **1** chapter; **2** episode (of a TV series).

capó noun Masc. bonnet (of a car).

a

b

c

d

e

f

g

h

i

j

k

l

m

n

ñ

o

p

q

r

s

t

u

v

w

x

y

z

capricornio noun Masc./Fem. Capricorn; **es capricornio** he's Capricorn.

Capricornio noun Masc. Capricorn.

cara noun Fem. **1** face; **tiene una cara bonita** she has a pretty face; **tienes cara de cansada** you look tired; **al oírlo puso cara de sorpresa** he looked surprised when he heard it; **tu hermana tenía mala cara** your sister looked ill; ★ **¡qué cara más dura tienes!** (informal) you've got some nerve! (literally: what a hard face you have!); **2** side; **la otra cara del disco** the other side of the record; **3** **¿cara o cruz?** heads or tails?

caracol noun Masc. **1** snail; **2** winkle.

carácter noun Masc. **1** character; **el carácter Latino** the Latin character; **2** **tiene muy mal carácter** he's got a very bad temper; **es una persona de buen carácter** she's a good-natured person; **3** **no tiene mucho carácter** he doesn't have much personality.

caramba exclamation **1** good heavens!; **2** damn it!.

caramelo noun Masc. **1** sweet; **un caramelo de menta** a mint; **2** caramel.

caravana noun Fem. **1** tailback; **hay caravana para entrar en Sevilla** there's a tailback into Seville; **una caravana de diez kilómetros** a ten-kilometre tailback; **2** caravan.

carbón noun Masc. coal; **carbón vegetal** charcoal.

cárcel noun Fem. jail; **meter a alguien en la cárcel** to put somebody in jail.

cardíaco/cardíaca adjective heart; **un ataque cardíaco** a heart attack.

careta noun Fem. mask.

carga noun Fem. **1** burden; **no quiero ser una carga para nadie** I don't want to be a burden on anybody; **2** freight, cargo; **3** load; **carga máxima** maximum load; **4** refill (for a pen); **5** **¡a la carga!** charge!

cargado/cargada adjective **1** loaded; **la pistola estaba cargada** the gun was loaded; **vas muy cargada** you're loaded down; **iba cargado de paquetes** he was loaded down with parcels; **2** **un café cargado** a strong coffee.

cargar verb [28] **1** to load (a lorry or weapon); **2** to fill (a pen).

cargo noun Masc. **1** position; **un cargo de responsabilidad** a position of responsibility; **2** **a cargo de** in charge of; **estoy a cargo del departamento** I'm in charge of the department; **dejó los niños a mi cargo** she left the children in my care.

Caribe noun Masc. **el Caribe** the Caribbean; **el mar Caribe** the Caribbean Sea.

caribeño/caribeña noun Masc., Fem., adjective Caribbean.

cariño noun Masc. **1** affection; **tenerle cariño a** to be fond of; **les**

tengo cariño I'm fond of them; **tomarle cariño a** to become fond of; **les tomó cariño** he became fond of them; **2 con cariño, Maya** love, Maya (*in letters*); **3 dear; ven, cariño** come here, dear.

cariñoso/cariñosa *adjective* **1** affectionate, loving (*a person*); **2** warm; **un cariñoso saludo** warm regards (*in a letter*).

carmín *noun Masc.* lipstick.

carnaval *noun Masc.* carnival.

carné, carnet *noun Masc.* card; **carné de identidad** identity card; **carné de estudiante** student card; **carné de conducir** driving licence.

carne *noun Fem.* **1** meat; **carne de vaca** beef; **carne de cerdo** pork; **carne de cordero** lamb; **carne de ternera** veal; **2** flesh.

carnicería *noun Fem.* butcher's.

carnicero/carnicera *noun Masc./Fem.* butcher.

carnívoro/carnívora *adjective* carnivorous.

caro/cara *adjective* expensive; **cuesta muy caro** it's very expensive; **eso lo vas a pagar caro** you're going to pay dearly for this.

carpeta *noun Fem.* folder; **carpeta de anillas** ring binder.

carpintero/carpintera *noun Masc./Fem.* carpenter.

carrera *noun Fem.* **1** race; **una carrera automovilística** a car race; **las carreras de caballos** the races; **una carrera de obstáculos** a steeplechase; **una carrera de** **relevos** a relay race; **2 echar una carrera** to have a race (*against somebody*); **echamos una carrera** let's have a race; **te echo una carrera** I'll race you; **3 echar una carrera** to run; **eché una carrera y alcancé el autobús** I ran and got the bus; **4** degree course; **hacer una carrera** to study for a degree; **no quiero hacer una carrera** I don't want to go to university; **está haciendo la carrera de medicina** she's studying medicine.

carreta *noun Fem.* cart.

carretera *noun Fem.* road; **carretera nacional** A-road; **carretera comarcal** B-road; **carretera de circunvalación** ringroad.

carretilla *noun Fem.* wheelbarrow.

carril *noun Masc.* lane; **carril bus** bus lane.

carrito *noun Masc.* trolley.

carro *noun Masc.* cart.

carta *noun Fem.* **1** letter; **mandar una carta** to send a letter; **echar una carta al correo** to post a letter; **una carta certificada** a registered letter; **2** menu; **¿nos puede traer la carta, por favor?** could you bring us the menu, please?; **3** card (*in a pack*); **jugar a las cartas** to play cards.

cartel *noun Masc.* **1** poster (*for publicity*); **2** sign; **¿qué dice el cartel?** what does the sign say?

cartelera *noun Fem.* **la cartelera de cine** 'what's on' at the cinema; **la obra lleva tres años en**

cartelera the play has been running for three years; **la película sigue en cartelera** the film is still showing.

cartera noun Fem. **1** wallet; **2** briefcase; **3** satchel.

carterista noun Masc./Fem. pickpocket.

cartero/cartera noun Masc./Fem. postman/postwoman.

cartón noun Masc. cardboard.

casa noun Fem. **1** house; **una casa adosada** a semi-detached house; **una casa de campo** a country house; **una casa de huéspedes** guesthouse; **2** flat; **su casa está en la quinta planta** her flat's on the fifth floor; **3** home; **no están en casa** they're not at home; **estoy pasando unos días en casa de Juan** I'm staying at Juan's for a few days.

casado/casada adjective married; **estar casado/ser casado** to be married.

casarse reflexive verb [17] to get married; **se casó con mi primo** she married my cousin.

cascar verb [31] to crack.

cáscara noun Fem. **1** peel; **2** shell.

casco noun Masc. **1** helmet; **un casco protector** a safety helmet, crash helmet; **2** hoof (of a horse); **3** empty bottle; **guardo los cascos para reciclarlos** I keep the empty bottles for recycling; **4** cascos headphones.

caserío noun Masc. **1** farmhouse; **2** hamlet.

casero/casera noun Masc./Fem. landlord/landlady.

casero adjective homemade.

caseta noun Fem. **1** hut (for a watchman or guard); **2** stand (in an exhibition); **3** kennel.

casete[1] noun Masc. cassette recorder.

casete[2] noun Masc. or Fem. cassette.

casi adverb **1** almost; **casi me pierdo** I almost got lost; **¡casi, casi!** almost!; **2** hardly; **casi no había gente** there was hardly anybody there; **casi nunca** hardly ever.

casilla noun Fem. **1** square (in a crossword); **2** box (on a form).

caso noun Masc. **1** case; **en ese caso** in that case; **en caso de accidente** in case of accident; **en todo caso/en cualquier caso** in any case; **en el peor de los casos** if the worst comes to the worst; **2 el caso es que ... the** thing is ...; **3** hacer caso de to pay attention to; **haz caso de las señales** pay attention to the signs; **no me hace caso** he pays no attention to me.

cassette noun Masc. or Fem. cassette.

castaña[1] noun Fem. chestnut.

castaño/castaña[2] adjective chestnut brown.

castañuelas plural noun Fem. castanets.

castellano[1] noun Masc. **1** Castilian; **2** Castilian Spanish (as opposed to other varieties of Spanish, particularly those of

*Spanish-speaking America;
Castilian Spanish generally means
the Spanish spoken in Spain).*

castellano[2]/**castellana** *noun
Masc./Fem., adjective* Castilian.

castigar *verb* [28] **1** to punish;
2 castigar a alguien sin salir to
ground somebody; **3** to give a
detention (*at school*); **la profesora
me dejó castigado** the teacher
gave me a detention.

castigo *noun Masc.* punishment.

Castilla *noun Fem.* Castile.

castillo *noun Masc.* castle; **castillo
de arena** sandcastle.

casualidad *noun Fem.* **1** chance;
de casualidad by chance; **lo vi por
casualidad** I saw it by chance; **2 da
la casualidad de que ...** it so
happens that ...; **dio la casualidad
de que llevaba las señas en mi
bolso** it so happened that I had the
address in my bag; **3 ¡qué
casualidad!** what a coincidence!.

catalán[1] *noun Masc.* Catalan (*the
language*).

catalán[2]/**catalana** *noun Masc./
Fem., adjective* Catalan.

Cataluña *noun Fem.* Catalonia.

catarata *noun Fem.* **1** waterfall;
2 cataract (*of the eye*).

catarro *noun Masc.* cold; **coger un
catarro** to catch a cold.

catear *verb* [17] (*informal*) to fail;
he cateado las mates I've failed
maths; **me han cateado en inglés**
the English teacher has failed me.

catedral *noun Fem.* cathedral.

categoría *noun Fem.* **1** category;
2 de primera categoría first class;
un hotel de mucha categoría a
top-quality hotel; **un restaurante
de poca categoría** a second-rate
restaurant.

católico/católica *noun Masc./
Fem., adjective* Catholic.

catorce *number* **1** fourteen; **tiene
catorce años** he's fourteen (years
old); **2** fourteenth (*in dates*); **el
catorce de mayo** the fourteenth of
May.

caucho *noun Masc.* rubber.

causa *noun Fem.* **1** cause; **sin
causa** without cause; **2 a causa
de** because of; **a causa de esto lo
despidieron** they sacked him
because of it.

causar *verb* [17] to cause.

cautiverio *noun Masc.* captivity;
mantener a alguien en cautiverio
to keep someone in captivity .

cautivo/cautiva *noun* prisoner.

cava *noun Masc.* cava (*sparkling
wine*).

cavar *verb* [17] to dig.

caverna *noun Fem.* cave.

cayendo SEE **caer**.

caza *noun Fem.* hunting; **ir de caza**
to go hunting.

cazar *verb* [22] to hunt.

cazuela *noun Fem.* casserole.

cebada *noun* barley *Fem.*

cebolla *noun Fem.* onion.

cebolleta *noun Fem.* spring onion.

cebollino *noun Masc.* chives .

ceder *verb* [18] **1** to give in;
finalmente cedí I finally gave in;

2 ceder el paso to give way; **3 le cedí mi asiento a un anciano** I gave up my seat to an elderly man.

ceguera noun Fem. blindness.

ceja noun Fem. eyebrow.

celda noun Fem. cell (in a prison).

celebración noun Fem. celebration.

celebrar verb [17] **1** to celebrate; **2** to hold (a meeting).
celebrarse reflexive verb [17] to take place; **la boda se celebró el sábado pasado** the wedding took place last Saturday.

célebre adjective famous.

celo noun Masc. Sellotape™.

celos plural noun Masc. **1** jealousy; **2 tener celos de alguien** to be jealous of somebody; **tiene celos de su hermana pequeña** she's jealous of her little sister; **3 darle celos a alguien** to make somebody feel jealous; **lo hace para darte celos** he does it to make you feel jealous.

celoso/celosa adjective jealous.

cementerio noun Masc. cemetery.

cemento noun Masc. cement.

cena noun Fem. **1** dinner (evening meal); **2** supper; **¿qué hay de cena?** what's for supper?

cenar verb [17] to have dinner; **normalmente cenamos a las nueve** we normally have dinner at nine; **salimos a cenar fuera** we went out for dinner.

cenicero noun Masc. ashtray.

ceñido/ceñida adjective tight; **una camiseta muy ceñida** a very tight T-shirt.

ceniza noun Fem. ash.

ceño noun Masc. **fruncir el ceño** to frown.

centavo noun Masc. **1** one hundredth; **2** cent (in the dollar system).

centenar noun Masc. hundred; **un centenar de libros** (about) a hundred books; **centenares de cartas** hundreds of letters.

centenario noun Masc. centenary.

centeno noun Masc. rye.

centésima noun Fem. hundredth; **una centésima de segundo** a hundredth of a second.

centésimo/centésima[2] adjective hundredth.

centígrado adjective centigrade.

centímetro noun Masc. centimetre.

céntimo noun **1** cent (in the euro system); **el euro se divide en cien céntimos** the euro is divided into a hundred cents; **2** penny; **no tengo ni un céntimo** I am penniless.

central noun Fem. **1** head office; **2 central telefónica** telephone exchange; **central de correos** general post office; **3** power station; **central nuclear** nuclear power station.

central adjective central.

céntrico/céntrica adjective central; **un barrio céntrico** an area in the centre of town.

centrifugar *verb* [28] to spin-dry.

centro *noun Masc.* **1** centre; **el centro de la ciudad** the town/city centre; **un centro cultural** a cultural centre; **estaba justo en el centro** it was right in the middle; **2 un centro comercial** a shopping mall.

cepillar *verb* [17] to brush. **cepillarse** *reflexive verb* [17] to brush; **cepillarse los dientes** to brush your teeth; **cepillarse el pelo** to brush your hair.

cepillo *noun Masc.* brush; **un cepillo de dientes** a toothbrush; **un cepillo del pelo** a hairbrush.

cera *noun Fem.* wax.

cerámica *noun Fem.* pottery.

cerca *adverb* **1** near, close; **viven aquí cerca** they live near here; **ponlos cerca el uno del otro** put them close to each other; **2** nearby; **mi casa está cerca** my house is nearby; **3 cerca de** near; **se sentó cerca de mí** he sat near me; **está cerca de la estación** it's near the station; **vive muy cerca de mí** she lives very near me; **4 cerca de** almost; **cerca de diez mil personas** almost ten thousand people.

cercanía *noun Fem.* proximity.

cercanías *plural noun Fem.* **1** surrounding area; **Barcelona y sus cercanías** Barcelona and the surrounding area; **en las cercanías del aeropuerto** in the area around the airport; **2** vicinity; **en las cercanías del bar** in the vicinity of the bar.

cercano/cercana *adjective* **1** nearby; **las casas cercanas** the nearby houses; **2 cercano a algo** near something; **los pueblos cercanos al aeropuerto** the villages near the airport; **3** near; **en un futuro cercano** in the near future.

cerdo[1] *noun Masc.* pork; **no como cerdo** I don't eat pork.

cerdo[2]**/cerda** *noun Masc./Fem.* pig.

cereales *plural noun Masc.* cereals.

ceremonia *noun Fem.* ceremony.

cereza *noun Fem.* cherry.

cerilla *noun Fem.* match.

cero *noun Masc.* **1** zero; **tres grados bajo cero** three degrees below zero; **mi prefijo en Londres es cero, dos, cero** my dialling code in London is 020; **2** love (*in tennis*); **3** nil (*in football*).

cerrado/cerrada *adjective* **1** closed; **la ventana está cerrada** the window's closed; **mi coche está cerrado con llave** locked; **cerrado con cerrojo** bolted; **el grifo está cerrado** the tap's turned off.

cerradura *noun Fem.* **1** lock; **2 el ojo de la cerradura** the keyhole.

cerrar *verb* [29] **1** to close; **cierrra la puerta** close the door; **cerramos a las ocho** we close at eight; **han cerrado la fábrica** the factory has been closed; **2 cerrar algo de un portazo** to slam something; **cerró la puerta de un portazo** he slammed the door shut; **3 cerrar con llave** to lock; **no te olvides de**

a
b
c
d
e
f
g
h
i
j
k
l
m
n
ñ
o
p
q
r
s
t
u
v
w
x
y
z

cerrar con llave don't forget to lock up; **4 cerrar con cerrojo** to bolt; **5 cerrar el grifo** to turn off the tap; **6 cierra la botella** put the top on the bottle; **¿has cerrado el frasco?** have you put the lid on the jar?; **7 cerrar una carta** to seal a letter.

cerrarse *reflexive verb* [29] to close; **la puerta se cerró** the door closed; **cerrarse de un portazo** to slam shut.

certificado¹ *noun Masc.* certificate.

certificado²/certificada *adjective* registered (*a letter or parcel*).

certificar *verb* [31] to certify.

cervecería *noun Fem.* **1** brewery; **2** bar (*selling lots of different beers*).

cerveza *noun Fem.* beer; **¿quieres una cerveza?** do you want a beer?; **cerveza de barril** draught beer; **cerveza negra** stout; **cerveza rubia** lager.

césped *noun Masc.* lawn; **'prohibido pisar el césped'** 'keep off the grass'.

cesta *noun Fem.* **1** basket; **una cesta de mimbre** a wicker basket; **2 una cesta de Navidad** a Christmas hamper.

cesto *noun Masc.* basket.

chalado/chalada *adjective* (*informal*) crazy.

chalé, chalet *noun Masc.* **1** villa; **2** detached house (*on estate*); **3** semi-detached house (*on estate*).

chaleco *noun Masc.* waistcoast; **un chaleco de punto** a sleeveless sweater.

champán *noun Masc.* champagne.

champaña *noun m or Fem.* champagne.

champiñón *noun Masc.* mushroom.

champú *noun Masc.* shampoo.

chanclas *noun Fem.* (*plural*) flip-flops.

chándal *noun Masc.* tracksuit.

chapa *noun Fem.* **1** top (*of a bottle*); **2** badge; **una chapa de policía** a police badge.

chapapote *noun Masc.* oil (*washed up on a beach*).

chaparrón *noun Masc.* downpour.

chaqueta *noun Fem.* jacket; **chaqueta de punto** cardigan.

charca *noun Fem.* pond.

charco *noun Masc.* puddle; **no pises los charcos** don't walk in the puddles.

charcutería *noun Fem.* delicatessen (*specializing in pork products*).

charlar *verb* [17] to chat.

chasco *noun Masc.* disappointment; **me llevé un chasco** I felt really disappointed.

chat *noun Masc.* chatroom.

cheque *noun Masc.* cheque; **extender un cheque** to write out a cheque; **me puedes extender un cheque a mi nombre** you can make out a cheque to me; **un cheque a nombre de Alberto López** a cheque payable to Alberto

López; **cobrar un cheque** to cash a cheque; **un cheque de viaje/un cheque de viajero** a traveller's cheque.

chequeo noun Masc. checkup; **hacerse un chequeo** to have a checkup.

chica noun Fem. girl.

chichón noun Masc. bump; **me di un golpe en la frente y me ha salido un chichón** I banged my forehead and now I've got a bump.

chicle noun Masc. chewing gum; **¿quieres un chicle?** do you want some chewing gum?

chico noun Masc. **1** boy; **2 unos chicos** some children; **había unos chicos jugando en la calle** there were some children playing in the street; **3** guy; **sale con un chico** she's going out with a guy.

chiflado/chiflada adjective (informal) crazy.

Chile noun Masc. Chile.

chile noun Masc. chilli.

chileno/chilena noun Masc./Fem., adjective Chilean.

chillar verb [17] to shout.

chimenea noun Fem. **1** chimney; **2** fireplace.

China noun Fem. **(la) China** China.

chincheta noun Fem. drawing pin.

chino[1] noun Masc. Chinese (the language).

chino[2]**/china** noun Masc./Fem. Chinese man/Chinese woman.

chino adjective Chinese.

Chipre noun Fem. Cyprus.

chirriar verb [32] to squeak (a door).

chis exclamation **1** shush!; **2** ¡**chis, chis!** hey! (calling somebody in the street, for example).

chisme noun Masc. **1** piece of gossip; **siempre está contando chismes** he's always gossiping; **2** thing; **¿para qué sirve este chisme?** what's this thing for?; **tiene un montón de chismes que no sirven para nada** he's got all sorts of useless stuff.

chispa noun Fem. **1** spark; **saltaron chispas del fuego** sparks flew out of the fire; **2 una chispa de** (informal) a drop of; **una chispa de ginebra** a drop of gin; **pon una chispa de sal** add a tiny bit of salt.

chispa adjective (informal) tipsy; **estaba un poco chispa** she was a bit tipsy.

chiste noun Masc. joke; **contar un chiste** to tell a joke; **un chiste verde** a dirty joke.

chocar verb [31] **1** to crash; **dos coches chocaron en la autopista** two cars crashed on the motorway; **2 chocar con** to run into; **chocaron con una farola** they ran into a lamp-post; **me choqué con ella** I bumped into her.

chocolate noun Masc. chocolate; **chocolate con leche** milk chocolate; **chocolate negro** dark chocolate; **una barra de chocolate** a bar of chocolate.

chocolatina noun Fem. chocolate bar.

a b c d e f g h i j k l m n ñ o p q r s t u v w x y z

a
b
c
d
e
f
g
h
i
j
k
l
m
n
ñ
o
p
q
r
s
t
u
v
w
x
y
z

chollo noun Masc. (informal)
1 cushy job; **2** este chico es un
chollo, sabe hacer de todo this
guy's a real find, he can do
anything.

choque noun Masc. **1** crash; un
choque frontal a head-on
collision; **2** clash; choques entre
los manifestantes y la policía
clashes between demonstrators
and police.

chorizo noun Masc. chorizo (spicy
salami-shaped sausage).

chorrada noun Fem. (informal)
eso es una chorrada that's
nonsense; decir chorradas to talk
nonsense; se enfada por
cualquier chorrada he gets upset
over the smallest thing.

chubasco noun Masc. **1** shower;
2 downpour.

chuchería noun Fem. trinket.

chuleta noun Fem. chop; una
chuleta de cerdo a pork chop.

chupar verb [17] **1** to suck; **2** to
absorb; este papel chupa la tinta
this paper absorbs ink.

chuparse reflexive verb [17] to
suck; chuparse el dedo to suck
your thumb.

churro noun Masc. **1** fritter;
2 (informal) botched job; ¡vaya
churro ha salido! it's turned out a
real mess!.

chutar verb [17] to shoot (at goal).

cibercafé noun Masc. Internet
café; ¿dónde hay un cibercafé?
where is there an Internet café?

cibernauta noun Masc./Fem.
surfer.

cicatriz noun Fem. scar.

ciclismo noun Masc. cycling.

ciclista noun Masc./Fem. cyclist.

ciego/ciega noun Masc./Fem.
blind person; los ciegos the blind.

ciego adjective blind; quedarse
ciego to go blind.

cielo noun Masc. **1** sky; **2** heaven; ir
al cielo to go to heaven; ¡cielos!
good heavens!

cien number hundred (see also
'ciento'); cien personas a hundred
people; el cien por cien a hundred
per cent; cien mil euros a hundred
thousand euros.

ciencia noun Fem. **1** science;
ciencia ficción science fiction;
2 ciencias (subject at
school); ciencias naturales
natural science; Ciencias
Económicas Economic Sciences;
Ciencias Empresariales Business
Studies; Ciencias de la
Información Media Studies.

cieno noun Masc. silt.

científico/científica noun
Masc./Fem. scientist.

científico adjective scientific.

ciento number **1** hundred; ciento
cinco one hundred and five; dos
cientos diez two hundred and ten;
cientos de cartas hundreds of
letters; **2** por ciento per cent;
cinco por ciento five per cent;
tanto por ciento percentage.

cierra, cierro, etc. verb SEE
cerrar.

cierto/cierta adjective **1** true;
eso no es cierto that's not true;
2 certain; cierta clase de

negocios certain types of business; **en cierta ocasión** on a certain occasion; **3 en cierto modo** in a way; **en cierto modo, lo entiendo** in a way, I understand; **4 hasta cierto punto** up to a point; **5 por cierto** by the way; **por cierto, ¿se lo has preguntado?** by the way, did you ask him?.

ciervo noun Masc. **1** deer; **2** stag.

cifra noun Fem. figure; **una cifra muy alta** a very high figure.

cigarrillo noun Masc. cigarette.

cigüeña noun Fem. stork.

cilindro noun Masc. cylinder.

cima noun Fem. top (of a mountain).

cinco number **1** five; **Julia tiene cinco años** Julia's five (years old); **2** fifth (in dates); **hoy es día cinco** today is the fifth; **3** five (in clock time); **son las cinco** it's five o'clock; **a las dos y cinco** at five past two.

cincuenta number fifty; **mi madre tiene cincuenta años** my mum's fifty (years old); **cincuenta y ocho** fifty-eight; **los años cincuenta** the fifties.

cine noun Masc. cinema; **ir al cine** to go to the cinema; **¿qué ponen en el cine?** what's on at the cinema?; **cine de barrio** local cinema; **la cartelera de cine** 'what's on' at the cinemas.

cineasta noun Masc./Fem. film-maker.

cinta noun Fem. **1** ribbon; **una cinta para el pelo** a hair ribbon; **2** tape; **una cinta de vídeo** a video tape; **grabar una cinta** to record on tape; **una cinta virgen** a blank tape; **cinta magnetofónica** magnetic tape; **cinta adhesiva** adhesive tape; **cinta métrica** tape measure.

cintura noun Fem. waist; **¿cuánto tienes de cintura?** what's your waist measurement?

cinturón noun Masc. belt; **cinturón de seguridad** seatbelt; **es cinturón negro de karate** he's a karate black belt; ★ **apretarse el cinturón** to tighten one's belt.

circo noun Masc. circus.

circulación noun Fem. **1** circulation; **2** traffic.

circular noun Fem.,

circular adjective circular.

circular verb [17] **1** to flow (blood or water); **2** to drive; **circulen por la derecha** drive on the right; **el coche circulaba a mucha velocidad** the car was travelling very fast.

círculo noun Masc. circle.

circunferencia noun Fem. circumference.

circunstancia noun Fem. **1** reason; **por alguna circunstancia no pudo hacerlo** he couldn't do it for some reason; **2** circumstances; **bajo ninguna circunstancia** under no circumstances; **en estas circunstancias** in these circumstances; **dadas las circunstancias** given the circumstances.

cirio noun Masc. candle.

a b c d e f g h i j k l m n ñ o p q r s t u v w x y z

ciruela noun Fem. plum; **ciruela pasa** prune.

cirugía noun Fem. surgery; **cirugía estética** plastic surgery; **cirugía láser** laser surgery.

cirujano/cirujana noun Masc./ Fem. surgeon.

cisne noun Masc. swan.

cita noun Fem. **1** appointment; **tengo cita con el médico** I've got an appointment to see the doctor; **el dentista me ha dado cita para el jueves** the dentist has given me an appointment for Thursday; **pedir cita** to make an appointment; **llamé al abogado para pedir cita** I phoned the lawyer to make an appointment; **2** date; **esta noche tengo una cita** I've got a date tonight, I'm meeting somebody tonight; **3** quotation.

citar verb [17] **1** to quote (a writer or book); **2** to mention; **citó algunos casos** he mentioned a few cases; **3** to give an appointment; **el médico me ha citado para esta tarde** the doctor's given me an appointment for this afternoon.

citarse reflexive verb [17] to arrange to meet; **se citaron para las cinco** they arranged to meet at five.

ciudad noun Fem. **1** town; **ciudad dormitorio** dormitory town; **2** city; **3 ciudad universitaria** university campus.

ciudadano/ciudadana noun Masc./Fem. citizen.

civil adjective **1** civil; **un matrimonio civil** a civil marriage;

2 civilian; **la población civil** the civilian population.

civil noun Masc./Fem. civilian.

clarinete noun Masc. clarinet.

claro adjective **1** light; **un verde claro** a light green; **un chico de ojos claros** a guy with light-coloured eyes (blue, green, or grey: opposite of 'dark eyes'); **2** bright; **un día claro** a bright, sunny day; **3** clear; **está muy claro** it's very clear; **no lo tengo muy claro** I'm not very clear about it.

claro adverb **1** clearly; **no habla claro** he doesn't speak clearly; **lo veo claro** I can see it clearly; **2** ¡claro! of course!; **claro que sí** of course; **claro que no** of course not.

clase noun Fem. **1** kind, type; **¿qué clase de material?** what kind of material?; **2 de primera clase** top-quality; **3** class; **la clase de matemáticas** the maths class; **entro en clase a las nueve** I start my classes at nine; **toda la clase ha ido al museo** the whole class has gone to the museum; **4 dar clase de algo** to teach something; **da clase de física en un colegio** he teaches physics in a school; **dar clase a alguien** to give somebody lessons; **me da clases de inglés** he gives me English lessons; **5 dar clase de algo** to have lessons in something; **da clases de música por las tardes** she has music lessons in the evenings; **6** classroom; **¿en qué clase están?** what classroom are they in?; **7 clase social** social class; **familia de clase media** a middle-

class family; **8** class (*of travel*);
viajar en primera clase to travel
first class; **clase turista** economy
class; **clase ejecutiva/clase
preferente** business class; **9** class
(*elegance*); **tener clase** to have
class.

clásico/clásica *adjective*
1 classical (*decoration*);
2 traditional (*method*); **3** classic; **la
clásica broma** the classic joke.

clasificación *noun Fem.*
1 classification; **2** qualifying (*in
sports*); **sin posibilidades de
clasificación** with no chance of
qualifying; **3** placings (*in sports*);
la clasificación es la siguiente ...
the placings are as follows ....

clasificar *verb* [31] to sort into
order (*papers, for example*).
clasificarse *reflexive verb* [17]
to qualify; **clasificarse para la
final** to qualify for the final.

clavar *verb* [17] to hammer; **clavar
un clavo en la pared** to hammer a
nail into the wall.

clave *noun Fem.* **1** key (*to a
mystery or problem*); **la clave es ...**
the key to it is ...; **2** code; **mensaje
en clave** coded message; **3** clef (*in
music*); **clave de sol** treble clef.
clave *adjective* key; **un factor
clave** a key factor.

clavija *noun Fem.* **1** peg; **2** plug (*for
an electrical appliance*).

clavo *noun Masc.* **1** nail; **2** clove
(*spice*).

claxon *noun Masc.* horn.

clic *noun Masc.* click; **un doble clic**
a double click; **hacer doble clic** to

double-click; **haz clic dos veces
en el icono** click the icon twice.

cliente/clienta *noun Masc./Fem.*
1 customer; **2** client (*of a company
or a lawyer*); **3** guest (*in a hotel*).

clima *noun Masc.* climate.

climatizado/climatizada
adjective air-conditioned.

clínica *noun Fem.* private hospital.

clip *noun Masc.* **1** paper clip; **2** un
clip para el pelo a hairgrip; **3** de
clip clip-on.

club *noun Masc.* club; **club de
jóvenes** youth club.

coartada *noun Fem.* alibi.

cobarde *noun Masc./Fem.* coward.
cobarde *adjective* cowardly.

cobrador/cobradora *noun
Masc./Fem.* conductor.

cobrar *verb* [17] **1** to get paid;
**cobro mil cuatro cientos euros al
mes** I get paid one thousand four
hundred euros a month; **cobramos
a fin de mes** we get paid at the end
of the month; **cobra el paro** he's on
unemployment benefit; **cobra
bastante pensión** he gets a
good pension; **2** to charge; **me
cobraron sesenta euros por todo**
they charged me sixty euros for
everything; **cobrar de más** to
overcharge; **cobrar de menos** to
undercharge; **3** to collect; **han
venido a cobrar la deuda** they've
come to collect the money owing;
4 to draw; **cobrar un cheque** to
draw a cheque; **cuando vengas a
cobrar tu pensión** when you come
to draw your pension.

cobre *noun Masc.* copper.

a b c d e f g h i j k l m n ñ o p q r s t u v w x y z

a
b
c
d
e
f
g
h
i
j
k
l
m
n
ñ
o
p
q
r
s
t
u
v
w
x
y
z

cocaína noun Fem. cocaine.

cocer verb [41] **1** to boil (in water); **cocer algo a fuego lento** to simmer something over a low heat; **2** to bake.

coche noun Masc. **1** car; **he venido en coche** I came by car; **coche bomba** car bomb; **coche de alquiler** hire car; **coche de carreras** racing car; **coche patrulla** patrol car; **2** carriage, coach (on a train); **¿qué número de coche es?** what coach number is it?; **coche cama** sleeping car; **coche restaurante** restaurant car; **3** **coche de bomberos** fire engine.

cochecito de bebé noun Masc. pram.

cochera noun Fem. bus depot.

cocido noun Masc. stew (made with chickpeas).

cocina noun Fem. **1** kitchen; **¿dónde está la cocina?** where's the kitchen?; **2** cooker; **cocina de gas** gas cooker; **cocina eléctrica** electric cooker; **3** cooking; **la cocina española** Spanish cooking; **un libro de cocina** a cookery book.

cocinar verb [17] to cook; **cocinar algo a fuego lento** to cook something on a low heat.

cocinero/cocinera noun Masc./Fem. cook.

coco noun Masc. **1** coconut; **2** (informal) head; **me duele el coco** I've got a headache; ★ **darle al coco** (informal) to think; ★ **comerse el coco** (informal) to worry your head off;; **no te comas**

el coco don't worry your head about it; ★ **comerle el coco a alguien** (informal) to try to convince somebody.

cocodrilo noun Masc. crocodile.

cóctel noun Masc. **1** cocktail; **2** cocktail party.

código noun Masc. code; **código de barras** bar code; **código postal** postcode.

codo noun Masc. elbow.

codorniz noun Fem. quail.

coger verb [3] **1** to take; **voy a coger el autobús** I'm going to take the bus; **¿has cogido los paquetes que había aquí?** have you taken the parcels that were here?; **la cogí del brazo** I took her by the arm; **2** to get; **cogió un resfriado** he got a cold; **coger una insolación** to get sunstroke; **voy a coger entradas para el teatro** I'll get tickets for the theatre; **3** **coger el teléfono** to answer the phone; **4** to catch; **no pudo coger la pelota** he couldn't catch the ball; **¡a que no me coges!** I bet you can't catch me!; **cogieron al asesino** they caught the murderer; **no me dio tiempo a coger el tren** I didn't have time to catch the train; **5** to pick; **coger fresas** to pick strawberries; **coger algo del suelo** to pick something up from the floor.

cogerse reflexive verb [3] **1** **cogerse de algo** to hold on to something; **cógete de la barra** hold on to the rail; **2** **se cogieron de la mano** they held hands.

cogido/cogida adjective **1** taken; **esta silla ya está cogida** this chair is already taken; **2 ir cogidos de la mano** to walk hand in hand; **ir cogidos del brazo** to walk arm in arm.

cohibido/cohibida adjective **1** self-conscious; **2** shy.

coincidencia noun Fem. coincidence; **¡qué coincidencia!** what a coincidence!; **dio la coincidencia de que ...** it so happened that ....

coincidir verb [19] to coincide.

coja, cojo, etc. verb SEE **coger.**

cojín noun Masc. cushion.

cojo/coja adjective **1** lame; **es cojo** he's lame; **2 está cojo** he has a limp; **3 andar a la pata coja** to hop.

col noun Fem. cabbage; **coles de Bruselas** Brussels sprouts.

cola noun Fem. **1** tail; **2** queue; **hacer cola** to queue up; **saltarse la cola** to jump the queue; **me puse a la cola** I joined the queue; **3** glue; **cola de carpintero** wood glue; **lo pegué con cola** I glued it.

colada noun Fem. laundry; **hacer la colada** to do the washing.

colador noun Masc. strainer.

colar verb [24] to strain (vegetables).
  colarse reflexive verb [24] **1** to jump the queue; **esa señora se ha colado** that lady has jumped the queue; **2 colarse en un sitio** to get in somewhere without paying; **se coló en el cine** he got into the cinema without paying.

colcha noun Fem. bedspread.

colchón noun Masc. mattress.

colección noun Fem. collection.

coleccionar verb [17] to collect.

coleccionista noun collector.

colega noun Masc./Fem. colleague.

colegial/colegiala noun Masc./Fem. schoolboy/schoolgirl.

colegio noun Masc. school; **colegio público** state school; **colegio privado** private school; **un colegio de curas** a catholic boys' school.

coleta noun Fem. ponytail.

colgado/colgada adjective **1 colgado de algo** hanging from something; **2 el teléfono está mal colgado** the phone's off the hook; **¿tienes el teléfono bien colgado?** have you put the phone down properly?

colgar verb [23] **1** to hang; **2 colgar la ropa** to hang out the washing; **3 colgar un cuadro** to put up a picture; **4** to put down (telephone); **cuelga el teléfono** put the phone down; **me ha colgado** she's hung up on me; **no cuelgue, por favor** hold the line, please.
  colgarse reflexive verb [23] **colgarse de algo** to hang from something.

coliflor noun Fem. cauliflower.

colilla noun Fem. cigarette end.

colina noun Fem. hill.

collar noun Masc. **1** necklace; **un collar de perlas** a string of pearls; **2** collar; **el collar del perro** the dog's collar.

a
b
c
d
e
f
g
h
i
j
k
l
m
n
ñ
o
p
q
r
s
t
u
v
w
x
y
z

a
b
c
d
e
f
g
h
i
j
k
l
m
n
ñ
o
p
q
r
s
t
u
v
w
x
y
z

colmo noun Masc. **1** el colmo de la incompetencia the height of incompetence; **2** ¡esto es el colmo! this is the limit!; ¡y para colmo ... ! and to cap it all ... !; **sería el colmo que no viniesen** it would be the limit if they didn't come.

colocación noun Fem. job; **está buscando colocación** he's looking for a job.

colocar verb [31] **1** to put; **colócalo ahí** put it there; ¿dónde coloco esta silla? where should I put this chair?; **2** aún tenemos que colocar los muebles we still have to arrange the furniture; **3 colocar a alguien** to get somebody a job; **su tío lo ha colocado** his uncle's got him a job.

colocarse reflexive verb [31] to find a job; **se ha colocado muy bien** she's found a very good job.

Colombia noun Fem. Colombia.

colombiano/colombiana noun Masc./Fem., adjective Colombian.

colonia noun Fem. **1** (eau de) cologne; **2** colony; **3 una colonia de vacaciones** a summer camp.

coloquial adjective colloquial.

coloquio noun Masc. discussion.

color noun Masc. colour; ¿de qué color es? what colour is it?; **colores claros** light colours; **es de color azul** it's blue; **telas de colores** coloured fabrics; **televisión en color** colour television.

colorado/colorada adjective red; **ponerse colorado** to go red;

¡te has puesto colorado! you've gone red!

colorante noun Masc. colouring.

colorear verb [17] to colour; **colorear algo de rojo** to colour something red.

colorete noun Masc. blusher.

columna noun Fem. **1** column; **2** spine; **la columna vertebral** the spine.

columpiar verb [17] to push (on a swing).
columpiarse reflexive verb [17] to swing.

columpio noun Masc. swing.

coma noun Fem. **1** comma; **2** decimal point; **dos coma cinco** two point five.

coma noun Masc. coma; **entrar en coma** to go into a coma.

comadrona noun Fem. midwife.

comandante noun Masc./Fem. major.

comba noun Fem. skipping rope; **saltar a la comba** to skip; **jugar a la comba** to skip.

combate noun Masc. **1** combat; **2** fight.

combinación noun Fem. combination.

combinar verb [17] to combine.

comedia noun Fem. comedy; **una comedia musical** a musical.

comedor noun Masc. **1** dining-room; **2** dining hall; **3** canteen.

comentar verb [17] **1** to talk about; **comentamos un poco la noticia** we talked a bit about the news; **2** to mention; **me lo**

comentó de pasada he mentioned it to me in passing; **3** to remark; **comentó que ...** he remarked that ....

comentario noun Masc. comment; **sin comentarios** no comment.

comenzar verb [25] to begin.

comer verb [18] **1** to eat; **2** to have lunch; **normalmente comemos a las dos** we normally have lunch at two; **¿qué había de comer?** what was for lunch?; **3** to take (a piece in chess or draughts); **te como el caballo** I take your knight.

comercial adjective commercial; **el centro comercial de la ciudad** the commercial centre of the town; **un centro comercial** a shopping centre.

comerciante noun Masc./Fem. **1** shopkeeper; **2** trader.

comercio noun Masc. **1** trade; **el comercio de animales exóticos** the trade in exotic animals; **2** shop; **un comercio pequeño** a small shop.

comestibles plural noun Masc. foodstuffs.

cometa noun Fem. **1** kite; **hacer volar una cometa** to fly a kite; **2** comet.

cometer verb [18] **1** to commit (a crime); **2** to make (a mistake); **he cometido un error** I've made a mistake.

cómic noun Masc. comic.

cómico/cómica adjective **1** funny (a situation or face); **2** comedy (actor).

cómico noun Masc./Fem. **1** comedian; **2** comedy actor/ comedy actress.

comida noun Fem. **1** food; **tenemos suficiente comida** we have enough food; **la comida rápida** fast food; **2** lunch; **a la hora de la comida** at lunch time; **3** meal; **cuatro comidas al día** four meals a day; **mi comida fuerte es a mediodía** I have my main meal at midday.

comienza, comienzo[1], etc. verb SEE **comenzar.**

comienzo[2] noun Masc. beginning; **al comienzo** in the beginning.

comillas plural noun Fem. inverted commas; **poner algo entre comillas** to put something in inverted commas.

comino noun Masc. cumin; ★ **me importa un comino** (informal) I couldn't care less.

comisaría noun Fem. police station.

comisión noun Fem. commission.

cómo adverb **1** how; **¿cómo estás?** how are you?; **¿cómo se dice 'mesa' en francés?** how do you say 'table' in French?; **¿cómo se escribe tu nombre?** how do you write your name?; **no sé cómo se enteraron** I don't know how they found out; **2** **¿cómo es?** what's it like?; **¿cómo es tu casa?** what's your house like?; **3** **¿cómo?** pardon? (when you haven't heard properly); **4** (in exclamations) **¡cómo quema!** it's so hot!; **¡cómo se parecen!** they are so like each other!; ¡cómo no! of course!; ¡cómo! ¿no la has visto aún? what, you haven't seen her yet?

como *adverb* **1** like; **uno como éste** one like this; **ser como** to be like; **eres como tu padre** you're like your father; **pienso como tú** I agree with you; **2** as; **negro como el carbón** as black as coal; **3** such as; **metales como el hierro** metals such as iron; **4** around; **eran como cincuenta personas** there were around fifty people; **como a las dos y media** around half past two; **5** como mucho at the most; **como poco** at least; **serán como poco quince niños** there will be at least fifteen children.

como *conjunction* **1** since; **como estaba cerca de su casa, me pasé a verla** since I was near her house, I went to see her; **2** if; **como no tengas cuidado te vas a caer** if you're not careful you'll fall; **3** como si as if; **como si no me importase** as if I didn't care; **4** the way; **así es como lo hizo** that's the way he did it; **5** como quieras whatever you want, however you want; **hazlo como quieras** do it however you want.

cómoda[1] *noun Fem.* chest of drawers.

comodín *noun Masc.* joker (*in cards*).

cómodo/cómoda[2] *adjective* comfortable; **¿estás cómodo?** are you comfortable?; **un sillón muy cómodo** a very comfortable armchair; **ponerse cómodo** to make yourself comfortable.

compact disc, compacto *noun Masc.* **1** CD; **2** CD player.

compañero/compañera *noun Masc./Fem.* **1** colleague; **mis compañeros de trabajo** my colleagues at work; **2** un compañero de clase a school mate; **su compañero de piso** her flatmate; **3** partner (*in a relationship*).

compañía *noun Fem.* company; **hacerle compañía a alguien** to keep somebody company; **el director de la compañía** the company director.

comparación *noun Fem.* comparison; **hacer una comparación** to make a comparison; **en comparación con** in comparison with.

comparar *verb* [17] to compare.

compartir *verb* [19] to share; **compartir algo con alguien** to share something with somebody; **compartieron su comida conmigo** they shared their food with me.

compás *noun Masc.* **1** time, rhythm; **llevar el compás** to keep time; **2** pair of compasses.

compensar *verb* [29] to compensate.

competencia *noun Fem.* competition; **nos hacen la competencia** they're in competition with us.

competición *noun Fem.* competition (*in a magazine, for example*).

competir *verb* [57] to compete.

compita, compito, etc. *verb* SEE **competir**.

completar *verb* [17] to complete.

completo/completa *adjective*
1 complete; **2** full; **el hotel está completo** the hotel is full; **'completo'** 'no vacancies'.

complicado/complicada *adjective* complicated.

complicar *verb* [31] to complicate. **complicarse** *reflexive verb* [31] to become complicated; **la situación se ha complicado** the situation has become complicated.

componer *verb* [11] **1** to make up; **el equipo está compuesto de once jugadores** the team is made up of eleven players; **2** to compose (*music or a poem*).
componerse *reflexive verb* [11] **componerse de** to be made up of.

comportamiento *noun Masc.* behaviour; **mal comportamiento** bad behaviour.

comportarse *reflexive verb* [17] to behave; **comportarse mal** to misbehave.

composición *noun Fem.* composition.

compositor/compositora *noun Masc./Fem.* composer.

compra *noun Fem.* purchase; **fue una buena compra** it was a good buy; **ir de compras** to go shopping; **hacer la compra** to do the shopping.

comprador/compradora *noun Masc./Fem.* buyer.

comprar *verb* [17] **1** to buy; **2 comprar algo a alguien** to buy

something for somebody (*as a present*); **le he comprado un jersey por su cumpleaños** I've bought him a jumper for his birthday; **3 comprar algo a alguien** to buy something from somebody; **voy a comprarle su bicicleta** I'm going to buy his bike from him.

comprender *verb* [18] to understand; **no me comprenden** they don't understand me; **no comprendo su actitud** I don't understand his attitude.

comprensión *noun Fem.* comprehension; **un ejercicio de comprensión** a comprehension test.

compresa *noun Fem.* sanitary towel.

comprimido *noun Masc.* pill.

comprobar *verb* [24] to check; **creo que sí, pero voy a comprobarlo** I think so, but I'm going to check it.

compromiso *noun Masc.* **1** commitment; **compromiso político** political commitment; **2** obligation; **sin compromiso** without obligation; **3 poner a alguien en un compromiso** to put somebody in an awkward situation; **ahora me has puesto en un compromiso** now you've put me in an awkward situation.

computador/computadora *noun Masc./Fem.* computer (*large, mainframe machine*).

común *adjective* common; **en común** in common; **no tenemos**

a
b
c
d
e
f
g
h
i
j
k
l
m
n
ñ
o
p
q
r
s
t
u
v
w
x
y
z

nada en común we have nothing in common; **trabajar en común** to work together.

comunicación *noun Fem.*
1 communication; **2 ponerse en comunicación con alguien** to get in touch with someone; **3 cortarse la comunicación** to be cut off (*on the phone*); **se ha cortado la comunicación** I've been cut off; **4** (*in transport*) **las comunicaciones son buenas** the communications are good; **un barrio con buena comunicación** an area with good public transport services.

comunicar *verb* [31] **1** to inform; **debo comunicarles que ...** I must inform you that ...; **2** to be engaged (*a telephone*); **estaba comunicando** it was engaged.
comunicarse *reflexive verb* [31] **1** to communicate; **comunicarse por carta** to communicate by letter; **2** to be connected.

comunidad *noun Fem.* community; **la Comunidad Europea** the European Community.

comunión *noun Fem.* communion; **hacer la primera comunión** to take communion for the first time.

con *preposition* **1** with; **lo hice con un cuchillo** I did it with a knife; **2** to; **hablar con alguien** to speak to somebody; **estar casado con alguien** to be married to somebody; **3** and; **bistec con patatas** steak and chips; **pan con mantequilla** bread and butter; **4 con tal de que** as long as; **te lo**

dejo, con tal de que lo cuides I'll lend it to you as long as you look after it.

concejal/concejala *noun Masc./Fem.* councillor; **su tío es concejal** her uncle is a councillor.

concentración *noun Fem.* concentration.

concentrar *verb* [17] to concentrate.
concentrarse *reflexive verb* [17] to concentrate; **me concentré en mi trabajo** I concentrated on my work.

concha *noun Fem.* shell.

concienzudo/concienzuda *adjective* conscientious.

concierto *noun Masc.* concert.

conclusión *noun Fem.* conclusion; **llegar a una conclusión** to reach a conclusion.

concurrido/concurrida *adjective* **1** busy (*bar or street*); **2** well-attended (*concert or exhibition*).

concurso *noun Masc.* competition; **concurso hípico** show-jumping competition; **programa concurso** quiz show.

conde *noun Masc.* count.

condesa *noun Fem.* countess.

condición *noun Fem.* condition; **a condición de que/con la condición de que** on condition that.

condón *noun Masc.* condom.

conducir *verb* [60] **1** to drive; **yo conduzco** I'll drive; **2** to lead; **el**

camino que conduce al pueblo the road that leads to the village.

conductor/conductora noun Masc./Fem. driver.

conduje, **condujo** verb SEE **conducir**.

conduzca, **conduzco**, etc. verb SEE **conducir**.

conectar verb [17] to connect; **el teléfono aún no está conectado** the telephone's not connected yet.

conejillo de Indias noun Masc. guinea pig.

conejo/coneja noun Masc./Fem. rabbit.

conexión noun Fem. connection.

conferencia noun Fem. **1** lecture; **una conferencia de prensa** a press conference; **2** long-distance call; **poner una conferencia a alguien** to make a long distance call to somebody.

confesar verb [29] to confess.

confianza noun Fem. **1** trust; **una persona de confianza** a trustworthy person; **2 tener confianza en alguien** to have confidence in somebody; **tiene mucha confianza en sí mismo** he's very self-confident; **3 tener confianza con alguien** to know somebody very well; **tenemos mucha confianza** we know each other very well.

confiar verb [32] to trust; **confío en ti** I trust you.

confidencia noun Fem. confidence; **hacerle una confidencia a alguien** to tell somebody something in confidence.

confirmar verb [17] to confirm.

confitería noun Fem. patisserie.

confitura noun Fem. fruit preserve.

conforme adjective **1 estar conforme** to agree; **no estoy conforme** I don't agree; **¿conforme?** do you agree?; **2 ¡conforme!** ok!; **estar conforme con algo** to be happy with something.

confortable adjective comfortable.

confortar verb [17] to comfort.

confundir verb [19] **1** to confuse; **no me confundas** don't confuse me; **2** to get mixed up; **he confundido las fechas** I've got the dates mixed up; **3** confundir a alguien con alguien to mistake somebody for somebody; **la confundí con Cristina** I mistook her for Cristina.

confundirse reflexive verb [19] **1** to make a mistake; **creo que te has confundido con la cuenta** I think you've made a mistake with the bill; **2 se confundió de carpeta** he got the wrong folder.

confusión noun Fem. confusion.

confuso/confusa adjective **1** confused; **estaba confuso** he was confused; **2** confusing; **esto es muy confuso** this is very confusing.

congelado/congelada adjective **1** frozen; **¡estoy congelada!** I'm freezing!;

a b c d e f g h i j k l m n ñ o p q r s t u v w x y z

alimentos congelados frozen food; **2 murió congelado** he died from exposure; **3 tenía un dedo congelado** he had frostbite in one finger.

congelador noun Masc. **1** freezer compartment; **2** deep freezer.

congelar verb [17] to freeze. **congelarse** reflexive verb [17] to freeze; **¡me estoy congelando!** I'm freezing!.

conjugar verb [28] to conjugate.

conjunto¹/**conjunta** adjective joint; **un esfuerzo conjunto** a joint effort.

conjunto² noun Masc. **1** group; **un conjunto de personas** a group of people; **un conjunto de música** a pop group; **2** collection; **un conjunto de cosas** a collection of things; **3** outfit; **¡qué conjunto más bonito!** what a nice outfit!; **un conjunto de falda y chaleco** a matching skirt and waistcoat; **hacer conjunto con algo** to match something; **4 en conjunto** as a whole.

conmigo pronoun **1** with me; **ven conmigo** come with me; **2** to me; **no habló conmigo** he didn't talk to me; **3 conmigo mismo/misma** with myself; **no estoy contento conmigo mismo** I'm not happy with myself.

conocer verb [35] **1** to know; **conozco la historia** I know that story; **los conozco de vista** I know them by sight; **se conocen bien** they know each other well; **2** to meet; **¿conoces a su hermana?**

have you met her sister?; **aún no conozco al nuevo profesor** I haven't met the new teacher yet; **3 ¿conoces España?** have you been to Spain?; **4** to recognize; **te conocí por la forma de andar** I recognized you by the way you walk.

conocido/**conocida** noun Masc./Fem. acquaintance.

conocido adjective **1** well-known (actor or song); **2** familiar; **una cara conocida** a familiar face.

conocimiento noun Masc. knowledge.

conozca, conozco, etc. verb SEE **conocer**.

conque conjunction so; **conque esta es tu novia** so, this is your girlfriend.

conseguir verb [64] **1** to achieve; **han conseguido su objetivo** they've achieved their objective; **2** to get; **he conseguido un trabajo** I've got a job.

consejero/**consejera** noun Masc./Fem. **1** adviser; **2** minister (in certain autonomous Spanish regions); **3** board member (of a company); **consejero/consejera delegado/delegada** managing director.

consejo noun Masc. **1** piece of advice; **te voy a dar un consejo** I'm going to give you a piece of advice; **2 consejos** advice; **no hacen caso de mis consejos** they aren't following my advice; **3** board; **el consejo de administración** the board of directors; **consejo escolar** board

of governors (*of a school*);
4 meeting; **un consejo de
ministros** a cabinet meeting;
5 council; **el Consejo de Europa**
the Council of Europe.

conserje *noun Masc./Fem.*
1 caretaker (*in a school or a public
building*); **2** receptionist (*in a
hotel*).

conservador/conservadora
noun Masc./Fem.,

conservador *adjective*
conservative.

conservar *verb* [17] **1** to preserve
(*food*); **2** to keep up (*traditions*);
3 to keep; **conservo todas tus
cartas** I keep all your letters;
intenta conservar la calma try to
keep calm.

conservarse *reflexive verb* [17]
to keep (*food*); **las manzanas se
conservan bien** apples keep well.

conservas *plural noun Fem.*
tinned food.

considerable *adjective*
considerable; **un número
considerable de estudiantes** a
considerable number of students.

consideración *noun Fem.*
consideración; **tomar algo en
consideración** to take something
into consideration.

considerar *verb* [17] to consider.

consiga, consigo[1],
consiguiendo, *etc. verb* SEE
conseguir.

consigna *noun Fem.* left-luggage
office.

consigo[2] *pronoun* **1** with him/
her; **lo trae consigo** he's bringing

it with him/she's bringing it with
her; **2 consigo mismo** with
himself; **consigo misma** with
herself; **no está contento consigo
mismo** he is not happy with
himself; **3 consigo mismo** to
himself; **consigo misma** to
herself; **estaba hablando consigo
misma** she was talking to herself;
4 with them; **el dinero que tenían
consigo** the money they had with
them; **5** with you (*talking politely
to somebody*); **si usted quiere lo
puede traer consigo** if you wish,
you can bring it with you.

consistir *verb* [19] **consistir en
algo** to consist of something;
**consiste en tres piezas de
madera** it consists of three pieces
of wood; **el trabajo consiste en ...**
the job involves ....

consonante *noun Fem.*
consonant.

constante *adjective* constant.

constipado[1]**/constipada**
adjective **estar constipado** to have
a cold.

constipado[2] *noun Masc.* cold;
coger un constipado to catch a
cold.

constructor/constructora
noun Masc./Fem. builder.

construir *verb* [54] to build.

**construya, construyendo,
construyo,** *etc. verb* SEE
construir.

cónsul *noun Masc.* consul.

consulado *noun Masc.* consulate.

consulta *noun Fem.* **1 hacer una
consulta** to ask something; **2 de**

consulta reference; **libro de consulta** reference book; **3** surgery; **tiene su consulta en esta calle** his surgery is in this street; **horas de consulta** surgery hours.

consultar *verb* [17] **1** to consult; **consultarle algo a alguien** to consult somebody about something; **2 tengo que consultarlo en diccionario** I have to look it up in the dictionary.

consultorio *noun Masc.* surgery.

consumición *noun Fem.* drink (*in bar, café*); **consumición mínima cuatro euros** minimum charge four euros.

consumo *noun* consumption.

contable *noun Masc./Fem.* accountant.

contacto *noun Masc.* **1** contact; **estar en contacto** to be in contact; **2** ignition (*in a car*).

contado *noun Masc.* **al contado** cash; **pagar al contado** to pay cash; **lo compré al contado** I paid for it in cash.

contador *noun Masc.* meter.

contagiar *verb* [17] to pass on (*an illness*); **no me beses, no quiero contagiarte el resfriado** don't kiss me, I don't want to give you my cold.

contagiarse *reflexive verb* [17] to become infected; **se ha contagiado de su hermana** she's got it from her sister.

contaminación *noun Fem.* **1** pollution; **2** contamination (*by radioactivity*).

contaminar *verb* [17] **1** to pollute (*air or water; for example*); **2** to contaminate (*with radioactivity*).

contar *verb* [24] **1** to count; **cuenta el dinero** count the money; **2 contar con alguien** to count on somebody; **nunca puedo contar contigo** I can never count on you; **3** to tell; **cuéntamelo** tell me about it; **le conté el secreto** I told him the secret; **4** to count; **eso no cuenta** that doesn't count; **el trabajo cuenta para mi nota final** the essay counts towards my final mark.

contenedor *noun Masc.* **1** container; **2** skip; **3 un contenedor de vidrio** a bottle bank.

contener *verb* [9] **1** to contain; **no contiene conservantes** it does not contain preservatives; **2 contener las lágrimas** to hold back the tears; **contener la risa** to stop yourself laughing; **contener la respiración** to hold your breath.

contenido *noun Masc.* **1** contents; **el contenido de la botella** the contents of the bottle; **2** content; **el contenido del libro** the content of the book.

contento/contenta *adjective* **1** happy; **los niños estaban muy contentos** the children were very happy; **2** pleased; **estoy contento de verte** I'm pleased to see you.

contestación *noun Fem.* **1** answer; **no nos dio una contestación** he didn't give us an answer; **2** reply; **quedo a la**

espera de su contestación looking forward to your reply.

contestador (automático) noun Masc. answering machine.

contestar verb [17] **1** answer; **contestar el teléfono** to answer the phone; **no contestó** he didn't answer; **2** reply; **no ha contestado a mi carta** he hasn't replied to my letter.

contexto noun Masc. context.

contigo pronoun **1** with you; **yo voy contigo** I'll go with you; **2** to you; **no estoy hablando contigo** I'm not talking to you; **3** contigo mismo/misma with yourself; **¿estás contento contigo mismo?** are you pleased with yourself?

continente noun Masc. continent.

continuación noun Fem. continuation; **a continuación** ... next ....

continuar verb [20] to continue; **continuaron hablando** they went on talking; **continuará** to be continued.

continuo/continua adjective constant.

contra preposition **1** against; **se apoyó contra la pared** he leant against the wall; **son dos contra uno** it's two against one; **estar en contra de algo** to be against something; **2** chocar contra algo to run into something.

contrabandista noun Masc./Fem. smuggler.

contrabando noun Masc. **1** smuggling; **pasar algo de**

contrabando to smuggle something; **2** smuggled goods.

contrario¹/contraria adjective **1** opposite; **la dirección contraria** the opposite direction; **soy contrario a las reformas** I'm opposed to the reforms; **pasarse al bando contrario** to change sides; **todo lo contrario** quite the opposite; **2** de lo contrario otherwise.

contrario² noun Masc. **1** opposite; **al contrario** on the contrary; **al contrario, me gusta mucho** on the contrary, I like it a lot; **es al contrario** it's the opposite way round; **2** por el contrario on the other hand.

contrarreloj adjective a **contrarreloj** against the clock.

contrato noun Masc. contract.

contribución noun Fem. **1** contribution; **2** tax.

control noun Masc. **1** control; **bajo control** under control; **control de pasaportes** passport control; **control remoto** remote control; **2** llevar el control de algo to keep a check on something; **3** test.

control noun Masc. control de la natalidad birth control.

controlar verb [17] **1** to control; **2** to keep a check on; **3** controlar la línea to watch you weight.

controvertido/controvertida adjective controversial; **una decisión controvertida** a controversial decision.

convencer verb [44] **1** to convince; **2** to persuade; **le**

a b c d e f g h i j k l m n ñ o p q r s t u v w x y z

convencimos para que fuera we persuaded him to go; **3 no me convence mucho la idea** I'm not sure about the idea.

conveniente *adjective* **1** convenient; **2** advisable.

convenir *verb* [15] **1 te conviene preguntar** you should ask; **te conviene descansar** you should rest; **conviene informarse antes** it's advisable to find out in advance; **2** (*in negative sentences*) **no te conviene cansarte** you should avoid tiring yourself out; **por ese sueldo no te conviene** for that salary it's not worth your while; **3 convenir en algo** to agree on something; **4 sueldo a convenir** salary negotiable.

convento *noun Masc.* convent.

convenza, convenzo, etc. *verb* SEE **convencer.**

conversación *noun Fem.* conversation.

convertir *verb* [14] **1 convertir algo en algo** to turn something into something; **convertir agua en vino** to turn water into wine; **convertir libras en euros** to convert pounds into euros; **2** to convert (*to a religion*).

convertirse *reflexive verb* [14] **1 convertirse en algo** to turn into something; **2** to convert; **convertirse al budismo** to convert to Buddhism.

convierta, convierto, etc. *verb* SEE **convertir.**

coñac *noun Masc.* brandy.

cooperar *verb* [17] to cooperate.

copa *noun Fem.* **1** wine glass; **una copa de vino** a glass of wine; **2** drink; **te invito a una copa** I'll buy you a drink; **tomar una copa** to have a drink.

copia *noun Fem.* copy; **copia de seguridad** back-up copy.

copiar *verb* [17] **1** to copy; **2** to make a copy of; **3** to copy down.

coraje *noun Masc.* courage.

corazón *noun Masc.* heart; **un ataque al corazón** a heart attack; **una persona de buen corazón** a kind-hearted person; ★ **partirle el corazón a alguien** to break someone's heart.

corbata *noun Fem.* tie.

corcho *noun Masc.* cork.

cordero *noun Masc.* lamb; **una pierna de cordero** a leg of lamb; **una chuleta de cordero** a lamb chop.

cordón *noun Masc.* string; **un cordón de zapato** a shoelace.

coro *noun Masc.* choir; **a coro** in chorus.

corona *noun Fem.* **1** crown; **2** wreath; **una corona de flores** a wreath of flowers.

coronel *noun Masc.* colonel.

corral *noun Masc.* farmyard.

correa *noun Fem.* **1** strap; **correa de reloj** watchstrap; **2** lead (*for a dog*).

correctamente *adverb* **1** politely; **2** correctly; **¿has rellenado el formulario correctamente?** have you filled in the form correctly?

correcto/correcta adjective
1 correct; **la respuesta correcta**
the correct answer; **2** polite;
siempre es muy correcto he's
always very polite.

corrector ortográfico noun
Masc. spelling checker.

corredor/corredora noun
Masc./Fem. **1** runner; **corredor de
fondo** long-distance runner;
2 corredor de coches racing
driver.

corregir verb [48] to correct.

correo noun Masc. post; **mandar
algo por correo** to send something
by post; **echar algo al correo** to
post something; **correo aéreo**
airmail; **correo electrónico**
electronic mail; **(la oficina de)
correos** the post office; **correo
urgente** special delivery.

correr verb [18] **1** to run; **crucé la
calle corriendo** I ran across the
street; **salió corriendo de la
habitación** she ran out of the
room; **bajar las escaleras
corriendo** to run down the stairs;
echar a correr to start running;
correr mucho to run very fast (a
person), to drive very fast (a
driver), to go very fast (a car or
bike); **2 ¡corre, vístete!** hurry up
and get dressed!; **hice la comida
corriendo** I made dinner quickly;
vino corriendo a verme he
rushed to see me; **se tiene que
marchar corriendo** he has to rush
off; **3 correr las cortinas** to draw
the curtains; **4 no debemos
correr riesgos** we shouldn't take

any risks; **5 correr peligro** to be in
danger.

correspondiente adjective
corresponding.

corresponsal noun Masc./Fem.
correspondent (in journalism).

corrida noun Fem. bullfight.

corrido/corrida adjective
embarrassed.

corriente noun Fem. **1** current
(water or electricity); **me ha dado
la corriente** I got an electric
shock; **no hay corriente** there's no
electricity; **2** draught; **hace
corriente** there's a draught.

corriente adjective **1** common; **un
error muy corriente** a very
common mistake; **una chica
normal y corriente** an ordinary
kind of girl; **lo más corriente es ...**
the most usual thing is ...; **2 agua
corriente** running water; **3 estar
al corriente de algo** to be aware of
something; **mantener a alguien al
corriente de algo** to keep
somebody up to date about
something.

corrija, corrijo, etc. verb SEE
corregir.

corrompido/corrompida
adjective corrupt.

corrupto/corrupta adjective
corrupt.

cortacésped noun Masc.
lawnmower.

cortado¹ noun Masc. small coffee
(with a dash of milk).

cortado²**/cortada** adjective
1 closed (a road or street); **2 la
leche está cortada** the milk is

sour; **la mayonesa está cortada** the mayonnaise has separated; **3 ser muy cortado** (*informal*) to be very shy; **ser un poco cortado** (*informal*) to be a bit shy; **4 estar cortado** (*informal*) to be embarrassed.

cortar *verb* [17] **1** to cut; **cortar un pastel** to cut a cake; **cortar algo por la mitad** to cut something in two; **cortar algo a rodajas** to slice something; **2 cortar el césped** to mow the lawn; **cortar leña** to chop wood; **cortar un árbol** to chop down a tree; **4** to cut off; **nos han cortado la luz** our electricity has been cut off; **corta esa punta** cut this end off.

cortarse *reflexive verb* [17] **1** to cut oneself; **me he cortado la mano** I've cut my hand; **2 cortarse el pelo** to have your hair cut; **mañana me voy a cortar el pelo** I'm going to have my hair cut tomorrow; **se ha cortado el agua** the water's been cut off; **4** to curdle; **5** (*informal*) to get embarrassed; **¡no te cortes!** don't get embarrassed.

cortaúñas *noun Masc.* nail clippers.

corte[1] *noun Masc.* **1** cut; **hacerse un corte** to cut yourself; **se hizo un corte en el dedo** he cut his finger; **un corte de pelo** a haircut; **ha habido un corte de agua** the water's been cut off; **2 corte y confección** dressmaking; **3** (*informal*) embarrassment; **me da corte preguntar** I'm embarrassed to ask; **¡qué corte!** how embarrassing!

corte[2] *noun Fem.* **1** court; **2 las Cortes** the Spanish Parliament.

cortés *adjective* polite.

corteza *noun Fem.* **1** bark (*of a tree*); **2** rind (*of cheese*); **3** crust (*of bread*); **4** peel (*of an orange or a lemon*).

cortina *noun Fem.* curtain.

corto/corta *adjective* short.

cosa *noun Fem.* **1** thing; **te he comprado una cosa** I've bought something for you; **¿qué tal van las cosas?** how are things going?; **se llevó todas sus cosas** he took all his things; **¡qué cosa más rara!** how strange!; **2 cualquier cosa** anything; **3 alguna cosa** something; **por si pasa alguna cosa** in case something happens; **4 alguna cosa** anything (*in questions*); **¿buscas alguna cosa en especial?** are you looking for anything in particular?; **¿quiere alguna otra cosa?** do you want anything else?

cosecha *noun Fem.* **1** harvest; **2** crop; **3** vintage.

cosechar *verb* [17] to harvest.

coser *verb* [18] to sew.

cosmético[1] *noun Masc.* cosmetic.

cosmético[2]**/cosmética** *adjective* cosmetic.

cosquillas *plural noun Fem.* **hacerle cosquillas a alguien** to tickle somebody; **tener cosquillas** to be ticklish.

Costa Rica *noun Fem.* Costa Rica.

costa noun Fem. coast.

costado noun Masc. side.

costar verb [24] **1** to cost; ¿cuánto cuesta? how much is it?; cuesta muy caro it's very expensive; la comida cuesta poco food is cheap; me costó barato it didn't cost me very much; **2** to be hard; cuesta mucho entenderlo it's very hard to understand; cuesta un poco acostumbrarse it takes a bit of getting used to; me costó hacerlo I found it difficult to do.

costarricense noun Masc., Fem., adjective Costa Rican.

coste noun Masc. cost.

costilla noun Fem. rib.

costoso/costosa adjective expensive.

costra noun Fem. scab.

costumbre noun Fem. **1** habit; coger la costumbre de hacer algo to get into the habit of doing something; tengo la costumbre de leer un poco antes de dormir I normally read for a bit before I go to sleep; por costumbre out of habit; **2** de costumbre usual; el lugar de costumbre the usual place; **3** custom (in a country or place).

costura noun Fem. **1** needlework; **2** seam.

cotilla noun Masc./Fem., adjective gossip; es muy cotilla he's such a gossip.

cotillear verb [17] to gossip.

cráneo noun Fem. skull.

creación noun Fem. creation.

creador/creadora noun Masc./Fem. creator.

creador adjective creative.

crear verb [17] to create.

crecer verb [35] **1** to grow; ¡cuánto has crecido! you've really grown!; **2** to grow up; creció en Escocia she grew up in Scotland.

crédito noun Masc. **1** credit (in a shop, for example); tengo crédito aquí they give me credit here; **2** loan; me han concedido el crédito they've granted me the loan; crédito hipotecario mortgage.

creer verb [37] **1** to think; creo que se llama Nekane I think she's called Nekane; ¿crees que me llamará? do you think he'll phone me?; creo que sí I think so; no creo I don't think so; **2** to believe; no creo en el destino I don't believe in fate; ¡no lo puedo creer! I don't believe it!

creíble adjective believable.

crema noun Fem. cream; crema hidratante moisturiser; crema bronceadora suntan lotion.

cremallera noun Fem. zip; subirse la cremallera to do up your zip.

crepúsculo noun Masc. twilight.

creyendo, creyó, etc. verb SEE creer.

crezca, crezco, etc. verb SEE crecer.

cría noun Fem. baby animal; una cría de leopardo a baby leopard.

criada noun Fem. maid.

criado noun Masc. servant.

a
b
c
d
e
f
g
h
i
j
k
l
m
n
ñ
o
p
q
r
s
t
u
v
w
x
y
z

a
b
c
d
e
f
g
h
i
j
k
l
m
n
ñ
o
p
q
r
s
t
u
v
w
x
y
z

criar verb [17] **1** to bring up; **lo crió su tía** he was brought up by his aunt; **2** to raise; **criar ganado** to raise cattle.

criarse reflexive verb [17] to grow up; **se crió en un pueblo** he grew up in a village.

crimen noun Masc. **1** crime; **cometer un crimen** to commit a crime; **2** murder.

criminal noun Masc./Fem. criminal.

crisis noun Fem. crisis; **estar en crisis** to be in crisis; **sufrir una crisis nerviosa** to have a nervous breakdown.

cristal noun Masc. **1** glass; **viene en botella de cristal** it comes in a glass bottle; **2** cristal; **cristal tallado** cut glass; **3** window pane; **tengo que limpiar los cristales del salón** I've got to clean the sitting-room windows; **la pelota rompió un cristal** the ball broke a window; **4** piece of broken glass; **el suelo estaba lleno de cristales** the floor was covered with broken glass.

cristianismo noun Christianity Masc.

cristiano/cristiana noun Masc./ Fem., adjective Christian.

Cristo noun Masc. Christ.

criterio noun Masc. **1** criterion; **2** judgement.

crítica noun Fem. **1** criticism; **recibió duras críticas** he's come in for a lot of harsh criticism; **2** review; **la película ha recibido muy buenas críticas** the film has had very good reviews.

criticar verb [31] **1** to criticize; **2** to review.

cromo noun Masc. sticker.

cruce noun (plural **cruces**) Masc. **1** crossroads; **2** 'cruce peligroso' 'dangerous junction'; **3** crossing; **cruce de peatones** pedestrian crossing.

crucero noun Masc. cruise.

crucigrama noun Masc. crossword.

crudo/cruda adjective **1** raw; **una zanahoria cruda** a raw carrot; **2 la verdura aún está cruda** the vegetables aren't cooked yet; **3** harsh; **la cruda realidad** the harsh reality.

cruel adjective cruel.

crueldad noun cruelty; **los trataron con gran crueldad** they were treated with great cruelty.

Cruz Roja noun Fem. Red Cross.

cruz noun Fem. **1** cross; **2** ¿cara o cruz? heads or tails?

cruzar verb [22] to cross; **ten cuidado al cruzar** be careful when you cross the road; **crucé la calle corriendo** I ran across the road; **cruzar los brazos** to cross your arms.

cruzarse reflexive verb [22] **1** to intersect (roads, for example); **2** to pass each other; **los dos coches se cruzaron** the two cars passed each other; **3 me crucé con ella en la calle** I met her in the street.

cuaderno noun Masc. **1** exercise book; **2** notebook.

cuadra noun Fem. stable.

cuadrado[1]/**cuadrada** adjective square; **de forma cuadrada** square-shaped.

cuadrado[2] noun Masc. square.

cuadro noun Masc. **1** painting; **2** picture; **3 a cuadros/de cuadros** checked; **una tela a cuadros** a piece of checked material.

cual pronoun **1 el cual/la cual/los cuales/las cuales** who; **pregunté a mi hermano, el cual me dio las señas** I asked my brother, who gave me the address; **2 el cual/la cual/los cuales/las cuales** whom; **los familiares a los cuales invité** the relatives whom he invited; **3 el cual/la cual/los cuales/las cuales** which; **los instrumentos con los cuales se hace la operación** the instruments with which the operation is carried out; **4 lo cual** which; **no ha llamado, lo cual es extraño** he hasn't rung, which is strange; **5 cada cual** everybody; **6 por lo cual** therefore.

cuál pronoun **1** which; **¿cuál te gusta?** which do you like?; **2** what; **¿cuál es el problema?** what's the problem?

cualesquiera adjective, pronoun SEE **cualquiera**.

cualidad noun Fem. quality.

cualquier adjective SEE **cualquiera**.

cualquiera (plural **cualesquiera**) adjective ('cualquiera' becomes 'cualquier' before a singular noun) any; **en un país cualquiera** in any country;

cualquier cosa anything; **cualquier persona** anybody; **si por cualquier motivo** if for any reason.

cualquiera pronoun **1** anybody, anyone; **cualquiera sabe algo así** anybody knows that sort of thing; **2** either, both; **'¿cuál de los dos quieres?' - 'cualquiera'** 'which of the two do you want?' – 'either'; **3** whichever (when referring to more than two people or things); **coge cualquiera de los que hay ahí** pick whichever you want from the ones that are there.

cuando conjunction when; **cuando estuve en Barcelona** when I was in Barcelona; **cuando la vea la próxima semana** when I see her next week.

cuándo adverb when?; **¿cuándo la conociste?** when did you meet her?; **¿desde cuándo?** since when?

cuanto[1]/**cuanta** adjective **1** as much as; **cuanta tela necesites** as much fabric as you need; **2** cuantos/cuantas as many as; **compra cuantos libros necesites** buy as many books as you need; **3 unos cuantos** a few; **unos cuantos empleados** a few employees.

cuanto pronoun **1 tengo cuanto necesito** I've got everything I need; **2 cuantos/cuantas** as many as; **coge cuantas quieras** take as many as you want; **3 unos cuantos** a few.

cuánto[1]/**cuánta** adjective **1 cuánto/cuánta** how much; **¿cuánto café quieres?** how much

a
b
c
d
e
f
g
h
i
j
k
l
m
n
ñ
o
p
q
r
s
t
u
v
w
x
y
z

a
b
c
d
e
f
g
h
i
j
k
l
m
n
ñ
o
p
q
r
s
t
u
v
w
x
y
z

coffee do you want?; **2 cuántos/cuántas** how many; **¿cuántas tazas saco?** how many cups should I put out?; **3** (*in exclamations*) **¡cuántas personas hay!** there are so many people!; **¡cuánta comida has hecho!** you've made so much food!; **4** (*in time*) **¿cuanto tiempo has tardado en hacerlo?** how long did you take to do it?; **¡cada cuánto tiempo la ves?** how often do you see her?

cuánto *pronoun* **1 cuánto/cuánta** how much; **'pon agua'** – **'¿cuánta?'** 'add some water' – 'how much?'; **2 cuántos/cuántas** how many; **dime cuántos necesitas** tell me how many you need; **3** how long (*in time*) **¿cuánto se tarda en llegar?** how long does it take to get there?; **¿cada cuánto la llamas?** how often do you call her?; **4** (*in exclamations*) **¡cuántas hay!** there are so many!; **¡cuánto ha quedado!** there's so much left!; **¡cuánto has tardado!** you've taken so long!

cuanto² *adverb* **1** as much as; **llama cuanto quieras** phone as much as you want; **2 cuanto más** the more; **cuanto más insiste, menos quiero** the more he insists, the less I want to; **cuanto menos ruido hagas mejor** the less noise you make, the better; **3 cuanto antes** as soon as possible; **4 en cuanto pueda** as soon as I can.

cuánto² *adverb* **1** how much; **¿cuánto cuesta?** how much is it?; **no sabes cuánto te he echado de**

menos you don't know how much I've missed you; **2 ¿cuánto mide la mesa?** what's the size of the table?; **¿cuánto mide de ancho?** how wide is it?; **3** (*in exclamations*) **¡cuánto te quiero!** I love you so much!

cuarenta *number* forty; **mi madre tiene cuarenta años** my mum's forty; **cuarenta y siete** forty-seven.

cuaresma *noun Fem.* Lent.

cuarta *noun Fem.* fourth gear; **meter la cuarta** to change into fourth.

cuartel *noun* barracks; **el cuartel general** the headquarters.

cuarto¹ *noun Masc.* **1** room; **el cuarto de estar** the living room; **el cuarto de baño** the bathroom; **el cuarto de los niños** the children's bedroom; **2** quarter (*in clock time*); **son las dos y cuarto** it's quarter past two; **a las doce menos cuarto** at quarter to twelve; **3** quarter; **corté la tarta en cuatro cuartos** I cut the cake into four quarters; **un cuarto de kilo** a quarter of a kilo; **4 los cuartos de final** the quarter finals.

cuarto²/**cuarta** *adjective* fourth; **en el cuarto piso** on the fourth floor; **llegar en cuarto lugar** to finish in fourth position.

cuatro *number* **1** four; **Juan tiene cuatro años** Juan's four (years old); **2** fourth (*in dates*); **el cuatro de mayo** the fourth of May; **3** four (*in clock time*); **son las cuatro** it's four o'clock.

cuatrocientos/
cuatrocientas *number* four
hundred; **cuatrocientos quince**
four hundred and fifteen.

Cuba *noun Fem.* Cuba.

cubano/cubana *noun Masc./*
Fem., *adjective* Cuban.

cubierto[1]**/cubierta** *adjective*
covered.

cubierto[2] *noun Masc.* **1 los**
cubiertos the cutlery; **pon los**
cubiertos en la mesa put the
knives and forks on the table;
cubiertos de plata silver cutlery;
2 poner otro cubierto en la mesa
to lay another place at the table.

cubo *noun Masc.* **1** cube; **2** bucket;
un cubo de agua a bucket of
water; **3 el cubo de la basura** the
bin.

cubrecama *noun Masc.*
bedspread.

cubrir *verb* [46] to cover.
cubrirse *reflexive verb* [46] **1** to
cover yourself; **me cubrí las**
rodillas I covered my legs; **2** to
cloud over; **esta mañana hacía**
sol, pero ahora se ha cubierto
this morning it was sunny, but now
it's clouded over.

cucaracha *noun Fem.* cockroach.

cuchara *noun Fem.* spoon;
cuchara de postre dessert spoon;
cuchara sopera soup spoon.

cucharada *noun Fem.* spoonful.

cucharadita *noun Fem.*
teaspoonful.

cucharilla, **cucharita** *noun*
Fem. teaspoon; **una cucharilla de**

café/una cucharita de café a
coffee spoon.

cuchichear *verb* [17] to whisper.

cuchilla *noun Fem.* blade; **una**
cuchilla de afeitar a razor blade.

cuchillo *noun Masc.* knife.

cuelga, cuelgo, etc. *verb* SEE
colgar.

cuello *noun Masc.* **1** neck; **2** collar;
el cuello de la camisa the shirt
collar; **un jersey de cuello**
redondo a round-neck jumper; **un**
jersey de cuello alto a polo-neck
jumper.

cuenco *noun Masc.* bowl.

cuenta[1]**, cuento**[1], *etc. verb* SEE
contar.

cuenta[2] *noun Fem.* **1** bill; **¿nos**
puede traer la cuenta, por favor?
could you bring us the bill, please?;
2 sum; **hacer una cuenta** to do a
sum; **hacer cuentas** to work
something out; **haz las cuentas de**
lo que te debo work out how much
I owe you; **3 llevar la cuenta de**
algo to keep count of something;
perder la cuenta de algo to lose
count of something; **4** account;
cuenta corriente current account;
cuenta de ahorros savings
account; **abrir una cuenta** to open
an account; **5 tener algo en**
cuenta to bear something in mind;
6 darse cuenta de algo to realize
something; **me di cuenta de que**
había perdido la cartera I realized
I'd lost my wallet; **7 trabajar por**
su cuenta to be self-employed;
trabajo por mi cuenta I'm self-
employed; **montar una tienda por**

a
b
c
d
e
f
g
h
i
j
k
l
m
n
ñ
o
p
q
r
s
t
u
v
w
x
y
z

su cuenta to set up your own shop; **8 más de la cuenta** too much; **bebieron más de la cuenta** they drank too much; **9 cuenta atrás** countdown; **10 bead** (*of necklace*).

cuento[2] *noun Masc.* **1** short story; **2** tale; **un cuento de hadas** a fairy tale; **3 eso no viene a cuento** that has nothing to do with it; ★ **¡eso es un cuento chino!** (*informal*) that's a load of rubbish!

cuerda *noun Fem.* **1** rope; **2 saltar a la cuerda** to skip; **3 dar cuerda a un juguete** to wind up a toy; **dar cuerda a un reloj** to wind a watch.

cuerno *noun Masc.* **1** horn; **2** antler.

cuero *noun Masc.* leather; **un bolso de cuero** a leather bag; **el cuero cabelludo** the scalp.

cuerpo *noun Masc.* body.

cuervo *noun Masc.* crow.

cuesta[1], **cueste**, *etc. verb* SEE **costar.**

cuesta[2] *noun Fem.* **1** slope; **subir una cuesta** to go up a slope; **ir cuesta arriba** to go uphill; **ir cuesta abajo** to go downhill; **2 llevar algo a cuestas** to carry something on your back.

cuestión *noun Fem.* **1** matter; **en la reunión se hablará de esta cuestión** this matter will be discussed in the meeting; **2 la cuestión es …** the thing is ….

cueva *noun Fem.* cave.

cueza, cuezo, *etc. verb* SEE **cocer.**

cuidado *noun Masc.* **1 tener cuidado con** to be careful with;

ten cuidado con los vasos be careful with the glasses; **¡cuidado con el escalón!** mind the step!; **¡cuidado con el perro!** beware of the dog!; **2 hacer algo con cuidado** to do something carefully; **lo cogí con cuidado** I picked it up carefully; **3 care; el cuidado de las manos es muy importante** hand care is very important; **4 cuidados intensivos** intensive care.

cuidado *exclamation* **¡cuidado!** watch out!

cuidadoso/cuidadosa *adjective* careful.

cuidar *verb* [17] **1** to look after; **yo me quedo cuidando a los niños** I'll stay and look after the children; **cuidan de su padre enfermo** they look after their sick father; **2** to take care of; **sé cuidar de mí misma** I can take care of myself.

culebra *noun Fem.* snake.

culebrón *noun Masc.* (*informal*) soap opera.

culo *noun Masc.* (*informal*) **1** bum; **2 el culo del vaso** the bottom of the glass.

culpa *noun Fem.* **1** fault; **no es mi culpa** it's not my fault; **es su culpa si se queda sin ir** it's his fault if he ends up not going; **no lo terminamos a tiempo por tu culpa** it's your fault we didn't finish it on time; **¿y qué culpa tengo yo?** and why is it my fault?; **2 echarle la culpa a alguien** to blame someone; **me echan la culpa de lo sucedido** they blame me for what happened; **3** guilt;

sentimiento de culpa guilty feelings.

culpable *noun Masc./Fem.* **él es el único culpable de todo esto** he's the only one to blame for all this.

culpable *adjective* **1** guilty; **sentirse culpable de algo** to feel guilty about something; **2 ser culpable de algo** to be to blame for something; **yo no soy culpable de la situación** I'm not to blame for the situation; **3 ser culpable de algo** to be guilty of something (*a crime*).

culpar *verb* [17] to blame; **culpar a alguien de algo** to blame somebody for something.

cultivar *verb* [17] **1** to grow (*fruit or vegetables*); **2** to cultivate (*land*).

culto *noun Masc.* **1** cult; **2** worship; **la libertad de culto** the freedom of worship.

cultura *noun Fem.* **1** culture; **2** knowledge; **preguntas de cultura general** general knowledge questions.

culturismo *noun Masc.* bodybuilding.

cumpleaños *noun Masc.* birthday; **fiesta de cumpleaños** birthday party; **¿cuándo es tu cumpleaños?** when's your birthday?; **¡feliz cumpleaños!** Happy Birthday!

cumplir *verb* [19] **1 ¿cuándo cumples años?** when's your birthday?; **mañana cumplo quince años** I'll be fifteen tomorrow; **¡que cumplas muchos más!** many happy returns!;

2 cumplir una promesa to keep a promise; **no has cumplido con tu palabra** you haven't kept your word; **3** to fulfil (*conditions*); **4** to carry out (*a task or an order*); **5 cumplir una condena** to serve a sentence.

cuna *noun Fem.* **1** cradle; **2** cot.

cuñada *noun Fem.* sister-in-law.

cuñado *noun Masc.* brother-in-law.

cupe, cupiera, cupo, etc. *verb* SEE **caber.**

cura[1] *noun Masc.* priest.

cura[2] *noun Fem.* cure.

curar *verb* [17] **1** to cure (*an illness or sick person*); **2** to dress (*a wound*).

curarse *reflexive verb* [17] to get better.

curioso/curiosa *noun Masc./ Fem.* busybody.

curioso *adjective* **1** nosy; **¡qué curiosa eres!** you're so nosy!; **2 lo curioso es que** ... the funny thing is ...; **es curioso que** ... it's strange that ....

cursillo *noun Masc.* (short) course.

cursiva *noun Fem.* italics; **en cursiva** in italics.

curso *noun Masc.* **1** year; **¿en qué curso estás?** what year are you in?; **mi hermana está en el primer curso** my sister's in first year; **el curso escolar** the academic year; **2** course; **un curso intensivo** an intensive course.

cursor *noun Masc.* cursor.

curva[1] *noun Fem.* bend; **curva peligrosa** sharp bend; **tomar una curva** to take a bend.

a b c d e f g h i j k l m n ñ o p q r s t u v w x y z

a

b

c

d

curvo/curva² *adjective* curved.

cuyo/cuya *adjective* whose; **el amigo cuyo ordenador utilicé** the friend whose computer I used.

e

f

Dd

g

h

i

j

k

l

m

n

ñ

o

p

q

r

s

t

u

v

w

x

y

z

dabuten *adjective* (*informal*) fantastic, cool; **unos pantalones dabuten** a fantastic pair of trousers.

dabuten *adverb* **lo pasé dabuten** I had a fantastic time.

dabuti *adjective* (*informal*) SEE **dabuten**.

dado *noun Masc.* dice; **tirar los dados** to throw the dice.

dama *noun Fem.* lady; **damas y caballeros** ladies and gentlemen; **una dama de honor** a bridesmaid.

danés¹ *noun Masc.* Danish (*the language*).

danés²/danesa *noun Masc./Fem.* Dane.

danés/danesa *adjective* Danish.

danza *noun Fem.*,

danza *noun Fem.* dance; **estudiar danza** to study dance.

dañar *verb* [17] to damage.

dañino/dañina *adjective* harmful.

daño *noun Masc.* **1 hacerse daño** to hurt yourself; **te vas a hacer daño** you are going to hurt yourself; **¿se hizo daño al caer?** did she hurt herself when she fell?; **me hice daño en la pierna** I hurt my leg; **2 hacerle daño a alguien** to hurt someone; **no quiero hacerte daño** I don't want to hurt you; **3 daños y perjuicios** damages.

dar *verb* [4] **1** to give; **me dio su número de teléfono** he gave me his telephone number; **dale esta carta a María** give this letter to María; **dale recuerdos** give him my regards; **dame un beso** give me a kiss; **2 ¿me da un kilo de tomates?** can I have a kilo of tomatoes?; **3 me dieron un premio** I got a prize; **4** to turn on; **dar la luz** to turn on the light; **5 darle a un botón** to press a button; **darle a un interruptor** to flick a switch; **6 el reloj dio las doce** the clock struck twelve; **7 dar una fiesta** to have a party; **8** to say; **dar las gracias** to say thank you; **dar los buenos días** to say good morning; **darle la bienvenida a alguien** to welcome someone; **9 dar un grito** to shout; **10 darle la mano a alguien** to shake somebody's hand; **11 dar un paseo** to go for a walk; **fuimos a dar una vuelta** we went for a walk; **12 dar de comer a alguien** to feed somebody; **dar de beber a alguien** to give somebody something to drink; **13 me dio miedo** it scared me; **las patatas fritas le dieron sed** the crisps made him feel thirsty; **este jersey da mucho calor** this jumper is very warm; **14 da lo mismo** it doesn't matter; **da lo mismo si lo hacemos luego** it doesn't matter if we do it later; **15 me da lo mismo** I don't mind; **si te da lo mismo, te hago un**

cheque if you don't mind, I'll write you a cheque; **16 el hotel da al mar** the hotel faces the sea; **la puerta da al salón** the door opens onto the living room.

darse *reflexive verb* [4] **1** to have; **darse un baño** to have a bath; **darse una ducha** to have a shower; **2 darse un golpe** to bump yourself; **me di con el pie en el bordillo** I hit my foot on the kerb; **3 darse prisa** to hurry up; **4 darse cuenta de algo** to realize something; **me di cuenta de que se me habían olvidado las llaves** I realized I'd forgotten my keys; **5 se le dan bien las matemáticas** she's good at maths; **no se me da bien pintar** I'm not good at painting.

dardo *noun Masc.* dart.

dársena *noun Fem.* **1** bay (*in bus station*); **2** (*for ships*) dry dock.

dC *abbreviation* (*short for: después de Cristo*) AD.

d. de J.C. *abbreviation* (*short for: después de Jesucristo*) AD.

de *preposition* (*note that 'de' + 'el' becomes 'del'*) **1 el coche de mis padres** my parent's car; **esto es de Juan** this is Juan's; **fuimos a casa de Isa** we went to Isa's; **2** of; **el nombre del libro** the name of the book; **el respaldo del asiento** the back of the chair; **3** from; **soy de Sevilla** I'm from Sevilla; **de Madrid a Bilbao** from Madrid to Bilbao; **de la cabeza a los pies** from head to toe; **no hemos tenido noticias de María** we haven't heard from María; **4 una silla de madera** a wooden chair; **flores de plástico** plastic flowers; **5** of (*in quantities*); **un vaso de leche** a glass of milk; **una caja de naranjas** a box of oranges; **6 una clase de conducir** a driving lesson; **los vasos del vino** the wine glasses; **una moneda de dos euros** a two-euro coin; **el cubo de la basura** the rubbish bin; **una película de miedo** a scary film; **7 la estación de Victoria** Victoria Station; **la ciudad de Barcelona** Barcelona; **el mes de marzo** the month of March; **8** (*describing people*) **un hombre de cincuenta años** a fifty-year-old man; **una niña de pelo corto** a girl de + 'el' becomes 'del'rl with short hair; **es la chica del jersey a rayas** it's the girl with a striped jumper; **yo iba vestida de rojo** I was dressed in red; **9 el mejor de todos** the best of all; **el más bonito de los tres** the nicest of the three; **más de quince** more than fifteen; **el más inteligente de la clase** the cleverest in the class; **10 un tercio del total** a third of the total; **el doble de lo que yo gano** twice what I earn; **poco a poco** little by little; **de tres en tres** three at a time; **11 a las dos de la tarde** at two in the afternoon; **de noche** by night; **trabajan de noche** they work at night; **viajaron de día** they travelled by day; **12 trabajar de algo** to work as something; **trabajo de enfermera** I work as a nurse.

dé *verb* SEE **dar.**

debajo *adjective* (*note that*) **1** underneath; **pon un plato**

a
b
c
d
e
f
g
h
i
j
k
l
m
n
ñ
o
p
q
r
s
t
u
v
w
x
y
z

a
b
c
d
e
f
g
h
i
j
k
l
m
n
ñ
o
p
q
r
s
t
u
v
w
x
y
z

debajo put a plate underneath; **2 el que está debajo** the one underneath; **el de debajo del todo** the one right at the bottom; **3 debajo de** under; **está debajo de la caja** it's under the box; **4 por debajo de** under; **pasé por debajo de la valla** I went under the fence; **por debajo de los diez grados** below ten degrees.

deber[1] noun Masc. **1** duty; **cumplir con tu deber** to do your duty; **2 deberes** homework; **hacer los deberes** to do your homework; **aún no he hecho los deberes** I haven't done my homework yet.

deber[2] verb [18] **1** to owe; **te debo veinte euros** I owe you twenty euros; **2** must; **debes intentarlo** you must try; **deberás estudiar mucho** you will have to study hard; **3 deberías descansar** you should have a rest; **deberías haber seguido mis consejos** you should have followed my advice.

debido/debida adjective **1** due; **a su debido tiempo** in due course; **con el debido respeto** with due respect; **con el debido cuidado** with the necessary care; **2 como es debido** properly; **pórtate como es debido** behave properly; **3 debido a** due to; **debido al accidente** due to the accident.

débil adjective weak.

década noun Fem. decade; **la década de los sesenta** the sixties.

decena noun Fem. **una decena de libros** about ten books; **divídelos por decenas** divide them into tens.

decente adjective decent.

decepción noun Fem. disappointment.

decepcionar verb [17] to disappoint; **la película nos decepcionó** the film disappointed us.

decidir verb [19] to decide; **decidí quedarme** I decided to stay.

decidirse reflexive verb [19] to make up your mind; **aún no se ha decidido del todo** she hasn't completely made up her mind.

décimo/décima adjective tenth; **el décimo piso** the tenth floor.

decir verb [5] **1** to say; **¿qué has dicho?** what did you say?; **aquí dice que ...** here it says that ...; **2** to tell; **me ha dicho que no viene** he's told me he's not coming; **dime lo que quieres** tell me what you want; **3** to mean; **¿qué quieres decir?** what do you mean?; **¿qué quiere decir 'paloma'?** what does 'paloma' mean?; **4 no digas tonterías** don't talk nonsense; **5 ¿diga?** hello? (on the phone); **6 dime** yes? (when somebody says your name); **'¡mamá!' – '¿dime?'** 'Mum!' – 'yes?'.

decisión noun Fem. decision; **tomar una decisión** to make a decision.

declarar verb [17] **1** to declare; **declarar la guerra** to declare war; **¿algo que declarar?** anything to declare? (at customs); **2** to give evidence; **se ha negado a declarar** he's refused to give evidence.

85 **delgado**

declararse *reflexive verb* [17]
declararse culpable to plead
guilty; **declararse inocente** to
plead not guilty.

decorador/decoradora *noun*
Masc./Fem. interior designer.

decorar *verb* [17] to decorate.

dedo *noun Masc.* **1** finger; **dedo
índice** index finger; **dedo anular**
ring finger; **dedo meñique** little
finger; **dedo pulgar** thumb; **dedo
corazón** middle finger; **2 dedo del
pie** toe; **el dedo gordo del pie** the
big toe; **3 hacer dedo** to hitchhike.

defecto *noun Masc.* flaw, defect.

defectuoso/defectuosa
adjective faulty.

defender *verb* [36] to defend.

defenderse *reflexive verb* [36]
1 to defend yourself; **2 me
defiendo en ingles** I get by in
English.

defensa *noun Fem.* **1** defence;
defensa personal self-defence;
2 defender (*in sport*).

defensor/defensora *noun*
Masc./Fem. defender; **el defensor
del pueblo** the ombudsman.

deficiente *adjective* **1** deficient;
2 inadequate.

definición *noun Fem.* definition.

definitivo/definitiva *adjective*
definitive.

dejar *verb* [17] **1** to leave; **quiere
dejar el colegio** she wants to leave
school; **ha dejado a su novia** he's
left his girlfriend; **¡déjala en paz!**
leave her alone!; **2** to let; **no la
dejan salir los domingos** they
don't let her go out on Sundays;

¡déjame entrar! let me in!; **3** to
lend; **le he dejado mis apuntes**
I've lent him my notes; **¿me dejas
un boli?** can you lend me a pen?;
4 dejar caer algo to drop
something; **5 dejar paso** to give
way; **6 dejar de hacer algo** to stop
doing something; **¡deja de
molestar!** stop being a nuisance!;
dejar de fumar to give up smoking;
**7 no dejes de llamarme cuando
llegues** make sure you phone me
when you get there.

dejarse *reflexive verb* [17] **1** to
leave; **me he dejado las gafas en
el coche** I left my glasses in the
car; **2 dejarse el pelo largo** to
grow your hair long; **dejarse
barba** to grow a beard.

del (*formed by 'de + el'; look under
'de' for more examples*) **el dedo
gordo del pie** the big toe.

delantal *noun Masc.* apron.

delante *adverb* **1 delante de** in
front of; **delante de la iglesia** in
front of the church; **delante de mí**
in front of me; **2 el asiento de
delante** the front seat; **la parte de
delante** the front; **3 ir delante** to
go ahead; **4 lleva un bolsillo por
delante** it has a pocket at the front;
entraron por delante they came in
through the front.

delantero/delantera *noun*
Masc./Fem. forward (*in sport*).

delantero *adjective* front; **la
rueda delantera** the front wheel.

deletrear *verb* [17] to spell.

delfín *noun Masc.* dolphin.

delgado/delgada *adjective* thin.

a
b
c
d
e
f
g
h
i
j
k
l
m
n
ñ
o
p
q
r
s
t
u
v
w
x
y
z

delicado/delicada *adjective*
1 delicate; **una situación delicada**
a delicate situation; **2** fragile (*a
piece of china, etc.*); **3** sensitive
(*skin*).

delicioso/deliciosa *adjective*
delicious.

delincuente *noun Masc./Fem.*
criminal.

delito *noun Masc.* crime; **cometer
un delito** to commit a crime.

demás *adjective* **los demás
alumnos** the rest of the pupils; **las
demás cartas** the rest of the
letters.

demás *pronoun* **1 lo demás** the
rest; **lo demás lo traigo mañana**
I'll bring the rest tomorrow; **aquí
está todo lo demás** here's
everything else; **2 los/las demás**
the rest, the others; **los demás
pueden venir conmigo** the rest
can come with me; **los problemas
de los demás** other people's
problems.

demasiado¹/demasiada
adjective, pronoun **1** too much;
gasta demasiado dinero he
spends too much money; **2** too
many; **hay demasiadas personas
aquí** there are too many people
here; **3 demasiadas veces** too
often; **4 hacía demasiado calor** it
was too hot.

demasiado² *adverb* **1** too much;
gasta demasiado he spends too
much; **no trabajes demasiado**
don't work too hard; **2** too; **los
billetes eran demasiado caro** the
tickets were too expensive.

democracia *noun Fem.*
democracy.

demoler *verb* [38] to demolish.

demolición *noun Fem.*
demolition.

demonio *noun Masc.* devil.

demora *noun Fem.* delay; **sin
demora** without delay.

demos, dan, den, etc. *verb* SEE
dar.

densidad *noun Fem.* **1** density;
2 denseness.

dentado/dentada *adjective*
jagged.

dentífrico *noun Masc.* toothpaste.

dentista *noun Masc./Fem.* dentist.

dentro *adverb* **1** inside; **pasar
dentro** to go inside; **desde dentro**
from inside; **2 aquí dentro** in here;
allí dentro in there; **ponlo aquí
dentro** put it in here; **3 dentro de**
inside, in; **dentro del edificio**
inside the building; **dentro de la
caja** in the box; **dentro de** on
the inside; **por dentro es verde** it's
green on the inside; **lo limpié por
dentro** I've cleaned the inside.

denunciar *verb* [17] to report (*a
person or crime*).

departamento *noun Masc.*
department.

depender *verb* [18] to depend;
depender de algo to depend on
something; **depende del
resultado** it depends on the result;
'¿se lo vas a decir?' – 'depende'
'are you going to tell him?' – 'it
depends'.

dependiente/dependienta
noun Masc./Fem. shop assistant.

deporte *noun Masc.* sport; **hacer deporte** to play sports; **me gusta hacer deporte** I like playing sports; **los deportes acuáticos** water sports; **los deportes de invierno** winter sports.

deportista *noun Masc./Fem.* sportsman/sportswoman.

deportista *adjective* sporty; **soy muy deportista** I do a lot of sport; **Jack es muy buen deportista** Jack's very good at games.

deportivo[1] *noun Masc.* sports car.

deportivo[2]/**deportiva** *adjective* sports; **club deportivo** sports club; **ropa deportiva** sports clothes, casual clothes.

depositar *verb* [17] **1** to place; **deposite su solicitud en esta caja** place your application in this box; **2** to deposit (*money in an account*).

depósito *noun Masc.* deposit.

deprimido/deprimida *adjective* depressed.

deprimirse *reflexive verb* [19] to get depressed.

deprisa *adverb* fast, quickly; **no lo hagas tan deprisa** don't do it so quickly; **andaba muy deprisa** he was walking very fast; **¡deprisa, vístete!** hurry up and get dressed!

derecha[1] *noun Fem.* **1** right; **gira a la derecha** turn right; **conducir por la derecha** to drive on the right; **la segunda calle a la derecha** the second road on the right; **2** right hand; **escribo con la derecha** I write with my right hand; **3 la derecha** the right (*in politics*); **ser de derechas** to be right-wing.

derecho[1] *noun Masc.* **1** right; **tener derecho a** to have a right to; **tienes derecho a reclamar** you've got the right to claim; **los derechos humanos** human rights; **2** law; **estudiar derecho** to study law; **derecho penal** criminal law; **3 derechos de autor** royalties.

derecho[2] *adverb* straight; **ponlo derecho** put it straight; **siga todo derecho** go straight on; **siéntate derecho** sit up straight.

derecho[3]/**derecha**[2] *adjective* **1** right; **el guante derecho** the right glove; **en la esquina superior derecha** in the top right-hand corner; **2** straight; **no está derecho** it's not straight.

derramar *verb* [17] to spill; **he derramado el café en la alfombra** I've spilt the coffee on the carpet.

derramarse *reflexive verb* [7] to spill; **se derramó la leche** the milk has spilt.

derribar *verb* [17] **1** to demolish (*a building or wall, for example*); **2** to break down (*a door*); **3** to shoot down (*a plane*).

derrotar *verb* [17] to defeat.

des *verb* SEE **dar**.

desabrochar *verb* [17] to undo (*a jacket or shirt*).

desabrocharse *reflexive verb* [17] to undo; **se desabrochó la chaqueta** he undid his jacket.

a b c d e f g h i j k l m n ñ o p q r s t u v w x y z

desafilado/desafilada *adjective* blunt.

desafortunadamente *adverb* unfortunately.

desafortunado/ desafortunada *adjective*
1 unlucky (*a person*);
2 unfortunate (*an event*).

desagradable *adjective* unpleasant.

desanimado/desanimada *adjective* discouraged.

desaparecer *verb* [35] 1 to disappear; **la tradición está desapareciendo** the tradition is dying out; 2 to go missing.

desaparición *noun Fem.* disappearance.

desaprovechar *verb* [17] to waste; **han desaprovechado mucho papel** they've wasted a lot of paper.

desarrollo *noun Masc.* development.

desastre *noun Masc.* disaster.

desatar *verb* [17] to untie. **desatarse** *reflexive verb* [17] to come undone.

desatornillar *verb* [17] to unscrew.

desayunar *verb* [17] 1 to have breakfast; **desayuné muy temprano** I had breakfast very early; 2 to have for breakfast; **desayuno café y tostadas** I have coffee and toast for breakfast.

desayuno *noun Masc.* breakfast; **tomar el desayuno** to have breakfast.

desbordar *verb* [17] to exceed. **desbordarse** *reflexive verb* [17] to overflow; **el río se desbordó** the river overflowed its banks.

descafeinado/descafeinada *adjective* decaffeinated.

descalificar *verb* [31] to disqualify.

descalzarse *reflexive verb* [22] to take your shoes off.

descalzo/descalza *adjective* barefoot.

descansado/descansada *adjective* rested.

descansar *verb* [17] 1 to rest; **necesitas descansar** you need to rest; **descansar la vista** to give your eyes a rest; 2 **que descanses** sleep well; 3 **¡descansen!** at ease! (*in the army*).

descansillo *noun Masc.* landing (*on stairs*).

descanso *noun Masc.* 1 rest; 2 half-time.

descapotable *noun Masc.*, **descapotable** *adjective* convertible.

descargar *verb* [28] to unload.

descender *verb* [36] 1 to go down (*a mountaineer*); 2 to descend (*a plane*); 3 to fall (*prices or temperature, for example*).

descolgar *verb* [23] 1 to pick up (*the phone*); 2 **han dejado el teléfono descolgado** they've left the phone off the hook; 3 to take down (*a picture, for example*).

desconectar *verb* [17] to disconnect; **¿has desconectado**

el ordenador? have you disconnected the computer?

desconfiar verb [32] to mistrust; **desconfiar de alguien** to mistrust someone.

descongelar verb [17] to defrost (the fridge or food).

descongelarse reflexive verb [17] to defrost (the fridge or food).

desconocido/desconocida noun Masc./Fem. stranger.

desconocido adjective unknown.

descontento[1] noun Masc. dissatisfaction.

descontento[2]/**descontenta** adjective dissatisfied; **quedar descontento con algo** to be dissatisfied with something.

describir verb [52] to describe.

descripción noun Fem. description.

descrito verb SEE **describir**.

descubrir verb [53] **1** to discover; **2** to unveil (a statue).

descuento noun Masc. discount.

descuidado/descuidada adjective **1** careless (a person); **2** neglected; **el jardín está muy descuidado** the garden is very neglected.

desde preposition **1** since; **desde la semana pasada** since last week; **desde que nos conocimos** since we met; **2** from; **mídelo desde este extremo hasta el otro** measure it from this end to the other; **puedo mandarlo desde Madrid** I can send it from Madrid; **desde el principio** from the beginning; **desde el primer momento** right from the start; **3 desde hace** for; **no les veo desde hace años** I haven't seen them for years; **trabajo allí desde hace tres meses** I've been working there for three months; **4 desde luego** of course.

desear verb [17] **1** to wish; **te deseo lo mejor** I wish you all the best; **te deseo un feliz cumpleaños** wishing you a happy birthday (in a card); **2 ¿qué desea?** can I help you? (in a shop, for example); **3 estoy deseando verte** I'm looking forward to seeing you; **están deseando que llegue el verano** they can't wait for the summer to come.

desembarcar verb [31] **1** to unload; **2** to disembark.

desempleado/desempleada noun Masc./Fem. unemployed person.

desempleado adjective unemployed.

desempleo noun Masc. unemployment; **cobrar subsidio de desempleo** to get unemployment benefit.

desenchufar verb [17] to unplug.

desenvolver verb [45] to unwrap.

deseo noun Masc. **1** wish; **pedir un deseo** to make a wish; **se cumplió mi deseo** my wish came true; **2 con mis mejores deseos** best wishes; **3** desire.

desfavorable adjective unfavourable.

a
b
c
d
e
f
g
h
i
j
k
l
m
n
ñ
o
p
q
r
s
t
u
v
w
x
y
z

desfile noun Masc. **1** parade; **2 un desfile de modelos** a fashion show.

desgracia noun Fem. misfortune; **por desgracia** unfortunately; ★ **las desgracias nunca vienen solas** it never rains but pours.

desgraciado/desgraciada adjective **1** unhappy; **soy muy desgraciado** I'm very unhappy; **2** ill-fated; **aquel desgraciado día** that ill-fated day.

deshacer verb [7] **1** to undo (a knot); **2** to unwrap (a parcel); **3** to take apart (a mechanism); **4** to crumble (a biscuit or stock cube, for example); **5** deshacer las maletas to unpack.

deshacerse reflexive verb [7] **1** to come undone (a knot or seam); **2** to melt (ice); **3** to come apart; **se deshizo en mis manos** it came apart in my hands; **4 deshacerse de algo** to get rid of something; **voy a deshacerme de este sofá** I'm going to get rid of this sofa.

deshielo noun Masc. thaw.

desierto[1] noun Masc. desert.

desierto[2]/**desierta** adjective deserted.

designar verb [17] to appoint.

desigual adjective **1** uneven (a surface or road); **2** unequal (a fight).

desmaquillarse reflexive verb [17] to remove your make-up.

desmayarse reflexive verb [17] to faint.

desmontar verb [17] **1** to take apart; **2** to take down (a tent).

desnudar verb [17] to undress. **desnudarse** reflexive verb [17] to take your clothes off, to undress.

desnudo/desnuda adjective **1** naked; **2** bare; **con los hombros desnudos** with bare shoulders.

desobedecer verb [35] to disobey; **desobedeció el reglamento** she disobeyed the rules.

desobedezca, desobedezco, etc. verb SEE **desobedecer**.

desobediente noun Masc./Fem. **eres un desobediente** you are very disobedient.

desobediente adjective disobedient.

desodorante noun Masc. deodorant; **desodorante en barra** stick deodorant.

desorden noun Masc. mess.

desorganizado/ desorganizada adjective disorganized.

despacho noun Masc. **1** office; **2** study (at home); **3 despacho de billetes** ticket office; **despacho de lotería** lottery agency.

despacio adverb slowly; **hazlo despacio** do it slowly; **¡más despacio!** slower!

despedida noun Fem. farewell; **una cena de despedida** a farewell dinner.

despedir verb [57] **1** to dismiss; **lo han despedido del trabajo** they've sacked him; **2** to lay off; **han tenido que despedir a algunos empleados** they've had to lay off some employees; **3** to say

goodbye; **fuimos todos a despedirla** we all went to say goodbye to her; **¿vendrás a despedirme a la estación?** will you come to see me off at the station?
despedirse reflexive verb [57] to say goodbye; **despedirse de alguien** to say goodbye to someone.
despegar verb [28] **1** to take off (a plane); **2** to peel off (a label or a sticker).
despegarse reflexive verb [28] to come unstuck.
despegue noun Masc. takeoff (of a plane).
despejado/despejada adjective clear (sky or a day, for example).
despejar verb [17] to clear.
desperdiciar verb [17] to waste.
desperdicio noun Masc. **1** waste; **no tiene desperdicio** it's excellent; **2 desperdicios** scraps.
despertador noun Masc. alarm (clock); **poner el despertador** to set the alarm.
despertar verb [29] to wake up; **¿puedes despertarme a las siete?** can you wake me up at seven?
despertarse reflexive verb [29] to wake up; **me desperté a las diez** I woke up at ten.
despida, despido, etc. verb SEE despedir.
despierta¹, despierto¹, etc. verb SEE despertar.
despierto²/despierta² adjective awake.

despistado/despistada noun Masc./Fem. scatterbrain.
despistado adjective absent-minded.
desplegar verb [30] to unfold.
despliega, despliego, etc. verb SEE desplegar.
después adverb **1** afterwards; **después me arrepentí** I regretted it afterwards; **poco después** shortly afterwards; **2** later; **lo haré después** I'll do it later; **se vieron mucho después** they saw each other much later; **3 después de** after; **después de las clases** after school; **4 después de todo** after all.
destino noun Masc. **1** destination; **¿qué destino tiene?** what's its destination?; **el vuelo con destino a Milán** the plane to Milan; **2** fate.
destornillador noun Masc. screwdriver.
destrucción noun Fem. destruction.
destruir verb [54] to destroy.
desván noun Masc. attic.
desventaja noun Fem. disadvantage; **estar en desventaja** to be at a disadvantage.
desvestirse reflexive verb [57] to undress.
desviar verb [32] to divert (a plane or traffic).
desvío noun Masc. diversion; **tomar un desvío** to make a detour.
detalle noun Masc. detail; **describir algo con todo detalle** to describe something in great detail.

a **detective** noun Masc./Fem.
detective; **detective privado**
private detective.

b

c **detener** verb [9] **1** to stop (traffic);
2 to arrest; **¡queda detenido!**
you're under arrest!

d

detenerse reflexive verb [9] to
stop; **detenerse a hacer** to stop to
do; **me detuve a descansar** I
stopped to rest.

e

f

g **detergente** noun Masc.
1 washing powder; **2** washing-up
liquid.

h

i **detestar** verb [17] to detest.

j **detrás** adverb **1** behind; **creo que
están detrás** I think they're
behind; **2 detrás de** behind; **ponte
detrás de mí** go behind me; **detrás
de la estación** behind the station;
3 se abrocha por detrás it buttons
up at the back; **entraron por
detrás** they got in through the
back.

k

l

m

n

ñ

o **deuda** noun Fem. debt; **tiene
muchas deudas** he has a lot of
debts.

p

q

r **devolver** verb [45] **1** to bring back;
te devolveré el libro mañana I'll
bring you the book back tomorrow;
2 to take back; **he devuelto la
camisa** I've taken the shirt back;
3 to return; **lo devolví a su dueño**
I returned it to its owner; **4** to
refund (money); **5** to be sick
(vomit); **creo que voy a devolver** I
think I'm going to be sick.

s

t

u

v

w

x **devuelto, devuelvo,** etc. verb
SEE **devolver**.

y

z **di** verb SEE **dar**.

día noun Masc. **1** day; **el día
siguiente** the following day; **el día
anterior** the previous day; **el día
tres de mayo** the third of May;
¿qué día es hoy? what day is it
today?; **todos los días** every day;
cada día every day; **un día festivo**
a public holiday; **se ha tomado el
día libre** he's taken the day off; **día
de Reyes** Twelfth Night (the 6th of
January, which is when people get
Christmas presents in Spain); **el
día de los Inocentes** the 28th of
December (equivalent to April
Fool's Day in Spain); **el día de los
enamorados** St Valentine's Day;
día del padre Father's Day;
2 buenos días good morning;
3 hacerse de día to get light (in the
morning); **aún no se ha hecho de
día** it's not light yet; **en pleno día**
in broad daylight; **4 estar al día** to
be up to date; **poner a alguien al
día** to bring someone up to date.

diabético/diabética noun
Masc./Fem.,

diabético adjective diabetic.

diablo noun Masc. devil.

diagnóstico noun Masc.
diagnosis; **emitir un diagnóstico**
to make a diagnosis.

diagonal noun Fem.,

diagonal adjective diagonal.

diagrama noun Masc. diagram.

dial noun Masc. dial.

diálogo noun Masc.
1 conversation; **2** dialogue.

diamante noun Masc. diamond.

diámetro noun Masc. diameter.

diapositiva noun Fem. slide.

diario[1] *noun Masc.* **1** diary; **llevar un diario** to keep a diary; **2** newspaper.

diario[2]/**diaria** *adjective* **1** daily; **la rutina diaria** the daily routine; **a diario** every day; **se escriben a diario** they write to each other every day; **2** a day; **ensayan dos horas diarias** they practise two hours a day; **3 de diario** everyday; **ropa de diario** everyday clothes.

diarrea *noun Fem.* diarrhoea.

dibujar *verb* [17] to draw.

dibujo *noun Masc.* **1** drawing; **hacer un dibujo** to do a drawing; **dibujo técnico** technical drawing; **2 dibujos animados** cartoons; **una película de dibujos animados** an animated cartoon film.

diccionario *noun Masc.* dictionary.

dice, dicho, etc. *verb* SEE **decir.**

diciembre *noun Masc.* December.

dictado *noun Masc.* dictation.

diecinueve *number* **1** nineteen; **tiene diecinueve años** she's nineteen (years old); **2** nineteenth (*in dates*); **el diecinueve de agosto** the nineteenth of August.

dieciocho *number* **1** eighteen; **tiene dieciocho años** she's eighteen (years old); **2** eighteenth (*in dates*); **el dieciocho de agosto** the eighteenth of August.

dieciséis *number* **1** sixteen; **tiene dieciséis años** she's sixteen (years old); **2** sixteenth (*in dates*); **el dieciséis de agosto** the sixteenth of August.

diecisiete *number* **1** seventeen; **tiene diecisiete años** she's seventeen (years old); **2** seventeenth (*in dates*); **el diecisiete de agosto** the seventeenth of August.

diente *noun Masc.* **1** tooth; **se le ha caído un diente** she's lost a tooth; **ya le están saliendo los dientes** he's already teething; **2 un diente de ajo** a clove of garlic.

diera, dieras, etc. *verb* SEE **dar.**

diesel *noun Masc.,*
diesel *adjective* diesel.

dieta *noun Fem.* diet; **estar a dieta** to be on a diet; **ponerse a dieta** to go on a diet.

diez *number* **1** ten; **tiene diez años** she's ten (years old); **2** tenth (*in dates*); **el diez de agosto** the tenth of August; **3** ten (*in clock time*); **son las diez** it's ten o'clock; **a las diez y cinco** at five past ten.

diferencia *noun Fem.*
1 difference; **hay poca diferencia de precio** there's not much difference in price; **2 a diferencia de** unlike; **a diferencia de su padre** unlike his father.

diferente *adjective* different; **ser diferente a/de** to be different from.

difícil *adjective* difficult.

dificultad *noun Fem.* difficulty; **con muchas dificultades** with great difficulty.

diga, digo, etc. *verb* SEE **decir.**

diluir *verb* [54] **1** to dilute; **2** to thin (*paint*).

dimensión *noun Fem.* dimension.

a
b
c
d
e
f
g
h
i
j
k
l
m
n
ñ
o
p
q
r
s
t
u
v
w
x
y
z

a **dimisión** noun Fem. resignation;
presentar la dimisión to hand in
b your resignation.

c **dimitir** verb [19] to resign.

d **dimos** verb SEE **dar**.

Dinamarca noun Fem. Denmark.

e **dinero** noun Masc. money; **dinero**
de bolsillo pocket money; **dinero**
f **en efectivo** cash; **dinero suelto**
change; **no tengo dinero suelto** I
g haven't got any change.

h **dinosaurio** noun Masc. dinosaur.

i **dio** verb SEE **dar**.

dios noun Masc. god.
j
Dios noun Masc. God; **gracias a**
k **Dios** thank heavens; **¡por Dios!** for
heaven's sake!; **¡Dios mío!** oh, my
l God!; **¡sabe Dios!** God knows!

m **diploma** noun Masc. diploma.

diplomático/diplomática
n noun Masc./Fem. diplomat.

ñ **diplomático** adjective
diplomatic.
o
diputado/diputada noun Masc./
p Fem. member of parliament.

q **dirá, diré, etc.** verb SEE **decir**.

dirección noun Fem. **1** address; **mi**
r **dirección es ...** my address is ...;
2 direction; **¿en qué dirección se**
s **fueron?** what direction did they go
in?; **venían en dirección contraria**
t they were coming the other way;
3 'dirección prohibida' 'no entry';
u 'dirección obligatoria' 'one way';
4 management (of a company).
v
directo[1]/**directa** adjective
w **1** direct; **¿hay un vuelo directo a**
Santiago? is there a direct flight to
x Santiago?; **2 un tren directo** a
through train; **3 en directo** live;
y
z

retransmisión en directo live
broadcast.

directo[2] adverb direct; **el autobús**
va directo al aeropuerto the bus
goes direct to the airport.

director/directora noun Masc./
Fem. **1** headmaster/headmistress;
2 manager (of a company);
3 director (of a film or play);
4 conductor (of an orchestra);
5 editor (of a newspaper).

dirigir verb [49] **1** to manage (a
company); **2** to direct (a film or
play); **3** to conduct (an orchestra);
4 no me dirigió la palabra en toda
la tarde he didn't say a word to me
all afternoon.

dirigirse reflexive verb [49]
dirigirse a hacia algo to head
towards something; **se dirigió**
hacia la puerta he headed towards
the door.

discapacidad noun Fem.
disability; **¿tiene alguna**
discapacidad? does she have a
disability?

disciplina noun Fem. discipline.

disco noun Masc. **1** record; **grabar**
un disco to make a record; **disco**
sencillo single; **disco compacto**
compact disc; **disco compacto**
interactivo interactive compact
disc; **2** disk; **disco duro** hard disk;
disco flexible floppy disk; **3** traffic
light; **el disco se ha puesto rojo**
the lights are red.

discoteca noun Fem. disco.

disculpa noun Fem. apology; **pedir**
disculpas a alguien por algo to

apologize to someone for something.

disculparse *reflexive verb* [17] to apologize.

discusión *noun Fem.* **1** argument; **2** discussion.

discutir *verb* [19] **1** to argue; **ha discutido con su novio** she's had an argument with her boyfriend; **2** to discuss.

diseñador/diseñadora *noun Masc./Fem.* designer; **diseñador/ diseñadora gráfico/gráfica** graphic designer.

diseñar *verb* [17] to design.

diseño *noun Masc.* design.

disfraz *noun Masc.* **1** disguise; **2** costume, fancy dress outfit; **un disfraz de pirata** a pirate outfit; **una fiesta de disfraces** a fancy dress party.

disfrazarse *reflexive verb* [22] to dress up; **me disfracé de bruja** I dressed up as a witch.

disfrutar *verb* [17] to enjoy yourself; **disfrutar de algo** to enjoy something; **he disfrutado mucho de las vacaciones** I really enjoyed my holiday.

disgustar *verb* [17] to upset. **disgustarse** *reflexive verb* [17] to get upset.

disgusto *noun Masc.* **tengo un disgusto enorme** I'm very upset.

disminución *noun Fem.* decrease.

disminuir *verb* [54] **1** to decrease; **el número de visitantes ha diminuido** the number of visitors

has decreased; **2** to reduce (*speed, costs*).

disolvente *noun Masc.* solvent.

disolver *verb* [45] to dissolve. **disolverse** *reflexive verb* [45] to dissolve.

disparar *verb* [17] **1** to fire; **2** to shoot.

disparo *noun Masc.* shot.

disposición *noun Fem.* **1** arrangement; **2** aptitude; **3 estoy a tu disposición** I'm at your disposal.

dispuesto/dispuesta *adjective* **1** arranged; **2** ready; **ya está todo dispuesto** everything's ready; **3 estar dispuesto a hacer** to be prepared to do; **no estoy dispuesto a esperar** I'm not prepared to wait.

disputa *noun Masc.* **1** dispute; **2** argument.

disputarse *reflexive verb* [17] **1** to compete for (*title, cup*); **2** to fight over (*inheritance*).

disquete *noun Masc.* diskette, floppy disk.

disquetera *noun Fem.* disk drive.

distancia *noun Fem.* distance; **¿a qué distancia está el colegio de tu casa?** how far is the school from your house?; **los dos postes están a una distancia de dos metros** the two posts are two metres apart; **está a poca distancia** it's quite near.

diste *verb* SEE **dar**.

distinguir *verb* [50] to distinguish. **distinguirse** *reflexive verb* [50]

a
b
c
d
e
f
g
h
i
j
k
l
m
n
ñ
o
p
q
r
s
t
u
v
w
x
y
z

1 distinguirse por algo to distinguish yourself by something; **2 distinguirse de algo** to be different from something.

distintivo/distintiva *adjective* distinctive.

distinto *adjective* different; **ser distinto a** to be different from; **es distinto al resto** it's different from the rest.

distracción *noun Fem.* **1** entertainment; **es su distracción favorita** it's his favourite entertainment; **la tele sirve de distracción** television is a way of passing the time for him; **2 se lo quitaron en un momento de distracción** they stole it from her when she wasn't paying attention.

distraer *verb* [42] **1** to distract; **distraer a alguien de algo** to distract somebody from something; **2 la costura me distrae** sewing gives me somthing to do.

distraerse *reflexive verb* [42] **1** to get distracted; **2 se distrae con la jardinería** gardening gives him something to do.

distribuidor/distribuidora *noun Masc./Fem.* distributor.

distribuir *verb* [54] to distribute.

distrito *noun Masc.* district; **distrito postal** postal area.

diversión *noun Fem.* **1** fun; **por diversión** for fun; **2 un lugar lleno de diversiones** a place with plenty of things to do.

divertido/divertida *adjective* **1** funny; **es un chico muy divertido** he's really funny; **2 la fiesta fue muy divertida** the party was real fun.

divertir *verb* [14] to amuse. **divertirse** *reflexive verb* [14] **1** to amuse yourself; **2 to have fun; ¡que te diviertas!** have fun!

dividir *verb* [19] to divide.

divisa *noun Fem.* currency; **divisas extranjeras** foreign currency.

división *noun Fem.* division.

divorciado/divorciada *noun Masc./Fem.* divorcee.

divorciado *adjective* divorced; **mis padres están divorciados** my parents are divorced.

divorciarse *reflexive verb* [17] to get divorced; **se divociaron en México** they got divorced in Mexico.

divorcio *noun Masc.* divorce.

DNI *abbreviation Masc.* (*short for: Documento Nacional de Identidad*) identity card.

doblar *verb* [17] **1** to fold (*a piece of paper or clothes*); **2** to bend (*a piece of metal or your leg*); **3** to double (*an offer or amount*); **4 doblar la esquina** to turn the corner.

doble *noun Masc.* **1 el doble de personas** twice as many people; **el doble de harina que de azúcar** twice as much flour as sugar; **el doble de peso** twice the weight; **el doble de largo** twice the length; **2 dobles** doubles (*in tennis*).

doble *adjective* double.

doce number **1** twelve; **tiene doce años** she's twelve (years old); **2** twelfth (*in dates*); **el doce de enero** the twelfth of January; **3** twelve (*in clock time*); **a las doce** at twelve o'clock; **son las doce del mediodía** it's twelve noon; **a las doce de la noche** at midnight.

doceavo/doceava adjective twelfth.

docena noun Fem. dozen; **una docena de huevos** a dozen eggs.

doctor/doctora noun Masc./Fem. doctor.

documentación noun Fem. **1** papers; **no llevaba mi documentación** I didn't have my papers on me; **2** documents (*for a car*).

documental noun Masc. documentary.

documental adjective **un programa documental** a documentary.

documento noun Masc. document; **mi documento de identidad** my identity card.

dólar noun Masc. dollar.

doler verb [38] **1** to hurt; **2 me duele el tobillo** my ankle hurts; **¿te duele mucho?** does it hurt a lot?; **me duele la cabeza** I've got a headache; **le dolía el estómago** he had stomachache.

dolor noun Masc. pain; **tengo dolor de garganta** I have a sore throat; **tengo dolor de muelas** I have toothache; **con dolor de estómago** with a stomachache.

doméstico/doméstica adjective domestic.

domicilio noun Masc. **¿cuál es su domicilio?** what's your address?; **en su domicilio particular** in his own home.

domingo noun Masc. Sunday; **domingo de Resurrección** Easter Sunday; **vienen el domingo** they're coming on Sunday; **el domingo pasado** last Sunday; **el domingo por la mañana** on Sunday morning; **un domingo sí y otro no** every other Sunday; **cierran los domingos** they close on Sundays.

dominical noun Masc. **1** Sunday newspaper; **2** Sunday supplement.

dominó noun Masc. dominoes; **jugar al dominó** to play dominoes.

don noun Masc. Mr; **Don Juan Pozo** Mr Juan Pozo.

doña noun Fem. Mrs, Ms; **Doña María del Valle** Mrs María del Valle.

donación noun Fem. donation.

donde adverb where; **el sitio donde nací** the place where I was born; **el lugar a donde nos dirigimos** the place we're going to; **iré a donde quiera** I'll go wherever I want; **ponlo donde sea** put it down anywhere.

dónde adverb where; **¿dónde está mi abrigo?** where's my coat?; **¿de dónde eres?** where are you from?; **no sé dónde lo guarda** I don't know where he keeps it; **¿por dónde se va a la oficina de**

a b c **d** e f g h i j k l m n ñ o p q r s t u v w x y z

a
b
c
d
e
f
g
h
i
j
k
l
m
n
ñ
o
p
q
r
s
t
u
v
w
x
y
z

correos? what's the way to the post office?

donut™ noun Masc. doughnut.

dorado/dorada adjective gold, golden.

dormido/dormida adjective asleep; **estar dormido** to be asleep; **quedarse dormido** to fall asleep.

dormir verb [51] **1** to sleep; **¿has dormido bien?** did you sleep well?; **no he dormido nada** I couldn't sleep at all; **2 ¡a dormir!** time for bed!; **ya es hora de irse a dormir** it's time to go to bed; **3** to get to sleep; **no puedo dormir** I can't get to sleep; **4 estar durmiendo** to be asleep; **Juan está todavía durmiendo** Juan is still asleep; **5 dormir la siesta** to have a nap.

dormirse reflexive verb [51] **1** to fall asleep; **no puedo dormirme** I can't get to sleep; **2** to oversleep; **me dormí y llegué tarde al trabajo** I overslept and was late for work.

dormitorio noun Masc. **1** bedroom; **2** dormitory.

dorso noun Masc. back; **el dorso de la mano** the back of the hand.

dos number **1** two; **tiene dos años** she's two (years old); **2** second (in dates); **el dos de enero** the second of January; **3** two (in clock time); **son las dos** it's two o'clock.

doscientos/doscientas number two hundred; **doscientos veinte** two hundred and twenty.

doy verb SEE **dar**.

dragón noun Masc. dragon.

drama noun Masc. drama.

dramático/dramática adjective dramatic.

droga noun Fem. drug.

droguería noun Fem. **1** hardware shop (specializing in household items); **2** chemist's.

drogadicto/drogadicta noun Masc./Fem. drug addict.

ducha noun Fem. shower; **pegarse una ducha** to have a shower.

ducharse reflexive verb [17] to have a shower.

duda noun Fem. **1** doubt; **sin duda es el mejor** it's undoubtedly the best; **no me queda la menor duda** I have no doubts whatsoever; **2** query; **¿tienes alguna duda?** do you have any queries?; **tengo algunas dudas** I have a few queries.

dudar verb [17] to doubt; **no lo dudo** I don't doubt it; **dudo que sepa hacerlo** I doubt he knows how to do it.

duela, duelo, etc. verb SEE **doler**.

dueño/dueña noun Fem. **1** owner; **¿quién es el dueño de este coche?** who's the owner of this car?; **se lo devolví a la dueña** I returned it to its owner; **2** landlord/landlady (of a pub or a guesthouse).

duerma, duermo, etc. verb SEE **dormir**.

dulce noun Masc. **no me gustan los dulces** I don't like sweet things.

dulce adjective sweet.

duna noun Fem. dune.

duodécimo/duodécima
adjective twelfth.

duque *noun Masc.* duke.

duquesa *noun Fem.* duchess.

duración *noun Fem.* **1** length; **la duración de la película** the length of the film; **2 disco de larga duración** LP.

durante *preposition* **1** during; **durante aquel tiempo** during that time; **lo haré durante las vacaciones** I'll do it during the holidays; **2** for; **no se vieron durante tres semanas** they didn't see each other for three weeks; **3** throughout; **durante todo el partido** throughout the match.

durar *verb* [17] to last; **la guerra duró tres años** the war lasted three years; **¿cuánto dura?** how long is it?; **no dura mucho** it's not very long.

dureza *noun Fem.* hardness.

duro¹/dura *adjective* **1** hard; **al secarse se pone duro** it goes hard when it dries; **fue un golpe muy duro para todos** it was a hard blow for all of us; **un profesor muy duro** a very strict teacher; **2** tough *(meat)*; **3** stale *(bread)*; **4 un huevo duro** a hard-boiled egg; **5 ser duro de oído** to be hard of hearing.

duro *adverb* hard; **estudiar duro** to study hard.

duro²/dura *noun Masc.* five-peseta coin.

Ee

e *conjunction* and ('y' becomes 'e' before words beginning with 'i-' or 'hi-'); **padres e hijos** parents and children.

echar *verb* [17] **1** to put; **echa más sal a la sopa** put more salt in the soup; **eché el monedero en la bolsa** I put my purse in my bag; **tengo que echar gasolina al coche** I have to put some petrol in the car; **2** to give; **¿te echo un poco de salsa?** shall I give you some sauce?; **3** to throw; **eché agua al fuego** I threw water on the fire; **4 echar a alguien** to throw someone out; **los eché de mi casa** I threw them out of my house; **5 echar a alguien del trabajo** to sack someone; **lo han echado del trabajo** he's been sacked; **6** to show; **echan una película en la tele** they're showing a film on the television; **¿qué echan en el cine?** what's on at the cinema?; **7 echar una carta (al correo)** to post a letter; **8 echar de menos a alguien** to miss somebody; **echo de menos a mi hermana** I miss my sister; **te echo mucho de menos** I miss you a lot.

echarse *verb reflexive* [17] **1 echarse al suelo** to throw yourself on the ground; **2 echarse a la derecha** to move to the right; **echarse para atrás** to move backwards; **me eché a un lado** I moved to one side; **3 echarse una siesta** to have a nap.

a b c d e f g h i j k l m n ñ o p q r s t u v w x y z

a **eclipse** noun Masc. eclipse.

b **eco** noun Masc. echo.

ecológico/ecológica adjective
ecological.

c

d **ecologista** noun Masc./Fem.
ecologist.

e **economía** noun Fem. economics.

f **económico/económica**
adjective 1 economic; **una crisis
económica** an economic crisis;
g **2** financial; **los problemas
económicos** financial problems;
h **3** cheap; **un hotel muy
económico** a very cheap hotel;
i **4** thrifty (person).

ecuación noun Fem. equation.

j

k **ecuador** noun Masc. equator.

Ecuador noun Masc. Equador.

l

m **ecuatoriano/ecuatoriana**
noun, adjective Ecuadorian.

n **edad** noun Fem. age; **¿qué edad
tienes?** how old are you?; **Carmen
ñ y yo tenemos la misma edad**
Carmen and I are the same age;
o **tendrá tu edad más o menos** he
must be around the same age as
p you; **una mujer de unos treinta
años de edad** a woman of about
q thirty; **la edad de piedra** the Stone
Age; **la edad media** the Middle
r Ages; **está en la edad del pavo**
he's at that awkward age.

s

edición noun Fem. **1** publication;
t **2** edition; **edición de bolsillo**
pocket edition.

u

edificio noun Masc. building.

v

w **editar** verb [17] **1** to publish; **2** to
edit (a text).

x

y

z

edredón noun Masc. quilt; **un
edredón nórdico** a duvet.

educación noun Fem.
1 education; **educación física**
physical education; **educación
secundaria** secondary education;
educación a distancia distance
learning; **2** upbringing;
3 manners; **tiene mucha
educación** she's very polite; **eso
es de mala educación** that's bad
manners.

educado/educada adjective
polite; **una persona mal educada**
a rude person.

educar verb [31] **1** to educate; **2** to
bring up.

EE.UU. abbreviation (short for:
Estados Unidos) USA.

efectivo[1] noun Masc. cash; **un
millón de euros en efectivo** a
million euros in cash; **pagar en
efectivo** to pay cash.

efectivo[2]**/efectiva** adjective
effective (remedy or method).

efecto noun Masc. effect; **la
pastilla no me hizo efecto** the pill
didn't have any effect on me;
efectos secundarios side effects;
efectos especiales special effects;
el efecto invernadero the
greenhouse effect.

efectuar verb [20] **1** to carry out;
efectuar un registro to carry out a
search; **2** to effectuar un viaje** to go
on a trip; **3 el tren efectuará su
salida a las nueve treinta** the
train will depart at 9:30; **4** efectuar
un disparo** to fire a shot.

eficaz adjective effective.

egoísta noun Masc./Fem. **eres un egoísta** you're really selfish.

egoísta adjective selfish.

ejecutar verb [17] to execute.

ejecutivo/ejecutiva noun Masc./Fem., adjective executive.

ejemplar noun Masc. **1** copy (of a book); **2** issue (of a magazine); **3** specimen (of an animal or a plant).

ejemplo noun Masc. example; **por ejemplo** for example; **no puedes poner ese caso como ejemplo** you can't take that case as an example; **dar buen ejemplo** to set a good example.

ejercicio noun Masc. exercise; **hacer ejercicio** to do exercise.

ejército noun Masc. army; **el ejército de tierra** the army; **el ejército de aire** the air force; **alistarse en el ejército** to join the army.

el definite article ('el' is used before masculine singular nouns; see also 'la', 'los' and 'las') **1** the; **el libro blanco** the white book; **el sol** the sun; **2** ('el' is also used before feminine nouns that start with stressed 'a' or 'ha') **el águila** the eagle; **el hada** the fairy; **3** ('a' followed by 'el' becomes 'al') **le llevaron al hospital** they took him to hospital; **4** (sometimes 'el' is not translated) **el caviar es muy caro** caviar is very dear; **éste es el señor Martínez** this is Mr Martínez; **el coche de Juan** Juan's car; **5** (with parts of the body or personal belongings) **se rompió el brazo** she broke her arm; **se**

afeitó el bigote he shaved off his moustache; **me quité el abrigo** I took my coat off; **6** (talking about dates and days of the week) **el dos de mayo** the second of May; **iré el próximo lunes** I'll go next Monday; **el miércoles abren a las diez** they open at ten on Wednesdays; **7 me gustó el rojo** I liked the red one; **8 el mío es mejor** mine is better; **el suyo es más caro** his is more expensive; **9 el mío y el de usted** mine and yours; **éste es el de María** this one is María's; **me gusta más el de Toni** I like Toni's better; **10 el que** the one (that); **el que yo compré** the one I bought; **el que quieras** whichever you want.

él pronoun **1** he; **él no lo sabe** he doesn't know; **estaba hablando con él** I was talking to him; **pregúntale a él** ask him; **iba detrás de él** I was behind him; **3 es de él** it's his; **4 él mismo** he himself.

elástico/elástica adjective elastic.

elección noun Fem. **1** choice; **no tener elección** to have no choice; **2** him; **las elecciones** the election; **convocar elecciones** to call an election.

electorado noun Masc. electorate.

electoral adjective **campaña electoral** election campaign.

electricidad noun Fem. electricity.

electricista noun Masc./Fem. electrician.

a b c d e f g h i j k l m n ñ o p q r s t u v w x y z

a
b
c
d
e
f
g
h
i
j
k
l
m
n
ñ
o
p
q
r
s
t
u
v
w
x
y
z

eléctrico/eléctrica *adjective* 1 electric; 2 electrical.

electrocutar *verb* [17] to electrocute.

electrodoméstico *noun* Masc. electrical appliance.

electrónico/electrónica *adjective* electronic.

elefante *noun* Masc. elephant.

elegante *adjective* 1 elegant; 2 smart; **siempre va muy elegante** he's always very smartly dressed.

elegir *verb* [48] to choose.

elemento *noun* Masc. element.

elepé *noun* Masc. LP.

elija, elijo *verb* SEE **elegir**.

eliminar *verb* [17] 1 to eliminate; 2 to remove.

eliminatorio/eliminatoria *adjective* qualifying (round or match).

ella *pronoun* 1 she; **ella no lo sabe** she doesn't know; 2 her; **estaba hablando con ella** I was talking to her; **pregúntale a ella** ask her; **yo iba detrás de ella** I was behind her; 3 **es de ella** it's hers; 4 **ella misma** she herself.

ellas *pronoun* ('ellas' is the feminine plural form of the pronoun; it is used to refer to two or more females) 1 they; **ellas no lo saben** they don't know; 2 them; **estaba hablando con ellas** I was talking to them; **pregúntales a ellas** ask them; **iba detrás de ellas** I was behind them; 3 **es de ellas** it's theirs; 4 **ellas mismas** they themselves.

ello *pronoun* 1 it; **se beneficiaron de ello** they benefited from it; 2 this; **para ello es necesario ...** for this, it is necessary ....

ellos *pronoun* ('ellos' is the masculine plural form of the pronoun; it is used to refer to two or more males or a group of mixed sex) 1 they; **ellos no lo saben** they don't know; 2 them; **estaba hablando con ellos** I was talking to them; **pregúntales a ellos** ask them; **iba detrás de ellos** I was behind them; 3 **es de ellos** it's theirs; 4 **ellos mismos** they themselves.

embajada *noun* Fem. embassy.

embajador/embajadora *noun* Masc./Fem. ambassador.

embalse *noun* Masc. reservoir.

embarazada *noun* Fem. pregnant woman.

embarazada *adjective* pregnant; **quedarse embarazada** to get pregnant; **estoy embarazada de tres meses** I'm three months pregnant.

embarazo *noun* Masc. 1 pregnancy; 2 embarrassment.

embarcación *noun* Fem. vessel (boat).

embarcadero *noun* Masc. wharf.

embarcar *verb* [31] 1 to board (a plane); 2 to embark (on a boat); 3 to load (goods or luggage).

embarcarse *reflexive verb* [31] 1 to board (a plane); 2 to embark (*on a boat*); **3 embarcarse en algo** to get involved in something.

emboscada *noun Fem.* ambush.

embotellamiento *noun Masc.* traffic jam.

embrague *noun Masc.* clutch.

embrujado/embrujada *adjective* **1** haunted; **2** bewitched.

emergencia *noun Fem.* emergency.

emigrar *verb* [17] to emigrate.

emisión *noun Fem.* emission.

emisora *noun Fem.* radio station.

emoción *noun Fem.* **1** emotion; **2** excitement; **¡qué emoción!** how exciting!; **un espectáculo lleno de emoción** a really exciting show.

emocionado/emocionada *adjective* **1** moved; **2** excited.

emocional *adjective* emotional.

emocionante *adjective* **1** moving; **2** exciting; **¡qué emocionante!** how exciting!

emoticon *noun Masc.* smiley, emoticon.

empacho *noun Masc.* (*informal*) **tener empacho** to have a stomach-ache (*from eating too much*); **se cogió un empacho de pasteles** he ate so many cakes he had a stomachache.

empalme *noun Masc.* junction (*on railway*).

empanada *noun Fem.* pie; **empanada de atún** tuna pie.

empapado/empapada *adjective* soaking wet; **venían empapados** they were soaking wet.

empaparse *verb* [17] to get soaking wet.

empastar *verb* [17] to fill (*a tooth*).

empaste *noun Masc.* filling (*in a tooth*).

empatar *verb* [17] to draw; **empataron a dos** they drew two all.

empate *noun Masc.* draw (*in sports*).

empecé *verb* SEE **empezar**.

empeorar *verb* [17] **1** to get worse; **la situación ha empeorado** things have got worse; **2** to make worse; **va a empeorar las cosas** it's going to make things worse.

emperador *noun Masc.* emperor.

emperatriz *noun Fem.* empress.

empezar *verb* [25] **1** to begin; **el colegio empieza el quince de septiembre** school begins on the fifteenth of September; **2** to start; **tendré que empezar otra vez** I'll have to start again; **empezó a llover** it started raining.

empiece, empieza, empiezo, etc. *verb* SEE **empezar**.

empinado/empinada *adjective* steep (*a road or street*).

empleado/empleada *noun Masc./Fem.* **1** employee; **2** clerk (*in a bank or office*); **3** shop assistant; **4 los empleados** the staff (*in a company*); **todos los empleados se beneficiarán** all the staff will benefit.

emplear *verb* [17] **1** to employ; **2** to use; **emplearon materiales viejos** they used old materials.

a b c d e f g h i j k l m n ñ o p q r s t u v w x y z

a b c d e f g h i j k l m n ñ o p q r s t u v w x y z

empleo noun Masc. **1** employment; **2** job; **buscar empleo** to look for a job; **3** estar sin empleo to be unemployed.

emprendedor/ emprendedora adjective enterprising.

empresa noun Fem. company.

empujar verb [17] to push.

en preposition **1** in; **ponlo en el cajón** put it in the drawer; **vivo en Londres** I live in London; **en español** in Spanish; **en invierno** in winter; **2** into; **entró en la casa** he went into the house; **3** on; **está en la mesa** it's on the table; **en el segundo piso** on the second floor; **4** at; **estaré en casa toda la tarde** I'll be at home all afternoon; **es muy buena en inglés** she's very good at English; **5 nunca he estado en París** I've never been to Paris; **6** by; **ir en coche** to go by car.

enagua noun Fem. petticoat.

enaguas noun Fem. (plural) petticoat.

enamorado/enamorada adjective in love; **estar enamorado de alguien** to be in love with someone.

enamorarse reflexive verb [17] to fall in love; **enamorarse de alguien** to fall in love with someone.

enano/enana noun Masc./Fem. dwarf.

encantado/encantada adjective **1** delighted; **están encantados con la casa** they're delighted with the house;

2 ¡encantado de conocerte! pleased to meet you!; **3** enchanted.

encantador/encantadora noun Masc./Fem. magician; **encantador de serpientes** snake-charmer.

encantador adjective **1** lovely (thing); **2** charming (person).

encantar verb [17] **me encantó el libro** I loved the book; **nos encantó el hotel** we loved the hotel; **le encantaría venir a verte** he'd love to come and see you.

encargado/encargada noun Masc./Fem. manager.

encargado adjective **encargado de algo** responsible for something; **la persona encargada del reparto** the person responsible for the delivery.

encendedor noun Masc. lighter.

encender verb [36] **1** to light; **2** to turn on.

encendido/encendida adjective **1** on; **2** alight.

encerado noun Masc. blackboard.

enchufar verb [17] **1** to plug in; **2** to turn on.

enchufe noun Masc. plug.

enciclopedia noun Fem. encyclopedia.

encienda, **enciendo**, **etc.** verb SEE **encender**.

encima adverb **1** on; **pon un plástico encima** put a piece of plastic on it; **ponlo ahí encima** put it on there; **el piso de encima** the flat above; **no llevaba el carnet de identidad encima** he didn't have his identity card on him; **2** encima de on, on top of; **está encima de la cama** it's on the bed; **encima del armario** on top of the wardrobe; **llevaba una gabardina encima de la chaqueta** I was wearing a raincoat over my jacket; **el niño estaba sentado encima de su madre** the baby was sitting on his mother's lap; **3 el/la encima de** the top one; **4 por encima de** over; **5 encima de llegar tarde aún se queja** he arrives late and on top of that he complains; **¡y encima no me lo devolvió!** and on top of that he didn't give it back to me!

encontrar verb [24] to find; **no he encontrado cerillas en ninguna parte** I couldn't find any matches anywhere.

encontrarse reflexive verb [24] **1** to meet; **me encontré con Carmen en la calle** I met Carmen in the street; **2** to find; **me encontré un billete de diez euros** I found a ten-euro note; **3** to be; **el pueblo se encuentra situado en la montaña** the village is situated in the mountains.

encuentra, encuentro, etc. verb SEE **encontrar**.

encuesta noun Fem. survey; **encuesta de opinión** opinion poll.

enemigo/enemiga noun Masc./Fem. enemy.

energía noun Fem. energy.

enérgico/enérgica adjective energetic.

enero noun Masc. January.

enfadado/enfadada adjective **1** angry; **2** annoyed.

enfadar verb [17] **1** to make angry; **2** to annoy.

enfadarse reflexive verb [17] **1** to get angry; **se enfadó muchísimo** he got really angry; **2** to get annoyed; **se enfadó conmigo** he got annoyed with me; **3** to get cross; **mamá se va a enfadar** Mum's going to get cross.

énfasis noun Masc. emphasis.

enfermar verb [17] to fall ill.

enfermedad noun Fem. illness.

enfermería noun Fem. **1** nursing; **2** infirmary.

enfermero/enfermera noun Masc./Fem. nurse.

enfermo/enferma noun Masc./Fem. sick person; **los enfermos** sick people.

enfermo adjective ill; **está gravemente enferma** she's seriously ill; **caer enfermo** to fall ill.

enfrente adverb opposite; **la tienda está justo enfrente de la casa** the shop is just opposite the house.

engañar verb [17] **1** to deceive; **2** to cheat, swindle; **3** to be unfaithful to.

engañarse reflexive verb [17] to fool yourself.

engaño noun Masc. **1** deception; **2** swindle.

engordar verb [17] **1** to put on weight; **2** to be fattening.

enhorabuena noun Fem. **¡enhorabuena por tu trabajo nuevo!** congratulations on your

a b c d e f g h i j k l m n ñ o p q r s t u v w x y z

a
b
c
d
e
f
g
h
i
j
k
l
m
n
ñ
o
p
q
r
s
t
u
v
w
x
y
z

new job!; **darle la enhorabuena a alguien** to congratulate someone.

enjuagar verb [28] to rinse.

enjuagarse reflexive verb [28] **enjuagarse el pelo** to rinse your hair.

enmohecerse reflexive verb [35] to go mouldy.

enojado/enojada adjective **1** angry; **2** annoyed.

enorme adjective huge.

enormemente adverb extremely, a lot; **enormemente preocupado** extremely worried.

enrollar verb [17] to roll up.

enroscar verb [31] **1** to wind; **2** to screw on.

ensaimada noun Fem. light round cake covered in icing sugar.

ensalada noun Fem. salad; **ensalada mixta** mixed salad; **ensalada de frutas** fruit salad.

ensaladera noun Fem. salad bowl.

ensaladilla, ensaladilla rusa noun Fem. potato salad.

ensanchar verb [17] to widen.

ensayo noun Masc. rehearsal; **ensayo general** dress rehearsal.

enseguida adverb right away; **enseguida lo hago** I'll do it right away.

enseñanza noun Fem. **1** teaching; **me gusta la enseñanza** I like teaching; **2** education; **enseñanza primaria** primary education; **enseñanza secundaria** secondary education; **enseñanza superior** higher education.

enseñar verb [17] **1** to teach; **le enseñé a montar en bicicleta** I taught him to ride a bike; **2** to show; **nos enseñó la casa** he showed us the house.

ensuciar verb [17] to make dirty; **no ensucies la mesa** don't make the table dirty; **ensucié el mantel de salsa de tomate** I got tomato sauce on the tablecloth.

ensuciarse reflexive verb [17] to get dirty; **te vas a ensuciar las manos** you'll get your hands dirty; **me he ensuciado las botas de barro** I've got mud on my boots.

entender verb [36] **1** to understand; **entiendo un poco de español** I can understand a little bit of Spanish; **entiendo lo que dices** I understand what you are saying; **no te entiendo** I can't understand you; **2 entender algo mal** to misunderstand something; **la entendí mal** I misunderstood her; **3 dar a entender algo** to imply something; **4 entender de algo** to know about something; **entiendo un poco de fontanería** I know a bit about plumbing.

entenderse reflexive verb [36] **1 entenderse con alguien** to communicate with someone; **nos entendimos por señas** we communicated with each other by signs; **2 entenderse con alguien** to get along with someone; **se entiende muy bien con su hermana** she gets along very well with her sister.

entendido/entendida adjective **1** understood; **queda bien**

entendido it's clearly understood; ¿**entendido**? is that clear?; **2 ser entendido en algo** to know about something.

entero/entera adjective **1** whole; **un día entero** a whole day; **2 leche entera** full-cream milk.

enterrar verb [29] to bury.

entienda, entiendo, etc. verb SEE **entender**.

entonces adverb **1** then; **desde entonces** since then; **entonces llegó Carlos** then Carlos arrived; **2** so; **entonces nos vemos mañana** so we'll see each other tomorrow.

entrada noun Fem. **1** entrance; ¿**dónde está la entrada?** where is the entrance?; **2** ticket (for the cinema or theatre); **ya he comprado las entradas para el teatro** I've already bought the tickets for the theatre; ¿**cuánto cuesta la entrada?** how much is a ticket?; **los niños pagan media entrada** it's half-price for children; **3 'entrada libre'** 'admission free'; **4** deposit; **pagué la entrada para el coche** I put down a deposit on the car; **5** tackle (in football).

entrar verb [17] **1** to get in; **no puedo entrar** I can't get in; **entraron por una ventana** they got in through a window; **2** to go in; **han entrado en esa tienda** they've gone into that shop; **entraron en la clase corriendo** they ran into the classroom; **3** to come in; ¡**entra!** come in!; **4 dejar entrar a alguien** to let someone in; **5 hacer entrar a alguien** to show

someone in; **6** to fit; **no entra por la puerta** it doesn't fit through the door; **7** to join; **entrar en la ONU** to join UN; **8 me entró hambre** I got hungry; **te va a entrar frío si te sientas ahí** you'll get cold if you sit there; **9** to be included; **el desayuno no entra en el precio** breakfast is not included in the price; **10 no me entra** (informal) I don't get it; **no le entran las matemáticas** (informal) he just can't get to grips with maths.

entre preposition **1** between; **estaba sentado entre Jaime y Margarita** I was sitting between Jaime and Margarita; **2** among; **lo encontré entre mis papeles** I found it among my papers; **3 lo hicimos entre todos** we did it all together; **4** by; **nueve dividido entre tres** nine divided by three; **5 entre paréntesis** in brackets; **6 cerrado entre semana** closed during the week.

entreabierto/entreabierta adjective half-open.

entreacto noun Masc. interval.

entrega noun Fem. **1** delivery (of goods); **2** presentation (of a prize or award); **3 la fecha límite para la entrega de formularios** the deadline for handing in the forms.

entregar verb [28] **1** to deliver; **vino a entregar una carta** he came to deliver a letter; **2** to give, to hand; **me entregó los documentos** he handed me the documents; **tenemos que entregar el trabajo el próximo lunes** we have to hand in the essay next Monday; **3** to present (*a prize or award*); **4** to surrender (*a town or weapons*); **5** to turn in (*a criminal*).

entregarse *reflexive verb* [28] to give yourself up; **se entregó a la policía** he gave himself up to the police.

entremés *noun Masc.* starter (*in a meal*).

entrenador/entrenadora *noun Masc./Fem.* trainer.

entrenamiento *noun Masc.* training.

entrenar *verb* [17] to train. **entrenarse** *reflexive verb* [17] to train.

entretanto *adverb* in the meantime.

entretenido/entretenida *adjective* entertaining.

entrevista *noun Fem.* interview; **una entrevista de trabajo** a job interview.

entrevistar *verb* [17] to interview.

entumecido/entumecida *adjective* numb.

entusiasmar *verb* [17] **me entusiasmó la idea** I loved the idea; **le entusiasma el deporte** she's really keen on sports; **no me entusiasma viajar** I'm not very keen on travelling.
entusiasmarse *reflexive verb* [17] **entusiasmarse con algo/por algo** to get excited about something.

entusiasmo *noun Masc.* enthusiasm.

enviar *verb* [32] to send.

envidia *noun Fem.* **1** envy; **se muere de envidia** he's green with envy; **2** jealousy; **tenerle envidia a alguien** to be jealous of someone; **me tienen envidia** they're jealous of me; **le da envidia que yo tenga una bici mejor** she's jealous because I've got a better bike.

envidia *noun Fem.* envy; **tiene envidia de su hermana** she's envious of her sister.

envidiar *verb* [17] to be envious of; **me envidia el resultado de los exámenes** she's envious of my exam results.

envidioso/envidiosa *adjective* envious.

envolver *verb* [45] to wrap up.

envuelto¹/envuelta *adjective* **1** wrapped; **envuelto para regalo** gift-wrapped; **2 envuelto en algo** involved in something.

envuelto² *verb* SEE **envolver.**

epidemia *noun Fem.* epidemic.

episodio *noun Masc.* episode.

época *noun Fem.* **1** age; **era otra época** it was a different age; **2** time; **en aquella época** at that time; **3** times; **en la época de los romanos** in Roman times.

equilibrio *noun Masc.* balance; **estar en equilibrio** to be balanced; **perder el equilibrio** to lose your balance.

equipaje *noun Masc.* luggage; **equipaje de mano** hand luggage.

equipo *noun Masc.* **1** team; **formar un buen equipo** to make a good team; **el equipo visitante** the away team; **trabajo en equipo** team work; **2** equipment; **3 equipo de música** sound system; **equipo de alta fidelidad** hi-fi system.

equis noun Fem. the Spanish name for the letter 'x'.

equitación noun Fem. horse riding.

equivaler verb [43] **equivaler a algo** to be equivalent to something.

equivocado/equivocada adjective wrong.

equivocarse reflexive verb [31] **1** to make a mistake; **creo que me he equivocado** I think I've made a mistake; **2** to be wrong; **te equivocas si piensas eso** you're wrong if you think like that; **3 me equivoqué de carpeta** I picked up the wrong folder; **se equivocó de calle** he took the wrong street.

era, érais, eras, eres, etc. verb SEE **ser**.

error noun Masc. mistake; **cometer un error** to make a mistake; **un error tipográfico** a typing error; **un error de cálculo** a miscalculation.

eructar verb [17] to burp.

eructo noun Masc. burp.

es verb SEE **ser**.

esa[1] adjective that (see 'ese'/'esa' for examples).

esa[2], **ésa** pronoun that one (see 'ese'/'esa' for examples).

esas[1] adjective those (see 'esos'/'esas' for examples).

esas[2], **ésas** pronoun those ones (see 'esos'/'esas' for examples).

escala noun Fem. **1** stopover; **hacer escala en París** to stop over in Paris; **2** scale (of a map or measurements); **hacer algo a escala** to do something to scale; **a gran escala** on a large scale; **3** scale (in music).

escalada noun Fem. **1** (rock) climbing; **2** climb.

escalador/escaladora noun Masc./Fem. climber.

escalar verb [17] to climb.

escalera noun Fem. staircase; **subir las escaleras** to go up the stairs; **una escalera de caracol** a spiral staircase; **una escalera mecánica** an escalator; **una escalera de incendios** a fire escape; **una escalera de mano** a ladder.

escalofrío noun Masc. shiver; **tener escalofríos** to be shivering.

escalón noun Masc. step.

escalope noun Masc. escalope.

escándalo noun Masc. **1** scandal; **un escándalo político** a political scandal; **¡su comportamiento fue un escándalo!** his behaviour was really outrageous!; **2** racket; **armar un escándalo** to make a racket; **¡qué escándalo están armando!** what a racket they are making!.

escandaloso/escandalosa adjective **1** shocking (behaviour or clothes); **2** noisy (people).

Escandinavia noun Fem. Scandinavia.

a
b
c
d
e
f
g
h
i
j
k
l
m
n
ñ
o
p
q
r
s
t
u
v
w
x
y
z

escandinavo/escandinava noun Masc./Fem. Scandinavian; **los escandinavos** Scandinavians.
escandinavo adjective Scandinavian.

escáner noun Masc. **1** scanner; **2** scan.

escapar verb [17] to escape; **escapar de algo** to escape from something.

escaparse reflexive verb [17] **1** to escape; **se ha escapado de la cárcel** he's escaped from prison; **2** to run away; **escaparse de casa** to run away from home; **3** to leak (gas or water).

escaparate noun Masc. shop window.

escarabajo noun Masc. beetle.

escarcha noun Fem. frost.

escasez noun Fem. shortage; **hay escasez de agua** there's a water shortage.

escena noun Fem. scene.

escenario noun Masc. stage.

esclavo/esclava noun Masc./Fem. slave.

esclusa noun Fem. lock (on a canal).

escoba noun Fem. broom.

escocés/escocesa noun Masc./Fem. Scot.

escocés/escocesa adjective Scottish.

Escocia noun Fem. Scotland.

escoger verb [3] to choose.

escoja, escojo, etc. verb SEE **escoger**.

escolar noun Masc./Fem. schoolboy/schoolgirl.

escolar adjective school; **la vida escolar** school life.

esconder verb [18] to hide.
esconderse reflexive verb [18] to hide; **esconderse de algo** to hide from something.

escondido/escondida adjective hidden.

escorpión[1], **escorpio** noun Masc./Fem. Scorpio; **soy escorpión** I'm Scorpio.

escorpión[2] noun Masc. scorpion.

Escorpión, Escorpio noun Masc. Scorpio.

escribir verb [52] **1** to write; **escribir una novela** to write a novel; **le escribí una carta** I wrote a letter to him; **2 escribir a máquina** to type; **3** to spell; **¿cómo se escribe tu nombre?** how do you spell your name?

escrito verb SEE **escribir**.

escritor/escritora noun Masc./Fem. writer.

escritorio noun Masc. desk.

escuchar verb [17] **1** to listen; **escuchamos atentamente** we listen carefully; **2** to listen to; **escucha bien lo que digo** listen carefully to what I say; **escúchame** listen to me.

escuela noun Fem. school; **escuela primaria** primary school; **escuela nocturna** night school.

escultor/escultora noun Masc./Fem. sculptor.

escultura noun Fem. sculpture.

escupir verb [19] **1** to spit; **escupir a alguien** to spit at someone; **2** to spit out; **escupió la comida** he spat out the food.

ese[1]**/esa** adjective that; **ese libro** that book; **esa chica** that girl.

ese[2]**/esa, ése/ésa** pronoun that one; **ese es más bonito** that one is nicer; **esa es tu bolsa** that one is your bag.

esfuerzo noun Masc. effort; **hacer un esfuerzo** to make an effort.

esguince noun Masc. sprain.

eslogan noun Masc. slogan.

eslovaco/eslovaca noun Masc./Fem., adjective Slovak.

Eslovaquia noun Fem. Slovakia.

Eslovenia noun Fem. Slovenia.

esloveno/eslovena noun Masc./Fem., adjective Slovene.

eso pronoun that; **eso no importa** that doesn't matter; **por eso** that's why.

ESO abbreviation Fem. (short for 'Educación Secundaria Obligatoria') compulsory secondary education programme in Spain for the 12–16 age group.

esos[1]**/esas** adjective those; **esos libros** those books; **esas chicas** those girls.

esos[2]**/esas, ésos/ésas** pronoun those ones; **esos son más bonitos** those ones are nicer.

espabilado/espabilada adjective alert.

espacio noun Masc. **1** space; **la conquista del espacio** the conquest of space; **dejar un espacio** leave a space; **2** room; **no tengo mucho espacio para**

ponerlo I haven't got much room for it.

espaguetis plural noun Masc. spaghetti.

espalda noun Fem. back; **ser ancho de espaldas** to be broad-shouldered; **darle la espalda a alguien** to have your back to somebody, to turn your back on somebody; **nos daba la espalda** he had his back to us; **nadar de espaldas** to swim backstroke; **tumbarse de espaldas** to lie on your back.

España noun Fem. Spain.

español[1] noun Masc. Spanish (the language).

español[2]**/española** noun Masc./Fem. Spaniard; **los españoles** the Spanish.

español adjective Spanish.

espantapájaros noun Masc. scarecrow.

espantoso/espantosa adjective **1** horrific (crime); **2** horrible; **un vestido espantoso** a horrible dress; **tiene un gusto espantoso** he has a horrible sense of taste; **3** **hacía un frío espantoso** it was terribly cold; **tengo un sueño espantoso** I'm terribly sleepy.

esparadrapo noun Masc. sticking plaster.

esparcimiento noun Masc. Masc. relaxation.

espárrago noun Masc. asparagus.

especia noun Fem. spice.

especial adjective special.

a b c d e f g h i j k l m n ñ o p q r s t u v w x y z

especialidad noun Fem. speciality.

espectáculo noun Masc. **1** sight; **era un espectáculo espantoso** it was a terrible sight; **2** show; **el mundo del espectáculo** show business.

espectador/espectadora noun Masc./Fem. spectator.

espejo noun Masc. mirror; **espejo retrovisor** rear-view mirror.

espera noun Fem. wait; **una corta espera** a short wait; **estar a la espera de algo** to be waiting for something.

esperanza noun Fem. hope; **darle esperanzas a alguien** to build up somebody's hopes; **hay pocas esperanzas de encontrarlos** there's little hope of finding them.

esperar verb [17] **1** to wait; **espera aquí** wait here; **2** to wait for; **te he estado esperando más de una hora** I've been waiting for you for more than an hour; **3** to hope; **espero que vengas** I hope you'll come; **espero que sí/eso espero** I hope so; **4** to expect; **no esperaba esa respuesta** I didn't expect that answer.

espeso/espesa adjective thick.

espesor noun Masc. thickness.

espesura noun Fem. thickness; **tiene diez centímetros de espesura** it's ten centimetres thick.

espía noun Masc./Fem. spy.

espiar verb [32] to spy on.

espina noun Fem. thorn.

espinaca noun Fem. spinach.

espionaje noun Masc. spying, espionage.

espléndido/espléndida adjective **1** splendid (a party, day, or house); **2** generous (a person).

espliego noun Masc. lavender.

esponja noun Fem. sponge.

esposa noun Fem. **1** wife; **la esposa de Juan** Juan's wife; **2** esposas handcuffs.

esposo noun Masc. husband; **el esposo de mi hermana** my sister's husband.

espuma noun Fem. **1** foam; **espuma de afeitar** shaving foam; **2** lather (of soap); **3** froth (of beer); **4** espuma para el pelo styling mousse.

espumoso/espumosa adjective **1** foaming; **2** frothy (beer); **3** vino espumoso sparkling wine.

esqueleto noun Masc. skeleton; ★ **estar hecho un esqueleto** to be all skin and bones.

esquí noun Masc. **1** ski; **2** skiing; **practicar el esquí** to go skiing; **esquí acuático** waterskiing; **esquí nórdico/esquí de fondo** cross-country skiing.

esquiador/esquiadora noun Masc./Fem. skier.

esquiar verb [32] to ski.

esquimal noun Masc./Fem., **esquimal** adjective Eskimo.

esquina noun Fem. corner; **doblar la esquina** to turn the corner; **vivo en la esquina de la calle León con la calle Viriato** I live on the corner of León Street and Viriato Street.

esta[1] *adjective* this (*see 'este/esta' for examples*).

esta[2], **ésta** *pronoun* this one (*see 'este/esta' for examples*).

está *verb* SEE **estar**.

estación *noun Fem.* **1** station; **la estación de autobuses** the bus station; **una estación de servicio** a petrol station; **2** season; **el otoño es mi estación preferida** autumn is my favourite season; **la estación de las lluvias** the rainy season; **3 una estación de esquí** a ski resort.

estacionar *verb* [17] to park; **estacionar en doble fila** to double park.

estacionario/estacionaria *adjective* stationary.

estadio *noun Masc.* stadium; **el estadio de fútbol** the football stadium.

estado *noun Masc.* **1** state; **estado de guerra** state of war; **2 en buen estado** in good condition (*a picture, table, etc.*); **3 estado civil** marital status; **4 estar en estado** to be pregnant; **5 un estado de cuenta** a bank statement.

Estados Unidos *plural noun Masc.* United States.

estafa *noun Fem.* swindle; **¡qué estafa!** what rip-off!

estáis *verb* SEE **estar**.

estallar *verb* [17] **1** to explode (*a bomb*); **2** to burst (*a balloon*); **3** to blow out (*a tyre*).

estancia *noun Fem.* stay; **su estancia en Madrid durará tres días** his stay in Madrid will last three days.

estanco *noun Masc.* tobacconist's.

estanque *noun Masc.* pond.

estante *noun Masc.* shelf.

estantería *noun Fem.* **1** shelves; **2** bookcase.

estar *verb* [2] **1** (*location*) to be; **¿dónde está mi abrigo?** where's my coat?; **¿has estado en Buenos Aires?** have you been to Buenos Aires?; **estaré en Leeds un mes** I'll be in Leeds for a month; **2** (*state*) to be; **estoy contento** I'm happy; **está casado** he's married; **¿cómo estás?** how are you?; **desde que hablé con él está más simpático** he's nicer since I had a chat with him; **3** (*appearance, taste*) **esta paella está muy buena** this paella is very nice; **con ese vestido estás muy guapa** you look very nice in that dress; **4** (*with dates*) **estamos a tres de julio** it's the third of July today; **5 estar de** to be; **estar de viaje** to be away on a trip; **están de vacaciones** they're on holiday; **6** (*with a gerund or past participle*) to be; **están trabajando en Soria** they're working in Soria; **está nevando** it's snowing; **estaban sentados allí** they were sitting over there; **aún no está terminado** it's not finished yet; **7** (*talking about how clothes fit*) **la chaqueta no me está bien** the jacket doesn't fit me; **esa falda te está corta** this skirt is too short for you; **me está grande** it's

a
b
c
d
e
f
g
h
i
j
k
l
m
n
ñ
o
p
q
r
s
t
u
v
w
x
y
z

a
b
c
d
e
f
g
h
i
j
k
l
m
n
ñ
o
p
q
r
s
t
u
v
w
x
y
z

too big for me; **8 lo firmas y ya está** you sign it and that's that; **¿están ya las fotocopias?** are the photocopies ready?; **las patatas ya están** the potatoes are done.

estarse *reflexive verb* [2] **1** to be; **se estuvo sentado toda la tarde** he was sitting down all afternoon; **2** to stay; **se está horas mirando la tele** he stays in front of the TV for hours; **¡estate quieto!** keep still!

estatua *noun Fem.* statue.

estatus *noun Masc.* status.

este[1] *noun Masc.* east.

este[2]/**esta** *adjective* this; **este libro** this book; **esta chica** this girl.

este[3]/**esta, éste/ésta** *pronoun* this one; **este es más bonito** this one is nicer; **esta es tu bolsa** this one is your bag.

esté, estén *verb* SEE **estar.**

estera *noun Fem.* **1** rush matting; **2** rush mat; **3** beach mat.

estéreo *noun Masc.* stereo.

estés *verb* SEE **estar.**

esteticista *noun Masc./Fem.* beautician.

estilo *noun Masc.* **1** style; **2 ni nada por el estilo** or anything like that; **o algo por el estilo** or something of the kind.

estilográfica *noun Fem.* fountain pen.

estirar *verb* [17] to stretch.

esto *pronoun* this; **¿qué es esto?** what is this?; **esto es lo más**

importante this is the most important thing.

estofado *noun Masc.* stew.

estómago *noun Masc.* stomach; **me duele el estómago** I've got stomachache.

Estonia *noun Fem.* Estonia.

estonio/estonia *noun Masc./Fem., adjective* Estonian.

estornudar *verb* [17] to sneeze.

estornudo *noun Masc.* sneeze.

estoy *verb* SEE **estar.**

estrecho/estrecha *adjective* **1** narrow; **una calle estrecha** a narrow street; **2** tight; **me queda muy estrecho** it's too tight for me.

estrella *noun Fem.* star; **estrella fugaz** shooting star; **estrella de cine** film star.

estrellarse *reflexive verb* [17] to crash; **estrellarse contra algo** to crash into something.

estrenar *verb* [17] **1 la película se estrena el próximo lunes** the film comes out next Monday; **2 el domingo estrenaré los zapatos** I'll wear my new shoes on Sunday; **aún no he estrenado la bici** I haven't used the new bike yet.

estresado/estresada *adjective* stressed.

estricto/estricta *adjective* strict.

estropear *verb* [17] **1** to break; **vas a estropear la tele si sigues haciendo eso** you'll wreck the TV if you carry on doing that; **2** to spoil; **el tiempo nos estropeó las vacaciones** the weather spoiled our holidays; **3** to damage; **me estropeó el coche** he damaged my car; **4** to ruin (*a carpet or dress, for example*).

estropearse *reflexive verb* [17] **1** to break down; **se ha estropeado el coche otra vez** the car's broken down again; **2** to go off (*fruit*); **3** to go bad (*milk or fish*); **4** to get ruined (*a carpet or dress, for example*).

estructura *noun Fem.* structure.

estuche *noun Masc.* case (*for glasses, pencils etc*).

estudiante *noun Masc./Fem.* student.

estudiar *verb* [17] **1** to study; **estudiar medicina** to study medicine; **2** to learn; **tenemos que estudiar dos temas para mañana** we have to study two topics for tomorrow.

estudio *noun Masc.* **1** studio (*in a house*); **2** studio flat; **3** study; **el estudio de la naturaleza** the study of nature.

estudios *plural noun Masc.* studies; **estudios de medicina** medical studies; **estudios de mercado** market research.

estufa *noun Fem.* heater, fire.

estupendo/estupenda *adjective* great; **¿ganaste? ¡estupendo!** did you win? great!

estúpido/estúpida *noun Masc./ Fem.* stupid person; **es un estúpido** he's really stupid.

estúpido *adjective* stupid.

estuve, estuvo, etc. *verb* SEE **estar.**

etapa *noun Fem.* stage; **por etapas** in stages.

etcétera *noun Masc.* etcetera.

eternidad *noun Fem.* eternity.

ética *noun Fem.* ethics.

etiqueta *noun Masc.* **1** label; **2** price tag.

euro *noun Masc.* euro; **el euro se divide en cien céntimos** the euro is divided in a hundred cents.

Europa *noun Fem.* Europe.

europeo/europea *noun Masc./ Fem., adjective* European.

eurozona *noun Fem.* eurozone.

Euskadi *noun Fem.* the Basque Country.

euskera *noun Masc.* Basque (*the language*).

euskera *adjective* Basque.

evaluación *noun Fem.* assessment.

evaporarse *reflexive verb* [17] to evaporate.

evidencia *noun Fem.* evidence.

evidente *adjective* obvious.

evidentemente *adverb* obviously.

evitar *verb* [17] **1** to avoid; **evitan tomar la responsabilidad** they avoid taking responsibility; **2** to prevent; **evitar un accidente** to prevent an accident.

evolución *noun Fem.* evolution.

exactamente *adverb* exactly.

exacto/exacta *adjective* **1** exact; **2** accurate.

exagerar *verb* [17] to exaggerate.

a
b
c
d
e
f
g
h
i
j
k
l
m
n
ñ
o
p
q
r
s
t
u
v
w
x
y
z

a b c d e f g h i j k l m n ñ o p q r s t u v w x y z

examen noun Masc. exam; **hacer un examen** to take an exam; **presentarse a un examen** to sit an exam; **aprobar un examen** to pass an exam; **un examen oral** an oral exam.

examinar verb [17] to examine. **examinarse** reflexive verb [17] to take an exam.

excelente adjective excellent.

excepción noun Fem. exception; **hacer una excepción** to make an exception; **a excepción de** with the exception of.

excepcional adjective exceptional.

excepcionalmente adverb exceptionally.

excepto preposition except for.

excursión noun Fem. trip; **ir de excursión al campo** to go on a trip to the countryside.

excusa noun Fem. excuse; **poner excusas** to make excuses.

exigente adjective demanding.

exigir verb [49] to demand.

existir verb [19] 1 to exist; 2 **existen motivos para pensarlo** there are reasons to think that.

éxito noun Masc. success; **tener éxito** to be successful.

experiencia noun Fem. experience.

experimentado/ experimentada adjective experienced.

experimento noun Masc. experiment.

experto/experta noun Masc./ Fem. expert.

explicación noun Fem. explanation.

explicar verb [31] to explain.

explotar verb [17] to explode.

exportación noun Fem. export; **la lana es la exportación más importante** wool is the most important export.

exportar verb [17] to export; **Rusia exporta mucha madera y petróleo** Russia exports a lot of oil and timber.

exposición noun Fem. exhibition.

expresar verb [17] to express.

expresión noun Fem. expression.

expreso[1] noun Masc. 1 express train; 2 espresso (coffee).

expreso[2]**/expresa** adjective express; **correo expreso** express mail.

exterior noun Masc. 1 exterior, outside; **el exterior de la casa** the outside of the house; 2 outward appearance; **en su exterior estaba tranquilo** his outward appearance was calm.

exterior adjective 1 outer (layer); 2 outside (temperature); 3 **la parte exterior de la casa** the outside of the house; 4 foreign; **política exterior** foreign policy.

externo/externa adjective 1 outward (appearance or signs); 2 external.

extinción noun Fem. extinction; **una especie en en vías de extinción** an endangered species.

extincto *adjective* extinct.

extintor *noun Masc.* **extintor (de incendios)** fire extinguisher.

extrañar *verb* [17] **me extraña que no hayan llamado** I'm surprised they haven't phoned; **le extrañó verla allí** he was surprised to see her there.

extranjero[1] *noun Masc.* **vivir en el extranjero** to live abroad; **viaja mucho al extranjero** he travels abroad a lot.

extranjero[2]/**extranjera** *noun Masc./Fem.* foreigner.

extranjero *adjective* foreign.

extraño/extraña *noun Masc./Fem.* stranger.

extraño *adjective* strange.

extraordinario/extraordinaria *adjective* extraordinary.

extraterrestre *noun Masc./Fem.* alien *(from outer space)*.

extremo[1] *noun Masc.* **1** extreme; **2** end.

extremo[2]/**extrema** *noun Masc./Fem.* winger *(in sports)*.

extremo *adjective* extreme.

extrovertido/extrovertida *adjective* extrovert.

Ff

fábrica *noun Fem.* factory.

fabricar *verb* [31] to manufacture.

fácil *adjective* easy; **es un trabajo fácil** it's an easy job; **fácil de hacer** easy to do; **es fácil de entender** it's easy to understand.

facilidad *noun Fem.* **1** ease; **lo hice con facilidad** I did it with ease; **2 tener facilidad de palabra** to have a way with words.

fácilmente *adverb* easily.

factura *noun Fem.* **1** invoice; **2** bill.

facultad *noun Fem.* **1** faculty; **perder facultades** to lose your faculties; **2 ir a la facultad** to go to college; **la Facultad de Medicina** the Faculty of Medicine.

facultativo/facultativa *adjective* **1** optional; **2** medical.

faena *noun Fem.* task; **las faenas de la casa/domésticas** the housework.

faisán *noun Masc.* pheasant.

falda *noun Fem.* skirt; **una falda escocesa** a tartan skirt, a kilt; **una falda de tubo** a straight skirt.

falla *noun Fem.* flaw.

fallar *verb* [17] **1** to fail *(equipment or brakes, for example)*; **2** to go wrong *(a plan)*; **algo ha fallado** something's gone wrong; **3 me falló la puntería** I missed *(the target)*.

fallo *noun Masc.* **1** fault; **el motor tiene un fallo** there's something wrong with the engine; **2** failure; **un fallo en el sistema** a failure in the system; **3 fallo humano** human error; **4** verdict *(in court or competition)*.

falsificación *noun Fem.* forgery; **el cuadro es una falsificación** the picture is a forgery.

falso/falsa *adjective* **1** false; **2** fake *(a diamond or picture, for example)*.

a
b
c
d
e
f
g
h
i
j
k
l
m
n
ñ
o
p
q
r
s
t
u
v
w
x
y
z

falta noun Fem. **1** lack; **falta de algo** lack of something; **por falta de dinero** due to lack of money; **falta de personal** staff shortage; **2 falta de educación** bad manners; **eso es una falta de educación** that's bad manners; **fue una falta de educación por su parte** it was really rude of him; **3** misdemeanour; **una falta grave** a serious misdemeanour; **4 falta de asistencia** absence (from school); **poner una falta a alguien** to mark someone absent; **ya tiene tres faltas** he's been absent three times already; **5 una falta de ortografía** a spelling mistake; **6** foul (in sport) **sacar la falta** to take the free kick; **7 hace falta lavarlo** it needs to be washed; **hace falta comprar pan** we need to buy bread; **no hace falta cambiarlo** it doesn't need to be changed; **no hace falta que me esperes** you don't need to wait for me; **8 me hace falta un bolígrafo** I need a pen; **no me hace falta nada más, gracias** I don't need any more, thank you.

faltar verb [17] **1** to be missing; **¿quién falta?** who's missing?; **2 faltar al colegio** to be absent from school; **3 nos falta práctica** we need practice; **nos faltan mil euros para poder comprarlo** we need a thousand euros to buy it; **le falta interés** he lacks interest; **4 sólo faltan tres días** there are only three more days to go; **faltan diez días para mi cumpleaños** it's ten days to my birthday; **falta**

poco para el verano it's almost summertime; **aún falta mucho para las doce** there's still a long way to go till twelve o'clock; **¿te falta mucho?** are you going to be long?; **no les falta mucho para terminar** they've almost finished; **nos faltó tiempo** we didn't have enough time.

fama noun Fem. **1** fame; **2** reputation; **tener buena fama** to have a good reputation; **tener fama de mentiroso** to have a reputation for being a liar.

familia noun Fem. family; **ser de familia numerosa** to be from a large family.

familiar noun Masc./Fem. relative.

familiar adjective **1** family; **tuve problemas familiares** I had family problems; **2** familiar.

famoso/famosa adjective famous.

fantasía noun Fem. **1** fantasy; **un mundo de fantasía** a fantasy world; **2** imagination; **tener mucha fantasía** to have a lot of imagination; **3 joyas de fantasía** costume jewellery.

fantasma noun Masc. ghost.

fantástico/fantástica adjective fantastic.

farmacéutico/farmacéutica noun Masc./Fem. chemist, pharmacist.

farmacéutico adjective pharmaceutical.

farmacia noun Fem. chemist's, pharmacy; **farmacia de guardia/ de turno** duty chemist.

farmacia noun Fem. chemist's; **farmacia de guardia/de turno** duty chemist.

faro noun Masc. **1** lighthouse; **2** headlamp.

farola noun Fem. **1** streetlight; **2** lamp post.

fascinar verb [17] to fascinate.

fastidiar verb [17] to annoy; **sólo lo hacen para fastidiar** they only do it to annoy; **¡deja de fastidiar!** stop being a pain!

fastidiarse reflexive verb [17] **¡que se fastidie!** he'll have to put up with it!; **¡te fastidias!** tough!

fastidio noun Masc. annoyance; **¡qué fastidio!** how annoying!

fatal adjective **1** (informal) awful; **sentirse fatal** to feel awful; **estar fatal** to be really ill, to be really badly done; **2** fatal (an accident or illness).

fatal adverb **canto fatal** I am hopeless at singing.

favor noun Masc. **1** favour; **hacerle un favor a alguien** to do someone a favour; **pedir un favor** to ask for a favour; **estar a favor de algo** to be in favour of something; **2 por favor** please.

favorito/favorita adjective favourite.

fax noun Masc. fax.

fe noun Fem. faith.

febrero noun Masc. February.

fecha noun Fem. date; **fecha de nacimiento** date of birth; **¿a qué fecha estamos hoy?** what's the date today?; **fecha de caducidad** expiry date (for medicines), use-by date (for food).

felicidad noun Fem. **1** happiness; **2 ¡felicidades!** happy birthday!, congratulations!.

felicitar verb [17] **felicitar a alguien** to wish someone happy birthday; to congratulate someone.

feliz adjective (plural **felices**) happy; **¡feliz Año Nuevo!** Happy New Year!; **¡feliz Navidad!** Merry Christmas!; **feliz cumpleaños** happy birthday; **felices Pascuas** Happy Easter.

felpudo noun Masc. doormat.

femenino[1] noun Masc. feminine.

femenino[2]/femenina adjective **1** woman's; **el equipo femenino** the women's team; **2** feminine (style, manners, or noun); **3** female; **el sexo femenino** the female sex.

fenomenal adjective (informal) great.

fenomenal adverb great; **pasarlo fenomenal** to have a great time.

feo/fea adjective ugly.

feria noun Fem. fair.

feroz adjective fierce.

ferretería noun Fem. ironmonger's.

ferrocarril noun Masc. railway.

ferry noun Masc. ferry.

festivo/festiva adjective **1** festive (atmosphere); **2 un día festivo** a public holiday.

fiable adjective reliable.

fiambre noun Masc. cold meats.

fiarse reflexive verb [32] **1 fiarse de** to believe; **no te fíes de los**

periódicos don't believe what the newspapers say; **2 fiarse de alguien** to trust someone.

fibra noun Fem. fibre.

ficción noun Fem. fiction.

ficha noun Fem. **1** card; **2 ficha médica** medical card; **ficha policial** police records; **3** token (for the telephone); **4** counter (in games).

fideo noun Masc. noodle.

fiebre noun Fem. **1** temperature; **tener fiebre** to have a temperature; **le ha subido la fiebre** his temperature has gone up; **2** fever; **fiebre del heno** hay fever.

fiel adjective **1** faithful; **no le es fiel a su mujer** he's not faithful to his wife; **2** loyal; **3** accurate (a translation or copy, for example).

fiesta noun Fem. **1** party; **2** public holiday; **mañana es fiesta** tomorrow's a holiday.

figura noun Fem. figure.

figurar verb [17] to appear.

figurarse reflexive verb [17] to imagine; **me figuro que sí** I imagine so.

fijar verb [17] to fix; **fijar una fecha** to fix a date.

fijarse reflexive verb [17] **1 fijarse en algo** to look at something; **2** to notice; **se fija en todo** she notices everything.

fijo/fija adjective **1** fixed; **precios fijos** fixed prices; **está fijo a la pared** it's fixed to the wall; **2** permanent (a job); **3 ¿está la escalera bien fija?** is the ladder steady?

fila noun Fem. **1** line; **hacer fila** to form a line; **en fila india** in single line; **2** row (of seats in the theatre or cinema).

filete noun Masc. **1** steak; **2** fillet (of fish).

filmar verb [17] **1** to shoot (a film); **2** to film.

filosofía noun Fem. philosophy.

fin noun Masc. **1** end; **llegar al fin** to get to the end; **el fin de semana** the weekend; **a fin de mes** at the end of the month; **fin de año** New Year's Eve; **2 al fin/por fin** at last; **3 en fin, ya te llamaré** anyway, I'll give you a ring.

final noun Masc. **1** end; **el final de las vacaciones** the end of the holidays; **2** ending; **una película con final feliz** a film with a happy ending; **3 al final** at the end; **al final del libro** at the end of the book; **4 al final** in the end; **al final lo conseguí hacer** I managed to do it in the end.

final noun Fem. final.

final adjective final.

finca noun Fem. **1** plot of land; **2** farm.

finlandés¹ noun Masc. Finnish (the language).

finlandés²/finlandesa noun Masc./Fem. Finn.

finlandés/finlandesa adjective Finnish.

Finlandia noun Fem. Finland.

fino¹ noun Masc. dry sherry.

fino²/fina adjective **1** fine (a line, for example); **2** thin (a layer or slice); **3** slender (waist or finger);

a b c d e f g h i j k l m n ñ o p q r s t u v w x y z

4 refined (*a person*); **5** subtle (*sense of humour*); **6** tener el oído muy fino to have a very acute sense of hearing; tener el olfato muy fino to have a very acute sense of smell.

firma *noun Fem.* **1** signature; **2** company.

firmar *verb* [17] to sign.

firme *adjective* **1** steady (*a ladder or chair, for example*); con pulso firme with a steady hand; **2** firm; **3** estudiar de firme to study hard.

física[1] *noun Fem.* physics.

físico[1] *noun Masc.* **1** physique; **2** appearance.

físico[3]/**física**[2] *noun Masc./Fem.* physicist.

físico *adjective* physical.

fisioterapia *noun Fem.* physiotherapy.

fitness *noun Masc.* fitness training.

flaco/flaca *adjective* thin.

flamenco[1] *noun Masc.* flamenco.

flamenco[2]/**flamenca** *adjective* flamenco; baile flamenco flamenco dancing.

flan *noun Masc.* caramel custard.

flauta *noun Fem.* flute; flauta dulce recorder.

flecha *noun Fem.* arrow.

flequillo *noun Masc.* fringe.

flexible *adjective* flexible.

flojo/floja *adjective* **1** loose (*a knot or screw*); **2** slack (*rope*); **3** weak (*coffee or tea*); **4** poor (*piece of work*).

flor *noun Fem.* flower; de flores flower-patterned; una falda de flores a flower-patterned skirt; estar en flor to be in flower.

florero *noun Masc.* flowerpot.

florista *noun Masc./Fem.* florist.

floristería *noun Fem.* florist's.

flota *noun Fem.* fleet.

flotar *verb* [17] to float.

fluido[1]/**fluida** *adj* fluid, freeflowing; la circulación está fluida the traffic is flowing freely.

fluido[2] *noun Masc.* fluid.

fluir *verb* [54] to flow.

flujo *noun Masc.* flow.

foca *noun Fem.* seal (*animal*).

foco *noun Masc.* **1** focus; el foco de atención the focus of attention; **2** spotlight.

folclórico/folclórica *adjective* folk; musica folclórica folk music.

folleto *noun Masc.* **1** leaflet; **2** brochure.

fondo *noun Masc.* **1** bottom; el fondo del lago the bottom of the lake; al fondo del baúl at the bottom of the trunk; llegar al fondo de la cuestión to get to the bottom of the matter; sin fondo bottomless; **2** back; está al fondo de la sala it's at the back of the room; **3** end; al fondo del pasillo at the end of the corridor; **4** kitty; hacer un fondo común to make a kitty; **5** fondos funds (*money*); **6** estudiar algo a fondo to study something in depth; prepararse a fondo to prepare thoroughly; **7** ruido de fondo background noise; música de fondo background music.

fontanero/fontanera noun
Masc./Fem. plumber.

footing noun Masc. jogging; **hacer footing** to go jogging.

forastero/forastera noun
Masc./Fem. stranger.

forma noun Fem. **1** shape; **con la forma de una hoja** leaf-shaped; **tiene forma cuadrada** it's square; **2** way; **es mi forma de ser** it's the way I am; **3 en forma** fit; **mantenerse en forma** to keep fit; **4 de todas formas** anyway.

formación noun Fem.
1 education; **un chico con una buena formación** a well-educated boy; **2** training; **formación profesional** vocational training.

formal adjective **1** reliable (person); **2** formal (dinner or invitation); **3** firm (offer).

formar verb [17] **1** to form; **formar un grupo de música** to form a band; **2** to make up; **el equipo está formado por doce miembros** the team's made up of twelve members; **3 formar parejas** to get into pairs (in class or games); **4** to educate (a person).

formarse reflexive verb [17] **1** to be educated; **2** to form; **formarse una opinión** to form an opinion; **se formó un atasco** a traffic jam formed.

formidable adjective formidable.

fórmula noun Fem. formula.

formulario noun Masc. form.

fortaleza noun Fem. fortress.

fortuna noun Fem. **1** fortune; **ganar una fortuna** to earn a

fortune; **2 por fortuna** fortunately; **3 tener la buena fortuna de hacer** to have the good fortune of doing; **tuve la buena fortuna de conocerlos** I had the good fortune of meeting them; **4 probar fortuna** to try your luck.

forzar verb [26] **1** to force; **me forzaron a aceptar** they forced me to accept; **2 forzar la vista** to strain your eyes.

forzarse reflexive verb [26]
forzarse a hacer to force yourself to do.

fosa noun Fem. pit; **las fosas nasales** the nostrils.

fósforo noun Masc. match (that you strike).

foto noun Fem. photo; **sacar/hacer una foto** to take a photo.

fotocopia noun Fem. photocopy.

fotocopiadora noun Fem. photocopier.

fotocopiar verb [17] to photocopy.

fotografía noun Fem.
1 photography; **2** photograph; **sacer una fotografía** to take a photograph.

fotógrafo/fotógrafa noun
Masc./Fem. photographer.

fracasar verb [17] to fail.

fracaso noun Masc. failure.

fractura noun Fem. fracture.

frágil adjective fragile.

frambuesa noun Fem. raspberry; **mermelada de frambuesas** raspberry jam.

francés[1] noun Masc. French (the language).

rancés²/francesa noun Masc./Fem. Frenchman/Frenchwoman.

rancés/francesa adjective French.

rancia noun Fem. France.

rasco noun Masc. **1** bottle; **2** jar; **un frasco de mermelada** a jar of jam.

rase noun Fem. **1** sentence; **2** phrase; **frase hecha** set phrase.

raude noun Masc. fraud.

recuencia noun Fem. frequency; **con frecuencia** often.

recuente adjective frequent.

recuentemente adverb often, frequently.

regadero noun Masc. sink.

regar verb [30] **1** to wash; **fregar los platos** to wash the dishes; **2 fregar el suelo** to mop the floor; **3** to scrub.

reír verb [53] to fry.

renar verb [17] **1** to brake; **2** to slow down (a process); **3** to curb (inflation).

reno noun Masc. brake.

rente noun Masc. **1** front; **2 al frente de la manifestación** at the head of the demonstration; **al frente de la patrulla** leading the patrol; **3 al frente del equipo** in charge of the team; **4 dar un paso al frente** to step forward; **5 hacer frente a** to face (a problem or attacker).

rente noun Fem. forehead.

resa noun Fem. strawberry; **mermelada de fresas** strawberry jam.

fresco¹ noun Masc. **1** fresh air; **tomar el fresco** to get some fresh

air; **estar al fresco** to be out in the fresh air; **2 hace fresco** it's chilly; **3** fresco (painting).

fresco²/fresca adjective **1** cool; **una bebida fresca** a cool drink; **una brisa fresca** a cool breeze; **2 hoy hace fresco** it's chilly today; **3** fresh; **pescado fresco** fresh fish; **4 pintura fresca** wet paint; **5 ¡qué fresco!** what a nerve!; **ser muy fresco** to have a nerve.

fría, frío, etc. verb SEE **freír**.

friega, friego, friegue, etc. verb SEE **fregar**.

frigorífico noun Masc. fridge.

frijol noun Masc. bean; **frijoles volteados** fried beans.

frío¹ noun Masc. cold; **hace frío** it's cold; **tengo frío** I'm cold; **un día frío** a cold day.

frío²/fría adjective cold.

frito/frita adjective **1** fried; **2 quedarse frito** (informal) to fall asleep.

frontera noun border Fem.; **cruzamos la frontera en Irún** we crossed the border at Irún.

frotar verb [17] to rub.

frotarse reflexive verb [17] to rub.

fruncir verb [66] **fruncir el ceño** to frown.

frustrante adjective frustrating.

frustrar verb [17] **1** to frustrate (person); **me frustra que ...** I find it frustrating that ...; **2** to thwart (plans).

fruta noun Fem. fruit.

a b c d e f g h i j k l m n ñ o p q r s t u v w x y z

frutería noun Fem. fruit shop.

frutero noun Masc. fruit bowl.

fruto noun Masc. fruit; **frutos secos** nuts and dried fruits.

fue verb SEE **ser, ir.**

fuego noun Masc. 1 fire; **encender el fuego** to light the fire; **prender fuego a algo** to set fire to something; 2 **¿tienes fuego?** have you got a light?; 3 **a fuego lento** on a low heat.

fuegos artificiales noun Masc. (plural) fireworks.

fuente noun Fem. 1 spring; 2 fountain; 3 large dish; **una fuente de servir** a serving dish; **una fuente de horno** an ovenproof dish.

fuera, fuéramos, etc. verb SEE **ser, ir.**

fuera adverb 1 out; **¡sal fuera!** go out!; **ahí fuera** out there; **salimos a cenar fuera** we went out for dinner; 2 outside; **están esperando fuera** they're waiting outside; **la parte de fuera de la maleta** the outside of the suitcase; **deja las cajas fuera** leave the boxes outside; **por fuera es plateado** it's silver on the outside; 3 away; **el jefe está fuera** the boss is away; 4 abroad; **están fuera del país** they're abroad; 5 **fuera de peligro** out of danger; **fuera de lugar** out of place; **fuera de serie** exceptional; 6 **fuera de juego** offside.

fueron verb SEE **ser, ir.**

fuerte adjective 1 strong; **ser fuerte** to be strong; **un olor fuerte** a strong smell; 2 loud; **no pongas la música tan fuerte** don't play the music so loud; 3 hard (blow); 4 big; **un beso fuerte** a big kiss; 5 substantial; **tomamos una comida fuerte al mediodía** we have a big meal at lunchtime; 6 **un dolor fuerte** an intense pain.

fuerte adverb 1 hard; **pegar fuerte** hit it hard; 2 tight; **agárralo fuerte** hold it tight.

fuerza noun Fem. 1 strength; **tener fuerza** to be strong; **no tuvo fuerza para levantarlo** he wasn't strong enough to lift it; 2 **hice fuerza y conseguí abrirlo** I used all my strength and I managed to open it; 3 **empujar con fuerza** to push hard; 4 **por la fuerza** by force; **lo obligaron a entrar en el coche por la fuerza** they forced him to get into the car; 5 **a fuerza de** by; **a fuerza de empujar** by pushing; 6 force; **fuerza aérea** air force; **fuerzas armadas** armed forces; 7 **fuerza de voluntad** willpower.

fuga noun Fem. 1 leak; **una fuga de gas** a gas leak; 2 **una fuga de prisioneros** a jailbreak; 3 **darse a la fuga** to flee.

fui, fuimos, fuiste, etc. verb SEE **ser, ir.**

fumador/fumadora noun Masc./Fem. smoker.

fumar verb [17] to smoke.

función noun Fem. 1 function; 2 performance; **función de noche** late-night performance; **función benéfica** charity performance.

funcionar verb [17] **1** to work; ¿cómo funciona? how does it work?; **'no funciona'** 'out of order'; **2** to run; funciona con electricidad it runs on electricity.

funcionario/funcionaria noun Masc./Fem. government employee.

funda noun Fem. **1** cover (for a cushion, pillow, etc.); **2** sleeve (of a record); **3** pillow case.

fundamental adjective fundamental.

fundir verb [19] to melt. **fundirse** reflexive verb [19] to melt.

funeral noun Masc. funeral.

funeraria noun Fem. funeral director's.

furgoneta noun Fem. van.

furia noun Fem. fury; **estar hecho una furia** (informal) to be furious.

furioso/furiosa adjective furious; **ponerse furioso** to get furious.

fusible noun Masc. fuse; **saltaron los fusibles** the fuses blew.

fusil noun Masc. rifle.

fusionar verb to merge.

futbito noun Masc. five-a-side football.

fútbol noun Masc. football; **jugar al fútbol** to play football.

futbolín noun Masc. **1** table football; **2** los futbolines the amusement arcade.

futbolista noun Masc./Fem. footballer.

fútbol sala noun Masc. indoor-football.

futuro[1] noun Masc. future.

futuro[2]/**futura** adjective future.

Gg

gafas plural noun Fem. glasses; **gafas de sol** sunglasses; **llevar gafas** to wear glasses.

galápago noun Masc. **1** giant turtle; **2** terrapin.

galaxia noun Fem. galaxy.

galería noun Fem. **1** gallery; **galería de arte** art gallery; **2 galería comercial** shopping arcade.

galés[1] noun Masc. Welsh (the language).

galés[2]/**galesa** noun Masc./Fem. Welshman/Welshwoman.

galés/galesa adjective Welsh.

Gales noun Masc. **el país de Gales** Wales.

gallego[1] noun Masc. Galician (the language).

gallego[2]/**gallega** noun Masc./Fem. Galician.

gallego adjective Galician.

galleta noun Fem. biscuit.

gallina noun Fem. hen.

gallo noun Masc. cockerel.

galopar verb [17] to gallop.

gamba noun Fem. prawn.

gamberro/gamberra noun Masc./Fem. **1** rowdy; **2** hooligan.

gamberro adjective **es muy gamberro** he's a real rowdy, he's a real hooligan.

a
b
c
d
e
f
g
h
i
j
k
l
m
n
ñ
o
p
q
r
s
t
u
v
w
x
y
z

a
b
c
d
e
f
g
h
i
j
k
l
m
n
ñ
o
p
q
r
s
t
u
v
w
x
y
z

gana noun Fem. **1 tener ganas de hacer algo** to feel like doing something; **no tengo ganas de ir al cine** I don't feel like going to the cinema; **2 tengo ganas de verlos** I'm looking forward to seeing them; **3** (informal) **no lo hace porque no le da la gana hacerlo** he doesn't do it because he doesn't want to; **voy porque me da la gana** I'm going because I feel like it; **hace siempre lo que le da la gana** she always does as she pleases; **4 hacer algo sin ganas** to do something half-heartedly; **hacer algo de buena gana** to do something willingly; **hacer algo de mala gana** to do something reluctantly.

ganador/ganadora noun Masc./Fem. winner.

ganador adjective winning (number).

ganancia noun Fem. profit.

ganar verb [17] **1** to win; **ganar una carrera** to win a race; **ganaron el primer premio** they won first prize; **2** to earn; **gano un buen sueldo** I earn a good salary.

ganarse reflexive verb [17] **1** to earn; **ganarse la vida** to earn your living; **se gana la vida pintando** he earns his living painting; **2** to win; **ganarse la confianza de alguien** to win someone's trust.

gancho noun Masc. hook.

ganga noun Fem. bargain.

ganso/gansa noun Masc./Fem. **1** goose; (informal) **ser un ganso** to be a clown; **hacer el ganso** to clown around.

garaje noun Masc. garage.

garantía noun Fem. guarantee; **bajo garantía** under guarantee.

garantizar verb [22] to guarantee.

garbanzo noun Masc. chickpea.

garganta noun Fem. throat; **me duele la garganta** I have a sore throat.

gas noun Masc. **1** gas; **una cocina a gas** a gas cooker; **2 gases tóxicos** toxic fumes.

gaseosa noun Fem. lemonade.

gasoil, gasóleo noun Masc. **1** heating oil; **2** diesel.

gasolina noun Fem. petrol; **voy a echar gasolina al coche** I'm going to put some petrol in the car; **gasolina sin plomo** unleaded petrol.

gasolinera noun Fem. petrol station.

gastar verb [17] **1** to spend; **gastar mucho en comida** they spend a lot of money on food; **2** to use; **mi coche gasta mucha gasolina** my car uses a lot of petrol; **me gastó todo el champú** she used up all my shampoo; **2 ¿qué número de pie gastas?** what shoe size do you take?

gastarse reflexive verb [17] to run out; **se han gastado las pilas** the batteries have run out.

gasto noun Masc. expense; **tenemos muchos gastos** we have a lot of expenses; **gastos de desplazamiento** travel expenses; **gastos de envío** postage and packing.

gatear verb [17] to crawl.

gato/gata noun Masc./Fem. cat.

gaviota noun Fem. seagull.

gazpacho noun Masc. gazpacho (*a chilled soup made with tomatoes, cucumber, and other vegetables*).

gel noun Masc. gel.

gelatina noun Fem. jelly.

gemelo/gemela noun Masc./Fem., adjective twin.

gemelos plural noun Masc. binoculars.

géminis noun Masc./Fem. Gemini; **soy géminis** I'm Gemini.

Géminis noun Masc. Gemini.

gemir verb [57] to groan; **gemir de dolor** to groan with pain.

generación noun Fem. generation.

general noun Masc./Fem. general; **el general Serrano** General Serrano.

general adjective general; **en general** in general; **por lo general** generally; **en líneas generales** broadly speaking.

generalmente adverb generally.

generoso/generosa adjective generous.

genética noun Fem. genetics.

genial adjective 1 brilliant; **una idea genial** a brilliant idea; 2 (*informal*) great, brilliant; **¡es genial!** it's great!

genio noun Masc. 1 genius; **Ana es un genio** Ana is a genius; 2 temper; **tener mal genio** to be bad-tempered; **¡vaya genio!** what a temper!

gente noun Fem. people; **vino mucha gente** a lot of people came; **la gente dice que ...** people say that ....

geografía noun Fem. geography.

geología noun Fem. geology.

geometría noun Fem. geometry.

gerente noun Masc./Fem. manager.

gestión noun Fem. 1 management; **la gestión de la empresa** the management of the company; 2 **tengo que hacer una gestión en el consulado** I have to sort things out at the consulate.

gesto noun Masc. gesture; **me hizo un gesto para que me acercara** he gestured to me to come over; **hice un gesto de asentimiento** I nodded.

Gibraltar noun Masc. Gibraltar.

gigabyte noun Masc. gigabyte; **un disco duro de veinte gigabytes** a twenty gigabyte hard disk.

gigante/giganta noun Masc./Fem. giant.

gimnasia noun Fem. 1 gymnastics; 2 exercise; **es bueno hacer gimnasia** it's good to get exercise; **gimnasia de mantenimiento** keep-fit; **clase de gimnasia** PE class.

gimnasio noun Masc. gym.

gin tonic noun Masc. gin and tonic.

ginebra noun Fem. gin.

girar verb [17] 1 to turn; **gira a la derecha en el semáforo** turn right at the traffic lights; **girar la cabeza** to turn your head; 2 to go

a b c d e f **g** h i j k l m n ñ o p q r s t u v w x y z

round; **la tierra gira alrededor del sol** the earth goes round the sun; **3** to spin; **4 girar un cheque** to draw a cheque; **5 girar dinero** to send money.

girasol *noun Masc.* sunflower.

gitano/gitana *noun Masc./Fem.* gypsy.

glaciar *noun Masc.* glacier.

globo *noun Masc.* **1** balloon; **2** lob (*in tennis*).

gloria *noun Fem.* glory.

glorieta *noun Fem.* **1** square (*in a town*); **2** roundabout (*on the road*).

glotón/glotona *adjective* greedy.

gobernar *verb* [17] **1** to rule; **2** to govern.

gobierno *noun Masc.* government.

gol *noun Masc.* goal; **marcar/meter un gol** to score a goal; **ganar/perder por tres goles a dos** to win/lose by three goals to two.

golf *noun Masc.* golf; **jugar al golf** to play golf.

golfista *noun Masc./Fem.* golfer.

golfo *noun Masc.* **1** gulf (*in geography*); **2** scoundrel; **eres un golfo** you're a scoundrel; **3** little rascal (*to a child*).

golondrina *noun Fem.* swallow.

golosina *noun Fem.* sweet; **no comas tantas golosinas** don't eat so many sweets.

golpe *noun Masc.* **1** knock; **darse un golpe** to knock yourself; **se dió un golpe en la pierna** he knocked his leg; **2** blow; **fue un duro golpe** it was a hard blow; **3 darle un golpe a alguien** to hit someone;

4 tap; **dar unos golpes en la mesa** to tap the table; **5 la ventana se cerró de golpe** the window slammed shut; **cerré el baúl de golpe** I slammed the trunk shut.

golpear *verb* [17] **1** to hit; **le golpeé el brazo con una revista** I hit him on the arm with a magazine; **2** to bang; **la ventana golpeaba por el viento** the window was banging in the wind; **3** to beat; **golpear un tambor** to beat a drum; **4** to tap.

golpearse *reflexive verb* [17] to bang; **se golpeó el brazo con la mesa** he banged his arm on the table.

goma *noun Fem.* **1** rubber; **botas de goma** rubber boots; **goma espuma** foam rubber; **2 una goma (de borrar)** a rubber; **3 una goma (elástica)** a rubber band.

gorda[1] *noun Fem.* fat woman.

gordo[1] *noun Masc.* **1** fat man; **2** jackpot (*in the state lottery*).

gordo[2]**/gorda**[2] *adjective* **1** fat; **ponerse gordo** to get fat; **2** thick (*book or jumper*); **3** serious (*problem or mistake*); ★ **me cae gordo** (*informal*) I can't stand him.

gorila *noun Masc.* gorilla.

gorra *noun Fem.* cap.

gorro *noun Masc.* cap.

gota *noun Fem.* drop.

gotear *verb* [17] **1** to drip; **2 una gota de** (*informal*) a drop of; **tomaré una gota de café** I'll have a drop of coffee; **no tiene ni una**

gota de paciencia he hasn't got the slightest bit of patience.

gozar verb [22] to enjoy; **gozo mucho oyendo música** I enjoy listening to music a lot; **todos gozamos del espectáculo** we all enjoyed the show.

grabación noun Fem. recording.

grabador noun Masc. tape recorder.

grabadora noun Fem. tape recorder.

grabar verb [17] to record.

gracia noun Fem. **1** joke; **hacer una gracia** to make a joke; **2 tener gracia** to be funny; **esa broma no tiene gracia** that joke isn't funny; **tiene mucha gracia contando cosas** she's very good at telling funny stories; **3 me hace gracia verlo** seeing it makes me laugh; **4 no me hace ninguna gracia ir** I don't like the idea of going at all.

gracias plural noun Fem. thank you; **muchas gracias** thank you very much; **darle las gracias a alguien** to thank someone; **gracias a ellos** thanks to them.

gracioso/graciosa adjective funny.

grado noun Masc. degree; **veinte grados centígrados** twenty degrees centigrade; **cinco grados bajo cero** five degrees below zero.

gradual adjective gradual.

graduarse reflexive verb [20] to graduate.

gráfico noun Masc. graph; **gráficos** graphics (in computing).

gramática noun Fem. grammar.

gramo noun Masc. gram.

gran adjective SEE **grande**.

Gran Bretaña noun Fem. Great Britain.

grande, gran adjective ('grande' becomes 'gran' before a singular noun) **1** big; **tienen una casa muy grande** they have a very big house; **la chaqueta me queda grande** the jacket's too big for me; **un gran número de personas** a great number of people; **2** great; **soy un gran admirador suyo** I'm a great admirer of hers; **es un gran actor** he's a great actor; **una gran oportunidad** a great opportunity; **3** grown-up; **cuando sea grande** when I grow up; **ya eres muy grande para hacer eso** you're too grown-up to do that; **4 grandes almacenes** department store.

granizado noun Masc. crushed ice drink; **granizado de limón** iced lemon drink.

granizar verb [22] to hail.

granizo noun Masc. hail.

granja noun Fem. farm.

granjero/granjera noun Masc./ Fem. farmer; **es granjero** he's a farmer.

grano noun Masc. **1** grain; **un grano de arena** a grain of sand; **2** (coffee) bean; **3** spot, pimple; **me ha salido un grano** I've got a spot.

grapa noun Fem. staple.

grapadora noun Fem. stapler.

grapar verb [17] to staple.

a
b
c
d
e
f
g
h
i
j
k
l
m
n
ñ
o
p
q
r
s
t
u
v
w
x
y
z

a

grasa noun Fem. **1** fat; **el contenido de grasa** the fat content; **2** grease; **el horno estaba lleno de grasa** the oven was covered in grease.

grasiento/grasienta adjective greasy.

gratis adjective free; **entrada gratis** free entry.

gratis adverb free; **los niños viajan gratis** children travel free.

gratuito/gratuita adjective free; **entrada gratuita** free entry.

grava noun Fem. gravel.

grave adjective serious; **está muy grave** he's seriously ill.

gravedad noun Fem. **1** gravity (in physics); **2** seriousness (of problem).

Grecia noun Fem. Greece.

griego[1] noun Masc. Greek (the language).

griego[2]**/griega** noun Masc./Fem., adjective Greek.

grifo noun Masc. tap; **abrir el grifo** to turn the tap on; **cerrar el grifo** turn the tap off.

grillo noun Masc. cricket.

gripe noun Fem. flu; **tener (la) gripe/estar con gripe** to have flu.

gris noun Masc., adjective grey.

gritar verb [17] to shout; **gritar de alegría** to shout for joy; **gritar de dolor** to scream with pain.

grito noun Masc. **1** shout; **dar un grito** to shout; **2** cry; **un grito de protesta** a cry of protest; **3** un **grito de dolor** a cry of pain; **un grito de horror** a scream of horror.

grosella noun Fem. redcurrant.

grosería noun Fem. **no digas groserías** don't be so rude; **¡qué grosería!** how rude!

grosero/grosera adjective rude.

grúa noun Fem. crane.

grueso/gruesa adjective **1** thick; **2** fat (person).

gruñón/gruñona adjective grumpy.

grupo noun Masc. group; **salir en grupo** to go out in a group; **un grupo musical** a group (playing music).

guante noun Masc. glove.

guapo/guapa adjective good-looking.

guarda noun Masc./Fem. **1** guard; **2** keeper (in museum).

guardabarros noun Masc. mudguard.

guardaespaldas noun Masc./Fem. bodyguard.

guardar verb [17] **1** to keep; **guardo todas sus cartas** I keep all his letters; **2** to put away; **guarda tus juguetes** put your toys away; **3** guardar cama to stay in bed.

guardería infantil noun Fem. nursery.

guardia[1] noun Masc./Fem. **1** policeman/policewoman; **2 la Guardia Civil** the Civil Guard; **3** guardia jurado security guard; **4** guardia urbano police officer (in local force).

guardián/guardiana noun Masc./Fem. **1** guard; **2** guardian.

guarnición noun Fem. **1** side dish; **2** topping.

guarro/guarra adjective (informal) **1** filthy; **2** disgusting (a person).

guarro/guarra noun Masc./Fem. (informal) filthy pig.

guatemalteco/guatemalteca noun Masc./Fem., adjective Guatemalan.

guau exclamation wow!

guay adjective (informal) fantastic, cool; **¡qué música más guay!** what cool music!

guay adverb **lo pasé guay** I had a fantastic time.

guerra noun Fem. war.

guerrilla noun Fem. guerrilla unit.

guerrillero/guerrillera noun Masc./Fem. guerrilla, guerrilla fighter.

guía noun Fem. **1** guide; **guía de restaurantes** restaurant guide; **2** map (of a city or town); **3 guía telefónica** telephone directory.

guía noun Masc./Fem. guide (person); **es guía turístico** he's a tourist guide.

guiar verb [32] to guide.
  guiarse reflexive verb [32] **guiarse por un mapa** to follow a map.

guijarro noun Masc. pebble.

guiñar verb [17] to wink.

guiño noun Masc. wink.

guión noun Masc. **1** dash; **2** hyphen; **una palabra con guión** a hyphenated word; **3** script (of a film).

guisante noun Masc. pea.

guisar verb [17] to cook; **guisa muy bien** he's a very good cook.

guitarra[1] noun Fem. guitar; **guitarra española** Spanish guitar.

guitarra[2] noun Masc./Fem. guitarist.

guitarrista noun Masc./Fem. guitarist.

gusano noun Masc. worm.

gustar verb [17] **me gusta mucho** I like it a lot; **me gustan los animales** I like animals; **no le gustó el libro** he didn't like the book; **a mi padre le gustan las fresas** my dad likes strawberries; **el que más me gusta** the one I like the best; **les gusta mirar la tele** they like watching telly; **¡así me gusta!** that's what I like to hear/see!

gusto noun Masc. **1** taste; **tiene gusto a menta** it tastes of mint; **tiene buen gusto** it tastes nice; **tengo mal gusto en la boca** I have a nasty taste in my mouth; **2 tiene muy buen gusto** she has very good taste; **3 mucho gusto en conocerle** pleased to meet you.

Hh

ha verb SEE **haber**.

haba noun Fem. **1** bean; **2** broad bean.

habéis verb SEE **haber**.

haber verb [6] **1** (used with another verb in the same way as 'have' in English to form past tenses); **he**

a b c d e f g h i j k l m n ñ o p q r s t u v w x y z

escrito a mi hermano I have written to my brother; **él no lo ha cogido** he hasn't taken it; **aún no había comido** I hadn't eaten yet; **después de haberlo pensado bien** after having thought about it properly; **2** there is; **aquí no hay suficiente** there's not enough here; **había un paquete en recepción** there was a parcel in reception; **3** there are; **hay varios errores** there are various mistakes; **había más de treinta personas en la sala** there were more than thirty people in the room; **4** ¿qué hay que hacer? what needs to be done?; **hay que limpiar la cocina** the kitchen needs to be cleaned; **hay que sacar dinero** we need to take some money out; **ahora hay que pintarlo** it needs painting now; **5** hola, ¿qué hay? hi, how are things?; **6** 'muchas gracias' – 'no hay de qué' 'thank you very much' – 'don't mention it'.

hábil adjective **1** skilful; **un jugador hábil** a skilful player; **2** clever; **es muy hábil para conseguir lo que quiere** he's very clever when it comes to getting what he wants.

habilidad noun Fem. skill.

habitación noun Fem. room; **una habitación sencilla/individual** a single room; **una habitación doble** a double room.

habitante noun Masc./Fem. inhabitant.

habla noun Fem. **1** speech; **se quedó sin habla** he was

speechless; **2** un país de habla hispana a Spanish-speaking country; **3** al habla speaking (on the phone); '¿el Señor López?' – 'al habla' 'Mr López?' – 'speaking'.

hablador/habladora noun Masc./Fem. **1** chatterbox; **2** gossip.

hablador adjective **1** talkative; **2** gossipy.

hablar verb [17] **1** to speak; **sabe hablar inglés** he speaks English; **¿hablas algún idioma?** do you speak any foreign languages?; **2** to talk; **no habla mucho** she doesn't talk very much; **hablar de** to talk about; **siempre habla mucho de ti** she's always talking about you; **me habló de sus proyectos** he talked to me about his plans.

habrán, habré, etc. verb SEE **haber**.

hacer verb [7] **1** to make; **hacer un pastel** to make a cake; **hacer la cama** to make the bed; **2** to do; **no sé qué hacer** I don't know what to do; **hacer los deberes** to do your homework; **¿qué haces?** what are you doing?; **estoy haciendo derecho** I'm doing law; **3** hacer la comida to cook lunch; **hacer la cena** to cook dinner; **4** to build (a house or road, for example); **5** hacer una visita to pay a visit; **6** hacer un regalo a alguien to give somebody a present; **7** hace (el papel) de Otelo he plays Othello; **8** (talking about the weather) hace frío it's cold; **hacía mucho viento** it was very windy; **este verano ha hecho muy mal tiempo** the weather's been very bad this summer; **9** (*talking about time*) **hace tres días** three days ago; **hace tres días que se fueron** they left three days ago; **eso pasó hace mucho tiempo** that happened a long time ago; **¿cuánto tiempo hace que vives aquí?** how long have you been living here?; **hacía dos meses que no iba a verlos** I hadn't been to see them for two months; **trabaja aquí desde hace tres meses** she's been working here for three months now; **10 hacer a alguien hacer algo** to make someone do something; **le hice repetirlo** I made him do it again; **eso me hizo pensar** that made me think.

hacerse *reflexive verb* [7] **1** to become; **hacerse famoso** to become famous; **se hicieron amigos** they became friends; **2 se están haciendo viejos** they're getting old; **3 hacerse daño** to hurt yourself; **me he hecho un corte en el dedo** I've cut my finger; **4 me he hecho un vestido** I've made myself a dress; **se ha hecho una mesa para la cocina** she's made a table for her kitchen; **5 ¿cómo se hace?** how do you do it?

hacha *noun Fem.* axe (*even though 'hacha' is feminine, it takes 'el' or 'un' in the singular*).

hacia *preposition* **1** towards; **vinieron hacia mí** they came towards me; **hacia el norte** northwards; **muévelo hacia abajo** move it down; **2** (*with time*) about; **llamaré hacia las dos de la tarde**

I'll call at about two o'clock; **te pagaré hacia final de mes** I'll pay you towards the end of the month.

hacienda *noun Fem.* estate, ranch.

hada *noun Fem.* fairy (*even though 'hada' is feminine, it takes 'el' or 'un' in the singular*).

haga, hago, etc. *verb* SEE **hacer.**

Haití *noun Masc.* Haiti.

haitiano/haitiana *noun Masc., Fem., adjective* Haitian.

halagar *verb* [28] to flatter.

halcón *noun Masc.* falcon.

hallar *verb* [17] to find; **no pudieron hallar una solución** they couldn't find a solution.

hallarse *reflexive verb* [17] **1** to be; **el pueblo se halla (situado) cerca del mar** the village is (situated) near the sea; **2** to feel; **me hallaba tranquilo** I was feeling calm.

hamaca *noun Fem.* hammock.

hambre *noun Fem.* hunger (*even though 'hambre' is feminine, it takes 'el' or 'un'*); **tener hambre** to be hungry; **me muero de hambre** (*informal*) I'm starving; **el aire del mar me da hambre** the sea air makes me feel hungry.

hamburguesa *noun Fem.* hamburger.

hamburguesería *noun Fem.* hamburger bar.

hámster *noun Masc.* hamster.

han *verb* SEE **haber.**

harán, haré, etc. *verb* SEE **hacer.**

harina *noun Fem.* flour; **harina integral** wholemeal flour.

a

b

c

d

e

f

g

h

i

j

k

l

m

n

ñ

o

p

q

r

s

t

u

v

w

x

hartarse *reflexive verb* [17] to get fed up; **me estoy hartando de este color** I'm getting fed up with this colour; **se hartó de esperar** he got fed up of waiting.

harto/harta *adjective* **estar harto de** to be fed up of/with; **están hartos de comer siempre lo mismo** they're fed up of always eating the same thing; **estoy harta de tus excusas** I'm fed up with your excuses.

has *verb* SEE **haber**.

hasta *preposition* **1** until; **me quedaré hasta la semana que viene** I'll stay until next week; **hasta que** until; **no lo mandes hasta que yo lo diga** don't send it until I tell you; **2** ¡hasta mañana! see you tomorrow!; **¡hasta luego!** see you later!; **¡hasta pronto!** see you soon!; **3** up to; **hasta ahora** up to now; **hasta hace tres meses** up to three months ago; **4 la falda me llega hasta los tobillos** the skirt goes down to my ankles; **5** as far as; **llegamos hasta Bilbao** we went as far as Bilbao.

hay *verb* SEE **haber**.

haz *verb* SEE **hacer**.

he *verb* SEE **haber**.

hechizo *noun Masc.* spell.

hecho[1] *noun Masc.* **1** fact; **el hecho es que ...** the fact is ...; **¿cuáles son los hechos?** what are the facts?; **2 tenemos que pasar de las palabras a los hechos** we must stop talking and do something; **3 de hecho** in fact.

hecho[2]**/hecha** *adjective* **1** made; **hecho a mano** hand-made; **un trabajo bien hecho** a job well done; **2 ¡bien hecho!** well done!

helada[1] *noun Fem.* frost.

heladería *noun Fem.* ice-cream parlour.

heladero/heladera *noun Masc./Fem.* ice cream seller.

helado[1] *noun Masc.* ice cream; **un helado de fresa** a strawberry ice cream.

helado[2]**/helada**[2] *adjective* **1** frozen; **el río estaba helado** the river was frozen; **la pobre chica estaba helada** the poor girl was frozen; **2** freezing; **tienes las manos heladas** your hands are freezing; **estoy helado** I'm freezing; **la casa está helada** the house is freezing.

helar *verb* [29] **esta noche va a helar** there's going to be a frost tonight.

helarse *reflexive verb* [29] to freeze; **el río se ha helado** the river has frozen over.

hélice *noun Fem.* propeller.

helicóptero *noun Masc.* helicopter.

hemos *verb* SEE **haber**.

heno *noun Masc.* hay; **fiebre del heno** hay fever.

heredar *verb* [17] **1** to inherit; **2 heredar el trono** to succeed to the throne.

heredero/heredera *noun Masc./Fem.* heir.

herida[1] *noun Fem.* injury.

herido/herida[2] *adjective*
1 injured; **estar seriamente herido** tó be seriously injured;
2 wounded; **resultó herido en la pelea** he was wounded in the fight.

herir *verb* [14] **1** to wound; **2** to hurt; **hirieron mis sentimientos** they hurt my feelings.

hermana *noun Fem.* sister;
hermana gemela twin sister;
hermana política sister-in-law.

hermanastro/hermanastra *noun Masc./Fem.* **1** stepbrother/stepsister; **2** half-brother/half-sister.

hermano *noun Masc.* **1** brother;
hermano gemelo twin brother;
hermano político brother-in-law;
2 hermanos brothers, brothers and sisters; **¿tienes hermanos?** do you have any brothers or sisters?

hermoso/hermosa *adjective* beautiful.

héroe *noun Masc.* hero.

heroína *noun Fem.* **1** heroine;
2 heroin.

herramienta *noun Fem.* tool.

hervir *verb* [14] to boil; **hervir unas patatas** to boil some potatoes.

hice *verb* SEE **hacer**.

hidratante *adjective* moisturizing.

hiedra *noun Fem.* ivy.

hielo *noun Masc.* ice; **cubito de hielo** ice cube.

hierba *noun Fem.* **1** grass; 'no pisar la hierba' 'do not walk on the grass'; **2** herb; **hierbas de cocina** (cooking) herbs; **3 una hierba mala** a weed.

hierro *noun Masc.* iron.

hígado *noun Masc.* liver.

higiénico/higiénica *adjective* hygienic.

higo *noun Masc.* fig.

hija *noun Fem.* daughter; **hija política** daughter-in-law.

hijo *noun Masc.* **1** son; **su hijo se llama Carlos** his son is called Carlos; **hijo político** son-in-law;
2 hijos children; **tienen tres hijos** they've got three children.

hilo *noun Masc.* thread.

himno *noun Masc.* hymn.

hincha *noun Masc./Fem.* supporter;
es hincha del Sevilla he's a Seville supporter.

hinchado/hinchada *adjective* swollen.

hinchar *verb* [17] **1** to blow up (*a balloon*); **2** to pump up (*a tyre*).

hincharse *reflexive verb* [17] to swell up; **se me ha hinchado el tobillo** my ankle has swollen up.

hinchazón *noun Fem.* swelling.

hipermercado *noun Masc.* hypermarket.

hipnotizar *verb* [25] hypnotize.

hipo *noun Masc.* hiccups; **tener hipo** to have hiccups.

hipoteca *noun Fem.* mortgage.

hispano/hispana *noun Masc./Fem.* Hispanic.

hispano *adjective* **1** Hispanic, Spanish; **países de habla hispana** Spanish-speaking countries;
2 Spanish American.

a
b
c
d
e
f
g
h
i
j
k
l
m
n
ñ
o
p
q
r
s
t
u
v
w
x
y
z

a
b
c
d
e
f
g
h
i
j
k
l
m
n
ñ
o
p
q
r
s
t
u
v
w
x
y
z

Hispanoamérica noun Fem. Spanish America.

hispanoamericano/ hispanoamericana noun Masc./Fem., adjective Spanish American.

hispanohablante noun Masc./ Fem. Spanish-speaker.

hispanohablante adjective Spanish-speaking.

historia noun Fem. **1** history; **la historia de Chile** the history of Chile; **2** story; **una historia de miedo** a horror story.

histórico/histórica adjective **1** historical; **2** historic.

historieta noun Fem. cartoon.

hizo verb SEE hacer.

hogar noun Masc. home; **éste es mi hogar** this is my home; **labores del hogar** housework.

hoguera noun Fem. bonfire.

hoja noun Fem. **1** leaf (of a tree or plant); **2** sheet (of paper or metal); **3** page (of a book).

hola exclamation hello.

Holanda noun Fem. Holland.

holandés[1] noun Masc. Dutch (the language).

holandés[2]**/holandesa** noun Masc./Fem. Dutchman/ Dutchwoman.

holandés/holandesa adjective Dutch.

holgado/holgada adjective loose-fitting.

hombre noun Masc. **1** man; **un hombre de negocios** a businessman; **el hombre del tiempo** the weatherman; **un**

hombre rana a frogman; **el hombre moderno es más alto que sus antepasados** modern man is taller than his ancestors; **2** ¡**hombre**! ¡**tú por aquí**! hey! look who's here!; ¡**no, hombre**! of course not!

hombro noun Masc. shoulder.

homenaje noun Masc. tribute; **un homenaje al autor** a ceremony to honour the author.

homosexual noun Masc./Fem., adjective homosexual.

hondo[1] adverb respirar hondo to breathe deeply.

hondo[2]**/honda** adjective **1** deep; **un pozo hondo** a deep well; **2** en **lo más hondo de mi corazón** deep in my heart.

hondureño/hondureña noun Masc./Fem., adjective Honduran.

honesto/honesta adjective honest.

hongo noun Masc. **1** fungus; **2 tener hongos** to have athlete's foot.

honor noun Masc. honour; **tener el honor de** to have the honour of; **en honor de** in honour of.

honra noun Fem. honour.

honradez noun Fem. honesty.

honrado/honrada adjective honest.

hora noun Fem. **1** hour; **la película dura dos horas** the film lasts two hours; **media hora** half an hour; **hora y media** an hour and a half; **a las quince horas** at fifteen hours; **la hora punta** the rush hour;

durante las horas de trabajo during working hours; **horas de visita** visiting hours (*at the hospital*); **hay un bus que sale cada hora** there is an hourly bus; **2** time; **¿qué hora es?** what's the time?; **¿a qué hora empieza?** what time does it start?; **¿tiene hora?** have you got the time?; **¿me puede dar la hora?** could you tell me what time it is?; **a la hora de comer** at lunchtime; **es hora de ir a la cama** it's bedtime; **ya es hora de entrar** it's time to go in; **en mis horas libres** in my free time; **hacer horas extra** to do overtime; **llegar a la hora** to arrive on time; **3 pedir hora** to make an appointment; **he pedido hora con el dentista** I made an appointment to see the dentist; **4 a primera hora de la mañana** first thing in the morning; **una noticia de última hora** a news flash.

horario noun Masc. **1** timetable; **el horario de clase** the school timetable; **2 horario de visitas** visiting hours (*at the hospital*).

horchata noun Fem. a cold drink made from tiger nuts.

horchatería noun Fem. refreshments stall (*selling horchata*).

horizontal adjective horizontal.

horizonte noun Masc. horizon.

hormiga noun Fem. ant.

hormigón noun Masc. concrete.

horno noun Masc. **1** oven; **verduras al horno** roast vegetables; **un**

horno microondas a microwave oven; **2** kiln.

horóscopo noun Masc. horoscope.

horquilla noun Fem. hairpin.

horrible adjective horrible.

horror noun Masc. **1** horror; **2** (*informal*) **¡qué horror!** how awful!.

horrorizar verb [22] to horrify.

horroroso/horrorosa adjective **1** horrific (*crime*); **2** (*informal*) awful (*a dress, book or picture, for example*).

hospedar verb [17] to provide accommodation for.
hospedarse reflexive verb [17] to stay; **nos hospedamos en una pensión** we stayed in a guesthouse.

hospital noun Masc. hospital.

hospitalidad noun Fem. hospitality.

hostal noun Masc. hotel (*small and not expensive*).

hotel noun Masc. hotel.

hotelero/hotelera noun Masc./Fem. hotel manager.

hotelero adjective hotel.

hoy adverb **1** today; **hoy es mi cumpleaños** it's my birthday today; **¿a qué estamos hoy?** what day is it today?; **2 hoy en día** nowadays; **hoy en día son bastante comunes** nowadays they are quite common.

hoyo noun Masc. hole.

hube, hubo, etc. verb SEE **haber**.

hucha noun Fem. moneybox.

hueco¹ noun Masc. **1** hollow; **suena a hueco** it sounds hollow;

a b c d e f g h i j k l m n ñ o p q r s t u v w x y z

a

b

c

d

e

f

g

h

i

j

k

l

m

n

ñ

o

p

q

r

s

t

u

v

w

x

y

z

2 space; **hazme un hueco** make some room for me; **un hueco para aparcar** a parking space; **3 el hueco de la escalera** the stairwell; **el hueco del ascensor** the lift shaft; **4** gap (*in timetable*).

hueco³/hueca *adjective* hollow.

huela, huelo, etc. *verb* SEE **oler.**

huelga *noun Fem.* strike; **hacer huelga** to strike; **estar en huelga** to be on strike; **huelga de celo** work-to-rule.

huella *noun Fem.* **1** footprint; **2** track (*of an animal or tyre, for example*); **3 huellas dactilares** fingerprints.

huérfano/huérfana *noun Masc./Fem.* orphan.

huerto/huerta *noun Masc./Fem.* **1** vegetable garden; **2** orchard.

hueso *noun Masc.* **1** bone; **romperse un hueso** to break a bone; **2** stone (*in fruit*).

huésped *noun Masc./Fem.* guest.

huesudo *adjective* bony.

huevo *noun Masc.* egg; **huevo duro** hard-boiled egg; **huevo pasado por agua** soft-boiled egg; **huevo escalfado** poached egg; **huevo frito** fried egg; **huevos revueltos** scrambled eggs; **huevo de Pascua** Easter egg.

huir *verb* [54] to flee; **huir de la cárcel** to escape from prison.

humano/humana *noun Masc./Fem.* human being.

humano *adjective* **1** human; **la naturaleza humana** human nature; **2** humane.

humedad *noun Fem.* **1** dampness; **la casa tiene humedad** the house is damp; **2** humidity.

húmedo/húmeda *adjective* **1** damp; **2** wet; **3** moist.

humillar *verb* [17] to humiliate.

humo *noun Masc.* smoke.

humor *noun Masc.* **1** humour; **tener sentido del humor** to have a sense of humour; **2** mood; **estar de buen humor** to be in a good mood; **estar de mal humor** to be in a bad mood; **no estoy de humor para verlos** I'm not in the mood to see them.

hundir *verb* [19] to sink.

hundirse *reflexive verb* [19] to sink.

húngaro¹ *noun Masc.* Hungarian (*the language*).

húngaro²/húngara *noun Masc./Fem.*,

húngaro *adjective* Hungarian.

Hungría *noun Fem.* Hungary.

huracán *noun Masc.* hurricane.

hurra *exclamation* hurrah!

huyas, huyo, etc. *verb* SEE **huir.**

Ii

iba, iban, etc. *verb* SEE **ir.**

iceberg *noun Masc.* iceberg.

icono *noun Masc.* icon.

ida¹ *noun Fem.* departure; **un billete de ida** a single ticket; **un billete de ida y vuelta** a return ticket.

a
b
c
d
e
f
g
h
i
j
k
l
m
n
ñ
o
p
q
r
s
t
u
v
w
x
y
z

ida[2] *verb* SEE **ir.**

idea *noun* Fem. idea; '**¿a qué hora llegan?' – 'no tengo ni idea'** 'what time will they arrive?' – ' I haven't a clue'; **no tienen ni idea de cómo ir** they have no idea how to get there; **tengo una idea** I've got an idea.

ideal *adjective* ideal.

idéntico/idéntica *adjective* identical; **es idéntico a su padre** he's just like his father.

identidad *noun* Fem. identity; **un carné de identidad** an identity card.

identificación *noun* Fem. identification.

identificar *verb* [31] to identify. **identificarse** *reflexive verb* [31] **1** to identify yourself; **2 identificarse con** to identify with; **me identifico mucho con la protagonista del libro** I identify a lot with the heroine of the book.

idioma *noun* Masc. language; **hablar idiomas varios** to speak several foreign languages.

idiota *noun* Masc./Fem. idiot.

idiota *adjective* stupid.

ido *verb* SEE **ir.**

iglesia *noun* Fem. church.

ignorante *adjective* ignorant.

ignorar *verb* [17] **1** to ignore; **no me gusta que me ignoren** I don't like being ignored; **2** not to know; **ignoro las razones** I don't know the reasons.

igual *adjective* **1** same; **uno de igual tamaño** one of the same size; **parecen todos iguales** they all

look the same; **2 igual a/igual que** the same as; **era igual a éste** it was the same as this one; **no es igual que los demás** it's not the same as the others; **3 todo le da igual** he doesn't care about anything; **'¿quieres ir al cine o al teatro?' – 'me da igual'** 'do you want to go to the cinema or to the theatre?' – 'I don't mind'; **le da igual lo uno que lo otro** either way it makes no difference to them.

igual *adverb* **1** the same; **suenan igual** they sound the same; **2** equally; **los quiero a todos igual** I love them all equally; **los dos sistemas son igual de eficientes** both systems are equally efficient; **3** (*in comparisons*) **es igual de alto que su padre** he's as tall as his father; **es igual de ancho que la mesa** it's as wide as the table; **es Géminis, igual que yo** she's a Gemini, just like me; **4** maybe; **igual la vemos en la fiesta** maybe we'll see her at the party; **5 al igual que** just like.

igualdad *noun* Fem. equality; **igualdad de oportunidades** equal opportunities; **en igualdad de condiciones** on equal terms.

igualmente *adverb* **1** equally; **igualmente aburrido** equally boring; **2 'que pases una feliz Navidad' – 'igualmente'** 'have a good Christmas' – 'you too'.

ilegal *adjective* illegal.

ilegalmente *adverb* illegally.

ileso/ilesa *adjective* unhurt, uninjured.

a **ilimitado/ilimitada** adjective
unlimited.

b **iluminación** noun Fem. **1** lighting
(in a room or theatre);
c **2** illumination (of a building or
statue).

d **iluminar** verb [17] **1** to light (a
e room or theatre); **2** to illuminate (a
building or statue).

f **ilusión** noun Fem. **1** hope; **2 me
g hace ilusión ir** I'm excited about
going; **3** illusion.

h **ilustración** noun Fem.
i illustration.

j **ilustrar** verb [17] to illustrate.

k **imagen** noun Fem. **1** image; **es la
viva imagen de su madre** she's
l the image of her mother; **2** picture
(on a TV screen); **3** reflection (in a
m mirror).

n **imaginación** noun Fem.
imagination; **son imaginaciones
ñ suyas** he's just imagining things.

o **imaginar** verb [17] to imagine.

imaginarse reflexive verb [17]
p **1** to imagine; **me imaginaba que
sería más grande** I imagined it
q would be bigger; **2 me imagino
que no** I suppose not; **me imagino
r que sí** I imagine so.

s **imán** noun Masc. magnet.

imbécil noun Masc./Fem. idiot.

t **imbécil** adjective stupid.

u **imitar** verb [17] to imitate.

impacientar verb [17] to make
v impatient.

w **impacientarse** reflexive verb
[17] to get impatient.

x **impaciente** adjective impatient.

y **impacto** noun Masc. impact.

z

impar adjective odd.

impecable adjective impeccable.

impedir verb [57] **1** to prevent;
impedirle a alguien hacer algo to
prevent someone from doing
something; **2 impedir el paso** to
block the way.

imperativo noun Masc.
imperative.

imperdible noun Masc. safety pin.

imperfecto[1] noun Masc.
imperfect.

imperfecto[2]**/imperfecta**
adjective imperfect.

impermeable noun Masc.
raincoat.

impersonal adjective impersonal.

implicar verb [31] to involve.

imponer verb [11] to impose (a
condition or punishment).

importación noun Fem. import;
artículos de importación
imports.

importado/importada
adjective imported.

importancia noun Fem.
importance; **darle importancia a
algo** to attach importance to
something.

importante adjective
1 important; **lo importante es ...**
the important thing is ...;
2 considerable; **una importante
suma de dinero** a considerable
sum of money.

importar verb [17] **1** to matter; **no
importa, déjalo así** it doesn't
matter, leave it like this; **no
importa mucho el color** the

colour doesn't matter very much; **2 no me importa ayudarles** I don't mind helping them; **¿te importa que use el teléfono?** do you mind if I use your phone?; **¿le importaría comprobarlo?** would you mind checking it?; **3 ¿y a ti que te importa?** it's none of your business; **no me importa lo que diga** I don't care what he says; **4** to import (goods); ★ **me importa un comino/un rábano** (informal) I couldn't care less.

imposible adjective impossible.

impresión noun Fem. impression **1 causar una buena impresión** to make a good impression; **2 me da la impresión de que** ... I've got the feeling that...

impresionante adjective impressive.

impresionar verb [17] **1** to impress; **quiere impresionarte** she wants to impress you; **2** to affect; **me impresionó mucho verlos discutir** seeing them argue really affected me; **la violencia de la escena me impresionó mucho** the violence of the scene shocked me.

impreso[1] noun Masc. form; **impreso de solicitud** application form.

impreso[2]/**impresa** adjective printed.

impresora noun Fem. printer; **una impresora láser** a laser printer.

imprevisible adjective **1** unpredictable; **2** unforeseeable.

imprevisto[1] noun Masc. unforeseen event.

imprevisto[2]/**imprevista** adjective unforeseen, unexpected.

improvisado/improvisada adjective improvised.

improvisar verb [17] to improvise.

improviso in phrase **de improviso** unexpectedly, out of the blue.

imprudente noun Masc./Fem. **1** careless person; **2** reckless person; **es un imprudente conduciendo** he's a reckless driver.

imprudente adjective **1** careless; **2** reckless.

impuesto noun Masc. tax.

impulsivo/impulsiva adjective impulsive.

inaccesible adjective inaccessible.

inaceptable adjective unacceptable.

inadecuado/inadecuada adjective **1** inappropriate; **2** inadequate.

inadmisible adjective unacceptable.

inadvertido/inadvertida adjective **pasar inadvertido** to go unnoticed.

inalámbrico/inalámbrica adjective cordless.

incapaz adjective **es incapaz de hacer daño a nadie** he's incapable of harming anyone; **fui incapaz de entenderlo** I was unable to understand it.

incendio noun Masc. fire.

a
b
c
d
e
f
g
h
i
j
k
l
m
n
ñ
o
p
q
r
s
t
u
v
w
x
y
z

a b c d e f g h i j k l m n ñ o p q r s t u v w x y z

incertidumbre noun Fem.
uncertainty.

incierto/incierta adjective
uncertain.

incitar verb [17] **incitar a alguien
a hacer** to incite someone to do.

incluido/incluida adjective
included; **dos mil euros, todo
incluido** two thousand euros,
everything included; **seremos
diez personas, nosotros
incluidos** there will be ten people
including us.

incluir verb [54] to include.

inclusive adjective inclusive; **los
viernes inclusive** including
Fridays.

incluso adverb even; **es incluso
mejor** it's even better.

incluya, incluyo, etc. verb SEE
incluir.

incoloro/incolora adjective
colourless.

incómodo/incómoda adjective
uncomfortable.

incompetente adjective
incompetent.

incompleto/incompleta
adjective incomplete.

incomprensible adjective
incomprehensible.

incondicional adjective
unconditional.

inconsciente adjective
unconscious.

inconveniente noun Masc.
drawback, disadvantage.

inconveniente adjective
inconvenient.

incorporar verb [17] to
incorporate.

incorporarse reflexive verb [17]
to sit up.

incorrecto/incorrecta
adjective incorrect.

increíble adjective unbelievable,
incredible.

indecente adjective indecent.

indeciso/indecisa adjective
1 indecisive; **2** undecided; **están
indecisos sobre la cantidad**
they're undecided about the
quantity.

indefenso/indefensa adjective
defenceless.

indefinidamente adverb
indefinitely, for good.

indefinido/indefinida adjective
1 indefinite; **2** vague (outline, for
example).

indemnizar verb [22] to
compensate; **los indemnizaron
con veinte mil euros** they received
twenty thousand euros in
compensation.

indemnzación noun Fem.
compensation; **le pagaron una
indemnización** they paid her
compensation.

independencia noun Fem.
independence.

independiente adjective
independent.

India noun Fem. **(la) India** India.

indicación noun Fem.
1 indication; **2** sign; **me hizo una
indicación para que lo siguiese**
he signalled to me to follow him;

hay una indicación en el camino there's a sign on the road.

indicar *verb* [31] **1** to indicate; **2** to point to.

índice *noun Masc.* index.

indiferente *adjective* **1** indifferent; **2 me es indiferente** it makes no difference to me.

indígena *adjective* native.

indigestión *noun Fem.* indigestion.

indigesto/indigesta *adjective* indigestible.

indignación *noun Fem.* **1** indignation; **2** outrage.

indignar *verb* [17] **1** to make angry; **2** to outrage. **indignarse** *reflexive verb* [17] **1** to get angry; **2** to be outraged.

indio/india *noun Masc./Fem.*, *adjective* Indian.

indirecta[1] *noun Fem.* hint.

indirecto/indirecta[2] *adjective* indirect.

indiscreto/indiscreta *adjective* indiscreet.

indispensable *adjective* essential.

indispuesto/indispuesta *adjective* **estar indispuesto** to be unwell.

individual *adjective* individual.

individuo *noun Masc.* **1** person; **un individuo con pelo largo** a person with long hair; **2** (*pejorative*) character; **un individuo con muy mal aspecto** a nasty looking character.

industria *noun Fem.* industry.

industrial *adjective* industrial.

ineficaz *adjective* **1** ineffective (*remedy, measure*); **2** inefficient (*person*).

inepto/inepta *noun Masc./Fem.*, **inepto** *adjective* incompetent.

inesperado/inesperada *adjective* unexpected.

inevitable *adjective* unavoidable; **era inevitable que pasase** it was bound to happen.

inexperto/inexperta *adjective* inexperienced.

infancia *noun Fem.* childhood.

infantil *adjective* **1** childish; **eres muy infantil** you're so childish; **2** childlike; **3 literatura infantil** children's books.

infarto *noun Masc.* heart attack; **le dio un infarto** he had a heart attack.

infección *noun Fem.* infection.

infectado/infectada *adjective* infected.

infectar *verb* [17] to infect. **infectarse** *reflexive verb* [17] to become infected.

infeliz *adjective* unhappy.

infiel *adjective* unfaithful; **serle infiel a alguien** to be unfaithful to someone.

infierno *noun Masc.* hell.

infinitivo *noun Masc.* infinitive.

infinito[1] *noun Masc.* infinity.

infinito[2]**/infinita** *adjective* infinite.

inflable *adjective* inflatable.

inflación *noun Fem.* inflation.

inflamable *adjective* flammable.

a

inflar verb [17] **1** to inflate (a tyre, for example); **2** to blow up (a balloon, for example).

b

c

influencia noun Fem. influence.

d

influir verb [54] to influence.

e

información noun Fem.
1 information; **'Información'** 'Information Desk' (on a sign); **2** news (in newspaper or TV news); **la información internacional** the foreign news; **3** directory enquiries (on the telephone); **llamar a información** to call directory enquiries.

f

g

h

i

j

k

informal adjective **1** informal (a chat or meal, for example); **2** casual (clothes); **3** unreliable (person).

l

m

informar verb [17] to inform; **me informaron mal** I was misinformed; **¿podría informarme sobre ... ?** could you give me information about ... ?.
informarse reflexive verb [17] to find out information; **me informaré sobre el horario** I'll find out about the timetable.

n

ñ

o

p

q

r

informática noun Fem. computer science, IT.

s

informe noun Masc. report.

t

infracción noun Fem. offence; **cometer una infracción** to commit an offence; **una infracción de tráfico** a traffic offence.

u

v

infusión noun Fem. herbal tea; **una infusión de menta** a peppermint tea.

w

x

ingeniero/ingeniera noun Masc./Fem. engineer.

y

z

ingenuo/ingenua noun Masc./ Fem. naive. **eres un ingenuo** you're so naive.

ingenuo adjective naive.

Inglaterra noun Fem. England.

inglés[1] noun Masc. English (the language).

inglés[2]**/inglesa** noun Masc./Fem. Englishman/Englishwoman; **los ingleses** the English, English people.

inglés/inglesa adjective English.

ingrato/ingrata adjective ungrateful.

ingrediente noun Masc. ingredient.

inicial noun Fem. initial.

inicial adjective initial.

iniciativa noun Fem. initiative; **por iniciativa propia** on her own initiative.

injusto/injusta adjective unfair.

inmediatamente adverb immediately.

inmediato/inmediata adjective immediate; **de inmediato** immediately.

inmenso/inmensa adjective **1** immense; **2** huge; **un salón inmenso** a huge living room.

inmigración noun Fem. immigration.

inmigrante noun Masc./Fem. immigrant.

inmobiliaria noun Fem. estate agent's.

inmoral adjective immoral.

inmueble noun Masc. property.

inmunizar verb [22] to immunize.

innecesario/innecesaria *adjective* unnecessary.

innovación *noun Fem.* innovation.

innovar *verb* [17] to innovate.

innumerable *adjective* innumerable.

inocentada *noun Fem.* practical joke (*this is also used for a joke played on someone on 28 December, which is the Spanish equivalent of April Fool's Day*) **gastarle una inocentada a alguien** to play a practical joke on someone.

inocente *adjective* **1** innocent; **2** naive; SEE **día**.

inofensivo/inofensiva *adjective* harmless.

inolvidable *adjective* unforgettable.

inoxidable *adjective* **acero inoxidable** stainless steel.

inquieto/inquieta *adjective* **1** worried; **2** restless.

inquietud *noun Fem.* **1** uneasiness; **2** interest.

inquilino/inquilina *noun Masc./Fem.* tenant.

inscribir *verb* [52] **1** to register (*on a course, for example*); **2** to engrave.

inscribirse *reflexive verb* [52] to register.

inscripción *noun Fem.* **1** registration (*on a course, for example*); **2** inscription.

insecto *noun Masc.* insect.

insertar *verb* [17] to insert.

insignificante *adjective* insignificant.

insistir *verb* [19] to insist; **insistir en algo** to insist on something.

insolación *noun Fem.* sunstroke; **coger una insolación** to get sunstroke.

insolente *adjective* rude.

insólito/insólita *adjective* unheard of.

insonorizado/insonorizada *adjective* soundproofed.

insoportable *adjective* unbearable.

inspección *noun Fem.* inspection.

inspeccionar *verb* [17] to inspect.

inspector/inspectora *noun Masc./Fem.* inspector.

inspiración *noun Fem.* inspiration.

inspirar *verb* [17] to inspire. **inspirarse** *reflexive verb* [17] **inspirarse en algo** to be inspired by something.

instalación *noun Fem.* installation.

instalar *verb* [17] to install (*a washing machine or a computer, for example*). **instalarse** *reflexive verb* [17] to install yourself.

instantáneo/instantánea *adjective* **1** instant; **2** immediate.

instante *noun Masc.* moment; **un instante, por favor** one moment, please.

a
b
c
d
e
f
g
h
i
j
k
l
m
n
ñ
o
p
q
r
s
t
u
v
w
x
y
z

instinto noun Masc. instinct;
instinto de conservación survival
instinct; **por instinto** instinctively.

instituto noun Masc. institute;
instituto de bachillerato
secondary school.

instrucción noun Fem.
1 education; **2** training;
instrucción militar military
training; **3 instrucciones**
instructions (for a computer, for
example).

instructor/instructora noun
Masc./Fem. instructor; **instructor
de autoescuela** driving
instructor; **instructor de esquí** ski
instructor.

instruir verb [54] **1** to instruct; **2** to
educate.

instrumento noun Masc.
instrument; **tocar un instrumento**
to play an instrument.

insuficiente noun Masc. fail (at
school).

insuficiente adjective
inadequate.

insultar verb [17] to insult.

insulto noun Masc. insult.

intacto/intacta adjective intact.

integral adjective
1 comprehensive; **2 pan integral**
wholemeal bread.

íntegro/íntegra adjective **la
versión íntegra de la película** the
full-length version of the film; **el
texto íntegro** the unabridged text.

intelectual noun Masc./Fem.,
intelectual adjective intellectual.

inteligencia noun Fem.
intelligence.

inteligente adjective intelligent.

intención noun Fem. intention; **no
fue mi intención** it wasn't my
intention; **no era mi intención
ofenderla** I didn't mean to offend
her; **tiene buenas intenciones** she
means well; **lo preguntó con mala
intención** he asked the question to
cause trouble.

intensivo/intensiva adjective
intensive.

intenso/intensa adjective
1 intense; **2** deep (feeling).

intentar verb [17] to try; **¡inténtalo
otra vez!** try again!; **intentar
hacer** to try to do; **intenté cerrarlo**
I tried to shut it; **intenta llegar
temprano** try to arrive early.

intercambiar verb [17] **1** to
exchange; **2** to swap.

intercambiarse reflexive verb
[17] to swap; **se intercambiaron
las revistas** they swapped their
magazines.

intercambio noun Masc.
1 exchange; **2** swap.

interés noun Masc. interest; **es de
gran interés para mí** it's of great
interest to me; **su interés por la
historia** her interest in history.

interesante adjective
interesting; **un película
interesante** an interesting film;
resulta interesante que ... it's
interesting that ....

interesar verb [17] **no me
interesa el deporte** I'm not
interested in sport; **¿te interesa la
historia?** are you interested in
history?

interesarse *reflexive verb* [17]
interesarse en algo/interesarse por algo to take an interest in something.

interfono *noun Masc.*
1 entryphone; **2** intercom.

interior *noun Masc.* **1** inside; **el interior de la caja** the inside of the box; **2 en mi interior, tenía miedo** deep down inside, I was afraid.

interior *adjective* **1** interior; **escalera interior** interior staircase; **2 un piso interior** a flat with windows facing into an inner courtyard; **3** inside; **en la parte interior** on the inside.

intermediario/intermediaria *noun Masc./Fem.* intermediary.

intermedio[1] *noun Masc.* interval.

intermedio[2]**/intermedia** *adjective* **1** intermediate (*level or stage, for example*); **2** medium; **de tamaño intermedio** medium-sized.

intermitente *adjective* **1** flashing (*a light*); **2** intermittent.

internacional *adjective* international.

internado[1] *noun Masc.* boarding school.

internado[2]**/internada** *adjective* **está internado** he's been taken into hospital.

internauta *noun Masc./Fem.* surfer (*on the Internet*).

Internet *noun Masc.* Internet (*Spanish omits 'el' with Internet*); **en Internet** on the Internet.

interno/interna *noun Masc./Fem.* boarder (*in a school*).

interno *adjective* internal.

interpretar *verb* [17] **1** to interpret; **2 interpretar un papel** to play a part (*in a play or film*); **interpretar una pieza de música** to perform a piece of music; **interpretar una canción** to sing a song.

intérprete *noun Masc./Fem.*
1 interpreter; **2** performer (*of a piece of music*); **3** singer (*of a song*).

interrogación *noun Fem.* interrogation.

interrogante *noun Masc. or Fem.*
1 question; **quedan muchos interrogantes sin responder** there are many questions left unanswered; **2** question mark; **pon un interrogante** write a question mark.

interrogar *verb* [28] to question (*a suspect*).

interrumpir *verb* [19] to interrupt.

interrupción *noun Fem.* interruption.

interruptor *noun Masc.* switch.

interurbano/interurbana *adjective* **1** long-distance; **una llamada interurbana** a long-distance call; **2 un tren interurbano** an intercity train.

intervalo *noun Masc.* interval.

intervención *noun Fem.* intervention.

intervenir *verb* [15] **1** to take part; **intervenir en las negociaciones** to take part in the negociations; **2** to intervene; **no quiero intervenir** I don't want to

a b c d e f g h i j k l m n ñ o p q r s t u v w x y z

a intervene; **3 intervenir a alguien** to operate on somebody.

b **interviú** *noun Fem.* interview.

c **intimidar** *verb* [17] to intimidate.

íntimo/íntima *adjective*
d **1** private; **mi vida íntima** my
private life; **2** intimate; **un**
e **ambiente íntimo** an intimate
atmosphere; **un** **amigos**
f **íntimos** my close friends; **4 una**
cena íntima a candlelit dinner.

g
intolerante *adjective* intolerant.

h **intoxicación** *noun Fem.*
poisoning; **intoxicación**
i **alimenticia** food poisoning.

j **intransitivo/intransitiva**
adjective intransitive.

k
intriga *noun Fem.* intrigue.

l **introducir** *verb* [60] **1** to
introduce; **introducir cambios** to
m introduce changes; **2** to insert;
introducir la moneda en la ranura
n insert the coin in the slot.
introducirse *reflexive verb* [60]
ñ **1** to be introduced; **2** to get in; **el**
ladrón se introdujo por la
o **ventana** the burglar got in through
the window.

p
intruso/intrusa *noun Masc./Fem.*
q intruder.

r **intuitivo/intuitiva** *adjective*
intuitive.

s
inundación *noun Fem.* flooding;
t **ha habido inundaciones en**
Cataluña there's been flooding in
u Cataluña.

v **inútil** *noun Masc./Fem.* **es una inútil**
she's useless.

w
inútil *adjective* **1** useless; **2 es**
x **inútil intentarlo** it's useless trying.

y

z

invadir *verb* [19] to invade.

inválido/inválida *noun Masc./*
Fem. disabled person.

invasión *noun Fem.* invasion.

inventar *verb* [17] **1** to invent; **2** to
make up (*a story or game*).

inventarse *reflexive verb* [17] to
invent, to make up; **se inventó una**
excusa he made up an excuse.

invento *noun Masc.* invention.

invernadero *noun Masc.*
greenhouse.

inversión *noun Fem.* investment.

inverso/inversa *adjective*
reverse.

investigación *noun Fem.*
1 investigation (*of a crime or*
accident, for example); **2** research;
investigación de mercado market
research.

invierno *noun Masc.* winter; **en**
invierno in winter; **el invierno**
pasado last winter.

invisible *adjective* invisible.

invitación *noun Fem.* invitation.

invitado/invitada *noun Masc./*
Fem. guest.

invitar *verb* [17] **1** to invite; **invitar**
a alguien a una fiesta to invite
someone to a party; **me han**
invitado a su casa they've invited
me to their house; **2 te invito a**
cenar I'll take you out for dinner;
nos invitó a una copa he bought
us a drink; **¡yo invito!** it's on me!

involuntario/involuntaria
adjective involuntary.

inyección *noun Fem.* injection.

ir *verb* [8] **1** to go; **van a casa de Alicia** they're going to Alicia's; **iremos al museo** we'll go to the museum; **¿adónde vas?** where are you going?; **¿dónde van los platos?** where do the plates go?; **aún no va al colegio** she doesn't go to school yet; **2** to come; **¡ya voy!** I'm coming!; **3** (*talking about how things are progressing*) **¿cómo van las cosas?** how are things?; **¿cómo te va?** how are you doing?; **¿cómo va el enfermo?** how is the patient doing?; **le va muy bien en el trabajo** he's doing very well at work; **me fue muy mal en la entrevista** I did very badly at the interview; **el proyecto va bien** the project is going well; **4** (*talking about how something works*) **la lavadora no va bien** the washing machine is not working properly; **5** to be; **iba solo** he was alone; **ellos iban en la parte de delante** they were at the front; **yo iba de pie** I was standing up; **6** (*referring to the way you dress*) **iba con un abrigo marrón** he was wearing a brown coat; **iban bien vestidos** they were well dressed; **7** (*talking about whether something suits you*) **el negro te va bien** black suits you; **8** (*talking about an activity*) **ir de vacaciones** to go on holiday; **voy a ir a España de vacaciones** I'm going to Spain for my holidays; **ir de compras** to go shopping; **ir a la compra** to do the shopping; **siempre tengo yo que ir a la compra** I'm always the one who does the shopping; **9** (*talking about*

transport) **ir en coche** to go by car; **fueron en coche** they drove here; **ir en avión** to go by plane; **ir en bicicleta** to go by bike; **va en bicicleta a todas partes** she goes everywhere by bike; **ir a pie** to go on foot; **ir a caballo** to go on horseback; **10** **ir a por algo/alguien** to go to get something/someone; **voy a por pan** I'm going to buy some bread; **fuimos a por ella** we went to fetch her; **vete a por el médico** go and get the doctor; **11** **ir a hacer** to go to do; **fuimos a ver su casa nueva** we went to see their new house; **ve a recoger tu habitación** go and tidy up your room; **12** (*expressing the future*) **voy a comprar leche** I'm going to buy some milk; **voy a ser médico** I'm going to be a doctor; **iré a recogerla** I'll go to pick her up; **iba a mandártelo hoy** I was going to send it to you today; **13** **su salud va mejorando** her health is getting better; **iban acercándose** they were getting closer; **14** **¡vamos!** come on!; **15** (*expressing surprise or annoyance*) **¡vaya hombre, un billete de cincuenta euros!** hey look, a fifty-euro note!; **¡vaya, si es Carlos!** what a surprise, it's Carlos!; **¡vaya, se ha fundido la luz!** oh dear, the light has gone!; **¡vaya, no lo encuentro!** bother, I can't find it!; **16** **¿lo ha hecho él solo?' – '¡qué va!'** 'did he do it on his own?' – 'not likely!'; **'¿te molesta?' – '¡qué va!'** 'do you mind?' – 'not at all!'.

irse *reflexive verb* [8] **1** to leave; **nos fuimos pronto** we left early; **bueno, me voy** well, I'm off; **2** to go; **se fueron a casa** they went home; **3 ¿cómo se va a la estación?** which is the way to the station.

ira *noun Fem.* rage; **en un arrebato de ira** in a fit of rage; ★ **ciego de ira** in a blind rage.

Irlanda *noun Fem.* Ireland.

irlandés[1] *noun Masc.* Irish (*the language*).

irlandés[2]/**irlandesa** *noun Masc./ Fem.* Irishman/Irishwoman.

irlandés/irlandesa *adjective* Irish.

ironía *noun Fem.* irony.

irónico/irónica *adjective* ironic.

irreal *adjective* unreal.

irresponsable *adjective* irresponsible.

irritación *noun Fem.* irritation.

irritar *verb* [17] to irritate.

irritarse *reflexive verb* [17] **1** to get irritated (*a person*); **2** to become irritated.

isla *noun Fem.* island.

islámico/islámica *adjective* Islamic.

islandés/islandesa *noun Masc./ Fem.* Icelander.

Islandia *noun Fem.* Iceland.

Israel *noun Masc.* Israel.

israelí *noun Masc./Fem., adjective* Israeli.

Italia *noun Fem.* Italy.

italiano[1] *noun Masc.* Italian (*the language*).

italiano[2]/**italiana** *noun Masc./ Fem., adjective* Italian.

itinerario *noun Masc.* itinerary, route.

IVA *abbreviation Masc.* (*short for: Impuesto al Valor Agregado*) VAT.

izquierda[1] *noun Fem.* **1** left; **tuerce a la izquierda** turn left; **se sentaron a mi izquierda** they sat on my left; **2 está a la izquierda** it's on the left-hand side; **3 ser de izquierdas** to be left-wing (*in politics*).

izquierdo/izquierda[2] *adjective* left.

Jj

jabalí *noun Masc.* wild boar.

jabón *noun Masc.* soap; **una pastilla de jabón** a cake of soap.

jabonera *noun Fem.* soapdish.

Jamaica *noun Fem.* Jamaica.

jamaicano/jamaicana *noun Masc., Fem., adjective* Jamaican.

jamás *adverb* never; **no lo he visto jamás** I've never seen it; **nunca jamás volveré** I'll never ever go back again.

jamón *noun Masc.* ham; **jamón de York** cooked ham; **jamón serrano** cured raw ham.

Japón *noun Masc.* **(el) Japón** Japan.

jarabe *noun Masc.* syrup; **jarabe para la tos** cough mixture.

jardín *noun Masc.* **1** garden; **está en el jardín** she's in the garden;

2 jardín de infancia nursery (school).

jardinero/jardinera *noun Masc./ Fem.* gardener.

jarra *noun Fem.* SEE **jarro**.

jarro *noun Masc.* jug.

jarrón *noun Masc.* vase.

jaula *noun Fem.* cage.

jefe/jefa *noun Masc./Fem.* **1** boss (*at work*); **2** manager (*of a company*); **3** chief; **el jefe de policía** the chief of police; **el jefe de bomberos** the chief fire officer; **4** leader (*of a group*).

jengibre *noun Masc.* ginger.

jerez *noun Masc.* sherry.

jersey *noun Masc.* sweater.

Jesucristo *noun Masc.* Jesus Christ.

jinete *noun Masc.* **1** rider; **2** jockey.

JJ.OO. *abbreviation plural Masc.* (*short for: Juegos Olímpicos*) Olympic Games.

jornada *noun Fem.* day; **una jornada de trabajo** a working day; **trabajar media jornada** to work part time; **trabajar la jornada completa** to work full time.

joven *noun Masc./Fem.* **un joven** a young man; **una joven** a young woman.

joven *adjective* young; **moda joven** young fashion.

jovencito/jovencita *noun Masc./Fem.* young man/young woman.

joya *noun Fem.* **1** piece of jewellery; **no me gustan las joyas** I don't like

jewellery; **2 esa chica es una joya** that girl's a real gem.

joyería *noun Fem.* jeweller's.

joyero *noun Masc.* jeweller's.

jubilación *noun Fem.* retirement.

jubilado/jubilada *noun Masc./ Fem.* pensioner; **los jubilados** retired people.

jubilado *adjective* retired.

jubilarse *reflexive verb* [17] to retire.

judaísmo *noun Masc.* Judaism.

judía[1] *noun Fem.* bean; **judías blancas** haricot beans; **judías pintas** kidney beans; **judías verdes** green beans.

judío/judía[2] *noun Masc./Fem.* Jew.

judío *adjective* Jewish.

judo *noun Masc.* judo.

juega, juego[1], etc. *verb* SEE **jugar**.

juego[2] *noun Masc.* **1** game; **juegos de mesa** board games; **un juego de azar** a game of chance; **los Juegos Olímpicos** the Olympic Games; **los Juegos Paralímpicos** the Paralympic Games; **a los diez minutos de juego** ten minutes into the game; **2 un juego de manos** a conjuring trick; **3** gambling; **es aficionado al juego** he likes gambling; **4** play; **un juego de palabras** a play on words; **juego limpio** fair play; **5** set; **un juego de cacerolas** a set of pans; **un juego de llaves** a set of keys; **6 hacer juego con algo** to match something; **no hace juego con los pantalones** it doesn't match the trousers; **7 fuera de**

a b c d e f g h i j k l m n ñ o p q r s t u v w x y z

juego offside; ★ **es un juego de niños** it's child's play.

juegue verb SEE **jugar**.

juerga noun Fem. **ir de juerga** (*informal*) to go out on the town.

juerguista noun Masc./Fem. (*informal*) raver.

jueves noun Masc. Thursday; **el jueves** on Thursday; **el jueves por la mañana** on Thursday morning; **los jueves** on Thursdays.

juez noun Masc./Fem. **1** judge; **2** referee.

jugador/jugadora noun Masc./Fem. **1** player; **2** gambler.

jugar verb [27] **1** to play; **jugar al fútbol** to play football; **jugar a la pelota** to play ball; **¿a qué quieres jugar?** what do you want to play?; **2** to gamble; **3** to move (*in board games*); **te toca jugar a ti** it's your turn (to move).

jugo noun Masc. juice.

jugoso/jugosa adjective juicy.

juguete noun Masc. toy; **un coche de juguete** a toy car.

juguetería noun Fem. toyshop.

juicio noun Masc. **1** trial; **llevar a alguien a juicio** to take someone to court; **2** sense; **no tiene ningún juicio** he's not very sensible; **3** no **estar en su sano juicio** to be out of one's mind; **perder el juicio** to lose one's mind.

julio noun Masc. July; **en julio/en el mes de julio** in July.

jungla noun Fem. jungle.

junio noun Masc. June; **en junio/en el mes de junio** in June.

júnior adjective junior.

junta[1] noun Fem. **1** board, committee; **2** meeting.

juntar verb [17] **1** to put together; **2** to join.

juntarse *reflexive verb* [17] **1** to join; **2** to meet; **me junté con unos amigos** I met some friends; **3** to get closer; **juntaos más** come closer.

junto/junta[2] adjective **1** together; **ahora todos juntos** all together now; **no los pongas tan juntos** don't put them so close together; **2** junto a next to; **junto a la ventana** next to the window; **3** junto con with, together with.

jurado noun Masc. jury.

jurar verb [17] to swear; **te lo juro** I swear.

jurídico/jurídica adjective legal.

justamente adverb **1** fairly; **tratar a alguien justamente** to treat someone fairly; **2** exactly; **justamente eso es lo que yo quería decir** that's exactly what I meant; **¡justamente!** exactly!.

justicia noun Fem. justice.

justificar verb [31] to justify.

justo[1]**/justa** adjective **1** fair; **no has sido justo con él** you haven't been fair with him; **una sociedad justa** a fair society; **2** exact; **la cantidad justa** the exact amount; **son ciento cincuenta euros justos** it's exactly one hundred and fifty euros; **3** just enough; **tengo lo justo para el autobús** I have just enough for my bus fare; **viven con lo justo** they have just enough to live on; **4** tight; **te está un poco**

justo it's a bit tight on you; **los zapatos me quedan muy justos** the shoes are too tight on me.

justo² *adverb* **1** just; **justo a tiempo** just in time; **2 justo en el centro** right in the middle.

juvenil *adjective* **1** youthful (*appearance*); **2** young (*fashion*); **3** junior (*team or competition*).

juventud *noun Fem.* youth; **la juventud de hoy** today's youth.

juzgado *noun Masc.* court.

juzgar *verb* [28] **1** to judge (*people or behaviour*); **te he juzgado mal** I've misjudged you; **2** to try (*a case or person*).

Kk

kaki *adjective* khaki.

kárate *noun Masc.* karate.

karting *noun Masc.* karting.

ketchup *noun Masc.* ketchup *Masc.*

Kg. *abbreviation (short for: kilogramo)* kg.

kilo *noun Masc.* kilo.

kilogramo *noun Masc.* kilogram.

kilómetro *noun Masc.* kilometre.

kiosco *noun Masc.* **1** kiosk (*selling sweets, cigarrettes, etc*); **2** newspaper kiosk; **3** stand; **un kiosko de helados** an ice cream stand; **4 el kiosko de la orquesta** the bandstand.

kiwi *noun Masc.* **1** kiwifruit; **2** kiwi.

km. *abbreviation (short for: kilómetro)* km.

koala *noun Masc.* koala bear.

Ll

la¹ *definite article* ('*la*' *is used before feminine singular nouns; see also* '*el*', '*los*' *and* '*las*') **1** the; **la casa es grande** the house is big; **2** (*sometimes* '*la*' *is not translated*) **no me gusta la sandía** I don't like watermelon; **irse a la cama** to go to bed; **la maleta de Isabel** Isabel's suitcase; **esta es la señora Martínez** this is Mrs Martínez; **3** (*with parts of the body or personal belongings*) **se rompió la pierna** she broke her leg; **se afeitó la barba** he shaved his beard off; **me quité la chaqueta** I took my jacket off; **4** (*talking about time*) **iré la próxima semana** I'll go next week; **5 me gustó la verde** I liked the green one; **la mía es roja** mine is red; **esa es la tuya** that one is yours; **6 esta es la de Ana** this one is Ana's; **la mía y la de usted** mine and yours; **me gusta más la de Toni** I like Toni's better; **7 la que yo compré** the one I bought; **la que quieras** whichever you want.

la² *pronoun* **1** her; **la acompañé a casa** I took her home; **2** it (*referring to a Spanish feminine noun*); **compré una camiseta, pero la voy a cambiar** I bought a T-shirt, but I'm going to change it.

labio *noun Masc.* lip.

laborable *adjective* **día laborable** working day.

a
b
c
d
e
f
g
h
i
j
k
l
m
n
ñ
o
p
q
r
s
t
u
v
w
x
y
z

laboratorio noun Masc. laboratory.

laca noun Fem. **1** lacquer; **2** hairspray; **3** laca de uñas nail varnish.

ladera noun Fem. slope.

lado noun Masc. **1** side; **el otro lado** the other side; **hacerse a un lado** to move to the side; **al otro lado de la carretera** on the other side of the road; **2 al lado de** next to; **al lado de Miguel** next to Miguel; **se sentó a mi lado** he sat next to me; **viven en la casa de al lado** they live next door; **3 de lado** sideways; **ponlo de lado** put it sideways; **tumbarse de lado** to lie on your side; **4 en todos lados/por todos lados** everywhere; **he buscado por todos lados** I've looked everywhere; **5 en otro lado** somewhere else; **deben estar en otro lado** they must be somewhere else; **6 en cualquier lado** anywhere; **deja siempre sus cosas en cualquier lado** he always leaves his things all over the place; **7 en algún lado** somewhere; **debe estar en algún lado** it must be somewhere; **8 en ningún lado/por ningún lado** nowhere, not anywhere; **no está por ningún lado** it's nowhere; **no lo encuentro en ningún lado** I can't find it anywhere; **9 por un lado ... por otro ...** on the one hand ... on the other hand ....

ladrar verb [17] to bark.

ladrillo noun Masc. brick.

ladrón/ladrona noun Masc./Fem. **1** thief, burglar; **2** robber.

lagarto noun Masc. lizard.

lago noun Masc. lake.

lágrima noun Fem. tear.

laguna noun Fem. **1** lake; **2** lagoon.

lamentar verb [17] **1** to regret; **lamento tener que informarle de ...** I regret to have to inform you that ...; **2 lo lamento mucho** I'm very sorry; **lamento no poder ayudarle** I'm sorry I can't help you.

lamer verb [18] to lick.

lámpara noun Fem. lamp; **lámpara de pie** standard lamp.

lana noun Fem. wool; **una chaqueta de lana** a wool jacket; **pura lana virgen** pure new wool.

langosta noun Fem. lobster.

langostino noun Masc. king prawn.

lanza noun Fem. spear.

lanzamiento noun Masc. launch (of rocket, product).

lanzar verb [22] **1** to throw (a ball or stone); **2** to launch (a product or an attack).

lanzarse reflexive verb [22] **1** to throw yourself; **se lanzó al agua** he leapt into the water; **lanzarse en paracaídas** to parachute; **2 lanzarse sobre alguien** to pounce on someone.

lápiz noun Masc. **1** pencil; **2 un lápiz de color** a crayon; **3 lápiz de ojos** eyeliner; **lápiz de labios** lipstick.

largo[1] noun Masc. length; **¿cuánto mide de largo?** how long is it?;

cinco metros de largo five metres long.

largo[^1]/**larga** adjective **1** long; **una falda larga** a long skirt; **te está muy largo** it's too long for you; **2 a lo largo de** along; **a lo largo de la costa** along the coast; **3 a lo largo de** throughout; **a lo largo del día** throughout the day.

las[^1] definite article ('las' is used before feminine plural nouns; see also 'el', 'la' and 'los') **1** the; **deja las cajas ahí** leave the boxes there; **2** (sometimes 'las' is not translated) **no me gustan las naranjas** I don't like oranges; **las maletas de Isabel** Isabel's suitcases; **3** (with parts of the body or personal belongings) **se lavó las manos** she washed her hands; **me quité las botas** I took my boots off; **4 las mías son rojas** mine are red; **esas son las tuyas** those are yours; **me gustaron las verdes** I liked the green ones; **5 estas son las de Ana** these ones are Ana's; **las mías y las de usted** mine and yours; **me gustan más las de Toni** I like Toni's better; **6 las que yo compré** the ones I bought; **las que quieras** whichever you want.

las[^2] pronoun them (referring to a plural Spanish feminine noun); **las vi ayer** I saw them yesterday; **te las puedes llevar** you can take them with you.

láser noun Masc. laser; **un rayo láser** a laser beam.

lástima noun Fem. **1** shame; **es una lástima que no puedas venir** it's a shame you can't come; **¡qué lástima!** what a shame!; **2 sentir lástima de alguien** to feel sorry for someone; **su madre me da lástima** I feel sorry for her mother; **3 estar hecho una lástima** to be in a pitiful state.

lata noun Fem. **1** tin; **una lata de tomates** a tin of tomatoes; **en lata** tinned; **sardinas en lata** tinned sardines; **2** (informal) nuisance; **¡qué lata!** what a nuisance!; **es una lata tener que esperar** it's a nuisance having to wait; **2 dar la lata** (informal) to be a nuisance; **¡deja de dar la lata!** stop being a nuisance!; **siempre están dando la lata** they're always such a nuisance.

latín noun Masc. Latin.

Latinoamérica noun Fem. Latin America.

latinoamericano/ latinoamericana noun Masc./ Fem., adjective Latin American.

latón noun Masc. brass.

laurel noun Masc. **1** laurel; **2 una hoja de laurel** a bayleaf.

lavabo noun Masc. **1** washbasin; **2** toilet; **¿dónde están los lavabos?** where are the toilets?

lavado noun Masc. wash; **lavado en seco** dry cleaning; **lavado a mano** handwashing.

lavadora noun Fem. washing machine.

lavanda noun Fem. lavender.

lavandería noun Fem. **1** laundry; **2** laundrette.

lavaplatos noun Masc. (does not change in the plural) dishwasher.

lavar verb [17] **1** to wash; **lavar la ropa** to wash the clothes; **lavar los platos** to wash the dishes; **2 lavar algo en seco** to dry-clean something; **3** lavar y marcar wash and blow-dry.

lavarse reflexive verb [17] to wash; **lavarse las manos** to wash your hands; **lavarse la cabeza** to wash your hair; **me lavo la cabeza todos los días** I wash my hair everyday; **lavarse los dientes** to clean your teeth.

lavavajillas noun Masc. (does not change in the plural) dishwasher.

lazo noun Masc. ribbon.

le pronoun **1** him (as indirect object); **quedé con Carlos y le di las llaves** I met Carlos and gave him the keys; **le mandé el paquete el lunes** I sent him the parcel on Monday; **¿qué le quitaron?** what did they take from him?; **2** her (as indirect object); **quedé con Inés y le di las llaves** I met Inés and gave her the keys; **le mandé el paquete el lunes** I sent her the parcel on Monday; **¿qué le quitaron?** what did they take from her?; **3** you (polite form: as indirect object); **¿le llevo las maletas a su habitación?** shall I carry your suitcases to your room?; **le mandé el paquete el lunes** I sent you the parcel on Monday; **4** it (as indirect object); **le puse la tapa** I put the lid on it; **le puse una estantería** I added another shelf to it.

lección noun Fem. lesson.

leche noun Fem. milk; **leche desnatada/leche descremada** skimmed milk; **leche en polvo** powdered milk.

lechuga noun Fem. lettuce.

lectura noun Fem. reading.

leer verb [37] to read; **estoy leyendo una novela** I'm reading a novel; **¿has leído a Lorca?** have you read Lorca?

legal adjective legal.

legendario/legendaria adjective legendary.

lejano/lejana adjective distant; **son parientes lejanos** they are distant relatives; **el Lejano Oriente** the Far East.

lejía noun Fem. bleach.

lejos adverb **1** far; **no está muy lejos** it's not very far; **está demasiado lejos para ir andando** it's too far to walk; **2** a long way; **está lejos del centro** it's a long way from the centre; **viven lejos de aquí** they live a long way from here; **está muy lejos** it's a long way (away); **3 desde lejos** from a distance.

lengua noun Fem. **1** tongue; **morderse la lengua** to bite your tongue; **2** language; **una lengua muy difícil** a very difficult language; **mi lengua materna** my mother tongue.

lenguado noun Masc. sole.

lenguaje noun Masc. language; **lenguaje corporal** body language.

lente noun Fem. lens; **lentes de contacto** contact lenses.

lenteja noun Fem. lentil.

lentilla noun Fem. contact lens.

lento¹/lenta *adjective* slow; **son muy lentos** they're very slow; **cocinar algo a fuego lento** to cook something over a low heat.

lento² *adverb* slowly; **caminan muy lento** they're walking very slowly.

leña *noun Masc.* firewood.

leño *noun Masc.* log.

leo *noun Masc./Fem.* Leo; **es leo** she's Leo.

Leo *noun Masc.* Leo.

león *noun Masc.* lion.

leopardo *noun Masc.* leopard.

leotardos *plural noun Masc.* woollen tights.

les *pronoun* **1** them (*as indirect object*); **les di las llaves** I gave them the keys; **les mandé el paquete el lunes** I sent them the parcel on Monday; **¿qué les quitaron?** what did they take from them?; **les puse la tapa** I put the lids on them; **2** you (*polite form, talking to more than one person: as indirect object*); **les mandé el paquete el lunes** I sent you the parcel on Monday.

lesión *noun Fem.* injury.

letón/letona *noun Masc./Fem., adjective* Latvian.

Letonia *noun Fem.* Latvia.

letra *noun Fem.* **1** letter; **letras mayúsculas** capital letters; **letras minúsculas** lower case letters; **2** handwriting; **tiene muy buena letra** she has very nice handwriting; **casi no se le entiende la letra** you can hardly

read his handwriting; **3** lyrics (*of a song*); **4** instalment; **me quedan dos letras por pagar** I still have two instalments to pay.

letrero *noun Masc.* notice, sign.

levadura *noun Fem.* yeast.

levantar *verb* [17] **1** to lift; **levantar un peso** to lift a weight; **levantar la tapadera** to lift the lid; **2** to raise; **levantar la mano** to raise your hand; **3** to pick up; **levantamos a la niña del suelo** we picked the girl up from the floor; **4** **¡levanta ese ánimo!** cheer up!
levantarse *reflexive verb* [17] **1** to get up; **levantarse de la cama** to get out of bed; **2** **levántate del suelo** get up off the floor; **3** **levantarse de la mesa** to leave the table.

ley *noun Fem.* law.

leyenda *noun Fem.* legend.

leyó *verb* SEE **leer**.

libanés/libanesa *noun Masc./ Fem., adjective* Lebanese.

Líbano *noun Masc.* **(el) Líbano** Lebanon.

liberar *verb* [17] **1** to free; **2** to liberate.

libertad *noun Fem.* freedom; **libertad de expresión** freedom of speech; **libertad condicional** parole.

libra¹ *noun Fem.* pound; **diez libras esterlinas** ten pounds sterling.

libra² *noun Masc./Fem.* Libra; **Susana es libra** Susana's Libra.

Libra *noun Masc.* Libra.

a b c d e f g h i j k l m n ñ o p q r s t u v w x y z

a
b
c
d
e
f
g
h
i
j
k
l
m
n
ñ
o
p
q
r
s
t
u
v
w
x
y
z

librar verb [17] **librar a alguien de morir ahogado** to save someone from drowning.

librarse reflexive verb [17]
1 librarse de morir ahogado to save yourself from drowning; **me libré del castigo** I escaped punishment; **2 librarse de una obligación** to get out of an obligation; **se libró de lavar los platos** he got out of doing the dishes.

libre adjective **1** free; **dejar libre a alguien** to set someone free; **¿está libre este asiento?** is this seat free?; **quinientos metros libres** five hundred metres freestyle; **2 trabajar por libre** to work freelance; **3 al aire libre** in the open air.

librería noun Fem. **1** bookshop; **2** bookcase.

libreta noun Fem. notebook.

libro noun Masc. book; **libro de texto** textbook; **libro de bolsillo** paperback; **libro de consulta** reference book.

licencia noun Fem. licence, permit.

licenciado/licenciada noun Masc./Fem. graduate.

licor noun Masc. liqueur.

licuadora noun Fem. liquidizer.

líder noun Masc./Fem. leader.

liebre noun Fem. hare.

liga noun Fem. league; **la liga de fútbol** the football league.

ligeramente adverb slightly.

ligero/ligera adjective **1** light; **un paquete ligero** a light parcel; **tener el sueño ligero** to be a light sleeper; **2** slight; **hay un ligero problema** there's a slight problem; **un ligero sabor a almendras** a slight taste of almonds; **3** thin (fabric); **4** fast; **un caballo muy ligero** a very fast horse; **5** agile.

lima noun Fem. **1** file; **una lima de uñas** a nailfile; **2** lime.

limitar verb [17] **1** to limit; **2 limitar con algo** to border on something; **España limita con Francia** Spain has a border with France.

limitarse reflexive verb [17] **1 el problema no se limita a eso** the problem is not just that; **2 me limité a ayudarlos con el ordenador** I just helped them with the computer.

límite noun Masc. **1** limit; **el límite de velocidad** the speed limit; **hay un tiempo límite** there's a time limit; **2 la fecha límite** the deadline; **3 ¡todo tiene un límite!** enough is enough!; **4** border (of a country).

limón noun Masc. lemon.

limonada noun Fem. lemonade.

limonero noun Masc. lemon tree.

limosna noun Fem. **pedir limosna** to beg; **dar limosna** to give money to beggars.

limpiaparabrisas noun Masc. (does not change in the plural) windscreen wiper.

limpiar verb [17] **1** to clean; **limpiar la casa** to clean the house; **2** to clean off; **limpiar una mancha de la mesa** to clean a dirty mark off the table; **3** limpiar algo con un trapo to wipe something clean; **4** limpiar los zapatos to polish the shoes; **5** limpiar algo en seco to dry-clean something.

limpieza noun Fem. **1** hacer la limpieza to do the cleaning; **hacer una limpieza general** to do a spring-clean; **2** limpieza en seco dry-cleaning; **3** una limpieza de cutis a facial.

limpio/limpia adjective **1** clean (clothes, a house, or person, for example); **2** fair (a game or business deal, for example).

lindo/linda adjective lovely.

línea noun Fem. **1** line; **línea de llegada** finishing line; **línea de meta** goal line; **2** línea aérea airline; **línea regular** airline operating scheduled flights; **3** línea telefónica telephone line; **no me da línea** the line is dead; **4** escribirle unas líneas a alguien to drop someone a line; **leer entre líneas** to read between the lines; **5** un jugador de primera línea a top player; **productos de primera línea** top-quality products; **6** figure; **mantener la línea** to watch your figure.

lino noun Masc. linen.

linterna noun Fem. torch.

lío noun Masc. (informal) **1** mess; **¡vaya lío!** what a mess!; **2** hacerse un lío to get muddled up; **me hice un lío con las fechas** I got the dates all muddled up; **3** armar un

lío to kick up a fuss; **4** trouble; **¡no te metas en líos!** keep out of trouble!

liquidación noun Fem. **1** sale; **liquidación por cierre** closing-down sale; **liquidación total** clearance sale; **2** liquidation (of a business); **3** settlement (of a debt or an account).

líquido¹ noun Masc. liquid.

líquido²/líquida adjective liquid.

liso/lisa adjective **1** smooth; **piel lisa** smooth skin; **2** straight; **tiene el pelo liso** she's got straight hair; **3** flat (ground).

lista¹ noun Fem. **1** list; **una lista de espera** a waiting list; **una lista de bodas** a wedding list; **una lista de precios** a price list; **la lista de vinos** the wine list; **2** (at school) register; **pasar lista** to take the register.

listín noun Masc. listín telefónico/ listín de teléfonos telephone directory.

listo/lista² adjective **1** clever; **2** estar listo to be ready; **ya estamos listos para salir** we're ready to go now.

litera noun Fem. **1** bunk bed; **2** berth.

literatura noun Fem. literature.

litro noun Masc. litre.

Lituania noun Fem. Lithuania.

lituano/lituana noun Masc./Fem., adjective Lithuanian.

llama noun Fem. **1** flame; **2** llama.

llamada noun Fem. call; **una llamada telefónica** a telephone

a
b
c
d
e
f
g
h
i
j
k
l
m
n
ñ
o
p
q
r
s
t
u
v
w
x
y
z

a
b
c
d
e
f
g
h
i
j
k
l
m
n
ñ
o
p
q
r
s
t
u
v
w
x
y
z

call; **una llamada interurbana** a long-distance call; **una llamada urbana** a local call; **una llamada a cobro revertido** a reverse-charge call.

llamar *verb* [17] **1** to call; **te llama tu madre** your mother is calling you; **llamar al médico** to call the doctor; **llamamos a un taxi** we called a taxi; **la llamamos Tintina** we call her Tintina; **2** to phone; **¿cuándo llamarás?** when will you phone?; **le llamé por teléfono** I phoned him.

llamarse *reflexive verb* [17] to be called; **se llama Ángeles** she's called Ángeles; **¿cómo te llamas?** what's your name?

llano/llana *adjective* flat, level (*ground*).

llave *noun Fem.* **1** key; **una llave maestra** a master key; **la llave de contacto** the ignition key; **cerrar algo con llave** to lock something; **2 la llave del gas** the gas tap; **la llave del agua** the mains water tap; **3** switch (*for a light*); **4** spanner; **una llave inglesa** an adjustable spanner; **5** hold; **una llave de judo** a judo hold.

llavero *noun Masc.* keyring.

llegada *noun Fem.* arrival; **a su llegada al hotel** when he arrived at the hotel.

llegar *verb* [28] **1** to arrive; **llegan a las siete** they arrive at seven; **cuando lleguemos a casa** when we get home; **2** to come; **ya llega el invierno** winter is coming; **3 llegar pronto a un sitio** to get somewhere early; **siempre llegas tarde** you're

always late; **llegó justo a tiempo** he was just in time; **4** to reach; **no llego a la lámpara** I can't reach the lamp; **5 la hierba me llega hasta las rodillas** the grass comes up to my knees; **las cortinas llegan hasta el suelo** the curtains go down to the floor; **mi parte del jardín llega hasta la valla** my part of the garden goes up to the fence; **6** to be enough; **con tres litros de leche llega para todos** three litres of milk will be enough for everybody; **7 llegar a hacer** to get to do; **llegué a conocerlo** I got to meet him; **no llegué a verlo** I didn't get to see it; **8 llegar a ser** to become; **llegó a ser famoso** he became famous.

llenar *verb* [17] **1** to fill; **llenar la bañera** to fill the bath; **2** to fill up; **llene el depósito, por favor** fill up the tank, please; **3** fill in (*a form, for example*).

lleno/llena *adjective* **1** full; **la botella está llena de agua** the bottle is full of water; **2** covered; **el suelo estaba lleno de papeles** the floor was covered with papers.

llevar *verb* [17] **1** to take; **te lo puedes llevar** you can take it with you; **llevaré una botella de vino a la fiesta** I'll take a bottle of wine to the party; **yo te puedo llevar a la estación** I can take you to the station; **la llevé a comer a un restaurante** I took her for lunch to a restaurant; **2** to carry; **yo llevaba al niño en brazos** I was carrying the baby in my arms; **3 la llevé en coche a su casa** I drove her home;

4 to have; **¿qué llevas en el bolso?**
what have you got in your bag?; **no
llevo las llaves encima** I don't
have the keys on me; **5** to wear;
llevaba un vestido verde she was
wearing a green dress; **6 lleva
tiempo** it takes time; **me llevó dos
semanas terminarlo** it took me
two weeks to finish it; **le llevó
mucho hacerlo** it took her a lot of
time to do it; **lleva media hora
hablando por teléfono** he's been
on the phone for half an hour;
**¿cuánto tiempo llevas
trabajando aquí?** how long have
you been working here?; **llevamos
dos semanas en Londres** we've
been in London for two weeks; **7 le
llevo cuatro años** I'm four years
older than him; **8** to lead; **el
camino que lleva al río** the road
that leads to the river.

llevarse *reflexive verb* [17] **1** to
take (away); **se llevó los discos** he
took the records; **ya puedes
llevarte esto** you can take this
away now; **2 llevarse bien con
alguien** to get on with someone; **no
se llevan bien** they don't get on.

llorar *verb* [17] to cry.

llover *verb* [38] to rain; **está
lloviendo** it's raining; ★ **está
lloviendo a cántaros** it's pouring
down (*literally: it's raining in
jugfuls*).

llovizna *noun Fem.* drizzle.

llueva, llueve, etc. *verb* SEE
llover.

lluvia *noun Fem.* rain.

lluvioso/lluviosa *adjective*
rainy.

lo[1] *definite article* **1** the; **lo mejor**
... the best thing is ...; **lo curioso**
... the funny thing is ...; **prefiero lo
salado a lo dulce** I prefer savoury
things to sweet things; **2 lo mío**
mine; **esto es lo tuyo** that's yours;
lo vuestro está en la habitación
your things are in the bedroom;
3 esto es lo de mi madre this is
my mother's; **lo de Marta lo he
puesto en la mesa** I've put
Marta's things on the table;
4 ¿sabes lo de Eva? have you
heard about Eva?; **lo de Pablo es
muy raro** it's really strange this
thing with Pablo; **lo del accidente
fue horrible** that thing about the
accident was horrible; **le conté lo
tuyo** I told her about you; **5 lo que**
what; **eso es lo que yo compré**
that's what I bought; **coge lo que
quieras** take whatever you want;
dime todo lo que sepas tell me
everything you know.

lo[2] *pronoun* **1** him; **lo vi ayer** I saw
him yesterday; **2** it; **lo metí en tu
bolso** I put it in your bag; **3 ya lo
sé** I know.

lobo *noun Masc.* wolf.

local *noun Masc.* premises.

localidad *noun Fem.* **1** town; **una
pequeña localidad** a small town;
2 ticket; **'no hay localidades'** 'sold
out'.

loción *noun Fem.* lotion; **loción
para después del afeitado**
aftershave lotion; **loción
bronceadora** suntan lotion.

loco/loca *noun Masc./Fem.*
madman, madwoman.

a b c d e f g h i j k l m n ñ o p q r s t u v w x y z

loco adjective **1** mad; ¡tú estás loco! you're mad!; **2** estar loco por alguien to be crazy about somebody; **3** ¡este niño me va a volver loco! that child's going to drive me mad!; las fresas la vuelven loca she loves strawberries; ★ estar loco de remate (informal) to be completely bonkers; ★ hacer algo a lo loco to do something any old how.

locomotora noun Fem. engine (of a train).

locura noun Fem. **1** madness; **2** eso es una locura that's crazy; otra de sus locuras another one of his crazy ideas.

locutor/locutora noun Masc./Fem. **1** announcer; **2** newsreader; **3** locutor deportivo sports commentator.

lógico/lógica adjective logical.

lograr verb [17] **1** to achieve; lograr la victoria to achieve victory; **2** lograr hacer to manage to do; lograr que alguien haga to get someone to do.

lombriz noun Fem. worm.

lomo noun Masc. **1** back (of an animal); **2** spine (of a book); **3** lomo de cerdo loin of pork; **4** filete de lomo sirloin steak.

loncha noun Fem. slice; una loncha de jamón a slice of ham; una loncha de bacon a rasher of bacon.

londinense noun Masc./Fem. Londoner.

londinense adjective London.

Londres noun Masc. London.

longaniza noun Fem. spicy pork sausage.

longitud noun Fem. **1** length; tiene doce metros de longitud it's twelve metres long; **2** longitude; **3** longitud de onda wavelength.

loro/lora noun Masc./Fem. parrot; ★ hablar como un loro (informal) to be a chatterbox; ★ repetir algo como un loro to repeat something parrot-fashion.

los[1] definite article ('los' is used before masculine plural nouns; see also 'el', 'la' and 'las') **1** the; deja los libros ahí leave the books there; **2** (sometimes 'los' is not translated) no me gustan los tomates I don't like tomatoes; los discos de Isabel Isabel's records; **3** (with parts of the body or personal belongings) se frotó los ojos she rubbed her eyes; me quité los zapatos I took my shoes off; **4** los míos son rojos mine are red; ésos son los tuyos those are yours; me gustaron los verdes I liked the green ones; **5** éstos son los de Ana these ones are Ana's; los míos y los de usted mine and yours; me gustan más los de Toni I like Toni's better; **6** los que yo compré the ones I bought; los que quieras whichever you want.

los[2] pronoun them; los vi ayer I saw them yesterday; te los puedes llevar you can take them with you.

lote noun Masc. batch Masc.; a batch of letters un lote de cartas.

lotería noun Fem. lottery; **tocarle a alguien la lotería** to win the lottery.

luces plural noun SEE **luz.**

lucha noun Fem. fight.

luchar verb [17] **1** to fight; **luchar cuerpo a cuerpo** to fight hand to hand; **2** to struggle.

luego adverb **1** then; **luego vino su madre** then her mother came; **2** later; **luego te veo** I'll see you later; **¡hasta luego!** see you later!; **3** afterwards; **luego te arrepentirás** you'll be sorry afterwards; **luego podemos cenar** we can have dinner afterwards; **4** then; **primero está su casa y luego la mía** first comes her house and then mine; **primero iré al banco y luego a tu casa** I'll go to the bank first and then to your house; **5 desde luego** of course.

lugar noun Masc. **1** place; **un lugar precioso** a beautiful place; **lugar de nacimiento** place of birth; **me siento fuera de lugar** I feel out of place; **2 en cualquier lugar** anywhere; **por cualquier otro lugar** anywhere else; **3 en otro lugar** somewhere else; **4 yo en su lugar ... if I were him ...; 5** position (in a race or competition); **en primer lugar** in first position; **llegó en último lugar** he finished in last place; **6 en primer lugar** first of all; **en segundo lugar ...** second ...; **en último lugar** last of all; **7 en lugar de** instead of.

lúgubre adjective gloomy.

lujo noun Masc. luxury; **apartamentos de lujo** luxury apartments.

lujoso/lujosa adjective luxurious.

luminoso/luminosa adjective **1** bright; **2** luminous.

luna noun Fem. **1** moon; **esta noche hay luna** the moon is out tonight; **luna llena** full moon; **luna creciente** waxing moon; **luna menguante** waning moon; **luna de miel** the honeymoon; **2 una luna de espejo** a mirror; **la luna del escaparate** the shop window.

lunar noun Masc. **1** mole (on your skin); **2** polka-dot; **una camisa de lunares** a polka-dot shirt.

lunes noun Masc. Monday (see 'domingo' for examples).

lupa noun Fem. magnifying glass.

luto noun Masc. mourning; **ir de luto** to be in mourning; **ponerse de luto** to go into mourning.

Luxemburgo noun Masc. Luxembourg.

luz (plural **luces**) noun Fem. **1** light; **dar la luz** to switch on the light; **apagar la luz** to switch off the light; **la luz del sol** the sunlight; **2** electricity; **se ha ido la luz** the electricity's gone off; **3 luces de cruce/luces cortas** dipped headlights; **luces largas** full beam; **luces de freno** brake lights; **4 dar a luz** to give birth; ★ **tener pocas luces** to be a bit dim.

a
b
c
d
e
f
g
h
i
j
k
l
m
n
ñ
o
p
q
r
s
t
u
v
w
x
y
z

Mm

a
b
c
d
e
f
g
h
i
j
k
l
m
n
ñ
o
p
q
r
s
t
u
v
w
x
y
z

macarrones *plural noun Masc.* macaroni.

macedonia *noun Fem.* fruit salad.

maceta *noun Fem.* flowerpot.

machista *noun Masc./Fem.* male chauvinist.

machista *adjective* sexist.

macho *adjective* male.

madera *noun Fem.* **1** wood; **2** timber.

madrastra *noun Fem.* stepmother.

madre *noun Fem.* **1** mother; **ser madre soltera** to be a single mother; **madre política** mother-in-law; **2 ¡madre mía!** my goodness!.

Madrid *noun Fem.* Madrid.

madrileño/madrileña *noun Masc./Fem.* person from Madrid.

madrileño *adjective* of/from Madrid; **las iglesias madrileñas** the churches of Madrid.

madrina *noun Fem.* **1** godmother; **2** in Spanish weddings, the woman who accompanies the groom, usually his mother.

madrugada *noun Fem.* dawn; **de madrugada** at dawn; **nos levantamos de madrugada** we got up at dawn; **llegamos de madrugada** we arrived in the early hours of the morning; **a las cuatro de la madrugada** at four in the morning.

madurar *verb* [17] **1** to ripen; **2** to mature.

maduro/madura *adjective* **1** ripe; **2** mature; **es muy poco maduro** he's quite immature.

maestro/maestra *noun Masc./Fem.* **1** teacher (*primary school*); **2** master (*of a trade*).

magdalena *noun Fem.* fairycake.

magia *noun Fem.* magic.

mágico/mágica *adjective* magical.

magnético/magnética *adjective* magnetic.

magnetofón, magnetófono *noun Masc.* tape recorder.

magnífico/magnífica *adjective* **1** wonderful; **2** magnificent.

mago/maga *noun Masc./Fem.* **1** magician; **2** wizard.

mahonesa *noun Fem.* mayonnaise.

maíz *noun Masc.* **1** sweetcorn; **una mazorca de maíz** a corn on the cob; **2** maíze.

mal *noun Masc.* evil; **el bien y el mal** good and evil.

mal *adjective* **1** bad; **es un mal amigo** he's a bad friend; **vinieron en mal momento** they came at a bad time; **2** wrong; **la respuesta está mal** the answer's wrong; **está mal criticar** it's wrong to criticize; **3** ill; **¿te sientes mal?** do you feel ill?; **su padre está muy mal** his father's very ill.

mal *adverb* **1** badly; **está muy mal pintado** it's really badly painted; **lo leyó muy mal** she read it very badly; **le va muy mal en el trabajo** he's doing very badly at work; **el país marcha mal** the country's not doing well; **2** wrong; **lo hizo mal** he did it wrong; **hace mal en no pedir perdón** he's wrong not to apologize; **3 contestar mal a alguien** to answer someone back; **4 te oigo mal** I can't hear you very well; **5 la comida sabe mal** the food tastes horrible; **olía muy mal** there was a nasty smell; **6 portarse mal** to misbehave; **entender mal algo** to misunderstand something; **7 ¡menos mal!** thank goodness!

malabarismos *noun Masc.* (*plural*) **hacer malabarismos** to juggle.

malabarista *noun Masc./Fem.* juggler.

malcriado/malcriada *noun Masc./Fem.* **es un malcriado** he's really spoilt.

malcriado *adjective* **1** spoilt; **2** naughty

maldición *noun Fem.* **1** curse; **2 soltar una maldición** to swear; **3 ¡maldición!** damn!.

maleducado/maleducada *noun Masc./Fem.* **es una maleducada** she's really rude.

maleducado *adjective* rude.

malentendido *noun Masc.* misunderstanding.

maleta *noun Fem.* suitcase.

maletero *noun Masc.* boot (*of a car*).

maletín *noun Masc.* **1** briefcase; **2** overnight case; **3 el maletín del médico** the doctor's bag.

malhumor *noun Masc.* bad temper.

malla *noun Fem.* **1** mesh; **malla de alambre** wire mesh; **2** leotard; **3 mallas** leggings.

Mallorca *noun Fem.* Majorca.

mallorquín/mallorquina *noun Masc./Fem.*, *adjective* Majorcan.

malo/mala *adjective* **1** bad; **una mala costumbre** a bad habit; **es malo para la salud** it's bad for your health; **2** naughty; **¡qué niño más malo!** what a naughty child!; **3** nasty; **no seas mala y devuélveselo** don't be nasty and give it back to her; **4** poor; **de mala calidad** poor quality; **5 ayer hizo malo** the weather was bad yesterday; **nos hizo muy malo durante las vacaciones** we had horrible weather during the holidays; **6 estar malo** to be ill; **no puede venir porque está mala** she can't come because she's ill; **el pobre está muy malo** the poor thing is in a really bad way; **7 estar malo** to be off (*food*); **la leche está mala** the milk's gone off; **8 estar malo** to taste horrible; **la sopa estaba muy mala** the soup was horrible; **9 ser malo para** (*a person*) to be bad at; **soy malo para las matemáticas** I'm bad at maths; SEE **mal**[2].

mamá *noun Fem.* (*informal*) Mum.

mamífero *noun Masc.* mammal.

manada *n Fem.* **1** herd (*of cattle*); **2** pack (*of dogs*); **3** gang (*of young people*)

mancha *noun Fem.* **1** stain; **una mancha de chocolate** a chocolate stain; **quitar una mancha** to remove a stain; **2** mark; **3 mancha de petróleo** oil slick.

manchar verb [17] **1** to get (something) dirty; **mancharon la alfombra de barro** they got mud all over the carpet; **2** to stain.

mancharse reflexive verb [17] to get yourself dirty; **cuidado, no te manches** careful, don't get yourself dirty; **se manchó los pantalones de barro** he got mud all over his trousers.

manchón noun Fem. stain.

mandar verb [17] **1** to order; **2 le gusta mandar** she likes to give the orders; **3** mandar a alguien hacer to tell somebody to do; **me mandó recoger la habitación** she told me to tidy my bedroom; **haz lo que te mandan** do as you're told; **4** to send; **mandar una carta a alguien** to send somebody a letter; **los mandé a comprar fruta** I sent them to buy some fruit; **5 mandar llamar a alguien** to send for someone.

mandarina noun Fem. mandarin, tangerine.

mando noun Masc. **1** command; **estar al mando de** to be in charge of; **2** control (of a machine or a television, for example); **mando a distancia** remote control.

manejar verb [17] **1** to use (a computer, dictionary); **2** to operate (a machine); **3** to manage (a business).

manera noun Fem. **1** way; **lo hice a mi manera** I did it my way; **no hubo manera de arreglarlo** there

was no way of fixing it; **es su manera de ser** it's the way he is; **2 de alguna manera** somehow; **me las arreglaré de alguna manera** I'll do it somehow; **3 de cualquier manera**; any old how; **puedes decorarlo de cualquier manera** you can decorate it any way you want; **4 de una manera u otra** one way or another; **5 ¡de ninguna manera!** no way!; **¿me dejas el coche? ' – '¡de ninguna manera!'** 'can I borrow your car?' – 'no way'; **6 de todas maneras** anyway; **de todas maneras no pensaba comprarlo** I wasn't thinking of buying it anyway; **7 de manera que** so; **de manera que al final no la vi** so I didn't see her in the end.

manga noun Fem. **1** sleeve; **una camisa de manga corta** a short-sleeved shirt; **sin mangas** sleeveless; **2** hose (for watering).

mango noun Masc. **1** handle (of a knife or tool); **2** mango.

manguera noun Fem. hosepipe.

manía noun Fem. **1 tiene la manía del orden** he's obsessed with tidiness; **es maja pero tiene sus manías** she's nice but she has her funny little ways; **2 tenerle manía a alguien** to have it in for somebody.

maniático/maniática noun Masc./Fem. **es una maniática de la limpieza** she's obsessed with cleanliness.

maniático adjective fussy.

manifestación noun Fem. **1** demonstration; **2** sign (of

disapproval, for instance);
3 manifestaciones statements.

manifestar *verb* [29] **1** to express (*disapproval or an opinion*); **2** to show (*emotions*).

manifestarse *reflexive verb* [29] **1** to demonstrate; **2** to become evident; **3 manifestarse en contra de algo** to come out against something.

manillar *noun Masc.* handlebars.

manipular *verb* [17] **1** to operate (*a machine*); **2** to manipulate (*data or information*).

maniquí *noun Masc.* mannequin.

manivela *noun Fem.* handle.

mano *noun Fem.* **1** hand; **levantar la mano** to raise your hand; **ir de la mano** to go hand in hand; **coger a alguien de la mano** to take somebody's hand; **darle la mano a alguien** to give somebody your hand, to shake somebody's hand; **3 decir adiós con la mano** to wave goodbye; **4** coat; **una mano de pintura** a coat of paint.

manómetro *noun Masc.* pressure gauge.

mansión *noun Fem.* mansion.

manso/mansa *adjective* **1** tame (*an animal*); **2** gentle (*a person*).

manta *noun Fem.* blanket.

manteca *noun Fem.* lard.

mantecado *noun Masc.* almond delicacy (*eaten at Christmas*).

mantel *noun Masc.* tablecloth.

mantendrá, mantendría, etc. *verb* SEE **mantener.**

mantener *verb* [9] **1** to keep; **mantener la calma** to keep calm; **mantener el equilibrio** to keep your balance; **2** to support (*a family, for example*).

mantenerse *reflexive verb* [9] to keep; **mantenerse en equilibrio** to keep your balance; **mantenerse en contacto con alguien** to keep in touch with somebody.

mantengo, mantenga, etc. *verb* SEE **mantener.**

mantenimiento *noun Masc.* **1** maintenance; **2 ejercicios de mantenimiento** keep-fit exercises.

mantequilla *noun Fem.* butter.

mantilla *noun Fem.* mantilla (*a lace headscarf*).

mantuve, mantuvo, etc. *verb* SEE **mantener.**

manual *adjective* manual.

manzana *noun Fem.* **1** apple; **2** block (*in a town*); **dar una vuelta a la manzana** to go round the block.

manzanilla *noun Fem.* **1** camomile tea; **2** dry sherry.

manzano *noun Masc.* apple tree.

mañana *noun Fem.* morning; **a la mañana siguiente** the next morning; **por la mañana** in the morning; **a las once de la mañana** at eleven o'clock in the morning.

mañana *adverb* tomorrow; **pasado mañana** the day after tomorrow; **hasta mañana** see you tomorrow; **mañana por la tarde** tomorrow afternoon.

a
b
c
d
e
f
g
h
i
j
k
l
m
n
ñ
o
p
q
r
s
t
u
v
w
x
y
z

a **mapa** noun Masc. map; **un mapa de carreteras** a road map.

b **maquillaje** noun Masc. make-up.

c **maquillar** verb [17] to make up.
maquillarse reflexive verb [17] to put your make-up on; **apenas se maquilla** she hardly wears any make-up.

d

e **máquina** noun Fem. **1** machine; **una máquina de escribir** a typewriter; **escribir a máquina** to type; **una máquina de coser** a sewing machine; **2 una máquina de fotos** a camera; **3 una máquina de afeitar** an electric shaver.

f

g

h

i **maquinaria** noun Fem. machinery.

j

k **maquinilla** noun Fem. safety razor.

l

m **mar** noun Masc. sea; **viajar por mar** to travel by sea; **el mar Cantábrico** the Bay of Biscay.

n

ñ **maratón** noun m or Fem. marathon.

o

p **maravilla** noun Fem. wonder; **es una maravilla de casa** it's a wonderful house; **★ a las mil maravillas** (informal) wonderfully.

q

r **maravilloso/maravillosa** adjective wonderful.

s

t **marca** noun Fem. **1** mark; **el cuadro ha dejado una marca en la pared** the picture has left a mark on the wall; **2** brand; **artículos de marca** brand products; **ropa de marca** designer clothes; **3 marca registrada** registered trademark; **4** record (in sports); **establecer una nueva marca** to establish a

u

v

w

x

y

z

new record; **batir una marca** to break a record.

marcador noun Masc. scoreboard.

marcar verb [31] **1** to mark; **la experiencia me marcó mucho** the experience really marked me; **2 mi reloj marca las nueve** my watch says nine o'clock; **el termómetro marcaba cinco grados** the thermometer was registering five degrees; **3 marcar un número** to dial a number; **marca 00 44 para Gran Bretaña** dial 00 44 for Britain; **4 marcar un gol** to score a goal; **5 marcar el ritmo/marcar el compás** to beat time.

marcha noun Fem. **1** hike; **ir de marcha** to go hiking; **fuimos de marcha a la montaña** we went hiking in the mountains; **2** march (a demonstration); **3** gear (in a car); **marcha atrás** reverse; **meter la marcha atrás** to put the car into reverse; **4** speed; **disminuir la marcha** to reduce speed; **5 estar en marcha** to be running (a car engine, for example); **6 poner en marcha** to start (a car, for example); **7 ¡en marcha!** let's go!; **8** (informal) **una discoteca con mucha marcha** a really fun disco; **¡qué marcha tiene ese grupo!** this group's really wild!; **9** (informal) **ir de marcha** to go out partying.

marchar verb [17] **1** to work (a machine or a company); **esto no marcha** this isn't working; **2** to march; **3 ¡marchando dos cafés!** two coffees coming up!.

marcharse reflexive verb [17] to

leave; **nos marchamos mañana** we're leaving tomorrow.

marco noun Masc. **1** frame; **2** framework; **3** goal (in football).

marea noun Fem. tide; **está subiendo la marea** the tide's coming in; **cuando baje la marea** when the tide goes out; **marea negra** oil slick.

mareado/mareada adjective **1 estar mareado** to feel dizzy, to feel queasy; **me siento mareado/mareada** I'm feeling dizzy/queasy; **2 estar mareado** (informal) to be muddled up; **estoy mareado con tantos números** I'm all muddled up with all these numbers.

marear verb [17] **1** to make (somebody) feel dizzy, to make (somebody) feel queasy; **2** (informal) to confuse; **me marearon a preguntas** they asked me so many questions my head was spinning.

mareo noun Masc. **1** sick feeling; **me dan mareos si viajo en coche** I get carsick; **2** seasickness; **3** dizziness.

marfil noun Masc. ivory.

margarina noun Fem. margarine.

margarita noun Fem. **1** daisy; **2** marguerite.

margen noun Masc. margin; **escribir algo en el margen** to write something in the margin.

marido noun Masc. husband.

marina noun Fem. navy.

marinero noun Masc. sailor.

marioneta noun Fem. puppet.

mariposa noun Fem. butterfly.

mariquita noun Fem. ladybird.

marisco noun Masc. shellfish; **me gusto el marisco** I like shellfish.

mármol noun Masc. marble.

marrón noun Masc. brown.

marrón adjective brown; **zapatos marrones** brown shoes; **unos pantalones marrón claro** a pair of light brown trousers (note that 'marrón' does not change in the plural when used with another adjective).

martes noun Masc. Tuesday (see 'domingo' for examples).

martillo noun Masc. hammer.

marzo noun Masc. March; **en marzo/en el mes de marzo** in March.

más adverb, adjective, pronoun **1** more; **éste me gusta más** I like this one more; **pon más azúcar** add more sugar; **tres más** three more; **más o menos** more or less; **¿necesitas más?** do you need any more?; **no comas más** don't eat any more; **no lo hagas más** don't do it again; **2 es un poco más grande** it's a bit bigger; **tenemos que hacerlo más rápido** we have to do it faster; **3 es más interesante que su primer libro** it's more interesting than his first book; **más que nunca** more than ever; **me gusta más el de cuero que el de tela** I prefer the leather one to the cloth one; **más blanco que la nieve** as white as snow; **4 el de más peso** the heaviest one; **los de más prestigio** the most prestigious ones; **el libro con más páginas** the book with the most pages; **5 el que más me gusta** the one I like the most; **los que son más altos** the tallest ones; **6 más de** more than; **más de veinte kilos** more than twenty kilos; **vinieron más de veinte personas** more than twenty people came; **7 hay tres sillas de más** there are three chairs too many; **hay tres pasteles de más** there are three cakes left over; **si quieres venir, tengo un billete de más** I've got a spare ticket if you want to come; ★ **estar de más** to feel out of place;; **8** (*referring to time*) **no les he visto más** I've never seen them again; **no me quedo más** I won't stay any longer; **9** else; **¿esperas a alguien más?** are you expecting anybody else?; **nadie más** nobody else; **no quiero nada más** I don't want anything else; **¿querías algo más?** did you want anything else?; **10 no ... más** only; **no tardo más de diez minutos** I'll only take ten minutes; **no es más que un resfriado** it's only a cold; **11** (*in exclamations*) **¡es más bonito!** it's so beautiful!; **¡había más gente!** there were so many people!; **¡le gustó más!** he liked it a lot!

más *preposition* plus; **cinco más siete** five plus seven.

masa *noun Fem.* **1** dough; **masa de pan** bread dough; **2** pastry; **masa de hojaldre** puff pastry.

masaje *noun Masc.* massage.

máscara *noun Fem.* mask.

mascarilla *noun Fem.* mask.

masculino[1] *noun Masc.* masculine (*in grammar*).

masculino[2]**/masculina** *adjective* masculine.

masticar *verb* [31] to chew.

mástil *noun Masc.* **1** mast; **2** flagpole.

matador *noun Masc.* matador.

matanza *noun Fem.* **1** massacre (*of people*); **2** slaughter (*of animals*).

matar *verb* [17] to kill.
matarse *reflexive verb* [17] **1** to kill yourself; **2** to get killed; **si sigues conduciendo así, te vas a matar** if you carry on driving like that you're going to get killed.

mate *noun Masc.* **jaque mate** checkmate.

mate *adjective* matt.

matemáticas *plural noun Fem.* maths.

materia *noun Fem.* **1** material; **materia prima** raw material; **2 materia grasa** fat; **3** subject (*of study or of a book*).

material *noun Masc.*, *adjective* material.

maternal *adjective* maternal.

materno/materna *adjective* **1** motherly; **2** mother; **lengua materna** mother tongue; **3 abuelos maternos** grandparents on the mother's side.

matiz *noun Masc.* shade (*of a colour*).

matrícula *noun Fem.* **1** registration; **hacer la matrícula** to register; **2** registration number (*of a car*); **un coche con matrícula de Sevilla** a car with a Seville

number plate; 3 matrícula de honor distinction; **sacar matrícula en física** to get a distinction in physics.

matrimonio *noun Masc.*
1 marriage; **matrimonio civil** civil wedding; **2** married couple; **son un matrimonio muy unido** they're a very close couple.

máximo/máxima *adjective*
1 maximum; **2** top (*speed*);
3 highest; **el punto máximo** the highest point.

mayo *noun Masc.* May; **en mayo/en el mes de mayo** in May.

mayonesa *noun Fem.* mayonnaise.

mayor *noun Masc./Fem.* adult.

mayor *adjective* **1** greater;
2 greatest; **3** higher; **un número mayor que cien** a number higher than one hundred; **a la mayor altura** at the maximum height;
4 bigger; **¿tienes una talla mayor?** do you have a bigger size?;
5 biggest; **el de mayor tamaño** the biggest one; **6** older; **es cinco años mayor que su mujer** he's five years older than his wife; **7** oldest; **mi hermana mayor** my oldest sister; **soy el mayor de todos mis hermanos** I'm the oldest of my brothers and sisters; **8 cuando seas mayor** when you grow up; **las personas mayores** the grown-ups; **ya son muy mayores** they're quite old now; **9 la mayor parte de** most of; **la mayor parte de los estudiantes** most of the students;
10 ser mayor de edad to be of age.

mayores *plural noun Masc.* **los mayores** the grown-ups; the elderly.

mayoría *noun Fem.* majority; **la mayoría de** most of.

mayúscula[1] *noun Fem.* capital letter.

mayúsculo/mayúscula[2]
adjective **1** capital (*letter*);
2 (*informal*) terrible (*mistake or fright*).

mazapán *noun Masc.* marzipan.

me *pronoun* **1** me; **me invitaron a su fiesta** they invited me to their party; **no me han visto** they haven't seen me; **2** to me; **me lo dieron ellos** they gave it to me; **me mintió** he lied to me; **me lo ha comprado mi madre** my mother bought it for me; **3** myself; **me corté** I cut myself; **4** (*with reflexive verbs*) **me reí mucho** I laughed a lot; **voy a bañarme** I'm going for a swim; **me senté a la mesa** I sat at the table; **5** (*with parts of the body or clothes*) **me quité el abrigo** I took my coat off; **me limpié los pies al entrar** I wiped my feet at the door; **6** (*having things done*) **el sábado iré a cortarme el pelo** I'll go and have my hair cut on Saturday.

mecánico/mecánica[2] *noun Masc./Fem.* mechanic.

mecánico *adjective* mechanical.

mecanografía *noun Fem.* typing.

mecedora *noun Fem.* rocking chair.

mechero *noun Masc.* lighter.

medalla *noun Fem.* medal.

a b c d e f g h i j k l m n ñ o p q r s t u v w x y z

media[1] *noun Fem.* average; **la media de altura** the average height, average; **la media eúropea** the European average.

media[2] *noun Fem.* **1** stocking; **2 medias** tights; **3** (*telling the time*) **las dos y media** half past two; **dos horas y media** two hours and a half; **4 hacer algo a medias** to half-do something; **lo dejó a medias** he didn't finish it; **5 lo hicimos a medias** we did it between the two of us; **pagar a medias** to pay half each.

mediados *plural noun Masc.* **a mediados de semana** midweek; **a mediados de año** halfway through the year.

mediano/mediana *adjective* **1** medium; **de peso mediano** medium weight; **2** average; **3 de mediana calidad** mediocre.

medianoche *noun Fem.* midnight; **a media noche** at midnight.

medicamento *noun Masc.* medicine.

medicina *noun Fem.* medicine; **estudiar medicina** to study medicine; **tomarse la medicina** to take your medicine.

médico/médica *noun Masc./Fem.* doctor; **médico de cabecera** family doctor.

médico *adjective* medical.

medida *noun Fem.* **1** measure; **tomar medidas a algo** to measure something; **2** measurement; **¿qué medidas tiene la mesa?** what are the measurements of the table?;

3 traje a medida a made-to-measure suit; **4 a medida que** as; **a medida que pase el tiempo** as time goes by; **5 en gran medida** to a large extent; **en cierta medida** to a certain extent; **en la medida de lo posible** as far as possible.

medieval *adjective* medieval.

medio ambiente *noun Masc.* environment.

medio[1] *noun Masc.* **1** middle; **ponlo en el medio** put it in the middle; **la casa de en medio** the house in the middle; **2 quitarse de en medio** to get out of the way; **3** way; **es el mejor medio** it's the best way; **no hubo medio de localizarlo** there was no way of finding him; **lo intenté por todos los medios** I tried every possible way; **4** means; **por cualquier medio** by any means; **por todos los medios** by any possible means; **medios de transporte** means of transport; **5 por medio de** through; **por medio de un amigo** through a friend; **6 en medio de todo aquel jaleo** amidst all that racket; **7 los medios de comunicación** the media.

medio[2] *adverb* half; **ya está medio convencido** he's half convinced now.

medio[3]**/media** *adjective* **1** half; **medio kilo** half a kilo; **media docena** half a dozen; **media pensión** half board; **2** average; **de estatura media** of average height; **3** (*in time expressions*) half; **media hora** half an hour.

mediodía noun Masc. midday; **al mediodía** at midday.

medir verb [57] **1** to measure; **¿cuánto mide de ancho?** how wide is it?; **mide sesenta centímetros de largo** it's sixty centimetres long; **2 ¿cuánto mides?** how tall are you?

mediterráneo/**mediterránea** adjective Mediterranean.

Mediterráneo noun Masc. Mediterranean.

mejicano/**mejicana** noun Masc./Fem., adjective Mexican.

Méjico noun Masc. SEE **México**.

mejilla noun Fem. cheek.

mejillón noun Masc. mussel.

mejor noun Masc./Fem. **el/la mejor** the best one.

mejor adjective **1** better; **éste es de mejor calidad** this one is better quality; **cuanto antes mejor** the earlier the better; **es mejor que no vayamos** it's better if we don't go; **2** best; **la mejor forma es** ... the best way is ....

mejor adverb **1** better; **Isabel toca la guitarra mejor** Isabel plays the guitar better; **mejor que** better than; **mejor que el otro** better than the other one; **cada vez mejor** better and better; **2** best; **es la que mejor dibuja** she's the one that draws the best; **hazlo lo mejor que puedas** do your best; **3 a lo mejor** maybe; **a lo mejor es de Sara** maybe it's Sara's; **a lo mejor no voy** I might not go; **4 mejor no preguntes** it's better if you don't ask; **mejor déjalo así** it's better if

you leave it like this; **mejor venid en tren** you'd be better coming by train.

mejora noun Fem. improvement.

mejorar verb [17] **1** to improve; **2** to get better; **ha mejorado del estómago** he's got over his stomach problems.

mejorarse reflexive verb [17] to get better; **¡que te mejores!** get well soon!.

mellizo/**melliza** noun Masc./Fem., **mellizo** adjective twin.

melocotón noun Masc. peach.

melodía noun Fem. melody.

melón noun Masc. melon.

memoria noun Fem. **1** memory; **aprenderse algo de memoria** to learn something by heart; **2 memorias** memoirs.

mencionar verb [17] to mention.

mendigar verb [17] to beg.

mendigo/**mendiga** noun Masc./Fem. beggar.

menestra noun Fem. **menestra de verduras** vegetable stew.

meñique noun Masc. little finger.

menor noun Masc./Fem. **1 el/la menor** the younger; **2 un/una menor** a minor.

menor adjective **1** younger; **mi hermana menor** my younger sister; **soy menor que tú** I'm younger than you; **2** youngest; **el menor de la familia** the youngest of the family; **3** little; **con el menor esfuerzo posible** with as little effort as possible; **4** less; **su importancia es cada vez menor** it gets less and less important all the

a
b
c
d
e
f
g
h
i
j
k
l
m
n
ñ
o
p
q
r
s
t
u
v
w
x
y
z

a
b
c
d
e
f
g
h
i
j
k
l
m
n
ñ
o
p
q
r
s
t
u
v
w
x
y
z

time; **en menor grado** to a lesser extent; **5** minor; **de menor importancia** of minor importance; **6** smaller; **un número menor de alumnos** a smaller number of pupils; **7** smallest; **hasta el menor detalle** in the smallest detail; **8 no tengo la menor idea** I haven't got the slightest idea.

menos *adjective (does not change in the plural)* **1** less; **de menos peso** of less weight; **2** few; **había menos de cien personas** there were fewer than a hundred people.

menos *adverb* **1** less; **ahora sale menos** he goes out less now; **cada vez menos** less and less; **2** least; **los menos informados** the least well-informed; **es lo menos que esperaba** it's the least I expected; **3** el menos alto the shortest one; **el que corre menos** the slowest of all; **4** menos que less than, fewer than; **habla menos que yo** he speaks less than I do; **cuesta menos que el otro** it costs less than the other one; **había menos que ayer** there were fewer than yesterday; **5** menos de less than; **cuesta menos de cien libras** it costs less than a hundred pounds; **adultos de menos de treinta años** adults under thirty; **6** ahora los veo menos I don't see them as often now; **7** ahora sale menos she doesn't go out as much now.

menos *pronoun* **1 ahora compramos menos** now we don't buy as much; **2 cobrar de menos** to undercharge; **hay diez tarjetas de menos** there are ten cards too

few; **3 al menos/por lo menos** at least; **4 ¡menos mal!** thank goodness!

menos *preposition* except; **todos menos su madre** everybody except her mother.

mensaje *noun Masc.* message; **un mensaje de texto** a text message; **te mandaré un mensaje de texto mañana** I'll send you a text message tomorrow.

mensajero/mensajera *noun Masc./Fem.* **1** messenger; **2** courier; **servicio de mensajeros** courier service.

mensual *adjective* monthly; **dos cientos euros mensuales** two hundred euros a month.

mensualmente *adverb* monthly.

menta *noun Fem.* mint; **un caramelo de menta** a mint.

mental *adjective* mental.

mente *noun Fem.* mind; **se me quedó la mente en blanco** my mind went blank.

mentir *verb* [14] to lie.

mentira *noun Fem.* lie.

mentiroso/mentirosa *noun Masc./Fem.* liar.

mentón *noun Masc.* chin.

menú *noun Masc.* menu; **menú del día** set menu.

menudo/menuda *adjective* **1** small; **es muy menuda** she's quite small; **2 a menudo** often; **nos vemos a menudo** we see each other often; **3 ¡menudo problema!** what a problem!; **¡menuda moto!** what an incredible motorbike!

mercado noun Masc. market; **ir al mercado** to go to the market; **el Mercado Común** the Common Market.

mercancías plural noun Fem. goods.

mercería noun Fem. haberdashery.

merecer verb [35] 1 to deserve; **mereces un castigo** you deserve to be punished; 2 **merecer la pena** to be worthwhile; **la película merece la pena** the film is worth seeing.

merecerse reflexive verb [35] to deserve; **no me merezco que me traten así** I don't deserve to be treated like this.

merendar verb [29] to have a teatime snack; **siempre merienda pan y chocolate** he always has bread and chocolate in the afternoon; **¿quieres merendar algo?** do you want something to eat?; **¡a merendar!** teatime!

merezca, merezco, etc. verb SEE **merecer**.

meridional adjective southern.

merienda[1] noun Fem. 1 afternoon snack; 2 **merienda campestre** picnic; **ir de merienda** to go for a picnic.

merienda[2], **meriendo, etc.** verb SEE **merendar**.

mérito noun Masc. merit.

mermelada noun Fem. jam.

mes noun Masc. month; **el mes que viene** next month; **mil euros al mes** a thousand euros a month; **un**

bebé de siete meses a seven-month-old baby.

mesa noun Fem. table; **sentarse a la mesa** to sit at the table; **poner la mesa** to set the table; **quitar la mesa/recoger la mesa** to clear the table; **¡a la mesa!** food's ready!

mesita noun Fem. **mesita de noche** bedside table.

meta noun Fem. 1 finishing line; 2 aim; **tiene como meta ser actriz** her aim is to become an actress.

metal noun Masc. metal.

metálico/metálica adjective metallic.

meteorológico/ meteorológica adjective meteorological; **parte meteorológico** weather forecast.

meter verb [18] 1 to put (something) in; **metió la mano** he put his hand in; **métalo en la carpeta** put it in the folder; 2 to fit; **¿puedes meter algo más en la maleta?** can you fit anything else in the suitcase?; 3 **meter la primera** to put the car in first gear; **meter la marcha atrás** to put the car into reverse; 4 **meter un gol** to score a goal.

meterse reflexive verb [18] 1 **meterse en** to get in(to); **meterse en la cama** to get into bed; 2 **meterse en algo** to get involved in something; **no te metas en mis asuntos** mind your own business.

método noun Masc. method.

métrico adjective metric.

a b c d e f g h i j k l m n ñ o p q r s t u v w x y z

a **metro** noun Masc. **1** underground;
2 metre; **los cien metros libres**
the hundred metres freestyle.

b
c **mexicano/mexicana** noun
Masc./Fem., adjective Mexican.

d **México** noun Masc. Mexico.

e **mezcla** noun Fem. **1** mixture;
2 mix; **una mezcla de culturas** a
mix of cultures.

f
g **mezclar** verb [17] **1** to mix; **2** to
mix up; **has mezclado todos los
papeles** you've mixed up all the
papers.

h
mezclarse reflexive verb [17]
mezclarse en algo to get mixed up
in something.

i
j **mezquita** noun Fem. mosque.

k **mi** adjective my; **mis amigos** my
friends.

l
mí pronoun **1** me; **detrás de mí**
behind me; **se olvidaron de mí**
they forgot about me; **2** (as indirect
object) **me lo dio a mí** he gave it to
me; **3 a mí me gusta** I like it; **a mí
me parece que** ... I think that ...;
4 mí mismo/misma myself; **sé
cuidar de mí misma** I can look
after myself; **5 por mí** ... as far as
I'm concerned.

m

n

ñ

o
p **micrófono** noun Masc.
microphone.

q **microondas** noun Masc. (does not
change in the plural) microwave
(oven).

r
s **microscopio** noun Masc.
microscope.

t
u **mida**, **midiendo**, **midió**, **mido**,
etc. verb SEE medir.

v
w **miedo** noun Masc. **1** fear; **tener
miedo** to be scared; **tengo mucho**

x

y

z

miedo I'm really scared; **tengo
miedo de intentarlo** I'm afraid of
trying; **¡qué miedo!** how
frightening!; **miedo a algo** fear of
something; **2 me da miedo la
altura** I'm afraid of heights; **les da
miedo ir solos** they are afraid of
going on their own; **3 pasamos un
rato de miedo** (informal) we had a
great time.

miedoso/miedosa adjective **es
muy miedoso** he's afraid of
everything.

miel noun Fem. honey.

miembro noun Masc. **1** member;
2 limb.

mienta, miento, etc. verb SEE
mentir.

mientras adverb meanwhile;
mientras tanto in the meantime;
**mientras tanto él seguía
esperando en la estación** in the
meantime he was waiting at the
station.

mientras conjunction **1** while;
**pon la mesa mientras yo hago la
comida** lay the table while I cook
the meal; **2** as long as; **mientras yo
viva** as long as I'm alive.

miércoles noun Masc.
Wednesday; **el miércoles** on
Wednesday; **el miércoles por la
mañana** on Wednesday morning;
los miércoles on Wednesdays.

miga noun Fem. crumb.

mil number thousand; **mil
doscientos** one thousand two
hundred.

milagro noun Masc. miracle.

milenio noun Masc. millennium.

milésimo/milésima adjective thousandth.

mili noun Fem. (informal) military service.

milímetro noun Masc. milimetre.

militar noun Masc./Fem. soldier.

militar adjective military.

millón number million; **un millón de euros** a million euros; **un millón de gracias** thank you ever so much.

millonario/millonaria noun Masc./Fem. millionaire.

mina noun Fem. mine; **una mina de carbón** a coalmine.

mineral noun Masc., adjective mineral.

minero/minera noun Masc./Fem. miner.

minero adjective mining.

mini noun Fem. (informal) mini.

minifalda noun Fem. miniskirt.

mínimo[1] noun Masc. minimum.

mínimo[2]**/mínima** adjective minimum; **no me importa lo más mínimo** I couldn't care less.

ministerio noun Masc. ministry.

ministro/ministra noun Masc./Fem. minister.

minoría noun Fem. minority.

mintamos, mintió, etc. verb SEE mentir.

minúscula[1] noun Fem. small letter (not capital).

minúsculo/minúscula[2] adjective tiny.

minusválido/minusválida noun Masc./Fem. disabled person.

minusválido adjective disabled.

minuto noun Masc. minute.

mío/mía adjective mine; **un amigo mío** a friend of mine.

mío pronoun mine; **el mío es verde** mine is green.

miope adjective shortsighted.

mirada noun Fem. look; **una mirada alegre** a happy look; **dirigir una mirada a** to look at; **me dirigió una mirada** she looked at me; **bajar la mirada** to look down.

mirar verb [17] **1** to look; **miré afuera** I looked outside; **miré en el cajón** look in the drawer; **2 mirar algo** to look at something; **miró el cuadro con interés** he looked at the picture with interest; **me miró** he looked at me; **3** to watch; **mirar la tele** to watch TV; **4 mirar fijamente** to stare.

mirarse reflexive verb [17] **mirarse en el espejo** to look at yourself in the mirror; **mirarse las manos** to look at your hands.

mirlo noun Masc. blackbird.

misa noun Fem. mass; **ir a misa** to go to mass.

miserable adjective **1** miserable; **2** stingy.

miseria noun Fem. **1** misery; **2** poverty; **3** pittance.

misil noun Masc. missile.

mismo[1] adverb **1** right; **ahora mismo** right now; **en ese mismo momento** right at that moment; **está ahí mismo** it's right there; **al lado mismo de casa** right next to the house; **2** just; **lo mismo que yo** just like me; **eso mismo dije yo** that's just what I said.

mismo²/misma *adjective*
1 same; **al mismo tiempo** at the same time; **llevan los mismos zapatos** they have the same shoes; **lo mismo** the same; **2** very; **en este mismo lugar** in this very spot; **3** yo mismo I myself; **lo vi yo mismo** I saw it myself; **lo dijo ella misma** she said it herself.

mismo *pronoun* **1** el mismo the same one; **he usado la misma** I've used the same one; **Sara tiene los mismos** Sara has the same ones; **2** da lo mismo it doesn't matter; **me da lo mismo el color** I don't mind which colour.

misterio *noun Masc.* mystery.

misterioso/misteriosa *adjective* mysterious.

mitad *noun Fem.* **1** half; **la mitad del pastel** half the cake; **a mitad de precio** half-price; **2** halfway; **a mitad de camino paramos a comer** we stopped halfway to eat; **llenar algo hasta la mitad** to half fill something; **lo he leído hasta la mitad** I'm halfway through reading it; **3** cortar algo por la mitad to cut something in two.

mito *noun Masc.* myth.

mixto/mixta *adjective* mixed.

mobiliario *noun Masc.* furniture; **mobiliario de cocina** kitchen fittings.

mochila *noun Fem.* backpack.

mocos *plural noun Masc.* **tener mocos** to have a runny nose.

moda *noun Fem.* fashion; **la moda juvenil** young fashion; **estar de moda** to be in fashion; **pasarse de moda** to go out of fashion; **siempre va a la última moda** he's always wearing the latest fashion.

modales *plural noun Masc.* manners; **tener buenos modales** to have good manners.

modelo¹ *noun Masc.* model; **utilizar algo como modelo** to use something as a model.

modelo² *noun Masc./Fem.* model (*fashion*).

moderno/moderna *adjective* **1** modern; **2** trendy.

modesto/modesta *adjective* **1** modest; **2** humble.

modificar *verb* [31] to change.

modisto/modista *noun Masc./Fem.* **1** dressmaker; **2** (fashion) designer.

modo *noun Masc.* **1** way; **lo haré a mi modo** I'll do it my way; **a mi modo de ver** to my way of thinking; **no hubo modo** there was no way (of doing it); **2** lo hizo de cualquier modo he did it any old way; **3** de cualquier modo te llamaré antes in any case, I'll phone you first; **4** ¡de ningún modo! no way!; **5** de todos modos anyway; **de todos modos no iba a comprarlo** I wasn't going to buy it anyway; **6** de modo que so; **7** en cierto modo somehow; **8** modo de empleo instructions for use.

mohoso/mohosa *adjective* mouldy.

mojado/mojada *adjective* wet.

mojar *verb* [17] to wet.

mojarse *reflexive verb* [17] to get

wet; **se me mojó el pelo** my hair got wet.

moler *verb* [38] to grind.

molestar *verb* [17] **1** to disturb; 'no molestar' 'do not disturb'; **no molestes a tu madre, que está trabajando** don't disturb your mother, she's working; **2** to bother; **perdona que te moleste** sorry to bother you; **3** ¿**te molesta que ponga la tele?** do you mind if I put the TV on?; **4** to annoy; **me molesta que no me hayan invitado** I'm annoyed that they haven't invited me.

molestarse *reflexive verb* [17] **1** to get upset; **se molestó porque fuimos sin ella** she got upset because we went without her; **2 molestarse en hacer algo** to bother to do something; **no se molestó en preguntar** she didn't bother to find out.

molestia *noun Fem.* **1** trouble; **no es ninguna molestia** it's no trouble at all; **causar molestias a alguien** to inconvenience someone; **2 tomarse la molestia de hacer algo** to take the trouble to do something; **3 perdone la molestia** sorry to bother you; **4 si no es molestia** ... if you don't mind ....

molesto/molesta *adjective* **1** annoying; **2** uncomfortable; **3 estar molesto** to be upset; **sé que está molesto conmigo** I know he's upset with me.

momento *noun Masc.* moment; **justo en ese momento** right at that moment; **dentro de un**

momento in a moment; **¡un momento!** just a moment!; **de momento** at the moment; **en cualquier momento** any moment now; **en este momento** right now.

monarquía *noun Fem.* monarchy.

monasterio *noun Masc.* monastery.

moneda *noun Fem.* **1** coin; **2** currency.

monedero *noun Masc.* purse.

monja *noun Fem.* nun.

monje *noun Masc.* monk.

mono/mona *noun Masc./Fem.* monkey.

mono *adjective* **1** cute (*a puppy or baby, for example*); **2** pretty (*person, garment*).

monopatín *noun Masc.* skateboard.

monstruo *noun Masc.* monster.

montaña *noun Fem.* **1** mountain; **en la montaña** in the mountains; **2 la montaña rusa** the roller coaster.

montar *verb* [17] **1** to get on; **montar en el avión** to get on the plane; **2** to get in; **montar en el coche** to get in the car; **3** to ride; **montar a caballo** to ride a horse; **montar en la moto** get on the motorbike; **montar en bicicleta** to ride a bike; **4** to mount (*a horse*); **5** to set up (*a business or an exhibition*); **6** to put up (*a tent*); **7 montar claras a punto de nieve** to whisk the egg whites until stiff; **8 montar un escándalo** (*informal*) to cause a scene.

montarse *reflexive verb* [17] **1** to

a b c d e f g h i j k l **m** n ñ o p q r s t u v w x y z

a

get on; **se montó en el tren** he got on the train; **2** to get in; **montarse en un coche** to get in a car.

b

c **monte** noun Masc. mountain; scrubland; **monte de piedad** pawnbroker's shop.

d

e **montón** noun Masc. **1** pile; **puse todas las revistas en un montón** I put all the magazines in a pile; **2 un montón de** (informal) loads of; **había un montón de niños** there were loads of children; **montones de** (informal) loads of; **montones de dinero** loads of money; **3 me gusta un montón** (informal) I like it a lot; **4 del montón** (informal) ordinary; **un cantante del montón** an ordinary singer.

f

g

h

i

j

k

l

m **monumento** noun Masc. monument.

n **moqueta** noun Fem. fitted carpet.

ñ **mora** noun Fem. blackberry.

o **morado**[1] noun Masc. purple.

p **morado**[2]**/morada** adjective purple.

q **moral** noun Fem. **1** morals; **no tienen ninguna moral** they have no morals; **2** morale; **estar bajo de moral** to feel low.

r

s **moral** adjective moral.

t **morcilla** noun Fem. black pudding.

u **morder** verb [38] to bite.

v **mordisco** noun Masc. bite; **darle un mordisco a algo** to bite (on) something.

w

x

y **moreno/morena** adjective **1** dark (hair); **2 es morena** she's dark-haired; **3 estar moreno** to be

z

tanned; **ponerse moreno** to get tanned.

morir verb [55] to die; **morir ahogado** to drown; **morir en un accidente** to be killed in an accident.

morirse reflexive verb [55] to die; **me muero de hambre** I'm starving; **se muere por ir a la playa** he's dying to go to the beach.

moro/mora noun Masc./Fem. **1** Moor; **2** North African.

moro adjective Moorish.

mortal adjective **1** deadly, lethal; **2** fatal.

mosca noun Fem. fly; **★ por si las moscas** (informal) just in case; **★ ¿qué mosca le ha picado?** (informal) what's got into him? (literally: 'what fly has bitten him?').

mosquito noun Masc. mosquito.

mostaza noun Fem. mustard.

mostrador noun Masc. **1** counter (in a shop); **2** bar (in a pub); **3** check-in desk.

mostrar verb [24] to show.

mostrarse reflexive verb [24] **mostrarse interesado** to show interest; **mostrarse amable** to be kind; **mostrarse contento** to be happy.

motivo noun Masc. **1** cause; **el motivo del accidente** the cause of the accident; **2** reason; **por motivos personales** for personal reasons.

moto noun Fem. motorbike; **montar en moto** to ride a motorbike; **montar en la moto** to get on the motorbike; **moto acuática** jetski.

motocicleta noun Fem. motorbike.

motociclista noun Masc./Fem. motorcyclist.

motor noun Masc. engine; **motor a reacción** jet engine.

motora noun Fem. motorboat.

motorista noun Masc. motorcyclist.

mover verb [38] to move.
  moverse reflexive verb [38] to move; **no te muevas** don't move.

movimiento noun Masc. movement.

moza noun Fem. young girl.

mozo noun Masc. 1 young boy; 2 **mozo de estación** porter.

muchacha noun Fem. girl.

muchacho noun Masc. boy.

muchedumbre noun Fem. crowd.

mucho¹ adverb 1 a lot; **lo usan mucho** they use it a lot; **eso es mucho mejor** that's a lot better; **salen mucho** they go out a lot; 2 very; **lo siento mucho** I'm very sorry; **'¿te interesa?'** – **'mucho'** 'are you interested?' – 'very'; **trabajar mucho** to work very hard; **voy a estudiar mucho** I'm going to study very hard; 3 **mucho antes** long before; **mucho después** long after; 4 **como mucho** at the most; 5 **ni mucho menos** far from it.

mucho² pronoun 1 a lot; **tienes mucho que aprender** you have a lot to learn; 2 much; **no tengo mucho** I haven't got much;

3 many; **no quedan muchas** there aren't many left; **muchos se sorprendieron** many were surprised; 4 (talking about time) **tardan mucho** they are taking a long time; **¿hace mucho que ha llamado?** did she call a long time ago?; **hace mucho que no sé nada de ella** it's a long time since I last heard from her; **ya no falta mucho para mi cumpleaños** it's not long to my birthday now.

mucho³/**mucha** adjective 1 a lot of; **mucho tiempo** a lot of time; 2 much; **no tienen mucho interés** they haven't got much interest; 3 many; **¿había muchos niños?** were there many children?; **muchas veces** many times; 4 **hacía mucho frío** it was very cold; **tengo mucho sueño** I'm very sleepy; 5 **tengo mucha prisa** I'm in a real hurry; 6 **nos vimos hace mucho tiempo** we saw each other a long time ago; 7 **muchas gracias** thanks a lot; **mucho gusto** nice to meet you; **lo haré con mucho gusto** I'd be very pleased to do it.

mudanza noun Fem. removal; **camión de mudanzas** removal van; **estar de mudanza** to be in the process of moving.

mudar verb [17] to move (from one house to another).
  mudarse reflexive verb [17] 1 to change one's clothes; 2 to move; **mudarse de casa** to move house.

mueble noun Masc. piece of furniture; **muebles** furniture.

muela noun Fem. back tooth; **tener dolor de muelas** to have toothache.

muera, muero, etc. verb SEE **morir**.

muerda, muerdo, etc. verb SEE **morder**.

muerte noun Fem. death; **muerte repentina** sudden death; **estar condenado a muerte** to be sentenced to death.

muerto/muerta noun Masc./Fem. dead person; **no ha habido muertos** there were no casualties; **hubo un muerto** one person died.

muerto adjective dead; **muerto de sed** dying of thirst; **estoy muerto de frío** I'm freezing to death; **estoy muerto de hambre** I'm starving; **estábamos muertos de cansancio** we were dead tired.

muestra, muestro, etc. verb SEE **mostrar**.

mueva, muevo, etc. verb SEE **mover**.

mujer noun Fem. 1 woman; 2 wife; **mi mujer** my wife.

muleta noun Fem. crutch.

mulo/mula noun Masc./Fem. mule.

multa noun Fem. fine; **me pusieron una multa** I was fined.

multicolor adjective multicoloured.

multiplicación noun Fem. multiplication.

multiplicar verb [31] to multiply.

mundial noun Masc. **el mundial de fútbol** the World Cup.

mundial adjective world; **un récord mundial** a world record; **la economía mundial** the world economy; **de fama mundial** world-famous.

mundo noun Masc. world.

municiones noun Fem. (plural) ammunition.

municipal adjective 1 local; 2 municipal.

muñeca noun Fem. 1 doll; **jugar a las muñecas** to play dolls; **muñeca de trapo** rag doll; 2 wrist.

muñeco noun Masc. 1 toy; **muñeco de peluche** soft toy; 2 puppet.

muralla noun Fem. wall (fortified); **the Great Wall of China** la Gran Muralla de China.

murciélago noun Masc. bat.

muriendo, murió, etc. verb SEE **morir**.

murmullo noun Masc. 1 whispering; **hablar en un murmullo** to whisper; 2 murmur.

murmurar verb [17] 1 to whisper; 2 to murmur; 3 **murmurar sobre alguien** to gossip about someone; **se murmura que ...** the rumour is ....

muro noun Masc. wall.

músculo noun Masc. muscle.

museo noun Masc. museum; **un museo de pintura** a gallery; **un museo de arte moderno** a modern art museum.

música[1] noun Fem. music; **música en directo/música en vivo** live music; **música pop** pop music.

musical adjective musical.

músico/música[2] noun Masc./Fem. **1** musician; **2** composer.

muslo noun Masc. **1** thigh; **2** leg (of a chicken).

musulmán/musulmana noun Masc./Fem., adjective Muslim.

mutuo/mutua adjective mutual.

muy adverb **1** very; **es muy difícil** it's very difficult; **está muy bien** it's very good; **muy bien, sigamos** very good, let's continue; **2** too; **era muy pequeño para entenderlo** he was too small to understand it; **3** Muy señor mío Dear sir (in a letter).

Nn

nabo noun Masc. turnip.

nácar noun Masc. mother-of-pearl.

nacer verb [35] to be born; **nací en Valencia** I was born in Valencia; **¿dónde has nacido?** where were you born?

nacido/nacida adjective born; **nacido en Sevilla** born in Seville; **un niño recién nacido** a new-born baby.

nacimiento noun Masc. **1** birth; **es ciego de nacimiento** he was born blind; **2** crib (nativity scene).

nación noun Fem. nation.

nacional adjective national.

nacionalidad noun Fem. nationality; **¿de qué nacionalidad eres?** what nationality are you?

nada pronoun **1** nothing; **no hay nada nuevo** there's nothing new;

no hay nada como ... there's nothing like ...; **2** anything; **no me queda nada** I haven't got anything left; **yo no sé nada de eso** I don't know anything about that; **no me dijeron nada** they didn't say anything to me; **3 no tengo nada de dinero** I have no money at all; **4 nada más** nothing else; **sólo quiero hablar con ella, nada más** I only want to speak to her, nothing else; **nada más, gracias** that's all thank you; **5 nada más** nothing else; **no quiero nada más** I don't want anything else; **nada más que** only; **no quiero nada más que un kilo** I only want one kilo; **7 de nada** not at all (to someone who has said thank you); **8** love (in tennis); **treinta nada** thirty love.

nada adverb at all; **no me gusta nada** I don't like it at all; **no me ayudan nada** they don't help me at all.

nadar verb [17] to swim.

nadie pronoun **1** nobody; **al final nadie llamó** nobody phoned in the end; **2 no se lo dije a nadie** I didn't tell anybody.

nailon noun Masc. nylon.

naipe noun Masc. card.

nana noun Fem. lullaby.

naranja noun Fem. orange; **zumo de naranja** orange juice.

naranja noun Masc. orange (the colour).

naranja adjective orange (never changes); **unos pantalones naranja** orange trousers.

naranjada noun Fem. orangeade.

naranjo noun Masc. orange tree.

a b c d e f g h i j k l m n ñ o p q r s t u v w x y z

narcotraficante noun Masc./ Fem. drugs trafficker.

narcotráfico noun Masc. drugs trade.

nariz noun Fem. nose; **sonarse la nariz** to blow your nose; ★ **darse de narices con alguien** (informal) to bump into someone; ★ **en mis propias narices** (informal) right under my nose.

nata noun Fem. cream; **nata líquida** single cream; **nata para montar** double cream; **nata montada** whipped cream.

natación noun Fem. swimming.

natillas plural noun Fem. custard.

natural adjective natural.

naturaleza noun Fem. **1** nature; **respetar la naturaleza** to respect nature; **la naturaleza humana** human nature; **2 naturaleza muerta** still life.

naturalmente adverb naturally.

náusea noun Fem. nausea; **tener náuseas** to feel sick; **el olor me daba náuseas** the smell was making me feel sick.

nauseabundo/nauseabunda adjective nauseating.

navaja noun Fem. **1** penknife; **2 navaja de afeitar** razor.

nave noun Fem. **1** ship; **nave espacial** spaceship; **2** premises; **una nave industrial** industrial premises.

navegar verb [28] **1** to navigate; **2** to sail; **navegar en Internet** to surf the Internet.

navegar verb [28] to sail.

Navidad noun Fem. **1** Christmas; **el día de Navidad** Christmas Day; **feliz Navidad** Merry Christmas; **2 Navidades** Christmas time; **pasaré las Navidades con mi hermana** I'll spend Christmas with my sister.

nazca, nazco, etc. verb SEE **nacer.**

neblina noun Fem. mist.

necesario/necesaria adjective necessary.

necesidad noun Fem. need; **no hay necesidad de llamarlos** there's no need to call them; **en caso de necesidad** ... if necessary ....

necesitar verb [17] **1** to need; **no necesitas llevar el pasaporte** you don't need to take your passport; **2 'se necesitan camareros'** (on sign) 'waiters wanted'.

nectarina noun Fem. nectarine.

neerlandés[1] noun Masc. Dutch (the language).

neerlandés[2]**/neerlandesa** noun Masc./Fem. Dutchman/ Dutchwoman.

neerlandés/neerlandesa adjective Dutch.

nefasto/nefasta adjective **1** disastrous (consequences); **2** awful (weather or taste in clothes).

negar verb [30] **1** to deny; **lo niega todo** he denies everything; **2** to refuse; **nos negaron su ayuda** they refused to help us.

negarse reflexive verb [30] to

refuse; **se niega a colaborar** he refuses to colaborate.

negativo/negativa *adjective* negative.

negociación *noun Fem.* negotiation.

negociar *verb* [17] to negotiate.

negocio *noun Masc.* **1** business; **montar un negocio** to set up a business; **un viaje de negocios** a business trip; **2 negocios** business; **dedicarse a los negocios** to be in business; **3** deal; **hacer un buen negocio** to make a good deal.

negro/negra *noun Masc./Fem.* black man/black woman.

negro *adjective* black.

neozelandés/neozelandesa *noun* New Zealander.

neozelandé/neozolandesas *adjective* (from) New Zealand.

nervio *noun Masc.* nerve; **tengo muchos nervios** I'm very nervous; ★ **tener los nervios de punta** to be on edge.

nervioso/nerviosa *adjective* nervous; **ponerse nervioso** to get nervous.

neumático *noun Masc.* tyre.

neumonía atípica *noun Fem.* SARS (*the disease*).

neutro/neutra *adjective* **1** neutral; **2** neuter (*in grammar*).

nevada *noun Fem.* snowfall.

nevar *verb* [29] to snow; **está nevando** it's snowing.

nevasca *noun Fem.* snow storm.

nevera *noun Fem.* fridge.

nevisca *noun Fem.* snow flurry.

ni *conjunction* **1** not ... even; **ni lo he abierto** I haven't even opened it; **ni uno de ellos llamó** not even one of them called; **2 no ... ni** ... neither ... nor; **no vino él ni su hermana** neither he nor his sister came; **no es mío ni suyo** it's not mine and it's not hers either; **una casa sin luz ni agua corriente** a house with neither water nor electricity; **ni uno ni otro** neither one nor the other; **3 no es ni grande ni pequeño** it's neither big nor small; **4 ¡ni hablar!** no way!

nicaragüense *noun Masc./Fem.*, *adjective* Nicaraguan.

nido *noun Masc.* nest.

niebla *noun Fem.* fog; **había mucha niebla** it was very foggy.

nieta *noun Fem.* granddaughter.

nieto *noun Masc.* **1** grandson; **2 mis nietos** my grandchildren.

nieva, nieve[1], **etc.** *verb* SEE **nevar**.

nieve[2] *noun Fem.* **1** snow; **2 batir claras a punto de nieve** to beat eggwhites until stiff; ★ **blanco como la nieve** as white as snow.

niña *noun Fem.* girl.

niñera *noun Fem.* nanny.

ningún *adjective* SEE **ninguno**.

ninguno/ninguna *adjective* ('*ninguno*' becomes '*ningún*' before a masculine singular noun) **1** any; **no trajeron ninguna caja** they didn't bring any boxes; **no he comprado ningún libro** I didn't buy any books; **no hay ninguna necesidad** there's no need; **2 en**

a
b
c
d
e
f
g
h
i
j
k
l
m
n
ñ
o
p
q
r
s
t
u
v
w
x
y
z

a
b
c
d
e
f
g
h
i
j
k
l
m
n
ñ
o
p
q
r
s
t
u
v
w
x
y
z

ningún momento never; **en ningún lugar** nowhere; **no lo veo por ningún lado** I can't see it anywhere; **3 de ninguna manera** no way.

ninguno *pronoun* **1** neither; **ninguno de los dos vale** neither of them is suitable; **ninguno de los dos me gusta** I don't like either of them; **2** none; **ninguno de los que estaban allí** none of those who were there; **no compró ninguno** he didn't buy any of them; **3** nobody; **ninguno lo vio** nobody saw him.

niño *noun Masc.* **1** boy; **2** child; **van a tener un niño** they're going to have a baby; **3 niños** children; **ropa de niños** children's clothes.

nitrógeno *noun Masc.* nitrogen.

nivel *noun Masc.* **1** level; **el nivel del agua** the level of the water; **2** standard; **el nivel de vida** the standard of living.

no *adverb* **1** no; **'¿es tuyo?' – 'no'** is it yours?' – 'no'; **2** not; **no es mi amigo** he's not my friend; **no sabe nadar** he can't swim; **no se sabe** it's not known; **no mucho** not much; **ahí no** not there; **3 no comió nada** he didn't eat anything; **no voy nunca al cine** I never go to the cinema; **no se parecen en nada** they are not similar at all; **4 somos siete ¿no?** there are seven of us, aren't there?; **tú hablaste con ella, ¿no?** you spoke to her, didn't you?; **5 la no violencia** non-violence; **los nofumadores** non smokers; **6 ¡cómo no!** of course!

noche *noun Fem.* **1** evening; night; **a las ocho de la noche** at eight o'clock in the evening; **a las once de la noche** at eleven o'clock at night; **esta noche** this evening, tonight; **por la noche** in the evening, at night; **la noche anterior** the previous evening, the night before; **el lunes por la noche** Monday evening, Monday night; **de noche** in the evening, at night; **buenas noches** good evening, goodnight; **2 hacerse de noche** to get dark.

Nochebuena *noun Fem.* Christmas Eve.

Nochevieja *noun Fem.* New Year's Eve.

nocturno/nocturna *adjective* **1** nocturnal; **2** evening; **clases nocturnas** evening lessons.

nombrar *verb* [17] **1** to mention; **2** to appoint.

nombre *noun Masc.* **1** name; **¿qué nombre tiene el grupo?** what's the name of the group?; **¿qué nombre le van a poner al niño?** what are they going to call the baby?; **nombre de pila** first name; **2** (*on forms*) **'nombre'** 'first name'; **'nombre y apellidos'** 'full name'; **3** *noun* (*in grammar*).

nordeste, noreste *noun Masc.* northeast.

norma *noun Fem.* rule.

normal *adjective* **1** normal; **eso es normal** that's normal; **2 normal y corriente** ordinary.

normalmente *adverb* normally.

noroeste *noun Masc.* northwest.

norte noun Masc. north; **hacia el norte** northwards; **al norte del Madrid** to the north of Madrid.

norteamericano/ norteamericana noun Masc./ Fem., adjective North American.

Noruega noun Fem. Norway.

noruego[1] noun Masc. Norwegian (the language).

noruego[2]**/noruega** noun Masc./ Fem., adjective Norwegian.

nos pronoun **1** us; **nos invitaron a la fiesta** they invited us to the party; **2** to us; **nos mintió** he lied to us; **3** ourselves; **nos portamos bien** we behaved ourselves; **4** each other; **siempre nos ayudamos** we always help each other; **5** (with reflexive verbs) **nos reímos mucho** we laugh a lot; **vamos a bañarnos** let's go for a swim; **nos sentamos a la mesa** we sat at the table; **6** (with parts of the body or clothes) **nos quitamos los abrigos** we took our coats off; **nos limpiamos los pies al entrar** we wiped our feet at the door; **7** (having something done) **el sábado iremos a cortarnos el pelo** we'll go and get our hair cut on Saturday.

nosotros/nosotras pronoun **1** we; **lo hicimos nosotras** we did it; **2** us; **detrás de nosotros** behind us; **3** nosotros mismos ourselves.

nota noun Fem. **1** note; **tomar nota de algo** to write something down; **tomar notas** to take notes; **¿qué nota has sacado en física?** what did you get in physics?; **sacar**

buenas notas to get good marks; **3** nota musical note.

notable adjective noteworthy.

notable noun Masc. mark between 70% and 85%.

notar verb [17] to notice; **te noto preocupado** you look worried; **se nota que ...** you can tell that ....

notario/notaria noun Masc./Fem. notary public.

noticia noun Fem. **1** (noticia: singular) **una noticia interesante** an interesting piece of news; **la noticia me sorprendió** the news surprised me; **dar la noticia a alguien** to break the news to someone; **2** (noticias: plural) **tengo buenas noticias** I've got good news; **las noticias de las nueve** the nine o'clock news.

novecientos/novecientas number nine hundred; **novecientos veinte** nine hundred and twenty.

novela noun Fem. novel.

noveno/novena adjective ninth; **el noveno piso** the ninth floor.

noventa number ninety; **tiene noventa años** she's ninety (years old); **noventa y siete** ninety-seven; **los años noventa** the nineties.

novia noun Fem. **1** bride; **2** fiancée; **3** girlfriend.

noviembre noun Masc. November; **en noviembre/en el mes de noviembre** in November.

novillada noun Fem. bullfight for young bulls.

novillos plural noun Masc. **hacer novillos** to play truant.

a b c d e f g h i j k l m n ñ o p q r s t u v w x y z

novio noun Masc. **1** groom; **2** fiancé; **3** boyfriend.

nube noun Fem. cloud; **un cielo cubierto de nubes** a cloudy sky.

nublado/nublada adjective cloudy.

nublarse reflexive verb [17] to cloud over; **se nubló por la tarde** it clouded over in the afternoon.

nuclear noun Fem. nuclear power station.

nuclear adjective nuclear.

nudillo noun Masc. knuckle.

nudo noun Masc. knot.

nuera noun Fem. daughter-in-law.

nuestro/nuestra adjective our; **nuestra casa** our house; **un familiar nuestro** a relative of ours.

nuestro pronoun ours; **la nuestra es verde** ours is green; **los nuestros están en el salón** ours are in the living room; **aquél es el nuestro** that one is ours.

nueve number **1** nine; **Jaime tiene nueve años** Jaime's nine (years old); **2** ninth (in dates); **hoy estamos a nueve** it's the ninth today; **3** nine (in clock time).**son las nueve** it's nine o'clock.

nuevo/nueva **1** new; **mis zapatos nuevos** my new shoes; **2 de nuevo** once more; **3 ¿qué hay de nuevo?** (informal) what's new?

nuez noun Fem. **1** walnut; **2** Adam's apple; **3 nuez moscada** nutmeg.

número noun Masc. **1** number; **mi número de teléfono** my telephone number; **2** issue (of a magazine, for example); **3** size;

¿qué número de zapatos calzas? what size shoes do you take?

nunca adverb never; **nunca he estado en ese bar** I've never been to that bar; **nunca más** never again; **más que nunca** more than ever; **casi nunca** hardly ever.

nutritivo/nutritiva adjective nourishing.

Ññ

ñoño/ñoña adjective no seas ñoño don't be so wet.

Oo

o conjunction **1** or; **antes o después** sooner or later; (note that before a word beginning with 'o', it becomes 'u') **plata u oro** silver or gold; (note that when 'o' appears between numbers, it has an accent) **11 ó 12** 11 or 12; **2 o sea** que no te importa? so you don't mind?

oasis noun Masc. oasis.

obedecer verb [35] to obey; **tienes que obedecerme** you must do as I say.

obedezca, obedezco, etc. verb SEE **obedecer.**

obediencia noun Fem. obedience.

obediente adjective obedient.

obispo noun Masc. bishop.

objetivo[1] *noun Masc.* objective.

objetivo[2]/**objetiva** *adjective* objective.

objeto *noun Masc.* object; **objetos de valor** valuables.

obligar *verb* [28] **obligar a alguien a hacer algo** to make somebody do something.
    obligarse *reflexive verb* [28] **obligarse a hacer** to force yourself to do.

obligatorio/obligatoria *adjective* compulsory.

obra *noun Fem.* **1** deed; **una buena obra** a good deed; **2** play; **una obra de Shakespeare** a Shakespeare play; **3** work; **una obra de arte** a work of art; **4 una obra maestra** a masterpiece; **5** building site; **estar en obras** to be having some building work done.

obrero/obrera *noun Masc./Fem.* **1** worker; **2** labourer.

obsceno/obscena *adjective* obscene.

obscuridad *noun Fem.* darkness.

obscuro/obscura *adjective* dark; **a obscuras** in the dark.

observación *noun Fem.* **1** observartion; **2** remark.

observador/observadora *noun Masc./Fem.* observer.

observador *adjective* observant.

observar *verb* [17] **1** to observe; **2** to remark.

observatorio *noun Masc.* observatory.

obsesión *noun Fem.* obsession; **tiene una obsesión con la** limpieza he has an obsession with cleanliness; **tiene la obsesión de que la siguen** she's obsessed with the idea that she's being followed.

obstáculo *noun Masc.* obstacle; **superar un obstáculo** to overcome an obstacle.

obstante *in phrase* **no obstante** nevertheless.

obstinado/obstinada *adjective* obstinate.

obstinarse *reflexive verb* [17] **obstinarse en hacer** to insist on doing.

obtendré, obtendría, etc. *verb* SEE **obtener**.

obtener *verb* [9] **1** to obtain; **2 obtener un premio** to win a prize.

obtenga, obtengo, obtuve, etc. *verb* SEE **obtener**.

obvio/obvia *adjective* obvious.

oca *noun Fem.* goose.

ocasión *noun Fem.* **1** occasion; **2** opportunity; **si hay ocasión** if there's an opportunity; **3 precios de ocasión** bargain prices; **coches de ocasión** second-hand cars.

ocasionar *verb* [17] to cause.

occidental *adjective* Western.

Occidente *noun Masc.* the West.

océano *noun Masc.* ocean.

ochenta *number* eighty; **tiene ochenta años** she's eighty (years old); **ochenta y cinco** eighty-five; **los años ochenta** the eighties.

ocho *number* **1** eight; **tiene ocho años** she's eight (years old);

2 eighth (*in dates*); **estamos a ocho** it's the eighth today; **3** eight (*in clock time*); **son las ocho** it's eight o'clock.

ochocientos/ochocientas *number* eight hundred; **ochocientos siete** eight hundred and seven.

ocio *noun Masc.* spare time.

ocioso/ociosa *adjective* idle.

octavo/octava *adjective* eighth; **el octavo piso** the eighth floor.

octubre *noun Masc.* October; **en octubre/en el mes de octubre** in October.

ocupación *noun Fem.* occupation.

ocupado/ocupada *adjective*
1 busy; **está muy ocupado** he's very busy; **2** engaged; **la línea está ocupada** the line is engaged; **3** taken; **¿está ocupado este asiento?** is this seat taken?

ocupar *verb* [17] **1** ocupar un asiento to have a seat; **ocupa el asiento 11b** he's in seat 11b; **¿quién ocupa esa habitación?** who's in that room?; **2** to occupy (*land or a building*); **3** (*talking about time*) **ocupo mi tiempo libre leyendo** I spend my free time reading.

ocuparse *reflexive verb* [17] **ocuparse de algo** to take care of something.

ocurrir *verb* [19] to happen; **me ocurrió una cosa muy graciosa** something really funny happened to me; **¿qué le ocurre?** what's the matter with him?.

ocurrirse *reflexive verb* [19] **¿se**

te ocurre alguna idea? can you think of anything?; **se me ocurrió que podríamos** ... I thought we could ....

odiar *verb* [17] to hate.

odio *noun Masc.* hate, hatred.

oeste *noun Masc.* west; **hacia el oeste** westwards; **al oeste de Madrid** to the west of Madrid.

ofender *verb* [18] to offend.
ofenderse *reflexive verb* [18] to take offence.

oferta *noun Fem.* offer; **estar de/en oferta** to be on offer.

oficial *adjective* official.
oficial *noun Masc./Fem.* officer.

oficina *noun Fem.* office; **oficina de cambio** bureau de change; **oficina de objetos perdidos** lost property (office); **oficina de (información y) turismo** tourist (information) office.

oficinista *noun Masc./Fem.* office worker.

oficio *noun Masc.* **1** trade; **2** service (*in a church*).

ofrecer *verb* [35] to offer.

ofrezca, ofrezco, etc. *verb* SEE **ofrecer.**

oído *noun Masc.* **1** ear; **tener dolor de oídos** to have earache; **2** tener **buen oído** to have a good ear.

oiga, oigo, etc. *verb* SEE **oír.**

oír *verb* [56] **1** to hear; **no oigo nada** I can't hear anything; **2** listen to; **oír las noticias** to listen to the news; **oír música** to listen to music; **3** ¡**oye!** hey!

ojalá *exclamation* ¡ojalá me llame! I hope he rings me!; ¡ojalá pudiera! I wish I could!

ojo *noun Masc.* **1** eye; tiene los ojos verdes he's got green eyes; ojos claros light-coloured eyes (*blue, green, or grey as opposed to brown*); con los ojos cerrados with your eyes closed; **2** el ojo de la cerradura the keyhole; ★ no pegué ojo en toda la noche I didn't sleep a wink all night; ★ salir por un ojo de la cara (*informal*) to cost an arm and a leg.

ojo *exclamation* ¡ojo! careful!

ola *noun Fem.* wave; una ola de calor a heatwave; una ola de frío a cold spell.

ole, olé *exclamation* olé.

oler *verb* [39] to smell; oler una flor to smell a flower; oler a algo to smell of something; huele a lavanda it smells of lavender.

olimpiadas *plural noun Fem.* Olympic Games.

olímpico/olímpica *adjective* Olympic.

oliva *noun Fem.* olive; aceite de oliva olive oil.

olivo *noun Masc.* olive tree.

olla *noun Fem.* pan; olla a presión pressure cooker.

olor *noun Masc.* smell; tiene un olor raro it has a funny smell; tiene olor a almendras it smells of almonds.

olvidar *verb* [17] to forget; ¡olvídalo! forget it!
  olvidarse *reflexive verb* [17] to forget; se me olvidó llamarte I

forgot to ring you; se me olvidó la cartera I forgot my wallet.

ombligo *noun Masc.* navel.

omitir *verb* [19] to omit.

once *number* **1** eleven; tiene once años she's eleven (years old); **2** eleventh (*in dates*); hoy estamos a once it's the eleventh today; **3** eleven (*in clock time*); son las once it's eleven o'clock.

onceavo/onceava *adjective* eleventh.

onda *noun Fem.* wave; onda larga long wave; ★ estar en la onda (*informal*) to be trendy.

ondulado/ondulada *adjective* wavy.

ONU *abbreviation Fem.* (*short for: Organización de las Naciones Unidas*) UN.

opcional *adjective* optional.

ópera *noun Fem.* opera.

operación *noun Fem.* operation; ha sufrido una operación he's had an operation.

operador/operadora *noun Masc./Fem.* operator.

operar *verb* [17] **1** to operate on (*a person*); ¿tendrán que operarlo? will they have to operate on him?; **2** to produce (*a change*).
  operarse *reflexive verb* [17] to have an operation; se va a operar del corazón she's going to have a heart operation.

opinar *verb* [17] **1** to think; opino que ... I think that ...; ¿qué opinas del diseño? what do you think of the design?; prefiero no opinar I

a
b
c
d
e
f
g
h
i
j
k
l
m
n
ñ
o
p
q
r
s
t
u
v
w
x
y
z

prefer not to say what I think; **2** to express an opinion.

opinión *noun Fem.* opinion; **¿cuál es vuestra opinión?** what do you think?; **cambiar de opinión** to change your mind.

oponer *verb* [11] **1** to raise (*an objection*); **2 oponer resistencia** to put up a fight.

oponerse *reflexive verb* [11] **oponerse a algo** to oppose something; **se oponen a cualquier cambio de las reglas** they are opposed to any change in the rules.

oporto *noun Masc.* port.

oportunidad *noun Fem.* opportunity; **aprovechar una oportunidad** to make the most of an opportunity.

oposición *noun Fem.* **1** opposition; **2 oposiciones** competitive public exams for a government job.

optativo/optativa *adjective* optional.

óptico/óptica *noun Masc./Fem.* optician.

optimismo *noun Masc.* optimism.

optimista *noun Masc./Fem.* optimist.

optimista *adjective* optimistic.

opuesto/opuesta *adjective* **1** conflicting (*views or opinions*); **2** opposite; **venían en dirección opuesta** they were coming from the opposite direction.

oral *noun Masc.,*
oral *adjective* oral.

orden[1] *noun Masc.* order; **en orden alfabético** in alphabetical order;

en orden de importancia in order of importance; **puestos en orden de tamaño** arranged according to size; **ponlos en orden** put them in order; **mantener el orden** to keep order; **poner la habitación en orden** to tidy up the room; **¡orden!** order!

orden[2] *noun Fem.* order; **dar una orden** to give an order.

ordenado/ordenada *adjective* tidy; **es muy ordenado** he's very tidy.

ordenador *noun Masc.* computer.

ordenar *verb* [17] **1** to tidy up (*a room or house*); **2** to put in order; **ordenar algo alfabéticamente** to put something in alphabetical order; **3** to order; **nos ordenó seguir** he ordered us to carry on.

ordinario/ordinaria *adjective* **1** vulgar; **2** rude (*a person*); **3** ordinary, normal (*a method or system*).

oreja *noun Fem.* ear.

orgánico/orgánica *adjective* organic.

organización *noun Fem.* organization.

organizar *verb* [22] to organize.

órgano *noun Masc.* organ.

orgullo *noun Masc.* pride; **tiene mucho orgullo** he's very proud.

orgulloso/orgullosa *adjective* proud; **estar orgulloso de algo** to be proud of something.

orientación *noun Fem.* **1 ¿qué orientación tiene la casa?** which way does the house face?;

2 orientation; **3** bearings;
4 orientación profesional
careers guidance.

oriental noun Masc./Fem. Oriental.

oriental adjective **1** Eastern;
2 Oriental.

orientar verb [17] **1** to guide; **2** to
give guidance to (a young person
or student).
orientarse reflexive verb [17] to
get your bearings.

Oriente noun Masc. East; **el
Lejano Oriente** the Far East.

original noun Masc., adjective
original.

orilla noun Fem. **1** bank; **sentados
a la orilla del río** sitting on the
river bank; **2** shore; **una casa a
orillas del mar** a house by the sea.

ornamental adjective
ornamental.

oro noun Masc. gold; **un reloj de oro**
a gold watch.

orquesta noun Fem. orchestra;
una orquesta de jazz a jazz band.

ortiga noun Fem. nettle.

ortografía noun Fem. spelling.

oruga noun Fem. caterpillar.

os pronoun **1** you (talking to more
than one person); **os vimos desde
la ventana** we saw you from the
window; **¿os dieron suficiente
información?** did they give you
enough information?; **2** to you; **os
mintió** he lied to you;
3 yourselves; **os tenéis que
portar bien** you must behave
yourselves; **4** each other; **¿os
conocéis?** do you know each
other?; **5** (with a reflexive verb)

¿os divertisteis? did you have a
good time?; **iros a bañar** go for a
swim; **6** (with parts of the body or
clothes) **os podéis quitar los
abrigos** you can take your coats
off; **¿os habéis lavado las
manos?** have you washed your
hands?; **7** (having something
done) **os tenéis que cortar el
pelo** you have to have your hair
cut.

osado/osada adjective bold.

oscuridad noun Fem. darkness.

oscuro/oscura adjective dark; **a
oscuras** in the dark.

osito noun Masc. **un osito de
peluche** a teddy bear.

oso/osa noun Masc./Fem. bear.

ostra noun Fem. oyster.

OTAN abbreviation Fem. (short for:
Organización del Tratado del
Atlántico Norte) NATO.

otoño noun Masc. autumn.

otro/otra adjective **1** another; **¿te
has comprado otro casete?** did
you buy another cassette?; **añade
otros dos** add another two;
2 other; **en otros colores** in other
colours; **la otra tarde le vi** I saw
him the other evening; **¿no tienes
ningún otro color?** don't you have
any other colours?; **3 otra cosa**
something else; **me gustaría
comprarle otra cosa** I would like
to buy her something else; **eso es
otra cosa diferente** that's
something different; **¿quieres
alguna otra cosa?** do you want
something else?; **no me gusta
ninguna otra cosa** I don't like

a
b
c
d
e
f
g
h
i
j
k
l
m
n
ñ
o
p
q
r
s
t
u
v
w
x
y
z

anything else; **4 otra vez** again;
hazlo otra vez do it again.

otro *pronoun* **1** another one; **éste
no, dame otro** not this one, give
me another one; **2** (*talking about
people*) **los otros están en el cajón**
the other ones are in the drawer;
3 (*talking about people*) **los otros
vendrán en coche** the others will
come by car; **a otros les gustaría**
other people would like it; **4** (*talking
about time*) **un mes sí y otro no**
every other month; **de un día
para otro** from one day to the
next.

oveja *noun Fem.* sheep.

OVNI *abbreviation Masc.* (*short for:
objeto volante no identificado*)
UFO.

oxidado/oxidada *adjective*
rusty.

oxígeno *noun Masc.* oxygen.

oyendo, oyó *verb* SEE **oír**.

ozono *noun Masc.* ozone; **la capa
de ozono** the ozone layer.

Pp

pabellón *noun Masc.* pavilion.

paciencia *noun Fem.* patience;
tener paciencia to be patient.

paciente *noun Masc./Fem.*,
paciente *adjective* patient.

padecer *verb* [35] to suffer;
padecer de algo to suffer from
something.

padrastro *noun Masc.* stepfather.

padre *noun Masc.* **1** father; **2 mis
padres** my parents.

padrino *noun Masc.* **1** godfather;
2 mis padrinos my godparents.

padrino de boda *noun Masc.*
(*person who gives away the bride
and carries out duties of the best
man*).

paella *noun Fem.* paella.

paga *noun Fem.* **1** pay; **2** pocket
money.

pagar *verb* [28] **1** to pay; **2** to pay
off (*a debt*); **3** to pay for (*tickets, for
example*); **4** to repay (*a favour*).

página *noun Fem.* page.

pago *noun Masc.* payment; **pago
anticipado** payment in advance;
pago inicial down payment; **pago
al contado** payment in cash;
efectuar un pago to make a
payment.

país *noun Masc.* country.

paisaje *noun Masc.* landscape.

Países Bajos *plural noun Masc.*
los Países Bajos the Netherlands.

País de Gales *noun Masc.* **el País
de Gales** Wales.

País Vasco *noun Masc.* **el País
Vasco** the Basque Country.

paja *noun Fem.* **1** straw; **2 pajita**
drinking straw.

pajarita *noun Fem.* bow tie.

pájaro *noun Masc.* bird; ★ **matar
dos pájaros de un tiro** to kill two
birds with one stone.

pala *noun Fem.* **1** spade; **2** shovel;
3 bat (*for table tennis*); **4** slice (*in
cooking*).

palabra noun Fem. **1** word; **palabra compuesta** compound word; **no cumplió con su palabra** he didn't keep his word; **2** speech; **el don de la palabra** the gift of speech; **3** **pedir la palabra** to ask permission to speak.

palabrota noun Fem. swearword; **decir palabrotas** to swear.

palacio noun Masc. palace.

palanca noun Fem. **1** lever; **abrir algo haciendo palanca** to lever something open; **2** crowbar; **3** **palanca de cambios** gearstick; **palanca de mando** joystick.

paleta noun Fem. **1** palette; **2** spatula (for cooking); **3** trowel; **4** bat (in table tennis).

palidecer verb [35] to go pale.

pálido/pálida adjective pale.

palillo noun Masc. **1** chopstick; **2** drumstick; **3** **palillo de dientes** toothpick.

palma noun Fem. palm (of hand); **dar palmas** to clap your hands.

palmera noun Fem. palm tree.

palo noun Masc. **1** stick; **2** pole (for a tent); **3** **palo de escoba** broomstick.

paloma noun Fem. **1** dove; **la paloma de la paz** the dove of peace; **2** pigeon.

palomitas plural noun Fem. popcorn.

pan noun Masc. bread; **un pan de molde** a loaf of bread; **una barra de pan** a French loaf; **pan integral** wholewheat bread; **pan tostado** toast; **pan rallado** breadcrumbs.

pana noun Fem. corduroy.

panadería noun Fem. bakery.

panadero/panadera noun Masc./Fem. baker.

Panamá noun Masc. Panama; **el Canal de Panamá** the Panama Canal.

panameño/panameña noun Masc./Fem., adjective Panamanian.

pancarta noun Fem. banner.

panceta noun Fem. belly pork.

pandereta noun Fem. tambourine.

panecillo noun Masc. bread roll.

pánico noun Masc. panic.

panorama noun Masc. **1** panorama; **2** view.

pantalla noun Fem. **1** screen; **la pantalla grande** the big screen; **2** shade (of a lamp).

pantalón noun Masc. trousers; **un pantalón** a pair of trousers.

pantalones plural noun Masc. trousers; **un par de pantalones/ unos pantalones** a pair of trousers; **pantalones vaqueros** jeans; **pantalones cortos** shorts; **pantalones de peto** dungarees.

pantano noun Masc. **1** swamp; **2** reservoir.

pantanoso/pantanosa adjective swampy, marshy.

pantorrilla noun Fem. calf.

panty, panti noun Masc. tights.

pañal noun Masc. nappy.

paño noun Masc. cloth; **un paño** a piece of cloth; **un paño de cocina** a dishcloth; ★ **estar en paños**

menores (*informal*) to be in your undies.

pañuelo *noun Masc.*
1 handkerchief; **2** headscarf;
3 scarf.

papá *noun Masc.* daddy; **mis papás** my mum and dad.

papagayo *noun Masc.* parrot.

papel *noun Masc.* paper; **un trozo de papel** a piece of paper; **se encontró un papel en la mesa** he found a piece of paper on the table; **papel aluminio** aluminium foil; **papel higiénico** toilet paper; **papel pintado** wallpaper; **papel de envolver** wrapping paper; **papel de lija** sandpaper.

papelera *noun Fem.*
1 paperbasket; **2** litter bin (*in the street*).

papelería *noun Fem.* stationer's.

paperas *plural noun Fem.* mumps.

paquete *noun Masc.* **1** parcel; **mandar un paquete** to send a parcel; **2** packet; **un paquete de cigarrillos** a packet of cigarettes.

par *noun Masc.* **1** pair; **un par de zapatos** a pair of shoes; **2** couple; **un par de veces** a couple of times; **3 de par en par** wide open.

par *adjective* even; **un número par** an even number.

para *preposition* **1** for; **es para ti** it's for you; **sirve para limpiar** it's for cleaning; **¿para qué quieres la carpeta?** what do you want the folder for?; **hay suficiente para todos** there's enough for everybody; **estará terminado para el doce** it'll be finished for the

twelfth; **2** to; **se dijo para sí** he sa to himself; **es demasiado difíci para hacerlo** it's too difficult to d **3** (*direction*) **me voy para casa** I going home; **iban para la estació** they were going to the station; **4 para que** so that.

parabrisas *noun Masc.* (*does n change in the plural*) windscreer

paracaídas *noun Masc.* (*does n change in the plural*) parachute.

parachoques *noun Masc.* (*does not change in the plural*) bumper

parada[1] *noun Fem.* stop; **la parad del autobús** the bus stop; **parad de taxis** taxi rank.

parado/parada[2] *noun Masc./Fe* unemployed person.

parado *adjective* unemployed.

parador *noun Masc.* state-owned hotel.

paraguas *noun Masc.* (*does not change in the plural*) umbrella.

Paraguay *noun Masc.* Paraguay.

paraguayo/paraguaya *noun Masc./Fem., adjective* Paraguayan

paraíso *noun Masc.* paradise.

paralelo[1] *noun Masc.* parallel.

paralelo[2]**/paralela** *adjective* parallel; **paralelo a algo** parallel something.

parapente *noun Masc.* hang gliding.

parar *verb* [17] **1** to stop; **parar de hablar** to stop talking; **bailamos sin parar toda la noche** we didn' stop dancing all night; **paré el coche** I stopped the car; **2 para u momento** hang on a minute; **3** to save; **parar un gol** to make a save

(*in football, hockey*); **4 ir a parar** to
end up; **fueron a parar al hospital**
they ended up in hospital; **¡no sé a
donde vamos a ir a parar!** I don't
know what the world is coming to!

pararse *reflexive verb* [17] to
stop; **no te pares en medio de la
calle** don't stop in the middle of the
road; **se paró a pensar** he stopped
to think; **se me ha parado el reloj**
my watch has stopped.

pararrayos *noun Masc.* (*does not
change in the plural*) lightning
conductor.

parasol *noun Masc.* parasol.

parcela *noun Fem.* plot of land.

parche *noun Masc.* patch.

parchís *noun Masc.* ludo.

parecer *verb* [35] **1** to seem; **no
parece demasiado complicado** it
doesn't seem too complicated;
parece que ya no vienen it seems
they're not coming any more; **2** to
seem like, to look like; **parece de
madera** it looks as if it's made of
wood; **esa nube parece un pájaro**
that cloud looks like a bird; **parece
que está roto** it looks as though
it's broken; **parece que va a llover**
it looks like rain; **3 ¿qué te
pareció la película?** what did you
think of the film?; **me parece que
llegan hoy** I think they arrive
today; **me parece que no** I don't
think so; **le pareció muy mal que
no llamasen** he thought it was
really bad of them not to call;
4 según parece/al parecer
apparently.

parecerse *reflexive verb* [35]
1 to look like; **se parece mucho a**

su padre she looks very like her
father; **nos parecemos mucho** we
look very like each other; **2** to be
like (*in character*); **se parece
mucho a su madre** she is very like
her mother.

parecido[1] *noun Masc.*
1 similarity; **el parecido era
increíble** the similarity was
incredible; **2 ser bien parecido** to
be good-looking.

parecido[2]/**parecida** *adjective*
similar.

pared *noun Fem.* wall.

pareja *noun Fem.* **1** pair; **trabajar
en pareja** to work in pairs;
2 couple; **3 mi pareja** my partner.

paréntesis *noun Masc.* (*does not
change in the plural*) brackets.

parezca, parezco, etc. *verb*
SEE **parecer.**

pariente *noun Masc./Fem.* relative.

parking *noun Masc.* car park.

parlamento *noun Masc.*
parliament.

paro *noun Masc.* **1** unemployment;
estar en paro to be unemployed;
cobrar el paro to receive
unemployment benefit; **2** strike;
hicieron un paro de 24 horas they
went on a 24-hour strike; **3 un paro
cardíaco** heart failure.

parpadear *verb* [17] to blink.

párpado *noun Masc.* eyelid.

parque *noun Masc.* **1** park; **parque
nacional** national park; **parque
infantil** play park; **2 parque de
atracciones** amusement park;
parque temático theme park;

a
b
c
d
e
f
g
h
i
j
k
l
m
n
ñ
o
p
q
r
s
t
u
v
w
x
y
z

parque zoológico zoo; **3 parque de bomberos** fire station; **4 parque móvil** fleet (of cars, lorries etc); **5 parque eólico** wind farm.

parquímetro noun Masc. parking meter.

párrafo noun Masc. paragraph.

parrilla noun Fem. grill; **chuletas a la parrilla** barbecued chops.

parte[1] noun Fem. **1** part; **es parte de Asia** it's part of Asia; **una tercera parte de la herencia** a third of the inheritance; **la parte antigua de la ciudad** the old part of town; **2** share; **mi parte del trabajo** my share of the work; **3 la mayor parte de** most of; **la mayor parte de los alumnos** most of the students; **4 en/por alguna parte** somewhere; **en/por cualquier parte** anywhere; **en/por todas partes** everywhere; **5 en parte** partly; **en parte tienen razón** they're partly right; **6 en gran parte** largely; **7 de un tiempo a esta parte** for some time now; **8 ¿de parte de quién?** who shall I say is calling? (on the phone); **saludos de parte de Juan** Juan says hello; **felicítalos de mi parte** give them my congratulations; **9 yo por mi parte ...** as far as I'm concerned ....

parte[2] noun Masc. report; **el parte meteorológico** the weather report.

partera noun Fem. midwife.

participación noun Fem. **1** participation; **2** share in lottery ticket.

participar verb [17] to participate.

participio noun Masc. participle; **participio pasado** past participle.

particular adjective **1** private (lesson or teacher); **2** particular (feature, for example); **3 un colegio particular** a fee-paying school; **4 mi teléfono particular** my home telephone number; **nuestro domicilio particular** our home address; **5 es muy particular** (informal) he's very peculiar.

partida noun Fem. game; **una partida de ajedrez** a game of chess.

partido noun Masc. **1** party (political); **2** game, match.

partir verb [19] **1** to cut; **partir algo por la mitad** to cut something in two; **2** to break (a branch, for example); **3** to crack (a nut); **4** to leave (a train or person); **5 a partir de ese momento** from that moment on; **a partir de ahora** from now on.

partirse reflexive verb [19] to break (a branch, for example); **la rama se partió** the branch broke; **me partí un diente** I broke a tooth.

partitura noun Fem. score (music).

parto noun Masc. labour; **estar de parto** to be in labour.

pasa noun Fem. raisin.

pasado[1] noun Masc. past.

pasado[2]**/pasada** adjective **1** last; **el verano pasado** last summer; **2 pasados dos días, le llamé** after·

two days, I phoned him; **3 son las diez pasadas** it's past ten o'clock; **pasado mañana** the day after tomorrow; **4** off; **la leche está pasada** the milk is off; **5 quiero el filete muy pasado** I want my steak well done.

pasaje *noun Masc.* ticket.

pasajero/pasajera *noun Masc./ Fem.* passenger.

pasamanos *noun Masc. (does not change in the plural)* **1** banister; **2** handrail.

pasaporte *noun Masc.* passport.

pasar *verb* [17] **1** to go past; **pasaron por enfrente de mi casa** they went past my house; **pasar de largo** to go straight past; **me vió y pasó de largo** he saw me and walked straight past me; **2** to come past; **pasaron por aquí** they came past here; **3** to get past; **no podíamos pasar** we couldn't get past; **4 pásate por mi casa por la tarde** call round at my house in the evening; **el cartero pasa a las diez** the postman comes at ten; **pasaré por el banco para recoger los impresos** I'll call in at the bank to collect the forms; **5** to go in; **pasaron todos al salón** they all went into the living room; **6** to come in; **pase, por favor** please come in; **7 pasar de un lado a otro** to go from one side to the other; **8 pasar por** to go through; **pasar por la aduana** to go through customs; **el tren no pasa por Talavera** the train does not go through Talavera; **9 pasar algo por algo** to put something through

something; **10** to go by; **pasaron tres meses** three months went by; **11** to pass; **¿me pasas las tijeras?** could you pass me the scissors?; **me pasó el balón** he passed the ball to me; **12** to happen; **¿qué ha pasado?** what's happened?; **no le ha pasado nada** nothing has happened to him; **¿qué te ha pasado en la mano?** what's happened to your hand?; **¿qué te pasa?** what's the matter?; **13** to spend; **pasaremos las vacaciones en España** we'll spend our holidays in Spain; **pasé la noche en casa de un amigo** I spent the night at a friend's house; **14 pasarlo bien** to have a good time; **me lo pasé muy mal en las vacaciones** I didn't enjoy myself at all during the holidays; **15 pasar con** to put through; **le paso con el Señor Muñoz** I'll put you through to Mr Muñoz.

pasarse *reflexive verb* [17] **1** to go off *(milk or fish)*; **2** to go bad *(vegetables or fruit)*; **3 pasarse de un lado a otro** to go from one side to the other; **4** to come (by); **pásate por la oficina cuando quieras** come by my office whenever you want; **me pasaré por correos antes de ir a trabajar** I'll stop by the post office before going to work; **5** to go past; **nos pasamos de parada** we missed our stop.

pasatiempo *noun Masc.* pastime.

Pascua *noun Fem.* **1** Easter; **2** Christmas; **¡felices Pascuas!** Merry Christmas!.

a
b
c
d
e
f
g
h
i
j
k
l
m
n
ñ
o
p
q
r
s
t
u
v
w
x
y
z

pasear verb [17] **1** to go for a walk; **me gusta pasear por la playa** I like walking on the beach; **sacar al perro a pasear** to take the dog for a walk; **2 pasear en coche** to go for a drive; **fuimos a pasear en bicicleta** we went for a bike ride. **pasearse** reflexive verb [17] to go for a walk.

paseo noun Masc. **1** walk; **fuimos a dar un paseo** we went for a walk; **2** stroll; **3 ir a dar un paseo en coche** to go for a drive; **ir a dar un paseo en bicicleta** to go for a bike ride.

pasillo noun Masc. corridor.

pasión noun Fem. passion.

pasivo/pasiva adjective passive; **un fumador pasivo** a passive smoker.

paso noun Masc. **1** step; **dar un paso adelante** to take a step forward; **paso a paso** step by step; **2 oír pasos** to hear footsteps; **3 un paso a nivel** a level crossing; **un paso elevado** a flyover; **un paso subterráneo** a subway; **un paso de peatones** a pedestrian crossing; **un paso de cebra** a zebra crossing; **4 'ceda el paso'** 'give way'; **5 'prohibido el paso'** 'no entry'; **6 te viene de paso/te pilla de paso** it's on your way.

pasta noun Fem. **1** pasta; **prefiero el arroz a la pasta** I prefer rice to pasta; **2** paste; **3 pastas** biscuits; **4 pasta de dientes** toothpaste.

pastel noun Masc. cake.

pastelería noun Fem. cake shop.

pastilla noun Fem. **1** pill; **2 una pastilla de jabón** a bar of soap.

pastor/pastora noun Masc./Fem. shepherd/shepherdess.

pata[1] noun Fem. **1** leg; **2** paw; ★ **meter la pata** (informal) to put your foot in it.

patada noun Fem. kick; **dar una patada a alguien** to kick someone.

patata noun Fem. potato; **patatas fritas** chips, (potato) crisps.

paternal adjective paternal.

patín noun Masc. **1** roller skate; **2** ice skate; **3** skateboard; **4** pedalo.

patinador/patinadora noun skater.

patinaje noun Masc. **1** roller skating; **2** ice skating; **patinaje artístico** figure skating.

patinar noun 17 **1** to roller skate; **2** to ice skate; **3** to slip; **patiné en una mancha de aceite** I slipped on a patch of oil; **4** to skid (a car).

patio noun Masc. **1** patio; **2** playground.

pato/pata[2] noun Masc./Fem. duck; ★ **ser un pato** (informal) to be very clumsy.

patria noun Fem. homeland.

patrocinar verb [17] to sponsor.

patrón noun Masc. **1** boss; **2** landlord.

patrona noun Fem. landlady.

patrulla noun Fem. patrol; **patrulla de rescate** rescue party.

patrullera noun Fem. patrol boat.

patrullero noun Masc. **1** patrol boat; **2** patrol plane; **3** patrol car.

pausa noun Fem. pause; **hacer una pausa** to have a break.

pavo/pava noun Masc./Fem.
1 turkey; **2 pavo real** peacock.

payaso/payasa noun Masc./Fem. clown.

paz (plural **paces**) noun Fem.
1 peace; **2 hacer las paces** to make up; **nos peleamos pero al final hicimos las paces** we had a fight, but we made up in the end; **3 dejar en paz** to leave alone; **¡deja mi calculadora en paz!** leave my calculator alone!; **¡deja a tu hermano en paz!** leave your brother alone!; **¡estos niños nunca me dejan en paz!** these children never give me a moment's peace!; **4 en paz descanse** rest in peace.

PD abbreviation P.S. (at the end of a letter).

peaje noun Fem. toll; **carretera de peaje** toll road.

peatón noun Masc. pedestrian.

peca noun Fem. freckle.

pecado noun Masc. sin.

pecho noun Masc. **1** breast; **dar el pecho a un bebé** to breastfeed a baby; **2** chest.

pechuga noun Fem. breast; **pechuga de pollo** chicken breast.

pedal noun Masc. pedal; **pedal de arranque** kickstart.

pedazo noun Masc. piece; **un pedazo de queso** a piece of cheese; **hacer pedazos** to smash to pieces; **hizo pedazos el vaso** he smashed the glass to pieces; **el**

jarrón se cayó y se hizo pedazos the vase fell and smashed to pieces.

pedir verb [57] **1** to ask for; **pedir un favor** to ask for a favour; **pedir ayuda** to ask for help; **pedir consejo** to ask for advice; **2 pedir perdón** to apologize; **3 piden medio millón por el cuadro** they're asking half a million for the picture; **me pidió que le comprase un libro** he asked me to buy him a book; **4 pedir hora** to ask for an appointment; **5 pedir prestado** to ask to borrow; **me pidió prestada la moto** he asked to borrow my motorbike; **pedir dinero prestado** to ask to borrow some money, to ask for a loan; **6** to order (in a restaurant); **¿qué vas a pedir?** what are you going to order?

pegajoso/pegajosa adjective sticky.

pegamento noun Masc. glue.

pegar verb [28] **1** to hit; **me pegó** he hit me; **pegar una torta a alguien** to slap somebody; **pegar una patada a alguien** to kick somebody; **pegar una paliza a alguien** to give somebody a beating; **2 pegar un grito** to let out a yell; **3 pegar un salto** to jump; **pegar saltos de alegría** to jump for joy; **4 pegarle un susto a alguien** to give somebody a fright; **5** to stick; **he pegado una foto suya en la pared** I've stuck a picture of him on the wall; **6** to glue; **7** (informal) **me vas a pegar el resfriado** you're going to give me your cold.

a
b
c
d
e
f
g
h
i
j
k
l
m
n
ñ
o
p
q
r
s
t
u
v
w
x
y
z

pegarse *reflexive verb* [28] **1** to hit each other; **empezaron a pegarse** they started hitting each other; **2** to stick; **este sello no se pega** this stamp won't stick.

pegatina *noun Fem.* sticker.

peinado *noun Masc.* hairstyle.

peinar *verb* [17] **1** to comb; **2** to brush.

peinarse *reflexive verb* [17] **1** to comb your hair; **2** to brush your hair.

peine *noun Masc.* comb.

pela *noun Fem.* (*informal*) penny; **no me quedan pelas** I haven't got a penny.

pelar *verb* [17] **1** to peel (*a potato, for example*); **2** **pelar a alguien al cero** to cut somebody's hair very short.

pelarse *reflexive verb* [17] **1** to peel (*from sunburn*); **se me está pelando la nariz** my nose is peeling; **2** (*informal*) to have your hair cut.

peldaño *noun Masc.* **1** step; **2** rung.

pelea *noun Fem.* **1** fight; **2** row; **tuvo una pelea con su novio** she had a row with her boyfriend.

pelear *verb* [17] **1** to fight; **2** to quarrel.

pelearse *reflexive verb* [17] **1** to fight; **había dos hombres peleándose** there were two men fighting; **2** to quarrel; **se pelearon por dinero** they quarrelled over money; **siempre se está peleando con sus padres** she's always quarrelling with her parents.

película *noun Fem.* **1** film; **¿qué película ponen hoy?** what film are they showing today?; **una película de terror** a horror film; **una película de risa** a comedy film; **una película de suspense** a thriller; **2** film (*for a camera*).

peligro *noun Masc.* danger; **estar en peligro/correr peligro** to be in danger; **poner a alguien en peligro** to put somebody at risk; **fuera de peligro** out of danger; **un peligro para la salud** a health risk; **peligro de incendio** a fire hazard.

peligroso/peligrosa *adjective* dangerous.

pelirrojo/pelirroja *adjective* **1** red-haired; **2** **pelo pelirrojo** red hair.

pellizcar *verb* [31] to pinch.

pellizco *noun Masc.* pinch; **le di un pellizco en el brazo** I pinched her arm.

pelo *noun Masc.* **1** hair; **pelo liso/lacio** straight hair; **pelo rizado** curly hair; **tengo el pelo negro** I've got black hair; **2** **un pelo de la barba** a whisker; **3** fur (*of an animal*); ★ **salvarse por los pelos** (*informal*) to escape by the skin of your teeth; ★ **no se cayó por los pelos** he very nearly fell; ★ **ponerle a alguien los pelos de punta** (*informal*) to make somebody's hair stand on end; ★ **tomarle el pelo a alguien** (*informal*) to pull somebody's leg (*literally: to take somebody's hair*).

pelota *noun Fem.* ball; **una pelota de fútbol** a football.

peluca noun Fem. wig.

peluche noun Masc. **un juguete de peluche** a cuddly toy; **un osito de peluche** a teddy bear.

peludo/peluda adjective hairy.

peluquería noun Fem. hairdresser's.

peluquero/peluquera noun Masc./Fem. hairdresser.

pena noun Fem. **1** shame; **¡qué pena!** what a shame; **es una pena que no puedas venir** it's a shame you can't come; **me da pena verte llorar** it makes me sad to see you cry; **3 Sara me da mucha pena** I feel really sorry for Sara; **4** sentence; **pena de muerte** death penalty; **5 valer la pena** to be worth it; **no vale la pena** it's not worth it; **vale la pena ver la película** the film's worth seeing; **6 penas** problems; **cuéntame tus penas** tell me all your problems; ★ **a duras penas** with great difficulty.

penalti noun Masc. penalty.

pendiente noun Masc. earring.

pendiente noun Fem. slope.

pendiente adjective unresolved.

pene noun Masc. penis.

penetrar verb [17] to penetrate.

península noun Fem. peninsula.

penique noun Masc. penny.

pensamiento noun Masc. thought.

pensar verb [29] to think; **piénsalo bien antes de decidir** think about it carefully before deciding anything; **pensándolo bien ...** on second thoughts ...; **pensar en** to

think about; **estaba pensando en ti** I was thinking about you; **¿piensas llamarlo?** are you thinking of calling him?; **pensar mal de alguien** to think badly of someone; **¿qué piensas del nuevo entrenador?** what do you think of the new coach?

pensión noun Fem. **1** pension; **cobrar la pensión** to draw your pension; **pensión de viudedad** widow's pension; **2** guesthouse; **3 pensión completa** full board; **media pensión** half board.

pensionista noun Masc./Fem. pensioner.

peor noun Masc./Fem. **el/la peor** the worst one; **los/las peores** the worst ones.

peor adjective **1** worse; **éstas son peores que las de la otra tienda** these are worse than the ones in the other shop; **mucho peor** much worse; **2** worst; **mi peor enemigo** my worst enemy; **en el peor de los casos** in the worst scenario; **3 peor para ti** it's your loss.

peor adverb worse; **es aún peor** it's even worse; **cada vez peor** worse and worse; **de mal en peor** from bad to worse; **yo bailo peor que tú** I'm a worse dancer than you.

pepinillo noun Masc. gherkin.

pepino noun Masc. cucumber.

pequeño/pequeña noun Masc./Fem. small boy/small girl.

pequeño adjective **1** small; **una casa pequeña** a small house; **la chaqueta me está pequeña** the jacket's too small for me; **2** slight; **un pequeño esfuerzo** a slight

a b c d e f g h i j k l m n ñ o p q r s t u v w x y z

a effort; **3 young; mi hermana pequeña** my little sister.

b **pera** noun Fem. pear.

c **peral** noun Masc. pear tree.

d **percha** noun Fem. **1** hanger; **2** coat hook.

e **perder** verb [36] **1** to lose; **he perdido la cartera** I've lost my wallet; **perder la paciencia** to lose patience; **perder el conocimiento** to lose consciousness; **2** to miss; **perder el tren** to miss the train; **has perdido una gran oportunidad** you've missed a great opportunity; **3 perder la costumbre** to get out of the habit; **4 perder el tiempo** to waste time. **perderse** reflexive verb [36] to get lost; **me he perdido** I'm lost; **¿te has perdido?** are you lost?

k **pérdida** noun Fem. **1** loss; **2 es una pérdida de tiempo** it's a waste of time.

l **perdiz** noun Fem. partridge.

m **perdón** noun Masc. pardon.

n **perdón** exclamation excuse me.

ñ **perdonar** verb [17] **1** to forgive; **no la he perdonado** I haven't forgiven her; **2 te perdono el castigo** I'll let you off (without a punishment); **3 ¡perdona!/¡perdone!** sorry!, (more formal) excuse me!

p **peregrinación** noun Fem. pilgrimage; **irse de peregrinación** to go on a pilgrimage.

q **perejil** noun Masc. parsley.

r **pereza** noun Fem. laziness.

s **perezoso/perezosa** adjective lazy.

perfeccionar verb [17] **1** to improve; **2** to perfect.

perfectamente adverb perfectly.

perfecto/perfecta adjective perfect.

perfil noun Masc. profile; **visto de perfil** from the side.

perfume noun Masc. perfume.

perfumería noun Fem. perfume shop.

periódico noun Masc. newspaper.

periodista noun Masc./Fem. journalist.

período, periodo noun Masc. period (of time).

periquito noun Masc. budgie.

perla noun Fem. pearl.

permanecer verb [35] **1** to stay (in a place); **2** to remain; **permanecer callado** to remain silent.

permanente noun Fem. perm; **hacerse la permanente** to have your hair permed.

permanente adjective permanent.

permanezca, permanezco, etc. verb SEE permanecer.

permiso noun Masc. **1** permission; **darle permiso a alguien para hacer** to give someone permission to do; **2 con permiso** may I come in?, excuse me (to get past someone); **3** permit; **permiso de trabajo** work permit; **4** leave; **estar de permiso** to be on leave; **un permiso de una semana** a week's leave; **5 permiso de conducir** driving licence.

permitir verb [19] **1** to allow; **no nos permitieron pasar** they didn't allow us in; **2 no te permito que me contestes** I won't have you answering me back; **3** (when asking permission) **¿me permite?** may I?; **¿me permite una sugerencia?** may I make a suggestion?; **4** to make possible; **este proceso permite ...** this process makes it possible to ....

pero conjunction but.

perrito noun Masc. **1** puppy; **2 perrito caliente** hot dog.

perro/perra noun Masc./Fem. dog; **perro callejero** stray dog; ★ **estar de un humor de perros** (informal) to be in a foul mood.

persecución noun Fem. **1** pursuit; **salir en persecución de alguien** to set off in pursuit of someone; **2** persecution.

perseguir verb [64] to pursue.

persiana noun Fem. blind.

persistir verb [19] to persist.

persona noun Fem. **1** person; **una persona importante** an important person; **2 personas** people; **en la sala había diez personas** there were ten people in the room.

personaje noun Masc. **1** character (in a book, for example); **2** important figure; **un personaje del mundo de la música** an important figure in the music world.

personal noun Masc. staff.

personal adjective personal.

personalidad noun Fem. personality.

perspectiva noun Fem. **1** perspective; **2** prospect; **hay buenas perspectivas** there are good prospects.

persuadir verb [19] to persuade.

pertenecer verb [35] to belong.

pertenezca, pertenezco, etc. verb SEE **pertenecer**.

Perú noun Masc. Peru.

peruano/peruana noun Masc./ Fem., adjective Peruvian.

pesa noun Fem. weight; **hacer pesas** to do weightlifting.

pesadilla noun Fem. nightmare.

pesado/pesada noun Masc./Fem. **¡eres un pesado!** (informal) you're such a pain!

pesado adjective **1** heavy (a box or piece of furniture, for example); **2 ser muy pesado** (informal) to be a pain (a person); **3 ser muy pesado** to be boring (a job or book, for example).

pesar verb [17] **1** to weigh; **peso sesenta kilos** I weigh sixty kilos; **2 pesar mucho** to be very heavy; **puedo llevarlo, pesa poco** I can carry it, it's not very heavy; **¿te pesan mucho las bolsas?** are the bags too heavy for you?.

pesca noun Fem. fishing; **ir de pesca** to go fishing.

pescadería noun Fem. fishmonger's.

pescado noun Masc. fish.

pescador/pescadora noun Masc./Fem. fisherman/fisherwoman.

pescar verb [31] **1** to fish; **ir a pescar** to go fishing; **2** to catch; **no**

a

pescamos nada we didn't catch anything.

b

peseta noun Fem. peseta (former Spanish currency replaced by the euro; 500 pesetas = 3.00 euros).

c

pesimista noun Masc./Fem. pessimist.

d

pesimista adjective pessimistic.

e

peso noun Masc. weight; **perder peso** to lose weight; **ganar peso** to put on weight; **peso bruto** gross weight; **vender al peso** to sell by weight.

f

g

h

pestaña noun Fem. eyelash.

i

pétalo noun Masc. petal.

j

petardo noun Masc. banger.

k

petróleo noun Masc. oil.

l

petrolero noun Masc. oil tanker (ship).

m

pez (plural **peces**) noun Masc. fish (live); **un pez espada** a swordfish.

n

piano noun Masc. piano; **tocar el piano** to play the piano.

ñ

o

picado/picada adjective
1 decayed (tooth); **tengo una muela picada** I have a cavity in one of my back teeth; **2 carne picada** mince; **3 el mar estaba picado** the sea was choppy; **4** (informal) **estar picado** to be miffed (a person); **está picada porque no la llamaste** she's a bit miffed that you didn't call her.

p

q

r

s

picadura noun Fem. bite, sting.

t

picante adjective hot (spicy).

u

picaporte noun Masc. door handle.

v

w

x

picar verb [31] **1** to bite, to sting; **2** to mince (meat); **3** to chop

y

z

(vegetables); **4** to rot (teeth); **5** to be hot (spicy); **esta salsa pica mucho** this sauce is too hot; **6** to itch; **me pica la nariz** my nose is itching; **7 me pican los ojos** my eyes are stinging.

pico noun Masc. **1** beak; **2** pick; **3** peak (of a mountain); **4** corner (of a table, for example); **5 un cuello de pico** a V-neck; **6** ... **y pico** ... and something; **fueron tres mil y pico** it was three thousand and something; **llegaron a las cinco y pico** they arrived after five.

pida, pido, pidió, etc. verb SEE pedir.

pie noun Masc. **1** foot; **ir a pie** to go on foot; **2 de pie** standing; **estaban de pie** they were standing; **ponerse de pie** to stand up; **3** base (of a lamp or glass).

piedra noun Fem. **1** stone; **una mesa de piedra** a stone table; **piedra preciosa** precious stone; **tener piedras en el riñón** to have kidney stones; **2** flint (of a lighter).

piel noun Fem. **1** skin; **tener la piel seca** to have dry skin; **2** peel; **3** fur; **un abrigo de pieles** a fur coat; **4** leather; **bolsos de piel** leather bags.

piensa, pienso, etc. verb SEE pensar.

pierna noun Fem. leg.

pieza noun Fem. **1** piece; **2 pieza de recambio** spare part.

pijama noun Masc. pyjamas.

pila noun Fem. **1** pile; **una pila de libros** a pile of books; **2** battery; **3** (kitchen) sink.

píldora noun Fem. pill.

piloto noun Masc./Fem. pilot.

pimentón noun Masc. **1** paprika; **2** cayenne pepper.

pimienta noun Fem. pepper.

pimiento noun Masc. pepper; **un pimiento rojo** a red pepper.

pimpón noun Masc. table tennis.

pincel noun Masc. **1** paintbrush; **2** make-up brush.

pinchadiscos noun Masc./Fem. (informal) disc jockey.

pinchar verb [17] **1** to prick; **2** to be prickly; **3** to burst; **4** to puncture; **creo que hemos pinchado** I think we've got a flat tyre; **5** (informal) to give an injection to.

pincharse reflexive verb [17] **1** to burst; **2** to puncture; **se me ha pinchado una rueda** I've got a flat tyre; **3** to get miffed.

pinchazo noun Masc. puncture; **tuvimos un pinchazo** we had a puncture.

pingüino noun Masc. penguin.

pino noun Masc. pine tree; **muebles de pino** pine furniture.

pinta noun Fem. **1** tiene pinta de oficinista he looks like an office worker; **¡qué pinta más rara!** that looks very strange!; **la comida tiene muy buena pinta** the food looks delicious; **2** pint.

pintadas plural noun Fem. graffiti.

pintado/pintada adjective painted.

pintar verb [17] to paint.

pintor/pintora noun Masc./Fem. painter.

pintura noun Fem. **1** painting; **pintura al óleo** oil painting; **2** pinturas crayons.

pinza noun Fem. **1** clothes peg; **2** hairgrip; **3** pincer; **4** dart; **pantalón con pinzas** trousers with pleats.

pinzas plural noun Fem. tweezers.

piña noun Fem. **1** pineapple; **2** pine cone.

pipa noun Fem. pipe; **fumar en pipa** to smoke a pipe.

piragua noun Fem. canoe.

piragüismo noun Masc. canoeing.

pirámide noun Fem. pyramid.

Pirineos plural noun Masc. **los Pirineos** the Pyrenees.

pisar verb [17] **1** to step; **pisar a alguien** to step on somebody's foot; **2 'prohibido pisar el césped'** 'keep off the grass'.

piscina noun Fem. swimming pool; **la parte honda de la piscina** the deep end of the pool; **la parte poco profunda de la piscina** the shallow end of the pool.

piscis noun Masc./Fem. Pisces; **soy piscis** I'm Pisces.

Piscis noun Masc. Pisces.

piso noun Masc. **1** floor; **vivo en el tercer piso** I live on the third floor; **2** storey; **un edificio de cinco pisos** a five-storey building; **3 un autobús de dos pisos** a double-decker bus; **4** flat; **se han comprado un piso** they've bought a flat.

a b c d e f g h i j k l m n ñ o p q r s t u v w x y z

pista *noun Fem.* **1** track; **seguirle la pista a alguien** to be on somebody's trail; **2** racecourse; **3** (tennis) court; **4 pista de hielo** ice rink; **pista de patinaje** skating rink; **5 pista de esquí** sky slope; **6 pista de despegue** runway.

pistacho *noun Masc.* pistachio.

pistola *noun Fem.* gun.

pitar *verb* [17] **1** to blow a whistle; **2** to sound the horn, to hoot (*in a car*).

pito *noun Masc.* **1** whistle; **tocar el pito** to blow the whistle; **2** horn; **tocar el pito** to sound the horn.

pizarra *noun Fem.* **1** blackboard; **2** slate.

placa *noun Fem.* **1** plate, sheet (*of metal, for example*); **2 placa de matrícula** number plate; **3** badge.

placer *noun Masc.* pleasure.

plan *noun Masc.* **1** plan; **hacer planes** to make plans; **¿qué planes tienes para las vacaciones?** what are your plans for the holidays?; **2** (*informal*) **está en plan tirano** he's behaving like a tyrant; **3** (*informal*) **viajar en plan económico** to travel on the cheap.

plancha *noun Fem.* **1** iron; **2 a la plancha** grilled; **3** sheet; **una plancha de plástico** a sheet of plastic.

planchar *verb* [17] to iron.

planear *verb* [17] **1** to plan; **2** to glide.

planeta *noun Masc.* planet.

plano¹ *noun Masc.* **1** street map; **un plano de Madrid** a street map of Madrid; **2** plan (*of a building*).

plano²/plana *adjective* flat.

planta *noun Fem.* **1** plant; **2** floor; **la planta baja** the ground floor; **la sexta planta** the sixth floor.

plantar *verb* [17] to plant.

plástico *noun Masc.* plastic.

plata *noun Fem.* silver; **cubiertos de plata** silver cutlery.

plataforma *noun Fem.* **1** platform; **2 plataforma de lanzamiento** launching pad.

plátano *noun Masc.* banana.

platillo *noun Masc.* saucer.

plato *noun Masc.* **1** plate; **plato llano** dinner plate; **plato de postre** dessert plate; **lavar los platos** to wash the dishes; **2** dish; **plato del día** dish of the day; **plato combinado** complete meal served on a plate; **3** course; **tomé pescado de primer/segundo plato** I had fish for the first/second course.

playa *noun Fem.* **1** beach; **2** seaside; **veranear en la playa** to spend your summer holidays at the seaside.

playera *noun Fem.* canvas shoe.

plaza *noun Fem.* **1** square; **plaza mayor** main square; **2** market; **los martes hay plaza** there's a market on Tuesdays; **3** seat (*in a bus or train*); **4** position (*at work*); **hay plazas vacantes** there are vacancies; **5 plaza de toros** bullring.

plazo noun Masc. **1** period; **el plazo de entrega acaba el once** the deadline is the eleventh; **2 plazo de vencimiento** expiry date (of a passport, for example); **3 a corto plazo** in the short term; **a largo plazo** in the long term; **4 pagar algo a plazos** to pay for something in instalments.

plegar verb [30] to fold.

pleno/plena adjective **1** full; **2 en pleno verano** in the middle of summer; **en pleno centro** right in the centre.

pliega, pliego, pliegue, etc. verb SEE **plegar**.

plomo noun Masc. **1** lead; **2** (informal) **ser un plomo** to be really boring; **3** fuse; **se han fundido los plomos** the fuses have blown.

pluma noun Fem. **1** pen; **2** feather.

plumier noun Masc. pencil case.

plural noun Masc. plural; **en plural** in the plural.

plural adjective plural.

población noun Fem. population.

pobre noun Masc./Fem. poor person; **los pobres** the poor; **¡la pobre!** poor thing!

pobre adjective poor; **¡pobre Jaime!** poor Jaime!

pobreza noun Fem. poverty.

pocilga noun Fem. pigsty; **tu habitación está hecha una pocilga** your room is a pigsty.

poco¹/poca adjective **1** little; **con poco esfuerzo** with little effort; **hay poco pan** there's not much bread; **es poca cosa** it's not much;

2 few; **había pocas personas** there were only a few people; **pocos días más tarde** a few days later.

poco²/poca pronoun **1** little; **basta con poco** a little is enough; **queda poco** there's not much left; **2** few; **vinieron pocos** only a few came; **pon unos pocos aquí** put a few here; **3 un poco** a bit; **espera un poco** wait a bit; **me molesta un poco** it's a bit uncomfortable; **un poco de sal** a bit of salt; **4** (referring to time) **hace poco** not long ago; **hace poco que me escribió** he wrote to me not long ago; **aún voy a tardar un poco** it's going to take me a little while yet; **falta poco para las cinco** it's not long till five now; **dentro de poco** soon; **poco antes de comer** shortly before eating; **5 poco a poco** little by little.

poco³ adverb not very much; **habla poco** he doesn't talk very much; **soy muy poco paciente** I'm very impatient; **estaban poco interesados** they weren't very interested.

poder¹ noun Masc. power.

poder² verb [10] **1** to be able to (but often translated as 'can' in sentences); **no puedo levantarlo** I can't lift it; **no pude ir** I couldn't go; **pueden hacerlo solos** they can do it on their own; **lo mejor que puedas** the best you can; **¿podrás ayudarme?** will you be able to help me?; **¿pudiste encontrarlo?** were you able to find it?; **2** may (asking permission); **¿puedo abrir la**

a
b
c
d
e
f
g
h
i
j
k
l
m
n
ñ
o
p
q
r
s
t
u
v
w
x
y
z

a
b
c
d
e
f
g
h
i
j
k
l
m
n
ñ
o
p
q
r
s
t
u
v
w
x
y
z

ventana? may I open the window?; **¿se puede?** may I come in?; **¿podría usar tu ordenador?** may I use your computer?; **3** (*possibility*) **puede que lleguen más tarde** they might come later; **puede que se haya roto** it might have got broken; **podía suceder** it could happen; **has podido romperlo** you could have broken it; **¿crees que se habrán olvidado?** – 'puede ser' 'do you think they might have forgotten?' – 'they might have'; **puede ser que no lo sepan** it might be that they don't know; **puede ser que se hayan perdido** they might have got lost; **4** (*suggesting*) **podrías preguntar** you could ask; **podríamos comer fuera** we could eat out; **5** (*reproaching*) **¡podrías haberlo dicho!** you could have said!; **6 no puedo con tanto trabajo** I can't cope with so much work; **7 ¡ya no puedo más!** I can't carry on!; **8 si puede ser** if possible.

poderoso/poderosa *adjective* powerful.

podrá, podré, podría, etc. *verb* SEE **poder.**

podrido/podrida *adjective* rotten.

poema *noun Masc.* poem.

poesía *noun Fem.* poetry.

poeta *noun Masc./Fem.* poet.

póker *noun Masc.* poker (*card game*).

polaco[1] *noun Masc.* Polish (*the language*).

polaco[2]**/polaca** *noun Masc./Fem.* Pole.

polaco *adjective* Polish.

polémico/polémica *adjective* controversial; **una decisión polémica** a controversial decision.

policía *noun Masc./Fem.* police officer.

policía *noun Fem.* police.

policíaco/policíaca *adjective* **novela policíaca** detective novel.

polideportivo *noun Masc.* sports centre.

polilla *noun Fem.* moth.

política *noun Fem.* **1** politics; **2** policy (*of a government*).

político/política *noun Masc./Fem.* politician.

político *adjective* political.

póliza *noun Fem.* policy (*insurance document*).

pollito/pollita *noun Masc./Fem.* chick.

pollo *noun Masc.* chicken; **pollo asado** roast chicken.

polo *noun Masc.* **1** pole; **el Polo Norte** the North Pole; **2** ice-lolly.

Polonia *noun Fem.* Poland.

polución *noun Fem.* pollution.

polvo *noun Masc.* **1** dust; **quitar el polvo a los muebles** to dust the furniture; **2 polvos** face powder; **polvos de talco** talcum powder; **3 estar hecho polvo** (*informal*) to be all in; **después de la excursión nos quedamos hechos polvo** we were worn out after the trip; **este sofá está hecho polvo** this sofa's a wreck.

polvorón noun Masc. pastry (made with almonds; eaten at Christmas time).

pomada noun Fem. ointment.

pomelo noun Masc. grapefruit.

pondría, pondrías, etc. verb SEE **poner**.

poner verb [11] **1** to put; **ponlo encima de la mesa** put it on the table; **lo puse en el armario** I put it in the wardrobe; **pusimos diez euros cada uno** we put in ten euros each; **2** (with food) **¿te pongo más sopa?** shall I serve you more soup?; **3** (in a restaurant) **¿qué les pongo?** what can I get you?; **¿me pone un café?** can I have a coffee please?; **4** to put on; **le puso la silla al caballo** she put the saddle on the horse; **no le he puesto camiseta al niño** I haven't put a vest on the baby; **5** to put on (radio, hi-fi, etc.); **poner la tele** to put on the telly; **poner música** to put on some music; **pon el volumen más alto** turn the volume up; **6** poner el despertador to set the alarm clock; **puse el despertador a las ocho** I set the alarm clock for eight; **7** poner la mesa to lay the table; **8** to install; **9** to fit (a carpet); **10** (with names) **¿qué nombre le vais a poner al niño?** what are you going to call the baby?; **le pusieron el apodo de 'el Rubio'** they nicknamed him 'Blondy'; **11** poner una película to show a film; **¿qué ponen en el 'Maxin'?** what's on at the 'Maxin'?; **poner una obra de teatro** to put on a play; **12** poner una tienda to open a shop; **poner un negocio** to set up a business; **13** **¿me pone con el señor Sanz?** could you put me through to Mr Sanz? (on the telephone); **14** poner a alguien nervioso to make somebody nervous; **poner a alguien triste** to make somebody sad; **poner a alguien de mal humor** to put somebody in a bad mood; **15** poner atención to pay attention.

ponga, pongo, etc. verb SEE **poner**.

poni noun Masc. pony.

popular adjective popular.

por preposition **1** for; **por esa razón** for that reason; **por ejemplo** for example; **me ofrecieron dos mil euros por el coche viejo** they offered me two thousand euros for my old car; **lo hago por tu bien** I'm doing it for your own good; **2** through; **no entra por la ventana** it won't go in through the window; **me enteré por mi hermana** I heard through my sister; **pasamos por Toledo** we went through Toledo; **3** by; **mandar algo por correo** to send something by post; **viajar por carretera** to travel by road; **4** mide tres metros por cuatro it measures three metres by four; **cinco por tres son quince** five times three is fifteen; **5** por la mañana in the morning; **6** (place) **lo dejé por aquí** I left it around here somewhere; **viven por la Avenida Mayor** they live somewhere around Mayor Avenue;

a
b
c
d
e
f
g
h
i
j
k
l
m
n
ñ
o
p
q
r
s
t
u
v
w
x
y
z

¿por dónde queda la estación? whereabouts is the station?; **por todos lados** everywhere; **7** per; **treinta euros por persona** thirty euros per person; **a cien kilómetros por hora** at a hundred kilometres an hour; **8** in; **por escrito** in writing; **por adelantado** in advance; **9 preguntó por ti** he asked after you; **10 lo dijeron por la tele** they said so on the TV; **11 andar por la calle** to walk along the road; **caerse por la escalera** to fall down the stairs; **12 ¿por qué?** why?; **13 por supuesto** of course; **14 por eso no lo hice** that's why I didn't do it; **15 por cierto** by the way.

porcentaje *noun Masc.* percentage.

porche *noun Masc.* porch.

porción *noun Fem.* **1** portion; **una porción de tarta** a slice of cake; **2** share.

porque *conjunction* because.

porrón *noun Masc.* wine bottle (*with a long spout from which you drink, holding it as far away from your mouth as possible*).

portada *noun Fem.* **1** title page (*of a book*); **2** cover (*of a magazine*); **3** front page (*of a newspaper*).

portaequipajes *noun Masc.* (*does not change in the plural*) **1** roof rack; **2** luggage rack (*on a train*).

portarse *reflexive verb* [17] to behave; **portarse mal** to misbehave; **¡pórtate bien!** behave yourself!

portátil *adjective* portable.

portátil *noun Masc.* laptop (computer).

portazo *noun Masc.* **dar un portazo** to slam the door.

portería *noun Fem.* goal.

portero/portera *noun Masc./Fem.* **1** goalkeeper; **2** caretaker; **3** porter; **4 portero automático** entry-phone.

portorriqueño/ portorriqueña *noun Masc./Fem.*, *adjective* Puerto Rican.

Portugal *noun Masc.* Portugal.

portugués[1] *noun Masc.* Portuguese (*the language*).

portugués[2]**/portuguesa** *Masc./Fem.* Portuguese man/ woman.

portugués/portuguesa *adjective* Portuguese.

porvenir *noun Masc.* future.

posar *verb* [17] **1** to pose; **2** to lay (*hand or object*).

posarse *reflexive verb* [17] to land.

poseer *verb* [37] **1** to own; **2** to hold (*a title or record*).

posibilidad *noun Fem.* **1** possibility; **es una posibilidad** it's a possibility; **2 tener posibilidades de hacer** to have a good chance of doing; **no tienen muchas posibilidades de ganar** they don't have much chance of winning; **¿qué posibilidades tienen?** what are their chances?

posible *adjective* possible; **a ser posible** if possible; **no fue posible impedirlo** it was impossible to avoid it.

posible adverb **lo más tarde posible** as late as possible; **hazlo lo mejor posible** do the best you can.

posición noun Fem. **1** position; **en quinta posición** in fifth place; **2 posición social** social status.

positivo/positiva adjective positive.

postal noun Fem. postcard.

postal adjective postal.

poste noun Masc. **1** post; **2** pole.

póster noun Masc. poster.

posterior adjective **1** back; **el asiento posterior** the back seat; **la parte posterior de la casa** the back of the house; **2** subsequent, later.

postilla noun Fem. scab.

postizo/postiza adjective false; **dentadura postiza** false teeth.

postre noun Masc. pudding, dessert; **¿qué hay de postre?** what's for pudding?

potable adjective **agua potable** drinking water.

potencial adjective potential.

práctica noun Fem. practice; **lo aprenderás con la práctica** you'll learn with practice; **tener mucha práctica** to have a lot of practice; **he perdido la práctica** I'm out of practice; **en la práctica** in practice.

practicar verb [31] **1** to practise; **practicar el violín** to practise the violin; **2 practicar deportes** to do sports.

práctico/práctica adjective practical.

pradera noun Masc. grassland.

prado noun Masc. meadow.

precaución noun Fem. **1** precaution; **tomar precauciones** to take precautions; **2** caution; **actuar con precaución** to act with caution.

precedente adjective previous.

precio noun Masc. price; **¿qué precio tiene?** how much is it?; **precio fijo** fixed price; **precios de saldo** bargain prices; **los precios han subido mucho** prices have gone up a lot.

precioso/preciosa adjective **1** beautiful; **2** precious; **piedras preciosas** precious stones.

precipicio noun Masc. precipice.

precipitación noun Fem. **1** rush; **hacer algo con mucha precipitación** to do something in a rush; **salió con mucha precipitación** he rushed out; **2** precipitation; rainfall; **habrá precipitaciones moderadas** there will be moderate rainfall.

precipitarse reflexive verb [17] **1** to rush; **no te precipites** don't rush into anything; **2 precipitarse hacia algo** to rush towards something.

precisamente adverb precisely.

precisión noun Fem. precision.

preciso/precisa adjective **1** precise; **2 llegaron en el momento preciso** they arrived just in time; **en este preciso momento no puedo** I can't right now; **3** necessary; **si es preciso** if necessary; **no es preciso pagar por adelantado** you don't have to pay in advance; **es preciso que nos aseguremos** we must make sure.

predilecto/predilecta *adjective* favourite.

preescolar *adjective* preschool.

preferencia *noun Fem.*
1 preference; **2** right of way; **yo tenía preferencia** I had right of way; **3** priority; **tener preferencia** to have priority.

preferible *adjective* preferable; **ser preferible a algo** to be preferable to something.

preferido/preferida *adjective* favourite.

preferir *verb* [14] to prefer; **preferir algo a algo** to prefer something to something; **preferiría no tener que ir** I'd rather not have to go.

prefiera, prefiero, etc. *verb* SEE **preferir**.

prefijo *noun Masc.* **1** prefix; **2** dialling code; **el prefijo de España** the dialling code for Spain.

pregunta *noun Fem.* question; **hacer una pregunta** to ask a question.

preguntar *verb* [17] to ask; **preguntar acerca de/sobre algo** to ask about something; **preguntar por alguien** to ask about someone; **me preguntó por tus padres** he asked me about your parents.

preguntarse *reflexive verb* [17] to wonder; **me pregunto si dice la verdad** I wonder if he's telling the truth.

prejuicio *noun Masc.* prejudice; **tener prejuicios contra** to be prejudiced against.

prematuro/prematura *adjective* premature.

premiar *verb* [17] premiar a **alguien** to give somebody a prize.

premio *noun Masc.* prize; **dar un premio a alguien** to give someone a prize; **ganar un premio** to win a prize; **me tocó un premio en la rifa** I won a prize in the raffle; **¿qué dan de premio?** what's the prize?; **premio gordo** jackpot (*in the lottery*).

prender *verb* [18] **1** to catch (*a criminal*); **2** to light (*a cigarette or match*); **3** prenderle fuego a algo to set something on fire.

prensa *noun Fem.* la prensa the press; **leer la prensa** to read the newspapers.

preocupado/preocupada *adjective* worried; **estar preocupado por algo** to be worried about something.

preocupar *verb* [17] to worry; **me preocupan los exámenes** I'm worried about the exams.

preocuparse *reflexive verb* [17] to get worried; **se preocupó porque no la llamé** she got worried because I didn't phone her.

preparación *noun Fem.*
1 preparation; **2** training (*in sport*); **3** un trabajador con muy buena preparación a highly trained worker.

preparar verb [17] **1** to prepare; **preparar la cena** to prepare dinner; **preparar un examen** to prepare for an exam; **2** to train (*a player or athlete*); **3** to coach (*a student*); **4 preparar la cuenta** to draw up the bill.

prepararse *reflexive verb* [17] to get ready.

preparativos *plural noun Masc.* preparations.

preposición *noun Fem.* preposition.

presa *noun Fem.* **1** dam; **2** reservoir; **3** prey; **4 ser presa del terror** to be seized with panic.

presencia *noun Fem.* presence; **en presencia de sus padres** in front of his parents.

presentación *noun Fem.* **1** introduction; **hacer las presentaciones** to do the introductions; **2** presentation.

presentador/presentadora *noun Masc./Fem.* presenter.

presentar *verb* [17] **1** to introduce; **te presento a mi novio** this is my boyfriend; **les presentó a su jefe** he introduced them to his boss; **2** to present (*a programme, for example*); **3** to submit (*an application*).

presentarse *reflexive verb* [17] **1** to introduce yourself; **2** to turn up; **se presentaron sin avisar a nadie** they turned up without letting anybody know; **3 presentarse voluntario** to volunteer; **4 presentarse a un examen** to sit an exam;

5 presentarse a un concurso to enter a competition; **6 presentarse para un cargo** to apply for a post; **7 presentarse a la presidencia** to run for the presidency.

presente *noun Masc.* present.

preservativo *noun Masc.* condom.

presidencia *noun Fem.* presidency.

presidente/presidenta *noun Masc./Fem.* president.

presión *noun Fem.* **1** pressure; **2 cerveza a presión** draught beer.

preso/presa *noun Masc./Fem.* prisoner.

preso *adjective* **estar preso** to be in prison; **meter preso a alguien** to send somebody to prison.

préstamo *noun Masc.* loan; **préstamo hipotecario** mortgage.

prestar *verb* [17] **1** to lend; **le presté dinero para el coche** I lent him money for the car; **2 ¿me prestas tu abrigo?** can I borrow your coat?; **3 prestar atención** to pay attention.

prestidigitador/prestidigitadora *noun Masc./Fem.* conjurer.

presumido/presumida *noun Masc./Fem.* **es un presumido** he's so conceited.

presumido *adjective* conceited.

presumir *verb* [19] to show off; **presumen de casa grande** they like to boast about how big their house is; **presume de guapa** she thinks she's very good-looking.

a
b
c
d
e
f
g
h
i
j
k
l
m
n
ñ
o
p
q
r
s
t
u
v
w
x
y
z

presupuesto noun Masc. budget.

pretender verb [18] **1** to try; **¿qué pretendes conseguir?** what are you trying to achieve?; **pretendía que pagase yo** he was trying to make me pay for it; **2 pretender que alguien haga** to expect somebody to do; **pretende que yo le ayude** he expects me to help him.

pretexto noun Masc. pretext, excuse; **siempre tiene algún pretexto para no hacerlo** he always has some excuse or other not to do it.

prevenir verb [15] **1** to prevent; **2** to warn.

prever verb [16] to forsee.

previsto/prevista adjective **está previsto que vengan mañana** they're due to come tomorrow; **a la hora prevista** at the scheduled time.

primavera noun Fem. spring.

primer adjective first SEE **primero/ primera**.

primero¹/primera adjective, pronoun first; **primera clase** first class; **el primero de mayo** the first of May; *(note that 'primero' becomes 'primer' before a masculine singular noun)* **primer piso** first floor; **llegar en primer lugar** to finish in first position; **en primer lugar, no me interesa** first of all, I'm not interested.

primero² adverb first; **yo estaba primero** I was here first; **primero vamos a informarnos** first of all, let's find out.

primicia noun Fem. **1** scoop *(news story)*; **2** first showing *(of film)*.

primo/prima noun Masc./Fem. cousin.

princesa noun Fem. princess.

principal adjective main.

príncipe noun Masc. prince.

principiante/principianta noun Masc./Fem. beginner.

principio noun Masc. beginning; **a principios de mes** at the beginning of the month; **al principio de la temporada** at the beginning of the season; **un buen principio** a good start.

prisa noun Fem. **1** hurry; **tener prisa** to be in a hurry; **date prisa, que llegamos tarde** hurry up or we'll be late; **2 de prisa** fast; **hacer algo de prisa** to do something fast; **a toda prisa** in a hurry; **3 correr prisa** to be urgent; **este trabajo corre prisa** this job is urgent.

prisión noun Fem. prison.

prisionero/prisionera noun Masc./Fem. prisoner.

prismáticos plural noun Masc. binoculars.

privado/privada adjective private.

privar verb [17] **privar a alguien de algo** to deprive somebody of something.

privarse reflexive verb [17] **privarse de algo** to deprive yourself of something.

privilegiado/privilegiada adjective privileged.

privilegio noun Masc. privilege.

probable *adjective* probable.

probador *noun Masc.* changing room.

probar *verb* [24] **1** to try; **prueba a abrirlo con esta llave** try opening it with this key; **es la primera vez que pruebo la comida tailandesa** it's the first time I've tried Thai food; **probar no cuesta nada** there's no harm in trying; **2** to taste; **¿has probado la sopa?** have you tasted the soup?; **3** to test (*brakes, for example*); **4** to prove; **no pudo probar su inocencia** he could not prove his innocence. **probarse** *reflexive verb* [24] to try on; **¿quiere probárselo?** would you like to try it on?.

probeta *noun Fem.* test tube; **niño probeta** test-tube baby.

problema *noun Masc.* problem; **un problema muy importante** a major problem.

procedente *adjective* from; **el vuelo procedente de Londres** the flight from London.

proceder *verb* [18] **1 proceder de algo** to come from something; **2** to proceed; **procedieron con cautela** they proceeded with caution.

procesador *noun Masc.* **procesador de textos** word processor.

procesión *noun Fem.* procession.

proceso *noun Masc.* **1** process; **2** processing; **proceso de datos** data processing.

procurar *verb* [17] **procurar hacer** to try to do; **procura terminarlo**

para el viernes try to finish it by Friday.

producción *noun Fem.* production.

producir *verb* [60] **1** to produce; **producir coches** to produce cars; **2** to cause; **la tormenta produjo daños** the storm caused damage.

producto *noun Masc.* **1** product; **2** production.

productor/productora *noun Masc./Fem.* producer.

productor *adjective* producing; **países productores de petróleo** oil-producing countries.

produje, produzca, etc. *verb* SEE **producir.**

profe *noun Masc./Fem.* teacher (*informal*).

profesión *noun Fem.* profession.

profesional *adjective* professional.

profesor/profesora *noun Masc./Fem.* **1** professor, lecturer; **2** teacher (*in a secondary school*).

profundidad *noun Fem.* depth.

profundo/profunda *adjective* deep.

programa *noun Masc.* **1** programme; **2** program; **un programa informático** a computer program.

programador/programadora *noun Masc./Fem.* programmer.

programar *verb* [17] to program (*a computer*).

progresar *verb* [17] to progress.

a **progreso** noun Masc. progress;
hacer progresos to make
b progress.

c **prohibido/prohibida** adjective
forbidden; **está terminantemente
d prohibido** it's strictly forbidden;
'prohibido fumar' 'no smoking';
e **'prohibido el paso'/'prohibida la
entrada'** 'no entry'; **'prohibido
f pisar el césped'** 'keep off the
grass'.
g
prohibir verb [58] to prohibit; **se
h prohíbe la entrada a menores de
dieciséis años** no admission to
i persons under 16.

j **prolongar** verb [28] to prolong.
prolongarse reflexive verb [28]
k to go on (a meeting or party, for
example).
l
promedio noun Masc. average; **un
m promedio de quince libras por
semana** an average of fifteen
n pounds a week.

ñ **promesa** noun Fem. promise; **no
cumplió con su promesa** he
o didn't keep his promise.

p **prometer** verb [18] to promise; **te
lo prometo** I promise.
q
prometida noun Fem. fiancée.

r **prometido** noun Masc. fiancé.

s **promoción** noun Fem. promotion.

pronombre noun Masc. pronoun.
t
pronóstico noun Masc. 1 forecast;
u **pronóstico del tiempo** weather
forecast; 2 prognosis.
v
pronto[1] adverb 1 soon; **tan pronto
w como sea posible** as soon as
possible; 2 quickly; **respondieron
x muy pronto** they answered very
quickly; 3 early; **se marcharon
y
z

pronto they left early; **4 de pronto**
all of a sudden.

pronto[2]/**pronta** adjective
prompt; **una pronta respuesta** a
prompt reply.

pronunciación noun Fem.
pronunciation.

pronunciar verb [17] to
pronounce.

propaganda noun Fem.
1 advertising; **hacer propaganda
de un producto** to advertise a
product; 2 propaganda.

propiedad noun Fem. 1 property;
propiedad privada private
property; 2 **ser propiedad de
alguien** to belong to somebody.

propietario/propietaria noun
Masc./Fem. owner.

propina noun Fem. tip.

propio/propia adjective 1 own;
mi propio hermano my own
brother; 2 **la propia Elena lo
admitió** Elena herself admitted it.

proponer verb [11] 1 to suggest;
nos propuso ir a cenar fuera he
suggested we went out for dinner;
2 to propose; **proponer una idea** to
propose an idea; **proponer un
trato** to make a proposition; 3 to
put forward (a candidate).
proponerse reflexive verb [11]
1 to set yourself a goal; **me
propuse encontrar un trabajo** I
set myself the goal of finding a job;
**siempre consigue lo que se
propone** he always achieves what
he sets out to do; 2 to decide; **me
propuse ir a verlos** I decided to go
and see them.

proporción noun Fem.
1 proportion; **en proporción** in proportion; **2 proporciones** dimensions.

proposición noun Fem. proposal.

propósito noun Masc. intention.

prórroga noun Fem. **1** extension; **2** extra time (in sports).

prospecto noun Masc. **1** patient information leaflet (supplied with medicine); **2** advertising leaflet.

próspero/próspera adjective **1** prosperous; **2 ¡Próspero Año Nuevo!** Happy New Year!

prostituta noun Fem. prostitute.

protagonista noun Masc./Fem.
1 leading player; **2** leading character.

protección noun Fem. protection.
protector/protectora noun Masc./Fem. protector.
protector adjective **1** protective; **2 Sociedad Protectora de Animales** Society for the Prevention of Cruelty to Animals.

proteger verb [3] to protect.
protegerse reflexive verb [3] to protect yourself.

protesta noun Fem. protest; **en señal de protesta** in protest.

protestante noun Masc./Fem., **protestante** adjective Protestant.

protestar verb [17] to protest.

provecho noun Masc. **1** benefit; **sacar provecho de algo** to benefit from something; **2 siempre piensa primero en su propio provecho** he always thinks of himself first; **3 ¡buen provecho!** enjoy your meal!

proveniente adjective **personas provenientes de otros países** people from other countries.

proverbio noun Masc. proverb.

provincia noun Fem. province.

provisional adjective provisional.

provocador/provocadora noun Masc./Fem. political agitator.
provocador adjective provocative.

provocar verb [31] **1** to provoke (a person); **2** to cause (an explosion or fire).

proximidad noun Fem. proximity.

próximo/próxima adjective
1 next; **la próxima semana** next week; **2 en fecha próxima** in the near future.

proyecto noun Masc. **1** project; **2** plan; **¿qué proyectos tienes para el verano?** what are your plans for the summer?; **3 tengo varios trabajos en proyecto** I've got a few jobs lined up.

proyector noun Masc. projector.

prudente adjective sensible; **sé prudente conduciendo** drive carefully.

prueba¹ noun Fem. **1** proof; **no tienen pruebas** they have no proof; **2** test; **3 hacer la prueba** to try; **hice la prueba y funcionó** I tried it and it worked; **haz la prueba de limpiarlo con lejía** try cleaning it with bleach; **4 a prueba** on trial; **trabajadores a prueba** people working on a trial basis; **5 a prueba de balas** bullet-proof; **a prueba de agua** waterproof.

a

prueba², **pruebo, etc.** verb SEE probar.

psicólogo/psicóloga noun Masc./Fem. psychologist.

psiquiatra noun Masc./Fem. psychiatrist.

publicar verb [31] to publish.

publicidad noun Fem. **1** publicity; **2** advertising.

público¹ noun Masc. **1** public; **2** audience.

público²/pública adjective public.

pude, pudo, etc. verb SEE poder.

pudrir verb [59] to rot.

pudrirse reflexive verb [59] to rot.

pueblo noun Masc. **1** village; **2** small town; **3** people; **el pueblo español** the Spanish people.

puente noun Masc. **1** bridge; **2** puente aéreo shuttle service; **3** hacer puente take a long weekend (usually when the Thursday before or the Tuesday after is a public holiday).

puerco/puerca noun Masc./Fem. pig.

puerro noun Masc. leek.

puerta noun Fem. **1** door; **puerta principal** main door; **puerta giratoria** revolving door; **puerta trasera** back door; **quedamos en la puerta del cine** we arranged to meet outside the cinema; **2 puerta de embarque** gate (in an airport); **3 la puerta del jardín** the garden gate.

puerto noun Masc. **1** port; **un puerto pesquero** a fishing port;

2 harbour; **un puerto deportivo** a marina.

Puerto Rico noun Masc. Puerto Rico.

puertorriqueño/ puertorriqueña noun Masc./ Fem., adjective Puerto Rican.

pues conjunction **1 pues bien, como te iba diciendo ...** well, as I was telling you ...; **pues no estoy seguro** I'm not sure now; **pues mira, ahora no me acuerdo** well, look, I can't remember now; **2 ¡pues no vayas!** don't go then!; **pues si no te gusta el libro, no lo leas** if you don't like the book, don't read it then; **3 ¡pues claro!** of course!; **¡pues claro que no!** of course not!; **'¿lo querías tú?' – '¡pues sí!'** 'did you want it?' – 'yes, I did!'

puesto¹ noun Masc. **1** position; **llegar en primer puesto** to finish in first position; **sacar el primer puesto en un examen** to come top in an exam; **2** job; **puestos de trabajo** jobs; **perdió su puesto de trabajo** he lost his job; **puestos vacantes** vacancies; **un puesto fijo** a permanent job; **3** post; **un puesto de socorro** a first-aid post; **4** stall (in a market).

puesto conjunction **puesto que** since.

puesto²/puesta adjective **1 la mesa estaba puesta** the table was laid; **2 llevaba el abrigo puesto** I had my coat on.

pulga noun Fem. flea.

pulgada noun Fem. inch.

pulgar noun Masc. thumb.

pulir verb [19] to polish.

pulmón noun Masc. lung.

pulpo noun Masc. octopus.

pulsar verb [17] **1** to press (a key or button); **2** to pluck (a string).

pulsera noun Fem. **1** bracelet; **1** watchstrap.

pulso noun Masc. **1** pulse; **le tomó el pulso** he took his pulse; **2 tener buen pulso** to have a steady hand; **me temblaba el pulso** my hand was shaking; **3 levantar algo a pulso** to lift something with your bare hands; **dibujar algo a pulso** to draw something freehand; **4** arm-wrestling contest.

punta noun Fem. **1** point (of a knife or needle, for example); **acaba en punta** it's pointed; **2** tip (of pencil, tongue, finger, etc.); ★ **tener algo en la punta de la lengua** (informal) to have something on the tip of your tongue; **3** end; **a la otra punta del pasillo** at the other end of the corridor; **4 las puntas: cortarse las puntas** to have your hair trimmed; **tener las puntas abiertas** to have split ends; **5 sacar punta a un lápiz** to sharpen a pencil; **6 la hora punta** the rush hour.

puntada noun Fem. stitch.

puntapié noun Masc. kick; **darle un puntapié a algo** to kick something.

puntería noun Fem. aim; **tiene buena puntería** he's a good shot.

puntilla noun Fem. **1** lace edging; **2 ponerse de puntillas** to stand on tiptoe; **andar de puntillas** to walk on tiptoe.

punto noun Masc. **1** point; **un punto de vista** a point of view; **es mi punto débil** it's my weak point; **llevan tres puntos de ventaja** they're three points ahead; **hasta cierto punto** up to a point; **punto por punto** point by point; **2** dot; **el punto sobre la 'i'** the dot on the 'i'; **3** (in punctuation) **punto final** full stop; **punto y coma** semicolon; **4 en punto** on the dot; **las cinco en punto** five o'clock sharp; **a las dos en punto** at two on the dot; **llegar en punto** to arrive exactly on time; **5** stitch; **hacer punto** to knit; **de punto** knitted; **una falda de punto** a knitted skirt; **6 estar a punto de hacer** to be about to do; **7 estar algo en su punto** to be just right; **la carne está en su punto** the meat is just right; **8 batir las claras a punto de nieve** beat the egg whites until stiff; **9 punto muerto** neutral (gear); **10 punto negro** black spot (for accidents); black head (on skin).

puntocom noun Fem. **una puntocom** a dot-com company.

puntuación noun Fem. **1** punctuation; **2** score (in sports); **3** marks (in an exam).

puntual adjective punctual; **ser puntual** to be always on time; **llegaron puntuales** they arrived on time.

puñetazo noun Masc. punch; **me dio un puñetazo** he punched me; **di un puñetazo en la mesa** I banged the table with my fist.

a b c d e f g h i j k l m n ñ o p q r s t u v w x y z

puño *noun Masc.* **1** fist; **2** cuff; **3** handle (*of a tool*).

pupila *noun Fem.* pupil.

pupitre *noun Masc.* desk.

puré *noun Masc.* **1** purée; **2** thick soup; **puré de guisantes** pea soup; **3 puré de patatas** mashed potatoes.

puro[1] *noun Masc.* cigar.

puro[2]/**pura** *adjective* **1** pure; **2 la pura verdad** the simple truth; **3 de puro aburrimiento** out of sheer boredom.

púrpura *adjective* purple.

puse, puso, etc. *verb* SEE **poner.**

puzzle *noun Masc.* jigsaw puzzle.

Qq

que[1] *pronoun* **1** who; **el hombre que me lo dijo** the man who told me; **los que están interesados** those who are interested; **2** which, that; **el libro que recomendé** the book which I recommended; **la marca que me gusta** the brand (that) I like; **3 el que prefiero** the one (that) I prefer.

que[2] *conjunction* **1** that; **dijo que no lo necesitaba** she said (that) she didn't need it; **sé que le gusta** I know (that) he likes it; **nos pidió que le ayudásemos** he asked us to help him (*'que' is followed by the subjunctive in certain constructions*); **2** (*in comparisons*) than; **es más alto que yo** he's taller than me; **3** (*for emphasis*)

¡que te he dicho que sí me gusta! I've already told you that I like it!; **¡que es mío!** I'm telling you it's mine!; **'¿te importa?' – '¡que no!'** 'do you mind?' – 'I've already told you that I don't!'; **4** (*expressing surprise*) **¿que tiene veinte años?** she's twenty?; **5** (*expressing a wish*) **que te mejores pronto** get well soon; **que pases unas buenas vacaciones** have a nice holiday; **6** (*giving an order*) **¡que pasen!** show them in; **7 yo que tú** if I were you.

qué[1] *pronoun* **1** what; **¿qué es eso?** what's that?; **¿a qué te refieres?** what are you referring to?; **2 ¿qué?** what?; **3 ¿qué tal?** how are you doing?; **¿qué tal va?** how's it going?; **¿qué hay de nuevo?** what's new?; **4 ¡qué va!** no way!

qué[2] *adjective* **1** which; **¿qué abrigo es el tuyo?** which coat is yours?; **2** what (*in exclamations*); **¡qué casa tan grande!** what a big house!

qué[3] *adverb* **¡qué bonito!** how nice!; **¡qué egoísta eres!** you're so selfish!

quebradero *noun Fem.* worry.

quebrado *noun Masc.* fraction.

quebrar *verb* [29] to break.

quedar *verb* [17] **1** to be left; **quedan tres paquetes** there are three packets left; **¿te queda dinero?** do you have any money left?; **no queda leche** there's no milk; **2** (*in time expressions*) **aún quedan dos días** there are still two days to go; **quedaban quince minutos para el final de la clase** it was still fifteen minutes till the end of the class; **¿cuánto tiempo me queda?** how much time do I have left?; **aún queda tiempo** there's still time; **3** (with distances) **quedaban quince kilómetros** there were still fifteen kilometres to go; **4** (expressing a person's situation) **quedó viudo** he was widowed; **quedó ciego tras el accidente** he was left blind after the accident; **quedaron solos** they were left alone; **quedar en último lugar** to end up last; **5** (talking about the appearance of something) **así queda mejor** it's better like this; **queda muy feo con esa tela** it's horrible with that material; **6** (arranging meetings) **quedamos en la plaza** we arranged to meet in the square; **¿te apetece quedar?** would you like to meet?; **¿quedamos para el sábado?** shall we meet on Saturday?; **7** (when talking about clothes, hairstyles, etc.) **me queda apretado** it's too tight on me; **¿te queda bien?** does it fit you?; **esos pantalones te quedan fenomenal** those trousers look great on you; **ese color te queda muy bien** that colour really suits you; **8** (impressions) **quiere quedar bien con mi familia** she wants to make a good impression on my family; **9 va a quedar mal si no lo hacemos** it will look bad if we don't do it; **quedamos muy mal con sus padres** we made a bad impression on her parents;

10 quedar en algo to agree on something; **quedamos en vernos hoy** we agreed to see each other today; **11** (talking about location) to be; **queda cerca de mi casa** it's near my house; **queda bastante lejos** it's quite a long way away; **¿dónde queda la estación?** where is the station?

quedarse reflexive verb [17] **1** to stay; **prefiero quedarme en casa** I'd rather stay at home; **se quedó en la cama** he stayed in bed; **2** (expressing somebody's situation or state) **quedarse ciego** to go blind; **quedarse calvo** to lose your hair; **quedarse sin trabajo** to lose your job; **quedarse viudo** to be widowed; **quedarse soltero** to stay single; **quedarse dormido** to fall asleep; **quedarse callado** to remain silent; **3 quedarse con algo** to keep something.

queja noun Fem. complaint; **presentar una queja** to make a complaint; **presentó una queja al gerente por el mal servicio** he made a complaint to the manager about the bad service.

quejarse reflexive verb [17] to complain; **se quejan de la comida** they complain about the food; **se quejan de que tardamos mucho** they complain about how long we take.

quemado/quemada adjective burnt.

quemadura noun Fem. burn.

quemar verb [17] **1** to burn; **2** to scald; **3** to be very hot; **la sopa quema mucho** the soup's really hot; **4 quemar un motor** to burn out an engine; **5 quemar calorías** to burn up calories; **6 ¡cómo quema el sol!** the sun's scorching!

quemarse *reflexive verb* [17] **1** to burn yourself; **me quemé la mano** I burnt my hand; **2** to scald; **3** to get burned; **el mantel se quemó un poco** the tablecloth got slightly burnt; **¡cómo te has quemado!** you've really got burnt! (*in the sun*); **4** to burn down; **la casa se quemó toda** the house burned down.

querer *verb* [12] **1** to want; **¿qué quieres para tu cumpleaños?** what do you want for your birthday?; **no quiero ir al cine** I don't want to go to the cinema; **2** to love; **te quiero** I love you; **3** (*making an offer*) **¿quieres beber algo?** would you like something to drink?; **si quieres voy más tarde** if you like I'll go later; **4** (*asking for something in a shop, cafe, etc.*) **quisiera ver plumas** I would like to see some pens; **yo quiero un café** I'll have a coffee; **quisiera reservar una mesa para cuatro** I'd like to book a table for four; **5** (*asking somebody to do something*) **¿quieres apagar la tele, por favor?** would you mind switching off the television, please?; **6 querer decir** to mean; **¿qué quieres decir?** what do you mean?

quererse *reflexive verb* [17] to love each other.

querido/querida *adjective* dear; **Querido Pablo** Dear Pablo (*starting a letter*).

querrá, querré, querría, etc. *verb* SEE **querer.**

queso *noun Masc.* cheese; **queso rallado** grated cheese.

quiebra *noun Fem.* bankruptcy.

quien *pronoun* **1** who; **no fui yo quien lo dijo** it wasn't me who said it; **ellos son quienes no quisieron** they're the ones who didn't want to (*sometimes not translated*) **la persona con quien hablé** the person I spoke to; **2** whom, who; **Isabel, a quien vi ayer** Isabel, whom I saw yesterday.

quién *pronoun* **1** who; **¿quién es?** who is it?; **¡quién lo hubiese dicho!** who would have said!; **2** which; **¿quién de vosotros es Carlos?** which of you is Carlos?; **3 ¿de quién?** whose?; **¿de quién es esta cartera?** whose is this wallet?

quienquiera *pronoun* whoever.

quiera, quiere, etc. *verb* SEE **querer.**

quieto/quieta *adjective* still; **¡estate quieto!** keep still!

química[1] *noun Fem.* chemistry.

químico/química[2] *noun Masc./Fem.* chemist.

químico *adjective* chemical.

quince *number* **1** fifteen; **tiene quince años** he's fifteen (years old); **2 quince días** a fortnight; **3** fifteenth (*in dates*); **hoy estamos a quince** it's the fifteenth today.

quinceañero/quinceañera
noun Masc./Fem. teenager.

quincena *noun Fem.* **una quincena** a fortnight; **la primera quincena de mayo** the first two weeks in May.

quiniela *noun Fem.* pools coupon; **rellenar una quiniela** to fill in a pools coupon; **jugar a las quinielas** to do the pools.

quinientos/quinientas *number* five hundred; **quinientos cinco** five hundred and five.

quinto/quinta *adjective* fifth; **el quinto piso** the fifth floor; **llegar en quinto lugar** to finish in fifth position.

quiosco *noun Masc.* **1** news-stand; **2 el quiosco de los helados** the ice cream stand; **3 el quiosco de bebidas** the drinks stand; **4** kiosk.

quiosquero/quiosquera *noun Masc./Fem.* **1** newspaper vendor; **2** kiosk vendor.

quirúrgico/quirúrgica *adjective* surgical.

quise, quisiera, quiso, etc. *verb* SEE **querer**.

quitaesmalte *noun Masc.* nail varnish remover.

quitanieves *noun Masc.* snowplough.

quitar *verb* [17] **1** to take off; **quita los pies de la mesa** take your feet off the table; **no puedo quitar la tapa** I can't get the lid off; **2 le quité los zapatos al niño** I took the child's shoes off; **3 quitarle algo a alguien** to take something from someone; **le quitaron la**

cartera they took his wallet; **4** to take away; **le han quitado el carnet de conducir** they've taken his driving licence away; **quita esa silla de ahí** take that chair away from there; **5** to remove; **quitar la suciedad** to remove the dirt; **quitar el polvo** to dust.

quitarse *reflexive verb* [17] **1** to come out (*a stain, for example*); **2** to go away (*a pain*); **3 quitarse algo** to take something off; **se quitó el abrigo** he took his coat off.

quizá, quizás *adverb* perhaps.

Rr

rábano *noun Masc.* radish; ★ **me importa un rábano** (*informal*) I couldn't care less (*literally: it matters a radish to me*).

rabia *noun Fem.* **1** rabies; **2 me da mucha rabia** it really annoys me; **me da mucha rabia llegar tarde** I get very annoyed when I'm late; **le dio mucha rabia que no se lo dijeran** it really annoyed him that they didn't tell him; **3 tenerle rabia a alguien** to have it in for someone; **4 con rabia** angrily.

rabo *noun Masc.* tail.

racha *noun Fem.* **1 una racha de mala suerte** a spell of bad luck; **pasar una mala racha** to go through a bad patch; **tener una buena racha** to be on a winning streak; **2** gust (*of wind*).

a b c d e f g h i j k l m n ñ o p q r s t u v w x y z

a **racimo** noun Masc. bunch; **un racimo de uvas** a bunch of grapes.

b **ración** noun Fem. portion; **una ración de gambas** a portion of prawns (in a tapas bar).

c **racionar** verb [17] to ration.

d **racismo** noun Masc. racism.

e **racista** noun Masc./Fem., **racista** adjective racist.

g **radar** noun Masc. radar.

radiación noun Fem. radiation.

h **radiactivo/radiactiva** adjective radioactive.

i **radiador** noun Masc. radiator.

j **radio**[1] noun Fem. radio; **escuchar la radio** to listen to the radio; **poner la radio** to switch on the radio.

k **radio**[2] noun Masc. radius.

l **radiocassette** noun Masc. radio cassette player.

n **radiografía** noun Fem. X-ray; **hacerse una radiografía** to have an X-ray taken.

ñ **ráfaga** noun Fem. **1** gust; **una ráfaga de viento** a gust of wind; **2 una ráfaga de ametralladora** a burst of machine-gun fire.

o **raíz** noun Fem. **1** root; **echar raíces** to take root; **2 raíz cuadrada** square root; **3 a raíz de** as a result of.

p **rallado/rallada** adjective **1** grated; **2 pan rallado** breadcrumbs.

s **rallador** noun Masc. grater.

t **rallar** verb [17] to grate.

u **rama** noun Fem. branch; ★ **irse por las ramas** to beat about the bush.

ramo noun Masc. **1** bunch (of flowers); **2** bouquet.

rampa noun Fem. ramp; **rampa de lanzamiento** launch pad.

rana noun Fem. frog.

ranura noun Fem. coin slot.

rape noun Masc. **1** monkfish; **2 llevar el pelo cortado al rape** to have your hair closely cropped.

rápidamente adverb quickly.

rápido[1] noun Masc. express train.

rápido adverb fast, quickly; **todo lo rápido que podía** as fast as I possibly could.

rápido[2]**/rápida** adjective **1** quick, fast; **comida rápida** fast food; **2** rapid.

raqueta noun Fem. **1** racket; **2** snowshoe.

raro/rara adjective **1** strange; **¡qué raro que no hayan llamado!** how strange they haven't called!; **2** rare; **es raro que llueva en esa zona** it's rare for it to rain in that area.

rascacielos noun Masc. (does not change in the plural) skyscraper.

rascar verb [31] to scratch.

rascarse reflexive verb [31] to scratch yourself; **se rascó la nariz** he scratched his nose.

rasgar verb [28] to tear.

rasguño noun Masc. scratch.

rastrillo noun Masc. rake.

rastro noun Masc. **1** trail; **sin dejar rastro** without a trace; **2** flea market.

rata noun Fem. rat.

ratero/ratera noun Masc./Fem.
1 pickpocket; **2** petty thief.

rato noun Masc. **1** while; **tardaré un rato en hacerlo** it will take me a while to do it; **después de un rato** after a while; **dentro de un rato** in a while; **ya hace rato que se han ido** they went a while ago; **al rato** after a while; **al poco rato** soon afterwards; **2 pasar el rato** to kill time; **3 pasar un buen rato** to have a good time; **4 ratos libres** spare time.

ratón noun Masc. mouse.

raya noun Fem. **1** line; **2** dash (in punctuation); **3** parting (in your hair); **hacerse la raya** to part your hair; **a rayas** striped, stripy (a dress or material, for example); **una falda a rayas** a stripy skirt; **5** skate (fish).

rayar verb [17] **1** to scratch; **2 rayar en** to border on; **raya en lo ridículo** it's bordering on the ridiculous.

rayo noun Masc. **1** ray; **un rayo de luz** a ray of light; **2** flash of lightning; **3 un rayo láser** a laser beam; **4 rayos X** X-rays.

raza noun Fem. **1** race; **2** breed; **un perro de raza** a pedigree dog.

razón noun Fem. **1** reason; **por alguna razón** for some reason; **¿por qué razón se enfadó?** why did he get cross?; **con razón** with good reason; **por razones de salud** for medical reasons; **2 tener razón** to be right; **tienes razón** you're right; **no tienes razón en eso** you're wrong about that; **darle la razón a alguien** to agree that

somebody is right; **3** reason; **perder la razón** to lose your mind; **4 razón: 279452** call 279452 for information.

razonable adjective reasonable.

reacción noun Fem. reaction.

reacio/reacia adjective reluctant.

reactor noun Masc. **1** jet; **2** reactor.

real adjective **1** real; **2** true; **una historia real** a true story; **3** royal.

realidad noun Fem. **1** reality; **hacerse realidad** to become true; **2 en realidad** actually.

realista adjective **1** realistic; **es muy poco realista** he's very unrealistic; **2** royalist.

realizador/realizadora noun Masc./Fem. producer.

realizar verb [22] **1** to carry out (a task); **2** to make (a visit or trip); **3** to fulfil (a dream).

realizarse reflexive verb [22] **1** to come true (a dream); **2** to fulfil yourself.

rebaja noun Fem. **1** reduction; **hacer una rebaja** to give a reduction; **me hizo una rebaja de diez euros** he gave me a ten euro reduction; **lo rebajó a cuarenta euros** he reduced it to forty euros; **2 rebajas** sales; **esa tienda está de rebajas** this shop has a sale on.

rebajar verb [17] **1** to bring down (prices); **2** to reduce (an article); **todas las faldas están rebajadas** all the skirts are reduced; **3 rebajar peso** to lose weight.

rebanada noun Fem. slice.

a b c d e f g h i j k l m n ñ o p q r s t u v w x y z

rebaño noun Masc. **1** flock (*of sheep*); **2** herd (*of goats*).

rebeca noun Fem. cardigan.

rebelarse reflexive verb [17] to rebel.

rebelde noun Masc./Fem. rebel.

rebelde adjective **1** rebel; **2** unruly; **3 una tos rebelde** a persistent cough.

rebelión noun Fem. rebellion.

rebobinar verb [17] rewind.

rebotar verb [17] **1** to bounce; **la pelota rebotó en el poste** the ball bounced off the post; **2** to ricochet.

rebuznar verb [17] to bray.

recado noun Masc. **1** message; **no han dejado recado** they didn't leave a message; **2** errand; **hacer un recado** to run an errand.

recalentar verb [29] reheat.

recambio noun Masc. **1** spare part; **2** refill (*for a pen*).

recepción noun Fem. reception.

recepcionista noun Masc./Fem. receptionist.

receta noun Fem. **1** recipe; **2** prescription.

recetar verb [17] to prescribe.

recibidor noun Masc. entrance hall.

recibir verb [19] **1** to receive; **he recibido una carta de Lola** I've received a letter from Lola; **2** to get; **recibí una llamada del editor** I got a phone call from the editor; **3 recibir a alguien con los brazos abiertos** to welcome somebody with open arms; **4 ir a recibir a alguien** to go to meet somebody;

fuimos a recibirlos a la estación we went to meet them at the station; **5** (*ending a letter*) **recibe un fuerte abrazo** best wishes; **reciba un cordial saludo** yours sincerely.

recibo noun Masc. receipt.

reciclar verb [17] recycle.

recién adverb **1** pasteles recién hechos freshly baked cakes; **'recién pintado'** 'wet paint'; **2 un recién nacido** a newborn baby; **los recién casados** the newly-weds; **los recién llegados** the newcomers.

reciente adjective recent.

recientemente adverb recently.

recipiente noun Masc. container.

recitar verb [17] to recite.

reclamación noun Fem. **1** complaint; **hacer una reclamación** to make a complaint; **2** reclamación Fem.; **hacer una reclamación al seguro** to make a claim on insurance.

reclamar verb [17] **1** to complain; **2** to demand (*rights, money*).

recoger verb [3] **1** to pick up; **recoge ese papel del suelo** pick up that piece of paper off the floor; **fui a recogerlos a la estación** I went to pick them up from the station; **2** to tidy up; **tienes que recoger tu habitación** you have to tidy up your room; **3 recoger la mesa** to clear the table; **4** to collect (*money or signatures*); **5** to pick (*fruit or flowers*).

recogerse reflexive verb [3]

recogerse el pelo to tie your hair back.

recogida noun Fem. collection.

recomendación noun Fem. 1 recommendation; 2 reference (for a job).

recomendar verb [29] to recommend.

recompensa noun Fem. reward.

recompensar verb [17] to reward.

reconciliarse reflexive verb [17] **reconciliarse con alguien** to make it up with somebody.

reconocer verb [35] **1** to recognize; **al principio no la reconocí** I didn't recognize her to start with; **2** to admit (a mistake); **3** to examine (a patient).

reconocimiento noun Masc. **1 reconocimiento médico** medical examination; **2** reconnaissance.

reconozca, etc. verb SEE **reconocer**.

récord noun Masc. record.

recordar verb [24] **1** to remember; **si mal no recuerdo** if I remember rightly; **recuerdo que terminamos a las tres** I remember that we finished at three; **2** to remind; **me recuerda mucho a ella** he reminds me of her a lot; **3 recordarle a alguien que haga algo** to remind somebody to do something; **recuérdale que traiga los papeles** remind him to bring the papers.

recreo noun Masc. break (at school).

recta[1] noun Fem. straight line.

rectángulo noun Masc. rectangle.

recto/recta[2] adjective **1** straight; **2** honest.

recto adverb **seguir todo recto** to carry straight on.

recuerda, recuerdo[1]**, etc.** verb SEE **recordar**.

recuerdo[2] noun Masc. **1** memory; **tengo buenos recuerdos** I've got happy memories; **2** souvenir; **'recuerdo de España'** 'souvenir from Spain'; **3 recuerdos** regards; **dale recuerdos a tu hermana de mi parte** say hello to your sister from me.

recuperar verb [17] **1** to recover (money, strength); **2 recuperar tiempo** to make up for lost time.

recuperarse reflexive verb [17] **recuperarse de una enfermedad** to recover from an illness.

red noun Fem. **1** net; **2** network; **3 la Red** the Net (Internet); ★ **caer en las redes de alguien** to fall into somebody's clutches.

redacción noun Fem. **1** essay; **2** editorial team.

redactor/redactora noun Masc./Fem. editor.

redondo/redonda adjective round; **en números redondos** in round figures.

reducción noun Fem. reduction.

reducir verb [60] to reduce.

reduje, reduzca, reduzco, etc. verb SEE **reducir**.

reembolsar verb [17] to refund.

reembolso noun Masc. refund.

a **reemplazar** *verb* [22] **reemplazar a alguien** to stand in for somebody.

b **reemplazo** *noun Masc.* replacement.

c **referencia** *noun Fem.* reference; **hacer referencia a** to refer to.

d **referirse** *reflexive verb* [14] **referirse a** to refer to; **se refiere a ti** she's referring to you.

e **refiera, refiero, refiramos, refirió, etc.** *verb* SEE **referirse**.

f **reflejar** [17] to reflect. **reflejarse** *reflexive verb* [17] to be reflected.

g **reflejo** *noun Masc.* **1** reflection; **2** reflejos highlights; **3** reflejos reflexes.

h **reflexión** *noun Fem.* reflection.

i **reflexionar** *verb* [17] to reflect on; **después de reflexionarlo bien** after thinking it over.

j **reforestación** *Fem.* reforestation.

k **refrán** *noun Masc.* saying.

l **refrescante** *adjective* refreshing.

m **refrescar** *verb* [31] to refresh.

n **refresco** *noun Masc.* soft drink.

ñ **refrigerio** *noun Masc.* light refreshments.

o **refugiado/refugiada** *noun Masc./Fem.* refugee.

p **refugiarse** *reflexive verb* [17] **refugiarse de** to take refuge from.

q **refugio** *noun Masc.* shelter; **dar refugio a alguien** to give somebody shelter; **un refugio de montaña** a mountain refuge.

r **regadera** *noun Fem.* watering can; ★ **estar como una regadera**

s (*informal*) to be raving mad (*literally: to be like a watering can*).

regalar *verb* [17] **1** to give (*as a present*); **mis padrinos me han regalado un reloj** my godparents have bought me a watch; **¿qué vas a regalarle por Navidad?** what are you going to get her for Christmas?; **2** to give away; **me ha regalado su abrigo** he's given his coat to me; **¿te gusta? te lo regalo** do you like it? you can have it.

regalo *noun Masc.* **1** present; **regalo de cumpleaños** birthday present; **2** compre dos y llévese uno de regalo buy two and get one free.

regañar *verb* [17] **1** to tell off; **mi madre me regañó por llegar tarde** my mother told me off because I got home late; **2** regañar con alguien to quarrel with somebody; **ha regañado con su hermano** he's had an argument with his brother.

regar *verb* [30] to water.

régimen *noun Masc.* diet; **ponerse a régimen** to go on a diet.

región *noun Fem.* region.

regional *adjective* regional.

registrar *verb* [17] **1** to search; **nos registraron** we were searched; **la policía registró la casa** the police searched the house; **2** to go through; **me registró todos los papeles** he went through all my papers; **3** to register (*a birth, for example*); **4** to record (*temperature*).

registrarse *reflexive verb* [17]

1 to register; **2** to check in; **she checked in at five o'clock** se registró a las cinco.

registro noun Masc. **1** register; **2 el registro civil** the registry office; **3** search.

regla noun Fem. **1** ruler (for measuring); **2** rule; **por regla general** as a general rule; **3 estar con la regla** to have your period.

reglamento noun Masc. regulations.

regresar verb [17] to return.

regreso noun Masc. return.

regular adjective **1** regular; **2** poor (mark); **3** de tamaño regular medium-sized; **4** por lo regular as a general rule.

regular adverb '¿qué tal está tu padre?' – 'regular' 'how's your father?' – 'so-so'.

regularidad noun Fem. regularity; **con regularidad** regularly.

rehacer verb [7] **1 rehacer algo** to do something again; **2 rehizo su vida** she rebuilt her life.

reina noun Fem. queen.

reinado noun Masc. reign; **durante el reinado del rey Juan Carlos** during the reign of King Juan Carlos.

reinar verb [17] to reign.

reino noun Masc. kingdom.

Reino Unido noun Masc. United Kingdom.

reír verb [61] to laugh; **echarse a reír** to start laughing.

reírse reflexive verb [61] **reírse de** to laugh about; **siempre se están riendo de mí** they're always laughing at me; **reírse a carcajadas** to roar with laughter.

reja noun Fem. **1** railing; **2** grille; **estar entre rejas** to be behind bars.

relación noun Fem. **1** relationship; **2 relaciones públicas** public relations; **3** connection; **en relación con** mix with (people).

relacionado/relacionada adjective related.

relacionar verb [17] to relate; **relacionar algo con algo** to relate something to something.

relacionarse reflexive verb [17] to be related (facts, for example); **relacionarse con** to mix with (a person).

relajar verb [17] to relax.

relajarse reflexive verb [17] to relax.

relámpago noun Masc. flash of lightning; ★ **como un relámpago** like greased lightning.

religión noun Fem. religion.

religioso/religiosa adjective religious.

rellenar verb [17] **1 rellenar un impreso** to fill in a form; **2** to fill up; **3** to stuff (a chicken, for example).

relleno¹ noun Masc. **1** filling; **2** stuffing.

relleno²/rellena adjective **1** filled; **2** stuffed (peppers, for example).

reloj noun Masc. **1** clock; **un reloj despertador** an alarm clock; **2** watch; **un reloj de pulsera** a

a b c d e f g h i j k l m n ñ o p q r s t u v w x y z

a
b
c
d
e
f
g
h
i
j
k
l
m
n
ñ
o
p
q
r
s
t
u
v
w
x
y
z

wristwatch; **mi reloj va atrasado** my watch is slow.

relojería *noun Fem.* watchmaker's.

remar *verb* [17] to row.

remate *noun Masc.* **1** smash (*in tennis*); **2** finish (*in football*); **un remate de cabeza** a header; **3** end (*of a pole, for example*); **4** top (*of a tower, for example*); **5 y para remate** and to cap it all; ★ **loco de remate** (*informal*) completely nuts.

remediar *verb* [17] **1** to remedy; **2 no lo puede remediar** he can't help it; **no pudimos remediarlo** we couldn't do anything about it.

remedio *noun Masc.* **1** remedy; **remedios naturales** natural remedies; **2 si no queda más remedio** if there's no other alternative; **no queda más remedio que aguantarse** we had to put up with it, there was nothing else we could do; **no tuvimos más remedio que ir** we had no other option but to go; **¡qué remedio me queda!** what else can I do!; **eso ya no tiene remedio** there's nothing we can do about it now.

remendar *verb* [29] to mend.

remite *noun Masc.* return address.

remitente *noun Masc./Fem.* sender (*of a letter*).

remo *noun Masc.* oar.

remojar *verb* [17] to soak.

remojo *noun Masc.* **poner algo en remojo** to soak something.

remolacha *noun Fem.* beetroot.

remolcar *verb* [31] to tow.

remolino *noun Masc.* whirlpool.

remolque *noun Masc.* **1** trailer; **2 llevar algo a remolque** to tow something.

remorder *verb* [38] **aún me remuerde la conciencia** I still feel guilty about it.

remoto/remota *adjective* remote.

remover *verb* [38] **1** to stir (*a sauce, for example*); **2** to toss (*a salad*); **3** to turn over (*soil*).

remueva, remuevo, etc. *verb* SEE **remover.**

renacuajo *noun Masc.* tadpole.

rencor *noun Masc.* **guardarle rencor a alguien** to bear someone a grudge.

rendición *noun Fem.* surrender.

rendir *verb* [57] **1 rendirle homenaje a alguien** to pay tribute to someone; **2 ayer me rindió mucho en el trabajo** I managed to get a lot done yesterday at work. **rendirse** *reflexive verb* [57] to surrender.

RENFE *abbreviation Fem.* (*short for: Red Nacional de Ferrocarriles Españoles*) the Spanish national rail network.

renglón *noun Masc.* line.

renta *noun Fem.* **1** rent; **2** income.

rentable *adjective* profitable.

renunciar *verb* [17] **renunciar a** to renounce, to give up; **renunciar a un puesto** to resign from a job.

reparación noun Fem. repair; **taller de reparaciones** repair shop.

reparar verb [17] **1** to repair; **2** to mend.

repartir verb [19] **1** to deliver; **2** to hand out (*leaflets, for example*); **3** to distribute; **lo repartiremos entre todos nosotros** we'll share it between us.

reparto noun Masc. **1** delivery; **reparto a domicilio** home delivery service; **2** distribution; **hacer el reparto del dinero** to share out the money.

repasar verb [17] **1** to revise; **repasar los apuntes** to revise your notes; **2** to check through (*a list*).

repaso noun Masc. **1** revision; **dar un repaso a los apuntes** to revise your notes; **2** check (*for mistakes*).

repente in phrase **de repente** all of a sudden.

repentino/repentina adjective sudden.

repetición noun Fem. repetition.

repetición de la jugada noun Fem. action replay.

repetir verb [57] to repeat; **¿quieres repetir?** would you like a second helping?

repisa noun Fem. **1** ledge (*of window*); **2** mantelpiece (*of chimney*).

repita, repitió, repito, etc. verb SEE **repetir**.

repleto/repleta adjective full up; **estar repleto de algo** to be packed with something; **una sala repleta**

de gente a room packed with people.

repollo noun Masc. cabbage.

reponer verb [11] **1** to replace; **2** to repay; **3 reponer fuerzas** to get your strength back.

reponerse reflexive verb [11] to recover; **cuando me repuse del susto** when I recovered from the shock.

reportaje noun Masc. **1** article (*in a newspaper*); **2** report (*on TV*).

reportero/reportera noun Masc./Fem. reporter.

reposar verb [17] **1** to rest; **2 dejar reposar** to leave to stand.

reposo noun Masc. rest.

repostería noun Fem. confectionery.

representante noun Masc./Fem. representative.

representar verb [17] **1** to represent; **2 representar una obra** to perform a play; **representar un papel** to play a part.

reproducción noun Fem. reproduction.

reproducir verb [60] to reproduce. **reproducirse** reflexive verb [60] to reproduction.

reptil noun Masc. reptile.

república noun Fem. republic.

República Checa noun Fem. **la República Checa** the Czech Republic.

repugnante adjective disgusting.

repulsivo/repulsiva adjective repulsive.

reputación noun Fem. reputation.

a
b
c
d
e
f
g
h
i
j
k
l
m
n
ñ
o
p
q
r
s
t
u
v
w
x
y
z

a
b
c
d
e
f
g
h
i
j
k
l
m
n
ñ
o
p
q
r
s
t
u
v
w
x
y
z

requisito noun Masc. requirement.

resaca noun Fem. hangover.

resbaladizo/resbaladiza adjective slippery.

resbalar verb [17] to slip.
resbalarse reflexive verb [17] to slip.

rescatar verb [17] to rescue.

rescate noun Masc. rescue; **una operación de rescate** a rescue operation.

reserva noun Fem. 1 reservation; **hacer una reserva** to make a reservation; 2 reserve; **jugadores de reserva** reserve players; **una reserva natural** a nature reserve; 3 **tengo otro de reserva** I have a spare one; 4 **tengo mis reservas** I have my reservations.

reservado/reservada adjective reserved.

reservar verb [17] 1 to reserve; 2 to book.

resfriado noun Masc. cold; **tener un resfriado** to have a cold.

resfriarse reflexive verb [32] to catch a cold.

residencia noun Fem.
1 residence; **permiso de residencia** residence permit;
2 hall of residence; 3 **residencia de ancianos** old people's home.

residir verb [19] **residir en** to live in.

resistencia noun Fem.
1 resistance; 2 element (electrical);
3 **tener mucha resistencia** to have a lot of stamina.

resistir verb [19] 1 to resist; 2 to stand (pain or cold); **¡no puedo resistirlo!** I can't stand it!
resistirse reflexive verb [19] to resist.

resolver verb [45] 1 to solve; 2 to resolve.

resorte noun Masc. spring.

respaldo noun Masc. 1 back; 2 backing.

respecto noun Masc. **respecto a** ... regarding ....

respetable adjective respectable.

respetar verb [17] to respect.

respeto noun Masc. respect.

respiración noun Fem. breathing; **contener la respiración** to hold your breath.

respirar verb [17] to breathe.

responder verb [18] 1 to answer; **responder a algo** to answer something; 2 to respond; 3 to answer back; **¡a mí no me respondas!** don't answer back!

responsabilidad noun Fem. responsibility.

responsable noun Masc./Fem.
1 person in charge; **el responsable de ventas** the person in charge of sales; 2 person responsible.

responsable adjective responsible.

respuesta noun Fem. 1 answer; 2 response.

restante adjective remaining; **lo restante** the remainder.

restar verb [17] to subtract, to take away.

restaurante noun Masc.
restaurant.

restaurar verb [17] to restore.

resto noun Masc. **1** rest; **el resto de los libros** the rest of the books;
2 restos remains; **los restos del castillo** the remains of the castle;
3 restos leftovers (from a meal).

restricción noun Fem.
restriction.

restringir verb [49] to restrict.
restringirse reflexive verb [49]
to restrict yourself.

resultado noun Masc. **1** result;
2 outcome; **3 dar resultado** to
work (a plan or an idea).

resultar verb [17] **1** to work (a plan or an idea); **2 así resulta más fácil** it's easy this way; **resultó imposible convencerlo** it was impossible to convince him.

resumen noun Masc. summary.

resumir verb [19] **1** to summarize;
2 to sum up.

retener verb [9] **1** to retain; **2** to keep back.

retirar verb [17] **1** to withdraw;
2 to move back; **retira esa silla** move that chair back.
retirarse reflexive verb [17] **1** to withdraw; **2** to move back.
retrasado/retrasada noun Masc./Fem. mentally handicapped.
retrasado adjective **1** mentally handicapped; **2 vamos muy retrasados con el trabajo** we're very late with the job; **3 me reloj va retrasado** my watch is slow.

retrasar verb [17] **1** to delay (departure); **2** to postpone;

3 retrasar un reloj to put a clock back.
retrasarse reflexive verb [17]
1 to be late; **me retrasé diez minutos** I was ten minutes late;
2 to fall behind; **voy retrasado con mi trabajo** I'm behind with my work.

retraso noun Masc. **1** delay; **una media hora de retraso** a half-hour delay; **llevan retraso** they're late;
2 con retraso late; **llegaron con retraso** they arrived late.

retrato noun Masc. portrait; ★ **ser el vivo retrato de alguien** to be the spitting image of somebody.

retrovisor noun Masc. **1** rear-view mirror; **2** wing mirror.

reuma, reúma, reumatismo noun Masc. rheumatism.

reunión noun Fem. **1** meeting;
2 gathering; **3** reunion; **una reunión de antiguos alumnos** a reunion of former pupils.

reunir verb [62] **1** to gather (information, for example); **2** to have; **reúne los elementos que busco** it has everything I'm looking for; **no reúne los requisitos necesarios** it doesn't satisfy the necessary requirements; **3 reunir dinero** to raise money.
reunirse reflexive verb [62] to meet.

revancha noun Fem. **1** return game; **jugar la revancha** to play a rematch; **2 tomarse la revancha** to get your own back.

a b c d e f g h i j k l m n ñ o p q r s t u v w x y z

a

revelar verb [17] **1** to reveal; **2** to develop (a film).

reverencia noun Fem. bow, curtsey; **hacer una reverencia** to bow, to curtsey.

reverso noun Masc. back.

revés noun Masc. **1** back; **el revés de la página** the back of the page; **2** inside; **el revés del abrigo** the inside of the coat; **3 se puso el jersey al revés** he put his jumper on inside out, he put his jumper on back-to-front; **ese cuadro está al revés** that picture's upside down; **4 del revés** inside out.

revisar verb [17] **1** to check; **2** to revise; **3** to service.

revisión noun Fem. **1** (medical) checkup; **2** revision; **3** service (for a car or a machine).

revisor/revisora noun Masc./ Fem. ticket inspector.

revista noun Fem. magazine.

revolución noun Fem. revolution.

revolver verb [45] **1** to stir (soup or sauce); **2 me revolvieron todos los cajones** they went through all my drawers; **le habían revuelto todos sus papeles** they'd left all his papers in a mess.

revólver noun Masc. gun.

revuelto/revuelta adjective **1** in a mess; **los papeles estaban todos revueltos** all the papers were in a mess; **2** rough (sea); **3** unsettled (weather).

rey noun Masc. **1** king; **2 los reyes** the king and queen.

rezar verb [22] to pray.

ría, rían, etc. verb SEE **reír.**

riada noun Fem. flood.

ribera noun Fem. riverbank.

rico/rica noun Masc./Fem. rich person; **los ricos** the rich.

rico adjective rich.

ridículo[1] noun Masc. **hacer el ridículo** to make a fool of yourself; **dejar a alguien en ridículo** to make a fool of somebody.

ridículo[2]**/ridícula** adjective ridiculous.

ríe, ríen, etc. verb SEE **reír.**

riega, riego, riegue, etc. verb SEE **regar.**

rienda noun Fem. rein.

riesgo noun Masc. risk; **correr un riesgo** to run a risk; **voy a correr el riesgo** I'll take the risk; **un riesgo para la salud** a health hazard.

rifa noun Fem. raffle.

rímel noun Masc. mascara.

rincón noun Masc. **1** corner (of a room); **2 estará en algún rincón** it must be somewhere; **3 un rincón pintoresco** a lovely spot (in the country).

rinoceronte noun Masc. rhinoceros.

riña noun Fem. **1** fight; **una riña callejera** a street fight; **2** quarrel; **tuvo una riña con su novio** she had a quarrel with her boyfriend.

riñón noun Masc. **1** kidney; **2 tener dolor de riñones** to have backache.

río noun Masc. river; **ir río abajo** to go downstream.

rió verb SEE **reir**.

riqueza noun Fem. wealth.

risa noun Fem. **1** laugh; **una risa histérica** an hysterical laugh; **2 risas** laughter; **las risas del público** the laughter of the audience; **3 me dio risa verlo** seeing him made me laugh; **de repente le dio la risa** suddenly he got the giggles; **4 ¡qué risa!** how funny!; **5 morirse de risa** (informal) to die laughing.

ritmo noun Masc. rhythm; **llevar el ritmo** to keep time; **marcar el ritmo** to beat time.

rival noun Masc./Fem. rival.

rizado/rizada adjective curly.

rizo noun Masc. curl.

robar verb [17] **1** to steal; **robarle algo a alguien** to steal something from somebody; **2** to rob; **robar un banco** to rob a bank; **3 robar en una casa** to burgle a house; **les robaron mientras estaban de vacaciones** they were burgled while they were away; **4** to rip (somebody) off.

roble noun Masc. oak.

robo noun Masc. **1** theft; **2** robbery; **3** burglary; **4** break in; **5 ¡esto es un robo!** this is a rip-off!.

roca noun Fem. rock; ★ **firme como una roca** solid as a rock.

rocío noun Masc. dew.

rodaja noun Fem. slice; **cortar en rodajas** to slice.

rodar verb [24] **1** to roll (a ball, for example); **2** to turn (a wheel); **3** to shoot (a film).

rodeado/rodeada adjective surrounded; **rodeado de** surrounded by.

rodear verb [17] to surround.

rodilla noun Fem. knee; **ponerse de rodillas** to kneel down.

rogar verb [24] **1** to beg; **te ruego que me perdones** I beg you to forgive me; **2 'se ruega no fumar'** 'no smoking'.

rojo[1] noun Masc. red.

rojo[2]**/roja** adjective red; **ponerse rojo** to turn red.

rollo noun Masc. **1** roll; **un rollo de tela** a roll of fabric; **un rollo de papel higiénico** a toilet roll; **2** coil (of rope, wire); **3** (informal) bore; **¡vaya rollo de película!** what a boring film!; **4** (informal) business.

romántico/romántica adjective romantic.

rompecabezas noun Masc. (does not change in the plural) puzzle.

romper verb [40] **1** to break; **vas a romper la silla** you're going to break the chair; **2** to tear; **rompió la carta en pedazos** he tore up the letter; **3 romper algo en mil pedazos** to smash something to pieces.
romperse reflexive verb [40] to break; **la lámpara se ha roto** the lamp has broken; **romperse una pierna** to break your leg.

a
b
c
d
e
f
g
h
i
j
k
l
m
n
ñ
o
p
q
r
s
t
u
v
w
x
y
z

rompiente noun Masc. breaker (wave).

ron noun Masc. rum.

roncar verb [31] to snore.

ronco/ronca adjective hoarse; **quedarse ronco** to go hoarse.

ronda noun Fem. **1** round; **esta ronda la pago yo** it's my round; **2** patrol.

ronronear verb [31] to purr.

ropa noun Fem. **1** clothes; **tengo mucha ropa** I have a lot of clothes; **2 cambiarse de ropa** to get changed; **3 la ropa sucia** the dirty laundry; **4 ropa interior** underwear.

ropero noun Masc. wardrobe.

rosa[1] noun Fem. rose.

rosa[2] noun Masc., adjective pink.

rosado[1]**/rosada** adjective pink.

rosado[2] noun Masc. **1** rosé (wine); **2** pink.

rosario noun Masc. rosary.

rosbif noun Masc. roast beef.

rostro noun Masc. **1** face; **2** nerve; **¡vaya rostro que tiene!** (informal) he's got a nerve!.

roto/rota adjective **1** broken; **2** torn; **3** worn out (shoes).

rotulador noun Masc. felt-tip pen.

rubio/rubia adjective blonde.

ruborizarse reflexive verb [22] to blush.

rueda noun Fem. **1** wheel; **la rueda de repuesto** the spare wheel; **la rueda delantera** the front wheel; **2 una rueda de prensa** a press conference.

rugir verb [49] to roar.

ruido noun Masc. noise; **hacer ruido** to make a noise.

ruidoso/ruidosa adjective noisy.

ruina noun Fem. **1** ruin; **dejar a alguien en la ruina** to ruin somebody; **la empresa está en la ruina** the company is in a terrible state; **2 ruinas** ruins; **las ruinas del castillo** the ruins of the castle; **estar en ruinas** to be in ruins; ★ **estar hecho una ruina** (informal) to be a wreck.

ruiseñor noun Masc. nightingale.

rulo noun Masc. roller (curler).

Rumania, Rumanía noun Fem. Romania.

rumano/rumana noun Masc./ Fem., adjective Romanian.

rumbo noun Masc. **1** course; **poner rumbo a** to set a course for; **el rumbo que tomaron los acontecimientos** the course of events; **2** direction; **3 con rumbo a** to be heading for; **4 sin rumbo fijo** aimlessly.

rumor noun Masc. **1** rumour; **2** murmur.

Rusia noun Fem. Russia.

ruso[1] noun Masc. Russian (the language).

ruso[2]**/rusa** noun Masc./Fem., adjective Russian.

ruta noun Fem. route.

rutina noun Fem. routine; **por rutina** out of habit.

a
b
c
d
e
f
g
h
i
j
k
l
m
n
ñ
o
p
q
r
s
t
u
v
w
x
y
z

Ss

sábado noun Masc. Saturday (see 'domingo' for examples).

sábana noun Fem. sheet (for a bed).

saber noun Masc. knowledge.

saber verb [13] **1** to know; **ya lo sé** I know; **no sabe** he doesn't know; **sabía que no iba a querer hacerlo** I knew he wouldn't want to do it; **2 saber algo de memoria** to know something by heart; **3 ¿sabes montar en bicicleta?** can you ride a bike?; **sabe hablar inglés muy bien** she can speak English very well; **no sé alemán** I can't speak German; **4** to find out; **lo supe por su hermana** I found out through her sister; **5** to taste; **la comida sabía muy rica** the food tasted very nice; **¡qué mal sabe!** it tastes disgusting!; **6 saber a** to taste of; **sabe a fresa** it tastes of strawberry.

sabiduría noun Fem. wisdom.

sabio/sabia adjective wise.

sabor noun Masc. taste; **sabor a fresa** strawberry-flavoured.

sabrá, sabré, sabría, etc. verb SEE **saber**.

sabroso/sabrosa adjective tasty.

sacacorchos noun Masc. (does not change in the plural) corkscrew.

sacapuntas noun Masc. (does not change in the plural) pencil sharpener.

sacar verb [31] **1** to take out; **sacó su monedero del bolso** she took her purse out of her bag; **lo saqué de la caja** I took it out of the box; **sacar la basura** to take the rubbish out; **sacar al perro a pasear** to take the dog for a walk; **2 sacar la pistola** to draw a gun; **3** to get; **sacar entradas** to get tickets; **aún no he sacado los billetes** I haven't got the tickets yet; **4 sacar buenas notas** to get good marks; **he sacado un siete en matemáticas** I got seven (out of ten) in maths; **5 sacar una foto** to take a picture; **6 sacar una fotocopia** to make a photocopy; **7 sacar un libro** to publish a book; **sacar un disco** to release a record; **8 sacar la lengua** to stick your tongue out; **9** to serve (in tennis); **te toca a ti sacar** it's your service; **10** to kick off (in football).

sacarse reflexive verb [31] **1 sacarse una muela** to have a tooth out; **2 sacarse una foto** to have one's photograph taken; **me saqué una foto frente al palacio** I had my photograph taken in front of the palace.

sacerdote noun Masc. priest.

saco noun Masc. sack; **un saco de dormir** a sleeping bag.

sacrificar verb [31] to sacrifice.

sacrificio noun Masc. sacrifice.

sacudida noun Fem. **1** shake; **le di una sacudida** I gave it a shake; **2 el coche iba dando sacudidas** the car was jerking along.

sacudir verb [19] **1** to shake; **2** to shake off; **sacudió las migas del**

a
b
c
d
e
f
g
h
i
j
k
l
m
n
ñ
o
p
q
r
s
t
u
v
w
x
y
z

mantel she shook the crumbs off the tablecloth.

sacudirse *reflexive verb* [19] to shake off; **se sacudió el polvo de la chaqueta** he shook off the dust from his jacket.

sagaz *adjective* shrewd.

sagitario *noun Masc./Fem.* Sagittarius; **es sagitario** she's Sagittarius.

Sagitario *noun Masc.* Sagittarius.

sagrado/sagrada *adjective* **1** sacred; **2** holy.

sal *noun Fem.* salt; **sales de baño** bath salts.

sala *noun Fem.* **1** room; **una sala de estar** a living room; **una sala de espera** a waiting room; **2** hall; **una sala de exposiciones** an exhibition hall; **3** ward (*in a hospital*); **4 una sala de fiestas** a night club.

salado/salada *adjective* salted; **está muy salado** it's too salty; **agua salada** salt water.

salario *noun* **1** wages (*when weekly*); **2** salary (*when monthly*).

salchicha *noun Fem.* sausage.

salchichón *noun Masc.* salami sausage.

saldar *verb* [17] **1** to settle (*a debt*); **2** to sell off.

saldo *noun Masc.* **1** balance; **saldo positivo** credit balance; **saldo negativo** debit balance; **2** settlement; **3** saldos sales; **precios de saldo** sale prices.

saldrá, saldré, saldría, salga, salgo, etc. *verb* SEE **salir.**

salero *noun Masc.* **1** salt cellar; **2 tener mucho salero** (*informal*) to be very funny.

salida *noun Fem.* exit.

salir *verb* [63] **1** to go out; **salen mucho por la noche** they go out a lot in the evenings; **2** to come out; **salieron uno a uno** they came out one by one; **3** to get out; **no pude salir** I couldn't get out; **4** to leave; **el vuelo sale a las cinco** the flight leaves at five; **5 salgo de casa a las ocho** I leave home at eight; **no sale nunca de su habitación** he never leaves his room; **salió de la casa corriendo** he ran out of the house; **sal de debajo de la cama** come out from under the bed; **6 salir con alguien** to go out with someone; **sale con mi hermano** she's going out with my brother; **7 salir en la televisión** to appear on television; **la noticia salió en el periódico** the news was in the paper; **8** to turn out; **las cosas salieron mal** things turned out badly; **todo salió como esperábamos** everything turned out as we expected; **9 las vacaciones nos salieron muy caras** the holidays were very expensive in the end; **si compras tres, sale más barato** it's cheaper if you buy three; **10 ¿cómo te salieron las cosas en Inglaterra?** how did things turn out for you in England?; **le sale muy bien la tortilla de patatas** he can cook a really good Spanish omelette; **el retrato te ha salido perfecto** you've done a perfect portrait; **el**

examen me salió fatal I did terribly in the exam; **11 me ha salido un grano** I've got a spot; **le están saliendo canas** his hair's starting to go grey; **le salía sangre de la nariz** his nose was bleeding.

salirse *reflexive verb* [63] **1** to leave; **el cantante se ha salido del grupo** the singer has left the group; **salirse del colegio** to leave school; **2** to leak; **3 el agua se salió del fregadero** the sink overflowed; **se ha salido la leche** the milk has boiled over; **4 el coche se salió de la carretera** the car went off the road.

saliva *noun Fem.* saliva.

salmón *noun Masc.* salmon; **salmón ahumado** smoked salmon.

salmón *adjective* salmon-pink.

salón *noun Masc.* **1** living room; **2** function room; **3** salón de belleza beauty salon; **4** salón de actos assembly hall; **5** salón de fiestas reception room.

salpicar *verb* [31] to splash.

salsa *noun Fem.* **1** sauce; **salsa besamel** white sauce; **2** gravy; **3** salsa (*music*).

saltamontes *noun Masc.* grasshopper.

saltar *verb* [17] to jump; **saltar por encima de la verja** to jump over the fence; **saltar un muro** to jump over a wall; **saltar al suelo** to jump to the ground; **saltar de la cama** to jump out of bed.

saltarse *reflexive verb* [17] **1** to skip (*a page or an appointment*); **2 se saltaron un semáforo en rojo** they drove through a red light.

salto *noun Masc.* jump; **dar un salto** to jump; **ponerse de pie de un salto** to jump to your feet; **levantarse de un salto de la cama** to leap out of bed; **salto de altura** high jump.

salud *noun Fem.* health; **estar bien de salud** to be in good health.

salud *exclamation* cheers!; **¡a tu salud!** cheers!

saludable *adjective* healthy.

saludar *verb* [17] **1** to say hello; **nos saludó con la mano** she waved hello to us; **2 'le saluda atentamente'** 'Yours sincerely', 'Yours faithfully' (*ending a letter*).

saludo *noun Masc.* **1** greeting; **te envían sus saludos** they send their regards; **dale saludos de mi parte** give him my regards; **2 Un afectuoso saludo** Best wishes.

salvadoreño/salvadoreña *noun* Salvadorean.

salvadoreño *adjective* Salvadorean.

salvaje *adjective* **1** savage; **2** wild.

salvaje *noun Masc./Fem.* savage.

salvamanteles *noun Masc.* (*does not change in the plural*) table mat.

salvamento *noun Masc.* rescue; **bote de salvamento** lifeboat; **operación de salvamento** rescue operation.

salvar *verb* [17] to save.

salvarse *reflexive verb* [17] to survive.

salvavidas *noun Masc.* (*does not change in the plural*) life jacket.

a b c d e f g h i j k l m n ñ o p q r s t u v w x y z

salvo[1]/**salva** *adjective* safe.

salvo[2] *preposition, conjunction* except; **salvo que** unless.

salvo *in phrase* **estar a salvo** to be out of danger; **ponerse a salvo** to reach safety.

San *adjective* St (*Saint*).

San Salvador *noun Masc.* San Salvador.

sanar *verb* [17] **1** to recover (*patient*); **2** to heal (*injury*).

sandalia *noun Fem.* sandal.

sandía *noun Fem.* watermelon.

sándwich *noun Masc.* sandwich.

sangrar *verb* [17] to bleed.

sangre *noun Fem.* blood; **te sale sangre** you're bleeding.

sangría *noun Fem.* sangria (*a fruit punch made with red wine and lemonade*).

sano/sana *adjective* **1** healthy; **2** **sano y salvo** safe and sound.

santo[1] *noun Masc.* name day (*in Spain each day of the year is associated with the name of a saint and many people celebrate the day of the saint they are named after*).

santo[2]/**santa** *noun Masc./Fem.* saint; **tener la paciencia de un santo** to have the patience of a saint.

santo *adjective* holy.

santuario *noun* shrine.

sapo *noun Masc.* toad.

saque *noun Masc.* **1** serve (*in tennis*); **2** kick-off (*in football*); **saque de banda** throw in; **saque de esquina** corner kick.

sarampión *noun Masc.* measles.

sarcasmo *noun Masc.* sarcasm.

sardina *noun Fem.* sardine.

sargento *noun Masc./Fem.* sergeant.

sarpullido *noun Masc.* rash; **me ha salido un sarpullido** I've come out in a rash.

sartén *noun Fem.* frying pan.

sastre *noun Masc./Fem.* tailor.

satélite *noun Masc.* satellite.

satén *noun Masc.* satin.

satisfacción *noun Fem.* satisfaction.

satisfacer *verb* [7] to satisfy; **la calidad del producto no nos satisface** we are not satisfied with the quality of the product; **para satisfacer mi curiosidad** to satisfy my curiosity.

satisfacerse *reflexive verb* [7] to be satisfied.

satisfecho/satisfecha *adjective* satisfied; **estamos muy satisfechos con los resultados** we are very happy with the results.

sauce *noun Masc.* willow.

saxofón *noun Masc.* saxophone.

sazonado/sazonada *adjective* seasoned.

sazonar *verb* [17] to season.

se *pronoun* **1** himself/herself; **se cortó** he cut himself/she cut herself; **2** itself; **se desconecta solo** it disconnects itself; **3** themselves; **¿se han portado bien?** did they behave themselves?; **4** yourself (*polite form*); **espero que no se haya hecho daño** I hope you haven't hurt yourself; **5** yourselves (*polite form*); **¿se han divertido ustedes?** did you enjoy yourselves?; **6** him/her; **no se lo pregunté** I didn't ask him/I didn't ask her; **7** to him/to her; **se lo mandaré** I'll send it to him/I'll send it to her; **8** them; **cuando las vea se lo preguntaré** I'll ask them when I see them; **9** to them; **cuando las vea se lo daré** I'll give it to them when I see them; **10** you (*polite form*); **se lo dije a usted ayer** I told you yesterday; **11** to you (*polite form*); **se lo di a usted ayer** I gave it to you yesterday; **12** each other; **se quieren** they love each other; **se miraron** they looked at each other; **13** (*with parts of your body and personal belongings*); **se lavó las manos** he washed his hands/she washed her hands; **¿se ha cortado usted el dedo?** have you cut your finger?; **se pusieron la ropa** they put their clothes on; **14** (*the infinitives of many verbs in Spanish end in '-se' but are not reflexive in English*) **me reí mucho** I laughed a lot; **se cayó** he fell down/she fell down; **se han peleado** they've had a fight; **se levantaron** they stood up; **15** (*used in impersonal phrases*) **'se vende piso'** 'flat for sale'; **se habla inglés** English spoken here; **se hace así** it is done like this; **se corta la hoja en dos** cut the sheet in two.

sé *verb* SEE **saber**.

secador *noun Masc.* **secador de pelo** hairdryer.

secadora *noun Fem.* dryer.

secar *verb* [31] to dry.

secarse *reflexive verb* [31] **1** to dry; **¿cuánto tarda en secarse la pintura?** how long does the paint take to dry?; **la camisa ya se ha secado** the shirt's dry already; **2** to dry yourself; **secarse el pelo** to dry your hair; **secarse las lágrimas** to dry your tears; **sécate las manos con este trapo** dry your hands with this cloth; **3** to dry up.

sección *noun Fem.* **1** section; **2** department.

seco/seca *adjective* **1** dry; **limpieza en seco** dry-cleaning; **2** dried (*flowers, for example*).

secretaría *noun Fem.* secretary's office.

secretario/secretaria *noun Masc./Fem.* secretary.

secreto[1] *noun Masc.* secret.

secreto[2]**/secreta** *adjective* secret.

secuestrador/ secuestradora *noun Masc./ Fem.* **1** highjacker; **2** kidnapper.

secuestrar *verb* [17] **1** to kidnap; **2** to hijack.

secuestro *noun Masc.* **1** kidnapping; **2** hijacking.

secundario/secundaria *adjective* secondary.

sed *noun Fem.* thirst; **tenían sed** they were thirsty; **las patatas fritas me dan sed** crisps make me thirsty.

seda *noun Fem.* silk.

sedal *noun Masc.* fishing line.

a b c d e f g h i j k l m n ñ o p q r s t u v w x y z

sede noun Fem. **la sede de las Olimpiadas** the venue for the Olympics; **la sede de la compañía** the company's head office; **la sede del gobierno** the seat of government.

seguida[1] in phrase **en seguida** straight away; **voy en seguida** I'll be right there.

seguido[1]/**seguida**[2] adjective **1 tres días seguidos** three days in a row; **dan las dos películas seguidas** they show both films one after the other; **los tres autobuses vinieron seguidos** the three buses came one after the other; **2 seguido de** followed by.

seguido[2] adverb straight on; **vaya todo seguido** go straight on.

seguir verb [64] **1** to follow; **seguir a alguien** to follow somebody; **seguir una pista** to follow a trail; **seguir un consejo** to follow a piece of advice; **2** to carry on, to continue; **sigamos** let's carry on; **3 seguir haciendo** to carry on doing; **colgué el teléfono y seguí leyendo** I put down the telephone and carried on reading; **4 seguir haciendo** to be still doing; **siguen viviendo en Sevilla** they're still living in Seville; **5** to go on; **siga todo recto** go straight on; **siga por esta calle** go on down this street.

según preposition **1** according to; **según la ley** according to the law; **2 según parece** apparently; **3 según dijo él** from what he said.

según adverb '¿te interesa apuntarte?' – 'según' 'would you

be interested in enrolling?' – 'it depends'.

según conjunction as; **según los vayas terminando** as you finish them.

segunda[1] noun Fem. **la segunda** second gear.

segundo[1] noun Masc. **1** second; **espera un segundo** wait a moment; **no tardé ni un segundo en hacerlo** it didn't take me a minute to do it; **2 el segundo** the main course.

segundo[2]/**segunda**[2] adjective **1** second; **segunda clase** second class; **viven en el segundo piso** they live on the second floor; **llegar en segundo lugar** to finish in second position; **2 en segundo plano** in the background.

seguridad noun Fem. **1** security; **seguridad nacional** national security; **2** safety; **por razones de seguridad** for safety reasons; **3** certainty; **no lo sé con seguridad** I don't know for certain; **4 seguridad social** social security.

seguro[1] noun Masc. **1** insurance; **hacerse un seguro** to take out insurance; **seguro a todo riesgo** comprehensive insurance; **seguro contra incendios** fire insurance; **¿tienes seguro médico?** have you got medical insurance? **2** clasp (of a bracelet); **3** safety catch (on a weapon); **4 el Seguro Social** Social Security.

seguro[2]/**segura** adjective **1** safe; **la escalera no es muy segura** the ladder isn't very safe; **aquí me**

siento seguro I feel safe here; **2 seguro/segura de sí mismo/mismoes muy segura de sí misma** she's very self-confident; **3** sure; **¿estás seguro de que se pone así?** are you sure this is the way to put it?; **estoy completamente seguro** I'm absolutely certain; **4** definite; **no es seguro todavía** it's not definite yet; **5** reliable; **es un método muy seguro** it's a very reliable method.

seguro³ *adverb* definitely; **irán seguro** they'll definitely go; **seguro que no están** I bet they're not there.

seis *number* **1** six; **tiene seis años** he's six (years old); **2** sixth (*in dates*); **el seis de junio** the sixth of June; **3** six (*in clock time*); **son las seis** it's six o'clock.

seiscientos/seiscientas *number* six hundred; **seiscientos dos** six hundred and two.

selección *noun Fem.* **1** selection; **2 la selección nacional** the national team.

seleccionar *verb* [17] to select.

self-service *noun Masc.* self-service restaurant.

sello *noun Masc.* **1** stamp; **2 sello discográfico** record label.

selva *noun Fem.* **1** jungle; **2** forest; **la selva tropical** the tropical rainforest.

semáforo *noun Masc.* traffic lights; **saltarse un semáforo en rojo** to go through a red light; **cuando llegue al semáforo,** **tuerza a la derecha** when you get to the traffic lights, turn right.

semana *noun Fem.* week; **la próxima semana** next week; **entre semana** during the week; **Semana Santa** Easter; **en Semana Santa** at Easter.

semanal *adjective* weekly.

semanalmente *adverb* weekly.

sembrar *verb* [29] **1** to sow; **2** to plant.

semejante *adjective* similar; **semejante a** similar to.

semifinal *noun Fem.* semifinal.

semilla *noun Fem.* seed.

sémola *noun Fem.* semolina.

sencillo¹ *noun Masc.* **1** single (*record*); **2** single ticket.

sencillo²/sencilla *adjective* **1** simple; **2** modest.

senda *noun Fem.* path.

senderismo *noun Masc.* trekking.

senderista *noun Masc./Fem.* hiker.

seno *noun Masc.* **1** breast; **2** bosom.

sensación *noun Fem.* **1** feeling; **tengo la sensación de que ...** I have the feeling that ...; **una sensación de tristeza** a feeling of sadness; **2** sense; **una sensación de pérdida** a sense of loss; **3** sensation; **causar sensación** to cause a sensation; **su llegada causó sensación** her arrival caused a sensation.

sensacional *adjective* sensational; **una noticia sensacional** a sensational piece of news.

a b c d e f g h i j k l m n ñ o p q r s t u v w x y z

a

sensatez noun Fem. sense; **tener sensatez** to be sensible; **actuar con sensatez** to act sensibly.

b

c **sensato/sensata** adjective sensible.

d **sensibilidad** noun Fem. sensitivity.

e

f **sensible** adjective **1** sensitive; **2** noticeable (difference or change).

g **sensiblemente** adverb considerably.

h

i **sentado/sentada** adjective **estar sentado** to be sitting; **estaban sentados cerca de la puerta** they were sitting near the door; **estábamos sentados a la mesa** we were sitting at the table; **permanezcan sentados, por favor** please remain seated.

j

k

l

m

n **sentar** verb [29] **1** to sit; **senté al niño en su silla** I sat the baby on his chair; **2** to suit; **ese vestido se sienta muy bien** that dress really suits you; **el rojo me sienta fatal** red doesn't suit me at all; **3 los pimientos me sientan mal** peppers don't agree with me. **sentarse** reflexive verb [29] to sit down.

ñ

o

p

q

r

s

t **sentido** noun Masc. **1** sense; **sentido del deber** sense of duty; **sentido común** common sense; **2 no tiene sentido** it doesn't make sense; **en sentido literal** in the literal sense; **3** consciousness; **perder el sentido** to lose consciousness; **4** direction; **venían en sentido contrario** they were coming from the opposite direction; **en sentido de las**

u

v

w

x

y

z

agujas del reloj clockwise; **en el sentido contrario al de las agujas del reloj** anticlockwise; **5 calle de sentido único** one-way street.

sentimental adjective **1** sentimental; **2 ¿qué tal tu vida sentimental?** how's your love life?.

sentimiento noun Masc. **1** feeling; **2 te acompaño en el sentimiento** my condolences.

sentir verb [14] **1** to feel; **sentir dolor** to feel pain; **sentir sed** to feel thirsty; **sentir alegría** to feel happy; **2 sentir un ruido** to hear a noise; **3** (used to express apology) **lo siento mucho** I'm very sorry; **siento llegar tarde** sorry I'm late; **sentimos tener que comunicarle que ...** we regret to inform you that ....

sentirse reflexive verb [14] to feel; **¿cómo te sientes?** how do you feel?; **no se sentía bien y se fue a casa** he wasn't feeling well and he went home; **me siento un poco cansado** I feel a bit tired.

seña noun Fem. **1** sign; **hacer una seña** to make a sign; **me hizo señas para que entrase** he beckoned to me to come in; **2 señas** address; **¿quieres darme tus señas?** would you like to give me your address?.

señal noun Fem. **1** sign; **señal de tráfico** traffic sign; **2 en señal de amistad** as a token of friendship; **3** sign; **hacer una señal** to make a sign; **nos estaba haciendo señales** she was signalling to us; **4** deposit; **dar una señal** to pay a deposit.

señalar verb [17] **1** to point; **señaló hacia la casa** he pointed to the house; **no es de buena educación señalar con el dedo** it's bad manners to point at people; **2** to point out; **señaló que ...** she pointed out that ...; **3** to fix (a date or time).

señalarse reflexive verb [17] **se señaló la pierna** he pointed at his leg.

señor noun Masc. **1** gentleman; **había un señor esperando** there was a gentleman waiting; **2** sir; **perdone señor, ¿me deja pasar?** excuse me sir, could you let me through?; **3** Mr; **el señor Puyol** Mr Puyol; **los señores López** Mr and Mrs López; (note that sometimes 'señor' is used in Spanish before somebody's first name as a sign of respect, for example 'el señor Mateo' and also in front of titles) **el señor presidente** the President; **4 Muy señor mío** Dear Sir (in letters); **5** (for emphasis) **no señor, eso no se hace** you mustn't do that; **sí señor, es verdad** yes, that's quite right.

señora noun Fem. **1** lady; **una señora se me acercó** a lady came up to me; **2** madam; **perdone señora, ¿me deja pasar?** excuse me madam, could you let me through?; **3** Mrs, Ms; **la señora Frutos** Mrs Frutos (in Spain, women use their maiden name after they get married and not their husband's surname) **Doña Ana Villa, señora de García** Mrs Ana García (literally, Ms Ana Villa,

marrried to Mr García) (note that sometimes 'señora' is used in Spanish before somebody's first name as a sign of respect, for example 'la señora Juana'); **4** wife; **fui de vacaciones con mi señora** I went on holiday with my wife; **5** (for emphasis) **no señora, no fui yo** it was not me; **sí señora, es mío** it certainly is mine.

señorita noun Fem. **1** young lady; **le ha llamado una señorita** a young lady has called you; **2** Miss, Ms; **la señorita García** Miss García, Ms García ('señorita' is also used to address a teacher) **aquí están mis deberes, señorita** here's my homework, Miss; **3** (for emphasis) **no señorita, no se lo dejo** I am certainly not lending it to you.

sepa, sepan, etc. verb SEE **saber.**

separación noun Fem. **1** gap; **2** separation.

separado/separada adjective **1** separated; **2 por separado** separately.

separar verb [17] **1** to separate; **2** to move (something) away; **separa la silla de la chimenea** move the chair away from the fire.
separarse reflexive verb [17] **1** to separate (a couple); **2 nunca nos hemos separado antes** we've never been apart before.

septiembre noun Masc. September; **en septiembre/en el mes de septiembre** in September.

a

b

c

d

e

f

g

h

i

j

k

l

m

n

ñ

o

p

q

r

s

t

u

v

w

x

y

z

séptimo/séptima *adjective* seventh; **el séptimo piso** the seventh floor.

sequía *noun Fem.* drought.

ser *noun Masc.* **ser humano** human being.

ser *verb* [1] **1** to be; **es muy bonito** it's very beautiful; **es soltero** he's single; **es muy simpática** she's very friendly; **soy bastante alta** I'm quite tall; **¿quién es?** – **'soy yo'** 'who's that?' – 'it's me'; **mi madre es médico** my mother's a doctor; **estas naranjas son buenísimas** these oranges are really nice; **¿cuánto es?** how much is it?; **hoy es once** it's the eleventh today; **eran las seis y media** it was half past six; **2 ser de** to be from; **mi amiga es de Argentina** my friend is from Argentina; **3 el coche es de Juan** the car is Juan's; **era de mi hermano** it was my brother's; **4 ser de** to be made of; **es de madera** it's made of wood; **es de metal** it's made of metal; **5** (*passive use*) to be; **la propuesta ha sido rechazada** the proposal has been rejected; **6 cuando sea** whenever; **como sea** however; **donde sea** wherever; **7 lo que sea** whatever; **8 ya sea ... o ...** either ... or ...; **ya sea por carta o por teléfono** either by post or by telephone; **9 o sea, que no lo has terminado** so, you haven't finished; **dentro de una semana, o sea el próximo jueves** in a week, that is, next Thursday; **10 a no ser** unless; **a no**

ser que no le interese unless he's not interested.

será, seré, sería, etc. *verb* SEE ser.

serie *noun Fem.* **1** series; **fabricación en serie** mass production; **2 fuera de serie** out of this world.

serio/seria *adjective* **1** serious; **ponerse serio** to have a serious expression; **un problema serio** a serious problem; **2** reliable (*a person*); **3** reputable (*a company*); **4 lo digo en serio** I mean it.

serpiente *noun Fem.* snake.

servicio *noun Masc.* **1** service; **servicios públicos** public services; **servicio incluido** service included; **servicio de atención al cliente** customer services; **2 estar de servicio** to be on duty; **3 'servicios'** 'toilets'; **4 servicio militar** military service.

servilleta *noun Fem.* serviette.

servir *verb* [57] **1** to serve; **servir la sopa** to serve the soup; **¿te sirvo más vino?** shall I pour you some more wine?; **2** to be of use; **estas herramientas ya no sirven** these tools are no good any more; **3 servir para algo** to be used for; **¿para qué sirve este interruptor?** what's this switch for?; **esto no nos sirve para abrirlo** this is no use for opening it; **4 no sirves para nada** you're useless; **yo no sirvo para camarera** I'm no good as a waitress.

servirse *reflexive verb* [57] to help yourself to; **se sirvió**

ensalada she helped herself to some salad; **sírvete más** help yourself to some more.

sesenta *number* sixty; **tiene sesenta años** he's sixty (years old); **sesenta y dos** sixty-two; **los años sesenta** the sixties.

sesión *noun Fem.* **1** session; **2** performance; **la sesión de noche** the evening performance; **sesión continua** continuous performance.

seta *noun Fem.* **1** mushroom; **2** toadstool.

setecientos/setecientas *number* seven hundred; **setecientos ochenta** seven hundred and eighty.

setenta *number* seventy; **tiene setenta años** he's seventy (years old); **setenta y dos** seventy-two; **los años setenta** the seventies.

seto *noun Masc.* hedge.

severo/severa *adjective* **1** severe (*person, punishment*); **2** harsh (*climate*).

sexo *noun Masc.* sex.

sexto/sexta *adjective* sixth; **el sexto piso** the sixth floor.

sexual *adjective* sexual; **tener relaciones sexuales con alguien** to have sex with someone.

sí *adverb* yes; **sí, es cierto** yes, it's true; **¿lo vas a comprar?' – 'sí'** 'are you going to buy it? ' – 'yes I am'; **¿es suyo?' – 'creo que sí'** 'is it hers? ' – 'I think so'; **ellos no lo saben, pero yo sí** they don't know, but I do.

sí *pronoun* **1** himself/herself; **pensó para sí** he thought to himself/she thought to herself; **2** (*polite form*) yourself, (*polite form*) yourselves; **3** itself; **este problema es, en sí mismo ...** this problem is, in itself ...; **4** themselves; **los dos hermanos lo quieren todo para sí** both brothers want everything for themselves; **5** **sí mismo** himself; **sí misma** herself; **quiere hacerlo por sí mismo** he wants to do it by himself; **quiere hacerlo por sí misma** she wants to do it by herself; **6** **sí mismo/sí misma** yourself (*polite form*); **sí mismos/sí mismas** yourselves (*polite form*); **7** **sí mismo** oneself; **reírse de sí mismo** to laugh at oneself; **8** **entre sí** between themselves.

si *conjunction* **1** if; **si yo estuviera en tu lugar** if I were you; **si lo hubiese sabido ...** if I had known ...; **si tuviese dinero, lo compraría** if I had the money I would buy it; **2** whether; **no sé si podré** I don't know whether I'll be able to; **tanto si quiere como si no** whether he wants to or not.

Sicilia *noun Fem.* Sicily.

sida *noun Masc.* Aids.

sidra *noun Fem.* cider.

siempre *adverb* **1** always; **casi siempre** almost always; **desde siempre** always; **2** **para siempre** for ever; **¿te vas a quedar allí para siempre?** are you going to stay there for ever?; **3** **como siempre** as usual; **la historia de siempre** the usual story; **4** **siempre que**

whenever; **siempre que puedo** whenever I can.

sienta, siento, etc. *verb* SEE **sentar, sentir.**

sierra *noun Fem.* **1** saw; **2** range of mountains; **veranean en la sierra** they spend their summer holidays in the mountains.

siesta *noun Fem.* nap; **echarse una siesta** (*informal*) to have a nap; **está durmiendo la siesta** he's having a nap.

siete *number* **1** seven; **tiene siete años** she's seven (years old); **2** seventh (*in dates*); **hoy es siete de abril** today it's the seventh of April; **3** seven (*in clock time*); **son las siete** it's seven o'clock.

siga, sigan, etc. *verb* SEE **seguir.**

siglo *noun Masc.* century; **el siglo XIII** the 13th century (*centuries are always indicated in roman numbers in Spanish*); **hace un siglo que no nos vemos** (*informal*) we haven't seen each other for ages.

significado *noun Masc.* meaning.

significar *verb* [31] to mean; **¿qué significa esta palabra?** what does this word mean?; **eso no significa nada para él** that doesn't mean anything to him.

signo *noun Masc.* **1** sign; **signo del zodiaco** star sign; **¿de qué signo eres?** what sign are you?; **2** mark; **signo de exclamación** exclamation mark; **signo de interrogación** question mark.

sigo, sigue, etc. *verb* SEE **seguir.**

siguiente *noun Masc./Fem.* **el siguiente, por favor** next, please.

siguiente *adjective* next, following; **al día siguiente** ... the next day ....

siguió *verb* SEE **seguir.**

sílaba *noun Fem.* syllable.

silbar *verb* [17] to whistle.

silbato *noun Masc.* whistle; **tocar el silbato** to blow the whistle.

silbido *noun Masc.* whistle; **dar un silbido** to whistle.

silencio *noun Masc.* silence.

silenciosamente *adverb* quietly.

silencioso/silenciosa *adjective* quiet.

silla *noun Fem.* chair; **silla de montar** saddle (*for a horse*); **una silla de ruedas** a wheelchair.

sillín *noun Masc.* saddle (*on a bicycle*).

sillón *noun Masc.* armchair.

símbolo *noun Masc.* symbol.

similar *adjective* similar; **similar a** similar to.

similitud *noun Fem.* similarity.

simio *noun Masc./Fem.* ape.

simpático/simpática *adjective* nice; **me cae simpático** I think he's really nice.

simple *adjective* **1** simple; **2** mere; **una simple formalidad** a mere formality.

simplemente *adverb* simply.

simplificar *verb* [31] to simplify.

simular *verb* [17] **1** to feign; **2** to fake.

simultáneo/simultánea *adjective* simultaneous.

sin *preposition* **1** without; **sin esfuerzo** without effort; **lo hice sin pensar** I did it without thinking; **2 agua mineral sin gas** still mineral water; **cerveza sin alcohol** non-alcoholic beer; **3 está sin revisar** it hasn't been checked yet; **terminó sin amigos** he ended up with no friends; **nos quedamos sin dinero** we ran out of money; **estamos sin azúcar** we're out of sugar; **4 sin querer** unintentionally; **5 sin embargo** nevertheless.

sinagoga *noun Fem.* synagogue.

sinceramente *adverb* **1** sincerely; **2** quite honestly.

sinceridad *noun Fem.* sincerity.

sincero/sincera *adjective* sincere.

sindicalista *noun Masc./Fem.* trade unionist.

sindicato *noun Masc.* trade union.

singular *noun Masc.* singular; **en singular** in the singular.

siniestro[1] *noun Masc.* **1** accident; **2** disaster.

siniestro[2]**/siniestra** *adjective* sinister.

sino *conjunction* but; **no verde, sino amarillo** not green but yellow.

sinónimo *noun Masc.* synonym.

sinónimo *adjective* synonymous.

sintético/sintética *adjective* synthetic.

sintieron, sintió, etc. *verb* SEE **sentir.**

síntoma *noun Masc.* symptom.

sintonizar *verb* [22] to tune in.

sinvergüenza *noun Masc./Fem.* **1** swine; **2** crook; **3** rascal.

siquiera *adverb* **1** at least; **dales siquiera un poco de dinero** give them at least a bit of money; **2 ni siquiera** not even; **ni siquiera me di cuenta** I didn't even realise.

sirena *noun Fem.* **1** mermaid; **2** siren.

sistema *noun Masc.* system.

sitio *noun Masc.* **1** place; **ponlo otra vez en su sitio** put it back in its place; **2 room; no tengo sitio en la maleta** I haven't got any room in my suitcase; **hay sitio para uno más en el coche** there's room for one more in the car; **hacer sitio** to make room; **3 seat; hay un sitio al lado de la ventana** there's a seat by the window; **4 en cualquier sitio** anywhere; **en algún sitio** somewhere; **en ningún sitio** nowhere; **en otro sitio** somewhere else; **5 siege; 6 un sitio web** a web site.

situación *noun Fem.* **1** situation; **2** position; **la situación de la casa es buena** the house is in a good position.

situado/situada *adjective* situated.

situar *verb* [20] **1** to site (*a building*); **2** to set (*a plot in a novel*).

situarse *reflexive verb* [20] **1** to be situated; **2 situarse en primer puesto** to reach the first position;

a b c d e f g h i j k l m n ñ o p q r s t u v w x y z

a
3 situarse bien en la vida to do very well for yourself.

b
smoking noun Masc. dinner jacket.

c
sobaco noun Masc. armpit.

d
sobra in phrase **1 de sobra** to spare; **tenemos pan de sobra** we have plenty of bread; **hay una silla de sobra** there's a spare chair; **2 saber algo de sobra** to know something full well; **3 aquí estás de sobra** you're not wanted here; **como estaba de sobra me fui** I wasn't needed, so I left.

e

f

g

h

i

j
sobrar verb [17] **1 nos ha sobrado vino** we had a lot of wine left over; **¿te sobró algo de papel?** did you have any paper left over?; **va a sobrar dinero** there will be money left over; **2 le sobraba una entrada** he had a spare ticket; **3 aquí sobra dinero** there is too much money here; **sobran tres sillas** there are three chairs too many; **4 nos sobraba un sitio** we'd got an extra place; **5 nos sobra tiempo** we have plenty of time.

k

l

m

n

ñ

o
sobras plural noun Fem. leftovers.

sobre noun Masc. envelope.

sobre preposition **1** on; **lo dejó sobre la cama** he left it on the bed; **2** above; **la lámpara que está sobre el sofá** the lamp above the sofa; **sobre el nivel del mar** above sea level; **3** over; **el puente sobre el río** the bridge over the river; **4** about; **una conferencia sobre literatura** a lecture about literature; **5 sobre todo** especially.

p

q

r

s

t

u

v

w

x

y

z
sobredosis noun Fem. overdose.

sobrenatural adjective supernatural.

sobrepasar verb [17] to exceed.

sobresaliente noun Masc. mark between 8.5 and 10 (out of 10).

sobresaliente adjective outstanding, excellent.

sobresalir verb [63] **1 sobresalir en algo** to excel in something; **2** to overhang; **3** to protrude.

sobresalto noun Masc. fright; **llevarse un sobresalto** to get a fright.

sobreviviente noun Masc./Fem. survivor.

sobrevivir verb [19] to survive; **sobrevivir a algo** to survive something.

sobrina noun Fem. niece.

sobrino noun Masc. nephew; **sobrinos** nephews, nephews and nieces.

sociable adjective sociable.

social adjective social.

socialista noun Masc./Fem., **socialista** adjective socialist.

sociedad noun Fem. **1** society; **la sociedad de consumo** the consumer society; **2 sociedad anónima** public limited company.

socio/socia noun Masc./Fem. member; **hacerse socio de algo** to join something.

socorrer verb [18] to help.

socorrista noun Masc./Fem. lifeguard; **¿hay un socorrista en la playa?** is there a lifeguard at the beach?

socorro noun Masc. help; **pedir socorro** to ask for help.

socorro *exclamation* ¡socorro! help!

sofá *noun Masc.* sofa.

sofocar *verb* [31] to put out (*a fire*).
sofocarse *reflexive verb* [31] to get worked up.

sois *verb* SEE **ser**.

soja *noun Fem.* soya.

sol *noun Masc.* sun; **hacía sol** it was sunny; **un día de sol** a sunny day; **al ponerse el sol** at sunset; **el sol estaba saliendo** the sun was rising; **sentarse al sol** to lie in the sun.

solamente *adverb* only.

soldado *noun Masc./Fem.* soldier.

soleado/soleada *adjective* sunny.

soledad *noun Fem.* loneliness.

soler *verb* [38] **1** suele salir por las noches he usually goes out in the evenings; **suelen verse** they usually see each other; **no suele importarle** he usually doesn't mind; **2** solía escribirme de vez en cuando she used to write to me from time to time.

sólido/sólida *adjective* **1** solid; **2** sound.

solitario/solitaria *adjective* lonely.

solo/sola *adjective* **1** alone; **vive solo** he lives alone; **cuando me quedé solo** when I was left alone; **2** lonely; **está muy sola** she's very lonely; **sentirse solo** to feel lonely; **3** on your own; **desde que murió su madre está sola** she's been on her own since her mother died; **4** by yourself; **lo hice sola** I did it

by myself; **5** con una sola mano with one hand; **sin una sola queja** without a single complaint; **6** un café solo a black coffee; **una ginebra sola** a straight gin.

sólo *adverb* only.

solomillo *noun Masc.* fillet steak.

soltar *verb* [24] **1** to let go of; **le solté la mano** I let go of his hand; **¡suéltame!** let go of me!; **2** to release (*a prisoner*); **3** to untie; **soltar un nudo** to untie a knot; **4** soltar al perro to let the dog off the lead; **5** soltar un grito to let out a cry; **soltar una carcajada** to let out a laugh; **soltar una palabrota** to come out with a swearword.
soltarse *reflexive verb* [24] **1** no te sueltes de la barandilla don't let go of the banister; **se soltó de mi mano** he let go of my hand; **2** soltarse el pelo to let your hair down; **3** to come undone (*a knot*).

soltero/soltera *noun Masc./Fem.* **1** bachelor (*male*); **2** single woman.
soltero *adjective* single.

soltura *noun Fem.* hablar español con soltura to speak Spanish fluently; **moverse con soltura** to move with ease.

soluble *adjective* soluble.

solución *noun Fem.* solution.

solucionar *verb* [17] **1** to solve; **2** to settle (*a conflict*).

sombra *noun Fem.* **1** shadow; **2** shade; **sentarse en la sombra** to sit in the shade; **dar sombra** to give shade; **3** sombra de ojos eye shadow.

sombrero noun Masc. hat.

sombrilla noun Fem. **1** parasol; **2** sunshade.

sombrío/sombría adjective **1** dark (street or room); **2** gloomy (face or look).

somos, son verb SEE **ser.**

sonar verb [24] **1** to sound; **suena a hueco** it sounds hollow; **sonó un ruido** there was a noise; **2** to ring (a doorbell or telephone); **3 el despertador no ha sonado** the alarm clock hasn't gone off; **4 me suena mucho su cara** her face is very familiar to me; **¿Carlos Ramírez? no me suena** Carlos Ramírez? it doesn't ring any bells.

sonarse reflexive verb [24] **sonarse la nariz** to blow one's nose.

soñar verb [24] to dream.

sondeo noun Masc. survey.

sonido noun Masc. sound.

sonreír verb [61] to smile; **me sonrió** he smiled at me.

sonreírse reflexive verb [61] to smile.

sonría, sonríe, sonrío, etc. verb SEE **sonreír.**

sonrisa noun Fem. smile.

sonrojarse verb [17] to blush.

sopa noun Fem. soup.

soplar verb [17] **1** to blow; **2** to blow off; **soplar el polvo de la mesa** to blow the dust off the table; **3 soplarle la respuesta a alguien** (informal) to whisper the answer to someone (in an exam).

soportar verb [17] **1** to put up with (situation); **2** to bear (pain or heat); **3 no puedo soportar a Rafael** I can't stand Rafael; **4** to withstand.

soporte noun Masc. support.

sorbete noun Masc. sorbet.

sorbo noun Masc. **1** sip; **beber a sorbos** to sip; **2** gulp; **beberse algo de un sorbo** to drink something in one gulp.

sordo/sorda noun Masc./Fem. deaf person.

sordo adjective deaf.

sordomudo/sordomuda noun Masc./Fem. deaf mute.

sordomudo adjective deaf and dumb.

sorprendente adjective surprising.

sorprender verb [18] to surprise; **me sorprende que se retrase** I'm surprised he's late.

sorprenderse reflexive verb [18] to be surprised.

sorprendido/sorprendida adjective surprised.

sorpresa noun Fem. surprise.

soso/sosa adjective **1** dull; **2** bland.

soso noun bore.

sospecha noun Fem. suspicion; **tengo la sospecha de que ...** I have a feeling that ...

sospechar verb [17] to suspect.

sospechoso/sospechosa adjective suspicious; **me parece sospechoso** I find it suspicious.

sostén *noun Masc.* **1** support; **2** bra.

sostener *verb* [9] **1** to support (*arch, ceiling, or family*); **2** to bear (*a weight or load*).

sótano *noun Masc.* **1** basement; **2** cellar.

soy *verb* SEE ser.

Sr. *abbreviation* (*short for: Señor*) Mr.

Sra. *abbreviation* (*short for: Señora*) Mrs, Ms.

Sres. *abbreviation* (*short for: Señores*) Messrs.

Srta. *abbreviation* (*short for: Señorita*) Miss, Ms.

su *adjective* **1** his/her; **¿es su falda como ésta?** is her skirt like this one?; **ahí está Carlos con sus padres** there's Carlos with his parents; **2** its; **el perro duerme en su caseta** the dog sleeps in its kennel; **3** their; **mis padres viven allí y éste es su coche** my parents live there and that's their car; **4** your (*polite form*); **¿son éstos sus zapatos?** are these your shoes?

suave *adjective* **1** soft; **2** smooth; **3** gentle (*voice*); **4** mild (*weather*).

suavizante *noun Masc.* **1** fabric softener; **2** hair conditioner.

subestimar *verb* [17] understimate.

subida *noun Fem.* **1** rise (*in temperature or price, for example*); **2** climb.

subir *verb* [19] **1** to go up; **el ascensor está subiendo** the lift is going up; **subir al tercer piso** to go up to the third floor; **la temperatura ha subido tres grados** the temperature has gone up three degrees; **2** to come up; **¡sube!** come up!; **3** to bring up; **sube estas cajas al segundo piso** bring these boxes up to the third floor; **súbeme un vaso de agua** bring a glass of water up for me; **4** to take up; **¿le subo las maletas a su habitación?** shall I take the luggage up to your room?; **5** to put up; **han vuelto a subir el precio de la gasolina** they've put up the price of petrol again; **6** subir al **tren** to get on the train; **subir a un coche** to get into a car; **subir a bordo** to board; **7** to turn up (*volume*); **subió un poco la música** he turned up the music a bit; **8** to raise; **subir una persiana** to raise a blind; **9** to rise; **el nivel del agua ha subido** the water level has risen; **10** to come in (*the tide*).

subirse *reflexive verb* [19] **1** subirse al **tren** to get on the train; **subirse a un coche** to get into a car; **subirse a bordo** to board; **2** subirse a un árbol to climb up a tree; **3** subirse los calcetines to pull up your socks.

súbitamente *adverb* suddenly.

súbito/súbita *adjective* sudden.

subjuntivo *noun Masc.* subjunctive.

submarinismo *noun Masc.* scuba diving.

submarinista *noun Masc./Fem.* scuba diver.

a b c d e f g h i j k l m n ñ o p q r s t u v w x y z

a

submarino noun Masc.
submarine.

b

subrayar verb [17] to underline.

c

subsidio noun Masc. **1** subsidy;
2 subsidio de desempleo
unemployment benefit; **subsidio
de invalidez** disability allowance.

d

e

f

subterráneo[1] noun Masc.
subway.

g

subterráneo[2]/**subterránea**
adjective underground.

h

i

suburbio noun Masc. **1** slum area
(on the outskirts of a town);
2 suburb.

j

subvención noun Fem. subsidy.

k

subvencionar verb [17] to
subsidize.

l

m

suceder verb [18] **1** to happen;
¿qué le ha sucedido? what's
happened to him?; **sucedió todo
muy rápido** it all happened very
quickly; **2** to succeed (to the
throne).

n

ñ

o

suceso noun Masc. **1** event;
2 incident; **'página de sucesos'**
'accidents and crimes report' (in a
newspaper).

p

q

r

suciedad noun Fem. **1** dirt;
2 dirtiness.

s

t

sucio/sucia adjective **1** dirty;
tienes la cara sucia your face is
dirty; **2 primero hice el trabajo en
sucio** I did the essay in rough first.

u

sucursal noun Fem. **1** branch (of a
bank); **2** office (of a company).

v

w

sudadera noun Fem. sweatshirt.

x

Sudamérica noun Fem. South
America.

y

z

**sudamericano/
sudamericana** noun Masc./
Fem., adjective South American.

sudar verb [17] to sweat.

sudeste noun Masc. southeast.

sudoeste noun Masc. southwest.

sudor noun Masc. sweat.

Suecia noun Fem. Sweden.

sueco[1] noun Masc. Swedish (the
language).

sueco[2]/**sueca** noun Masc./Fem.
Swede.

sueco adjective Swedish.

suegra noun Fem. mother-in-law.

suegro noun Masc. **1** father-in-law;
2 mis suegros my parents in law.

suela[1] noun Fem. sole.

suela[2], **suelas**, **etc.** verb SEE
soler.

sueldo noun Masc. **1** salary;
2 wage; **3 aumento de sueldo** pay
rise.

suelo[1] noun Masc. **1** floor;
2 ground; **tirarse al suelo** to throw
yourself to the ground.

suelo[2] verb SEE **soler.**

suelta[1], **suelte**, **suelto**[1], **etc.**
verb SEE **soltar.**

suelto[2] noun Masc. small change;
¿tienes suelto? do you have any
small change?.

suelto[3]/**suelta**[2] adjective **1** loose;
el tornillo está suelto the screw is
loose; **2 dinero suelto** small
change.

suena, **suene**, **sueno**, **etc.**
verb SEE **sonar.**

sueña, **sueñe**, **sueño**[1], **etc.**
verb SEE **soñar.**

sueño² noun Masc. **1** dream; **2** tener sueño to be sleepy; tener el sueño ligero to be a light sleeper.

suerte noun Fem. luck; tener suerte to be lucky; traer mala suerte to bring bad luck; ¡qué mala suerte! what bad luck!

suéter noun Masc. sweater.

suficiente noun Masc. pass (equivalent to 5 out of 10).

suficiente adjective enough.

sufrir verb [19] **1** to suffer; sufre mucho he's suffering a lot; **2** to have; sufrir un accidente to have an accident; sufre una grave enfermedad he has a serious illness.

sugerencia noun Fem. suggestion.

sugerir verb [14] to suggest.

sugestión noun Fem. suggestion.

sugiera, sugiero, sugirieron, etc. verb SEE sugerir.

suicidarse reflexive verb [17] to commit suicide.

suicidio noun Masc. suicide.

Suiza noun Fem. Switzerland.

suizo/suiza noun Masc./Fem., adjective Swiss.

sujetador noun Masc. bra.

sujeto/sujeta adjective **1** secure; está bien sujeto it's really secure; **2** tener sujeto a to have hold of; **3** estar sujeto a algo to be subject to something.

suma noun Fem. **1** addition; **2** en suma in short.

sumar verb [17] to add.

supe, supiste, etc. verb SEE saber.

súper, super adjective (informal) super.

súper adverb (informal) really; cantan súper bien they sing really well; me lo pasé súper bien I had a great time.

superar verb [17] **1** to overcome (fear or a problem); **2** to get over (a shock); **3** to exceed.

superficie noun Fem. surface.

superior adjective **1** superior; es superior a los demás en calidad it's better quality than all the others; **2** top (floor or layer); **3** upper (lip); **4** higher (level or class).

supermercado noun Masc. supermarket.

superstición noun Fem. superstition.

supersticioso/supersticiosa adjective superstitious.

supervisar verb [17] supervise.

supervisor/supervisora noun Masc./Fem. supervisor.

superviviente noun Masc./Fem. survivor.

suplementario/suplementaria adjective additional.

suplemento noun Masc. supplement.

supondrá, supondré, supondría, etc. verb SEE suponer.

suponer verb [11] to suppose; supongo que sí I suppose so.

suponga, supongo, etc. *verb*
SEE **suponer.**

supositorio *noun Masc.*
suppository.

suprimir *verb* [19] **1** to suppress
(*news*); **2** to abolish; **3** to delete.

supuesto *in phrase* **por supuesto**
of course.

supuse, supuso *verb* SEE
suponer.

sur *noun Masc.* south.

Suramérica *noun Fem.* South
America.

**suramericano/
suramericana** *noun Masc./Fem.,*
suramericano *adjective* South
American.

sureste *noun Masc.* southeast.

surf *noun Masc.* surfing; **practicar
el surf** to go surfing.

surfista *noun Masc./Fem.* surfer (*in
the sea*).

suroeste *noun Masc.* southwest.

surtido[1] *noun Masc.* **1** assortment;
2 selection.

surtido[2]**/surtida** *adjective*
1 assorted; **2** **una tienda bien
surtida** a well-stocked shop.

surtidor *noun Masc.* petrol pump.

suspender *verb* [18] **1** to fail; **he
suspendido la física** I've failed
physics; **2** to suspend (*a payment
or service*); **3** **suspender un viaje**
to call off a trip.

suspense *noun Masc.* suspense;
película de suspense thriller
(*film*).

suspenso *noun Masc.* fail; **sacar
un suspenso en examen** to fail an
exam.

suspirar *verb* [17] to sigh.

suspiro *noun Masc.* sigh.

sustancia *noun Fem.* substance.

sustantivo *noun Masc.* noun.

sustituir *verb* [54] **1** to replace;
sustituir algo por algo to replace
something with something;
2 **sustituir a alguien** to stand in for
someone (*at work*), to come on as a
substitute for someone (*in football,
for example*).

sustituto/sustituta *noun Masc./
Fem.* **1** replacement; **2** substitute;
3 locum.

susto *noun Masc.* fright; **darle un
susto a alguien** to give someone a
fright; **¡qué susto me llevé!** I got
such a fright!

sustraer *verb* [42] to subtract.

susurrar *verb* [17] to whisper.

sutil *adjective* subtle.

suyo/suya *adjective* **1** his/hers;
(*goes after the noun*) **un conocido
suyo** a friend of his/hers; **2** theirs;
venían con un amigo suyo they
came with a friend of theirs;
3 yours (*polite form*).

suyo *pronoun* **1** his/hers; **el suyo
es gris** his/hers is grey; **las suyas
son mejores** his/hers are better;
2 yours (*friend of theirs*); **3** theirs; **no
es el de mis hijos, el suyo es más
grande** it's not my children's,
theirs is bigger.

Tt

tabaco noun Masc. **1** tobacco; **2** cigarettes; **tengo que comprar tabaco** I've got to buy some cigarettes.

taberna noun Fem. bar (selling wine).

tabla noun Fem. **1** plank; **2** board; **una tabla de planchar** an ironing board; **una tabla de picar** a chopping board; **3 tabla de multiplicar** multiplication table; **4 tabla de gimnasia** circuit training; **5** pleat.

tablao noun Masc. **un tablao flamenco** a flamenco bar.

tablero noun Masc. **1** board (for a game); **un tablero de damas** a draughtboard; **2** noticeboard.

tablón noun Masc. **1** plank; **2 tablón de anuncios** noticeboard.

taburete noun Masc. stool.

tacaño/tacaña noun Masc./Fem. miser.

tacaño adjective stingy.

tachar verb [17] to cross out.

taco noun Masc. **1** cue (in billiards); **2** stud (on a sports boot); **3** (informal) swearword.

tacón noun Masc. heel; **zapatos de tacón alto** high-heeled shoes; **tacón de aguja** stiletto heel.

táctica noun Fem. **1** tactic; **2** tactics.

tacto noun Masc. **1** sense of touch; **2** feel; **3** tact; **fue una falta de tacto** it was really tactless.

tal adjective **1** such; **tal cosa es imposible** such a thing is impossible; **2** tenía tal preocupación que ...** I was so worried that ...; **había tal cantidad de cajas que ...** there were so many boxes that ...; **3 en tal caso** in that case.

tal adverb **1 ¿qué tal estás?** (informal) how are you doing?; **¿qué tal van las cosas?** (informal) how are things?; **2 tal vez** maybe; **3 con tal de que** as long as; ★ **son tal para cual** one is as bad as the other.

talco noun Masc. talc; **polvos de talco** talcum powder.

talento noun Masc. talent.

TALGO abbreviation Masc. (short for: Tren Articulado Ligero Goicoechea Oriol) express train.

talla noun Fem. size; **¿qué talla de pantalones tienes?** what size of trousers do you take?

taller noun Masc. **1** workshop; **2** garage; **llevar el coche al taller** to take the car to the garage.

talón noun Masc. heel.

talonario noun Masc. chequebook.

tamaño noun Masc. size; **hay de todos los tamaños** they come in all sizes.

también adverb too; **ella también vive allí** she lives there too; **'tengo quince años' – 'yo también'** 'I'm fifteen' – 'so am I'; **'yo quiero tarta' – 'yo también'** 'I want some cake' – 'so do I'.

tambor noun Masc. drum.

tampoco adverb **él tampoco irá** he won't go either; **'a mí no me gusta' - 'a mí tampoco'** 'I don't like it' - 'neither do I'.

tampón noun Masc. tampon.

tan adverb **1** so; **no es fácil** it's not so easy; **2** such; **es una persona tan egoísta** he's such a selfish person; **3** (in comparisons) **es tan alto como su padre** he's as tall as his father; **no era tan caro como el otro** it wasn't as expensive as the other one; **4** ¡qué **casa tan grande!** what a big house!

tanque noun Masc. tank.

tanto[1] noun Masc. **1** tanto por **ciento** percentage; **gano un tanto por ciento de las ventas** I get a percentage on the sales; **2** point, goal; **marcar un tanto** to score a point, to score a goal.

tanto[2] adverb **1** so; **tanto mejor** so much the better; **no corras tanto** don't go so fast; **se enfadó tanto** he got so upset; **2** so much; **no deberías gastar tanto** you shouldn't spend so much; **3** so often; **yo no les visito tanto** I don't visit them all that often; **4** so long; **lleva tanto hacerlo** it takes so long to do; **5** **pesa tanto como éste** it's as heavy as this one.

tanto[3]/**tanta** adjective **1** so much; **tanto dinero** so much money; **tanta sal** so much salt; **2** so many; **tantos libros** so many books; **tantas cajas** so many boxes; **había tanta gente que no cabíamos** there were so many people that there wasn't room for us; **3** tanto/

tanta ... como ... as much ... as ...; **no gasta tanta gasolina como el coche viejo** it doesn't use as much petrol as the old car; **4** tantos/ **tantas ... como ...** as many ... as ...; **no hay tantos alumnos como antes** there aren't as many students as before.

tanto pronoun **1** tanto/tanta so much; **no hace falta tanto/tanta** we don't need so much; **2** tantos/ **tantas** so many; **vinieron tantos que no había sillas libres** so many came that there weren't any chairs left; **3** tanto (referring to time) so long; **no tardes tanto como ayer** don't take as long as yesterday; **'me llevará dos días hacerlo' - ¿tanto?** 'it'll take me two days to do it' - 'as long as that?'; **4** por lo **tanto** therefore; **5** mientras tanto in the meantime; **entre tanto** in the meantime.

tapa noun Fem. **1** lid; **2** top; **tapa de rosca** screw top; **3** tapa (a small snack chosen from a selection in a tapas bar); **un bar de tapas** a tapas bar; **comer de tapas** to eat tapas for lunch, supper, etc.

tapar verb [17] **1** to cover; **2** to put the top on; **3** tapar un agujero to fill a hole; **4** to block (a road or door).

tapón noun Masc. **1** cork; **2** top (of a bottle); **3** plug (of a sink or bath).

taquilla noun Fem. **1** box office; **éxito de taquilla** box office hit; **2** ticket office.

tardar verb [17] to take a long time; **tardó mucho en contestarme** she took a long time to answer;

¿cuánto se tarda de Sevilla a Córdoba? how long does it take from Seville to Cordoba?; **¡no tardes!** don't be long!; **no tardes en volver** come back soon; **a las cuatro a más tardar** at four o'clock at the latest.

tarde *noun Fem.* afternoon, evening; **buenas tardes** good afternoon, good evening; **por la tarde** in the afternoon, in the evening.

tarde *adverb* late; **llegar tarde** to be late; **se hizo tarde** it got late; **tarde o temprano** sooner or later.

tarea *noun Fem.* **1** task; **2 las tareas de la casa** the housework; **3** homework.

tarifa *noun Fem.* **1** price list; **2 tarifa telefónica** telephone charges.

tarjeta *noun Fem.* card; **una tarjeta (postal)** a postcard; **una tarjeta de crédito** a credit card; **una tarjeta telefónica** a telephone card; **una tarjeta de embarque** a boarding card; **una tarjeta de cumpleaños** a birthday card; **una tarjeta de Navidad** a Christmas card; **una tarjeta de fidelidad** a loyalty card; **sacarle a alguien la tarjeta amarilla/roja** to show somebody the yellow/red card.

tarrina *noun Fem.* tub (*for food*).

tarro *noun Masc.* jar.

tarta *noun Fem.* cake; **una tarta de cumpleaños** a birthday cake; **tarta helada** ice-cream cake.

tartera *noun Fem.* sandwich box.

tasa *noun Fem.* **1** rate; **la tasa de interés** the interest rate; **la tasa de desempleo** the level of unemployment; **2** valuation; **3** tax.

tatuaje *noun Masc.* tatoo.

tauro *noun Masc./Fem.* taurus; **es tauro** he's Taurus.

Tauro *noun Masc.* Taurus.

taxi *noun Masc.* taxi.

taxista *noun Masc./Fem.* taxi driver.

taza *noun Fem.* **1** cup; **taza de café** coffee cup, cup of coffee; **2** (toilet) pan.

tazón *noun Masc.* bowl.

te *pronoun* **1** you; **te quiero** I love you; **te vi ayer** I saw you yesterday; **2** to you; **te lo mandaré por correo** I'll post it to you; **3** (*with parts of the body and personal belongings*) **¿te has cortado el dedo?** have you cut your finger?; **¿quieres quitarte los zapatos?** do you want to take your shoes off?; **4** (*having things done*) **¿te has cortado el pelo?** have you had your hair cut?; **5** yourself; **cuídate mucho** look after yourself; **6 siéntate** sit down.

té *noun Masc.* tea; **voy a tomar un té** I'm going to have a cup of tea.

teatro *noun Masc.* theatre.

tebeo *noun Masc.* comic (*for children*).

techo *noun Masc.* **1** ceiling; **2 techo corredizo/solar** sunroof; **3 sin techo** homeless.

tecla *noun Fem.* key.

teclado *noun Masc.* keyboard.

técnica[1] *noun Fem.* technique.

técnico/técnica[2] *noun Masc./Fem.* technician.

técnico *adjective* technical.

tecnología *noun Fem.* technology.

teja *noun Fem.* tile.

tejado *noun Masc.* roof.

tejanos *plural noun Masc.* jeans.

tejer *verb* [18] **1** to weave; **2** to knit.

tela *noun Fem.* **1** fabric; **tela de algodón** cotton fabric; **2** canvas (*for painting*).

telaraña *noun Fem.* **1** spider's web; **2** cobweb; **3** spider diagram.

tele *noun Fem.* (*informal*) telly, TV; **ver la tele** to watch telly; **poner la tele** to switch on the telly.

telediario *noun Masc.* television news.

telefonear *verb* [17] to telephone.

telefónico/telefónica *adjective* telephone; **conversación telefónica** telephone conversation; **listín telefónico** telephone book.

teléfono *noun Masc.* telephone; **llamar por teléfono a alguien** to phone somebody; **no tengo teléfono** I'm not on the phone (*I don't have a phone*); **contestar el teléfono** to answer the phone; **colgar el teléfono** to put down the phone; **estaba hablando por teléfono** I was on the phone; **no has colgado bien el teléfono** you've left the phone off the hook; **teléfono celular/móvil** mobile phone.

telegrama *noun Masc.* telegram.

telenovela *noun Fem.* TV series.

telescopio *noun Masc.* telescope.

televisión *noun Fem.* television; **ver la televisión** to watch television; **poner la televisión** to switch on the television; **hoy ponen una película en la televisión** there's a film on the television today.

televisor *noun Masc.* television set.

tema *noun Masc.* **1** subject; **2** topic.

temblar *verb* [29] **1** to shiver; **2** to shake; **le temblaban las manos** his hands were shaking.

temer *verb* [18] **1** to fear (*danger or punishment*); **2 temer a alguien** to be afraid of somebody.

temerse *reflexive verb* [18] **1** to fear; **2 me temo que no podré acudir** I'm afraid I won't be able to come.

temperatura *noun Fem.* temperature; **ha bajado la temperatura** the temperature has dropped.

tempestad *noun Fem.* storm.

templado/templada *adjective* **1** mild (*climate*); **2** warm; **3** lukewarm.

temporada *noun Fem.* season; **fuera de temporada** out of season.

temprano[1] *adverb* early; **llegar temprano** to arrive early.

temprano[2]**/temprana** *adjective* early.

tendencia *noun Fem.* tendency.

tender *verb* [36] **1 tender a** to tend to; **tienden a molestarse** they tend to get upset; **2 tender la ropa** to hang out the washing.

tenderse *reflexive verb* [36] to lie down; **tenderse al sol** to lie down in the sun.

tendero/tendera *noun Masc./Fem.* shopkeeper.

tendrá, tendré, tendría, etc. *verb* SEE **tener.**

tenedor *noun Masc.* fork.

tener *verb* [9] **1** to have; **tengo dos hermanas** I've got two sisters; **tiene los ojos marrones** he's got brown eyes; **tener dolor de cabeza** to have a headache; **no tengo tiempo** I haven't got the time; **¿tienes hora?** have you got the time?; **ha tenido un niño** she had a baby; **2 tener sed** to be thirsty; **tener frío** to be cold; **¡qué calor tengo!** I'm really hot!; **ten cuidado** be careful; **3 tener sueño** to feel sleepy; **tener envidia de alguien** to be jealous of somebody; **4 tener que hacer** to have to do; **no puedo, tengo que estudiar** I can't, I have to study; **tienes que obedecerme** you must do as I tell you; **tengo que ir a verla un día** I must go and see her one day; **tendrían que ayudarme** they would have to help me; **tendría que ir al banco** I should go to the bank; **5 tiene que haberse perdido** he must have got lost; **6 tener que ver con alguien:** **no tiene nada que ver con él** it has nothing to do with him; **7 lo tengo hecho** I've done it; **lo tienen solucionado** they've sorted it out; **tenía pensado invitarlos** I'd thought about inviting them.

tenga, tengo, etc. *verb* SEE **tener.**

teniente *noun Masc./Fem.* lieutenant.

tenis *noun Masc.* tennis; **tenis de mesa** table tennis.

tenista *noun Masc./Fem.* tennis player.

tensión *noun Fem.* **1** tension; **2** stress; **3** blood pressure; **tomarse la tensión** to have your blood pressure taken.

tentación *noun Fem.* temptation.

tentar *verb* [29] to tempt.

teñir *verb* [65] to dye.

teñirse *reflexive verb* [65] to dye; **teñirse el pelo** to have your hair dyed.

tercer *adjective* third (*see also* '*tercero/tercera*').

tercero/tercera *adjective* (*note that 'tercero' becomes 'tercer' before a masculine singular noun*) third; **la tercera puerta a la derecha** the third door on the right; **el tercer piso** the third floor; **llegar en tercer lugar** to finish in third position; **el Tercer Mundo** the Third World.

terminado/terminada *adjective* finished.

terminal *noun Fem.* **1** terminal; **2** bus station.

terminal *adjective* terminal.

terminar *verb* [17] **1** to finish; **¿cuándo termina el colegio?** when does school finish; **aún no he terminado** I haven't finished yet; **no he terminado de revisarlo** I haven't finished checking it;

a b c d e f g h i j k l m n ñ o p q r s t u v w x y z

2 terminar con to finish with; **¿has terminado con el libro?** have you finished with the book?; **ha terminado con su novio** she's broken up with her boyfriend; **3** to end up; **terminamos en una discoteca** we ended up in a disco; **terminó harta** she was fed up in the end; **terminaron por pelearse** they ended up having a fight; **4** to end in; **su nombre termina en 'l'** her name ends in 'l'; **termina en punta** it's pointed; **termina en una cruz** it's got a cross at the end. **terminarse** *reflexive verb* [17] **1** to be over; **la clase se terminó a las cinco** the lesson was over at five; **2 se ha terminado la leche** we've run out of milk; **se me terminó la tinta del boli** my pen ran out (of ink).

termo™ *noun Masc.* Thermos™.

termómetro *noun Masc.* thermometer.

ternera[1] *noun Fem.* veal.

ternero/ternera[2] *noun Masc./Fem.* calf.

terraza *noun Fem.* **1** balcony; **2** terrace (*of a café or bar*).

terremoto *noun Masc.* earthquake.

terreno *noun Masc.* **1** plot of land; **2** field; **3** land; **la casa tiene mucho terreno** the house has a lot of land; **4 terreno de juego** football pitch.

terrible *adjective* terrible.

territorio *noun Masc.* territory.

terrón *noun Masc.* lump (*of sugar, earth*).

terror *noun Masc.* terror.

terrorismo *noun Masc.* terrorism.

terrorista *noun Masc./Fem.,*

terrorista *adjective* terrorist.

tesoro *noun Masc.* treasure.

test *noun Masc.* **1** test; **2 examen tipo test** multiple-choice exam.

testamento *noun Masc.* will; **hacer testamento** to make your will.

testigo *noun Masc./Fem.* witness.

tétano *noun Masc.* tetanus.

tetera *noun Fem.* teapot.

texto *noun Masc.* text.

ti *pronoun* **1** you; **detrás de ti** behind you; **se olvidaron de ti** they forgot about you; **a mí no me dijo nada, ¿y a ti?** he hasn't told me anything – has he told you?; **2** to you; **te lo dio a ti** he gave it to you; **3 ¿a ti te gusta?** do you like it?; **¿a ti qué te parece?** what do you think?; **4 ti mismo/misma** yourself; **sabes cuidar de ti misma** you can look after yourself.

tía *noun Fem.* aunt.

tibio/tibia *adjective* lukewarm.

tiburón *noun Masc.* shark.

tiembla, tiemblo, etc. *verb* SEE **temblar.**

tiempo *noun Masc.* **1** time; **llegar a tiempo** to be on time; **tiempo libre** spare time; **ha pasado mucho tiempo desde entonces** it's been a long time since then; **hace mucho tiempo que no la veo** I haven't seen her for a long time; **¿cuánto tiempo hace que se fueron?** how long ago did they go?; **al mismo**

tiempo at the same time; **la mayor parte del tiempo** most of the time; **2 ¿cada cuánto tiempo?** how often?; **cada cierto tiempo** every so often; **3 por un tiempo** for a while; **4 a su debido tiempo** in due course; **5 trabajar a tiempo completo** to work full time; **trabajar a tiempo parcial** to work part time; **6 en aquellos tiempos** in those days; **corren otros tiempos** things are different now; **7** weather; **el pronóstico del tiempo** the weather forecast; **nos hizo buen tiempo** we had nice weather; **8 el primer tiempo** the first half (*of a match*); **9** tense (*in grammar*).

tienda¹ *noun Fem.* **1** shop; **una tienda de discos** a record shop; **una tienda de recuerdos** a souvenir shop; **una tienda de comestibles** a grocer's; **2 una tienda de campaña** a tent.

tienda², **tiendo**, etc. *verb* SEE **tender.**

tierno/tierna *adjective* **1** tender (*meat*); **2** affectionate.

tierra *noun Fem.* **1** land; **tierra adentro** inland; **viajar por tierra** to travel overland; **2** earth; **3** ground; **tierra firme** solid ground; **4 tomar tierra** to land.

tiesto *noun Masc.* flowerpot.

tigre *noun Masc.* tiger.

tijeras *plural noun Fem.* scissors; **un par de tijeras/unas tijeras** a pair of scissors.

timbre *noun Masc.* bell, doorbell; **tocar el timbre** to ring the bell.

tímido/tímida *adjective* shy.

tinta *noun Fem.* ink.

tinto *noun Masc.* red wine.

tinto *adjective* red (*wine*).

tintorería *noun Fem.* dry cleaner's.

tiña, tiñeron, tiño, tiñó, etc. *verb* SEE **teñir.**

tío *noun Masc.* **1** uncle; **2 mis tíos** my uncles; my aunt and uncle; **3** (*informal*) guy.

tiovivo *noun Masc.* merry-go-round.

típico/típica *adjective* typical.

tipo *noun Masc.* **1** type; **2** figure, physique; **tiene buen tipo** she's got a good figure; **3 tipo de cambio** exchange rate; **tipo de interés** interest rate.

tirantes *noun Masc.* (*plural*) braces.

tirar *verb* [17] **1** to throw; **tirar algo al suelo** to throw something on the floor; **2 tirarle algo a alguien** to throw something at somebody; **tírame ese boli** throw me that pen; **3** to throw away; **no tires esos papeles** don't throw those papers away; **tirar algo a la basura** to throw something out (*that you no longer want*); **4** to pull; **tira un poco más** pull a bit more; **5 tirar de algo** to pull something; **tira de la cuerda cuando yo te diga** pull the rope when I tell you; **6 tirarle de las orejas a alguien** to tweak somebody's ear (*in Spain you do this when you wish somebody happy birthday*); **7** to shoot; **tirar una flecha** to shoot an arrow; **tirar**

a b c d e f g h i j k l m n ñ o p q r s t u v w x y z

a **una bomba** to drop a bomb; **8** to knock over; **tiré una silla sin querer** I accidentally knocked a chair over; **9** to knock down; **tiraron la puerta abajo** they knocked the door down.

b

c

d **tirarse** *reflexive verb* [17] **tirarse al suelo** to throw yourself to the ground; **tirarse al agua** to dive into the water; **tirarse en paracaídas** to parachute, to bale out.

e

f

g **tirita™** *noun Fem.* sticking plaster.

h **tiritar** *verb* [17] to shiver; **tiritar de frío** to shiver with cold.

i

j **tiro** *noun Masc.* **1** shot; **disparar un tiro** to fire a shot; **matar a alguien de un tiro** to shoot somebody dead; **tiro al blanco** target shooting; **2** shot (*in sport*); **un tiro a portería** a shot at goal; **un tiro libre** a free kick.

k

l

m

n **tirón** *noun Masc.* pull; **dar un tirón a algo** to pull something; ★ **de un tirón** (*informal*) in one go.

ñ

o **títere** *noun Masc.* **1** puppet; **2 títeres** puppet show.

p **título** *noun Masc.* **1** title; **2** heading; **3** degree; **título universitario** university degree; **4** certificate; **5 título nobiliario** title (*such as 'duke' or 'duchess'*).

q

r

s **tiza** *noun Fem.* chalk; **una tiza** a piece of chalk.

t

u **toalla** *noun Fem.* towel.

tobillo *noun Masc.* ankle.

v **tobogán** *noun Masc.* slide.

w **tocador** *noun Masc.* dressing table.

x **tocar** *verb* [31] **1** to touch; **me tocó el hombro** he touched me on the shoulder; **toqué la escultura** I

y

z

touched the sculpture; **tocar un tema** to touch on a subject; **2 tocar el timbre** to ring the bell; **3 tocar la bocina** to blow the horn; **4** to play (*an instrument*); **tocar el violín** to play the violin; **5 tocarle a alguien hacer** to be somebody's turn to do; **te toca jugar** it's your turn to play; **6 les ha tocado un viaje** they've won a trip; **nunca me ha tocado la lotería** I've never won the lottery.

tocarse *reflexive verb* [31] to touch; **se tocó la cabeza** he touched his head; **los dos cables se están tocando** the two cables are touching.

tocino *noun Masc.* bacon.

todavía *adverb* **1** still; **todavía nos vemos** we still see each other; **2** yet; **todavía no han llegado** they haven't arrived yet; **3** even; **todavía más tarde** even later.

todo /**toda** *adjective* **1** all; **todos mis amigos** all my friends; **viajar por todo el mundo** to travel all over the world; **2** whole; **toda la semana** the whole week; **se comieron toda la caja de bombones** they ate the whole box of chocolates; **3 todos los días** every day; **hay que revisar todas las carpetas** we have to check every folder; **4 a toda velocidad** at top speed.

todo *pronoun* **1** everything; **se lo conté todo** I told him everything; **a pesar de todo** despite everything; **2** all; **todo o nada** all or nothing; **vinieron todos** they all came; **todos estábamos de**

acuerdo we were all in agreement; **3 ante todo** above all; **4 con todo** even so; **5 de todo** everything; **tienen de todo** they've got everything; **6 sobre todo no te olvides del billete** above all, don't forget the ticket; **se divertieron mucho, sobre todo Ana** they enjoyed themselves a lot, specially Ana.

todo *adverb* **1** all; **estaba todo nervioso** he was all nervous; **2** completely; **está todo roto** it's completely had it; **3 seguir todo derecho** to carry straight on.

todo[2] *noun Masc.* **el todo** the whole.

tomar *verb* [17] **1** to take; **tomar el autobús** to take the bus; **me tomó del brazo** she took me by the arm; **2** to have; **tomar el desayuno** to have breakfast; **¿quieres tomar un café?** would you like a coffee?; **3 toma, tu billete** here's your ticket; **4 tomar el sol** to sunbathe; **5 tomar el aire** to get some fresh air; **6 tomar algo en serio** to take something seriously; **tomar algo a mal** to take something the wrong way; **tomar algo mal/bien** to take something badly/well.

tomarse *reflexive verb* [17] **1** to take; **tomarse unas vacaciones** to take some holiday; **tomarse la molestia de hacer** to take the trouble to do; **2** to have; **se tomó un helado** she had an ice cream; **3 tomarse la tensión** to have your blood pressure taken; ★ **tomarle el pelo a alguien** to pull somebody's leg (*literally: to take somebody's hair*).

tomate *noun Masc.* tomato; **salsa de tomate** tomato sauce; ★ **ponerse (colorado) como un tomate** to go as red as a beetroot.

tonelada *noun Fem.* ton.

tónica *noun Fem.* tonic water.

tono *noun Masc.* **1** tone; **en tono serio** in a serious tone; **2** shade; **telas de tonos suaves** materials in soft shades; **3** tone of marcar dial tone; **tono de ocupado** engaged tone; ★ **fuera de tono** inappropriate (*a comment*).

tontería *noun Fem.* **vaya tontería** how silly; **no te enfades por esa tontería** don't get upset over such a silly thing; **decir tonterías** to talk nonsense.

tonto/tonta *noun Masc./Fem.* idiot; ★ **hacerse el tonto** (*informal*) to play the fool; ★ **hacer el tonto** (*informal*) to act dumb.

tonto *adjective* silly.

topo *noun Masc.* mole (*animal*).

torbellino *noun Masc.* whirlwind.

torcer *verb* [41] **1** to turn; **tuerce a la derecha al final de la calle** turn right at the end of the road; **torcer la esquina** to turn the corner; **torcer la cabeza** to turn your head; **2** to twist.

torcerse *reflexive verb* [41] **1** to twist; **torcerse el tobillo** to twist your ankle; **2** to twist.

torcido/torcida *adjective* **1** twisted; **tiene el tobillo torcido** he's twisted his ankle; **2** crooked; **una línea torcida** a crooked line; **3** bent.

a
b
c
d
e
f
g
h
i
j
k
l
m
n
ñ
o
p
q
r
s
t
u
v
w
x
y
z

a

torero/torera noun Masc./Fem.
bullfighter.

b

tormenta noun Fem. storm;
tormenta de nieve snowstorm.

c

tornado noun Masc. tornado.

d

torneo noun Masc. tournament.

e

tornillo noun Masc. screw; ★ **le**
falta un tornillo (informal) he's
got a screw loose.

f

g

toro noun Masc. **1** bull; **2 los toros**
bullfighting; **ir a los toros** to go to
a bullfight; **¿te gustan los toros?**
do you like bullfighting?.

h

i

torpe adjective **1** clumsy;
2 awkward.

j

k

torre noun **1** tower; **torre de alta**
tensión pylon; **2** rook, castle (in
chess).

l

m

torta noun Fem. **1** cake; **2 darle**
una torta a alguien to slap
somebody; **3 me pegué una torta**
con la farola I banged into the
streetlamp (on foot), I crashed into
the streetlamp (in a car); ★ **no**
entiendo ni torta (informal) I
don't understand a thing.

n

ñ

o

p

tortilla noun Fem. omelette;
tortilla francesa French omelette;
tortilla española Spanish
omelette, tortilla.

q

r

tortuga noun Fem. **1** tortoise;
2 turtle.

s

t

torturar verb [17] to torture.

u

tos noun Fem. cough; **tener tos** to
have a cough; **le dio la tos** he
started coughing.

v

w

toser verb [18] to cough.

x

y

tostada noun Fem. **una tostada** a
piece of toast; **tomo tostadas para**

z

desayunar I have toast for
breakfast.

tostador noun Masc. toaster.

tostadora noun Fem. toaster.

tostar verb [24] **1** to toast (bread);
2 to roast (coffee).

tostarse reflexive verb [24] to
tan, to go brown.

total noun Masc. total; **¿cuánto es**
el total? how much is the total?;
son cinco mil quinientas en total
it's five thousand five hundred in
total.

total adjective total.

totalidad noun Fem. **la totalidad**
del colegio the whole school; **la**
totalidad de los alumnos all the
pupils.

tóxico/tóxica adjective tóxico/
tóxica; **residuos tóxicos** toxic
waste.

trabajador/trabajadora noun
Masc./Fem. worker.

trabajador adjective hard-
working.

trabajar verb [17] to work; **trabaja**
de camarera she works as a
waitress; **trabaja de canguro** she's
a babysitter; **trabajar a tiempo**
completo to work full time;
trabajar a tiempo parcial to work
part time.

trabajo noun Masc. **1** work; **estar**
sin trabajo to be out of work;
trabajo a tiempo completo full-
time work; **trabajo a tiempo**
parcial part-time work; **el trabajo**
de la casa the housework; **2** job;
buscar trabajo to look for a job;
quedarse sin trabajo to lose your
job; **un trabajo fijo** a steady job;

3 trabajos manuales handicrafts; **4** piece of work; **un trabajo sobre la contaminación** an essay on pollution.

tractor noun Masc. tractor.

tradición noun Fem. tradition.

tradicional adjective traditional.

traducción noun Fem. translation.

traducir verb [60] to translate.

traductor/traductora noun Masc./Fem. translator.

traduje, traduzca, traduzco, etc. verb SEE **traducir**.

traer verb [42] **1** to bring; **he traído algo de comida** I've brought some food; **me trae un café, por favor** would you bring me a coffee, please?; **la traerá en coche a la estación** he'll bring her to the station in his car; **traer buena suerte** to bring good luck, to be lucky; **2** to carry; **la traía en brazos** he was carrying her in his arms.

traficante noun Masc./Fem. dealer; **traficante de armas** arms dealer.

tráfico noun Masc. **1** traffic; **2** trade; **tráfico de armas** arms trade; **tráfico de drogas** drug dealing.

tragaperras noun Masc./Fem. (does not change in the plural) (informal) slot machine.

tragar verb [28] to swallow.

tragarse reflexive verb [28] to swallow; **se tragó un hueso de aceituna** he swallowed an olive stone.

tragedia noun Fem. tragedy.

trágico/trágica adjective tragic.

traición noun Fem. **1** treason; **2 una traición** an act of treachery.

traidor/traidora noun Masc./Fem. traitor.

traiga, traigo, traje[1], etc. verb SEE **traer**.

traje[2] noun Masc. **1** suit; **2 traje de baño** swimsuit, swimming trunks; **3** costume; **un traje de luces** a bullfighter's costume; **4** dress; **en traje típico** in traditional dress.

trampa noun Fem. trap; **tenderle una trampa a alguien** to set a trap for somebody.

trampilla noun Fem. trapdoor.

trampolín noun Masc. **1** springboard, diving board; **2** trampoline; **3** ski jump.

tranquillo noun Masc. knack; **coger el tranquillo a algo** to get the knack of something.

tranquilo/tranquila adjective **1** quiet; **una calle tranquila** a quiet street; **2** relaxed; **se le ve tranquilo** he looks relaxed; **¡tranquilo!** relax!; **3** calm; **un ambiente tranquilo** a calm environment; **4 ¡déjame tranquilo!** leave me alone!; **5 tengo la conciencia tranquila** my conscience is clear.

transbordador noun Masc. **1** ferry; **2 transbordador espacial** space shuttle.

transbordar verb [17] **1** to transfer (luggage or goods); **2** to change (trains, for example).

a
b
c
d
e
f
g
h
i
j
k
l
m
n
ñ
o
p
q
r
s
u
v
w
x
y
z

a **transbordo** noun Masc. change;
hacer transbordo to change
(trains, buses); **haz transbordo en
Sol** change at Sol.

b
c **transeúnte** noun Masc./Fem.
passer-by.

d
e **transferencia** noun Fem.
transfer; **transferencia bancaria**
bank transfer.

f
g **transformar** verb [17] **1** to
transform; **2** to convert;
tranformar algo en algo to
convert something into something.
transformarse reflexive verb
[17] **1** to be transformed; **2** to be
converted.

h
i
j
k **transfusión** noun Fem.
transfusion.

l **transmisión** noun Fem.
broadcast; **transmisión en directo**
live broadcast; **transmisión en
diferido** pre-recorded broadcast.

m
n
ñ **transparente** adjective
transparent.

o
p **transportar** verb [17] to
transport, to carry (people).

q **transporte** noun Masc. transport.

tranvía noun Masc. tram.

r **trapo** noun Masc. cloth; **un trapo
del polvo** a duster; **un trapo de
cocina** a tea towel.

s
t **tras** preposition **1** behind; **tras de
mí** behind me; **2** after; **hora tras
hora** hour after hour; **tras
despedirme, subí al coche** after
saying goodbye, I got in the car.

u
v
w
x **trasero/trasera** adjective
1 back; **la puerta trasera** the back
door; **2** rear; **la rueda trasera** the
rear wheel.

y
z

traslado noun Masc. transfer (of
an employee).

trasnochar verb [17] to stay up
late; **anoche trasnochamos** we
had a late night last night.

trasplante noun Masc. transplant.

tratado noun Masc. treaty.

tratamiento noun Masc.
treatment; **estar en tratamiento** to
be undergoing medical treatment.

tratar verb [17] **1** to treat; **no me
trataron bien** they didn't treat me
very well; **2 no trata sus libros
con cuidado** she's not careful with
her books; **3 tratar a alguien de
usted** to address somebody using
the polite 'usted' form; **tratar a
alguien de tú** to address somebody
using the less formal 'tú' form;
4 tratar de hacer to try to do; **trató
de impedirlo** he tried to stop it;
5 tratar de algo to be about
something; **¿de qué trata la
película?** what's the film about?
tratarse reflexive verb [17]
1 tratarse de algo to be about
something; **2 tratarse de usted** to
address each other using the polite
'usted' form; **tratarse de tú** to
address each other using the less
formal 'tú' form.

través in phrase **a través de algo**
through something (from one side
to the other), across something.

travieso/traviesa adjective
naughty; **no seas travieso** don't be
naughty.

trayecto noun Masc. **1** journey;
cubrir un trayecto to make a
journey; **2** road; **3 final de**

trayecto end of the line (*on public transport*).

trazar *verb* [22] **1** to trace; **2** to draw (*a map*); **3** to draw up (*a plan*).

trece *number* **1** thirteen; **tiene trece años** she's thirteen (years old); **2** thirteenth (*in dates*); **el trece de mayo** the thirteenth of May.

treinta *number* **1** thirty; **tiene treinta años** she's thirty (years old); **treinta y siete** thirty-seven; **2** thirtieth (*in dates*); **el treinta de mayo** the thirtieth of May.

tremendo/tremenda *adjective* tremendous; **una tremenda victoria/derrota** a tremendous victory/defeat.

tren *noun Masc.* **1** train; **coger el tren** to catch the train; **ir en tren** to go by train; **un tren directo** a through train; **un tren de cercanías** a local train; **un tren de largo recorrido** a long-distance train; **un tren de alta velocidad** a high-speed train; **2 tren de aterrizaje** landing gear; **3 tren de montaje** assembly line.

trepar *verb* [17] to climb; **trepar a un árbol** to climb a tree.

tres *number* **1** three; **tiene tres años** she's three (years old); **2** third (*in dates*); **el tres de mayo** the third of May; **3** three (*in clock time*); **son las tres** it's three o'clock.

trescientos/trescientas *number* three hundred;

trescientos veinte three hundred and twenty.

triángulo *noun Masc.* triangle.

tribu *noun Fem.* tribe.

tribunal *noun Masc.* **1** court; **2** tribunal.

trigo *noun Masc.* wheat.

trillizos/trillizas *plural noun Masc./Fem.* triplets.

trimestre *noun Masc.* **1** term (*in school*); **2** quarter (*three months*).

trineo *noun Masc.* sledge.

Trinidad *noun Fem.* Trinidad.

triniteño/triniteña *adjective, noun* Trinidadian.

trinitense *adjective, noun* Trinidadian.

tripa *noun Fem.* **1** (*informal*) belly; **2** gut; **3 tripas** innards.

triple *noun Masc.* **el triple del precio original** three times the original price; **es el triple de ancho** it's three times as wide; **subió al triple** it tripled.

triple *adjective* triple.

triplicarse *reflexive verb* [31] to triple; **el precio se ha triplicado** the price has tripled.

tripulación *noun Fem.* crew.

tripulante *noun Masc./Fem.* crew member.

triste *adjective* **1** sad; **2** gloomy.

tristeza *noun Fem.* sadness.

triunfar *verb* [17] to triumph.

triunfo *noun Masc.* **1** victory; **2** triumph.

trivial *adjective* trivial.

trofeo *noun Masc.* trophy.

a **trombón** noun Masc. trombone.

b **trompeta** noun Fem. trumpet.

tronar verb [24] to thunder.

c **tronco** noun Masc. **1** trunk; **2** log;
★ **dormir como un tronco** to sleep
d like a log.

e **trono** noun Masc. throne.

f **tropezar** verb [25] to trip; **tropezar
con algo** to trip over something.

g **tropezarse** reflexive verb [25] to
trip; **tropezarse con algo** to trip
h over something, to come up
against something (a problem).

tropezón noun Masc. stumble; **dar
j un tropezón** to stumble.

k **trópico** noun Masc. tropic.

l **tropiece, tropiezo, etc.** verb
SEE **tropezar.**

m **trotar** verb [17] to trot.

n **trozo** noun Masc. piece; **un trozo de
tela** a piece of cloth.

ñ **trucha** noun Fem. trout.

o **truco** noun Masc. trick; **el truco
está en hacerlo despacio** the
p trick is to do it slowly.

q **trueno** noun Masc. thunder.

r **tu** adjective your; **tu casa** your
house; **tus amigos** your friends.

s **tú** pronoun **1** you; **tú no lo sabes**
you don't know it; **2 tú mismo/
t misma** yourself; **hazlo tú mismo**
do it yourself; **3 tratar a alguien
u de tú** to address somebody using
the 'tú' form (rather than the more
v formal 'usted').

w **tubo** noun Masc. **1** tube; **2 tubo de
escape** exhaust pipe.

x
tuerca noun Fem. nut.
y

z **tuerza, tuerzo, etc.** verb SEE
torcer.

tuesta, tueste, tuesto, etc.
verb SEE **tostar.**

tulipán noun Masc. tulip.

tumba noun Fem. **1** grave; **2** tomb.

tumbar verb [17] to knock down;
tumbar a alguien de un puñetazo
to floor somebody (with a punch).

tumbarse reflexive verb [17] to
lie down; **se tumbó en el sofá** he
lay down on the sofa.

tumbona noun Fem. deckchair.

tunecino/tunecina noun Masc./
Fem., adjective Tunisian.

túnel noun Masc. tunnel.

Túnez noun Masc. Tunisia.

turbante noun Masc. turban.

turco/turca noun Masc./Fem.,
adjective Turkish.

turismo noun Masc. **1** tourism;
oficina de turismo tourist office;
hacer turismo to travel around, to
go sightseeing; **2** saloon car.

turista noun Masc./Fem. tourist.

turístico/turística adjective
tourist.

turnarse reflexive verb [17] to take
turns.

turno noun Masc. **1** turn; **tocarle el
turno a alguien** to be somebody's
turn; **te toca el turno a ti** it's your
turn; **2** shift; **turno de noche** night
shift; **hacer turnos trabajo** to
work shifts.

Turquía noun Fem. Turkey.

turrón noun Masc. nougat (a special
sort traditionally eaten in Spain at
Christmas).

tutear verb [17] **tutear a alguien** to address somebody using the familiar 'tú' form (*rather than the more formal 'usted'*).

tutearse *reflexive verb* [17] to address each other using the familiar 'tú' form (*see note above*).

tutor/tutora noun Masc./Fem.
1 tutor; **2** class teacher.

tutoría noun Fem. **1** study period; **2** tutorship.

tuvo, tuvieron, tuviste, etc. verb SEE **tener**.

tuyo/tuya adjective yours (*goes after the noun*); **un amigo tuyo** a friend of yours; **una vecina tuya** a neighbour of yours.

tuyo pronoun yours; **el tuyo es verde** yours is green; **las tuyas son mejores** yours are better.

Uu

u conjunction or ('*o*' *becomes* '*u*' *before words beginning with* '*o-*' *or* '*ho-*'); **uno u otro** one or the other.

Ucrania noun Fem. Ukraine.

ucraniano/ucraniana noun Masc./Fem., adjective Ukrainian.

Ud. abbreviation (*short for:* usted) you.

Uds. abbreviation (*short for:* ustedes) you.

UE abbreviation Fem. (*short for:* Unión Europea) EU.

úlcera noun Fem. ulcer.

últimamente adverb lately.

último/última noun Masc./Fem. **el último** the last one; **esta es la última que queda** this is the last one left; **coge el último del montón** take the one at the bottom of the pile.

último adjective **1** last; **el último día fuimos a la playa** on the last day we went to the beach; **2** latest; **su última película** her latest film; **lo último en equipo audio** the latest in audio equipment; **3** top; **el último libro del montón** the book at the bottom of the pile.

ultramarinos noun Masc. (*does not change in the plural*) grocer's shop.

un/una[1] indefinite article **1** a, an; **un hombre** a man; **una manzana** an apple; **tiene un año** she's a year old/one year old ('*un' is used before feminine nouns starting with stressed 'a' or 'ha'*) **un ala** a wing; **un hacha** an axe; **2** (*plural*) **unos/unas** some, a few; **compré unos sobres** I bought some envelopes; **se quedarán unas horas** they will stay for a few hours; **3 cuesta unas tres mil euros** it costs about three thousand euros; **llevará unos treinta minutos hacerlo** it'll take about thirty minutes to do it.

único/única noun Masc./Fem. **el único/la única** the only one; **el único que funciona** the only one that works.

único adjective **1** unique; **2** only; **su único hijo** her only child; **3 talla única** one size.

unidad noun Fem. **1** unit; **unidad de cuidados intensivos, unidad**

a b c d e f g h i j k l m n ñ o p q r s t u v w x y z

de vigilancia intensiva intensive care unit; **2** unity.

unido/unida *adjective* **1** united; **2** joined; **3** close; **las dos hermanas están muy unidas** the two sisters are very close.

uniforme *noun Masc.* uniform.

uniforme *adjective* **1** uniform; **2** even.

Unión Europea *noun Fem.* European Union.

unir *verb* [19] **1** to join; **2** to combine; **el diseño une la elegancia con la eficacia** the design combines elegance and efficiency; **3** to merge (*companies, for example*).

unirse *reflexive verb* [19] **1** to join together; **2** to combine; **3** to merge.

universidad *noun Fem.* university; **universidad a distancia** open university; **universidad laboral** technical college; **estar en la universidad** to be at university.

universitario/universitaria *noun Masc./Fem.* university student.

universitario *adjective* university; **profesores universitarios** university teachers.

universo *noun Masc.* universe.

uno¹/**una** *number* **1** one; **compré sólo uno** I bought only one; **hay una razón** there is one reason; **2** one (*in clock time*); **la una** one o'clock; **es la una** it's one o'clock; **llegaron a la una** they arrived at one o'clock; **3** first (*in dates*); **el uno de enero** the first of January.

uno²/**una** *pronoun* **1** one; **de uno en uno** one by one (*note that 'uno' becomes 'un' before a masculine singular noun*); **2 unos/unas** some; **unos saben y otros no** some know and some don't.

unos/unas SEE **un/una**¹, **uno/una**².

uña *noun Fem.* nail (*of finger, toe*); **una uña del dedo del pie** a toe nail.

urbano/urbana *adjective* urban.

urgencia *noun Fem.* **1** urgency; **2** (*in hospital*) **'urgencias'** 'accident and emergency'; **sala de urgencias** accident and emergency department.

urgente *adjective* **1** urgent; **2** express (*post*).

urgentemente *adverb* urgently; **quiere verte urgentemente** she wants to see you urgently.

Uruguay *noun Masc.* Uruguay.

uruguayo/uruguaya *noun Masc./Fem., adjective* Uruguayan.

usado/usada *adjective* **1** used; **2** second-hand; **ropa usada** second-hand clothes.

usar *verb* [17] **1** to use; **¿qué champú usas?** what shampoo do you use?; **2** to take (*clothes size*).

uso *noun Masc.* use; **instrucciones de uso** instructions for use.

usted *pronoun* you (*the formal, polite form: talking to one person*); **usted mismo/misma** yourself.

ustedes *pronoun* you (*the formal, polite form: talking to more than one person*); **ustedes mismos/ mismas** yourselves.

usual *adjective* usual.

usuario/usuaria *noun Masc./Fem.* user.

utensilio *noun Masc.* **1** tool; **2** utensil.

útil *adjective* useful.

utilizar *verb* [22] to use.

uva *noun Fem.* grape; **las uvas de la suerte** the twelve grapes (*one for each month of the year*) eaten traditionally in Spain at midnight on New Year's Eve; **tomar las uvas** to eat grapes (*at midnight on New Year's Eve*).

Vv

vaca *noun Fem.* cow.

vacaciones *plural noun Fem.* holiday, holidays; **irse de vacaciones** to go on holiday; **tomarse unas vacaciones** to take a holiday; **las vacaciones de Navidad** the Christmas holidays; **estar de vacaciones** to be on holiday.

vaciar *verb* [32] to empty.

vacilar *verb* [17] **1** to hesitate; **sin vacilar** without hesitating; **vacilaba entre quedarse o no** she was hesitating whether to stay or not; **2** to falter; **3** (*informal*) to joke; **¡deja de vacilar!** stop fooling about!

vacío/vacía *adjective* empty.

vacío *noun Masc.* vacuum.

vacuna *noun Fem.* vaccine.

vacunar *verb* [17] to vaccinate.

vagabundo/vagabunda *noun Masc./Fem.* vagrant.

vagabundo *adjective* **un perro vagabundo** a stray dog.

vago/vaga *noun Masc./Fem.* layabout.

vago *adjective* lazy.

vagón *noun Masc.* **1** carriage; **2** wagon.

vainilla *noun Fem.* vanilla.

valdrá, valdré, valdría, etc. *verb* SEE **valer.**

vale *noun Masc.* **1** voucher; **2** credit slip.

vale *exclamation* okay; '**¿vamos a cenar fuera?**' – '**¡vale!**' 'shall we go out for dinner?' – 'okay!'

valer *verb* [43] **1** to cost; **¿cuánto vale?** how much is it?; **vale trescientos cincuenta euros** it's three hundred and fifty euros; **2** to be worth; **vale bastante dinero** it's worth quite a lot of money; **3** valer **la pena** to be worth it; **no vale la pena** it's not worth it; **no vale la pena enfadarse por ello** it's not worth getting upset about; **vale la pena el esfuerzo** it's worth the effort; **4** to be valid (*a ticket or coupon*); **5** to be allowed; **no vale preguntar** you can't ask; **eso no vale, tú ya lo habías visto** that's not fair, you'd already seen it.

valga, valgo, etc. *verb* SEE **valer.**

válido/válida *adjective* valid.

valiente *adjective* brave.

a
b
c
d
e
f
g
h
i
j
k
l
m
n
ñ
o
p
q
r
s
t
u
v
w
x
y
z

valioso/valiosa *adjective* valuable.

valle *noun Masc.* valley.

valor *noun Masc.* courage.

valorar *verb* [17] to value.

vals *noun Masc.* waltz.

vamos *verb* SEE **ir.**

vandalismo *noun Masc.* hooliganism.

vanidoso/vanidosa *adjective* vain.

vano/vana *adjective* **1** futile; **2** pointless.

vapor *noun Masc.* steam; **al vapor** steamed.

vaquero *noun Masc.* jeans; **vaqueros** jeans.

variado/variada *adjective* varied.

variar *verb* [32] **1** to vary; **2** to change.

varicela *noun Fem.* chicken pox.

variedad *noun Fem.* variety.

varios/varias *pronoun, adjective* several; **varias veces** several times.

varón *noun Masc.* male.

varón *adjective* male.

varonil *adjective* manly.

vasco[1] *noun Masc.* Basque (*the language*).

vasco[2]**/vasca** *noun Masc./Fem., adjective* Basque.

vasija *noun Fem.* vessel.

vaso *noun Masc.* glass; **un vaso de agua** a glass of water; **un vaso de papel** a paper cup.

Vd. *abbreviation* (*short for: usted*) you.

Vds. *abbreviation* (*short for: ustedes*) you.

vecindad *noun Fem.* neighbourhood.

vecino/vecina *noun Masc./Fem.* neighbour.

vecino *adjective* neighbouring.

vegetariano/vegetariana *noun Masc./Fem., adjective* vegetarian.

vehículo *noun Masc.* vehicle; **vehículo espacial** spacecraft.

veía, veían, etc. *verb* SEE **ver.**

veinte *number* **1** twenty; **tiene veinte años** she's twenty (years old); **veintidós** twenty-two; **2** twentieth (*in dates*); **el veinte de diciembre** the twentieth of December; **3** twenty (*in clock time*); **a las veinticinco** at twenty-five past.

vejez *noun Fem.* old age.

vela *noun Fem.* **1** candle; **2** sail; **3** sailing; **4** **pasar la noche en vela;** **he pasado toda la noche en vela** I've been awake all night.

velero *noun Masc.* sailing ship, sailing boat.

velocidad *noun Fem.* **1** speed; **el coche iba a mucha velocidad** the car was going very fast; **disminuir la velocidad** to slow down; **2** gear (*in a car*); **la cuarta velocidad** fourth gear.

vena *noun Fem.* vein.

vencedor/vencedora *adjective* winning.

vencer verb [44] **1** to defeat; **vencer a alguien** to defeat somebody; **2** to win; **3** to overcome; **4** to expire (*a passport, for example*).

vencido/vencida adjective defeated.

venda noun Fem. bandage.

vendar verb [17] **1** to bandage; **2** **vendar los ojos a alguien** to blindfold somebody.

vendaval noun Masc. gale.

vendedor/vendedora noun **1** shop assistant; **2** salesman/saleswoman; **3** seller; **un vendedor ambulante** a street seller.

vender verb [18] to sell; **le he vendido mi coche** I've sold him my car; **los venden a ciento ochenta euros** they're selling them for a hundred and eighty euros; **'se vende'** 'for sale'.

vendimia noun Fem. wine harvest.

vendrá, vendré, vendría, etc. verb SEE **venir**.

veneno noun Masc. poison, venom.

venenoso/venenosa adjective poisonous.

venezolano/venezolana noun Masc./Fem., adjective Venezuelan.

Venezuela noun Fem. Venezuela.

venga, vengo, etc. verb SEE **venir**.

venganza noun Fem. revenge. **vengarse** reflexive verb [28] **vengarse de alguien** to get one's revenge on someone.

venir verb [15] **1** to come; **sus padres no vinieron** her parents didn't come; **ven a las siete** come at seven; **2** **venir de** to come from; **viene de Italia** it comes from Italy; **3** **venir a hacer** to come to do; **yo vendré a buscarte** I'll come and collect you; **4** **venir a por algo** to come to fetch something; **vengo a por el paquete** I've come to fetch the parcel; **venir a por alguien** to come to collect somebody; **yo vendré a buscarte** I'll come and collect you; **5** to be; **la noticia viene en la primera página** the news is on the front page; **6** **venirle bien a alguien** to suit someone; **mañana no les viene bien** tomorrow doesn't suit them; **¿te viene bien quedar en la entrada?** is it okay for you if we meet at the entrance?; **esta parada de metro me viene muy bien** this tube station's very convenient for me; **7** **que viene: la semana que viene** next week; **el domingo que viene** next Sunday; **8** **¡venga!** come on!

venta noun Fem. sale; **estar en venta** to be for sale; **'prohibida su venta'** 'not for sale'.

ventaja noun Fem. advantage.

ventana noun Fem. window.

ventanilla noun Fem. **1** window (*in a train or car*); **2** box office; **3** **horario de ventanilla** opening hours (*at a consulate, for example*).

ventilación noun Fem. ventilation.

ventilador noun Masc. fan.

ventisca noun Fem. blizzard.

a b c d e f g h i j k l m n ñ o p q r s t u v w x y z

a
b
c
d
e
f
g
h
i
j
k
l
m
n
ñ
o
p
q
r
s
t
u
v
w
x
y
z

ver *verb* [16] **1** to see; **los vi ayer** I saw them yesterday; **la vi cogerlo** I saw her take it; **no veo nada desde aquí** I can't see anything from here; **no veo bien de lejos** I'm shortsighted; **ya veo cuál es el problema** I can see the problem; **ya veremos lo que hacemos** we'll see what we do; **2** to watch; **ver la tele** to watch TV; **anoche vimos una película muy buena** we watched a very good film last night; **3** to think; **lo que ha hecho no lo veo bien** I don't think what he's done is right; **4 tener que ver con algo** to have something to do with something; **eso no tiene nada que ver** that has nothing to do with it; **5 a ver, ¿qué te pasa?** okay, what's the matter with you?; **'mira lo que he encontrado' – '¿a ver?'** 'look what I've found' – 'let's see'.

verse *reflexive verb* [16] **1** to see yourself; **verse en el espejo** to see yourself in the mirror; **2** to see each other; **se ven todas las semanas** they see each other every week; **3** to meet; **¿nos vemos a la entrada del cine?** shall we meet outside the cinema?; ★ **verse en un aprieto** to find yourself in a tight spot.

veraneante *noun Masc./Fem.* holidaymaker.

veranear *verb* [17] **veranear en** to spend your summer holidays in; **veranean en la montaña** they spend their summer holidays in the mountains.

veras *in phrase* **¡de veras!** really!; **una moto de veras** a real motorbike.

verbena *noun Fem.* festival (*held to celebrate the Saint's Day of a town or village*); dance (*in the open air*).

verbo *noun Masc.* verb.

verdad *noun Fem.* **1** truth; **dime la verdad** tell me the truth; **la pura verdad** the absolute truth; **la verdad, no me acuerdo** I don't remember, honestly; **la verdad es que ... the truth is that ...; **2 a decir verdad ...** to tell the truth ...; **3 de verdad** really; **de verdad que no me importa** I don't mind, really; **4 de verdad** real; **un amigo de verdad** a real friend.

verdadero/verdadera *adjective* **1** real; **su verdadero nombre** his real name; **es un verdadero idiota** he's a real idiot; **2** true; **una historia verdadera** a true story.

verde *noun Masc.* **1** green; **verde botella** bottle-green; **2 los Verdes** the Greens (*in politics*).

verde *adjective* **1** green; **tiene los ojos verdes** she has green eyes; **una blusa verde oscuro** a dark green blouse; **2** smutty; **un chiste verde** a dirty joke.

verdulería *noun Fem.* greengrocer's.

verdura *noun Fem.* vegetable; **cómete la verdura** eat your vegetables; **un puesto de verduras** a vegetable stall.

vergonzoso/vergonzosa *adjective* 1 timid; 2 shameful.

vergüenza *noun Fem.* 1 shame; **tener vergüenza** to be ashamed; **¡qué poca vergüenza tienes!** have you no shame at all?; 2 **darle vergüenza a alguien** to be ashamed; **me da vergüenza haberme portado de esa forma** I'm ashamed of behaving the way I did; 3 embarrassment; **pasar vergüenza** to feel embarrassed; 4 **me da vergüenza hablar en público** I feel embarrassed when I have to speak in public.

verruga *noun Fem.* 1 wart; 2 verruca.

versión *noun Fem.* version; **una película en versión original** a film which has not been dubbed (*a foreign film, usually with subtitles*).

verso *noun Masc.* 1 verse; **en verso** in verse; 2 poem; 3 line of a poem; **el tercer verso** the third line of the poem.

vertical *adjective* 1 vertical; 2 down (*in crosswords*); **ocho vertical** eight down.

vertiente *noun Fem.* slope.

vértigo *noun Masc.* vertigo; **me da vértigo mirar abajo** looking down makes me dizzy.

vestíbulo *noun Masc.* 1 hall; 2 foyer.

vestido[1] *noun Masc.* dress; **un vestido de noche** an evening dress; **un vestido de novia** a wedding dress.

vestido[2]**/vestida** *adjective* dressed; **ir bien vestido** to be well dressed; **iba vestida con un traje azul** she was wearing a blue suit; **tenemos que ir al colegio vestidos de uniforme** we have to wear school uniform.

vestir *verb* [57] to dress; **vestir bien** to dress well.

vestirse *reflexive verb* [57] 1 to get dressed; **voy a vestirme** I'm going to get dressed; 2 to dress; **se viste a la última moda** she wears the latest fashions; **me gusta vestirme de azul** I like wearing blue.

vestuario *noun Masc.* 1 wardrobe; 2 changing room.

veterinario/veterinaria *noun Masc./Fem.* veterinary surgeon.

vez (*plural* **veces**) *noun Fem.* 1 time; **la primera vez que fui a Inglaterra** the first time I went to England; **por última vez** for the last time; **algunas veces** sometimes; **¿has estado alguna vez en Italia?** have you ever been to Italy?; **a veces** sometimes; **tal vez** perhaps, maybe; **de vez en cuando** ocasionally, from time to time; **de vez en cuando nos manda una carta** occasionally he sends us a letter; **a la vez** at the same time, at once; 3 **cada vez** each time; **cada vez más** more and more; **hay cada vez más turistas** there are more and more tourists; 4 **cada vez menos** less and less, fewer and fewer; 5 **muchas veces** often; **pocas veces** not very often; **rara vez** seldom; 6 **una vez** once; **dos veces** twice; **tres veces al año**

three times a year; **7 otra vez** again; **8 en vez de** instead of; **9 érase una vez** ... once upon a time ....

vía *noun Fem.* **1** track; **la vía férrea** the railway track; **2 por vía aérea** by air; **por vía marítima** by sea; **3 vía de acceso** slip road; **4 Vía Láctea** Milky Way.

viajar *verb* [17] to travel; **viajar en avión** to travel by plane.

viaje *noun Masc.* journey, trip; **estar de viaje** to be away; **hacer un viaje** to go on a journey, to go on a trip; **salir de viaje** to go on a journey, to go on a trip; **¡buen viaje!** have a good journey!; **viaje de negocios** business trip; **viaje organizado** package tour; **viaje de novios** honeymoon.

viajero/viajera *noun Masc./Fem.* **1** traveller; **2** passenger.

víbora *noun Fem.* viper.

vibrar *verb* [17] to vibrate.

vicio *noun Masc.* **1** vice; **2** bad habit; **tengo el vicio de morderme las uñas** I have the bad habit of biting my nails.

víctima *noun Fem.* victim; **el número de víctimas mortales asciende a 25** the death toll has risen to 25.

victoria *noun Fem.* victory.

vid *noun Fem.* vine.

vida *noun Fem.* life; **¡esto es vida!** this is the life!; **la vida está muy cara** the cost of living is very high; **una cuestión de vida o muerte** a matter of life or death; **llevar una vida muy ajetreada** to lead a very

busy life; **ganarse la vida** to earn a living.

vídeo *noun Masc.* video; **en vídeo** on video.

videocámara *noun Fem.* video camera.

videoclub *noun Masc.* video shop.

videojuego *noun Masc.* video game.

vidrio *noun Masc.* glass.

viejo/vieja *noun Masc./Fem.* old man/old woman.

viejo *adjective* old.

viento *noun Masc.* **1** wind; **hace viento** it's windy; **2** guy rope (*of tent*).

vientre *noun Masc.* **1** belly; **2** womb.

viernes *noun Masc.* Friday; **Viernes Santo** Good Friday (*see* 'domingo' *for more examples*).

vigésimo/vigésima *adjective* twentieth.

villancico *noun Masc.* Christmas carol.

vinagre *noun Masc.* vinegar.

vine, viniste, vino, etc. *verb* SEE **venir**.

viñedo *noun Masc.* vineyard.

vino *noun Masc.* wine; **vino tinto** red wine; **vino blanco** white wine; **vino de mesa** table wine.

violar *verb* [17] to rape.

violencia *noun Fem.* violence.

violento/violenta *adjective* **1** violent; **2** embarrassing (*situation*); **3** embarrassed.

violeta noun Fem., **violeta** adjective violet.

violín noun Masc. violin; **tocar el violín** to play the violin.

violoncelo, violonchelo noun Masc. cello.

virar verb [17] to swerve; **el coche viró brucamente para esquivar al perro** the car swerved sharply to avoid the dog.

virgen noun Fem. virgin.

virgo noun Masc./Fem. Virgo; **es virgo** he's Virgo.

Virgo noun Masc. Virgo.

virtud noun Fem. virtue.

virus noun Masc. virus; **software anti virus** anti-virus software.

visado noun Masc. visa.

visibilidad noun Fem. visibility.

visible adjective visible.

visión noun Fem. **1** vision; **2** sight; **perder la visión** to lose your sight.

visita noun Fem. **1** visit; **una visita al museo** a visit to the museum; **hacer una visita a alguien** to visit somebody; **2** visitor; **tienes una visita** you have a visitor; **3** hit (on web site).

visitar verb [17] to visit.

víspera noun Fem. **la víspera** the day before; **la víspera del partido** the day before the match.

vista[1] noun Fem. **1** eyesight; **tener buena vista** to have good eyesight; **perder la vista** to lose your sight; **el sol me hace daño a la vista** the sun's hurting my eyes; **conocer a**

alguien de vista to know someone by sight; **2** **estar a la vista** to be within sight; **no estar a la vista** to be out of sight; **3** view; **el hotel tiene unas vistas preciosas** the hotel has beautiful views; **4** **con vistas a** with a view to; **5** **¡hasta la vista!** see you!

vistieron, vistió, etc. verb SEE vestir.

visto[1] verb SEE ver.

visto[2] adjective **1** clear; **está visto que ...** it's clear that ...; **2** **por lo visto** apparently; **3** **estar bien visto** to be acceptable; **está mal visto** it's not the done thing; **4** **eso está muy visto** that's not very original.

vitamina noun Fem. vitamin.

viudo/viuda noun Fem. widow/widower.

viva[1] exclamation **¡viva!** hurray!; **¡viva la novia!** three cheers for the bride!

vivienda noun Fem. **1** housing; **el problema de la vivienda** the housing problem; **2** flat, house; **un bloque de viviendas** a block of flats.

vivir verb [19] to live; **vive en casa de su hermana** she lives with her sister; **vive de las traducciones** she makes her living from translation; **vive de su pensión** she lives off her pension.

vivo/viva[2] adjective **1** alive; **2** **actuación en vivo** live performance.

a **vocabulario** noun Masc. vocabulary.

b **volante** noun Masc. steering wheel.

c **volante** adjective flying.

d **volar** verb [24] **1** to fly; **2** to blow up; **volar un edificio** to blow up a building.

e **volcán** noun Masc. volcano.

f **volcar** verb [24] **1** to turn over; **el camión volcó** the lorry turned over; **2 volcar el contenido de algo** to empty something; **3** to knock over.

g **volcarse** reflexive verb [24] **1** to turn over (a vehicle); **2 volcarse en algo** to throw yourself into something.

h **vóleibol, voleibol** noun Masc. volleyball; **jugar al vóleibol** to play volleyball.

i **voltereta** noun Fem. somersault.

j **volumen** noun Masc. volume; **subir el volumen** to turn up the volume.

k **voluntad** noun Fem. **1** will; **fuerza de voluntad** will power; **lo hice por mi propia voluntad** I did it of my own free will; **2** wish; ★ **siempre hace su santa voluntad** she always does exactly as she pleases.

l **voluntario/voluntaria** noun Masc./Fem. volunteer.

m **voluntario** adjective voluntary.

n **volver** verb [45] **1** to turn; **volver la página** to turn the page; **volvió la cabeza** she turned her head; **al volver la esquina ...** when I turned the corner ...; **2** to come back; **aún**

no ha vuelto he hasn't come back yet; **¿cuándo volverás?** when will you come back?; **3** to go back; **volver al colegio** to go back to school; **¿quieres que volvamos a casa?** do you want us to go back home?; **ha vuelto con su novia** he's gone back to his girlfriend; **4** to be back; **volveré a eso de las siete** I'll be back by about seven; **no había vuelto a Sevilla desde el verano pasado** I hadn't been back to Seville since last summer; **5** to get back; **¿cuándo volviste de tu viaje?** when did you get back from your trip?; **6** volver a hacer to do again; **volví a revisarlo** I checked it again; **¡no lo vuelvas a hacer!** don't do it again!; **tenemos que volver a empezar** we have to start again; **7** volver loco a alguien to drive someone mad; **me está volviendo loca con tantas preguntas** she's driving me mad with all her questions; **8** volver en sí to come round (recover consciousness).

volverse reflexive verb [45] **1** to turn around; **me volví para mirar** I turned around to see; **2** volverse de espaldas to turn your back; **¡no te vuelvas de espaldas cuando te estoy hablando!** don't turn your back on me when I'm talking to you!; **3** volverse boca abajo to turn over onto your stomach; **volverse boca arriba** to turn over onto your back; **4** to become; **se ha vuelto muy vanidosa** she's turned very vain; **la situación se ha vuelto insoportable** the situation

283

has become unbearable; **volverse loco** to go mad.

vomitar verb [17] to be sick; **tener ganas de vomitar** to feel sick.

vosotros/vosotras pronoun you (talking to more than one person); **¿vosotras queréis ir?** do you want to go?; **vosotros mismos/ vosotras mismas** yourselves.

votar verb [17] **1** to vote on (a measure); **2** to vote for (a party, a candidate); **siempre vota a los verdes** she always votes for the Greens; **¿por quién votaste?** who did you vote for?.

voto noun Masc. **1** vote; **un voto a favor** a vote for; **un voto en contra** a vote against; **un voto secreto** a secret ballot; **un voto en blanco** a blank ballot paper; **un voto de censura** a vote of no confidence; **2** vow.

voy verb SEE **ir.**

voz (plural **voces**) noun Fem. voice; **oír voces** to hear voices; **tener la voz tomada** to be hoarse; **en voz baja** quietly; **hablar en voz alta** to speak loudly; **leer algo en voz alta** to read something out loud.

vuelo noun Masc. flight; **un vuelo regular** a scheduled flight.

vuelta noun Fem. **1** turn; **una vuelta a la derecha** a turn to the right; **2** return; **a la vuelta podemos visitar el museo** we can visit the museum on our way back; **'vuelta al colegio'** 'back to school' (after the summer holidays); **3 dar la vuelta a algo** to turn something; **dar la vuelta a la página** to turn

the page; **dale la vuelta al cuadro** turn the picture round the other way; **dar la vuelta a un disco** to turn a record over; **4 dar la vuelta a la esquina** to turn the corner; **5 dar la vuelta al mundo** to go round the world; **dar una vuelta a la manzana** to go round the block; **6 dar una vuelta** to go for a walk; **¿te vienes a dar una vuelta?** are you coming for a walk?; **dar una vuelta en coche** to go for a drive; **7 dar una vuelta alrededor de algo** to go around something.

vuelva, vuelvo, etc. verb SEE **volver.**

vuestro/vuestra adjective your (talking to more than one person); **vuestra casa** your house; **un familiar vuestro** a relative of yours.

vuestro pronoun yours; **la vuestra es verde** yours is green; **los vuestros están en el salón** yours are in the living room; **aquel es el vuestro** that one is yours.

vulgar adjective **1** vulgar; **2** common.

Ww

walkman™ noun Masc. personal stereo.

wáter noun Masc. toilet.

whisky noun Masc. whisky.

windsurf noun Masc. **hacer windsurf** to go windsurfing.

windsurf noun Masc. windsurfing.

Xx

xilófono noun Masc. xylophone.

Yy

y conjunction ('y' becomes 'e' before a word beginning with 'i-' or 'hi-') **1** and; **Amanda y yo** Amanda and I; **2** (with numbers and times) **treinta y siete** thirty-seven; **3** (with clock time) **las dos y media** half past two; **a las diez y cinco** at five past ten; **4 ¿y a mí qué?** so what's it to me?

ya adverb **1** already; **ya está hecho** it's already done; **¿has comido ya?** have you already eaten? **2** yet; **¿han llegado ya?** have they arrived yet? **3** any more; **ya no importa** it doesn't matter any more; **4** now; **antes no quería, pero ya ha cambiado de idea** he didn't want to before but he's changed his mind now; **tenemos que decidirnos ya** we must decide now; **5** (in the future) **ya veremos** we'll see; **ya te contaré** I'll tell you about it; **6** (not translated but used to stress what you are saying) **ya lo sé** I know; **ya entiendo** I understand; **ya era hora** it's about time too; **¡ya está!** that's it!; **¡ya estoy!** I'm ready!; **¡ya voy!** I'm just coming!; **¡ya lo creo!** you bet!; **preparados, listos, ¡ya!** ready, steady, go!; **7 'esto es de Juan'** – **'ya'** 'this is Juan's' – 'I know'; **8 'yo**

no he sido' – **'ya, ya'** 'it wasn't me' – 'yeah, yeah!'; **9 ya que** since; **ya que vas a estar aquí** since you're going to be here.

yate noun Masc. yacht.

yedra noun Fem. ivy.

yegua noun Fem. mare.

yema noun Fem. **1** yolk; **2 la yema del dedo** the fingertip.

yerno noun Masc. son-in-law.

yo pronoun **1** I; **yo no lo sé** I don't know; **2** me; **soy yo** it's me; **3 yo mismo/misma** myself; **lo haré yo mismo** I'll do it myself.

yoga noun Fem. yoga.

yogur noun Masc. yoghurt.

yudo noun Masc. judo.

Yugoslavia noun Fem. Yugoslavia.

yugoslavo/yugoslava noun Masc./Fem., adjective Yugoslavian.

Zz

zanahoria noun Fem. carrot.

zapatería noun Fem. shoe shop.

zapatero/zapatera noun Masc./Fem. **1** shoemaker; **2** shoe repairer's.

zapatilla noun Fem. **1** slipper; **2** canvas shoe; **3 zapatilla de deporte** trainer; **4 zapatilla de esparto** espadrille; **5 zapatilla de ballet** ballet shoe.

zapato noun Masc. shoe; **zapato de tacón** high heeled shoe; **zapato bajo** flat shoe.

zarzamora *noun Fem.* blackberry.

zarzuela *noun Fem.* Spanish light opera.

zodíaco, **zodiaca** *noun Masc.* zodiac.

zona *noun Fem.* area; **viven en la zona** they live locally; **zona peatonal** pedestrian precinct; **zona comercial** commercial district.

zoo *noun Masc.* zoo.

zoológico *noun Masc.* zoo.

zorro *noun Masc.* fox.

zueco *noun Masc.* clog.

zumo *noun Masc.* juice; **zumo de fruta** fruit juice; **zumo de naranja** orange juice.

zurdo/zurda *noun Masc./Fem.* left-handed person.

a
b
c
d
e
f
g
h
i
j
k
l
m
n
ñ
o
p
q
r
s
t
u
v
w
x
y
z

VERB TABLES AND FORMS

Spanish verb tables
The following verb tables show you how Spanish verbs are formed. They fall into three categories – main irregular verbs, the three regular verb patterns using **hablar**, **comer**, and **vivir** as models, and other irregular verbs.

Main Spanish irregular verbs (pages 288–303)
The following Spanish verbs are unlike any others – they are irregular. The way that they are formed is given in the following section. When you look up a verb in this dictionary, you will see that it has a number in square brackets ([1], [2] etc.) This number tells you which verb to look up in this section.

[1]	**ser**	to be	[9]	**tener**	to have
[2]	**estar**	to be	[10]	**poder**	to be able
[3]	**coger**	to take	[11]	**poner**	to put
[4]	**dar**	to give	[12]	**querer**	to want, to love
[5]	**decir**	to say, to tell	[13]	**saber**	to know (facts)
[6]	**haber**	to have	[14]	**sentir**	to feel
[7]	**hacer**	to make, to do	[15]	**venir**	to come
[8]	**ir**	to go	[16]	**ver**	to see

Regular Spanish verbs (pages 304–306)
All other Spanish verbs belong to verb families. These are the **–ar**, **-er**, and **–ir** verbs. The ones with regular patterns follow the ones given in full here. In this dictionary, the numbers in square brackets ([17], [18] or [19]) tell you which verb pattern to follow.

-ar verbs	[17]	**hablar**	to speak, to talk
-er verbs	[18]	**comer**	to eat
-ir verbs	[19]	**vivir**	to live

Other irregular verbs (pages 307–317)
However, some of the verbs in the **-ar**, **-er**, and **–ir** regular verb families have differences from the regular patterns. These verbs are also numbered in the dictionary to tell you where to find them in this centre section. These verbs follow the regular verb patterns, apart from the forms that are given on pages 307-317.

Reflexive verbs
Many Spanish verbs may also be used reflexively with the appropriate pronouns (**me/te/se/nos/os/se**) for each person. Remember that when a verb is used reflexively its meaning may change, so check carefully in the dictionary. A typical example is [14] **sentir** on page 301.

1

ser
to be

Gerund
siendo   being

Past participle
sido   been

Present indicative

soy   I am
eres
es
somos
sois
son

Imperfect indicative

era   I was or I used to be
eras
era
éramos
erais
eran

Past simple indicative

fui   I was
fuiste
fue
fuimos
fuisteis
fueron

Future indicative

seré   I will be
serás
será
seremos
seréis
serán

Conditional (present)

sería   I would be
serías
sería
seríamos
seríais
serían

Present subjunctive

sea   I am
seas
sea
seamos
seáis
sean

Imperfect subjunctive

fuera   I was or I were
fueras
fuera
fuéramos
fuerais
fueran

Imperative

sé (tú)   be (singular)
sea (usted)   be (sing formal)
seamos   let us be or
(nosotros)   let's be
sed (vosotros)   be (plural)
sean (ustedes)   be (pl formal)

Gerund		Past participle	
estando	being	estado	been

2

estar
to be

Present indicative

estoy	I am
estás	
está	
estamos	
estáis	
están	

Imperfect indicative

estaba	I was or I used to be
estabas	
estaba	
estábamos	
estabais	
estaban	

Past simple indicative

estuve	I was
estuviste	
estuvo	
estuvimos	
estuvisteis	
estuvieron	

Future indicative

estaré	I will be
estarás	
estará	
estaremos	
estaréis	
estarán	

Conditional (present)

estaría	I would be
estarías	
estaría	
estaríamos	
estaríais	
estarían	

Present subjunctive

esté	I am
estés	
esté	
estemos	
estéis	
estén	

Imperfect subjunctive

estuviera	I was or I were
estuvieras	
estuviera	
estuviéramos	
estuvierais	
estuvieran	

Imperative

está (tú)	be (singular)
esté (usted)	be (sing formal)
estemos (nosotros)	let us be or let's be
estad (vosotros)	be (plural)
estén (ustedes)	be (pl formal)

3

coger
to take

Gerund		Past participle	
cogiendo	taking	cogido	taken

Present indicative

cojo	I take or I am taking
coges	
coge	
cogemos	
cogéis	
cogen	

Imperfect indicative

cogía	I was taking or I used to take
cogías	
cogía	
cogíamos	
cogíais	
cogían	

Past simple indicative

cogí	I took
cogiste	
cogió	
cogimos	
cogisteis	
cogieron	

Future indicative

cogeré	I will take
cogerás	
cogerá	
cogeremos	
cogeréis	
cogerán	

Conditional (present)

cogería	I would take
cogerías	
cogería	
cogeríamos	
cogeríais	
cogerían	

Present subjunctive

coja	I take
cojas	
coja	
cojamos	
cojáis	
cojan	

Imperfect subjunctive

cogiera	I took or I were to take
cogieras	
cogiera	
cogiéramos	
cogierais	
cogieran	

Imperative

coge (tú)	take (singular)
coja (usted)	take (sing formal)
cojamos (nosotros)	let us take or let's take
coged (vosotros)	take (plural)
cojan (ustedes)	take (pl formal)

Gerund		Past participle		**4**
dando	giving	dado	given	

dar
to give

Present indicative

doy   I give
das
da
damos
dais
dan

Conditional (present)

daría   I would give
darías
daría
daríamos
daríais
darían

Imperfect indicative

daba   I gave or I used to give
dabas
daba
dábamos
dabais
daban

Present subjunctive

dé   I give
des
dé
demos
deis
den

Past simple indicative

di   I gave
diste
dio
dimos
disteis
dieron

Imperfect subjunctive

diera   I gave or I were to give
dieras
diera
diéramos
dierais
dieran

Future indicative

daré   I will give
darás
dará
daremos
daréis
darán

Imperative

da (tú)	give (singular)
de (usted)	give (sing formal)
demos (nosotros)	let us give or let's give
dad (vosotros)	give (plural)
den (ustedes)	give (pl formal)

5
decir
to say *or* to tell

Gerund		**Past participle**
diciendo	saying	dicho	said

Present indicative
digo — I say or I am saying
dices
dice
decimos
decís
dicen

Imperfect indicative
decía — I was saying or I used to say
decías
decía
decíamos
decíais
decían

Past simple indicative
dije — I said
dijiste
dijo
dijimos
dijisteis
dijeron

Future indicative
diré — I will say
dirás
dirá
diremos
diréis
dirán

Conditional (present)
diría — I would say
dirías
diría
diríamos
diríais
dirían

Present subjunctive
diga — I say
digas
diga
digamos
digáis
digan

Imperfect subjunctive
dijera — I said or I were to say
dijeras
dijera
dijéramos
dijerais
dijeran

Imperative
di (tú) — say (singular)
diga (usted) — say (sing formal)
digamos (nosotros) — let us say or let's say
decid (vosotros) — say (plural)
digan (ustedes) — say (pl formal)

Gerund	Past participle
habiendo having	habido been

6
haber
to have

Present indicative

he	I have
has	
ha	
hemos	
habéis	
han	

Imperfect indicative

había	I was having or
	I used to have
habías	
había	
habíamos	
habíais	
habían	

Past simple indicative

hube	I had
hubiste	
hubo	
hubimos	
hubisteis	
hubieron	

Future indicative

habré	I will have
habrás	
habrá	
habremos	
habréis	
habrán	

Conditional (present)

habría	I would have
habrías	
habría	
habríamos	
habríais	
habrían	

Present subjunctive

haya	I have
hayas	
haya	
hayamos	
hayáis	
hayan	

Imperfect subjunctive

hubiera	I had or I were to have
hubieras	
hubiera	
hubiéramos	
hubierais	
hubieran	

Imperative

he (tú)	have (singular)
haya (usted)	have (sing formal)
hayamos (nosotros)	let us have or let's have
habed (vosotros)	have (plural)
hayan (ustedes)	have (pl formal)

7

hacer
to make *or* to do

Gerund
haciendo
making *ord* oing

Past participle
hecho
made *or* done

Present indicative

hago	I make *or* I am making *or* I do *or* I am doing
haces	
hace	
hacemos	
hacéis	
hacen	

Imperfect indicative

hacía	I was making *or* I used to make *or* I was doing *or* I used to do
hacías	
hacía	
hacíamos	
hacíais	
hacían	

Past simple indicative

hice	I made *or* I did
hiciste	
hizo	
hicimos	
hicisteis	
hicieron	

Future indicative

haré	I will make *or* I will do
harás	
hará	
haremos	
haréis	
harán	

Conditional (present)

haría	I would make *or* I would do
harías	
haría	
haríamos	
haríais	
harían	

Present subjunctive

haga	I make *or* I do
hagas	
haga	
hagamos	
hagáis	
hagan	

Imperfect subjunctive

hiciera	I made *or* I were to make *or* I did *or* I were to do
hicieras	
hiciera	
hiciéramos	
hicierais	
hicieran	

Imperative

haz (tú)	make *or* do (singular)
haga (usted)	make *or* do (sing formal)
hagamos (nosotros)	let us make *or* let's make *or* let us do *or* let's do
haced (vosotros)	make *or* do (plural)
hagan (ustedes)	make *or* do (pl formal)

Gerund		Past participle	
yendo	going	ido	gone

Present indicative

voy	I go or I am going
vas	
va	
vamos	
vais	
van	

Imperfect indicative

iba	I was going or I used to go
ibas	
iba	
íbamos	
ibais	
iban	

Past simple indicative

fui	I went
fuiste	
fue	
fuimos	
fuisteis	
fueron	

Future indicative

iré	I will go
irás	
irá	
iremos	
iréis	
irán	

Conditional (present)

iría	I would go
irías	
iría	
iríamos	
iríais	
irían	

Present subjunctive

vaya	I go
vayas	
vaya	
vayamos	
vayáis	
vayan	

Imperfect subjunctive

fuera	I went or I were to go
fueras	
fuera	
fuéramos	
fuerais	
fueran	

Imperative

ve (tú)	go (singular)
vaya (usted)	go (sing formal)
vamos (nosotros)	let us go or let's go
id (vosotros)	go (plural)
vayan (ustedes)	go (pl formal)

9
tener
to have

Gerund	**Past participle**
teniendo	tenido had
having	

Present indicative

tengo	I have or I am having
tienes	
tiene	
tenemos	
tenéis	
tienen	

Imperfect indicative

tenía	I was having or I used to have
tenías	
tenía	
teníamos	
teníais	
tenían	

Past simple indicative

tuve	I had
tuviste	
tuvo	
tuvimos	
tuvisteis	
tuvieron	

Future indicative

tendré	I will have
tendrás	
tendrá	
tendremos	
tendréis	
tendrán	

Conditional (present)

tendría	I would have
tendrías	
tendría	
tendríamos	
tendríais	
tendrían	

Present subjunctive

tenga	I have
tengas	
tenga	
tengamos	
tengáis	
tengan	

Imperfect subjunctive

tuviera	I have
tuvieras	
tuviera	
tuviéramos	
tuvierais	
tuvieran	

Imperative

ten (tú)	have (singular)
tenga (usted)	have (sing formal)
tengamos (nosotros)	let us have or let's have
tened (vosotros)	have (plural)
tengan (ustedes)	have (pl formal)

Gerund pudiendo being able to	**Past participle** podido been able to	**10** **poder** to be able

Present indicative

puedo	I am able to or I can
puedes	
puede	
podemos	
podéis	
pueden	

Imperfect indicative

podía	I was able to or I used to be able to
podías	
podía	
podíamos	
podíais	
podían	

Past simple indicative

pude	I was able to to or I could
pudiste	
pudo	
pudimos	
pudisteis	
pudieron	

Future indicative

podré	I will be able to
podrás	
podrá	
podremos	
podréis	
podrán	

Conditional (present)

podría	I would be able to
podrías	
podría	
podríamos	
podríais	
podrían	

Present subjunctive

pueda	I am able to or I can
puedas	
pueda	
podamos	
podáis	
puedan	

Imperfect subjunctive

pudiera	I was able to or I were able to
pudieras	
pudiera	
pudiéramos	
pudierais	
pudieran	

Imperative

The imperative is not used with
poder

11

poner
to put

Gerund	Past participle
poniendo	puesto put
putting	

Present indicative

pongo	I put or I am putting
pones	
pone	
ponemos	
ponéis	
ponen	

Imperfect indicative

ponía	I was putting or I used to put
ponías	
ponía	
poníamos	
poníais	
ponían	

Past simple indicative

puse	I put
pusiste	
puso	
pusimos	
pusisteis	
pusieron	

Future indicative

pondré	I will put
pondrás	
pondrá	
pondremos	
pondréis	
pondrán	

Conditional (present)

pondría	I would put
pondrías	
pondría	
pondríamos	
pondríais	
pondrían	

Present subjunctive

ponga	I put
pongas	
ponga	
pongamos	
pongáis	
pongan	

Imperfect subjunctive

pusiera	I put or I were to put
pusieras	
pusiera	
pusiéramos	
pusierais	
pusieran	

Imperative

pon (tú)	put (singular)
ponga (usted)	put (sing formal)
pongamos (nosotros)	let us put or let's put
poned (vosotros)	put (plural)
pongan (ustedes)	put (pl formal)

Gerund	Past participle
queriendo	querido loved
wanting to *or* loving	

12

querer
to want *or* to love

Present indicative

quiero	I want to *or* I love
quieres	
quiere	
queremos	
queréis	
quieren	

Imperfect indicative

quería	I wanted to *or* I used to want to *or* I loved or I used to love
querías	
quería	
queríamos	
queríais	
querían	

Past simple indicative

quise	I wanted to *or* I loved
quisiste	
quiso	
quisimos	
quisisteis	
quisieron	

Future indicative

querré	I will want to *or* I will love
querrás	
querrá	
querremos	
querréis	
querrán	

Conditional (present)

querría	I would want to *or* I would love
querrías	
querría	
querríamos	
querríais	
querrían	

Present subjunctive

quiera	I want to *or* I love
quieras	
quiera	
queramos	
queráis	
quieran	

Imperfect subjunctive

quisiera	I wanted to *or* I were to want to *or* I loved *or* I were to love
quisieras	
quisiera	
quisiéramos	
quisierais	
quisieran	

Imperative

quiere (tú)	want (singular)
quiera (usted)	want (sing formal)
queramos (nosotros)	let us put *or* let's put
quered (vosotros)	want (plural)
quieran (ustedes)	want (pl formal)

13
saber
to know

	Gerund		Past participle	
	sabiendo	knowing	sabido	known

Present indicative

sé	I know
sabes	
sabe	
sabemos	
sabéis	
saben	

Imperfect indicative

sabía	I knew or I used to know
sabías	
sabía	
sabíamos	
sabíais	
sabían	

Past simple indicative

supe	I knew
supiste	
supo	
supimos	
supisteis	
supieron	

Future indicative

sabré	I will know
sabrás	
sabrá	
sabremos	
sabréis	
sabrán	

Conditional (present)

sabría	I would know
sabrías	
sabría	
sabríamos	
sabríais	
sabrían	

Present subjunctive

sepa	I know
sepas	
sepa	
sepamos	
sepáis	
sepan	

Imperfect subjunctive

supiera	I knew
supieras	
supiera	
supiéramos	
supierais	
supieran	

Imperative

sabe (tú)	know (singular)
sepa (usted)	know (sing formal)
sepamos (nosotros)	let us know or let's know
sabed (vosotros)	know (plural)
sepan (ustedes)	know (pl formal)

Gerund	Past participle	**14**
sintiendo feeling	sentido felt	**sentir** to feel

Present indicative

siento I feel
sientes
siente
sentimos
sentís
sienten

Imperfect indicative

sentía I felt or I used to feel
sentías
sentía
sentíamos
sentíais
sentían

Past simple indicative

sentí I felt
sentiste
sintió
sentimos
sentisteis
sintieron

Future indicative

sentiré I will feel
sentirás
sentirá
sentiremos
sentiréis
sentirán

Conditional (present)

sentiría I would feel
sentirías
sentiría
sentiríamos
sentiríais
sentirían

Present subjunctive

sienta I feel
sientas
sienta
sintamos
sintáis
sientan

Imperfect subjunctive

sintiera I felt or I were to feel
sintieras
sintiera
sintiéramos
sintierais
sintieran

Imperative

siente (tú)	feel (singular)
sienta (usted)	feel (sing formal)
sintamos (nosotros)	let us feel or let's feel
sentid (vosotros)	feel (plural)
sientan (ustedes)	feel (pl formal)

15
venir
to come

Gerund
viniendo
coming

Past participle
venido
come

Present indicative
vengo   I come or I am coming
vienes
viene
venimos
venís
vienen

Imperfect indicative
venía   I was coming or I used to
         come
venías
venía
veníamos
veníais
venían

Past simple indicative
vine   I came
viniste
vino
vinimos
vinisteis
vinieron

Future indicative
vendré   I will come
vendrás
vendrá
vendremos
vendréis
vendrán

Conditional (present)
vendría   I would come
vendrías
vendría
vendríamos
vendríais
vendrían

Present subjunctive
venga   I come
vengas
venga
vengamos
vengáis
vengan

Imperfect subjunctive
viniera   I came or I were to come
vinieras
viniera
viniéramos
vinierais
vinieran

Imperative
ven (tú)   come (singular)
venga (usted)   come
                     (sing formal)
vengamos (nosotros) let us come or
                     let's come
venid (vosotros)   come (plural)
vengan (ustedes)   come (pl formal)

Gerund		Past participle		**16**
viendo	seeing	visto	seen	**ver** to see

Present indicative

veo — I see *or* I am seeing
ves
ve
vemos
veis
ven

Imperfect indicative

veía — I saw *or* I used to see
veías
veía
veíamos
veíais
veían

Past simple indicative

vi — I saw
viste
vio
vimos
visteis
vieron

Future indicative

veré — I will see
verás
verá
veremos
veréis
verán

Conditional (present)

vería — I would see
verías
vería
veríamos
veríais
verían

Present subjunctive

vea — I see
veas
vea
veamos
veáis
vean

Imperfect subjunctive

viera — I saw *or* I were to see
vieras
viera
viéramos
vierais
vieran

Imperative

ve (tú)	see (singular)
vea (usted)	see (sing formal)
veamos (nosotros)	let us see *or* let's see
ved (vosotros)	see (plural)
vean (ustedes)	see (pl formal)

17
hablar
to talk *or* to speak

regular *-ar*

Gerund
hablando
speaking

Past participle
hablado
spoken

Present indicative
hablo	I speak
hablas	
habla	
hablamos	
habláis	
hablan	

Imperfect indicative
hablaba	I was speaking or I used to speak
hablabas	
hablaba	
hablábamos	
hablabais	
hablaban	

Past simple indicative
hablé	I spoke
hablaste	
habló	
hablamos	
hablasteis	
hablaron	

Future indicative
hablaré	I will speak
hablarás	
hablará	
hablaremos	
hablaréis	
hablarán	

Conditional (present)
hablaría	I would speak
hablarías	
hablaría	
hablaríamos	
hablaríais	
hablarían	

Present subjunctive
hable	I speak
hables	
hable	
hablemos	
habléis	
hablen	

Imperfect subjunctive
hablara	I spoke or I were to speak
hablaras	
hablara	
habláramos	
hablarais	
hablaran	

Imperative
habla (tú)	speak (singular)
hable (usted)	speak (sing formal)
hablemos (nosotros)	let us speak or let's speak
hablad (vosotros)	speak (plural)
hablen (ustedes)	speak (pl formal)

Gerund	Past participle	**18**
com**iendo** eating	com**ido** eaten	**comer** to eat
		regular -er

Present indicative

como   I eat or I am eating
comes
come
comemos
coméis
comen

Imperfect indicative

comía   I was eating or I used to eat
comías
comía
comíamos
comíais
comían

Past simple indicative

comí   I ate
comiste
comió
comimos
comisteis
comieron

Future indicative

comeré   I will eat
comerás
comerá
comeremos
comeréis
comerán

Conditional (present)

comería   I would eat
comerías
comería
comeríamos
comeríais
comerían

Present subjunctive

coma   I eat
comas
coma
comamos
comáis
coman

Imperfect subjunctive

comiera   I ate or I were to eat
comieras
comiera
comiéramos
comierais
comieran

Imperative

come (tú)	eat (singular)
coma (usted)	eat (sing formal)
comamos (nosotros)	let us eat or let's eat
comed (vosotros)	eat (plural)
coman (ustedes)	eat (pl formal)

19
vivir
to live

regular -ir

	Gerund		Past participle	
	viviendo	living	vivido	lived

Present indicative
vivo   I live or I am living
vives
vive
vivimos
vivís
viven

Imperfect indicative
vivía   I lived or I used to live
vivías
vivía
vivíamos
vivíais
vivían

Past simple indicative
viví   I lived
viviste
vivió
vivimos
vivisteis
vivieron

Future indicative
viviré   I will live
vivirás
vivirá
viviremos
viviréis
vivirán

Conditional (present)
viviría   I would live
vivirías
viviría
viviríamos
viviríais
vivirían

Present subjunctive
viva   I live
vivas
viva
vivamos
viváis
vivan

Imperfect subjunctive
viviera   I lived or I were to live
vivieras
viviera
viviéramos
vivierais
vivieran

Imperative
vive (tú)	live (singular)
viva (usted)	live (sing formal)
vivamos (nosotros)	let us live or let's live
vivid (vosotros)	live (plural)
vivan (ustedes)	live (pl formal)

20 **actuar** - like **17 hablar** except:

Present indicative	Present subjunctive
actúo	actúe
actúas	actúes
actúa	actúe
actuamos	actuemos
actuáis	actuéis
actúan	actúen

Imperative

actúa (tú)
actúe (usted)
actuemos (nosotros)
actuad (vosotros)
actúen (ustedes)

21 **andar** - like **17 hablar** except:

Past simple indicative	Imperfect subjunctive
anduve	anduviera
anduviste	anduvieras
anduvo	anduviera
anduvimos	anduviéramos
anduvisteis	anduvierais
anduvieron	anduvieran

22 **cazar** - like **17 hablar** except:

Past simple indicative	Present subjunctive
cacé	cace
cazaste	caces
cazó	cace
cazamos	cacemos
cazasteis	cacéis
cazaron	cacen

Imperative

caza (tú)
cace (usted)
cacemos (nosotros)
cazad (vosotros)
cacen (ustedes)

23 **colgar** - like **17 hablar** except:

Present indicative	Present subjunctive
cuelgo	cuelgue
cuelgas	cuelgues
cuelga	cuelgue
colgamos	colguemos
colgáis	colguéis
cuelgan	cuelguen

Past simple indicative	Imperative
colgué	cuelga (tú)
colgaste	cuelgue (usted)
colgó	colguemos (nosotros)
colgamos	colgad (vosotros)
colgasteis	cuelguen (ustedes)
colgaron	

24 **contar** - like **17 hablar** except:

Present indicative	Present subjunctive
cuento	cuente
cuentas	cuentes
cuenta	cuente
contamos	contemos
contáis	contéis
cuentan	cuenten

Imperative

cuenta (tú)
cuente (usted)
contemos (nosotros)
contad (vosotros)
cuenten (ustedes)

25 empezar - like 17 hablar except:

Present indicative	Present subjunctive
empiezo	empiece
empiezas	empieces
empieza	empiece
empezamos	empecemos
empezáis	empecéis
empiezan	empiecen

Past simple indicative	Imperative
empecé	empieza (tú)
empezaste	empiece (usted)
empezó	empecemos (nosotros)
empezamos	empezad (vosotros)
empezasteis	empiecen (ustedes)
empezaron	

26 forzar - like 17 hablar except:

Present indicative	Present subjunctive
fuerzo	fuerce
fuerzas	fuerces
fuerza	fuerce
forzamos	forcemos
forzáis	forcéis
fuerzan	fuercen

Past simple indicative	Imperative
forcé	fuerza (tú)
forzaste	fuerce (usted)
forzó	forcemos (nosotros)
forzamos	forzad (vosotros)
forzasteis	fuercen (ustedes)
forzaron	

27 jugar - like 17 hablar except:

Present indicative	Present subjunctive
juego	juegue
juegas	juegues
juega	juegue
jugamos	juguemos
jugáis	juguéis
juegan	jueguen

Past simple indicative	Imperative
jugué	juega (tú)
jugaste	juegue (usted)
jugó	juguemos (nosotros)
jugamos	jugad (vosotros)
jugasteis	jueguen (ustedes)
jugaron	

28 pagar - like 17 hablar except:

Past simple indicative	Present subjunctive
pagué	pague
pagaste	pagues
pagó	pague
pagamos	paguemos
pagasteis	paguéis
pagaron	paguen

	Imperative
	paga (tú)
	pague (usted)
	paguemos (nosotros)
	pagad (vosotros)
	paguen (ustedes)

29 **pensar** - like **17 hablar** except:

Present indicative	Present subjunctive
pienso	piense
piensas	pienses
piensa	piense
pensamos	pensemos
pensáis	penséis
piensan	piensen

Imperative

piensa (tú)
piense (usted)
pensemos (nosotros)
pensad (vosotros)
piensen (ustedes)

30 **regar** - like **17 hablar** except:

Present indicative	Present subjunctive
riego	riegue
riegas	riegues
riega	riegue
regamos	reguemos
regáis	reguéis
riegan	rieguen

Past simple indicative	Imperative
regué	riega (tú)
regaste	riegue (usted)
regó	reguemos (nosotros)
regamos	regad (vosotros)
regasteis	rieguen (ustedes)
regaron	

31 **sacar** - like **17 hablar** except:

Past simple indicative	Imperative
saqué	saca (tú)
sacaste	saque (usted)
sacó	saquemos (nosotros)
sacamos	sacad (vosotros)
sacasteis	saquen (ustedes)
sacaron	

Present subjunctive

saque
saques
saque
saquemos
saquéis
saquen

32 **vaciar** - like **17 hablar** except:

Present indicative	Present subjunctive
vacío	vacíe
vacías	vacíes
vacía	vacíe
vaciamos	vaciemos
vaciáis	vaciéis
vacían	vacíen

Imperative

vacía (tú)
vacíe (usted)
vaciemos (nosotros)
vaciad (vosotros)
vacíen (ustedes)

33 **caber** - like **18 comer** except:

Present indicative	Conditional (present)
quepo	cabría
cabes	cabrías
cabe	cabría
cabemos	cabríamos
cabéis	cabríais
caben	cabrían

Past simple indicative	Present subjunctive
cupe	quepa
cupiste	quepas
cupo	quepa
cupimos	quepamos
cupisteis	quepáis
cupieron	quepan

Future indicative	Imperfect subjunctive
cabré	cupiera
cabrás	cupieras
cabrá	cupiera
cabremos	cupiéramos
cabréis	cupierais
cabrán	cupieran

Imperative
cabe (tú)
quepa (usted)
quepamos (nosotros)
cabed (vosotros)
quepan (ustedes)

34 **caer** - like **18 comer** except:

Gerund cayendo
Past participle caído

Present indicative	Present subjunctive
caigo	caiga
caes	caigas
cae	caiga
caemos	caigamos
caéis	caigáis
caen	caigan

Past simple indicative	Imperfect subjunctive
caí	cayera
caiste	cayeras
cayó	cayera
caimos	cayéramos
caisteis	cayerais
cayeron	cayeran

Imperative
cae (tú)
caiga (usted)
caigamos (nosotros)
caed (vosotros)
caigan (ustedes)

35 **conocer** - like **18 comer** except:

Present indicative	Present subjunctive
conozco	conozca
conoces	conozcas
conoce	conozca
conocemos	conozcamos
conocéis	conozcáis
conocen	conozcan

Imperative
conoce (tú)
conozca (usted)
conozcamos (nosotros)
conoced (vosotros)
conozcan (ustedes)

36 **entender** - like **18 comer** except:

Present indicative	Present subjunctive
entiendo	entienda
entiendes	entiendas
entiende	entienda
entendemos	entendamos
entendéis	entendáis
entienden	entiendan

Imperative

entiende (tú)
entienda (usted)
entendamos
(nosotros)
entended (vosotros)
entiendan (ustedes)

37 **leer** - like **18 comer** except:

Gerund leyendo

Past participle leído

Past simple indicative	Imperfect subjunctive
leí	leyera
leíste	leyeras
leyó	leyera
leímos	leyéramos
leísteis	leyerais
leyeron	leyeran

38 **mover** - like **18 comer** except:

Present indicative	Present subjunctive
muevo	mueva
mueves	muevas
mueve	mueva
movemos	movamos
movéis	mováis
mueven	muevan

Imperative

mueve (tú)
mueva (usted)
movamos
(nosotros)
moved (vosotros)
muevan (ustedes)

39 **oler** - like **18 comer** except:

Present indicative	Present subjunctive
huelo	huela
hueles	huelas
huele	huela
olemos	olamos
oléis	oláis
huelen	huelan

Imperative

huele (tú)
huela (usted)
olamos (nosotros)
oled (vosotros)
huelan (ustedes)

40 **romper** - like **18 comer** except:

Past participle roto

41 **torcer** - like **18 comer** except:

Present indicative	Present subjunctive
tuerzo	tuerza
tuerces	tuerzas
tuerce	tuerza
torcemos	torzamos
torcéis	torzáis
tuercen	tuerzan

Imperative

tuerce (tú)
tuerza (usted)
torzamos (nosotros)
torced (vosotros)
tuerzan (ustedes)

42 **traer** - like **18 comer** except:

Gerund trayendo
Past participle traído

Present indicative	Imperfect subjunctive
traigo	trajera
traes	trajeras
trae	trajera
traemos	trajéramos
traéis	trajerais
traen	trajeran

Present subjunctive	Past simple indicative
traiga	traje
traigas	trajiste
traiga	trajo
traigamos	trajimos
traigáis	trajisteis
traigan	trajeron

Imperative
trae (tú)
traiga (usted)
traigamos (nosotros)
traed (vosotros)
traigan (ustedes)

43 **valer** - like **18 comer** except:

Present indicative	Present subjunctive
valgo	valga
vales	valgas
vale	valga
valemos	valgamos
valéis	valgáis
valen	valgan

Future indicative	Imperfect subjunctive
valdré	valiera
valdrás	valieras
valdrá	valiera
valdremos	valiéramos
valdréis	valierais
valdrán	valieran

Conditional (present)	Imperative
valdría	vale (tú)
valdrías	valga (usted)
valdría	valgamos (nosotro
valdríamos	valed (vosotros)
valdríais	valgan (ustedes)
valdrían	

44 **vencer** - like **18 comer** except:

Present indicative	Present subjunctive
venzo	venza
vences	venzas
vence	venza
vencemos	venzamos
vencéis	venzáis
vencen	venzan

Imperative
vence (tú)
venza (usted)
venzamos (nosotros)
venced (vosotros)
venzan (ustedes)

45 **volver** - like **18 comer** except:

Past participle vuelto

Present indicative	Present subjunctive
vuelvo	vuelva
vuelves	vuelvas
vuelve	vuelva
volvemos	volvamos
volvéis	volváis
vuelven	vuelvan

Imperative
vuelve (tú)
vuelva (usted)
volvamos (nosotros)
volved (vosotros)
vuelvan (ustedes)

46 **abrir** - like **19 vivir** except:

Past participle abierto

47 **adquirir** - like **19 vivir** except:

Present indicative	Present subjunctive
adquiero	adquiera
adquieres	adquieras
adquiere	adquiera
adquirimos	adquiramos
adquirís	adquiráis
adquieren	adquieran

	Imperative
	adquiere (tú)
	adquiera (usted)
	adquiramos (nosotros)
	adquirid (vosotros)
	adquieran (ustedes)

48 **corregir** - like **19 vivir** except:

Present indicative	Present subjunctive
corrijo	corrija
corriges	corrijas
corrige	corrija
corregimos	corrijamos
corregís	corrijáis
corrigen	corrijan

Past simple indicative	Imperative
corregí	corrige (tú)
corregiste	corrija (usted)
corrigió	corrijamos (nosotros)
corregimos	
corregisteis	corregid (vosotros)
corrigieron	corrijan (ustedes)

49 **dirigir** - like **19 vivir** except:

Present indicative	Present subjunctive
dirijo	dirija
diriges	dirijas
dirige	dirija
dirigimos	dirijamos
dirigís	dirijáis
dirigen	dirijan

	Imperative
	dirige (tú)
	dirija (usted)
	dirijamos (nosotros)
	dirigid (vosotros)
	dirijan (ustedes)

50 **distinguir** - like **19 vivir** except:

Present indicative	Present subjunctive
distingo	distinga
distingues	distingas
distingue	distinga
distinguimos	distingamos
distinguís	distingáis
distinguen	distingan

	Imperative
	distingue (tú)
	distinga (usted)
	distingamos (nosotros)
	distinguid (vosotros)
	distingan (ustedes)

51 **dormir** - like **19 vivir** except:

Gerund durmiendo

Past participle dormido

Present indicative	Past simple indicative
duermo	dormí
duermes	dormiste
duerme	durmió
dormimos	dormimos
dormís	dormisteis
duermen	durmieron

Imperfect subjunctive	Imperative
durmiera	duerme (tú)
durmieras	duerma (usted)
durmiera	durmamos
durmiéramos	(nosotros)
durmierais	dormid (vosotros)
durmieran	duerman (ustedes)

	Present subjunctive
	duerma
	duermas
	duerma
	durmamos
	durmáis
	duerman

52 **escriber** - like **19 vivir** except:

Past participle excrito

53 **freír** - like **19 vivir** except:

Gerund friendo
Past participle frito

Present indicative	Present subjunctive
frío	fría
fríes	frías
fríe	fría
freímos	friamos
freís	friáis
fríen	frían

Past simple indicative	Imperfect subjunctive
freí	friera
freíste	frieras
frió	friera
freímos	friéramos
freísteis	frierais
frieron	frieran

	Imperative
	fríe (tú)
	fría (usted)
	friamos (nosotros)
	freíd (vosotros)
	frían (ustedes)

54 **huir** - like **19 vivir** except:

Gerund huyendo
Past participle huido

Present indicative	Present subjunctive
huyo	huya
huyes	huyas
huye	huya
huimos	huyamos
huis	huyáis
huyen	huyan

Past simple indicative	Imperfect subjunctive
huí	huyera
huiste	huyeras
huyó	huyera
huimos	huyéramos
huisteis	huyerais
huyeron	huyeran

	Imperative
	huye (tú)
	huya (usted)
	huyamos (nosotros)
	huid (vosotros)
	huyan (ustedes)

55 **morir** - like **19 vivir** except:

Gerund muriendo
Past participle muerto

Present indicative	Present subjunctive
muero	muera
mueres	mueras
muere	muera
morimos	muramos
moris	muráis
mueren	mueran

Past simple indicative	Imperfect subjunctive
morí	muriera
moriste	murieras
murió	muriera
morimos	muriéramos
moristeis	murierais
murieron	murieran

56 oír - like 19 vivir except:

Gerund oyendo

Past participle oído

Present indicative	Imperfect indicative
oigo	oía
oyes	oías
oye	oía
oímos	oíamos
oís	oíais
oyen	oían

Past simple indicative	Present subjunctive
oí	oiga
oíste	oigas
oyó	oiga
oímos	oigamos
oísteis	oigáis
oyeron	oigan

Future indicative	Imperfect subjunctive
oiré	oyera
oirás	oyeras
oirá	oyera
oiremos	oyéramos
oiréis	oyerais
oirán	oyeran

Conditional (present)	Imperative
oiría	oye (tú)
oirías	oiga (usted)
oiría	oigamos (nosotros)
oiríamos	oíd (vosotros)
oiríais	oigan (ustedes)
oirían	

57 pedir - like 19 vivir except:

Present indicative	Present subjunctive
pido	pida
pides	pidas
pide	pida
pedimos	pidamos
pedís	pidáis
piden	pidan

Past simple indicative	Imperfect subjunctive
pedí	pidiera
pediste	pidieras
pidió	pidiera
pedimos	pidiéramos
pedisteis	pidierais
pidieron	pidieran

Imperative

pide (tú)
pida (usted)
pidamos (nostros)
pedid (vosotros)
pidan (ustedes)

58 prohibir - like 19 vivir except:

Present indicative	Present subjunctive
prohíbo	prohíba
prohíbes	prohíbas
prohíbe	prohíba
prohibimos	prohibamos
prohibís	prohibáis
prohíben	prohíban

Imperative

prohíbe (tú)
prohíba (usted)
prohibamos (nosotros)
prohibid (vosotros)
prohíban (ustedes)

59 **pudrir** - like **19 vivir** except:

Past participle podrido

60 **reducir** - like **19 vivir** except:

Present indicative	Present subjunctive
reduzco	reduzca
reduces	reduzcas
reduce	reduzca
reducimos	reduzcamos
reducís	reduzcáis
reducen	reduzcan

Past simple indicative	Imperfect subjunctive
reduje	redujera
redujiste	redujeras
redujo	redujera
redujimos	redujéramos
redujisteis	redujerais
redujeron	redujeran

Imperative

reduce (tú)
reduzca (usted)
reduzcamos (nosotros)
reducid (vosotros)
reduzcan (ustedes)

61 **reír** - like **19 vivir** except:

Present indicative	Conditional (present)
río	reiría
ríes	reirías
ríe	reiría
reímos	reiríamos
reís	reiríais
ríen	reirían

Imperfect indicative	Present subjunctive
reía	ría
reías	rías
reía	ría
reíamos	riamos
reíais	riáis
reían	rían

Past simple indicative	Imperfect subjunctive
reí	riera
reíste	rieras
rió	riera
reímos	riéramos
reísteis	rierais
rieron	rieran

Future indicative	Imperative
reiré	ríe (tú)
reirás	ría (usted)
reirá	riamos (nosotros)
reiremos	reíd (vosotros)
reiréis	rían (ustedes)
reirán	

62 **reunir** - like **19 vivir** except:

Present indicative	Imperative
reúno	reúne (tú)
reúnes	reúna (usted)
reúne	reunamos (nosotros)
reunimos	reunid (vosotros)
reunís	reúnan (ustedes)
reúnen	

Present subjunctive

reúna
reúnas
reúna
reunamos
reunáis
reúnan

63 **salir** - like **19 vivir** except:

Present indicative	Present subjunctive
salgo	salga
sales	salgas
sale	salga
salimos	salgamos
salís	salgáis
salen	salgan

Future indicative	Imperfect subjunctive
saldré	saliera
saldrás	salieras
saldrá	saliera
saldremos	saliéramos
saldréis	salierais
saldrán	salieran

Conditional (present)	Imperative
saldría	sal (tú)
saldrías	salga (usted)
saldría	salgamos (nosotros)
saldríamos	salid (vosotros)
saldríais	salgan (ustedes)
saldrían	

64 **seguir** - like **19 vivir** except:

Present indicative	Past simple indicative
sigo	seguí
sigues	seguiste
sigue	siguió
seguimos	seguimos
seguís	seguisteis
siguen	siguieron

Present subjunctive	Imperfect subjunctive
siga	siguiera
sigas	siguieras
siga	siguiera
sigamos	siguiéramos
sigáis	siguierais
sigan	siguieran

Imperative

sigue (tú)
siga (usted)
sigamos (nosotros)
seguid (vosotros)
sigan (ustedes)

65 **teñir** - like **19 vivir** except:

Gerund tiñendo

Present indicative	Present subjunctive
tiño	tiña
tiñes	tiñas
tiñe	tiña
teñimos	tiñamos
teñís	tiñáis
tiñen	tiñan

Past simple indicative	Imperfect subjunctive
teñí	tiñera
teñiste	tiñeras
tiñó	tiñera
teñimos	tiñéramos
teñisteis	tiñerais
tiñeron	tiñeran

Imperative

tiñe (tú)
tiña (usted)
tiñamos (nosotros)
teñid (vosotros)
tiñan (ustedes)

Aa

a *indefinite article* **1** (*before a noun which is masculine in Spanish*) un; **a tree** un árbol; **2** (*before a noun which is feminine in Spanish*) una; **a table** una mesa; **3** (*before professions, occupations, etc. 'a' is not translated*) **I'm a doctor** soy médico; **4 five euros a kilo** cinco euros el kilo; **5 fifty kilometres an hour** cincuenta kilómetros por hora; **6 three times a day** tres veces al día.

abandon *verb* abandonar [17].

abbey *noun* abadía *Fem.*; **Westminster Abbey** la abadía de Westminster.

abbreviation *noun* abreviatura *Fem.*

abide *verb* **I can't abide** ... no puedo soportar ....

ability *noun* **1** capacidad *Fem.*; **the ability to do** la capacidad de hacer; **2 do it to the best of your ability** hazlo lo mejor que puedas; **I did it to the best of my ability** lo hice lo mejor que pude.

able *adjective* **to be able to do** poder [10] hacer; **she wasn't able to come** no pudo venir.

abnormal *adjective* anormal.

abolish *verb* abolir [19].

abortion *noun* aborto *Masc.*

about *preposition* **1** (*on the subject of*) sobre; **a film about Picasso** una película sobre Picasso; **2 what's it about?** ¿de qué trata?; **3** (*concerning or in relation to*) acerca de; **he wants to talk to you about your exam** quiere hablarte acerca de tu examen; **4 to talk about something** hablar de algo; **what is she talking about?** ¿de qué está hablando?; **5 to think about something/somebody** pensar en algo/alguien; **I'm thinking about you** estoy pensando en ti.

about *adverb* **1** (*approximately*) **there are about sixty people** hay unas sesenta personas; **2** (*when talking about time*) **at about three o'clock** como a las tres; **about three weeks/a month ago** hace cosa de tres semanas/de un mes; **3 to be about to do** estar a punto de hacer; **I'm (just) about to leave** estoy a punto de marcharme.

above *preposition* **1** encima de; **above the sink** encima del fregadero; **2 above all** sobre todo.

above *adverb* **1** de arriba; **the flat above** el piso de arriba.

abroad *adverb* **to go abroad** irse al extranjero; **to live abroad** vivir en el extranjero.

abscess *noun* flemón *Masc.*

abseiling *noun* rappel *Masc.*

absent *adjective* ausente; **to be absent from** faltar a; **he was absent from the lesson** faltó a clase; **she's often absent from meetings** falta a menudo a las reuniones; (*when referring to the present moment, 'to be absent' is translated by the present perfect*) **he's absent from school today** hoy ha faltado a clase.

a b c d e f g h i j k l m n o p q r s t u v w x y z

a
b
c
d
e
f
g
h
i
j
k
l
m
n
o
p
q
r
s
t
u
v
w
x
y
z

absent-minded *adjective*
despistado/despistada.

absolute *adjective* absoluto/
absoluta; **an absolute disaster** un
desastre absoluto.

absolutely *adverb* **1** (*completely*)
totalmente; **I'm absolutely certain**
estoy totalmente segura; **2** (*extremely*) realmente; **it's
absolutely dreadful** es realmente
terrible; **3 you're absolutely right**
tienes toda la razón; **4 absolutely!**
¡por supuesto!

absorb *verb* absorber [18].

abuse *noun* **1 alcohol abuse**
alcoholismo *Masc.*; **drug abuse**
consumo *Masc.* de drogas;
2 (*violent treatment of a person*)
malos tratos *Masc. plural*;
3 (*insults*) insultos *Masc. plural*.

abuse *verb* **to abuse somebody**
maltratar [17] a alguien.

academic *adjective* académico/
académica; **the academic year** el
año académico.

accelerate *verb* acelerar [17].

accelerator *noun* acelerador
Masc.

accent *noun* acento *Masc.*; **she
has a Spanish accent** tiene
acento español.

accept *verb* aceptar [17].

acceptable *adjective* aceptable.

access *noun* acceso *Masc.*

access *verb* **to access
something** obtener [9] acceso a
algo.

accessory *noun* accesorio *Masc.*

accident *noun* **1** (*an unfortunate
happening*) accidente *Masc.*; **to**

have an accident tener [9] un
accidente; **a road accident** un
accidente de carretera; **a car
accident** un accidente de coche;
2 (*chance*) casualidad *Fem.*; **it's no
accident** no es casualidad; **3 by
accident** (*by chance*) por
casualidad(*without meaning to*)
sin querer; **I found it by accident**
lo encontré por casualidad; **she
broke it by accident** lo rompió sin
querer.

accidental *adjective* fortuito/
fortuita; **an accidental discovery**
un descubrimiento fortuito.

accident & emergency *noun*
urgencias *Fem. plural.*

accidentally *adverb* **1** (*without
meaning to*) sin querer; **I
accidentally knocked over his
glass** le tiré el vaso sin querer;
2 (*by chance*) por casualidad; **I
accidentally discovered that ...**
descubrí por casualidad que ....

accommodation *noun*
alojamiento *Masc.*; **I'm looking for
accommodation** estoy buscando
alojamiento; **hotel
accommodation** alojamiento en
hotel.

accompany *verb* **to accompany
somebody** acompañar [17] a
alguien.

according *in phrase* **according
to** según; **according to Sophie**
según Sophie.

accordion *noun* acordeón *Masc.*

account *noun* **1** (*in a bank, shop,
or post office*) cuenta *Fem.*; **a bank
account** una cuenta bancaria; **to**

open an account abrir [46] una cuenta; **I have fifty pounds in my account** tengo cincuenta libras en mi cuenta; **2** (*a description of an experience or event*) relato *Masc.*; **3 on account of** debido a; **the station is closed on account of the strike** la estación está cerrada debido a la huelga; **4 to take something into account** tener [9] algo en cuenta; **we will take his illness into account** tendremos en cuenta su enfermedad.

accountant *noun* contable *Masc./Fem.*; **she's an accountant** es contable.

accuracy *noun* precisión *Fem.*

accurate *adjective* preciso/precisa.

accurately *adverb* con precisión.

accuse *verb* acusar [17]; **to accuse somebody of something** acusar a alguien de algo; **to accuse somebody of doing something** acusar a alguien de hacer algo; **she accused me of stealing her pen** me acusó de haber robado su pluma.

accustomed to *adjective* **to be accustomed to something** estar [2] acostumbrado/acostumbrada a algo; **she's accustomed to having lots of homework** está acostumbrada a tener muchos deberes.

ace *noun* as *Masc.*; **the ace of hearts** el as de corazones.

ace *adjective* de primera (*informal*); **he's an ace drummer** es un batería de primera.

ache *verb* **my arm aches** me duele el brazo; **my head aches** me duele la cabeza.

achieve *verb* **1** conseguir [64]; **she's achieved a great deal** consiguió mucho; **2 to achieve an ambition** hacer [7] realidad una ambición; **3 to achieve an aim** lograr [17] un objetivo; **4 to achieve success** tener [9] éxito.

achievement *noun* **1** éxito *Masc.*; **it's a great achievement** es un gran éxito; **2 a sense of achievement** un sentimiento de satisfacción.

acid *noun* ácido *Masc.*

acid rain *noun* lluvia *Fem.* ácida.

acne *noun* acné *Masc.*

acorn *noun* bellota *Fem.*

acrobat *noun* acróbata *Masc./Fem.*

across *preposition* **1** (*over to the other side of*) **to walk across something** cruzar [22] algo; **we walked across the park** cruzamos el parque; **to run across the road** cruzar la calle corriendo; **2** (*on the other side of*) al otro lado de; **the house across the street** la casa de enfrente; **3 across from** en frente de; **she was sitting across from me** estaba sentada en frente de mí.

acrylic *noun* acrílica *Fem.*

act *noun* acto *Masc.*

act *verb* actuar [20].

acting *noun* actuación *Fem.*; **she wants to go into acting** quiere ser actriz.

action *noun* acción *Fem.*

action replay *noun* repetición *Fem.* de la jugada.

active *adjective* activo/activa.

activity *noun* actividad *Fem.*

activity holiday *noun* vacaciones *Fem. plural* con actividades programadas.

actor *noun* actor *Masc.*; **who's your favourite actor?** ¿quién es tu actor favorito?

actress *noun* actriz *Fem.* (*plural* actrices); **who's your favourite actress?** ¿quién es tu actriz favorita?

actual *adjective* **1** his actual words sus palabras textuales; **2** actual cases casos reales; **3** in actual fact de hecho.

actually *adverb* **1** (*in fact, as it happens*) la verdad es que; **actually, I've changed my mind** la verdad es que he cambiado de idea; **he's not actually here at the moment** la verdad es que no está aquí en este momento; **2** (*really and truly*) de verdad; **did she actually say that?** ¿dijo eso de verdad?

acupuncture *noun* acupuntura *Fem.*

acute *adjective* **1** (*pain*) agudo/aguda; **2** an acute accent un acento agudo.

ad *noun* anuncio *Masc.*; **to put an ad in the paper** poner un anuncio en el periódico; **the small ads** los anuncios por palabras.

AD d. de C. (*después de Cristo*); **in 400 AD** en el año 400 d. de C.

adapt *verb* **1** to adapt something adaptar [17] algo; **2** to adapt to something adaptarse [17] a algo; she's adapted to the new system se adaptó al nuevo sistema.

adaptor *noun* adaptador *Masc.*

add *verb* añadir [19]; **add three eggs** añadir tres huevos.

● **to add something up** sumar [17] algo.

addict *noun* **1** (*drug addict*) drogadicto *Masc.*, drogadicta *Fem.*; **2** (*of television, chocolate, for example*) adicto *Masc.*, adicta *Fem.*; **she's a telly addict** es una adicta a la televisión; **3** (*of sport*) fanático *Masc.*, fanática *Fem.*; **he's a football addict** es un fanático del fútbol.

addicted *adjective* **1** (*to drugs, television, computer games, etc.*) adicto/adicta; **she's addicted to heroin** es adicta a la heroína; **he's addicted to the Net** es un adicto a Internet; **2** (*to food*) **I'm addicted to tomatoes** los tomates son mi vicio (*informal*); **3** to become addicted to something (*to drugs*) hacerse adicto a algo (*to television, chocolate*) enviciarse con algo.

addition *noun* **1** (*adding up*) suma *Fem.*; **2** in addition además; **3** in addition to además de.

additional *adjective* adicional; **additional costs** costes *Masc. plural* adicionales.

additive *noun* aditivo *Masc.*

address *noun* **1** (*of person, house, office*) dirección *Fem.*; **what's your address?** ¿cuál es tu dirección?; **2** (*on a form*) domicilio *Masc.*; **3** to change address cambiar [17] de domicilio.

address book noun libreta Fem. de direcciones.

adequate adjective suficiente.

adhesive noun pegamento Masc.

adhesive adjective adhesivo/ adhesiva; **adhesive tape** cinta Fem. adhesiva.

adjective noun adjetivo Masc.

adjust verb 1 regular [17] (volume, temperature), ajustar [17] (height, width); 2 **to adjust to something** adaptarse [17] a algo.

adjustable adjective regulable.

administration noun administración Fem.

admiral noun almirante Masc./ Fem.

admiration noun admiración Fem.

admire verb admirar [17].

admission noun entrada Fem.; 'no admission' prohibida la entrada; 'admission free' entrada gratuita.

admit verb 1 (confess) admitir [19]; **she admits she lied** admite que mintió; 2 (concede) reconocer [35]; **I must admit that ...** debo reconocer que ...; 3 (allow to enter) dejar [17] entrar; **to admit somebody to a restaurant** dejar entrar a alguien en un restaurante.

adolescence noun adolescencia Fem.

adolescent noun adolescente Masc./Fem.

adopt verb adoptar [17].

adopted adjective adoptado/ adoptada.

adoption noun adopción Fem.

adore verb adorar [17].

Adriatic Sea noun the Adriatic Sea el mar Adriático.

adult noun adulto Masc., adulta Fem.

adult adjective adulto/adulta; **the adult population** la población adulta.

Adult Education noun educación Fem. para adultos.

advance noun avance Masc.; **advances in technology** avances en tecnología.

advance verb avanzar [22].

advanced adjective avanzado/ avanzada.

advantage noun 1 ventaja Fem.; **there are several advantages** hay varias ventajas; 2 **to take advantage of something** aprovechar [17] algo; **I took advantage of the sales to buy myself some shoes** aproveché las rebajas para comprarme unos zapatos; 3 **to take advantage of somebody** (unfairly) aprovecharse [17] de alguien.

adventure noun aventura Fem.

adventurous adjective 1 (person) aventurero/aventurera; 2 (design, designer, composer, etc.) innovador/ innovadora.

adverb noun adverbio Masc.

advert, advertisement noun 1 (on television, in a newspaper) anuncio Masc.; 2 (small ad in a newspaper advertising a job, an article for sale, etc.) anuncio Masc. por palabras.

a
b
c
d
e
f
g
h
i
j
k
l
m
n
o
p
q
r
s
t
u
v
w
x
y
z

advertise verb **1** to advertise a product hacer [7] publicidad de un producto; **2** to advertise something in the newspaper anunciar [17] algo en el periódico; I saw it advertised on telly lo vi anunciado en la tele; I saw a bike advertised in the paper (in the small ads) vi un anuncio (por palabras) de una bicicleta en el periódico.

advertising noun publicidad Fem.

advice noun **1** consejos Masc. plural; his advice is good sus consejos son buenos; **2** a piece of advice un consejo; **3** to give somebody advice aconsejar [17] a alguien; they gave me good advice me aconsejaron bien; **4** to ask for advice about something pedir [57] consejo sobre algo.

advise verb aconsejar [17]; to advise somebody to ... aconsejar a alguien que ... (followed by the subjunctive); I advised him to study more le aconsejé que estudiase más; I advised her not to wait le aconsejé que no esperase.

adviser noun asesor Masc., asesora Fem.

aerial noun antena Fem.

aerobics noun aerobic Masc.; to do aerobics hacer [7] aerobic.

aeroplane noun avión Masc.

aerosol noun an aerosol (can) un aerosol.

affair noun **1** asunto Masc.; international affairs asuntos

internacionales; **2** a love affair una aventura amorosa.

affect verb afectar [17].

affectionate adjective cariñoso/cariñosa.

afford verb to be able to afford to do tener [9] dinero para hacer; I can't afford to go out much no tengo dinero para salir mucho; I can't afford a new bike no tengo dinero para una bicicleta nueva.

afraid adjective **1** to be afraid tener [9] miedo; I'm afraid tengo miedo; **2** (with 'of') I'm afraid of dogs me dan miedo los perros; Dan's afraid of spiders a Dan le dan miedo las arañas; he's afraid of flying le da miedo volar; she's afraid of failing the exam le da miedo suspender el examen; **3** I'm afraid there's no milk left me temo que no queda leche; I'm afraid so me temo que sí; I'm afraid not me temo que no.

Africa noun África Fem.

African noun africano Masc., africana Fem.

African adjective africano/africana.

after preposition, adverb

after conjunction **1** (later in time) después de; after 10 o'clock después de las diez en punto; after lunch después de comer; after school después del colegio; after I've finished my homework después de terminar mis deberes; **2** soon after poco después; **3** the day after tomorrow pasado mañana.

- **to run after somebody** correr [18] tras alguien.

after all *adverb* después de todo; **after all, she's only six** después de todo, sólo tiene seis años.

afternoon *noun* tarde *Fem.*; **this afternoon** esta tarde; **tomorrow afternoon** mañana por la tarde; **yesterday afternoon** ayer por la tarde; **on Saturday afternoon** el sábado por la tarde; **on Saturday afternoons** los sábados por la tarde; **at four o' clock in the afternoon** a las cuatro de la tarde; **every afternoon** todas las tardes.

afters *noun* postre *Masc.*

aftershave *noun* loción *Fem.* para después del afeitado.

afterwards *adverb* después; **shortly afterwards** poco después.

again *adverb* **1** (*one more time*) otra vez; **try again** inténtalo otra vez; **I've forgotten it again** se me ha olvidado otra vez; **you should ask again** deberías preguntar otra vez; **2** (*with a negative verb*) **I don't want to see her again** no quiero volver a verla; **don't do it again** no lo vuelvas a hacer; **3 never again!** ¡nunca más!

against *preposition* contra; **against the wall** contra la pared; **to lean against the wall** apoyarse contra la pared; **I'm against the idea** estoy en contra de la idea; **to fight against racism** luchar contra el racismo.

age *noun* **1** edad *Fem.*; **at the age of fifteen** a la edad de quince años; **she's the same age as me** tiene

mi misma edad; **to be under age** ser menor de edad; **2 I haven't seen Johnny for ages** hace siglos que no he visto a Johnny (*informal*); **I haven't been to London for ages** hace un montón de tiempo que no voy a Londres (*informal*).

agenda *noun* agenda *Fem.*

agent *noun* agente *Masc./Fem.*

aggressive *adjective* agresivo/agresiva.

ago *adverb* **an hour ago** hace una hora; **three days ago** hace tres días; **five years ago** hace cinco años; **a long time ago** hace mucho tiempo; **not long ago** no hace mucho (tiempo); **how long ago was it?** ¿cuánto tiempo hace de eso?

agree *verb* **1 to agree with somebody** estar [2] de acuerdo con alguien; **I agree with Laura** estoy de acuerdo con Laura; **I don't agree** no estoy de acuerdo; **2 I agree that ...** estoy de acuerdo en que ...; **I agree that it's too late now** estoy de acuerdo en que ya es muy tarde; **3 to agree to do something** [18] hacer; **Steve's agreed to help me** Steve ha aceptado ayudarme; **4 coffee doesn't agree with me** el café no me sienta bien.

agreement *noun* acuerdo *Masc.*

agricultural *adjective* agrícola.

agriculture *noun* agricultura *Fem.*

ahead *adverb* **1 go ahead!** ¡adelante!; **2 straight ahead** todo recto; **go straight ahead until you**

a b c d e f g h i j k l m n o p q r s t u v w x y z

get to the crossroads sigue todo recto hasta que llegues al cruce; **3 our team was ten points ahead** nuestro equipo llevaba diez puntos de ventaja; **I'll go ahead** yo voy delante; **4 to be ahead of time** ir [8] adelantado.

aid noun **1** ayuda Fem.; **aid to developing countries** ayuda a los países en vías de desarrollo; **2 in aid of** en beneficio de; **in aid of the homeless** en beneficio de la gente sin hogar.

Aids noun sida Masc. (síndrome de inmunodeficiencia adquirida); **to have Aids** tener [9] el sida.

aim noun objetivo Masc.; **their aim is to control pollution** su objetivo es controlar la contaminación.

aim verb **1 to aim to do** proponerse [11] hacer; **we're aiming to finish it today** nos proponemos terminarlo hoy; **2 a campaign aimed at young people** una campaña dirigida a los jóvenes; **3 to aim a gun at somebody** apuntar [17] una pistola a alguien.

air noun **1** aire Masc.; **in the open air** al aire libre; **to go out for a breath of air** salir [8] a tomar el aire; **2 to travel by air** viajar [8] en avión.

airbag noun airbag Masc.

air-conditioned adjective con aire acondicionado.

air conditioning noun aire Masc. acondicionado.

air force noun fuerza Fem. aérea.

air hostess noun azafata Fem.; **she's an air hostess** es azafata.

airline noun compañía Fem. aérea.

airmail noun correo Masc. aéreo; **by airmail** por correo aéreo.

airport noun aeropuerto Masc.

aisle noun (in theatre, on plane) pasillo Masc.

alarm noun alarma Fem.; **a fire alarm** una alarma contra incendios; **a burglar alarm** una alarma antirrobo.

alarm clock noun reloj Masc. despertador.

album noun álbum Masc.

alcohol noun alcohol Masc.

alcoholic noun alcohólico Masc., alcohólica Fem.

alcoholic adjective alcohólico/ alcohólica; **alcoholic drinks** bebidas alcohólicas.

alert adjective espabilado/ espabilada.

alert noun **to be on the alert** estar [2] al alerta; **be on the alert for pickpockets** hay que estar al tanto con los carteristas.

A levels noun selectividad Fem. (Students take 'la selectividad' at the same age as A levels are taken in Britain.) You can explain A levels briefly as follows: Son exámenes que se realizan a dos niveles, AS y A2. Los exámenes AS se hacen después de un año de preparación, generalmente en cuatro o cinco asignaturas; los A2 abarcan un número menor de asignaturas que ya se hayan estudiado para el nivel AS. Ambos exámenes se califican desde A (nota máxima), a N (sin calificar). La calificación de los A *levels se toma en cuenta para ingresar a la universidad)* SEE **selectividad**.

alibi *noun* coartada Fem.

alien *noun* **1** *(foreigner)* extranjero Masc., extranjera Fem.; **2** *(from outer space)* extraterrestre Masc./Fem.

alike *adjective* **1** parecido/parecida; **they're all alike** son todos parecidos; **2 to look alike** parecerse [35]; **the two brothers look alike** los dos hermanos se parecen.

alive *adjective* vivo/viva.

all *adjective, pronoun* **1** todo/toda; **all the knives** todos los cuchillos; **all the cups** todas las tazas; **all the time** todo el tiempo; **all day** todo el día; **2 they've eaten it all** se lo han comido todo; **after all** después de todo; **not at all** de nada *(to somebody who's said 'thank you')*; **they're all there** están todos allí; **3 it's all I have** es todo lo que tengo; **4** *(in scores)* **three all** tres iguales.

all *adverb* completamente; **all alone** completamente solo; **she's all alone at the moment** ahora está completamente sola.

all along *adverb* desde el primer momento; **I knew it all along** lo supe desde el primer momento.

allergic *adjective* alérgico/alérgica; **to be allergic to something** ser [13] alérgico a algo.

allergy *noun* alergia Fem.

alligator *noun* caimán Masc.

allow *verb* **1 to allow somebody to do** permitir [19] a alguien hacer; **the teacher allowed them to go out** el maestro les permitió salir; **2** *(to do)* **I'm not allowed to go out during the week** no me dejan salir durante la semana; **they are allowed to watch TV in the evenings** les dejan ver la tele por las noches.

all right *adverb* **1** *(showing agreement)* de acuerdo, vale *(informal)*; **'come round to my house around six'** – **'all right'** 'ven a mi casa a eso de las seis' – 'de acuerdo', 'ven a mi casa a eso de las seis' – 'vale'; **it's all right by me** por mí de acuerdo, por mí vale *(informal)*; **2** *(fine)* **is everything all right?** ¿va todo bien?; **3** *(talking about health, wellbeing)* bien; **are you all right?** ¿estás bien?; **she's all right now** ya está bien; **4** *(not bad)* **the meal was all right** la comida no estuvo mal; **5 is it all right to leave the door open?** ¿puedo dejar la puerta abierta?

ally *noun* aliado Masc., aliada Fem.

almond *noun* almendra Fem.

almost *adverb* casi; **almost every day** casi cada día; **almost everybody** casi todo el mundo; **she's almost five** tiene casi cinco años.

alone *adjective* **1** solo/sola; **he lives alone** vive solo; **2 leave me alone!** ¡déjame en paz!; **3 leave these papers alone!** ¡deja esos papeles!

along *preposition* **1** a lo largo de; **there are trees all along the road**

hay árboles a lo largo de toda la carretera; **2** (there is often no direct translation for 'along' so the sentence has to be expressed differently) **she lives along the street from me** vive en mi misma calle; **to go for a walk along the beach** pasear por la playa; **a bit further along** un poco más adelante.

aloud adverb en voz alta; **to read something aloud** leer [37] algo en voz alta.

alphabet noun alfabeto Masc.

alphabetical adjective alfabético/alfabética; **in alphabetical order** por orden alfabético.

Alps plural noun **the Alps** los Alpes.

already adverb ya; **they've already left** ya han salido; **it's six o'clock already!** ¡ya son las seis!

Alsatian noun pastor Masc. alemán.

also adverb también; **I've also invited Karen** he invitado también a Karen.

alter verb cambiar [17].

alternate adjective **on alternate days** un día sí y otro no.

alternative noun alternativa Fem.; **we have no alternative** no tenemos alternativa.

alternative adjective otro/otra; **to find an alternative solution** encontrar otra solución.

alternatively adverb o bien; **alternatively, we could go**

together on Saturday o bien podríamos ir juntos el sábado.

alternative medicine noun medicina Fem. alternativa.

although conjunction aunque; **although she's ill, she's willing to help us** aunque está enferma, está dispuesta a ayudarnos.

altitude noun altitud Fem.

altogether adverb **1** en total; **I've spent thirty pounds altogether** he gastado treinta libras en total; **2** (completely) totalmente; **I'm not altogether convinced** no estoy totalmente convencido.

aluminium noun aluminio Masc.

always adverb siempre; **I always leave at five** siempre salgo a las cinco.

am verb SEE **be**.

a.m. abbreviation de la mañana; **at 8 a.m.** a las ocho de la mañana.

amateur noun amateur Masc./Fem. (plural amateurs); **amateur dramatics** teatro Masc. de amateurs.

amaze verb asombrar [17]; **what amazes me is** ... lo que me asombra es ....

amazed adjective asombrado/asombrada; **I was amazed to see her** me me quedé asombrado al verla; **he'll be amazed to find out** se quedará asombrado al enterarse.

amazement noun asombro Masc.; **to my amazement she agreed** para mi gran sorpresa aceptó.

amazing adjective increíble; **they've got an amazing house** tienen una casa increíble; **she has an amazing number of friends** tiene un número increíble de amigos.

ambassador noun embajador Masc., embajadora Fem.

ambition noun ambición Fem.

ambitious adjective ambicioso/ ambiciosa.

ambulance noun ambulancia Fem.

ambulance driver noun conductor/conductora Masc./Fem. de ambulancia.

amenities plural noun servicios Masc. plural públicos.

America noun América Fem.

American noun americano Masc., americana Fem.

American adjective americano/ americana.

ammunition noun municiones Fem. plural.

among, amongst preposition entre; **I found it among my books** lo encontré entre mis libros; **you can decide amongst yourselves** podéis decidirlo entre vosotros.

amount noun **1** cantidad Fem.; **an enormous amount of bread** una enorme cantidad de pan; **a huge amount of work** una enorme cantidad de trabajo; **2** (of money) suma Fem.; **a large amount of money** una gran suma de dinero.

amount to verb ascender [36] a; **the bill amounts to five hundred**

euros la cuenta asciende a quinientos euros.

amp noun **1** amperio Masc.; **2** (amplifier) amplificador Masc.

amplifier noun amplificador Masc.

amuse verb divertir [14].

amusement arcade noun salón Masc. de juegos recreativos.

amusement park noun parque Masc. de atracciones.

amusing adjective divertido/ divertida.

an article SEE **a**.

anaesthetic noun anestesia Fem.

analyse verb analizar [22].

analysis noun análisis Masc.

ancestor noun antepasado Masc., antepasada Fem.

anchor noun ancla Fem.

anchovy noun anchoa Fem.

ancient adjective **1** (historic) antiguo/antigua; **an ancient abbey** una antigua abadía; **2** (very old) viejísimo/viejísima; **an ancient pair of jeans** unos vaqueros viejísimos; **3** ancient **Greece** la Grecia antigua.

and conjunction **1** y; **Sean and Anna** Sean y Anna; **your shoes and socks** tus calcetines y tus zapatos ('y' becomes 'e' before a word that starts with 'i' or 'hi') **Spain and Italy** España e Italia; **2** (with numbers) **three hundred and six** trescientos seis; **five hundred and thirty-one** quinientos treinta y uno; **3 fish and chips** pescado con patatas

a b c d e f g h i j k l m n o p q r s t u v w x y z

a

b

c

d

e

f

g

h

i

j

k

l

m

n

o

p

q

r

s

t

u

v

w

x

y

z

fritas; **4 bigger and bigger** cada vez más grande.

Andalusia noun Andalucía Fem.

Andalusian noun andaluz, andaluza Masc./Fem.

Andalusian adjective andaluz/andaluza.

angel noun ángel Masc.

anger noun ira Fem.

angle noun ángulo Masc.

angrily adverb con enfado.

angry adjective **to be angry** estar [2] enfadado/enfadada; **she was angry with me** estaba enfadada conmigo; **to get angry** (about something) enfadarse [17] (por algo).

animal noun animal Masc.

ankle noun tobillo Masc.; **to break your ankle** romperse [40] el tobillo.

anniversary noun aniversario Masc.; **a wedding anniversary** un aniversario de boda.

announce verb anunciar [17].

announcement noun anuncio Masc.

annoy verb **to be annoyed** estar [2] enfadado/enfadada; **to get annoyed (about something)** enfadarse [17] (por algo); **she got annoyed** se enfadó.

annoying adjective **1** (person) pesado/pesada; **2** (noise or habit) irritante; **3** **how annoying!** ¡qué rabia!; **the whole thing's really annoying** todo es un verdadero fastidio.

annual adjective anual.

anorak noun anorak Masc. (plural anoraks).

anorexia noun anorexia Fem.

another adjective otro/otra; **would you like another cup of tea?** ¿quieres otra taza de té?; **another two years** otros dos años; **we need another three chairs** necesitamos otras tres sillas; **I'll come another time** vendré en otro momento.

answer noun **1** respuesta Fem.; **the right answer** la respuesta correcta; **the wrong answer** la respuesta equivocada; **2** **the answer to a problem** la solución a un problema.

answer verb **1** contestar [17]; **he hasn't answered your letter** no ha contestado a nuestra carta; **to answer the phone** contestar el teléfono; **2** **to answer the door** abrir [46] la puerta.

answering machine noun contestador Masc. automático; **to leave a message on the answering machine** dejar [17] un mensaje en el contestador.

ant noun hormiga Fem.

Antarctic noun **the Antarctic** la Antártida.

anthem noun **the national anthem** el himno nacional.

antibiotic noun antibiótico Masc.

anticlockwise adverb en el sentido contrario al de las agujas del reloj; **it turns anticlockwise** gira en el sentido contrario al de las agujas del reloj.

antique noun antiques las antigüedades.

antique adjective antiguo/ antigua; **an antique table** una mesa antigua.

antique shop noun tienda Fem. de antigüedades.

antiseptic noun antiséptico Masc.

anxious adjective preocupado/ preocupada.

anxiously adverb con preocupación.

any pronoun 1 (in negative sentences) ninguno/ninguna; **I don't want any** no quiero ninguno/ninguna; **2** (in questions) alguno/alguna; **do you want any?** ¿quieres alguno/alguna?

any adjective, adverb 1 (when followed by a noun 'any' is not translated) **is there any butter?** ¿hay mantequilla?; **have you got any glasses?** ¿tienes vasos?; **there isn't any flour** no hay harina; **I haven't got any glasses** no tengo vasos; **2 is there any more?** (followed by a singular) ¿queda más? (followed by a plural) ¿quedan más?; **there isn't any more butter** no me queda más mantequilla; **I haven't got any more glasses** no me quedan más vasos; **3** (referring to time) **I don't go there any more** ya no voy nunca; **I used to phone her but not any more** solía llamarla, pero ya no.

anybody, anyone pronoun 1 (in questions and after 'if') alguien; **does anybody want some tea?** ¿alguien quiere té?; **is anybody**

home? ¿hay alguien en casa?; **if anybody wants some beer, it's in the fridge** si alguien quiere cerveza, está en la nevera; **2 not ... anybody** no ... nadie; **there isn't anybody in her office** no hay nadie en su oficina; **I don't know anybody there** no conozco a nadie allí; **3** (absolutely anybody) cualquiera; **anybody can go** puede ir cualquiera.

anyhow adverb SEE anyway.

anyone pronoun SEE anybody.

anything pronoun 1 (in questions) algo; **is there anything I can do to help?** ¿puedo hacer algo para ayudar?; **2 not ... anything** no ... nada; **there isn't anything on the table** no hay nada en la mesa; **3** (anything at all) cualquier cosa; **anything could happen** puede pasar cualquier cosa.

anyway, anyhow adverb de todos modos; **anyway, I'll ring you before I leave** de todos modos te llamaré antes de salir.

anywhere adverb 1 (in questions) **have you seen my keys anywhere?** ¿has visto mis llaves por algún lado?; **are you going anywhere tomorrow?** ¿vas a algún lado mañana?; **2 not ... anywhere** por ningún lado; **I can't find my keys anywhere** no puedo encontrar mis llaves por ningún lado; **I'm not going anywhere tonight** esta noche no voy a ningún lado; **3** (absolutely anywhere) donde sea; **put your cases down anywhere** pon las maletas donde sea.

a b c d e f g h i j k l m n o p q r s t u v w x y z

apart *adjective, adverb* **1** (*separate*) separado/separada; **we don't like being apart** no nos gusta estar separados; **they're too far apart** están demasiado separados; **2 to be two metres apart** estar [2] a dos metros de distancia; **3 apart from** aparte de; **apart from Judy everybody was there** aparte de Judy, todo el mundo estaba allí.

apartheid *noun* apartheid *Masc.*

apartment *noun* apartamento *Masc.*

ape *noun* simio *Masc./Fem.*

apologize *verb* **1** disculparse [17]; **he apologized for his behaviour** se disculpó por su comportamiento; **2 to apologize to somebody** pedirle [57] perdón a alguien; **he apologized to Tanya** le pidió perdón a Tanya.

apology *noun* disculpa *Fem.*

apostrophe *noun* apóstrofe *Masc.*

apparent *adjective* aparente.

apparently *adverb* al parecer.

appeal *noun* **1** (*call*) **an appeal for calm** un llamamiento a la calma; **2 an appeal for help** una solicitud de ayuda.

appeal *verb* **to appeal to somebody** atraer [42] a alguien; **horror films don't appeal to me** las películas de miedo no me atraen.

appear *verb* **1** aparecer [35]; **Mick appeared at the door** Mick apareció en la puerta; **2 to appear on television** salir [63] en televisión; **3** (*seem*) parecer [35]; **it appears that somebody has**

stolen the key parece que alguien ha robado la llave; **he appears to be calm** parece que está tranquilo.

appendicitis *noun* apendicitis *Fem.*

appendix *noun* apéndice *Masc.*

appetite *noun* apetito *Masc.*; **it'll spoil your appetite** te quitará el apetito.

applaud *verb* aplaudir [19].

applause *noun* aplausos *Masc. plural.*

apple *noun* manzana *Fem.*

apple tree *noun* manzano *Masc.*

applicant *noun* candidato *Masc.*, candidata *Fem.*

application *noun* **a job application** una solicitud de trabajo.

application form *noun* impreso *Masc.* de solicitud.

apply *verb* **1 to apply for a job** solicitar [17] un trabajo; **2 I've applied for the course** he solicitado que me admitan en el curso; **3 to apply to** aplicarse [31] a; **that doesn't apply to students** eso no se aplica a los estudiantes.

appointment *noun* cita *Fem.*; **to make a dental appointment** pedir [57] cita en el dentista; **I've got a hair appointment at 4 o'clock** tengo cita en la peluquería para las cuatro.

appreciate *verb* agradecer [35]; **I appreciate your advice** te agradezco tus consejos; **I'd appreciate it if you could tidy up**

afterwards te agradecería que luego recogieses.

apprentice noun aprendiz Masc., aprendiza Fem.

apprenticeship noun aprendizaje Masc.

approach verb 1 (come near to) acercarse [31] a; **we were approaching Madrid** nos acercábamos a Madrid; 2 (tackle) abordar [17] (a problem, task).

appropriate adjective apropiado/apropiada.

approval noun aprobación Fem.

approve verb I don't approve of her friends no gustan sus amigos; I don't approve of his methods no estoy de acuerdo con sus métodos; does he approve of the idea? ¿le parece bien la idea?

approximate adjective aproximado/aproximada.

approximately adverb aproximadamente; **approximately fifty people** aproximadamente cincuenta personas.

apricot noun albaricoque Masc.

apricot tree noun albaricoquero Masc.

April noun abril Masc.; **in April** en abril.

April Fool noun inocente Masc./Fem. (see the entry for 'April Fool's Day').

April Fool's Day noun el día de los Santos Inocentes (the rough equivalent of April Fool's Day, but on the 28 December).

apron noun delantal Masc.

aquarium noun acuario Masc.

Aquarius noun Acuario Masc.; **Sharon's Aquarius** Sharon es Acuario.

Arab noun árabe Masc./Fem..

Arab adjective árabe; **the Arab countries** los países árabes.

arch noun arco Masc.

archaelogist noun arqueólogo Masc., arqueóloga Fem.; **she's an archeologist** es arqueóloga.

archaeology noun arqueología Fem.

archbishop noun arzobispo Masc.

architect noun arquitecto Masc., arquitecta Fem.; **he's an architect** es arquitecto.

architecture noun arquitectura Fem.

Arctic noun the Arctic el Ártico.

are verb SEE **be**.

area noun 1 (part of a town) barrio Masc.; **a nice area** un buen barrio; **a rough area** un barrio peligroso; 2 (region) zona Fem.; **in the Leeds area** en la zona de Leeds; 3 (of square, circle) superficie Fem.

Argentina noun Argentina Fem.

Argentinian noun argentino Masc., argentina Fem.

Argentinian adjective argentino/argentina.

argue verb discutir [19]; **there's no point in arguing** no tiene sentido discutir; **to argue about something** discutir sobre algo; **they're arguing about the result** están discutiendo sobre el resultado.

a b c d e f g h i j k l m n o p q r s t u v w x y z

a
b
c
d
e
f
g
h
i
j
k
l
m
n
o
p
q
r
s
t
u
v
w
x
y
z

argument noun discusión Fem.; **to have an argument** discutir [19].

Aries noun Aries Masc.; **Pauline's Aries** Pauline es Aries.

arithmetic noun aritmética Fem.

arm noun brazo Masc.; **he took my arm** me cogió del brazo; **to fold your arms** cruzar los brazos; **to go arm in arm** ir [8] del brazo; **to break your arm** romperse [40] el brazo.

armchair noun sillón Masc.

armed adjective armado/armada.

armpit noun axila Fem.

arms plural noun armas Fem. plural.

army noun ejército Masc.; **to join the army** alistarse en el ejército.

around preposition, adverb **1** (with time) alrededor de; **we'll be there around ten** estaremos allí alrededor de las diez; **2** (with amounts, age) **we need around six kilos** necesitamos unos seis quilos; **she's around fifteen** tiene unos quince años; **3** (surrounding) alrededor de; **the countryside around Edinburgh** el campo de alrededor de Edinburgo; **we sat around the table** nos sentamos alrededor de la mesa; **4** (near) por aquí; **is there a post office around here?** ¿hay una oficina de correos por aquí?; **is Phil around?** ¿está Phil por aquí?; **5** (wrapped around) **she had a scarf around her neck** tenía una bufanda alrededor del cuello; **6 around the corner** a la vuelta de

la esquina; **7 to travel around the world** viajar por el mundo.

arrange verb **to arrange to do** quedar [17] en hacer; **we've arranged to see a film on Saturday** quedamos en ver una película el domingo.

arrangement noun **1** (of things) disposición Fem.; **2** (agreement) acuerdo Masc.

arrest noun **he's under arrest** está detenido; **you're under arrest** queda detenido.

arrest verb arrestar [17].

arrival noun llegada Fem.

arrive verb llegar [17]; **they arrived at three** llegaron a las tres.

arrow noun flecha Fem.

art noun **1** arte Masc. (plural artes) (note that the plural 'artes' is feminine); **modern art** arte moderno; **the arts** las artes; **2** (school subject) dibujo Masc.; **the art class** la clase de dibujo.

art school noun escuela Fem. de Bellas Artes.

artery noun arteria Fem.

art gallery noun (public) museo Masc. de arte.

article noun artículo Masc.

artichoke noun alcachofa Fem.

artificial adjective artificial.

artist noun artista Masc./Fem.; **he's an artist** es artista.

artistic adjective artístico/artística.

as conjunction, adverb **1** como; **as you know** como sabes; **as usual** como siempre; **as I told you** como te dije; **2** (*because*) como; **as there were no trains, we took the bus** como no había trenes, cogimos el autobús; **3 as ... as** tan ... como; **he's as tall as his brother** es tan alto como su hermano; **you must be as tired as I am** debes estar tan cansado como yo; **I did it as quickly as I could** lo hice tan rápido como pude; **4 as much ... as** tanto/tanta ... como; **you have as much time as I do** tienes tanto tiempo como yo; **5 as many ... as** tantos/tantas ... como; **we have as many problems as he does** tenemos tantos problemas como él; **6 as long as** siempre que (*followed by the subjunctive*); **we'll go tomorrow, as long as it's a nice day** iremos mañana, siempre que haga buen tiempo; **7 you can stay for as long as you like** puedes quedarte todo el tiempo que quieras; **8 as soon as possible** lo más pronto posible; **9 to work as** trabajar [17] de; **he works as a taxi driver in the evenings** trabaja de taxista por las noches.

asbestos *noun* asbestos *Masc.*

ash *noun* ceniza *Fem.*

ashamed *adjective* **to be ashamed** estar [2] avergonzado; **you should be ashamed of yourself!** ¡debería darte vergüenza!

ashtray *noun* cenicero *Masc.*

Asia *noun* Asia *Fem.*

Asian *noun* asiático *Masc.*, asiática *Fem.*

Asian *adjective* asiático/asiátia.

ask *verb* **1** (*inquire*) preguntar [17]; **you can ask at reception** puedes preguntar en recepción; **to ask somebody something** preguntarle algo a alguien; **I asked him where he lived** le pregunté dónde vivía; **2** (*request*) pedir [57]; **to ask for something** pedir algo; **I asked for three coffees** pedí tres cafés; **to ask somebody to do** pedirle a alguien que haga (*note that 'que' is followed by subjunctive*) **ask Danny to give you a hand** pídele a Danny que te eche una mano; **3 to ask somebody a question** hacerle una pregunta a alguien; **I asked you a question!** ¡te he hecho una pregunta!; **4** invitar [17]; **they've asked us to a party at their house** nos han invitado a una fiesta en su casa; **5 Paul's asked Janie out on Friday** Paul invitó a Janie a salir el viernes.

asleep *adjective* dormido/ dormida; **to be asleep** estar [2] dormido; **the baby's asleep** el niño está dormido; **to fall asleep** quedarse [17] dormido.

asparagus *noun* espárrago *Masc.*

aspirin *noun* aspirina *Fem.*

assignment *noun* (*at school, college*) tarea *Fem.*

assist *verb* ayudar [17].

assistance *noun* ayuda *Fem.*

assistant *noun* **1** (*at work*) ayudante *Masc./Fem.*; **2 a shop assistant** un dependiente/una dependienta.

a

association noun asociación Fem.

assorted adjective variado/variada.

assortment noun surtido Masc.

assume verb suponer [11].

assure verb asegurar [17]; **I assure you** te lo aseguro.

asterisk noun asterisco Masc.

asthma noun asma Fem.; **she has asthma** tiene asma.

astonishing adjective asombroso/asombrosa; **her knowledge is astonishing** sus conocimientos son asombrosos.

astrologer noun astrólogo Masc., astróloga Fem.

astrology noun astrología Fem.

astronaut noun astronauta Masc./Fem.

astronomer noun astrónomo Masc., astrónoma Fem.

astronomy noun astronomía Fem.

at preposition **1** (in a place) en; **at home** en casa; **at school** en el colegio; **at my office** en mi oficina; **I'll be at work** estaré en el trabajo; **2** (talking about the time) a; **at eight o'clock** a las ocho; **3** **at night** por la noche; **I'll be there at the weekend** estaré allí el fin de semana; **4** **at Emma's house** en casa de Emma; **she's at her brother's this evening** esta noche está en casa de su hermano; **at the hairdresser's** en la peluquería; **5** **at last** por fin; **he's found a job at last** por fin ha encontrado un trabajo; **6** (in email addresses) arroba Fem.; **john.smith@easycom.com** john-punto-smith-arroba-easycom-punto-com.

athlete noun atleta Masc./Fem.

athletic adjective atlético/atlética.

athletics noun atletismo Masc.

Atlantic noun **the Atlantic** el Atlántico.

atlas noun atlas Masc.

atmosphere noun atmósfera Fem.

atom noun átomo Masc.

atomic adjective atómico/atómica.

attach verb **1** (fasten) sujetar [17]; **2** (tie) atar [17]; **3** (glue) pegar [28].

attached adjective **to be attached to** (be fond of) tenerle cariño a.

attachment noun **1** (to letter) documento Masc. adjunto; **2** (in e-mail) archivo Masc. adjunto.

attack noun ataque Masc.

attack verb atacar [31].

attacker noun agresor Masc., agresora Fem.

attempt noun intento Masc.; **at the first attempt** al primer intento.

attempt verb **to attempt to do** intentar [17] hacer.

attend verb asistir [19] a; **to attend a class** asistir a clase.

attention noun atención Fem.; **to pay attention to** prestar atención a; **I wasn't paying atttention** no estaba prestando atención.

attic noun desván Masc.

attitude noun actitud Fem.

attract verb atraer [42].

attraction noun atracción Fem.

attractive adjective atractivo/atractiva.

aubergine noun berenjena Fem.

auction noun subasta Fem.

audience noun público Masc.

August noun agosto Masc.

aunt, auntie noun tía Fem.

au pair noun au pair Masc./Fem.; I'm looking for a job as an au pair estoy buscando un trabajo de au pair.

Australia noun Australia Fem.

Australian noun australiano Masc., australiana Fem.

Australian adjective australiano/australiana.

Austria noun Austria Fem.

Austrian noun austriaco Masc., austriaca Fem.

Austrian adjective austriaco/austriaca.

author noun autor Masc., autora Fem.

autobiography noun autobiografía Fem.

autograph noun autógrafo Masc.

automatic adjective automático/automática.

automatically adverb automáticamente.

autumn noun otoño Masc.

availability noun disponibilidad Fem.

available adjective disponible.

avalanche noun avalancha Fem.

avenue noun avenida Fem.

average noun **1** media Fem.; above average por encima de la media; **2 on average** como promedio.

average adjective medio/media; of average height de estatura media.

avocado noun aguacate Masc.

avoid verb evitar [17]; she avoided me me evitó; to avoid doing evitar hacer; I avoid speaking to him evito hablar con él.

awake adjective to be awake estar [2] despierto/despierta; is Lola awake? ¿está despierta Lola?

award noun premio Masc.; to win an award ganar [17] un premio.

aware adjective to be aware of a problem ser [1] consciente de un problema; to become aware of something darse [4] cuenta de algo; as far as I'm aware que yo sepa; to be aware of a noise oír [56] un ruido.

away adverb **1 to be away** estar [2] fuera; I'll be away next week estaré fuera la próxima semana; **2 to go away** irse [8]; Laura's gone away for a week Laura se ha ido por una semana; go away! ¡vete!; **3 to run away** escaparse [17]; the thieves ran away los ladrones se escaparon; **4 the school is two kilometres away** el colegio está a dos kilómetros; how far away is it? ¿a qué distancia está?; not far away no muy lejos; a long way away muy lejos; **5 to put**

a b c d e f g h i j k l m n o p q r s t u v w x y z

something away guardar [17] algo; **I'll just put my books away** voy a guardar mis libros; **6 to give something away** regalar [17] algo; **she's given away all her tapes** ha regalado todas sus cintas.

away match *noun* partido *Masc.* fuera de casa.

awful *adjective* **1** horrible; **the film was awful!** la película era horrible; **2** (*ill*) **I feel awful** me siento fatal; **3** (*guilty*) **I feel awful about it** me siento muy culpable; **4 an awful lot of** un montón de; **5 how awful!** ¡qué horror!

awkward *adjective* **1** difícil; **it's an awkward situation** es una situación difícil; **it's a bit awkward** es un poco delicado; **an awkward child** un niño difícil; **2 an awkward question** una pregunta comprometida.

axe *noun* hacha *Fem.* (even though *'hacha'* is feminine, it takes *'el'* and *'un'* in the singular).

Bb

baby *noun* bebé *Masc.*

babysit *verb* hacer [7] de canguro.

babysitter *noun* canguro *Masc./ Fem.*

babysitting *noun* hacer [7] de canguro.

bachelor *noun* soltero *Masc.*

back *noun* **1** (*of a person or garment*) espalda *Fem.*; **to do something behind somebody's** **back** hacer [7] algo a espaldas de alguien; **2** (*of an animal*) lomo *Masc.*; **3** (*of a piece of paper or your hand*) dorso *Masc.*; **on the back** en el dorso; **4** (*of a car, a plane, or a hall*) fondo *Masc.*; **we have seats at the back** tenemos asientos al fondo; **the children are at the back of the room** los niños que están al fondo de la habitación; **5** (*of a building*) parte *Fem.* de atrás; **a garden at the back of the house** un jardín en la parte de atrás de la casa; **6** (*of a chair or sofa*) respaldo *Masc.*; **7** (*in football or hockey*) defensa *Masc., Fem.*

back *adjective* **1** trasero/trasera (*a wheel or seat*); **the back seat of the car** el asiento trasero del coche; **2 the back garden** el jardín de atrás; **the back gate** la verja de atrás.

back *adverb* **1 to go back** volver [45]; **to go back to school** volver al colegio; **Lisa's gone back to London** Lisa ha vuelto a Londres; **2 to come back** volver [45]; **they've come back from Italy** han vuelto de Italia; **she's back at work** ha vuelto al trabajo; **Sue's not back yet** Sue no ha vuelto aún; **she went by bus and walked back** fue en autobús y volvió andando; **3 to phone back** volver [45] a llamar; **I'll ring back later** te volveré a llamar más tarde; **4 to give something back to somebody** devolverle [45] algo a alguien; **I gave him back his cassettes** le devolví sus cintas; **give it back!** ¡devuélvemelo!

back verb **1** apoyar [17] (a candidate); **2** apostar [24] por (a horse).
● **to back up** (on a computer) **to back up a file** hacer [7] una copia de seguridad de un archivo.
● **to back somebody up** apoyar [17] a alguien.

backache noun dolor Masc. de espalda.

backbone noun columna Fem. vertebral.

back door noun **1** (of a building) puerta Fem. de atrás; **2** (of a car) puerta Fem. trasera.

backfire verb (turn out badly) salir [63] mal.

background noun **1** (of a person) origen Masc.; **2** (of events or a situation) contexto Masc.; **3** (in a picture or view) fondo Masc.; **the trees in the background** los árboles del fondo; **4 background music** música de fondo; **background noise** ruido de fondo.

backhand noun revés Masc.

backing noun (moral support) apoyo Masc.

backpack noun mochila Fem.

backpack verb **to go backpacking** viajar con mochila.

back seat noun asiento Masc. trasero.

backside noun trasero Masc.

backstroke noun estilo Masc. espalda; **to swim backstroke** nadar a espalda.

back to front adverb al revés; **your jumper's back to front** te has puesto el jersey al revés.

backup noun **1** (support) apoyo Masc.; **2** (in computing) **a backup disk** un disco de seguridad.

backwards adverb (to lean or fall) hacia atrás.

bacon noun bacon Masc.; **bacon and eggs** huevos con bacon.

bad adjective **1** (not good) malo/mala ('malo' becomes 'mal' before a masculine singular noun) **a bad moment** un mal momento; **it's bad for your health** es malo para la salud; **2** grave (an accident, a mistake); **a bad accident** un accidente grave; **3** fuerte (a headache, a cold); **a bad cold** un resfriado fuerte; **4** (rotten) podrido/podrida; **a bad apple** una manzana podrida; **to go bad** estropearse [17]; **5** (rude) **bad language** lenguaje grosero; **6** (naughty) malo/mala; **bad dog!** ¡(perro) malo!; **7 to be bad at something** dársele [4] algo mal a alguien; **I'm bad at physics** se me da mal la física; **8 it's not bad** no está mal; **his new film's not bad** su nueva película no está mal; ★ **too bad!** (I'm sorry for you) ¡qué rabia!, (I don't care) ¡y a mí qué!

badge noun **1** (pin-on) chapa Fem.; **2 a policeman badge** una placa de policía.

badly adverb **1** mal; **he writes badly** escribe mal; **I slept badly** dormí mal; **my exam went badly** el examen me fue mal; **2 badly hurt** gravemente herido; **3 the car**

a
b
c
d
e
f
g
h
i
j
k
l
m
n
o
p
q
r
s
t
u
v
w
x
y
z

a
b
c
d
e
f
g
h
i
j
k
l
m
n
o
p
q
r
s
t
u
v
w
x
y
z

was badly damaged el coche quedó muy estropeado.

bad-mannered adjective maleducado/maleducada.

badminton noun bádminton Masc.; **to play badminton** jugar al bádminton.

bad-tempered adjective
1 (answer, look) malhumorado/malhumorada; **2 to be bad-tempered** (for a while) estar de mal humor (always) tener mal genio.

bag noun 1 (plastic, paper) bolsa Fem.; **2** (handbag) bolso Masc.

bags plural noun maletas Fem. plural; **to pack your bags** hacer las maletas; ★ **to have bags under your eyes** tener ojeras.

baggage noun equipaje Masc.

baggage allowance noun franquicia Fem. de equipaje.

baggage reclaim noun recogida Fem. de equipaje.

bagpipes plural noun gaita Fem.; **to play the bagpipes** tocar la gaita.

Bahamas plural noun **the Bahamas** las Bahamas; **the Bahama Islands** las islas Bahamas.

Bahamian noun bahameño Masc., bahameña Fem.

Bahamian adjective bahameño/bahameña.

bake verb **to bake a cake** hacer [7] un pastel; **to bake potatoes** asar [17] patatas.

baked adjective 1 (fruit or vegetables) asado/asada; **baked apples** manzanas asadas; **a baked**

potato una patata asada; **2** (fish) al horno.

baked beans plural noun judías Fem. plural en salsa de tomate.

baker noun panadero Masc., panadera Fem.; **to go to the baker's** ir a la panadería.

bakery noun panadería Fem.

balance noun 1 equilibrio Masc.; **to lose your balance** perder el equilibrio; **2** (money in your bank account) saldo Masc.

balanced adjective equilibrado/equilibrada.

balcony noun balcón Masc.

bald adjective calvo/calva.

Balearic Islands plural noun las Islas Baleares.

ball noun 1 (for tennis or golf) pelota Fem.; **2** (for football or volleyball) balón Masc.; **3** (of string or wool) ovillo Masc.

ballet noun ballet Masc.

ballet dancer noun bailarín Masc. de ballet, bailarina Fem. de ballet.

ballet shoe noun zapatilla Fem. de ballet.

balloon nosun globo Masc.

ballot noun votación Fem.

ballpoint (pen) noun boli Masc. (informal), bolígrafo Masc.

ban noun prohibición Fem.; **to put a ban on smoking** prohibir fumar.

ban verb prohibir [58].

banana noun plátano Masc.; **a banana yoghurt** un yogur de plátano.

band noun **1** (*playing music*) grupo Masc.; **a rock band** un grupo de rock; **2 a jazz band** (*big*) una orquesta de jazz, (*small*) un conjunto de jazz; **3 a brass band** una banda de música; **4 a rubber band** una goma elástica.

bandage noun venda Fem.

bandage verb vendar [17].

bang noun **1** (*noise*) estallido Masc.; **2** (*of a window*) golpe Masc.; **3** (*of a door*) portazo Masc.

bang verb **1** (*to hit*) golpear [17] (*a drum, for example*); **he banged his fist on the table** golpeó la mesa con el puño; **2** (*to knock*) dar [4] golpes a; **to bang on the door** dar golpes a la puerta; **I banged my head on the door** me di un golpe en la cabeza con la puerta; **I banged into the table** me choqué con la mesa; **3 to bang the door** aporrear [17] la puerta.

bang exclamation (*like a gun*) ¡pum!

bangle noun pulsera Fem.

banister(s), bannister(s) plural noun barandilla Fem. (*singular*).

bank noun **1** (*for money*) banco Masc.; **I'm going to the bank** voy al banco; **2** (*of a river or lake*) orilla Fem.

bank account noun cuenta Fem. bancaria.

bank balance noun saldo Masc.

bank card noun tarjeta Fem. bancaria.

bank holiday noun día Masc. festivo.

banking noun banca Fem.

banknote noun billete Masc. de banco.

bank statement noun extracto Masc. de cuenta.

baptize verb bautizar [22].

bar noun **1** (*selling drinks*) bar Masc.; **Janet works in a bar** Janet trabaja en un bar; **2** (*the counter in a bar*) barra Fem.; **on the bar** en la barra; **3 a bar of chocolate** una tableta de chocolate; **4 a bar of soap** una pastilla de jabón; **5** (*made of wood or metal*) barra Fem.; **a metal bar** una barra de metal; **6** (*in music*) compás Masc.

bar verb (*to block physically*) bloquear [17]; **to bar someone's way** bloquear el paso a alguien.

Barbadian noun barbadense Masc./Fem.

Barbadian adjective barbadense.

barbecue noun barbacoa Fem.; **there's a barbecue tonight** hay una barbacoa esta noche.

barbecue verb **to barbecue a chicken** asar [17] un pollo a la parrilla; **barbecued chicken** pollo a la parrilla.

barbed wire noun alambre Masc. de púas.

bare adjective desnudo/desnuda.

barefoot adjective descalzo/descalza; **to be barefoot** estar descalzo/descalza.

bargain noun (*a good buy*) ganga Fem.; **I got a bargain** conseguí una ganga; **it's a bargain!** ¡es una ganga!

barge noun barcaza Fem.

a b c d e f g h i j k l m n o p q r s t u v w x y z

bark

bark noun 1 (of a tree) corteza Fem.; 2 (of a dog) ladrido Masc.

bark verb ladrar [17].

barley noun cebada Fem.

barmaid noun camarera Fem.

barman noun camarero Masc.

barn noun granero Masc.

barometer noun barómetro Masc.

barrel noun tonel Masc.

barrier noun barrera Fem.

base noun base Fem.

baseball noun baloncesto Masc.

based adjective 1 to be based on estar basado en; the film is based on a true story la película está basada en una historia real; 2 to be based in (a company) tener su base en, (a person) vivir en; he's based in Bristol vive en Bristol.

basement noun sótano Masc.; in the basement en el sótano.

bash noun 1 golpe Masc.; it's got a bash on the bumper tiene un golpe en el guardabarros; 2 I'll have a bash voy a probar.

bash verb I bashed my head me di un golpe en la cabeza.

basic adjective 1 básico/básica; basic knowledge conocimientos básicos; 2 the basic facts los hechos fundamentales; 3 basic salary sueldo base; 4 (not luxurious) sencillo/sencilla; the flat's a bit basic el piso es bastante sencillo.

basically adverb 1 fundamentalmente; it's basically all right fundamentalmente está bien;

2 basically, I don't really want to go en pocas palabras, no quiero ir.

basics noun rudimentos Masc. plural.

basin noun (washbasin) lavabo Masc.

basis noun 1 base Fem.; on the basis of en base a; 2 on a regular basis regularmente.

basket noun 1 cesta Fem.; a shopping basket una cesta de la compra; a linen basket una cesta de ropa sucia; 2 a waste-paper basket una papelera.

basketball noun baloncesto Masc.; to play basketball jugar al baloncesto.

Basque noun 1 (the language) euskera Masc., vasco Masc.; 2 (person) vasco Masc., vasca Fem.

Basque adjective vasco/vasca; the Basque Country el País Vasco, Euskadi Masc.

bass noun 1 bajo Masc.; to play bass tocar el bajo; 2 a double bass un contrabajo.

bass drum noun bombo Masc.

bass guitar noun bajo Masc.

bassoon noun fagot Masc.; to play the bassoon tocar el fagot.

bat noun 1 (for cricket or baseball) bate Masc.; 2 (for table tennis) paleta Fem.; 3 (animal) murciélago Masc.

batch noun lote Masc.; a batch of letters un lote de cartas.

bath noun 1 baño Masc.; I was in the bath estaba en el baño; 2 (bathtub) bañera Fem.; the bath's

beak

pink la bañera es rosa; **3 to have a bath** bañarse [17].

bathe verb **1** lavar [17] (a wound); **2** (go swimming) bañarse [17].

bathroom noun cuarto Masc. de baño.

bath towel noun toalla Fem. de baño.

batter noun **1** (for frying) rebozado Masc.; **fish in batter** pescado rebozado; **2** (for pancakes) masa Fem.

battery noun **1** (for a torch or radio, for example) pila Fem.; **2** (for a car) batería Fem.

battle noun batalla Fem.

bay noun **1** (on coast) bahía Fem.; **the Bay of Biscay** el Golfo de Vizcaya; **2** (for bus) dársena Fem.

B.C. a.de C. (antes de Cristo).

be verb **1** (referring to permanent characteristics) ser [1]; **it's beautiful** es precioso; **she's very tall** es muy alta; **honey is sweet** la miel es dulce; **2** (referring to changeable emotions and situations) estar [2]; **she's angry** está enfadada; **I'm tired** estoy cansada; **the soup is cold** la sopa está fría; **this cake is too sweet** este pastel está demasiado dulce; **3** (in a place) estar [2]; **Melanie is in the kitchen** Melanie está en la cocina; **¿where's the butter?** ¿dónde está la mantequilla?; **when we were in France** cuando estábamos en Francia; **4 there is** hay; **there are hay; there's more here** aquí hay más; **there are two children outside** hay dos niños

fuera; **is there any problem?** ¿hay algún problema?; **5** (with jobs and professions) ser [1] (note that 'a' is not translated) **she's a teacher** es profesora; **he's a taxi driver** es taxista; **6** (marital status) estar [2] es [1]; **she's married** está casada; **he's single** está/es soltero; **7** (in clock times) ser [1]; **it's one o'clock** es la una en punto; **it's half past five** son las cinco y media; **8** (for days of the week and dates) ser [1]; **what day is it today?** ¿qué día es hoy?; **it's Tuesday today** hoy es martes; **it's the twentieth of May** es veinte de mayo; **9** (talking about age) tener [9]; **to be fifteen** tener quince años; **how old are you?** ¿cuántos años tienes?; **Samuel's two** Samuel tiene dos años; **10** (feeling cold, hot, hungry) tener [9]; **I'm hot** tengo calor; **I'm cold** tengo frío; **I'm hungry** tengo hambre; **11** (talking about weather) **it's cold today** hoy hace frío; **it's a nice day** hace buen día; **12** (to a country or town) estar [2]; **I've never been to Paris** nunca he estado en París; **have you been to Spain before?** ¿has estado en España antes?; **13 to be loved** ser [1] amado (but note that often the passive is translated by the third person plural) **he has been killed** lo han matado (literally: they have killed him).

beach noun playa Fem.; **on the beach** en la playa.

bead noun cuenta Fem.

beak noun pico Masc.

a b c d e f g h i j k l m n o p q r s t u v w x y z

beam noun **1** (of light) rayo Fem.; **2** (for a roof) viga Fem.

bean noun alubia Fem., judía Fem.; **baked beans** alubias en salsa de tomate; **green beans** judías verdes.

bear noun oso Masc.

bear verb **1** soportar [17]; **I can't bear him** no puedo soportarlo; **I can't bear the idea** no puedo soportar la idea; **2 to bear something in mind** tener [9] algo en cuenta; **I'll bear it in mind** lo tendré en cuenta.

beard noun barba Fem.

bearded adjective barbudo/barbuda.

bearings plural noun **to get your bearings** orientarse [17].

beast noun **1** (animal) bestia Fem.; **2 you beast!** ¡bruto!

beat noun ritmo Masc.

beat verb **1** (defeat) ganarle a [17]; **we beat them!** ¡les hemos ganado!; **he beat me at chess** me ganó al ajedrez [17]; **3** batir [19]; **to beat the eggs** batir los huevos; **4 you can't beat a good meal** no hay nada mejor que una buena comida.

● **to beat somebody up** darle [4] una paliza a alguien (informal).

beautician noun esteticista Masc./Fem.

beautiful adjective precioso/preciosa; **a beautiful day** un día precioso; **how beautiful!** ¡qué precioso!

beautifully adverb maravillosamente.

beauty noun belleza Fem.

beauty spot noun (for tourists) lugar Masc. pintoresco.

because conjunction **1** porque; **because it's you** porque eres tú; **because it's cold** porque hace frío; **2 because of** a causa de; **because of the accident** a causa del accidente.

become verb **1** hacerse [7]; **I want to become a lawyer** quiero hacerme abogado; **she became famous** se hizo famosa; **we became friends** nos hicimos amigos; **2** ('become' with an adjective is sometimes translated by a reflexive verb in Spanish) **to become bored** aburrirse [19]; **to become tired** cansarse [17].

bed noun **1** cama Fem.; **a double bed** una cama de matrimonio; **in bed** en la cama; **to go to bed** ir a la cama; **2** (flower bed) macizo Masc.

bedclothes plural noun ropa Fem. de cama (singular).

bedding noun ropa Fem. de cama.

bedroom noun habitación Fem.; **my bedroom window** la ventana de mi habitación.

bedside table noun mesilla Fem. de noche.

bedsit, bedsitter noun habitación Fem. amueblada de aquiler.

bedspread noun colcha Fem.

bedtime noun **it's bedtime** es hora de acostarse.

bee noun abeja Fem.

beech noun haya Fem.

beef noun carne Fem. de vaca; **a roast of beef** un rosbif.

beefburger noun hamburguesa Fem.

beer noun cerveza Fem.; **two beers please** dos cervezas, por favor; **a beer can** una lata de cerveza.

beetle noun escarabajo Masc.

beetroot noun remolacha Fem.

before preposition, adverb **1** antes de; **before Monday** antes del lunes; **2 before somebody** antes que alguien; **he left before me** se fue antes que yo; **3 the day before** el día anterior; **the day before the wedding** el día anterior a la boda; **the day before yesterday** anteayer; **the week before** la semana anterior; **4** (already) ya; **I've seen him before somewhere** ya le he visto en algún sitio; **I had seen the film before** ya había visto la película; **she'd never tried before** nunca lo había intentado antes.

before conjunction **1** antes de; **before doing** antes de hacer; **I closed the windows before leaving** cerré las ventanas antes de salir; **phone before you leave** llámame antes de salir; **2** antes de que (followed by the subjunctive); **phone me before they leave** llámame antes de que salgan; **oh, before I forget** ... ah, antes de que se me olvide ....

beforehand adverb antes; **phone beforehand** llama antes.

beg verb **1** (ask for money) mendigar [28]; **2** (ask) suplicarle a

[31]; **she begged me not to leave me** suplicó que no me marchase; **I beg your pardon** perdone.

begin verb **1** empezar [25]; **the meeting begins at ten** la reunión empieza a las diez; **the words beginning with P** las palabras que empiezan con P; **2 to begin to do** empezar a hacer; **I'm beginning to understand** empiezo a comprender.

beginner noun principiante Masc./Fem.

beginning noun **1** principio Masc.; **at the beginning** al principio; **at the beginning of the holidays** al principio de las vacaciones; **2** (with 'day', 'week', 'month', 'year') **at the beginning of** a principios de; **at the beginning of the month** a principios de mes.

behalf noun **on behalf of** en nombre de.

behave verb **1** portarse [17]; **he behaved badly** se portó mal; **2 to behave yourself** portarse bien; **behave yourselves!** ¡portaos bien!

behaviour noun comportamiento Masc.

behind noun trasero Masc.

behind preposition detrás de; **behind the sofa** detrás del sofá; **behind them** detrás de ellos.

behind adverb **1** detrás; **you go behind** tú vas detrás; **the car behind** el coche de detrás; **2 to leave something behind** olvidarse algo; **I've left my keys behind** me he olvidado las llaves; **to stay behind** quedarse ahí; **3** (not

a
b
c
d
e
f
g
h
i
j
k
l
m
n
o
p
q
r
s
t
u
v
w
x
y
z

making progress) **he's behind in class** va retrasado en clase.

beige *adjective* beige (*does not change*); **beige socks** calcetines beige.

Belgian *noun, adjective* belga *Masc./Fem.*

Belgium *noun Fem.* Bélgica.

belief *noun* creencia *Fem.*; **his political beliefs** sus creencias políticas.

believe *verb* **1** creer [37]; **I believe you** te creo; **they believed what I said** se creyeron lo que dije; **I don't believe you!** ¡no te creo!; **2 to believe in** creer en; **to believe in ghosts** creer en fantasmas; **to believe in God** creer en Dios.

bell *noun* **1** (*in a church*) campana *Fem.*; **2** (*on a door*) timbre *Masc.*; **ring the bell!** ¡toca el timbre!; **3** (*for a cat or toy*) cascabel *Masc.*; ★ **that name rings a bell** ese nombre me suena.

belong *verb* **1 to belong to** ser [1] de; **that belongs to Lucy** eso es de Lucy; **2 to belong to a club** pertenecer [35] a un club; **3** (*go*) ir [8]; **that chair belongs in the study** esa silla va en el estudio; **where does this vase belong?** ¿adónde va este jarrón?

belongings *plural noun* pertenencias *Fem. plural*; **all my belongings are in London** todas mis pertenencias están en Londres.

below *preposition* debajo de; **below the window** debajo de la

ventana; **the flat below yours** el piso de debajo del tuyo.

below *adverb* abajo; **shouts came from below** se oyeron gritos abajo; **the flat below** el piso de abajo.

belt *noun* cinturón *Masc.*

bench *noun* banco *Masc.*

bend *noun* (*in a road, river*) curva *Fem.*

bend *verb* **1** (*to make a bend in*) doblar [17] (*your arm or leg, or a wire*); **2** (*to curve*) (*a road or path*) torcer [41]; **the road bends to the right** la carretera tuerce a la derecha; **3 to bend down** agacharse [17]; **she bent down to look** se agachó para mirar.

beneath *preposition* bajo.

benefit *noun* **1** beneficio *Masc.*; **2 unemployment benefit** subsidio *Masc.* de desempleo.

bent *adjective* doblado/doblada.

beret *noun* boina *Fem.*

berry *noun* baya *Fem.*

berth *noun* litera *Fem.*

beside *preposition* (*next to*) al lado de; **it's beside the table** está al lado de la mesa; **she was sitting beside me** estaba sentada a mi lado; ★ **that's beside the point** eso no viene al caso.

besides *adverb* además; **besides, it's too late** además, es demasiado tarde; **four dogs, and six cats besides** cuatro perros y además seis gatos.

best *adjective* **1** mejor; **it's the best** es el mejor; **that's the best car** ese coche es el mejor; **the best song of the album** la mejor canción del álbum; **she's my best friend** es mi mejor amiga; **2 she's the best at tennis** es la mejor jugando al tenis; **he's the best at English** es el mejor en inglés; **the best thing to do is to phone them** lo mejor es llamarlos por teléfono; **its the best I can do** es lo más que puedo hacer; **I did my best to help her** hice todo lo posible para ayudarla.

best *adverb* **1 mejor; he plays best** es el que mejor juega; **best of all** lo mejor de todo; **I like Barcelona best** Barcelona es la ciudad que más me gusta.

best man *noun* padrino *Masc.* de boda.

bet *noun* apuesta *Fem.*

bet *verb* apostar [24]; **to bet on a horse** apostar por un caballo; **I bet you'll forget!** ¡te apuesto algo a que se le olvida!

better *adjective* **1 mejor; she's found a better flat** ha encontrado un piso mejor; **this road's better than the other one** esta calle es mejor que la otra; **this pen writes better** esta pluma escribe mejor; **2 even better** todavía mejor; **it's even better than before** es todavía mejor que antes; **3** (*less ill*) **to be better** estar [2] mejor; **to feel better** sentirse [14] mejor; **I feel better** hoy me siento mejor; **4 to get better** mejorar [17]; **my Spanish is getting better** mi español está mejorando; **I hope you get better soon** espero que te mejores pronto; **5 so much the**

better mucho mejor; **the sooner the better** cuanto antes mejor.

better *adverb* **you/she/etc. had better** más vale que (*followed by the subjunctive*); **you'd better phone at once** más vale que llames ahora mismo; **he'd better not go** más vale que no vaya; **I'd better go now** más vale que me vaya ahora.

better off *adjective* **1** (*richer*) **they're better off than us** tienen más dinero que nosotros; **2** (*more comfortable*) **mejor; you'd be better off in bed** estarás mejor en la cama.

between *preposition* **1 entre; between London and Dover** entre Londres y Dover; **I'll go sometime between Monday and Friday** iré entre el lunes y el viernes; **between you and me** entre tú y yo; **2 it's closed between 2 and 5** está cerrado de dos a cinco.

beware *verb* **beware of the dog!** ¡cuidado con el perro!

beyond *preposition* **1** (*in space and time*) **beyond the border** más allá de la frontera; **2 it's beyond me!** ¡no lo entiendo!

Bible *noun* **the Bible** la Biblia.

bicycle *noun* bicicleta *Fem.*; **by bicycle** en bicicleta.

bicycle lane *noun* carril *Masc.* de bicicletas.

big *adjective* **1 grande; a big house** una casa grande; **big cities** ciudades grandes; **it's too big for me** es demasiado grande para mí; (*'grande' becomes 'gran' when it*

a
b
c
d
e
f
g
h
i
j
k
l
m
n
o
p
q
r
s
t
u
v
w
x
y
z

comes before a singular noun **a big disappointment** una gran desilusión; **2** (*older*) mayor; **my big sister** mi hermana mayor.

bigheaded *adjective* creído/creída; **to be bigheaded** ser un creído/una creída.

big screen *noun* pantalla *Fem.* grande.

big toe *noun* dedo *Masc.* gordo del pie.

bike 1 (*with pedals*) bici *Fem.*; **by bike** en bici; **2** (*with motor*) moto *Fem.*; **by bike** en moto.

bikini *noun* bikini *Masc.*

bilingual *adjective* bilingüe.

bill *noun* **1** (*in a restaurant*) cuenta *Fem.*; **can I have the bill, please?** ¿me trae la cuenta por favor?; **2** (*for gas, electricity, or in a hotel*) factura *Fem.*

billiards *noun* billar *Masc.*; **to play billiards** jugar al billar.

billion *noun* mil millones *Masc. plural.*

bin *noun* **1** (*dustbin*) cubo *Masc.* de la basura; **2** (*wastepaper bin*) papelera *Fem.*

binoculars *plural noun* prismáticos *Masc. plural.*

biochemistry *noun* bioquímica *Fem.*

biography *noun* biografía *Fem.*

biologist *noun* biólogo *Masc.*, bióloga *Fem.*

biology *noun* biología *Fem.*

bird *noun* **1** (*small*) pájaro *Masc.*; **2** (*large*) ave *Fem.* (even though

'ave' is feminine, it takes 'el' and 'un' in the singular).

birdwatching *noun* **to go birdwatching** ir [8] a observar pájaros.

Biro™ *noun* boli *Masc.* (*informal*).

birth *noun* nacimiento *Masc.*

birth certificate *noun* certificado *Masc.* de nacimiento.

birth control *noun* control *Fem.* de la natalidad.

birthday *noun* cumpleaños *Masc.* (*does not change in the plural*); **a birthday present** un regalo de cumpleaños; **happy birthday!** ¡feliz cumpleaños!

birthday party *noun* fiesta *Fem.* de cumpleaños.

biscuit *noun* galleta *Fem.*

bishop *noun* obispo *Masc.*

bit *noun* **1** (*small piece*) trozo *Masc.*; **a bit of string** un trozo de cordón; **a bit of chocolate** un trozo de chocolate; **2** (*small quantity*) **a bit** of un poco de; **a bit of sugar** un poco de azúcar; **with a bit of luck** con un poco de suerte; **to have a bit of trouble with something** tener un pequeño problema con algo; **3** (*in a book or film, for example*) trozo *Masc.*; **this bit's brilliant!** ¡este trozo es genial!; **4 to fall to bits** hacerse pedazos; **5 a bit of news** una noticia; **a bit of advice** un consejo; **6 a bit** un poco; **wait a bit!** ¡espera un poco!; **a bit hot** un poco caliente; **a bit early** un poco pronto; **7** (*for a horse*) bocado *Masc.*; ★ **bit by bit** poco a poco.

bite noun 1 (snack) bocado Masc.; I'll just have a bite before I go voy a tomar un bocado antes de irme; 2 (from an insect) picadura Fem.; a mosquito bite una picadura de mosquito; 3 (from a dog) mordisco Masc.; it gave me a bite me dio un mordisco.

bite verb 1 (a person or a dog) morder [38]; to bite your nails morderse las uñas; 2 (an insect) picar [31].

bitter adjective (taste) amargo/amarga.

black adjective 1 negro/negra; my black jacket mi chaqueta negra; to turn black volverse negro/negra; 2 a Black man un negro; a Black woman una negra; 3 a black coffee un café solo.

blackberry noun mora Fem.

blackbird noun mirlo Masc.

blackboard noun pizarra Fem.

blackcurrant noun grosella Fem. negra.

black eye noun ojo Masc. morado.

black pudding noun morcilla Fem.

blade noun hoja Fem.

blame noun 1 culpa Fem.; to put the blame on somebody echarle la culpa a alguien; 2 to take the blame for something asumir la responsabilidad de algo.

blame verb culpar [17]; to blame somebody for something culpar a alguien de algo; they blamed him for the accident lo culparon por el accidente; she is to blame for it ella tiene la culpa; I blame the parents! ¡yo culpo a los padres!; I don't blame you! ¡no me extraña!

blank noun (empty space) espacio Masc. en blanco (on a form, for instance).

blank adjective 1 (a page or piece of paper, or a cheque, or a screen) en blanco (a tape or disk) virgen; 2 my mind went blank me quedé en blanco.

blanket noun manta Fem.

blast noun 1 (an explosion) explosión Fem.; 2 (of air) ráfaga Fem.; 3 to play music at full blast poner la música a todo volumen.

blaze noun incendio Masc.

blaze verb arder [18].

blazer noun blázer Masc.

bleach noun lejía Fem.

bleed verb sangrar [17]; my nose is bleeding me está sangrando la nariz.

blend noun mezcla Fem.

blend verb mezclar [17].

blender noun batidora Fem.

bless verb bendecir [5]; bless you! (after a sneeze) ¡Jesús!

blind noun (in a window) persiana Fem.

blind adjective ciego/ciega; to go blind quedarse ciego/ciega.

blindness noun ceguera Fem.

blink verb (a person) pestañear [17].

blister noun ampolla Fem.

blizzard noun tormenta Fem. de nieve.

block noun 1 bloque Masc.; a block of flats un bloque de pisos; an office block un bloque de oficinas; 2 (a group of buildings)

a b c d e f g h i j k l m n o p q r s t u v w x y z

manzana *Fem.*; **to run** (*or* **drive**) **round the block** dar la vuelta a la manzana.

block *verb* **1** bloquear [17] (*an exit or a road*); **2** atascar [31] (*a drain or a hole*); **the sink's blocked** el fregadero está atascado.

blond *adjective* rubio/rubia.

blood *noun* sangre *Fem.*

blood test *noun* análisis *Masc.* de sangre.

blossom *noun* flor *Fem.*; **to be in blossom** estar [2] en flor.

blot *noun* borrón *Masc.*

blouse *noun* blusa *Fem.*

blow *noun* golpe *Masc.*

blow *verb* **1** (*the wind or a person*) soplar [17]; **2 to blow off/away** salir [63] volando; **my hat blew off** mi sombrero salió volando; **3** (*in an explosion*) **the bomb blew a hole in the wall** la bomba hizo un agujero en la pared; **4 to blow your nose** sonarse [24] la nariz.

● **to blow something out** (*a candle or flames*) apagar [28] algo.

● **to blow up** (*explode*) explotar [17].

● **to blow something up** inflar [17] algo (*a balloon or tyre*), hacer [7] volar algo (*a building or car*); **they blew up the president's residence** hicieron volar la residencia del presidente.

blow-dry *noun* brushing *Masc.*; **to have a blow-dry** hacerse [7] el brushing.

blue *adjective* azul; **blue eyes** ojos azules.

bluebell *noun* jacinto *Masc.* silvestre.

blues *plural noun* (*jazz*) blues *Masc.* (*singular*).

blunder *noun* metedura *Fem.* de pata.

blunt *adjective* **1** (*a knife or scissors*) desafilado/desafilada; **2** (*a pencil*) sin punta; **3** (*a person*) directo/directa.

blurred *adjective* **1** (*vision or image*) borroso/borrosa; **2** (*photo*) movido/movida.

blush *verb* ponerse [11] colorado.

board *noun* **1** (*plank*) tabla *Fem.*; **2** (*blackboard*) pizarra *Fem.*; **3** (*notice board*) tablón *Masc.* de anuncios; **4** (*for a board game*) tablero *Masc.*; **a chess board** un tablero de ajedrez; **5** (*accommodation*) **full board** pensión completa; **half board** media pensión; **board and lodging** comida y alojamiento; **6 on board** a bordo; **on board the ferry** a bordo del ferry.

board *verb* embarcarse [31].

boarder *noun* (*in a school*) interno *Masc.*, interna *Fem.*

board game *noun* juego *Masc.* de mesa.

boarding *noun* embarque *Masc.*

boarding card *noun* tarjeta *Fem.* de embarque.

boarding school *noun* internado *Masc.*

boast *verb* presumir [19]; **he was boasting about his new bike** estaba presumiendo de su nueva bici.

boat noun **1** (in general) barco Masc.; **2** (rowing boat) barca Fem.

body noun **1** cuerpo Masc.; **2** (corpse) cadáver Masc.

bodybuilding noun culturismo Masc.

bodyguard noun guardaespaldas Masc./Fem.

boil noun (swelling) furúnculo Masc.

boil verb **1** hervir [14]; **the water's boiling** el agua está hirviendo; **I'm going to boil some water** voy a hervir un poco de agua; **2** to boil vegetables cocer [41] verduras; to boil an egg cocer un huevo.

● **to boil over** salirse [63].

boiled egg noun huevo Masc. pasado por agua.

boiler noun **1** (for central heating) caldera Fem.; **2** (for central heating) calentador Masc.

boiling adjective **1** (water) hirviendo; **2** it's boiling hot today! ¡hoy hace un calor espantoso!

Bolivia noun Bolivia Fem.

Bolivian noun boliviano Masc., boliviana Fem.

Bolivian adjective boliviano/ boliviana.

bolt noun **1** (large) cerrojo Masc.; **2** (small) pestillo Masc.

bolt verb (a door) cerrar [29] con cerrojo.

bombing noun **1** (in a war) bombardeo Masc.; **2** (a terrorist attack) atentado Masc. terrorista.

bomb noun bomba Fem.

bomb verb bombardear [17].

bone noun **1** hueso Masc.; **2** (of a fish) espina Fem.

bonfire noun hoguera Fem.

bonnet noun (of a car) capó Masc.

bony adjective **1** (fish) lleno/llena de espinas; **2** (body) huesudo/ huesuda.

boo verb abuchear [17]; **the crowd booed the referee** el público abucheó al árbitro.

book noun **1** (that you read) libro Masc.; **a book about dinosaurs** un libro sobre los dinosaurios; **a biology book** un libro de biología; **2 an exercise book** un cuaderno; **3 a book of tickets** un taco de billetes; **a book of stamps** un librito de sellos.

book verb reservar [17]; **I booked a table for 8 o'clock** reservé una mesa para las ocho.

bookcase noun estantería Fem.

booking noun reserva Fem.

booking office noun taquilla Fem.

booklet noun folleto Masc.

bookshelf noun estante Masc.

bookshop noun librería Fem.

boot noun **1** (item of clothing) bota Fem.; **walking boots** botas de montaña; **wellington boots** botas de agua; **2** (short fashion boot) botín Masc.; **3** (of a car) maletero Masc.

border noun (between countries) frontera Fem.; **we crossed the border at Irún** cruzamos la frontera en Irún.

bore noun 1 (a boring person) pesado Masc., pesada Fem. (informal); 2 (a nuisance) what a bore! ¡qué rollo! (informal).

bored adjective aburrido/ aburrida; to be bored estar aburrido; I'm bored estoy aburrido; to get bored aburrirse [19].

boring adjective aburrido/ aburrida.

born verb to be born nacer [35]; she was born in June nació en junio.

borrow verb can I borrow your bike? ¿me prestas tu bici?; to borrow something from someone pedirle algo prestado a alguien (literally, to ask somebody for something on loan); I'll borrow some money from Dad le pediré dinero prestado a papá.

boss noun jefe Masc., jefa Fem.

bossy adjective mandón/mandona (informal).

both pronoun, adjective los/las dos; they both came vinieron los dos; they're both sold los dos están vendidos; both sisters were there las dos hermanas estaban allí; both my feet mis dos pies.

both conjunction both ... and tanto ... como; both at home and at school tanto en casa como en colegio; both in summer and in winter tanto en verano como en el invierno.

bother noun problemas Fem. plural; I've had a lot of bother with the car he tenido muchos problemas con el coche; it's no bother no es ningún problema; without any bother sin ningún problema; it's too much bother no merece la pena molestarse.

bother verb 1 (disturb) molestar [17]; I'm sorry to bother you siento molestarte; 2 (worry) preocuparse [17]; that doesn't bother me at all no me preocupa en absoluto; don't bother about dinner no te preocupes de la cena; 3 (take the trouble) molestarse [17]; she didn't even bother to come ni siquiera se molestó en venir; don't bother! ¡no te molestes!

bottle noun botella Fem.

bottle bank noun contenedor Masc. de botellas.

bottle opener noun abrebotellas Masc. (does not change in the plural).

bottom noun 1 (of a page, a hill, a wall, or steps) pie Masc.; at the bottom of the ladder al pie de la escalera; at the bottom of the page al pie de la página; 2 (of a bag, a hole, a stretch of water, a street, or a garden) fondo Masc.; at the bottom of the lake en el fondo del lago; 3 (of a list) final Masc.; 4 (of a bottle) culo Masc.; 5 (buttocks) trasero Masc.

bottom adjective 1 (lowest) de abajo; the bottom shelf el estante de abajo; 2 (a team, or place) último/última; 3 the bottom sheet la sábana bajera; the bottom flat el piso bajo.

bounce verb rebotar [17].

bouncer noun gorila Masc. (informal).

bound adjective **he's bound to be late** seguro que llega tarde; **that was bound to happen** eso tenía que pasar.

boundary noun línea Fem. divisoria.

bow noun 1 (in a shoelace or ribbon) lazo Masc.; 2 (for playing the violin or shooting arrows) arco Masc.

bowl noun 1 (for cereal) bol Masc.; 2 (larger, for mixing) cuenco Masc.; 3 (for washing up) barreño Masc.; 4 **a salad bowl** una ensaladera; **a fruit bowl** un frutero.

bowl verb lanzar [22] (a ball).

bowling noun (tenpin) bolos Masc. plural; **to go bowling** ir a jugar a los bolos.

bow tie noun pajarita Fem.

box noun 1 caja Fem.; **a box of chocolates** una caja de bombones; **a cardboard box** una caja de cartón; 2 (of matches) cajetilla Fem.; 3 (on a form) recuadro Masc.

boxer noun 1 (fighter) boxeador Masc.; 2 (dog) bóxer Masc.

boxer shorts plural noun calzoncillos Masc. plural.

boxing noun 1 boxeo Masc.; 2 **a boxing match** un combate de boxeo.

Boxing Day noun fiesta del 26 de diciembre.

box office noun taquilla Fem.

boy noun niño Masc.; **a little boy** un niño pequeño.

boyfriend noun novio Masc.

bra noun sujetador Masc.

brace noun (for teeth) aparato Masc. de los dientes.

braces plural noun (for trousers) tirantes Masc. plural.

bracelet noun pulsera Fem.

bracket noun **in brackets** entre paréntesis.

brain noun cerebro Masc.

brainwave noun idea Fem. genial.

brake noun freno Masc.

brake verb frenar [17].

bramble noun zarzamora Fem.

branch noun 1 (of a tree) rama Fem.; 2 (of a shop, company or bank) sucursal Fem.; **our Oxford branch** nuestra sucursal de Oxford.

brand noun marca Fem.

brand new adjective nuevo/ nueva.

brandy noun coñac Masc.

brass noun 1 (the metal) latón Masc.; **a brass candlestick** un candelabro dorado; 2 (in an orchestra) **the brass** los metales.

brass adjective de latón.

brass band noun banda Fem. de música.

Brazil noun Brasil Masc.

Brazilian noun brasileño Masc., brasileña Fem.

Brazilian adjective brasileño/ brasileña.

brave adjective valiente.

bread noun pan Masc.; **a slice of bread** una rebanada de pan.

break noun 1 (a short rest) descanso Masc.; **a fifteen-minute break** un descanso de quince minutos; **to take a break** descansar un rato; **2** (*in school*) recreo *Masc.*; **3 the Christmas break** las vacaciones de Navidad.

break *verb* **1** (*a fire*) romper [40]; **he broke a glass** rompió un vaso; **2 to break your leg** romperse una pierna; **I broke my arm** me rompí un brazo; **3 to break your promise** romper una promesa; **to break the rules** infringir [49] las reglas; **you mustn't break the rules** no debes infringir las reglas; **4 to break a record** batir [19] un récord; **5 to break the news** dar [4] la noticia.

● **to break down** estropearse [17]; **the car broke down** el coche se estropeó.

● **to break in: the thief broke in through the window** el ladrón se metió en la casa por la ventana; **the house was broken into** entraron ladrones en la casa.

● **to break out 1** (*a fire*) declararse [17]; **2** (*a war or a storm*) estallar [17]; **3** (*a prisoner*) escaparse [17].

● **to break up 1** (*a family*) separarse [17]; **2** (*a couple*) romper [40]; **3** (*a crowd or clouds*) dispersarse [17]; **4** (*for the holidays*) **we break up on Thursday** empezamos las vacaciones el jueves.

breakdown *noun* **1** (*of a vehicle*) avería *Fem.*; **we had a breakdown on the motorway** tuvimos una avería en la autopista; **2** (*in talks or negotiations*) ruptura *Fem.*; **3** (*a nervous collapse*) crisis *Fem.* nerviosa; **to have a (nervous)** breakdown sufrir una crisis nerviosa.

breakdown truck *noun* grúa *Fem.* de recogida en carretera.

breakfast *noun* desayuno *Masc.*; **to have breakfast** desayunar [17]; **we have breakfast at eight** desayunamos a las ocho.

break-in *noun* robo *Masc.*

breast *noun* **1** (*a woman's*) pecho *Masc.*; **2** (*of a chicken or other fowl*) pechuga *Fem.*

breaststroke *noun* braza *Fem.*

breath *noun* aliento *Masc.*; **out of breath** sin aliento; **to get one's breath** recobrar el aliento; **to take a deep breath** respirar hondo.

breathe *verb* respirar [17].

breathing *noun* respiración *Fem.*

breed *noun* (*of animal*) raza *Fem.*

breed *verb* **1** criar [32] (*animals*); **2** (*to have babies*) reproducirse [60]; **rabbits breed fast** los conejos se reproducen mucho.

breeze *noun* brisa *Fem.*

brewery *noun* cervecería *Fem.*

bribe *noun* soborno *Masc.*

bribe *verb* sobornar [17].

brick *noun* ladrillo *Masc.*; **a brick wall** una pared de ladrillo.

bride *noun* novia *Fem.*; **the bride and groom** los novios, el novio y la novia.

bridegroom *noun* novio *Masc.*

bridesmaid *noun* dama *Fem.* de honor.

bridge *noun* **1** (*over a river*) puente *Masc.*; **a bridge over the Thames** un puente sobre el Támesis;

2 (*card game*) bridge Masc.; **to play bridge** jugar al bridge.

bridle noun brida Fem.

brief adjective breve.

briefcase noun maletín Masc.

briefly adjective brevemente.

briefs plural noun calzoncillos Masc. plural.

bright adjective **1** (*star, light*) brillante; **2** (*colour*) vivo/viva; **bright green socks** calcetines de un verde vivo; **3 bright sunshine** un sol radiante; **4** (*clever*) inteligente; **she's not very bright** no es muy inteligente; ★ **to look on the bright side** ver el lado bueno de las cosas.

brighten up verb **the weather's brightening up** el tiempo está aclarando.

brilliant adjective **1** (*very clever*) brillante; **a brilliant surgeon** un brillante cirujano; **he's brilliant at maths** es genial para las matemáticas; **2** (*wonderful*) fenomenal (*informal*); **the party was brilliant!** ¡la fiesta estuvo fenomenal!

bring verb **1** traer [42]; **they brought a present** trajeron un regalo; **bring your camera** trae tu cámara; **it brings good luck** trae buena suerte; **she's bringing all the children** trae a todos los niños; **2 to bring something back** devolver [45] algo; **3 to bring up** criar [32] (*children*); **he was brought up by his aunt** lo crió su tía.

bristle noun cerda Fem.

Britain noun Gran Bretaña Fem.

British plural noun **the British** los británicos.

British adjective británico/británica; **the British Isles** las islas británicas.

broad adjective (*wide*) ancho/ancha.

broad bean noun haba Fem.

broadcast noun emisión Fem.

broadcast verb emitir [19] (*a programme*).

broccoli noun brécol Masc.

brochure noun folleto Masc.

broke adjective **to be broke** (*no money*) no tener un duro (*informal*).

broken adjective roto/rota; **the window's broken** la ventana está rota; **to have a broken leg** tener una pierna rota.

bronchitis noun bronquitis Fem.

bronze noun bronce Masc.

bronze adjective de bronce.

brooch noun broche Masc.

broom noun **1** (*for sweeping*) escoba Fem.; **2** (*bush*) retama Fem.

brother noun hermano Masc.; **my little brother** mi hermano pequeño; **my mother's brother** el hermano de mi madre.

brother-in-law noun cuñado Masc.

brown adjective **1** marrón (*never changes*); **brown shoes** zapatos marrón; **2** castaño/castaña (*hair or eyes*); **3** (*tanned in the sun*) moreno/morena; **to go brown** ponerse moreno/morena.

a b c d e f g h i j k l m n o p q r s t u v w x y z

a

b

c

brown bread noun pan Masc. integral.

brown sugar noun azúcar Masc./ Fem. moreno/morena.

d

bruise noun 1 (on a person) moratón Masc.; 2 (on fruit) magulladura Fem.

e

f

g

h

brush noun 1 (for your hair, clothes, nails, or shoes) cepillo Masc.; **my hair brush** mi cepillo del pelo; 2 (for sweeping) escoba Fem.; 3 (paintbrush) brocha Fem.

i

j

k

l

brush verb 1 cepillar [17] (your hair or shoes); **to brush your hair** cepillarse el pelo; **she brushed her hair** se cepilló el pelo; 2 **to brush your teeth** limpiarse [17] los dientes; **I'm going to brush my teeth** voy a limpiarme los dientes.

m

Brussels noun Bruselas Fem.

n

Brussels sprouts noun coles Fem. plural de Bruselas.

o

bubble noun burbuja Fem.

p

bubble bath noun gel Masc. de baño.

q

bucket noun cubo Masc.

r

buckle noun hebilla Fem.

s

bud noun brote Masc.

Buddhism noun budismo Masc.

t

Buddhist noun budista Masc./Fem.

u

budget noun presupuesto Masc.

v

budgie noun periquito Masc.

w

buffet noun 1 (on train) bar Masc.; 2 (meal) buffet Masc.

x

buffet car noun coche Masc. restaurante.

y

z

bug noun 1 (insect) bicho Masc. (informal); 2 (virus) virus Masc.; a

stomach bug un virus en el estómago.

build verb construir [54].

builder noun albañil Masc./Fem.

building noun edificio Masc.

building site noun solar Masc.

building society noun sociedad Fem. de crédito hipotecario.

built-in adjective empotrado/ empotrada.

built-up adjective urbanizado/ urbanizada; **a built-up area** una zona urbanizada.

bulb noun 1 (for a light) bombilla Fem.; 2 (that you plant) bulbo Masc.

bulky adjective voluminoso/ voluminosa.

bull noun toro Masc.

bulldozer noun bulldozer Masc.

bullet noun bala Fem.

bulletin noun boletín Masc.; **a news bulletin** boletín de noticias.

bullfight noun corrida Fem. de toros.

bullfighter noun torero Masc. torera Fem.

bullfighting noun los toros; **do you like bullfighting?** ¿te gustan los toros?

bullring noun plaza Fem. de toros.

bully noun bravucón Masc., bravucona Fem.; **he's a bully** es un bravucón.

bully verb intimidar [17].

bum noun (bottom) trasero Masc. (informal).

bump noun 1 **a bump on the head** un chichón en la cabeza; 2 **a bump in the road** un bache en la carretera; **3** (*jolt*) sacudida *Fem.*; **4** (*noise*) golpe *Masc.*

bump *verb* **1** (*bang*) darse [4] un golpe; **I bumped my head** me di un golpe en la cabeza; **2 to bump into something** chocarse [31] con algo; **I bumped into the table** me choqué con la mesa; **3 to bump into somebody** (*meet by chance*) encontrarse [24] con alguien.

bumper *noun* parachoques *Masc.* (*does not change in the plural*).

bumpy *adjective* **1** lleno/llena de baches (*road*); **2** con muchas sacudidas (*plane landing*).

bun *noun* **1** (*for a burger*) panecillo *Masc.*; **2** (*sweet*) bollo *Masc.*

bunch *noun* **1** (*of flowers*) ramo *Masc.*; **2** (*of carrots, radishes or keys*) manojo *Masc.*; **3 a bunch of grapes** un racimo de uvas.

bundle *noun* **1** (*of clothes*) fardo *Masc.*; **2** (*of papers, letters*) paquete *Masc.*

bungalow *noun* casa *Fem.* de una planta.

bunk *noun* (*on a train or boat*) litera *Fem.*

bunk beds *plural noun* literas *Fem. plural.*

bureau *noun* **1** (*agency*) agencia *Fem.*; **2** (*desk*) escritorio *Masc.*

bureau de change *noun* casa *Fem.* de cambio.

burger *noun* hamburguesa *Fem.*

burglar *noun* ladrón *Masc.*, ladrona *Fem.*

burglar alarm *noun* alarma *Fem.* antirrobo.

burglary *noun* robo *Masc.*

burn *noun* quemadura *Fem.*

burn *verb* quemar [17]; **I've burned the rubbish** he quemado la basura; **she burnt herself on the grill** se quemó en la parrilla; **you'll burn your finger!** ¡te vas a quemar el dedo!; **Mum's burnt her cake** a mamá se le ha quemado el pastel; **I burn easily** (*in the sun*) me quemo fácilmente.

burnt *adjective* quemado/quemada.

burst *verb* **1** estallar [17] (*a balloon*); **2** reventar [29] (*a tyre or pipe*) **a burst tyre** una rueda con un reventón; **3 to burst out laughing** echarse [17] a reír; **to burst into tears** echarse [17] a llorar; **4 to burst into flames** empezar [25] a arder.

bury *verb* enterrar [29].

bus *noun* **1** (*for urban transport*) autobús *Masc.*, bus *Masc.*; **we'll take the bus** cogeremos el autobús; **we missed the bus** perdimos el autobús; **on the bus** en el autobús; **a bus ticket** un billete de autobús; **2** (*coach*) autocar *Masc.*; **to go to London by bus** ir [8] a Londres en autocar.

bus driver *noun* conductor *Masc.* de autobús, conductora *Fem.* de autobús.

bush *noun* arbusto *Masc.*

business *noun* **1** (*commercial dealings*) negocios *Masc. plural*; **he's in Leeds on business** está en Leeds de viaje de negocios; **a business letter** una carta de negocios; **2** (*firm or company*) negocio *Masc.*; **small businesses**

a b c d e f g h i j k l m n o p q r s t u v w x y z

las pequeñas empresas; **3 mind your own business!** ¡no te metas en lo que no te importa!; **that's my business!** ¡eso es asunto mío!.

business class noun clase Fem. preferente.

businessman noun hombre Masc. de negocios.

business trip noun viaje Masc. de negocios.

businesswoman noun mujer Fem. de negocios.

bus lane noun carril Masc. bus.

bus pass noun abono Masc. de autobús.

bus route noun línea Fem. de autobús.

bus shelter noun marquesina Fem.

bus station noun estación Fem. de autobús.

bust noun busto Masc.

bus stop noun parada Fem. del autobús.

busy adjective **1** ocupado/ocupada (a person); **don't disturb him, he's busy** no lo molestes, está ocupado; **2** ajetreado/ajetreada (a day or week); **a very busy day** un día muy ajetreado; **3** (full of cars or people) concurrido/concurrida (a road); **the shops were busy** las tiendas estaban muy concurridas; **4** (phone) **the line's busy** está comunicando.

but conjunction **1** pero; **small but strong** pequeño pero fuerte; **I'll try, but it's difficult** lo intentaré, pero es difícil; **2 not ... but ...** no ... sino

...; **not Thursday but Friday** no el jueves sino el viernes.

but preposition **1** menos; **anything but that** cualquier cosa menos eso; **everyone but Leah** todos menos Leah; **2 the last but one** el penúltimo.

butcher noun carnicero Masc., carnicera Fem.; **the butcher's** la carnicería.

butter noun mantequilla Fem.

butter verb untar [17] con mantequilla.

buttercup noun botón Masc. de oro.

butterfly noun mariposa Fem.

button noun botón Masc.; **the record button** el botón de grabar.

buttonhole noun ojal Masc.

buy noun **a good buy** una buena compra; **a bad buy** una mala compra.

buy verb comprar [17]; **I bought the cinema tickets** compré las entradas para el cine; **to buy something for somebody** comprarle algo a alguien; **Sarah bought him a sweater** Sarah le compró un jersey; **to buy something from someone** comprarle algo a alguien; **he bought his bike from Tim** le compré a Tom su bici.

buyer noun comprador Masc., compradora Fem.

buzz verb (a fly or bee) zumbar [17].

buzzer noun timbre Masc.

by preposition **1** por; **by telephone** por teléfono; **the thief came in by the window** el ladrón entró por la ventana; **eaten by a dog** comido por un perro; **it's two metres by four** mide dos metros por cuatro; **by mistake** por equivocación; **they pay by the hour** pagan por hora; **written by Lorca** escrito por Lorca; **2** (*travel*) en; **to come by bus** venir en autobús; **to leave by train** salir en tren; **by bike** en bicicleta; **3** (*near*) al lado de; **by the fire** al lado del fuego; **by the sea** al lado del mar; **close by** cerca; **4** (*before*) para; **it'll be ready by Monday** estará listo para el lunes; **Kevin was back by four** Kevin estaba de vuelta para las cuatro; **5 they should have finished by now** ya deberían haber terminado; **6 by yourself** solo/sola; **I was by myself in the house** estaba solo en la casa; **she did it by herself** lo hizo sola; **7 to take somebody by the hand** coger a alguien de la mano; **8 by the way** por cierto; **9 to go by** pasar.

bye *exclamation* adiós; **bye for now!** ¡hasta luego!

bypass *noun* carretera *Fem.* de circunvalación.

Cc

cab *noun* **1** taxi *Masc.*; **to call a cab** llamar un taxi; **2** (*on a lorry*) cabina *Fem.*

cabbage *noun* repollo *Masc.*

cabin *noun* **1** (*on lorry, plane*) cabina *Fem.*; **2** (*on ship*) camarote *Masc.*

cable *noun* cable *Masc.*

cable car *noun* funicular *Masc.*

cable television *noun* televisión *Fem.* por cable.

cactus *noun* cactus *Masc.*

café *noun* cafetería *Fem.*

cage *noun* jaula *Fem.*

cagoule *noun* canguro *Masc.*

cake *noun* pastel *Masc.*; **would you like a piece of cake?** ¿quieres un trozo de pastel?

calculate *verb* calcular [17].

calculation *noun* cálculo *Masc.*

calculator *noun* calculadora *Fem.*

calendar *noun* calendario *Masc.*

calf *noun* **1** (*animal*) ternero *Masc.*, ternera *Fem.*; **2** (*of your leg*) pantorrilla *Fem.*

call *noun* (*telephone*) llamada *Fem.*; **I had several calls this morning;** he tenido varias llamadas esta mañana; **thank you for your call** gracias por llamar; **a phone call** una llamada de teléfono; **to give somebody a call** llamar [17] a alguien.

call *verb* **1** (*telephone*) llamar [17]; **to call a taxi** llamar un taxi; **to call the doctor** llamar al médico; **call this number** llama a este número; **thank you for calling** gracias por llamar; **I'll call you back later** te llamo más tarde; **2** (*name*) **they've called the baby Julie** le han puesto Julie al bebé; **3 to be called** llamarse [17]; **she has a brother called Dan** tiene un hermano que se llama Dan; **what's he called?** ¿cómo se llama?

a
b
c
d
e
f
g
h
i
j
k
l
m
n
o
p
q
r
s
t
u
v
w
x
y
z

a
b
c
d
e
f
g
h
i
j
k
l
m
n
o
p
q
r
s
t
u
v
w
x
y
z

● **to call in** pasar [17]; **I'll call in on my way back** pasaré por tu casa cuando vuelvo.

call box noun cabina Fem. telefónica.

calm adjective calma Fem.

calm verb calmar [17].

● **to calm down** calmarse; **he's calmed down a bit** se ha calmado un poco.

● **to calm somebody down** calmar a alguien; **I tried to calm her down** intenté calmarla.

calmly adverb con calma.

calorie noun caloría Fem.

camcorder noun videocámara Fem.

camel noun camello Masc.

camera noun 1 (for photos) cámara Fem. de fotos; **2** (film or TV camera) cámara Fem.

cameraman noun cámara Masc./Fem.

camp noun campamento Masc.

camp verb acampar [17].

campaign noun campaña Fem.

camper noun campista Masc./Fem.

camper van noun caravana Fem.

camping noun camping Masc.; **to go camping** ir de camping; **we're going camping in Andalusia this summer** nos vamos de camping a Andalucía este verano.

campsite noun camping Masc.

can[1], **can** noun 1 lata Fem.; **a can of tomatoes** una lata de tomates; **2** (for petrol or oil) bidón Masc.

can[2], **can** verb 1 poder [10]; **I can't be there before ten** no puedo estar

allí antes de las diez; **you can leave your bag here** puedes dejar tu bolsa aquí; **can you open the door, please?** ¿me abres la puerta por favor?; **can I help you?** ¿qué desea?; **they couldn't come** no pudieron venir; **you could ring back tomorrow** podrías volver a llamar mañana; **you could have told me** me lo podrías haber dicho; **2** (with hear, see, remember, find, 'can' is not translated) **can you hear me?** ¿me oyes?; **I can't see her** no la veo; **I can't remember** no me acuerdo; **I can't find my keys** no encuentro mis llaves; **3** (know how to) saber [13]; **she can't drive** no sabe conducir; **can you play the piano?** ¿sabes tocar el piano?.

Canada noun Canadá Masc.

Canadian noun canadiense Masc./Fem.

Canadian adjective canadiense.

canal noun canal Masc.

canary noun canario Masc.

Canary Islands noun the Canary Islands las Islas Canarias.

cancel verb cancelar [17]; **the concert's been cancelled** han cancelado el concierto.

cancer noun cáncer Masc.; **to have lung cancer** tener cáncer de pulmón.

Cancer noun Cáncer Masc.; **I'm Cancer** soy Cáncer.

candidate noun candidato Masc., candidata Fem.

candle noun vela Fem.

candlestick noun candelabro Masc.

candyfloss noun algodón Masc. de azúcar.

canned adjective en lata; **canned tomatoes** tomates en lata.

cannon noun cañón Masc.

cannot verb SEE can².

canoe noun piragua Fem.

canoeing noun piragüismo Masc.; **to go canoeing** hacer piragüismo; **I like canoeing** me gusta hacer piragüismo.

can-opener noun abrelatas Fem. (does not change in the plural).

canteen noun cantina Fem.

canvas noun 1 (fabric) lona Fem.; 2 (painting) lienzo Masc.

cap noun 1 (hat) gorro Masc.; **a baseball cap** un gorro de béisbol; 2 (on a bottle or tube) tapón Masc.

capable adjective capaz.

capacity noun capacidad Fem.

capital noun 1 (city) capital Fem.; **Madrid is the capital of Spain** Madrid es la capital de España; 2 (letter) mayúscula Fem.; **in capitals** en mayúsculas.

capitalism noun capitalismo Masc.

Capricorn noun Capricornio Masc.; **Linda's Capricorn** Linda es Capricornio.

captain noun 1 (of a ship or a team) capitán Masc., capitana Fem.; 2 (of a plane) comandante Masc./Fem.

captivity noun cautiverio Masc.; **to keep someone in captivity** mantener [9] a alguien en cautiverio.

capture verb capturar [17].

car noun coche Masc.; **a car crash** un accidente de coche; **to park the car** aparcar el coche; **we're going by car** vamos en coche.

caramel noun caramelo Masc.

caravan noun caravana Fem.

card noun 1 (for a card game) carta Fem.; **a card game** un juego de cartas; **to have a game of cards** jugar a las cartas; 2 (greetings, phone, bank) tarjeta Fem.; **a birthday card** una tarjeta de cumpleaños.

cardboard noun cartón Masc.

cardigan noun rebeca Fem.

cardphone noun teléfono Masc. de tarjeta.

care noun 1 cuidado Masc.; **he took care opening it** tuvo cuidado al abrirlo; 2 **to take care to do** asegurarse [17] de hacer; 3 **to take care of somebody** cuidar a alguien; 4 **take care!** (be careful) ¡cuidado!, (when saying goodbye) ¡cuídate!

care verb 1 **to care about** preocuparse [17] por; **to care about pollution** preocuparse por la contaminación; 2 **she doesn't care** a ella no le importa; **I couldn't care less!** ¡no me importa en absoluto!

career noun carrera Fem.

careful adjective 1 cuidadoso/cuidadosa; **try to be more careful**

a b c d e f g h i j k l m n o p q r s t u v w x y z

a
b
c
d
e
f
g
h
i
j
k
l
m
n
o
p
q
r
s
t
u
v
w
x
y
z

procura ser más cuidadoso; **2 a careful driver** un conductor/una conductora prudente; **3 be careful!** ¡ten cuidado!

carefully adverb **1** read the instructions carefully lea las instrucciones atentamente; **listen carefully** escuchad atentamente; **2** (handle) con cuidado; **she put the vase down carefully** colocó el jarrón con cuidado; **3 drive carefully!** ¡conduce con precaución!

careless adjective **1** he's very careless no pone atención en lo que hace; **2 this is careless work** este trabajo está hecho sin cuidado; **a careless mistake** una falta de atención; **3 careless driving** conducción negligente.

caretaker noun (in block of flats) portero Masc., portera Fem.

car ferry noun ferry Masc.

cargo noun carga Fem.

car hire noun alquiler Masc. de coches.

Caribbean[1] noun **the Caribbean** el Caribe; **the Caribbean Sea** el mar Caribe.

Caribbean[2] noun caribeño Masc., caribeña Fem.

Caribbean adjective caribeño/ caribeña.

caricature noun caricatura Fem.

carnation noun clavel Masc.

carnival noun carnaval Masc.

car park noun aparcamiento Masc.

carpenter noun carpintero Masc., carpintera Fem.

carpentry noun carpintería Fem.

carpet noun **1** (fitted) moqueta Fem.; **2** (loose) alfombra Fem.

car phone noun teléfono Masc. de automóvil.

car radio noun radio Masc. de coche.

carriage noun vagón Masc.

carrier bag noun bolsa Fem.

carrot noun zanahoria Fem.

carry verb **1** llevar [17]; **she was carrying a parcel** llevaba un paquete; **2** (vehicle, plane) transportar [17]; **the coach was carrying schoolchildren** el autobús transportaba colegiales.

● **to carry on** seguir [64]; **they carried on talking** siguieron hablando.

carrycot noun cuna Fem. portátil.

carsick adjective **to be carsick** marearse [17] al viajar en coche.

cart noun carro Masc.

carton noun envase Masc.

cartoon noun **1** (a film) dibujos Masc. plural animados; **2** (a comic strip) tira Fem. cómica; **3** (an amusing drawing) chiste Masc.

cartridge noun **1** (for a pen) recambio Masc.; **2** (for a gun) cartucho Masc.

carve verb trinchar [17] (meat).

case[1] noun **1** (suitcase) maleta Fem.; **to pack a case** hacer una maleta; **2** (for wine bottles for example) caja Fem.; **3** (for spectacles or small things) estuche Masc.

case[2] noun **1** caso Masc.; **a case of flu** un caso de gripe; **in that case**

en ese caso; **that's not the case** no se trata de eso; **2 in case** en caso; **in case he's late** en caso de que llegue tarde; **check first, just in case** asegúrate, por si acaso; **3 in any case** de todas formas; **in any case, it's too late** de todas formas, es demasiado tarde.

cash noun **1** (*money in general*) dinero Masc.; **I haven't any cash on me** no llevo dinero encima; **2** (*money rather than a cheque*) dinero Masc. en efectivo; **to pay in cash** pagar en efectivo; **£50 in cash** cincuenta libras en efectivo.

cash card noun tarjeta Fem. de cajero automático.

cash desk noun caja Fem.; **pay at the cash desk** pagar en caja.

cash dispenser noun cajero Masc. automático.

cashew noun anacardo Masc.

cashier noun cajero Masc., cajera Fem.

cash point noun cajero Masc. automático.

cassette noun cinta Fem. de cassette.

cassette recorder noun cassette Masc.

cast noun los actores Masc. plural; **the cast were on stage** los actores estaban en el escenario.

castle noun **1** castillo Masc.; **2** (*in chess*) torre Fem.

casual adjective informal.

casualty noun **1** (*in an accident*) víctima Fem.; **2** (*hospital*

department) urgencias Fem. plural; **he's in casualty** está en urgencias.

cat noun gato Masc., (*female*) gata Fem.; ★ **it's raining cats and dogs** está lloviendo a cántaros (*literally: it's raining in jugfuls*).

Catalan noun **1** (*the language*) catalán Masc.; **2** (*person*) catalán Masc., catalana Fem.

Catalan adjective catalán/catalana.

Catalonia noun Cataluña Fem.

catalogue noun catálogo Masc.

catastrophe noun catástrofe Fem.

catch noun **1** (*on a door*) pestillo Masc.; **2** (*a drawback*) trampa Fem.; **what's the catch?** ¿dónde está la trampa?

catch verb **1** coger [3]; **Tom caught the ball** Tom cogió la pelota; **you can't catch me!** ¡no me coges!; **can you catch hold of the branch?** ¿puedes coger la rama?; **2 to catch somebody doing** coger [3] a alguien haciendo; **he was caught stealing money** lo cogieron robando dinero; **3** coger [3] (*a bus or plane*); **did Tim catch his bus?** ¿cogió Tim el autobús?; **4** coger [3] (*an illness*); **he's caught chickenpox** ha cogido la varicela; **I've caught a cold** he cogido un resfriado; **5** (*fishing or hunting*) **to catch a fish** pescar [31] un pez; **to catch a mouse** cazar [22] un ratón; **6** oír [56] (*what somebody says*); **I didn't catch your name** no he oído tu nombre.

a b c d e f g h i j k l m n o p q r s t u v w x y z

a b c d e f g h i j k l m n o p q r s t u v w x y z

● **to catch up with somebody** alcanzar [22] a alguien.

category noun categoría Fem.

catering noun catering Masc.

caterpillar noun oruga Fem.

cathedral noun catedral Fem.; **Seville cathedral** la catedral de Sevilla.

Catholic noun católico Masc., católica Fem.

Catholic adjective católico/ católica.

cattle plural noun ganado Masc. (singular).

cauliflower noun coliflor Fem.; **cauliflower cheese** coliflor con besamel.

cause noun causa Fem.; **the cause of the accident** la causa del accidente; **for a good cause** por una buena causa.

cause verb causar [17]; **to cause problems** causar problemas.

caution noun cautela Fem.

cautious adjective cauteloso/ cautelosa.

cave noun cueva Fem.

caving noun espeleología Fem.; **to go caving** hacer espeleología.

CD noun disco Masc. compacto, CD Masc.

CD player noun compacto Masc.

CD-ROM noun CD-ROM Masc.

ceiling noun techo Masc.; **on the ceiling** en el techo.

celebrate verb celebrar [17]; **I'm celebrating my birthday** estoy celebrando mi cumpleaños.

celebrity noun famoso Masc., famosa Fem.

celery noun apio Masc.

cell noun célula Fem.

cellar noun sótano Masc.

cello noun violonchelo Masc.; **to play the cello** tocar [31] el violonchelo.

cement noun cemento Masc.

cemetery noun cementerio Masc.

cent noun 1 (in the euro system) céntimo Masc.; 2 (in the dollar system) centavo Masc.

centenary noun centenario Masc.

centigrade adjective centígrado Masc.; **ten degrees centigrade** diez grados centígrados.

centimetre noun centímetro Masc.

central adjective central; **central London** el centro de Londres; **the office is very central** la oficina está en pleno centro.

Central America noun América Fem. Central.

central heating noun calefacción Fem. central.

centre noun centro Masc.; **in the centre of** en el centro de; **in the town centre** en el centro de la ciudad; **a shopping centre** un centro comercial.

century noun siglo Masc.; **in the twentieth century** en el siglo veinte; **the sixth century** el siglo seis; **the twenty-first century** el siglo veintiuno.

cereal noun **breakfast cereal** cereales Masc. plural para el desayuno; **to have cereal for breakfast** desayunar cereales.

ceremony *noun* ceremonia *Fem.*

certain *adjective* **1** (*sure*) seguro/segura; **are you certain of the address?** ¿estás seguro de las señas?; **I'm certain of it** estoy seguro; **to be certain that ...** estar seguro de que ...; **Nicky's certain (that) you're wrong** Nicky está segura de que estás equivocado; **nobody knows for certain** nadie lo sabe con seguridad; **2** (*particular*) cierto/cierta; **a certain number of** un cierto número de.

certainly *adverb* **certainly** ¡por supuesto!; **certainly not** desde luego que no.

certificate *noun* certificado *Masc.*; **a birth certificate** un certificado de nacimiento.

chain *noun* cadena *Fem.*

chair *noun* **1** (*upright*) silla *Fem.*; **a kitchen chair** una silla de cocina; **2** (*with arms*) butaca *Fem.*

chair lift *noun* telesilla *Fem.*

chalet *noun* **1** (*in the mountains*) chalet *Masc.*; **2** (*in a holiday camp*) bungalow *Masc.*

chalk *noun* tiza *Fem.*

challenge *noun* reto *Masc.*; **the exam was a real challenge** el examen fue un verdadero reto.

champion *noun* campeón/campeona *Masc./Fem.*; **world champion** campeón del mundo.

chance *noun* **1** (*an opportunity*) ocasión *Fem.*; **to have the chance to do** tener [9] ocasión de hacer; **if**

you have the chance to go to New York si tienes ocasión de ir a Nueva York; **I haven't had the chance to write to him** no he tenido ocasión de escribirle; **2** (*likelihood*) posibilidad *Fem.*; **there's a chance that she'll pass** existe la posibilidad de que apruebe (*'de que' is followed by the subjunctive*); **there's little chance of winning** hay pocas posibilidades de ganar; **3** (*luck*) **by chance** por casualidad; **do you have her address, by any chance?** ¿tienes sus señas por casualidad?

change *noun* **1** cambio *Masc.*; **a change of plan** un cambio de planes; **they've made some changes to the house** han hecho algunos cambios en la casa; **it makes a change from hamburgers** por lo menos, es algo distinto a las hamburguesas; **2** (*a change of clothes*) una muda de ropa; **3** (*cash*) cambio *Masc.*; **I haven't any change** no tengo cambio; **keep the change** quédese con el cambio; **4 for a change** para variar; **for a change, let's eat out** vamos a comer fuera, para variar.

change *verb* **1** (*transform completely*) cambiar [17]; **it changed my life** cambió mi vida; **Liz never changes** Liz no cambia; **2** (*to switch from one thing to another*) cambiar [17] de; **we changed trains at Crewe** cambiamos de tren a Crewe; **she's changed her address** ha cambiado de dirección; **to change**

a
b
c
d
e
f
g
h
i
j
k
l
m
n
o
p
q
r
s
t
u
v
w
x
y
z

your mind cambiar de opinión; **to change the subject** cambiar de tema; **they changed places** se cambiaron de sitio; **to change colour** cambiar de color; **3** (*to swap one for another*) cambiar [17]; **have you changed the towels?** ¿has cambiado las toallas?; **4** (*to exchange in a shop*) cambiar [17]; **can I change it for the larger size?** ¿puedo cambiarlo por una talla más grande?; **5** (*to change your clothes*) cambiarse [17]; **Mike's gone up to change** Mike ha ido a cambiarse; **I must change my shirt** tengo que cambiarme de camisa.

changing room noun **1** (*for sport or swimming*) vestuario Masc.; **2** (*in a shop*) probador Masc.

channel noun **1** (*on TV*) canal Masc.; **to change channels** cambiar [17] de canal; **2 the Channel** el Canal de la Mancha.

Channel Tunnel noun Eurotúnel Masc.

chaos noun caos Masc.; **it was chaos!** ¡fue un caos!

chapel noun capilla Fem.

chapter noun capítulo Masc.; **in chapter two** en el capítulo número dos.

character noun **1** (*personality*) carácter Masc.; **a house with a lot of character** una casa con mucho carácter; **2** (*in a book, play, or film*) personaje Masc.; **the main character** el personaje principal.

characteristic noun característica Fem.

charcoal noun **1** (*for burning*) carbón Masc. vegetal; **2** (*for drawing*) carboncillo Masc.

charge noun **1** (*what you pay*) precio Masc.; **admission charge** precio de admisión; **there's no charge** es gratis; **an extra charge** un suplemento; **2 to be in charge** ser responsable; **who's in charge?** ¿quién es el responsable?; **to be in charge of something/somebody** estar a cargo de algo/alguien; **who's in charge of these children?** ¿quién está a cargo de estos niños?; **3 to be accused of theft** estar acusado de robo.

charge verb **1** (*ask payment*) cobrar [17]; **they charge ten pounds an hour** cobran diez libras la hora; **how much do you charge for one day?** ¿cuánto cobráis por un día?; **we don't charge, it's free** no cobramos, es gratis; **they didn't charge me for the drinks** no me cobraron las bebidas; **2 to charge somebody with** acusar [17] a alguien de (*a crime*).

charity noun organización Fem. benéfica.

charm noun encanto Masc.

charming adjective encantador/encantadora.

chart noun **1** (*table*) tabla Fem.; **2 the weather chart** el mapa del tiempo; **3 the charts** las listas de éxitos; **number one in the charts** número uno en las listas de éxitos.

charter flight noun vuelo Masc. chárter.

chase *noun* persecución *Fem.*; a **car chase** una persecución en coche.

chase *verb* perseguir [64] (a person or animal).

chat *noun* charla *Fem.*; **to have a chat with somebody** charlar con alguien.

chatroom *noun* chat *Masc.*

chat show *noun* programa *Masc.* de entrevistas.

chatter *verb* **1** (talk) cotorrear [17] (informal); **2** my teeth are chattering me castañetean los dientes.

cheap *adjective* barato/barata; **cheap shoes** zapatos baratos; **that's very cheap!** ¡eso es muy barato!

cheaply *adverb* **to buy/sell cheaply** comprar/vender barato; **to eat/dress cheaply** comer/vestir con poco dinero.

cheap-rate *adjective* de tarifa reducida; **a cheap-rate phone call** una llamada de teléfono de tarifa reducida.

cheat *noun* tramposo *Masc.*, tramposa *Fem.*

cheat *verb* engañar [17].

check *noun* **1** (in a factory or at border controls) control *Masc.*; **2** (by a doctor) examen *Masc.* médico; **3** (in chess) **check!** ¡jaque!

check *verb* **1** (to make sure) comprobar [24]; **he checked the time** comprobó la hora; **check they're all back** comprueba que ya han llegado todos; **check with your father** pregunta a tu padre.

● **to check in 1** (for a flight) facturar [17] el equipaje; **2** (at a hotel) registrarse [17]; **she checked in at five o'clock** se registró a las cinco.

● **to check out** irse [17].

check-in *noun* facturación *Fem.* de equipajes.

checkout *noun* caja *Fem.*; **at the checkout** en caja.

checkup *noun* chequeo *Masc.*

cheek *noun* **1** (part of face) mejilla *Fem.*; **2** (nerve) **what a cheek!** ¡qué cara! (informal).

cheeky *adjective* **1** (mischievous) descarado/descarada; **2** (rude) impertinente.

cheer *noun* **1** three cheers for Tom! ¡tres hurras por Tom!; **2** (when you have a drink) **cheers!** ¡salud!

cheer *verb* (to shout hurray) vitorear [17].

● **to cheer on** animar [17].

● **to cheer somebody up** animar [17] a alguien; **cheer up!** ¡ánimo!.

cheerful *adjective* alegre.

cheese *noun* queso *Masc.*; **blue cheese** queso azul; **a cheese sandwich** un sandwich de queso.

cheesecake *noun* tarta *Fem.* de queso.

chef *noun* chef *Masc./Fem.*

chemical *noun* producto *Masc.* químico.

chemist *noun* **1** farmacéutico *Masc.*, farmacéutica *Fem.*; **2** chemist's farmacia *Fem.*; **at the chemist's** en la farmacia;

a b d e f g h i j k l m n o p q r s t u v w x y z

3 (*scientist*) químico *Masc.*, química *Fem.*

chemistry *noun* química *Fem.*

cheque *noun* cheque *Masc.*; **to pay by cheque** pagar [28] con cheque; **to write a cheque** extender [18] un cheque.

chequebook *noun* talonario *Masc.* de cheques.

cherry *noun* cereza *Fem.*

chess *noun* ajedrez *Masc.*; **to play chess** jugar [27] al ajedrez.

chessboard *noun* tablero *Masc.* de ajedrez.

chest *noun* **1** (*part of the body*) pecho *Masc.*; **2** (*box*) arcón *Masc.*

chestnut *noun* castaña *Fem.*

chestnut tree *noun* castaño *Masc.*

chest of drawers *noun* cómoda *Fem.*

chew *verb* masticar [31] (*food*).

chewing gum *noun* chicle *Masc.*

chick *noun* (*of a hen*) pollito *Masc.*

chicken *noun* pollo *Masc.*; **roast chicken** pollo asado; **chicken thighs** muslos de pollo.

chickenpox *noun* varicela *Fem.*

chicory *noun* endivia *Fem.*

chief *noun* jefe *Masc.*, jefa *Fem.*; **the chief of police** el jefe de policía.

child *noun* (*boy*) niño *Masc.*, (*girl*) niña *Fem.*; **Jenny's children** los niños de Jenny.

childish *adjective* infantil.

childminder *noun* niñero *Masc.*, niñera *Fem.*

Chile *noun* Chile *Masc.*

Chilean *noun* chileno *Masc.*, chilena *Fem.*

Chilean *adjective* chileno/chilena.

chilled *adjective* (*drink*) frío/fría.

chilli *noun* chile *Masc.*

chilly *adjective* frío/fría (*a room or the weather*); **it's chilly today** hoy hace fresco.

chimney *noun* chimenea *Masc.*

chimpanzee *noun* chimpancé *Masc.*

chin *noun* barbilla *Fem.*

china *noun* porcelana *Fem.*; **a china plate** un plato de porcelana.

China *noun* China *Fem.*

Chinese *noun* **1 the Chinese** (*people*) los chinos; **2** (*language*) chino *Masc.*

Chinese *adjective* chino/china; **a Chinese man** un chino; **a Chinese woman** una china; **a Chinese meal** una comida china.

chip *noun* **1** (*fried potato*) patata *Fem.* frita; **I'd like some chips** quiero unas patatas fritas; **2** (*microchip*) chip *Masc.*; **3** (*in glass or china*) desportilladura *Fem.*

chipped *adjective* desportillado/desportillada.

chives *noun* cebolletas *Fem.* plural.

chocolate *noun* **1** chocolate *Masc.*; **a chocolate ice-cream** un helado de chocolate; **hot chocolate** chocolate caliente; **milk chocolate** chocolate con leche; **dark chocolate** chocolate sin leche; **2 a chocolate** un bombón; **a box of chocolates** una caja de bombones.

choice noun elección Fem.; **freedom of choice** libertad de elección; **it was a good choice** fue una buena elección; **you have a choice of two flights** puede elegir entre dos vuelos; **I had no choice** no tuve más remedio.

choir noun coro Masc.

choke noun (on a car) estárter Masc.

choke verb atragantarse [17]; **she choked on a bone** se atragantó con un hueso.

choose verb elegir [48]; **you chose well** elegiste bien; **Cathy chose the red one** Cathy eligió el rojo; **it's hard to choose from all these colours** es difícil elegir entre todos estos colores.

chop noun chuleta Fem.; **a lamb chop** una chuleta de cordero.

chop verb **1** cortar [17] (wood); **2** cortar [17] en trozos pequeños (vegetables or meat); **3** picar [31] (onion).

chopstick noun palillo Masc. para comida china.

chord noun acorde Masc.

chorus noun **1** (of a song) estribillo Masc.; **2** (a group of singers) coro Masc.

Christ noun Cristo.

christening noun bautizo Masc.

Christian noun, adjective cristiano/cristiana.

Christianity noun cristianismo Masc.

Christian name noun nombre Masc. de pila.

Christmas noun Navidad Fem.; **at Christmas!** en Navidad; **Happy Christmas!** ¡Feliz Navidad!

Christmas card noun tarjeta Fem. de Navidad.

Christmas carol noun villancico Masc.

Christmas Day noun día Masc. de Navidad.

Christmas dinner noun cena Fem. de Navidad.

Christmas Eve noun Nochebuena Fem.; **on Christmas Eve** en Nochebuena.

Christmas present noun regalo Masc. de Navidad.

Christmas tree noun árbol Masc. de Navidad.

chunk noun trozo Masc.

church noun iglesia Fem.; **to go to church** ir a la iglesia.

churchyard noun cementerio Masc.

chute noun (for sliding down) tobogán Masc.

cider noun sidra Fem.

cigar noun puro Masc.

cigarette noun cigarrillo Masc.; **to light a cigarette** encender un cigarrillo.

cinema noun cine Masc.; **to go to the cinema** ir al cine.

circle noun círculo Masc.; **to sit in a circle** sentarse en círculo; **to go round in circles** dar vueltas.

circuit noun (racing track) pista Fem.

circular adjective circular.

a
b
c
d
e
f
g
h
i
j
k
l
m
n
o
p
q
r
s
t
u
v
w
x
y
z

circumference noun circunferencia Fem.

circumstances plural noun **under the circumstances** en estas circunstancias.

circus noun circo Masc.

citizen noun ciudadano Masc., ciudadana Fem.

city noun ciudad Fem.; **the city of Seville** la ciudad de Sevilla.

city centre noun centro Masc. de la ciudad; **in the city centre** en el centro de la ciudad.

civilian noun civil Masc./Fem.

civilization noun civilización Fem.

civil servant noun funcionario Masc., funcionaria Fem.; **she's a civil servant** es funcionaria.

civil service noun administración Fem. pública.

civil war noun guerra Fem. civil.

claim noun 1 (statement) afirmación Fem.; 2 (on insurance) reclamación Fem.; **to make a claim on insurance** hacer [7] una reclamación al seguro.

claim verb asegurar [17]; **he claimed to know** aseguró saberlo.

clap verb 1 aplaudir [19]; **everyone clapped** todo el mundo aplaudió; 2 **to clap your hands** dar [4] palmadas.

clapping noun aplausos Masc. plural.

clarinet noun clarinete Masc.; **to play the clarinet** tocar [31] el clarinete.

clash noun (violent incident) choque Masc.

clash verb 1 (rival groups) chocar [31]; 2 (colours) desentonar [17]; **the curtains clash with the wallpaper** las cortinas desentonan con el papel pintado.

clasp noun (of a necklace) broche Masc.

class noun clase Fem.; **she's in the same class as me** está en la misma clase que yo; **an art class** una clase de arte; **in class** en clase; **a social class** una clase social.

classic adjective clásico/clásica.

classical adjective clásico/clásica; **classical music** música clásica.

classmate noun compañero Masc. de clase, compañera Fem. de clase.

classroom noun clase Fem.

claw noun 1 (of a cat or dog) zarpa Fem.; 2 (of a crab) pinza Fem.

clay noun 1 (for modelling) arcilla Fem.; 2 **a clay court** (in tennis) una pista de tierra batida.

clean adjective 1 limpio/limpia; **a clean shirt** una camisa limpia; **my hands are clean** tengo las manos limpias; 2 (germ-free) puro/pura (air or water).

clean verb 1 limpiar [17]; **I cleaned the whole house** limpié toda la casa; 2 **to clean your teeth** lavarse [17] los dientes; **I'm going to clean my teeth** voy a lavarme los dientes.

cleaner noun 1 (in a public place) limpiador Masc., limpiadora Fem.; 2 (a cleaning lady) señora Fem. de la limpieza; 3 **a dry cleaner's** una tintorería.

cleaning noun to do the cleaning hacer [7] la limpieza.

cleanser noun 1 (for the house) producto Masc. de limpieza; 2 (for your face) crema Fem. limpiadora.

clear adjective 1 (that you can see through) transparente; **clear glass** cristal transparente; 2 (cloudless) despejado/despejada; 3 (easy to understand) claro/clara; **clear instructions** instrucciones claras; **is that clear?** ¿está claro?; **it's clear that ...** está claro que ....

clear verb 1 sacar [31] (papers, rubbish, or clothes); **have you cleared your stuff out of your room?** ¿has sacado todas tus cosas de tu habitación?; 2 recoger [3] (a table); **can I clear the table?** ¿puedo recoger la mesa?; 3 despejar [17] (a road or path); 4 (fog or smoke) disiparse [17]; **and then the fog cleared** y entonces la niebla se disipó; 5 to clear your throat aclararse [17] la voz.

● to clear something up recoger [3]; **I'll just clear up my books** voy a recoger mis libros.

clearly adverb 1 (to think, speak, or hear) con claridad; 2 (obviously) claramente; **she was clearly worried** estaba claramente preocupada.

clementine noun clementina Fem.

clever adjective 1 inteligente; **their children are all very clever** todos sus hijos son muy inteligentes; 2 (ingenious) ingenioso/ingeniosa; **a clever idea** una idea ingeniosa.

click noun clic Masc.; **a double click** un doble clic.

click verb hacer [7] clic en; **click on the icon twice** haz clic dos veces en el icono.

client noun cliente Masc./Fem.

cliff noun acantilado Masc.

climate noun clima Masc.

climb verb 1 subir [19] (stairs); 2 escalar [17] (a hill or a tree); **we climbed Mont Blanc** escalamos el Mont Blanc.

climber noun alpinista Masc./Fem.

climbing noun alpinismo Masc.; **they go climbing in Italy** practican el alpinismo en Italia.

clinic noun 1 (in a hospital) consultorio Masc.; 2 (a private hospital) clínica Fem.

clip noun 1 (from a film) clip Masc.; 2 (for your hair) horquilla Fem.

clip verb 1 (to cut) cortar [17]; 2 (to fasten) sujetar [17] con un clip.

cloakroom noun (for coats) guardarropa Masc.

clock noun reloj Masc.; **an alarm clock** un reloj despertador; **to put the clocks forward an hour** adelantar los relojes una hora; **to put the clocks back** atrasar los relojes.

clock radio noun radiodespertador Masc.

clockwise adverb en el sentido de las agujas del reloj Masc.; **it turns clockwise** gira en el sentido de las agujas del reloj; **anticlockwise** en el sentido contrario al de las agujas del reloj.

clog noun zueco Masc.

a
b
c
d
e
f
g
h
i
j
k
l
m
n
o
p
q
r
s
t
u
v
w
x
y
z

close[1] *adjective, adverb* **1** (*result*) reñido/reñida; **2** (*relation*) cercano/cercana; **3** (*friend or relationship*) she's a close friend of mine es muy amiga mía; **they are very close** están muy unidos; **4** (*near*) cerca; **the station's very close** la estación está muy cerca; **she lives close by** vive cerca; **not very close** no muy cerca; **close to the cinema** cerca del cine.

close[2] *verb* cerrar [29]; **close your eyes!** ¡cierra los ojos!; **she closed the door** cerró la puerta; **the post office closes at six** la oficina de correos cierra a las seis.

● **to close down** (*a shop or factory*) cerrar [29].

closed *adjective* cerrado/cerrada; **'closed on Mondays'** 'cerrado los lunes'.

closely *adverb* de cerca; **to examine something closely** examinar [17] algo de cerca.

closing date *noun* fecha *Fem.* límite; **the closing date for entries** la fecha límite para inscribirse.

closing-down sale *noun* liquidación *Fem.* por cierre de negocio.

closing time *noun* hora *Fem.* de cierre.

cloth *noun* **1** (*for the floor or wiping surfaces*) bayeta *Fem.*; **2** (*for polishing*) trapo *Masc.* del polvo; **3** (*for drying up*) paño *Masc.* de cocina; **4** (*fabric by the metre*) tela *Fem.*

clothes *plural noun* ropa *Fem.* (*singular*); **to put your clothes on** ponerse [11] la ropa; **to take your clothes off** quitarse [17] la ropa; **to change your clothes** cambiarse [17] de ropa.

clothes hanger *noun* percha *Fem.*

clothes line *noun* cuerda *Fem.* de tender.

clothes peg *noun* pinza *Fem.* para tender.

cloud *noun* nube *Fem.*.

● **to cloud over** nublarse [17]; **it clouded over in the afternoon** se nubló por la tarde.

cloudy *adjective* nublado/nublada.

clove *noun* **1** clavo *Masc.*; **2 a clove of garlic** un diente de ajo.

clown *noun* payaso *Masc.*, payasa *Fem.*

club *noun* **1** (*association*) club *Masc.*; **he's in the football club** está en el club de fútbol; **2** (*in cards*) trébol; **the four of clubs** el cuatro de tréboles; **3** (*golfing iron*) palo *Masc.* de golf.

clue *noun* **1** pista *Fem.*; **they have a few clues** tienen unas cuantas pistas; ★ **I haven't a clue** no tengo ni idea; **2** (*in a crossword*) clave *Fem.*

clumsy *adjective* torpe.

clutch *noun* (*in a car*) embrague *Masc.*

clutch *verb* **to clutch something** tener [9] algo firmemente agarrado.

coach *noun* **1** (*bus*) autobús *Masc.*; **by coach** en autobús; **on the**

coach en el autobús; **to travel by coach** viajar en autobús; **2** (*sports trainer*) entrenador *Masc.*, entrenadora *Fem.*; **3** (*railway carriage*) vagón *Masc.*

coach station *noun* estación *Fem.* de autobuses.

coach trip *noun* excursión *Fem.* en autobús; **to go on a coach trip** hacer una excursión en autobús.

coal *noun* carbón *Masc.*

coal mine *noun* mina *Fem.* de carbón.

coal miner *noun* minero *Masc.*, minera *Fem.*

coarse *adjective* basto/basta.

coast *noun* costa *Fem.*; **on the east coast** en la costa este.

coat *noun* **1** (*that you wear*) abrigo *Masc.*; **2 a coat of paint** una capa de pintura.

coat hanger *noun* percha *Fem.*

cobweb *noun* telaraña *Fem.*

cocaine *noun* cocaína *Fem.*

cockerel *noun* gallo *Masc.*

cocoa *noun* (*drink*) chocolate *Masc.*, (*powder*) cacao *Masc.*

coconut *noun* coco *Masc.*

cod *noun* bacalao *Masc.*

code *noun* **1** código *Masc.*; **the highway code** el código de la circulación; **2 the dialling code for Barcelona** el prefijo de Barcelona.

coffee *noun* café *Masc.*; **a cup of coffee** un café; **a black coffee, please** un café solo, por favor; **a white coffee** un café con leche.

coffee break *noun* pausa *Fem.* para el café.

coffee cup *noun* taza *Fem.* de café.

coffee machine *noun* **1** (*vending machine*) máquina *Fem.* de café; **2** (*electric*) cafetera *Fem.* eléctrica.

coffee pot *noun* cafetera *Fem.*

coffee table *noun* mesa *Fem.* de centro.

coffin *noun* ataúd *Masc.*

coin *noun* moneda *Fem.*; **a pound coin** una moneda de una libra.

coincidence *noun* coincidencia *Fem.*

Coke™ *noun* Coca-Cola™ *Fem.*; **two Cokes please** dos Coca-Colas, por favor.

colander *noun* colador *Masc.*

cold *noun* **1** (*cold weather*) frío *Masc.*; **I don't want to go out in this cold** no quiero salir con este frío; **come in out of the cold** entra, que hace frío; **she was shivering with cold** estaba temblando de frío; **2** (*illness*) resfriado *Masc.*; **to have a cold** estar resfriado/resfriada; **Carol's got a cold** Carol está resfriada; **a bad cold** un fuerte resfriado.

cold *adjective* **1** frío/fría; **your hands are cold** tienes las manos frías; **cold milk** leche fría; **2** (*weather, temperature*) **it's cold today** hoy hace frío; **it's cold in the kitchen** hace frío en la cocina; **3** (*feeling*) **I'm cold** tengo frío; **he was feeling very cold** tenía mucho frío.

a b c d e f g h i j k l m n o p q r s t u v w x y z

cold sore noun calentura Fem.

collapse verb 1 (a roof or a wall) derrumbarse [17]; 2 (a person) he collapsed in his office sufrió un desmayo en su oficina.

collar noun 1 (on a garment) cuello Masc.; 2 (for a dog) collar Masc.

collarbone noun clavícula Fem.

colleague noun compañero Masc., compañera Fem.

collect verb 1 (as a hobby) coleccionar [17]; I collect stamps colecciono sellos; 2 recoger [3] (a person or a thing); she collects the children from school ella recoge a los niños del colegio; to collect in the exercise books recoger los cuadernos; 3 cobrar [17] (fares or money); 4 reunir [62] (data or information).

collection noun 1 (of stamps, CDs, etc.) colección Fem.; 2 (of money) colecta Fem.

collector noun coleccionista Masc./Fem.

college noun 1 (for higher education) colegio Masc. universitario; to go to college ir a la universidad; 2 (for vocational training) escuela Fem. de formación profesional; 3 (a school) instituto Masc.

collie noun collie Masc./Fem.

collision noun choque Masc.

Colombia noun Colombia Fem.

Colombian noun colombiano Masc., colombiana Fem.

Colombian adjective colombiano/colombiana.

colonel noun coronel Masc.

colour noun color Masc.; what colour is your car? ¿de qué color es tu coche?; what colour is it? ¿de qué color es?; do you have it in a different colour? ¿lo tiene en otros colores?

colour verb (with paints or crayons) colorear [17]; to colour something red colorear algo de rojo.

colour blind adjective daltónico/daltónica.

colour film noun (for a camera) carrete Masc. de color.

colourful adjective de colores.

colouring book noun libro Masc. para colorear.

column noun columna Fem.

comb noun peine Masc.

comb verb to comb your hair peinarse [17]; I'll just comb my hair voy a peinarme.

combine verb combinar [17] (two separate things); they don't combine well no combinan bien.

combination noun combinación Fem.

come verb venir [15]; come quick! ¡ven rápido!; come and see! ¡ven a ver!; Nick came by bike Nick vino en bici; did Jess come to school yesterday? ¿vino Jess ayer a clase?; can you come over for a coffee? ¿puedes venir a tomar un café?; the bus is coming ya viene el autobús; come on! ¡venga!; coming! ¡ya voy!

● **to come apart** deshacerse [7]; it

came apart in my hands se
deshizo en mis manos.

- **to come back** volver [45]; **she's
coming back to collect us** volverá
para recogernos.

- **to come down** bajar [17] (*the
stairs or the street*).

- **to come for** venir [15] a por (*a
person*); **my father's coming for
me** mi padre va a venir a por mí.

- **to come from** ser [1] de; **Ian
comes from Scotland** Ian es de
Escocia; **the wine comes from
Spain** el vino es español.

- **to come in** entrar [17]; **come in!**
¡adelante!; **she came into the
kitchen** entró en la cocina.

- **to come off 1** (*a button*)
desprenderse [18], (*a handle*)
soltarse [24]; **2** (*a lid*) **I can't get
the lid to come off** no puedo
quitar la tapa.

- **to come out** salir [63]; **they
came out when I called** salieron
cuando los llamé; **the CD's coming
out soon** el compacto va a salir
pronto; **the sun hasn't come out
yet** el sol no ha salido aún.

- **to come to 1** (*get to*) llegar [28]
a; **when you come to the church
turn right** gira a la derecha cuando
llegues a la iglesia; **2** (*add up to*) **it
comes to 150 euros** suma ciento
cincuenta euros.

- **to come up** subir [19]; **can you
come up a moment?** ¿puedes
subir un momento?.

- **to come up to somebody**
acercarse [31] a alguien.

comedian *noun* cómico *Masc.*,
cómica *Fem.*

comedy *noun* comedia *Fem.*

comfortable *adjective* cómodo/
cómoda; **this chair's really
comfortable** esta silla es muy
cómoda; **to feel comfortable** (*a
person*) estar cómodo/cómoda; **are
you comfortable there?** ¿estás
cómodo ahí?

comfortably *adverb*
cómodamente.

comic *noun* (*magazine*) cómic
Masc.

comic strip *noun* tira *Fem.*
cómica.

comma *noun* coma *Fem.*

command *noun* orden *Fem.*

comment *noun* (*in a
conversation*) comentario *Masc.*; **he
made some rude comments
about my friends** hizo unos
comentarios groseros sobre mis
amigos.

commentary *noun* crónica *Fem.*;
the commentary of the match la
crónica del partido.

commentator *noun*
comentarista *Masc./Fem.*; **a sports
commentator** un comentarista
deportivo.

commercial *noun* anuncio *Masc.*
de televisión.

commercial *adjective* comercial.

commit *verb* **1** cometer [18] (*a
crime*); **2 to commit yourself**
comprometerse [18].

committee *noun* comité *Masc.*

common *adjective* **1** corriente; **it's
a common problem** es un
problema corriente; **2 in common**
en común; **they have nothing in**

a
b
c
d
e
f
g
h
i
j
k
l
m
n
o
p
q
r
s
t
u
v
w
x
y
z

common no tienen nada en común.

common sense *noun* sentido *Masc.* común.

communicate *verb* comunicar [31].

communication *noun* 1 (*message, letter etc*) comunicación *Fem.*; 2 (*in transport*) **communications are good** las comunicaciones son buenas.

communion *noun* comunión *Fem.*

communism *noun* comunismo *Masc.*

communist *noun* comunista *Masc./Fem.*

community *noun* comunidad *Fem.*; **the European Community** la comunidad europea.

commute *verb* **to commute between Oxford and London** viajar [17] todos los días de Oxford a Londres para ir a trabajar.

commuter *noun* trenes llenos de personas que van a trabajar (*Spanish does not have a word for 'commuters' so it has to be explained as 'people travelling to work'*).

compact disc *noun* disco *Masc.* compacto.

compact disc player *noun* compacto *Masc.*

company *noun* 1 compañía *Fem.*; **an insurance company** una compañía de seguros; **she's set up a company** ha montado una compañía; **an airline company**

una compañía aérea; **a theatre company** una compañía de teatro; 2 **to keep somebody company** hacer [7] compañía a alguien; **the dogs keep me company** los perros me hacen compañía.

comparatively *adverb* relativamente.

compare *verb* comparar [17]; **if you compare the Spanish with the English** si comparas los españoles con los ingleses; **our house is small compared with yours** nuestra casa es pequeña comparada con la tuya.

comparison *noun* comparación *Fem.*; **in comparison with** en comparación con.

compartment *noun* compartimento *Masc.*

compass *noun* brújula *Fem.*

compatible *adjective* (*computing*) compatible.

compensation *noun* indemnización *Fem.*

compete *verb* 1 **to compete in something** participar [17] en algo (*race, event*); 2 **to compete for something** competir [57] (*jobs, places*); **thirty people are competing for the job** treinta personas compiten por el puesto.

competent *adjective* competente.

competition *noun* 1 (*in a magazine or at school*) concurso *Masc.*; **a poetry competition** un concurso de poesía; 2 (*in sports*) competición *Fem.*; **a fishing competition** una competición de pesca; **3** (*in business*) competencia *Fem.*

competitor *noun* **1** (*in sports*) participante *Masc./Fem.*; **2** (*in business*) competidor *Masc.*, competidora *Fem.*

complain *verb* quejarse [17]; **we complained about the hotel and the meals** nos quejamos del hotel y de las comidas.

complaint *noun* queja *Fem.*; **to make a complaint** presentar [17] una queja; **she made a complaint to the manager about the bad service** presentó una queja al gerente por el mal servicio.

complete *adjective* completo/completa; **the complete collection** la colección completa.

complete *verb* (*to finish*) terminar [17].

completely *adverb* completamente.

complexion *noun* cutis *Masc.*

complicated *adjective* complicado/complicada.

complication *noun* complicación *Fem.*; **there were complications** hubo complicaciones.

compliment *noun* cumplido *Masc.*; **to pay somebody a compliment** hacer [7] un cumplido a alguien.

compose *verb* componer [11]; **composed of** compuesto de.

composer *noun* compositor *Masc.*, compositora *Fem.*

comprehension *noun* comprensión *Fem.*; a

comprehension test un ejercicio de comprensión.

compulsory *adjective* obligatorio/obligatoria.

computer *noun* ordenador *Masc.*; **to work on a computer** trabajar en ordenador.

computer engineer *noun* técnico *Masc.* en informática, técnica *Fem.* en informática.

computer game *noun* juego *Masc.* de ordenador.

computer program *noun* programa *Masc.* informático.

computer programmer *noun* programador *Masc.*, programadora *Fem.*

computer science *noun* informática *Fem.*

computing *noun* informática *Fem.*

conceited *adjective* engreído/engreída.

concentrate *verb* concentrarse [17]; **I can't concentrate** no puedo concentrarme; **I was concentrating on the film** me estaba concentrando en la película.

concentration *noun* concentración *Fem.*

concern *noun* (*worry*) preocupación *Fem.*; **there is no cause for concern** no hay razón para preocuparse.

concern *verb* **1** (*to affect*) concernir [14]; **this doesn't concern you** esto no te concierne; **2 as far as I'm concerned** por mi parte.

a

b

c

d

e

f

g

h

i

j

k

l

m

n

o

p

q

r

s

t

u

v

w

x

y

z

concert noun **1** concierto Masc.; **to go to a concert** ir [8] a un concierto; **2 a concert ticket** una entrada para un concierto.

conclusion noun conclusión Fem.

concrete noun cemento Masc.; **a concrete floor** un suelo de cemento.

condemn verb condenar [17].

condition noun condición Fem.; **in good condition** en buenas condiciones; **weather conditions** condiciones meteorológicas; **the conditions of sale** las condiciones de venta; **on one condition** con una condición; **on condition that you let me pay** a condición de que me dejes pagar.

conditional noun condicional Masc.

conditioner noun (for your hair) suavizante Masc.

condom noun condón Masc.

conduct noun conducta Fem.

conduct verb dirigir [49] (an orchestra or a piece of music).

conductor noun **1** (of an orchestra) director Masc. de orquesta directora Fem. de orquesta; **2** (on bus) cobrador Masc., cobradora Fem.

cone noun **1** (for ice cream) cucurucho Masc.; **2** (for traffic) cono Masc.

confectionery noun dulces Fem. plural; **she works in a confectionery shop** trabaja en una confitería.

conference noun conferencia Fem.

confess verb confesar [29].

confession noun confesión Fem.

confidence noun **1** (self-confidence) seguridad Fem. en sí mismo; **he has a lot of confidence** tiene mucha seguridad en sí mismo; **you're lacking in confidence** te falta seguridad en ti mismo; **2** (faith in somebody else) confianza Fem.; **to have confidence in somebody** tener [9] confianza en alguien.

confident adjective **1** (sure of yourself) seguro de sí mismo, segura de sí misma; **you look very confident** pareces muy seguro de ti mismo; **she's a confident young woman** es una joven segura de sí misma; **2** (sure that something will happen) **to be confident that** estar [2] seguro de que; **I'm confident that it will work out all right** estoy seguro de que saldrá bien.

confirm verb confirmar [17]; **we'll confirm the date** confirmaremos la fecha.

confuse verb confundir [19]; **I confuse him with his brother** lo confundo con su hermano.

confused adjective **1** (unclear) confuso/confusa; **he gave us a confused story** contó una historia muy confusa; **2** confundido/confundida; **now I'm completely confused** ahora estoy completamente confundida; **I'm confused about the holiday dates** no estoy segura de las fechas de las vacaciones; **3** **to get confused** confundirse [19]; **she got confused** se confundió.

confusing *adjective* poco claro/clara; **the instructions are confusing** las instrucciones son poco claras.

confusion *noun* confusión *Fem.*

congratulate *verb* felicitar [17]; **I congratulated Tim on his success** felicité a Tim por su éxito; **we congratulate you on winning** te felicitamos por haber ganado.

congratulations *plural noun* enhorabuena *Fem.*; **congratulations on the baby!** ¡enhorabuena por el bebé!

conjurer *noun* mago *Masc.*, maga *Fem.*

connect *verb* (*to plug in to the mains*) conectar [17] (*a dishwasher or TV, for example*).

connection *noun* conexión *Fem.*; **a faulty connection** una conexión defectuosa; **Sally missed her connection** Sally perdió su conexión; **there's no connection between his letter and my decision** no hay relación entre su carta y mi decisión.

conscience *noun* conciencia *Fem.*; **to have a guilty conscience** no tener la conciencia tranquila.

conscious *adjective* consciente.

consequence *noun* consecuencia *Fem.*

consequently *adverb* por consiguiente.

conservation *noun* (*of nature*) protección *Fem.* del medio ambiente.

conservative *noun, adjective* conservador/conservadora.

conservatory *noun* jardín *Masc.* de invierno.

consider *verb* **1** (*to give thought to*) considerar [17] (*a suggestion or idea*); **2** (*to think you might do*) plantearse [17]; **we're considering buying a flat** estamos planteándonos comprar un piso; **3 all things considered** bien considerado.

considerable *adjective* considerable; **a considerable number of students** un número considerable de estudiantes.

considerate *adjective* considerado/considerada (*a person*).

consideration *noun* consideración *Fem.*

considering *preposition* teniendo en cuenta; **considering her age** teniendo en cuenta su edad; **considering he did it all himself** teniendo en cuenta que lo hizo todo él solo.

consist *verb* **to consist of** consistir [19] en.

consistent *adjective* constante.

consonant *noun* consonante *Fem.*

constant *adjective* constante.

constantly *adverb* constantemente.

constipated *adjective* estreñido/estreñida.

construct *verb* construir [54].

construction *noun* construcción *Fem.*

consul noun cónsul Masc.

consulate noun consulado Masc.

consult verb consultar [17].

consumer noun consumidor Masc., consumidora Fem.

consumption noun consumo Masc.

contact noun contacto Masc.; **to be in contact with somebody** estar en contacto con alguien; **we've lost contact** hemos perdido contacto; **Rob has contacts in the music business** Rob tiene contactos en el mundo de la música.

contact verb ponerse [11] en contacto con; **I'll contact you tomorrow** me pondré en contacto contigo mañana.

contact lens noun lentilla Fem.

contain verb contener [9].

container noun recipiente Masc.

contaminate verb contaminar [17].

contemporary adjective contemporáneo/contemporánea.

contents plural noun contenido Masc.; **the contents of my suitcase** el contenido de mi maleta.

contest noun 1 concurso Masc.; 2 (in sport) competición Fem.

contestant noun concursante Masc./Fem.

context noun contexto Masc.

continent noun continente Masc.; **on the Continent** en Europa continental.

continental adjective a **continental holiday** unas vacaciones en Europa continental.

continue verb 1 continuar [20]; **we continued our journey** continuamos con nuestro viaje; **'to be continued'** 'continuará'; 2 to **continue doing** seguir [64] haciendo; **Jill continued talking** Jill siguió hablando.

continuous adjective continuo/ continua; **continuous assessment** evaluación Fem. continua.

contraception noun anticoncepción Fem.

contraceptive noun anticonceptivo Masc.

contract noun contrato Masc.

contradict verb contradecir [5].

contradiction noun contradicción Fem.

contrary noun the contrary lo contrario; **on the contrary** al contrario.

contrast noun contraste Masc.

contribute verb contribuir [54] (money).

contribution noun (to charity or an appeal) contribución Fem.

control noun (of a crowd or animals) control Masc.; **the police have lost control** la policía ha perdido el control; **everything's under control** todo está bajo control.

control verb 1 controlar [17] (a crowd, animals, or a fire, for example); 2 to control oneself controlarse [17].

controversial *adjective* controvertido/controvertida; **a controversial decision** una decisión controvertida.

convenient *adjective* **1** práctico/ práctica; **frozen vegetables are very convenient** las verduras congeladas son muy prácticas; **2 to be convenient for somebody** venirle [15] bien a alguien; **if that's convenient for you** si te va bien; **3 the house is convenient for shops and schools** la casa está bien situada respecto a tiendas y colegios.

convent *noun* convento *Masc.*

conventional *adjective* **1** convencional; **2** (*person*) tradicional.

conversation *noun* conversación *Fem.*

convert *verb* convertir [14]; **we're going to convert the garage into a workshop** vamos a convertir el garaje el un taller.

convince *verb* convencer [44]; **I'm convinced you're wrong** estoy convencido de que estás equivocado.

convincing *adjective* convincente.

cook *noun* cocinero *Masc.*, cocinera *Fem.*

cook *verb* **1** cocinar [17]; **who's cooking tonight?** ¿quién cocina esta noche?; **I like cooking** me gusta cocinar; **2** cocer [41] (*vegetables, pasta, etc*); **cook the carrots for five minutes** cuece las zanahorias durante cinco minutos;

3 hacer [7] (*a meal*); **Fran's busy cooking supper** Fran está haciendo la cena; **4** (*food*) hacerse [7]; **the sausages are cooking** las salchichas se están haciendo; **is the chicken cooked?** ¿está hecho el pollo?

cooker *noun* cocina *Fem.*; **an electric cooker** una cocina eléctrica; **a gas cooker** una cocina de gas.

cookery *noun* cocina *Fem.*

cookery book *noun* libro *Masc.* de cocina.

cooking *noun* cocina *Fem.*; **Italian cooking** la cocina italiana; **home cooking** la comida casera; **to do the cooking** cocinar [27].

cool *noun* **1** (*coldness*) fresco *Masc.*; **stay in the cool** quedarse [17] al fresco; **2** (*calm*) calma *Fem.*; **to lose one's cool** perder [36] la calma; **he kept his cool** mantuvo la calma.

cool *adjective* **1** (*cold*) fresco/ fresca; **a cool drink** una bebida fresca; **it's cool inside** dentro hace fresco; **2** (*laid-back*) tranquilo/ tranquila; **3 to be cool** (*a person*) estar en la onda (*informal*); **he's so cool** está muy en la onda (*informal*); **4** (*trendy*) molón/ molona (*informal*) (*a car or a jacket*).

cool *verb* **to cool (down)** enfriarse [32].

cooperate *verb* cooperar [17].

cop *noun* poli *Masc./Fem.* (*informal*).

cope *verb* **1** (*to manage*) defenderse [36]; **she copes well** se

a b c d e f g h i j k l m n o p q r s t u v w x y z

a b c d e f g h i j k l m n o p q r s t u v w x y z

defiende bien; **2 to cope with** ocuparse [17] de (*children or work*); **I'll cope with the dishes** yo me ocupo de los platos; **3** hacer [7] frente a (*problems*); **she's had a lot to cope with** ha tenido que hacer frente a muchos problemas; **he can't cope any more** ya no puede más.

copper noun cobre Masc.

copy noun **1** copia Fem.; **make ten copies of this letter** haz diez copias de esta carta; **2** (*of a book*) ejemplar Masc.

copy verb copiar [17]; **I copied (down) the address** copié las señas.

cord noun (*for a blind, for example*) cordón Masc.

cordless telephone noun teléfono Masc. inalámbrico.

core noun (*of an apple or a pear*) corazón Masc.

cork noun **1** (*in a bottle*) tapón Masc.; **2** (*material*) corcho Masc.

corkscrew noun sacacorchos Masc. (*does not change in the plural*).

corn noun **1** (*wheat*) trigo Masc.; **2** (*sweetcorn*) maíz Masc.

corner noun **1** (*of street or page*) esquina Fem.; **at the corner of the street** en la esquina de la calle; **it's just round the corner** está a la vuelta de la esquina; **in the bottom right-hand corner of the page** en la esquina inferior derecha de la página; **2** (*of room or cupboard*) rincón Masc.; **in a corner of the kitchen** en un rincón de la cocina;

3 out of the corner of your eye por el rabillo del ojo; **4** (*in football*) córner Masc.

cornflakes noun copos Masc. plural de maíz.

Cornwall noun Cornualles Masc.

corpse noun cadáver Masc.

correct adjective **1** correcto/correcta; **the correct sum** la cantidad total correcta; **the correct answer** la respuesta correcta; **the correct choice** la elección adecuada; **2 yes, that's correct** sí, así es.

correct verb corregir [48].

correction noun corrección Fem.

correctly adverb correctamente; **have you filled in the form correctly?** ¿has rellenado el formulario correctamente?.

correspond verb corresponder [18].

corridor noun pasillo Masc.

cosmetics plural noun cosméticos Masc. plural.

cost noun coste Masc.; **the cost of a new computer** el coste de un nuevo ordenador; **the cost of living** el coste de la vida.

cost verb costar [24]; **how much does it cost?** ¿cuánto cuesta?; **the tickets cost ten pounds** las entradas cuestan diez libras; **it costs too much** cuesta demasiado caro.

Costa Rica noun Costa Rica Fem.

Costa Rican noun costarricense Masc., Fem.

Costa Rican adjective costarricense.

costume noun **1** (fancy dress) disfraz Masc.; **2** (for an actor) traje Masc.

cosy adjective (a room) acogedor/ acogedora; **it's cosy by the fire** se está muy bien al lado del fuego.

cot noun cuna Fem.

cottage noun casita Fem. en el campo.

cotton noun **1** (fabric) algodón Masc.; **a cotton shirt** una camisa de algodón; **2** (thread) hilo Masc.

cotton wool noun algodón Masc. en rama.

couch noun sofá Masc.

cough noun tos Fem.; **a nasty cough** una tos mala; **to have a cough** tener [9] tos.

cough verb toser [18].

could verb **1** poder [10]; **if he could pay** si pudiese pagar; **I couldn't open it** no podía abrirlo; **they couldn't smoke there** no podían fumar allí; **she did all she could** hizo todo lo que pudo; **2** (knew how to) **he couldn't drive** no sabía conducir; **I couldn't swim** no sabía nadar; **3** (with see, hear, smell, remember, or understand, 'could' is not translated) **I could hear a police car** oí un coche de policía; **she couldn't see anything** no veía nada; **4** (talking about a possibility) **they could be home by now** puede que ya estén en casa; **you could be right** puede que tengas razón; **5** (in 'if' sentences 'could' is translated by the subjunctive) **I would buy it if I could afford it** lo compraría si

pudiese; **I could have gone if I'd wanted** hubiese podido ir si hubiese querido; **6** (asking permission or suggesting) **could I speak to David?** ¿podría hablar con David?; **you could try telephoning** podrías intentar llamar por teléfono.

council noun consejo Masc.; **the town council** el ayuntamiento.

councillor noun concejal Masc., concejala Fem.; **her uncle is a councillor** su tío es concejal.

count verb **1** (reckon up) contar [24]; **I counted my money** conté mi dinero; **thirty-five not counting the children** treinta y cinco sin contar a los niños; **2 to count as** considerarse [17] como; **children over twelve count as adults** los niños mayores de doce años se consideran como adultos; **3** (to be allowed) **that doesn't count** eso no vale.

counter noun **1** (in a shop) mostrador Masc.; **2** (in a café) barra Fem.; **3** (in a post office or bank) ventanilla Fem.; **4** (for board games) ficha Fem.

country noun **1** (Spain, Britain, etc) país Masc.; **a foreign country** un país extranjero; **from another country** de otro país; **2** (not town) campo Masc.; **to live in the country** vivir en el campo; **a country walk** un paseo por el campo; **a country road** un camino rural.

country dancing noun baile Masc. folklórico.

countryside noun campo Masc.

a

b

c

d

e

f

g

h

i

j

k

l

m

n

o

p

q

r

s

t

u

v

w

x

y

z

county noun condado Masc.

couple noun 1 (a pair) pareja Fem.; **a married couple** una pareja de casados; 2 **a couple of** un par de; **a couple of times** un par de veces; **I've got a couple of things to do** tengo que hacer un par de cosas.

courage noun valor Masc.

courgette noun calabacín Masc.

courier noun 1 (on a package holiday) guía Masc./Fem.; 2 (delivery service) mensajería Fem.; **by courier** por mensajería.

course noun 1 (lessons) curso Masc.; **a beginners' course** un curso para principiantes; **a computer course** un curso de informática; **to go on a course** asistir a un curso; 2 (part of a meal) plato Masc.; **the main course** el plato principal; 3 **a golf course** un campo de golf; 4 **of course** claro; **yes, of course!** ¡sí, claro!; **he's forgotten, of course** se ha olvidado, claro.

court noun 1 (for tennis, squash, or basketball) cancha Fem.; 2 (of law) tribunal Masc.

courtyard noun patio Masc.

cousin noun primo Masc., prima Fem.; **my cousin Sonia** mi prima Sonia.

cover noun 1 (for a book) tapa Fem.; 2 (for a duvet or cushion) funda Fem.; **a duvet cover** una funda de edredón.

cover verb 1 cubrir [46]; **to cover the wound** cubrir la herida; **the ground was covered with snow** el suelo estaba cubierto de nieve; **he**

was covered in mud estaba cubierto de barro; 2 (your face or eyes) cubrirse [46]; **she covered her face** se cubrió la cara.

cow noun vaca Fem.; **mad cow disease** la enfermedad de las vacas locas.

coward noun cobarde Masc./Fem.

cowboy noun vaquero Masc.

crab noun cangrejo Masc.

crack noun 1 (in a wall) grieta Fem.; 2 (in a cup or plate) raja Fem.; 3 (a cracking noise) crujido Masc.

crack verb 1 (to make a crack in) hacer [7] una raja en (a cup or a window); 2 fracturar [17] (a bone); 3 (break open) cascar [31] (a nut or an egg); 4 (split by itself: ice, for example) rajarse [17]; 5 (make a noise) (a twig) crujir [19].

cracker noun (biscuit) galleta Fem. salada.

crackle verb crujir [19].

craft noun (at school) trabajos Masc. plural manuales.

crafty adjective astuto/astuta; **that was very crafty of her** eso fue muy astuto por su parte.

cramp noun calambre Masc.; **I've got cramp in my leg** tengo un calambre en la pierna.

crane noun grúa Fem.

crash noun 1 (an accident) accidente Masc.; **a car crash** un accidente de coche; 2 (smashing noise) estrépito Masc.; **a crash of broken glass** un estrépito de cristales rotos.

crash verb 1 (a car or plane) tener [9] un accidente; **the plane**

crashed el avión tuvo un accidente; **2 to crash into something** chocar [31] con algo; **the car crashed into a tree** el coche chocó con un árbol.

crash course noun curso Masc. intensivo.

crash helmet noun casco Masc.

crate noun **1** (for china) cajón Masc. para embalar; **2** (for bottles or fruit) caja Fem.

crawl noun (in swimming) crol Masc.

crawl verb **1** (a person, a baby) ir [8] a gatas; **2** (cars in a jam) ir [8] muy despacio; **we were crawling along** íbamos muy despacio.

crayon noun **1** (wax) pintura Fem. de cera; **2** (coloured pencil) lápiz Masc. de color.

craze noun fiebre Fem.; **the craze for computer games** la fiebre de los juegos de ordenador.

crazy adjective loco/loca; **to go crazy** volverse loco/loca; **to be crazy about someone** estar loco/loca por alguien; **he's crazy about football** le encanta el fútbol.

creak verb (a hinge) chirriar [32], (a floorboard) crujir [19].

cream noun **1** (dairy cream) nata Fem.; **strawberries and cream** fresas con nata; **2** (for hands, face, etc.) crema Fem.

cream cheese noun queso Masc. para untar.

crease noun arruga Fem.

creased adjective arrugado/arrugada.

create verb crear [17].

creative adjective creativo/creativa (a person).

creature noun criatura Fem.

creche noun guardería Fem.

credit noun crédito Masc.; **to buy something on credit** comprar algo a crédito.

credit card noun tarjeta Fem. de crédito.

crew noun **1** (on a ship or plane) tripulación Fem.; **2** (rowing or filming) equipo Masc.

crew cut noun corte Masc. de pelo al rape.

cricket noun **1** (game) críquet Masc.; **to play cricket** jugar [27] al críquet; **2** (insect) grillo Masc.

cricket bat noun bate Masc. de críquet.

crime noun **1** delito Masc.; **theft is a crime** el robo es un delito; **2** (murder) crimen Masc.; **3** (within society) crimen Masc.; **the fight against crime** la lucha contra el crimen.

criminal noun criminal Masc./Fem..

criminal adjective criminal.

crisis noun crisis Fem.

crisp noun patata Fem. frita; **a packet of (potato) crisps** un paquete de patatas fritas.

crisp adjective crujiente.

critical adjective **1** crítico/crítica (a remark or somebody's condition); **2** decisivo/decisiva (a moment).

criticism noun crítica Fem.

criticize verb criticar [31].

Croatia noun Croacia Fem.

a b c d e f g h i j k l m n o p q r s t u v w x y z

crockery noun vajilla Fem.

crocodile noun cocodrilo Masc.

crook noun (criminal) granuja Masc./Fem.

crooked adjective torcido/torcida; **a crooked line** una línea torcida.

crop noun cosecha Fem.

cross noun cruz Fem.

cross adjective enfadado/enfadada; **she's very cross** está muy enfadada; **I'm cross with you** estoy enfadada contigo; **to get cross** enfadarse [17].

cross verb **1** (to cross over) cruzar [22]; **to cross the road** cruzar la calle; **2 to cross your legs** cruzar las piernas; **3 to cross into Spain** pasar [17] a España; **4** (to cross each other) cruzarse [22]; **the two roads cross here** las dos carreteras se cruzan aquí.

● **to cross out** tachar [17] (a word or sentence).

cross-Channel adjective **a cross-Channel ferry** un ferry que cruza el Canal de la Mancha.

cross-country noun **1** cross Masc.; **2 cross-country skiing** esquí Masc. de fondo.

crossing noun **1** (from one place to another) travesía Fem.; **a Channel crossing** una travesía por el Canal de la Mancha; **2 a pedestrian crossing** un cruce de peatones; **a level crossing** un paso a nivel.

cross-legged adjective **to sit cross-legged** sentarse con las piernas cruzadas.

crossroads noun cruce Masc.; **at the crossroads** en el cruce.

crossword noun crucigrama Masc.; **to do the crossword** hacer el crucigrama.

crouch verb ponerse [11] en cuclillas.

crow noun cuervo Masc.; ★ **as the crow flies** en línea recta.

crow verb (a cock) cacarear [17].

crowd noun multitud Fem.; **in the crowd** en la multitud; **a crowd of 5,000** una multitud de cinco mil personas.

crowd verb **to crowd into** (or **onto**) aglomerase [17] en (a room or bus, for example); **we all crowded into the train** nos aglomeramos en el tren.

crowded adjective lleno/llena de gente.

crown noun corona Fem.

crude adjective **1** (rough and ready) rudimentario/rudimentaria; **2** (vulgar) grosero/grosera.

cruel adjective cruel.

cruelty noun crueldad Fem.; **they were treated with great cruelty** los trataron con gran crueldad.

cruise noun crucero Masc.; **to go on a cruise** ir de crucero.

crumb noun miga Fem.

crumple verb arrugar [28].

crunchy adjective crujiente.

crush verb aplastar [17].

crust noun corteza Fem.

crutch noun muleta Fem.; **to be on crutches** andar con muletas.

cry noun grito Masc.

cry *verb* **1** (*weep*) llorar [17]; **2** (*call out*) gritar [17].

crystal *noun* cristal *Masc.*

cub *noun* **1** (*animal*) cachorro *Masc.*; **2** (*scout*) lobato *Masc.*

Cuba *noun* Cuba *Fem.*

Cuban *noun* cubano *Masc.*, cubana *Fem.*

Cuban *adjective* cubano/cubana.

cube *noun* cubo *Masc.*; **an ice cube** un cubito de hielo.

cubic *adjective* (*for measurements*) cúbico/cúbica; **three cubic metres** tres metros cúbicos.

cubicle *noun* **1** (*in a changing room*) vestuario *Masc.*; **2** (*in a public lavatory*) cubículo *Masc.*

cuckoo *noun* cuco *Masc.*

cucumber *noun* pepino *Masc.*

cuddle *noun* **to give somebody a cuddle** dar [4] un abrazo a alguien.

cuddle *verb* abrazar [22].

cue *noun* (*billiards, pool, snooker*) taco *Masc.*

cuff *noun* (*on a shirt*) puño *Masc.*

cul-de-sac *noun* callejón *Masc.* sin salida.

culture *noun* cultura *Fem.*

cunning *adjective* astuto/astuta.

cup *noun* **1** (*for drinking*) taza *Fem.*; **a cup of tea** una taza de té; **2** (*a trophy*) copa *Fem.*

cupboard *noun* armario *Masc.*; **in the kitchen cupboard** en el armario de la cocina.

cup tie *noun* partido *Masc.* de copa.

cure *noun* cura *Fem.*

cure *verb* curar [17].

curiosity *noun* curiosidad *Fem.*

curious *adjective* curioso/curiosa.

curl *noun* rizo *Masc.*

curl *verb* rizar [22] (*hair*).

curly *adjective* rizado/rizada.

currant *noun* pasa *Fem.* de Corinto.

currency *noun* moneda *Fem.*; **foreign currency** moneda extranjera.

current *noun* (*of electricity or water*) corriente *Fem.*

current *adjective* actual (*a situation, for example*).

current affairs *noun* sucesos *Masc.* plural de actualidad.

curriculum *noun* **1** (*national*) plan *Masc.* de estudios; **2** (*for a single course*) programa *Masc.* de estudios.

curry *noun* curry *Masc.*; **chicken curry** curry de pollo.

cursor *noun* cursor *Masc.*

curtain *noun* cortina *Fem.*

cushion *noun* cojín *Masc.*

custard *noun* **1** (*runny*) natillas *Fem.* (*plural*); **2** (*baked*) flan *Masc.*

custom *noun* costumbre *Masc.*

customer *noun* cliente *Masc.*, clienta *Fem.*; **customer services** atención al cliente.

customs *plural noun* aduana *Fem.*; **to go through customs** pasar por la aduana.

customs hall *noun* aduana *Fem.*

customs officer *noun* agente *Masc./Fem.* de aduana.

cut *noun* (*injury or haircut*) corte *Masc.*

a
b
c
d
e
f
g
h
i
j
k
l
m
n
o
p
q
r
s
t
u
v
w
x
y
z

a **cut** verb **1** cortar [17]; **I've cut the bread** he cortado el pan; **you'll cut yourself!** ¡te vas a cortar!; **Kevin's cut his finger** Kevin se ha cortado el dedo; **to cut the grass** cortar la hierba; **2 to get your hair cut** cortarse el pelo; **Ayesha's had her hair cut** Ayesha se ha cortado el pelo; **3 to cut prices** bajar [17] los precios.

● **to cut down something** cortar [17] algo (*a tree*).

● **to cut down on something: to cut down on fats** consumir [19] menos grasas.

● **to cut out something 1** recortar [17] algo (*a shape, a newspaper article*); **2** suprimir [19] algo (*sugar, fatty food, etc*).

● **to cut up something** cortar [17] algo en trocitos (*food*).

cute adjective mono/mona.

cutlery noun cubertería Fem.

CV noun currículum Masc. vitae.

cycle noun (*bike*) bicicleta Fem.

cycle verb montar [17] en bicicleta; **do you like cycling?** ¿te gusta montar en bicicleta?; **we cycle to school** vamos al colegio en bicicleta.

cycle lane noun carril Masc. de bicicletas.

cycle race noun carrera Fem. de ciclismo.

cycling noun ciclismo Masc.

cycling holiday noun vacaciones Fem. plural en bicicleta.

cyclist noun ciclista Masc./Fem.

cylinder noun cilindro Masc; **a gas cylinder** una bombona.

Dd

dad noun **1** (*father*) padre Masc.; **Anna's dad** el padre de Ana; **my dad works in a bank** mi padre trabaja en un banco; **2** (*daddy*) papá; **Dad's not home yet** papá no ha llegado a casa aún.

daffodil noun narciso Masc.

daily adjective diario/diaria; **his daily visit** su visita diaria.

daily adverb a diario; **she visits him daily** le visita a diario.

dairy products plural noun productos Masc. plural lácteos.

daisy noun margarita Fem.

dam noun presa Fem.

damage noun daño Masc.; **the damage is done** el daño ya está hecho; **there's no damage** no ha habido daños.

damage verb dañar [17].

damn noun **he doesn't give a damn** le importa un comino (*informal*).

damn exclamation **damn!** ¡maldita sea! (*informal*).

damp noun humedad Fem.; **because of the damp** a causa de la humedad.

damp adjective húmedo/húmeda.

dance noun baile Masc.; **a folk dance** un baile folklórico.

dance verb bailar [17]; **I like dancing** me gusta bailar.

dancer noun bailarín Masc., bailarina Fem.

dancing noun baile Masc.; **I love dancing** me encanta bailar.

dancing class noun clase Fem. de baile; **to go to dancing classes** ir a clase de baile.

dandruff noun caspa Fem.

danger noun peligro Masc.; **to be in danger** estar en peligro; **out of danger** fuera de peligro.

dangerous adjective peligroso/peligrosa; **it's dangerous to drive so fast** es peligroso conducir tan rápido.

Danish noun danés Masc., danesa Fem.

Danish adjective danés/danesa.

dare verb 1 atreverse [18]; **to dare to do** atreverse a hacer; **I didn't dare suggest it** no me atreví a sugerirlo; **how dare you!** ¡cómo te atreves!; 2 **don't you dare tell her I'm here!** ¡no se te ocurra decirle que estoy aquí!; 3 **I dare you!** ¡a que no te atreves! (informal); **I dare you to tell him!** ¡a que no te atreves a decírselo! (informal).

daring adjective osado/osada; **that was a bit daring!** ¡eso ha sido un poco osado!

dark noun in the dark en la oscuridad; **to be afraid of the dark** tener miedo de la oscuridad; **after dark** de noche.

dark adjective 1 (colour or room) oscuro/oscura; **a dark blue suit** un traje azul oscuro; **she has dark brown hair** tiene el pelo castaño oscuro; **the kitchen's a bit dark** la cocina es un poco oscura; **it's dark**

in here está oscuro aquí; 2 **it's dark already** ya es de noche; **to get dark** oscurecer; **it gets dark around five** oscurece a eso de las cinco.

darkness noun oscuridad Fem.

darling noun querido Masc., querida Fem.; **see you later, darling!** ¡te veo luego querido!

dart noun dardo Masc.; **to play darts** jugar a los dardos.

data noun información Fem.

database noun base Fem. de datos.

date noun 1 fecha Fem.; **the date of the meeting** la fecha de la reunión; **to fix a date for** fijar una fecha para; 2 **what's the date today?** ¿qué día es hoy?; 3 (when you go out) **I have a date with Jerry on Sunday** he quedado para salir con Jerry el domingo; 4 **out of date** (passport, driving licence, etc) caducado/caducada, (technology, method, information, etc) anticuado/anticuada, 5 (fruit) dátil Masc.

date of birth noun fecha Fem. de nacimiento.

daughter noun hija Fem.; **Tina's daughter** la hija de Tina.

daughter-in-law noun nuera Fem.

dawn noun amanecer Masc.

day noun 1 día Masc.; **three days later** tres días más tarde; **it rained all day** llovió todo el día; **it's going to be a nice day tomorrow** mañana va a hacer buen día; 2 **the day after** al día siguiente; **the day**

a
b
c
d
e
f
g
h
i
j
k
l
m
n
o
p
q
r
s
t
u
v
w
x
y
z

a
b
c
d
e
f
g
h
i
j
k
l
m
n
o
p
q
r
s
t
u
v
w
x
y
z

after the wedding el día después de la boda; **the day after tomorrow** pasado mañana; **my sister's arriving the day after tomorrow** mi hermana llega pasado mañana; **3 the day before** el día anterior; **the day before the wedding** el día antes de la boda; **the day before yesterday** anteayer; **my sister arrived the day before yesterday** mi hermana llegó anteayer; **4 every day** todos los días.

day off noun día Masc. libre.

dead adjective muerto/muerta; **her father's dead** su padre ha muerto.

dead adverb (really) super (informal); **he's dead nice** es super majo; **it's dead easy** es super fácil; **it was dead good** fue genial; **you're dead right** tienes toda la razón; **she arrived dead on time** llegó justo a la hora.

dead end noun callejón Masc. sin salida.

deadline noun fecha Fem. límite.

deaf adjective sordo/sorda; **to go deaf** quedarse sordo/sorda.

deafening adjective ensordecedor/ensordecedora.

deal noun **1** (involving money) negocio Masc.; **it's a good deal** es un buen negocio; **2** (pact) trato Masc.; **I'll make a deal with you** voy a hacer un trato contigo; **it's a deal!** ¡trato hecho!; **3 a great deal of** mucho/mucha; **I don't have a great deal of time** no tengo mucho tiempo; **a great deal of energy** mucha energía; **4 a great deal**

mucho; **it has improved a great deal** ha mejorado mucho.

deal verb (in cards) repartir [19].

● **to deal with something** ocuparse [17] de algo; **Linda deals with the accounts** Linda se ocupa de las cuentas; **I'll deal with it as soon as possible** me ocuparé de ello tan pronto como sea posible.

dear adjective **1** querido/querida; **Dear Jo** Querida Jo; **2** (expensive) caro/cara.

death noun muerte Fem.; **after his father's death** después de la muerte de su padre; ★ **you'll frighten him to death** vas a matarlo del susto; ★ **I'm bored to death** me muero de aburrimiento; ★ **I'm sick to death of his complaining** estoy harta de sus quejas.

death penalty noun pena Fem. de muerte.

debate noun debate Masc.

debate verb debatir [19].

debt noun deuda Fem.; **to get into debt** endeudarse [17].

decade noun década Fem.

decaffeinated adjective descafeinado/descafeinada.

deceive verb engañar [17].

December noun diciembre Masc.

decent adjective decente; **a decent salary** un sueldo decente; **a decent meal** una comida decente; **he seems a decent enough guy** parece un tipo decente.

decide verb decidir [19]; **to decide to do** decidir hacer; **she's decided to buy a car** ha decidido comprarse un coche; **they've decided not to go on holiday** han decidido non irse de vacaciones.

decimal *adjective* decimal.

decimal point *noun* decimal *Masc.*

decision *noun* decisión *Fem.*; **the right decision** la decisión acertada; **the wrong decision** la decisión errónea; **to make a decision** tomar una decisión.

deck *noun* (on a ship) cubierta *Fem.*

deckchair *noun* tumbona *Fem.*

declare *verb* declarar [17].

decorate *verb* **1** adornar [17]; **to decorate the Christmas tree** adornar el árbol de Navidad; **2** (a room) (with paint) pintar [17] (with wallpaper) empapelar [17].

decoration *noun* **1** decoración *Fem.*; **2** (ornament) adorno *Masc.*

decorator *noun* pintor *Masc.*, pintora *Fem.*

decrease *noun* disminución *Fem.*; **a decrease in the number of** una disminución en el número de.

decrease *verb* disminuir [54].

deduct *verb* deducir [60].

deep *adjective* profundo/profunda; **a deep feeling of gratitude** un profundo sentimiento de gratitud; **the river is very deep here** aquí el río es muy profundo; **how deep is the swimming pool?** ¿qué profundidad tiene la piscina?; **a hole two metres deep** un agujero de dos metros de profundidad.

deep end *noun* (of a swimming pool) **the deep end** la parte honda de la piscina.

deep freeze *noun* congelador *Masc.*

deeply *adverb* profundamente.

deer *noun* ciervo *Masc.*

defeat *noun* derrota *Fem.*

defeat *verb* derrotar [17].

defect *noun* defecto *Masc.*

defence *noun* defensa *Fem.*

defend *verb* defender [36].

defender *noun* **1** (of cause) defensor *Masc.*, defensora *Fem.*; **2** (in football) defensa *Masc./Fem.*

define *verb* definir [19].

definite *adjective* **1** (clear) claro/clara; **a definite improvement** una clara mejora; **a definite advantage** una clara ventaja; **it's a definite possibility** es claramente una posibilidad; **2** (certain) seguro/segura; **it's not definite yet** aún no es seguro; **3** (exact) preciso/precisa; **a definite answer** una respuesta precisa; **I don't have a definite idea of what I want** no tengo una idea precisa de lo que quiero.

definite article *noun* artículo *Masc.* definido.

definitely *adverb* **1** (when giving your opinion about something) sin ninguna duda; **the blue one is definitely the biggest** el azul es sin ninguna duda el más grande; **your French is definitely better than mine** hablas francés mejor que yo sin ninguna duda; **'are you sure you like this one better?'** – **'definitely'** ¿estás seguro de que te gusta más éste? - 'segurísimo'; **2** (for certain) **she's definitely**

a
b
c
d
e
f
g
h
i
j
k
l
m
n
o
p
q
r
s
t
u
v
w
x
y
z

a
b
c

going to be there es seguro que va a estar aquí; **I'm definitely not going** es seguro que no voy; **she definitely said she would do it** dijo que seguro que lo haría.

d

definition *noun* definición *Fem.*

e

degree *noun* **1** grado *Masc.*; **thirty degrees** treinta grados; **2 a university degree** un título universitario.

f
g

delay *noun* retraso *Masc.*; **a two-hour delay** un retraso de dos horas.

h
i

delay *verb* retrasar [17]; **the flight was delayed by bad weather** el mal tiempo retrasó el vuelo; **the decision has been delayed until Thursday** retrasaron la decisión hasta el jueves.

j
k
l

m

deliberate *adjective* deliberado/ deliberada.

n

deliberately *adverb* a propósito; **you did it deliberately** lo hiciste a propósito; **he left it there deliberately** lo dejó allí a propósito.

o
p
q

delicate *adjective* delicado/ delicada.

r
s

delicatessen *noun* charcutería *Fem.*

t

delicious *adjective* delicioso/ deliciosa.

u

delighted *adjective* encantado/ encantada; **they're delighted with their new flat** están encantados con su nuevo piso; **I'm delighted to hear you can come** estoy encantado de saber que puedes venir.

v
w
x
y
z

deliver *verb* **1** (*goods*) entregar [28]; **the person who delivered the parcel** la persona que entregó el paquete; **2** (*mail*) repartir [19].

delivery *noun* entrega *Fem.*

demand *noun* petición *Fem.*

demand *verb* exigir [49].

democracy *noun* democracia *Fem.*

democratic *adjective* democrático/democrática.

demolish *verb* destruir [54].

demonstrate *verb* **1** demostrar [24] (*a theory or a skill*); **2** hacer [7] una demostración de (*a machine, product, or technique*); **3** (*protest*) manifestarse [29]; **to demonstrate against something** manifestarse en contra de algo.

demonstration *noun* **1** (*of machine, product, technique*) demostración *Fem.*; **2** (*protest*) manifestación *Fem.*

demonstrator *noun* (*in protest*) manifestante *Masc./Fem.*

denim *noun* tela *Fem.* vaquera; **a denim jacket** una chaqueta vaquera.

Denmark *noun* Dinamarca *Fem.*

dense *adjective* denso/densa.

dent *noun* abolladura *Fem.*

dent *verb* abollar [17].

dental *adjective* **1** dental; **dental hygiene** higiene *Fem.* dental; **2 a dental appointment** una cita con el dentista.

dental floss *noun* hilo *Masc.* dental.

dental surgeon noun cirujano Masc. dentistacirujana Fem. dentista.

dentist noun dentista Masc./Fem.; **my mum's a dentist** mi madre es dentista.

deny verb negar [30].

deodorant noun desodorante Masc.

depart verb salir [63].

department noun 1 (in school, university) departamento Masc.; **the language department** el departamento de idiomas; 2 (in a shop) sección Fem.; **the men's department** la sección de caballeros.

department store noun grandes almacenes Masc. plural.

departure noun salida Fem.

departure gate noun puerta Fem. de embarque.

departure lounge noun sala Fem. de embarque.

depend verb to depend on depender [18] de; **it depends on the price** depende del precio; **it depends on what you want** depende de lo que tú quieras (note that 'que' is followed by the subjunctive); **it depends** depende.

deposit noun 1 (when renting, hiring, or making a booking) depósito Masc.; **to pay a deposit** pagar un depósito; 2 (when buying something) entrada Fem.

depressed adjective deprimido/deprimida.

depressing adjective deprimente.

depth noun profundidad Fem.

deputy noun segundo Masc., segunda Fem.

deputy head noun subdirector Masc., subdirectora Fem.

descend verb descender [36].

describe verb describir [52].

description noun descripción Fem.

desert noun desierto Masc.

desert island noun isla Fem. desierta.

deserve verb merecer [35].

design noun diseño Masc.; **the design of the plane** el diseño del avión; **fashion design** diseño de moda; **a floral design** un diseño de flores.

design verb diseñar [17].

designer noun diseñador Masc., diseñadora Fem.

desire noun deseo Masc.

desire verb desear [17].

desk noun 1 (in office or at home) escritorio Masc.; 2 (pupil's) pupitre Masc.; 3 **the reception desk** la recepción; **the information desk** información Fem.

despair noun desesperación Fem.

desperate adjective 1 desesperado/desesperada; **a desperate attempt** un intento desesperado; 2 **to be desperate to do** estar [2] deseando hacer; **I'm desperate to see you** estoy deseando verte.

despise verb despreciar [17].

a
b
c
d
e
f
g
h
i
j
k
l
m
n
o
p
q
r
s
t
u
v
w
x
y
z

dessert noun postre Masc.; **what's for dessert?** ¿qué hay de postre?

destination noun destino Masc.

destroy verb destruir [54].

destruction noun destrucción Fem.

detached house noun casa Fem. no adosada.

detail noun detalle Masc.

detailed adjective detallado/ detallada.

detective noun **1** (police) agente Masc./Fem.; **2** a private detective un detective privado/una detective privada.

detective story noun novela Fem. policiaca.

detention noun (in school) **to be in detention** estar [2] castigado/ castigada.

detergent noun detergente Masc.

determined adjective decidido/ decidida; **he's determined to leave** está decidido a irse.

detour noun rodeo Masc.

develop verb **1** (a film) revelar [17]; **to get a film developed** revelar un carrete de fotos; **2** desarrollarse [17]; **how children develop** cómo se desarrollan los niños.

developing country noun país Masc. en vías de desarrollo.

development noun desarrollo Masc.

devil noun diablo Masc.

devoted adjective **1** (couple or family) unido/unida; **2** (admirer) ferviente.

dew noun rocío Masc.

diabetes noun diabetes Fem.

diabetic noun diabético Masc., diabética Fem.

diabetic adjective diabético/ diabética; **to be diabetic** ser diabético/diabética.

diagonal adjective diagonal.

diagnosis noun diagnóstico Masc.

diagram noun diagrama Masc.

dial verb marcar [31]; **dial 00 34 for Spain** marca 00 34 para España.

dialling tone noun tono Masc. de marcar.

dialogue noun diálogo Masc.

diameter noun diámetro Masc.

diamond noun **1** diamante Masc.; **2** (in cards) diamonds diamantes; **the jack of diamonds** la jota de diamantes; **3** (shape) rombo Masc.

diarrhoea noun diarrea Fem.; **to have diarrhoea** tener [9] diarrea.

diary noun **1** (for dates) agenda Fem.; **I've noted the date of the meeting in my diary** he anotado la fecha de la reunión en mi agenda; **2** (personal) diario Masc. íntimo; **to keep a diary** tener [9] un diario íntimo.

dice noun dado Masc.; **to throw the dice** tirar [17] los dados.

dictation noun dictado Masc.

dictionary noun diccionario Masc.; **to look up a word in the dictionary** buscar [31] una palabra en el diccionario.

did verb SEE do.

die verb **1** morir [55]; **my grandmother died in January** mi abuela murió en enero; **2 to be dying to do something** estar [2] deseando hacer algo; **I'm dying to see them!** ¡estoy deseando verlos!.

● **die out** desaparecer [35]; **the tradition is dying out** la tradición está desapareciendo.

diesel noun **1** diesel Masc.; **2 a diesel engine** un motor diesel; **a diesel car** un diesel.

diet noun **1** dieta Fem.; **to have a healthy diet** llevar una dieta saludable; **2** (slimming or special) régimen Masc.; **to be on a diet** estar a régimen; **to go on a diet** ponerse a régimen; **a salt-free diet** un régimen sin sal.

difference noun **1** diferencia Fem.; **I can't see any difference between the two** no puedo ver ninguna diferencia entre los dos; **what's the difference between ... ?** ¿qué diferencia hay entre ... ?; **2 it makes a difference** eso cambia las cosas; **it makes no difference** da lo mismo; **it makes no difference what I say** da lo mismo lo que yo diga.

different adjective distinto/distinta; **the two sisters are very different** las dos hermanas son muy distintas; **she's very different from her sister** es muy distinta a su hermana.

difficult adjective difícil; **it's really difficult** es muy difícil; **it's difficult to decide** es difícil decidir.

difficulty noun **1** dificultad Fem.; **2 I had difficulty finding your house** me resultó difícil encontrar tu casa.

dig verb cavar [17]; **to dig a hole** cavar [17] un agujero.

digestion noun digestión Fem.

digital adjective digital; **a digital watch** un reloj digital.

dignity noun dignidad Fem.

dim adjective **1** tenue; **a dim light** una luz tenue; **2 she's a bit dim** es un poco tonta (informal).

dimension noun dimensión Fem.

din noun ruido Masc.; **they were making a dreadful din** estaban haciendo un ruido enorme; **stop making such a din!** ¡deja de hacer tanto ruido!

dinghy noun **1 a sailing dinghy** un bote; **2 a rubber dinghy** un bote neumático.

dining room noun comedor Masc.; **in the dining room** en el comedor.

dinner noun **1** (evening meal) cena Fem.; **to have dinner** cenar [17]; **to invite somebody to dinner** invitar [17] a alguien a cenar; **2** (midday meal) comida Fem.; **to have dinner** comer [18]; **to have school dinner** comer [18] en el colegio.

dinner party noun cena Fem.

dinner time noun **1** (evening) hora Fem. de cenar; **2** (midday) hora Fem. de comer.

dinosaur noun dinosaurio Masc.

diploma noun diploma Masc.

direct adjective directo/directa; **a direct flight** un vuelo directo.

a b c d e f g h i j k l m n o p q r s t u v w x y z

direct *adverb* directo; **the bus goes direct to the airport** el autobús va directo al aeropuerto.

direct *verb* **1** (*a programme, film, play or traffic*) dirigir [49]; **2** (*give directions to*) indicarle [31] el camino a; **I directed them to the station** les indiqué el camino a la estación.

direction *noun* **1** dirección *Fem.*; **in the direction of the church** en dirección a la iglesia; **in the other direction** en la otra dirección; **2** to ask somebody for directions pedir a alguien que te indique el camino; **3 directions for use** instrucciones *Fem. plural* de uso.

directly *adverb* **1** (*to go, fly, deal or ask*) directamente; **2** (*at once*) inmediatamente; **3 directly afterwards** inmediatamente después.

director *noun* director *Masc.*, directora *Fem.* (*of a company, programme, film or play*).

directory *noun* guía *Fem.* telefónica; **to be ex-directory** no estar en la guía telefónica.

dirt *noun* suciedad *Fem.*

dirty *adjective* sucio/sucia; **my hands are dirty** tengo las manos sucias; **to get something dirty** ensuciar [17] algo; **I got the floor dirty** ensucié el suelo; **you'll get your dress dirty** te vas a ensuciar el vestido; **to get dirty** ensuciarse [17]; **the curtains get dirty quickly** las cortinas se ensucian rápido.

disability *noun* discapacidad *Fem.*; **does he have a disability?** ¿tiene alguna discapacidad?

disabled *adjective* discapacitado/ discapacitada; **disabled people** los discapacitados.

disadvantage *noun* **1** desventaja *Fem.*; **2 to be at a disadvantage** estar en desventaja.

disagree *verb* **1 I disagree** no estoy de acuerdo; **I disagree with James** no estoy de acuerdo con James.

disappear *verb* desaparecer [35].

disappearance *noun* desaparición *Fem.*

disappointed *adjective* decepcionado/decepcionada; **I was disappointed with my marks** mis notas me decepcionaron.

disappointment *noun* decepción *Fem.*

disaster *noun* desastre *Masc.*; **it was a complete disaster** fue un completo desastre.

disastrous *adjective* desastroso/ desastrosa.

discipline *noun* disciplina *Fem.*

disc *noun* **1 a compact disc** un disco compacto; **2 a slipped disc** una hernia de disco.

discipline *noun* disciplina *Fem.*

disc-jockey *noun* disc-jockey *Masc./Fem.*

disco *noun* **1** baile *Masc.*; **they're having a disco** tienen un baile; **2** (*club*) discoteca *Fem.*

disconnect *verb* desconectar [17]; **have you disconnected the electricity?** ¿has desconectado la electricidad?

discount *noun* descuento *Masc.*

discourage verb **1** (depress) desanimar [17]; **2 to discourage somebody from doing** convencer a alguien de que no haga (note that 'que no' is followed by the subjunctive); **I tried to discourage her from buying it** intenté convencerla de que no lo comprase.

discover verb descubrir [46].

discovery noun descubrimiento Masc.

discreet adjective discreto/ discreta.

discrimination noun discriminación Fem.; **racial discrimination** discriminación racial.

discuss verb **1** (a subject or topic) hablar [17] de; **to discuss politics** hablar [17] de política; **I'm going to discuss it with Phil** voy a hablarlo con Phil; **2** (a problem or plan) discutir [19].

discussion noun discusión Fem.

disease noun enfermedad Fem.

disgraceful adjective vergonzoso/vergonzosa.

disguise noun disfraz Masc.; **to be in disguise** ir disfrazado.

disguise verb disfrazar [22]; **to disguise oneself as something** disfrazarse [22] de algo; **disguised as a woman** disfrazado de mujer.

disgust noun **1** (indignation) indignación Fem.; **2** (physical revulsion) asco Masc.

disgusted adjective **1** (indignant) indignado/indignada; **2** (physically sick) asqueado/ asqueada.

disgusting adjective asqueroso/ asquerosa.

dish noun **1** (plate or food) plato Masc.; **to do the dishes** lavar [17] los platos; **he cooked my favourite dish** cocinó mi plato favorito; **2** (serving dish) fuente Fem.; **a large white dish** una fuente grande blanca.

dishcloth noun (for drying up) paño Masc. de cocina.

dishonest adjective deshonesto/ deshonesta.

dishonesty noun falta Fem. de honradez.

dish towel noun paño Masc. de cocina.

dishwasher noun lavaplatos Masc. (does not change in the plural).

disinfect verb desinfectar [17].

disinfectant noun desinfectante Masc.

disk noun disco Masc.; **a floppy disk** un disquete; **the hard disk** el disco duro; **the disk drive** la disquetera.

diskette noun disquete Masc.

dislike verb **I dislike sport** no me gusta el deporte; **he dislikes my friends** no le gustan mis amigos.

dismay noun consternación Fem.

dismiss verb despedir [57] (an employee).

disobedient adjective desobediente.

disobey verb desobedecer [35]; **she disobeyed the rules** desobedeció el reglamento.

display noun **1** exposición Fem.; **a handicrafts display** una exposición de artesanía; **to be on display** estar expuesto; **2 a window display** un escaparate; **3 a firework display** fuegos Masc. plural artificiales.

display verb exponer [11].

disposable adjective desechable.

dispute noun **1** (quarrel) disputa Fem.; **2** (argument) polémica Fem.

disqualify verb descalificar [31].

dissolve verb disolver [45].

distance noun distancia Fem.; **from a distance** de lejos; **in the distance** a lo lejos; **it's within walking distance** se puede ir andando.

distant adjective distante.

distinct adjective claro/clara.

distinctly adverb **1** claramente; **2 it's distinctly odd** es realmente raro.

distract verb distraer [42].

distribute verb distribuir [54].

distribution noun distribución Fem.

district noun **1** (in town) barrio Masc.; **a poor district of Barcelona** un barrio pobre de Barcelona; **2** (in the country) región Fem.

disturb verb molestar [17]; **sorry to disturb you** perdona que te moleste; **do not disturb** se ruega no molestar.

ditch noun zanja Fem.

ditch verb **to ditch somebody** plantar [17] a alguien (informal).

dive noun zambullida Fem.

dive verb tirarse [17]; **to dive into the water** tirarse al agua.

diver noun (deep-sea) submarinista Masc./Fem.

diversion noun (for traffic) desvío Masc.

divide verb dividir [19].

diving noun **1** (from a board) saltos Masc. plural de trampolín; **2** (from the surface of the water) submarinismo Masc.

diving board noun trampolín Masc.

division noun división Fem.

divorce noun divorcio Masc.

divorce verb divorciarse [17]; **they divorced in Mexico** se divociaron en México.

divorced adjective divorciado/divorciada; **my parents are divorced** mis padres están divorciados.

DIY noun bricolaje Masc.; **to do DIY** hacer [7] bricolaje; **a DIY shop** una tienda de bricolaje.

dizzy adjective **to feel dizzy** estar [2] mareado/mareada; **I feel dizzy** estoy mareado.

DJ noun disc-jockey Masc./Fem.

do verb **1** hacer [7]; **what are you doing?** ¿qué estás haciendo?; **I'm doing my homework** estoy haciendo mis deberes; **what have you done with the hammer?** ¿qué has hecho con el martillo?; **2** (in questions, 'do' is not translated) **did Maria go to the party?** ¿fue María a la fiesta?; **do you want some strawberries?** ¿quieres fresas?; **when does it start?** ¿cuándo empieza?; **how did you open the door?** ¿cómo has abierto la puerta?; **3** (*in negative sentences*) (*the negative in Spanish is formed adding 'no' before the verb*) **I don't like this kind of music** no me gusta este tipo de música; **Rosie doesn't like spinach** a Rosie no le gustan las espinacas; **you didn't shut the door** no has cerrado la puerta; **it doesn't matter** no importa; **4** (*when it refers back to another verb, 'do' is not translated*) **'do you live here?' – 'yes, I do'** '¿vives aquí?' – 'sí'; **she has more money than I do** tiene más dinero que yo; **'I live in Oxford' – 'so do I'** 'vivo en Oxford' – 'yo también'; **'I didn't phone Gemma' – 'neither did I'** 'no he llamado a Gemma' – 'yo tampoco'; **5 don't you?, doesn't he?** etc. ¿no?; **you know Helen, don't you?** conoces a Helen, ¿no?; **she left on Thursday, didn't she?** se marchó el jueves , ¿no?; **6 that'll do** así basta; **it'll do** like that así vale.

● **do with 1** tener [9] que ver con; **it has nothing to do with him** no tiene nada que ver con él; **2 I could do with a rest** me vendría bien un descanso.

● **to do something up 1** atar [17] (*shoes*); **I did my shoes up** me até los zapatos; **2** abrochar [17] (*cardigan, jacket*); **do your jacket up** abróchate la chaqueta; **3** arreglar [17] (*house*).

● **to do without something** arreglarse [17] sin algo; **we can do**

without knives nos arreglaremos sin cuchillos.

doctor noun médico *Masc./Fem.*; **her mother's a doctor** su madre es médico.

document noun documento *Masc.*

documentary noun documental *Masc.*

dodgems plural noun the dodgems los cochecitos de choque.

dog noun perro *Masc.* perra *Fem.*.

do-it-yourself noun bricolage *Masc.*

dole noun paro *Masc.*; **to be on the dole** estar en el paro.

doll noun muñeca *Fem.*

dollar noun dólar *Masc.*

dolphin noun delfín *Masc.*

dominate verb dominar [17].

Dominican noun dominicano *Masc.*, dominicana *Fem.*

Dominican adjective dominicano/dominicana.

Dominican Republic noun República Dominicana *Fem.*

domino noun ficha *Fem.* de dominó; **to play dominoes** jugar al dominó.

donation noun donación *Fem.*

donkey noun burro *Masc.*

don't SEE do.

door noun puerta *Fem.*; **to open the door** abrir [46] la puerta; **to shut the door** cerrar [29] la puerta.

doorbell noun timbre *Masc.*; **to ring the doorbell** tocar [31] el timbre; **there's the doorbell** llaman a la puerta.

a b c d e f g h i j k l m n o p q r s t u v w x y z

doorstep noun umbral Masc. de la puerta.

dormitory noun dormitorio Masc.

dot noun 1 (written) punto Masc.; 2 (on fabric) lunar Masc.; 3 at ten on the dot a las diez en punto.

double adjective, adverb 1 doble; a double helping una ración doble; a double whisky un whisky doble; a double room una habitación doble; a double bed una cama de matrimonio; 2 el doble; double the time el doble de tiempo; double the price el doble del precio.

double bass noun contrabajo Masc.; to play the double bass tocar [31] el contrabajo.

double-breasted adjective a double-breasted jacket una chaqueta cruzada.

double-decker bus noun autobús Masc. de dos pisos.

double glazing noun doble ventana Fem.

doubles noun (in tennis) dobles Masc. plural; to play a game of doubles jugar un partido de dobles.

doubt noun duda Fem.; there's no doubt about it no hay ninguna duda al respecto; I have my doubts tengo mis dudas.

doubt verb to doubt something dudar [17] algo; I doubt it lo dudo; I doubt that dudo que (note that 'que' is followed by the subjunctive); I doubt they'll do it dudo que lo hagan.

doubtful adjective 1 it's doubtful that no es seguro que (note that 'que' is followed by the subjunctive); it's doubtful that she'll want to no es seguro que quiera; 2 to be doubtful about doing dudar [17] si hacer; I'm doubtful about inviting them together estoy dudando si invitarlos a los dos juntos.

dough noun masa Fem.

doughnut noun donut Masc.

down adverb, preposition 1 abajo; he's down in the cellar está abajo, en el sótano; 2 down the road (nearby) un poco más allá; there's a chemist's just down the road hay una farmacia un poco más allá; 3 to go down bajar [17]; I went down to the kitchen bajé a la cocina; to walk down the street bajar la calle; to run down the stairs bajar corriendo la escalera; 4 to come down bajar [17]; she came down from her bedroom bajó de la habitación; 5 to sit down sentarse [29]; she sat down on the sofa se sentó en el sofá.

downstairs adverb 1 abajo; she's downstairs in the sitting-room está abajo en el salón; the dog sleeps downstairs el perro duerme abajo; 2 (after a noun) de abajo; the flat downstairs el piso de abajo; the people downstairs la gente de abajo.

doze verb dormitar [17].

dozen noun docena Fem.; a dozen eggs una docena de huevos.

drag noun what a drag! ¡qué rollo! (informal); she's a bit of a drag es un poco pesada (informal).

drag verb arrastrar [17].

dragon noun dragón Masc.

drain noun 1 (plughole) desagüe Masc.; 2 (in street) alcantarilla Fem.

drain verb escurrir [19] (vegetables).

drama noun 1 (subject) arte Masc. dramático; 2 **he made a big drama about it** montó una escena por eso (informal).

dramatic adjective dramático/dramática.

draught noun corriente Fem. de aire.

draughts noun damas Fem. plural; **to play draughts** jugar a las damas.

draw noun 1 (in a match) empate Masc.; **it was a draw** fue un empate; 2 (lottery) sorteo Masc.

draw verb 1 dibujar [17]; **I can't draw horses** no sé dibujar caballos; **she can draw really well** dibuja muy bien; 2 **to draw a picture** hacer [7] un dibujo; 3 **to draw the curtains** correr [18] las cortinas; 4 **to draw a crowd** atraer [42] a una multitud; 5 (in a match) empatar [17]; **we drew three all** empatamos a tres; 6 **to draw lots for something** echar [17] algo a suertes.

drawback noun inconveniente Masc.

drawer noun cajón Masc.

drawing noun dibujo Masc.

drawing pin noun chincheta Fem.

dreadful adjective terrible.

dreadfully adverb 1 (to sing or act) espantosamente; 2 **I'm dreadfully late** llego tardísimo;

I'm dreadfully sorry lo siento muchísimo.

dream noun sueño Masc.; **to have a dream** tener [9] un sueño; **I had a horrible dream last night** tuve un sueño horrible anoche.

dream verb soñar [24]; **to dream about something** soñar con algo.

drenched adjective empapado/empapada; **to get drenched** empaparse [17]; **I got drenched on the way home** me empapé yendo a casa.

dress noun vestido Masc.

dress verb vestir [57]; **to dress a child** vestir a un niño.

● **to dress up** disfrazarse [22]; **to dress up as a vampire** disfrazarse de vampiro.

dressed adjective 1 vestido/vestida; **is Tom dressed?** ¿está Tom vestido?; **she was dressed in black trousers and a yellow shirt** iba vestida con unos pantalones negros y una blusa amarilla; 2 **to get dressed** vestirse [57].

dresser noun (for dishes) aparador Masc.

dressing gown noun bata Fem.

dressing table noun tocador Masc.

drier noun **a hair drier** un secador de pelo; **a tumble drier** una secadora.

drift noun **a snow drift** una ventisca de nieve.

drill noun 1 (tool) taladradora Fem.; 2 (in homework) ejercicio Masc.

drink noun 1 bebida Fem.; **a hot drink** una bebida caliente; **a cold**

a b c d e f g h i j k l m n o p q r s t u v w x y z

drink un refresco; **2 would you like a drink?** ¿te apetece beber algo?; **3 to go out for a drink** salir [63] a tomar una copa (*informal*).

drink *verb* beber [18]; **he drank a glass of water** bebió un vaso de agua.

drive *noun* **1 to go for a drive** ir [8] a dar una vuelta en coche; **2** (*up to a house*) entrada *Fem.* para coches.

drive *verb* **1** conducir [60]; **she drives very fast** conduce muy rápido; **to drive a car** conducir [60] un coche; **I'd like to learn to drive** me gustaría aprender a conducir; **can you drive?** ¿sabes conducir?; **2** ir [8] en coche; **we drove to Seville** fuimos en coche a Sevilla; **3 to drive somebody (to a place)** llevar [17] en coche a alguien (a un sitio); **Mum drove me to the station** mamá me llevó en coche a la estación; **to drive somebody home** llevar [17] a alguien a casa en coche; ★ **she drives me mad!** ¡me saca de quicio!

driver *noun* **1** (*of a car, taxi or bus*) conductor *Masc.*, conductora *Fem.*; **2** (*of a racing car*) piloto *Masc./Fem.*

driving instructor *noun* instructor *Masc.* de autoescuela, instructora *Fem.* de autoescuela.

driving lesson *noun* clase *Fem.* de conducir.

driving licence *noun* permiso *Masc.* de conducir.

driving school *noun* autoescuela *Fem.*

driving test *noun* examen *Masc.* de conducir; **to take your driving test** presentarse [17] al examen de

conducir; **Jenny's passed her driving test** Jenny ha aprobado el examen de conducir.

drop *noun* gota *Fem.*

drop *verb* **1 I dropped my glasses** se me cayeron las gafas; **careful, don't drop it!** ¡cuidado, que no se te caiga!; **2** (*a course, subject or topic*) dejar [17]; **I'm going to drop history next year** voy a dejar la historia el próximo año; **3** dejar [17] (*a person*); **could you drop me at the station?** ¿me podrías dejar en la estación?; **4 drop it!** ¡déjalo ya!

drought *noun* sequía *Fem.*

drown *verb* ahogarse [28]; **she drowned in the lake** se ahogó en el lago.

drug *noun* **1** (*medicine*) medicina *Fem.*; **2** (*illegal*) **drugs** las drogas; **to be on drugs** drogarse [28].

drug abuse *noun* consumo *Masc.* de drogas.

drug addict *noun* drogadicto *Masc.*, drogadicta *Fem.*

drug addiction *noun* drogadicción *Fem.*

drum *noun* **1** tambor *Masc.*; **2 drums** batería *Fem.*; **to play drums** tocar [31] la batería.

drum kit *noun* batería *Fem.*

drummer *noun* batería *Masc./Fem.*

drunk *noun* borracho *Masc.*, borracha *Fem.*

drunk *adjective* borracho/borracha.

dry *adjective* seco/seca.

dry *verb* **1** secar [31]; **to dry the dishes** secar los platos; **2 to let**

something dry dejar que algo se seque; **it took ages to dry** tardó muchísimo en secarse; **3 to dry oneself** secarse [31]; **to dry your hair** secarse [31] el pelo; **I'm going to dry my hair** me voy a secar el pelo.

dry cleaner's noun tintorería Fem.

dryer noun SEE **drier.**

dual carriageway noun autovía Fem.

dubbed adjective **a dubbed film** una película doblada.

duck noun pato Masc., pata Fem.

due adjective, adverb **1 to be due to do** tener [9] que hacer; **we're due to leave on Thursday** tenemos que salir el jueves; **Paul's due back soon** Paul tiene que volver pronto; **2 what time is the train due?** ¿cuándo llega el próximo tren?; **3 due to** debido a; **the match has been cancelled due to bad weather** el partido ha sido cancelado debido al mal tiempo.

duke noun duque Masc.

dull adjective **1 dull weather** tiempo gris; **it's a dull day today** hoy hace un día muy gris; **2** (boring) aburrido/aburrida.

dumb adjective **1** mudo/muda; **to be deaf and dumb** ser sordomudo/sordomuda; **2** (stupid) tonto/tonta; **he asked some dumb questions** hizo unas preguntas muy tontas.

dummy noun (for a baby) chupete Masc.

dump verb **1** tirar [17] (rubbish); **2** plantar [17] (a person) (informal); **she's dumped her boyfriend** ha plantado a su novio.

dune noun duna Fem.

dungarees plural noun pantalón Masc. de peto.

dungeon noun mazmorra Fem.

during preposition durante; **during the night** durante la noche; **I saw her during the holidays** la vi durante las vacaciones.

dusk noun anochecer Masc.; **at dusk** al anochecer.

dust noun polvo Masc.

dust verb quitar [17] el polvo; **to dust the table** quitarle el polvo a la mesa.

dustbin noun cubo Masc. de la basura; **to put something in the dustbin** tirar [17] algo al cubo de la basura.

dustman noun basurero Masc.

dusty adjective cubierto/cubierta de polvo.

Dutch noun **1** (language) holandés Masc.; **2 the Dutch** (people) los holandeses.

Dutch adjective holandés/holandesa.

duty noun **1** deber Masc.; **to have a duty to do** tener [9] el deber de hacer; **you have a duty to inform us** tienes el deber de informarnos; **2 to be on duty** (a nurse or doctor) estar [2] de guardia (a policeman) estar [2] de servicio; **to be on night duty** tener [9] el turno de noche.

duty-free adjective libre de impuestos; **the duty-free shops**

a b c d e f g h i j k l m n o p q r s t u v w x y z

las tiendas libres de impuestos; **duty-free purchases** artículos libres de impuestos.

duvet noun edredón Masc.

duvet cover noun funda Fem. de edredón.

dwarf noun enano Masc., enana Fem.

dye noun tinte Masc.

dye verb teñir [65]; **to dye your hair** teñirse [65] el pelo; **I'm going to dye my hair pink** me voy a teñir el pelo de rosa.

dynamic adjective dinámico/dinámica.

dyslexia noun dislexia Fem.

dyslexic adjective disléxico/disléxica.

Ee

each adjective cada; **each time** cada vez; **curtains for each window** cortinas para cada ventana.

each pronoun cada uno/una; **my sisters each have a computer** mis hermanas tienen un ordenador cada una; **she gave us an apple each** nos dio una manzana a cada uno; **each of you** cada uno de vosotros; **we each bought a book** cada uno de nosotros compró un libro; **the tickets cost ten pounds each** las entradas cuestan diez libras cada una.

each other pronoun ('each other' is usually translated using a

reflexive pronoun) **they love each other** se quieren; **we know each other** nos conocemos; **do you often see each other?** ¿os veis a menudo?

eagle noun águila Fem. (even though 'águila' is feminine, it takes 'el' and 'un' in the singular).

ear noun oreja Fem.

earache noun to have earache tener dolor de oídos.

earlier adverb 1 (a while ago) hace un rato; **your brother called earlier** tu hermano llamó hace un rato; 2 (not as late) más temprano; **we should have started earlier** deberíamos haber empezado más temprano; **earlier in the morning** por la mañana temprano.

early adverb 1 (in the morning) temprano; **I get up early** me levanto temprano; **it's too early** es demasiado temprano; 2 (for an appointment) pronto; **we're early, the train doesn't leave until ten** hemos llegado pronto, el tren no sale hasta las diez; **Grandma likes to be early** a la abuela le gusta llegar pronto.

early adjective 1 (one of the first) primero/primera; **in the early months** en los primeros meses; 2 **to have an early lunch** comer temprano; **Jan's having an early night** Jan se ha acostado temprano; **we're making an early start** vamos a salir temprano; 3 **in the early afternoon** a primera hora de la tarde; **in the early hours** de madrugada.

earn *verb* ganar [17] (*money*); **Richard earns four pounds an hour** Richard gana cuatro libras por hora.

earnings *plural noun* ingresos *Masc. plural*.

earphones *plural noun* auriculares *Masc. plural*.

earring *noun* pendiente *Masc.*

earth *noun* tierra *Fem.*; **life on earth** la vida en la tierra; ★ **what on earth are you doing?** ¿qué demonios estás haciendo?.

earthquake *noun* terremoto *Masc.*

easily *adverb* **1** (*to do something*) con facilidad; **2** (*by far*) con mucho; **he's easily the best** es con mucho el mejor.

east *noun* este *Masc.*; **in the east** en el este.

east *adjective, adverb* **the east side** el lado este; **an east wind** un viento del este; **east of Seville** al este de Sevilla.

Easter *noun* Semana *Fem.* Santa; **they're coming at Easter** vienen en Semana Santa.

Easter Day *noun* Domingo *Masc.* de Pascua.

Easter egg *noun* huevo *Masc.* de Pascua.

Eastern Europe *noun* Europa *Fem.* del Este.

easy *adjective* fácil; **it's easy!** ¡es fácil!; **it was easy to decide** fue fácil decidir.

eat *verb* **1** comer [18]; **he was eating a banana** estaba comiendo un plátano; **we're going to have**

something to eat vamos a comer algo; **2** tomar [17] (*a meal*); **we were eating breakfast** estábamos tomando el desayuno; **3 to eat out** comer [18] fuera.

EC *noun* CE *Fem.*, Comunidad *Fem.* Europea.

echo *noun* eco *Masc.*

echo *verb* hacer [7] eco.

eclipse *noun* eclipse *Masc.*

ecological *adjective* ecológico/ecológica.

ecologist *noun* ecologista *Masc.*, ecologista *Fem.*

ecology *noun* ecología *Fem.*

economic *adjective* **1** (*relating to economics*) económoco/económica; **2** (*profitable*) rentable.

economical *adjective* económico/económica (*way of doing something*); **it's more economical to buy a big one** sale más económico comprar uno grande.

economics *noun* economía *Fem.*

economy *noun* economía *Fem.*

Ecuador *noun* Ecuador *Masc.*

Ecuadorian *noun* ecuatoriano *Masc.*, ecuatoriana *Fem.*

Ecuadorian *adjectiv* ecuatoriano/ecuatoriana.

eczema *noun* eczema *Masc.*

edge *noun* **1** (*of table, plate, or cliff*) borde *Masc.*; **the edge of the table** el borde de la mesa; **2** (*of river or lake*) orilla *Fem.*; **at the edge of the lake** en la orilla del lago; **3 to be on edge** estar nervioso.

edible *adjective* comestible.

Edinburgh *noun* Edimburgo *Masc.*

a
b
c
d
e
f
g
h
i
j
k
l
m
n
o
p
q
r
s
t
u
v
w
x
y
z

edit *verb* editar [17].

editor *noun* (*of a newspaper*) redactor *Masc.*, redactora *Fem.*

educate *verb* (*a teacher*) educar [31].

education *noun* educación *Fem.*

educational *adjective* educativo/educativa.

effect *noun* efecto *Masc.*; **the effect of the accident** el efecto del accidente; **to have an effect on** afectar [17] a; **it had a good effect on the whole family** afectó positivamente a toda la familia; **special effects** efectos especiales.

effective *adjective* eficaz.

efficient *adjective* eficiente.

effort *noun* esfuerzo *Masc.*; **to make an effort** hacer [7] un esfuerzo; **Jess made an effort to help us** Jess hizo un esfuerzo para ayudarnos; **he didn't even make the effort to apologize** mi sí quiera se molestó en disculparse; **it's not worth the effort** no merece la pena.

e.g. *abbreviation* p.ej.

egg *noun* huevo *Masc.*; **a dozen eggs** una docena de huevos; **a fried egg** un huevo frito; **two boiled eggs** dos huevos pasados por agua; **a hard-boiled egg** un huevo duro; **scrambled eggs** huevos revueltos.

egg-cup *noun* huevera *Fem.*

eggshell *noun* cáscara *Fem.* de huevo.

egg-white *noun* clara *Fem.* de huevo.

egg-yolk *noun* yema *Fem.* de huevo.

eight *number* ocho *Masc.*; **Rosie's eight** Rosie tiene ocho años; **it's eight o'clock** son las ocho.

eighteen *number* dieciocho; **Kate's eighteen** Kate tiene dieciocho años.

eighth *noun* 1 (*fraction*) an eighth una octava parte; 2 **the eighth of July** el ocho de julio.

eighth *adjective* octavo/octava; **on the eighth floor** en la octava planta.

eighties *plural noun* **the eighties** los años ochenta; **in the eighties** en los años ochenta.

eighty *number* ochenta *Masc.*; **she's eighty** tiene ochenta años; **eighty-five** ochenta y cinco.

Eire *noun* Irlanda *Masc./Fem.*

either *pronoun* 1 (*one or the other*) choose either (of them) elige cualquiera (de los dos); **I don't like either (of them)** no me gusta ninguno (de los dos); 2 (*both*) **either is possible** las dos cosas son posibles.

either *conjunction* 1 either ... or o ... o; **you either pay or return it** o pagas o lo devuelves; **I'll phone either Thursday or Friday** llamaré o el jueves o el viernes ('o' becomes 'u' before a word starting with 'o' or 'ho') **either one or the other** o uno u otro; 2 (*with a negative*) **he doesn't want to go either** él tampoco quiere ir; **I don't know them either** yo tampoco los conozco.

elastic *noun* elástico *Masc.*

elastic *adjective* elástico/elástica.

elastic band *noun* goma *Fem.* elástica.

elbow *noun* codo *Masc.*

elder *adjective* mayor; **her elder brother** su hermano mayor.

elderly *adjective* **an elderly man** un anciano; **an elderly woman** una anciana; **an elderly couple** una pareja de ancianos; **the elderly** los ancianos.

eldest *adjective* mayor; **her eldest brother** su hermano mayor.

elect *verb* elegir [48]; **she has been elected** ha sido elegida.

election *noun* elecciones *Fem. plural*; **in the election** en las elecciones; **to call a general election** convocar [31] elecciones generales.

electric *adjective* eléctrico/eléctrica.

electrical *adjective* eléctrico/eléctrica.

electrician *noun* electricista *Masc./Fem.*

electricity *noun* electricidad *Fem.*; **to turn off the electricity** desconectar [17] la corriente.

electronic *adjective* electrónico/electrónica.

electronic mail *noun* correo *Masc.* electrónico.

electronics *noun* electrónica *Fem.*

elegant *adjective* elegante.

element *noun* elemento *Masc.*

elephant *noun* elefante *Masc.*

eleven *number* once *Masc.*; **Josh is eleven** Josh tiene once años; **it's eleven o'clock** son las once.

eleventh *noun* **the eleventh of May** el once de mayo.

eleventh *adjective* onceavo/onceava; **on the eleventh floor** en la onceava planta.

eliminate *verb* eliminar [17].

else *adverb* **1** (*in questions and negative sentences*) más; **who else?** ¿quién más?; **what else?** ¿qué más?; **nothing else** nada más; **I don't want anything else** no quiero nada más; **2 somebody else** otra persona; **somebody else must have done it** lo ha debido hacer otra persona; **3 something else** otra cosa; **would you like something else?** ¿quieres otra cosa?; **4 everybody else** todos los demás; **everything else** todo lo demás; **5 somewhere else** en otra parte; **6 or else** si no; **hurry up, or else we'll be late** date prisa, que si no vamos a llegar tarde.

e-mail *noun* correo *Masc.* electrónico.

embankment *noun* **1** (*by a river*) muro *Masc.* de contención; **2** (*by a railway*) terraplén *Masc.*

embarrassed *adjective* **I was terribly embarrassed** me daba mucha vergüenza; **she feels a bit embarrassed** le da un poco de vergüenza.

embarrassing *adjective* violento/violenta (*situation or silence*); **how embarrassing!** ¡qué vergüenza!

a b c d e f g h i j k l m n o p q r s t u v w x y z

a

b

c

d

e

f

g

h

i

j

k

l

m

n

o

p

q

r

s

t

u

v

w

x

y

z

embarrassment noun vergüenza Fem.

embassy noun embajada Fem.; **the Spanish Embassy** la embajada española.

embroider verb bordar [17].

embroidery noun bordado Masc.

emergency noun 1 emergencia Fem.; **in an emergency, break the glass** en caso de emergencia, rompa el cristal; **it's an emergency!** ¡es una emergencia!; 2 (medical) urgencia Fem.; **an emergency operation** una operación de urgencia.

emergency exit noun salida Fem. de emergencia.

emergency landing noun aterrizaje Masc. forzoso.

emotion noun emoción Fem.

emotional adjective 1 (person) to **be emotional** estar [2] emocionado/emocionada; **to get emotional** emocionarse [17]; **she got quite emotional** se emocionó mucho; 2 (a speech or an occasion) emotivo/emotiva.

emperor noun emperador Masc.

emphasis noun énfasis Masc.

emphasize verb recalcar [31]; **he emphasized that it wasn't compulsory** recalcó que no era obligatorio.

empire noun imperio Masc.; **the Roman Empire** el imperio romano.

employ verb 1 (have in employment) emplear [17]; 2 (give work to) dar [4] un trabajo a.

employee noun empleado Masc., empleada Fem.

employer noun patrón Masc., patrona Fem.

employment noun empleo Masc.

empress noun emperatriz Fem.

empty adjective vacío/vacía; **an empty bottle** una botella vacía; **the room was empty** la habitación estaba vacía.

empty verb vaciar [32]; **I emptied the teapot into the sink** vacié la tetera en el fregadero.

enchanting adjective encantador/encantadora.

enclose verb (in a letter) adjuntar [17]; **please find enclosed a cheque** se adjunta un cheque.

encore noun bis Masc.; **encore!** ¡otra!

encourage verb animar [17]; **to encourage somebody to do** animar a alguien a hacer; **Mum encouraged me to try again** mamá me animó a intentarlo otra vez.

encouragement noun ánimo Masc.

encouraging adjective alentador/alentadora.

encyclopedia noun enciclopedia Fem.

end noun 1 (last part) final Masc.; **at the end of the film** al final de la película; **by the end of the day** al final del día; **in the end I went home** al final me fui a casa; 2 **at the end of the year** a finales de año; **Sally's coming at the end of June** Sally viene a finales de junio;

3 'The End' (*in a book or film*) 'Fin'; **4** (*of a table, garden, or stick, for example*) Masc.; **hold the other end** sujeta el otro extremo; **5** (*of a street or road*) final Masc.; **at the end of the street** al final de la calle; **6** (*of a football pitch*) lado Masc.; **to change ends** cambiar [17] de lado.

end verb **1** (*put an end to*) poner [11] fin a (*an arrangement*); **they've ended the strike** han puesto fin a la huelga; **2** (*to come to an end*) terminar [17]; **the day ended with a dinner** el día terminó con una cena.

● **to end up** terminar [17]; **we ended up taking a taxi** terminamos cogiendo un taxi; **Ross ended up in San Francisco** Ross terminó en San Francisco.

endangered adjective en peligro; **an endangered species** una especie en en vías de extinción.

ending noun final Masc.

endless adjective interminable.

enemy noun enemigo Masc., enemiga Fem.; **to make enemies** hacer [7] enemigos.

energetic adjective energético/ energética.

energy noun energía Fem.

engaged adjective **1** (*to be married*) prometido/prometida; **they're engaged** están prometidos; **to get engaged** prometerse [18]; **2** (*a phone*) comunicando; **it's engaged, I'll ring later** está comunicando,

llamaré más tarde; **3** (*a toilet*) ocupado/ocupada.

engagement noun (*to marry*) compromiso Masc.

engagement ring noun anillo Masc. de compromiso.

engine noun **1** (*in a car*) motor Masc.; **2** (*locomotive*) locomotora Fem.

engineer noun **1** (*who does repairs*) técnico Masc./Fem.; **2** (*who builds roads and bridges*) ingeniero Masc., ingeniera Fem..

England noun Inglaterra Fem.; **I'm from England** soy inglés.

English noun **1** (*the language*) inglés Masc.; **do you speak English?** ¿hablas inglés?; **he answered in English** contestó en inglés; **2** (*English people*) the **English** los ingleses.

English adjective **1** (*of or from England*) inglés/inglesa; **the English team** el equipo inglés; **2 an English lesson** una clase de inglés; **our English teacher** nuestro profesor de inglés.

English Channel noun the **English Channel** el Canal de la Mancha.

Englishman noun inglés Masc.

Englishwoman noun inglesa Fem.

enjoy verb **1** disfrutar [17]; **did you enjoy the party?** ¿disfrutaste de la fiesta?; **we really enjoyed the concert** disfrutamos mucho del concierto; **2 I enjoy swimming** me gusta nadar; **do you enjoy living in York?** ¿te gusta vivir en York?; **3 to**

a

enjoy youself divertirse [14]; **we really enjoyed ourselves** nos divertimos muchísimo; **did you enjoy yourself?** ¿te divertiste?.

b

c

enjoyable *adjective* agradable.

d

enlarge *verb* ampliar [32].

enlargement *noun* (*of a photo*) ampliación *Fem*.

e

f

enormous *adjective* enorme.

g

enough *adverb, pronoun*

h

1 suficiente; **there's enough for everyone** hay suficiente para todos; **is there enough bread?** ¿hay pan suficiente?; **there weren't enough books** no había libros suficientes; **2** (*with an adjective or adverb*) lo suficientemente; **big enough** lo suficientemente grande; **slowly enough** lo suficientemente despacio; **3** **that's enough** ya basta.

i

j

k

l

m

n

o

enquire *verb* informarse [17]; **I'm going to enquire about the trains** voy a informarme sobre los trenes.

p

q

enquiry *noun* **to make enquiries about something** pedir [57] información sobre algo.

r

enrol *verb* matricularse [17]; **I want to enrol on the course** quiero matricularme en el curso.

s

t

u

enter *verb* **1** (*go inside*) entrar [17] en (*a room or building*); **we all entered the church** todos entramos en la iglesia; **2 to enter for** presentarse [17] a (*an exam*); tomar [17] parte en (*a race or competition*).

v

w

x

y

entertain *verb* **1** (*keep amused*) entretener [9]; **something to**

z

entertain the children algo para entretener a los niños; **2** (*have people round*) invitar [17] a gente; **they don't entertain much** no invitan a mucha gente.

entertaining *noun* **they do a lot of entertaining** invitan a mucha gente.

entertaining *adjective* entretenido/entretenida.

entertainment *noun* (*fun*) entretenimiento *Masc*.; **there wasn't much entertainment in the evenings** por las noches no había mucho entretenimiento.

enthusiasm *noun* entusiasmo *Masc*.

enthusiast *noun* **to be a rugby enthusiast** ser [1] un apasionado/ una apasionada del rugby.

enthusiastic *adjective* entusiasta.

entire *adjective* entero/entera; **the entire class** la clase entera.

entirely *adverb* completamente.

entrance *noun* entrada *Fem*.

entry *noun* (*the way in*) entrada *Fem*.; **'no entry'** 'prohibida la entrada'.

entry phone *noun* portero *Masc*. automático.

envelope *noun* sobre *Masc*.

envious *adjective* envidioso/ envidiosa; **he's envious of my exam results** tiene envidia de las notas de mis exámenes.

environment *noun* medio *Masc*. ambiente.

environmental *adjective* medioambiental.

environment-friendly
adjective ecológico/ecológica.

envy *noun* envidia Fem.

epidemic *noun* epidemia Fem.

epileptic *noun* epiléptico Masc.,
epiléptica Fem.

episode *noun* episodio Masc.

equal *adjective* igual; **in equal
quantities** en cantidades iguales.

equal *verb* ser [1] igual a.

equalize *verb* empatar [17]; **they
equalized in the last minute**
empataron en el último minuto.

equally *adjective* (*to share*) en
partes iguales; **we divided it
equally** lo dividimos en partes
iguales.

equality *noun* igualdad Fem.

equator *noun* ecuador Masc.

equip *verb* equipar [17]; **well
equipped for the walk** bien
equipado para la marcha.

equipment *noun* **1** (*for sport*)
artículos Masc. plural deportivos;
2 (*in office or lab*) material Masc.

equivalent *adjective* **to be
equivalent to** ser [1] equivalente a.

error *noun* **1** (*in spelling or typing*)
falta Fem.; **a spelling error** una
falta de ortografía; **2** (*in maths or
on a computer*) error Masc.

escalator *noun* escalera Fem.
mecánica.

escape *noun* (*from prison*) fuga
Fem.

escape *verb* **1** (*a person*) fugarse
[28]; **2** (*an animal*) escaparse [17].

escort *noun* escolta Fem.; **a police
escort** una escolta policial.

especially *adjective*
especialmente.

essay *noun* redacción Fem.; **an
essay on pollution** una redacción
sobre la contaminación.

essential *adjective* esencial; **it's
essential to reply quickly** es
esencial responder rápidamente.

estate *noun* **1** (*a housing estate*)
urbanización Fem.; **2** (*a big house
and grounds*) propiedad Fem.

estate agent's *noun* agencia
Fem. inmobiliaria.

estate car *noun* coche Masc.
ranchera.

estimate *noun* **1** (*a quote for
work*) presupuesto Masc.; **2** (*a
rough guess*) cálculo Masc.
aproximado.

estimate *verb* **1** calcular [17];
2 the estimated time of arrival la
hora prevista de llegada.

etc. *abbreviation* etc.

ethnic *adjective* étnico/étnica; **an
ethnic minority** una minoría
étnica.

EU *abbreviation* EU Fem., Unión
Fem. Europea.

euro *noun* euro Masc.; **the euro is
divided into a hundred cents** el
euro se divide en cien céntimos.

Europe *noun* Europa Fem.

European *noun* europeo Masc.,
europea Fem.

European *adjective* europeo/
europea.

European Union *noun* Unión
Fem. Europea.

eurozone *noun* eurozona Fem.

evaporate *verb* evaporarse [17].

a b c d e f g h i j k l m n o p q r s t u v w x y z

a

b

c

d

e

f

g

h

i

j

k

l

m

n

o

p

q

r

s

t

u

v

w

x

y

z

eve noun **Christmas Eve** Nochebuena Fem.; **New Year's Eve** Nochevieja Fem..

even[1] adverb **1** incluso; **even I could do it** incluso yo podría hacerlo; **2** (in comparisons) **even more difficult** aún más difícil; **even faster** aún más rápido; **even more than** aún más que; **I liked the song even more than their last one** la canción me gustó aún más que la anterior; **3** (in negative sentences or after 'without') ni siquiera; **even Lisa didn't like it** ni siquiera a Lisa le gustó; **without even asking** sin ni siquiera preguntar; **not even** ni siquiera; **I don't like animals, not even dogs** no me gustan los animales, ni siquiera los perros; **4 even if** incluso si; **even if they arrive** incluso si llegan; **5 even so** aun así; **even so, we had a good time** aun así lo pasamos bien; **6 even though** aunque.

even[2] adjective **1** (a surface or layer) plano/plana; **2** (a number) par; **six is an even number** seis es un número par; **3** (with the same score) igualado/igualada; **Lee and Tony are even** Lee y Tony están igualados.

evening noun **1** (before dark) tarde Fem. (after dark) noche Fem.; **this evening** (before dark) esta tarde (after dark) esta noche; **at six o'clock in the evening** a las seis de la tarde; **at ten in the evening** a las diez de la noche; **tomorrow evening** mañana por la tarde, mañana por la noche; **on Thursday evening** el jueves por la tarde, el jueves por la noche; **the evening before** la tarde anterior, la noche anterior; **every evening** cada tarde, cada noche; **good evening** buenas tardes, buenas noches; **I work in the evening(s)** trabajo por las noches; **2 the evening meal** la cena; **3** (event) velada Fem.; **an evening with Pavarotti** una velada con Pavarotti.

evening class noun clase Fem. nocturna.

event noun **1** (a happening) acontecimiento Masc.; **2** (in athletics) prueba Fem.; **track events** pruebas de atletismo.

eventful adjective lleno de incidentes.

eventually adverb finalmente.

ever adverb **1** (at any time) alguna vez; **have you ever been to Spain?** ¿has estado alguna vez en España?; **have you ever noticed that?** ¿lo notaste alguna vez?; **hardly ever** casi nunca; **no-one ever came** nunca vino nadie; **more slowly than ever** más despacio que nunca; **2** (always) siempre; **as cheerful as ever** tan contento como siempre; **the same as ever** como siempre; **3 ever since** desde entonces; **and it's been raining ever since** y ha estado lloviendo desde entonces.

every adjective **1** todos/todas; **have you ever been to Spain?** todas las casas tienen jardín; **every day** todos los días; **every Monday** todos los lunes; **I've seen every one of his films** he visto todas sus películas; **2** (repetition) cada; **every**

ten kilometres cada diez
kilómetros; **every time** cada vez;
3 every now and then de vez en
cuando; **every second day** un día
sí y otro no.

everybody, everyone *pronoun*
todo el mundo; **everybody knows
that ...** todo el mundo sabe que ...;
everyone else todos los demás.

everything *pronoun* todo;
everything's ready está todo listo;
everything's fine está todo bien;
everything else todo lo demás;
everything you said todo lo que
dijiste.

everywhere *adverb* **there was
mud everywhere** había barro por
todas partes; **everywhere she
went** a todos los sitios a que fue;
everywhere else is closed todos
los demás sitios están cerrados.

evidently *adverb* obviamente.

evil *noun* mal *Masc.*

evil *adjective* malvado/malvada.

exact *adjective* exacto/exacta; **the
exact amount** la cantidad exacta;
it's the exact opposite es
exactamente lo contrario.

exactly *adverb* exactamente;
they're exactly the same age
tienen exactamente la misma
edad; **yes, exactly** exacto.

exaggerate *verb* exagerar [17].

exaggeration *noun* exageración
Fem.

exam *noun* examen *Masc.*; **a
history exam** un examen de
historia; **to sit an exam**
presentarse [17] a un examen; **to
pass an exam** aprobar [24] un

examen; **to fail an exam**
suspender [18] un examen.

examination *noun* examen *Masc.*

examine *verb* examinar [17].

examiner *noun* examinador
Masc., examinadora *Fem.*

example *noun* ejemplo *Masc.*; **for
example** por ejemplo; **to set a
good example** dar [4] buen
ejemplo.

excellent *adjective* excelente.

except *preposition* excepto;
except in March excepto en
marzo; **except Tuesdays** excepto
los martes; **except when it rains**
excepto cuando llueve.

exception *noun* excepción *Fem.*;
without exception sin excepción;
with the exception of con la
excepción de.

exchange *noun* **1** (*of information
or students*) intercambio *Masc.*; **an
exchange visit** un viaje de
intercambio; **2 in exchange for**
his help a cambio de su ayuda.

exchange *verb* cambiar [17]; **can
I exchange this shirt for a smaller
one?** ¿puedo cambiar esta camisa
por una más pequeña?

exchange rate *noun* tipo *Masc.*
de cambio.

excited *adjective* **1** (*happy*)
entusiasmado/entusiasmada;
**they're really excited about the
idea** están entusiasmados con la
idea; **2** (*noisy, boisterous*)
alborotado/alborotada; **the
children were too excited** los
niños estaban demasiado
alborotados; **3 to get excited**

a b c d e f g h i j k l m n o p q r s t u v w x y z

(*happy*) entusiasmarse [17]; (*boisterous*) alborotarse [17]; **the dogs get excited when they hear the car** los perros se alborotan cuando oyen el coche.

excitement noun emoción Fem.

exciting adjective emocionante; **a really exciting film** una película realmente emocionante.

exclamation mark noun signo Masc. de admiración.

excursion noun excursión Fem.

excuse noun excusa Fem.; **Gary has a good excuse** Gary tiene una buena excusa; **that's no excuse** eso no es excusa; **to make excuses** poner [11] excusas.

excuse verb (*apologizing*) **excuse me!** ¡perdón!

exercise noun ejercicio Masc.; **a maths exercise** un ejercicio de matemáticas; **physical exercise** ejercicio físico.

exercise book noun cuaderno Masc.; **my Spanish exercise book** mi cuaderno de español.

exhausted adjective agotado/agotada.

exhaust fumes noun gases Masc. plural del tubo de escape.

exhaust (pipe) noun tubo Masc. de escape.

exhibition noun exposición Fem.; **the Cézanne exhibition** la exposición de Cézanne.

exist verb existir [19].

exit noun salida Fem.

expect verb **1** esperar [17] (*guests or a baby*); **we're expecting about thirty people** esperamos unas

treinta personas; **2** esperarse [17] (*something to happen*); **I didn't expect that** no me esperaba eso; **I didn't expect it at all** no me lo esperaba en absoluto; **3** (*to suppose*) suponer [11]; **I expect you're tired** supongo que estarás cansado; **I expect she'll bring her boyfriend** supongo que traerá a su novio; **yes, I expect so** supongo que sí.

expedition noun expedición Fem.

expel verb **to be expelled** (*from school*) ser [1] expulsado.

expenses noun gastos Masc. plural.

expensive adjective caro/cara; **those shoes are too expensive for me** esos zapatos son demasiado caros para mí; **the most expensive hotels** los hoteles más caros.

experience noun experiencia Fem.

experienced adjective con experiencia.

experiment noun experimento Masc.; **to do an experiment** hacer [7] un experimento.

expert noun experto Masc., experta Fem.; **he's a computer expert** es un experto en ordenadores.

expire verb caducar [31].

expiry date noun fecha Fem. de caducidad.

explain verb explicar [31].

explanation noun explicación Fem.

explode *verb* explotar [17].

explore *verb* explorar [17].

explosion *noun* explosión Fem.

export *verb* exportar [17].

export *noun* exportación Fem.; **wool is the most important export** el artículo de exportación más importante es la lana.

export *verb* exportar [17]; **Russia exports a lot of timber and oil** Rusia exporta mucha madera y petróleo.

exposure *noun* (*of a film*) exposición Fem.; **a 24-exposure film** un carrete de veinticuatro fotos.

express *noun* (*a train*) rápido Masc.

express *verb* **1** expresar [17]; **2 to express yourself** expresarse [17].

expression *noun* expresión Fem.

extend *verb* ampliar [32] (*a building*).

extension *noun* **1** (*to a house*) ampliación Fem.; **2** (*telephone*) extensión Fem.; **can I have extension 2347 please?** ¿me puede poner con la extensión veintitrés cuarenta y siete, por favor? (*note that in spoken Spanish telephone numbers are usually said in pairs; this also applies to long numbers*).

extension lead *noun* alargador Masc.

extension number *noun* número Masc. de extensión.

extinct *adjective* extinto/ extincta; **to become extinct** extinguirse [50].

extinguish *verb* apagar [28].

extinguisher *noun* (*fire extinguisher*) extintor Masc.

extra *adjective, adverb* **1 they gave us some extra homework** nos dieron más deberes; **2 you have to pay extra** tiene que pagar un suplemento; **to charge extra for something** cobrar [17] un suplemento por algo; **wine is extra** el vino se cobra aparte; **at no extra charge** sin coste suplementario; **3 extra hot** super picante; **extra large** super grande.

extraordinary *adjective* extraordinario/extraordinaria.

extra-special *adjective* super especial.

extra time *noun* (*in football*) prórroga Fem.

extravagant *adjective* derrochador/derrochadora (*a person*).

extreme *noun* extremo Masc.; **to go to extremes** llevar [17] las cosas al extremo.

extreme *adjective* extremo/ extrema.

extremely *adverb* **extremely difficult** dificilísimo; **extremely fast** rapidísimo.

eye *noun* ojo Masc.; **a girl with blue eyes** una niña con ojos azules; **shut your eyes!** ¡cierra los ojos!; ★ **to keep an eye on something** vigilar [17] algo; ★ **to make eyes at somebody** hacerle [7] ojitos a alguien (*informal*).

eyebrow *noun* ceja Fem.

a b c d e f g h i j k l m n o p q r s t u v w x y z

eyelash noun pestaña Fem.

eyelid noun párpado Masc.

eyeliner noun delineador Masc. de ojos.

eye make-up noun maquillaje Masc. de ojos.

eye shadow noun sombra Fem. de ojos.

eyesight noun vista Fem.

Ff

fabric noun tela Fem.

fabulous adjective fabuloso/fabulosa.

face noun 1 (of a person) cara Fem.; **on your face** en la cara; **2 to pull a face** hacer [7] muecas; **3** (of a clock or watch) esfera Fem.

face verb 1 (a person) enfrentarse [17] a; **2** (to be opposite) estar [2] frente a; **the hotel faces the sea** el hotel está frente al mar; **3 it faces south** está orientado hacia el sur; **4 I can't face going back** no soporto la idea de volver.

face cloth noun toalla Fem. de cara.

facilities plural noun 1 **sports facilities** instalaciones Fem. plural deportivas; **2 the flat has cooking facilities** el piso tiene cocina.

fact noun hecho Masc.; **in fact** de hecho; **is that a fact?** ¿es eso cierto?

factory noun fábrica Fem.

fail verb 1 (a test or exam) suspender [18]; **I failed my driving test** he

suspendido el examen de conducir; **three students failed** tres estudiantes suspendieron; **2 to fail to do** no hacer; **he failed to contact us** no se puso en contacto con nosotros; ★ **without fail** sin falta; **ring me without fail** llámame sin falta.

failure noun 1 fracaso Masc.; **it was a terrible failure** fue un fracaso terrible; **2 a power failure** un apagón.

faint adjective 1 **to feel faint** sentirse [14] mareado/mareada; **2** (slight) ligero/ligera; **a faint smell of gas** un ligero olor a gas; **I haven't the faintest idea** no tengo ni la más remota idea; **3** (a voice or sound) débil.

faint verb desmayarse [17]; **Lisa fainted** Lisa se desmayó.

fair noun feria Fem.

fair adjective 1 (not unfair) justo/justa; **it's not fair!** ¡no es justo!; **2** (hair) rubio/rubia; **he's fair-haired** tiene el pelo rubio; **3** (skin) blanco/blanca; **4** (fairly good) bastante bueno/buena.

fairground noun parque Masc. de atracciones.

fairly adverb (quite) bastante; **she's fairly happy** es bastante feliz.

fairy noun hada Fem. (even though 'hada' is feminine, it takes 'el' and 'un' in the singular).

fairy tale noun cuento Masc. de hadas.

faith noun 1 (trust) confianza Fem.; **to have faith in somebody** tener confianza en alguien; 2 (religious belief) fe Fem.

faithful adjective fiel.

faithfully adverb **yours faithfully** le saluda atentamente.

fall noun caída Fem.; **to have a fall** sufrir [19] una caída.

fall verb 1 caerse [34]; **mind, you'll fall** cuidado, te vas a caer; **Tony fell off his bike** Tony se cayó de la bici; **she fell downstairs** se cayó por las escaleras; **my jacket fell on the floor** mi chaqueta se cayó al suelo; 2 (the temperature or prices) bajar [17]; **it fell to minus eleven last night** la temperatura bajó a once grados bajo cero anoche.

false adjective falso/falsa; **a false passport** un pasaporte falso; **a false alarm** una falsa alarma.

false teeth plural noun dentadura Fem. (singular) postiza.

fame noun fama Fem.

familiar adjective familiar; **your face is familiar** tu cara me es familiar.

family noun familia Fem.; **a family of six** una familia de seis personas; **Ben's one of the family** Ben es uno de la familia; **the Bunting family** la familia Bunting.

family name noun apellido Masc.

famous adjective famoso/famosa.

fan noun 1 (of a pop group) fan Masc./Fem. (informal); **Sarah's an Oasis fan** Sarah es fan de Oasis;

2 (of a team) hincha Masc./Fem.; **Martin's a Chelsea fan** Martin es hincha del Chelsea; 3 (electric, for cooling) ventilador Masc.; 4 (that you hold in your hand) abanico Masc.

fanatic noun fanático Masc., fanática Fem.

fancy noun **the picture took his fancy** se encaprichó del cuadro.

fancy adjective (equipment) sofisticado/sofisticada, (hotel) de lujo.

fancy verb 1 (to want) **do you fancy a coffee?** ¿te apetece un café?; **I don't fancy going out** no me apetece salir; 2 **I really fancy him** me gusta mucho; 3 (just) **fancy that!** ¡imagínate!; **fancy you being here!** ¡qué casualidad que estés aquí!.

fancy dress noun disfraz Masc.; **in fancy dress** disfrazado/disfrazada; **a fancy-dress party** una fiesta de disfraces.

fantastic adjective estupendo/estupenda (informal); **really? that's fantastic!** ¿de verdad?¡ eso es estupendo!; **a fantastic holiday** unas vacaciones estupendas.

far adverb, adjective 1 lejos; **it's not far** no está lejos; **is it far to Cordoba?** ¿está muy lejos Córdoba?; **how far is it to Granada?** ¿a qué distancia está Granada?; **he took us as far as Bilbao** nos llevó hasta Bilbao; 2 **by far** con mucho; **the prettiest by far** es con mucho la más bonita; 3 (much) mucho; **far better** mucho mejor; **far faster** mucho más

a
b
c
d
e
f
g
h
i
j
k
l
m
n
o
p
q
r
s
t
u
v
w
x
y
z

rápido; **4 far too many people**
demasiada gente; **far too much
noise** demasiado ruido; **5 so far**
hasta ahora; **so far everything's
going well** hasta ahora todo va
bien; **as far as I know** que yo sepa.

fare noun precio Masc. del billete;
half fare medio billete Masc.; **full
fare** billete Masc. entero; **the
return fare to Barcelona** el billete
de ida y vuelta a Barcelona.

Far East noun Lejano Oriente
Masc.

farm noun granja Fem.

farmer noun agricultor Masc.,
agricultora Fem.

farmhouse noun casa Fem. de
labranza.

farming noun agricultura Fem.

farthest adjective más lejano/más
lejana; **the farthest hill** la colina
más lejana.

farthest pronoun lo más lejos; **the
farthest we went** lo más lejos que
fuimos aquel día.

fascinating adjective fascinante.

fashion noun moda Fem.; **in
fashion** de moda; **out of fashion**
pasado/pasada de moda.

fashionable adjective de moda.

fashion model noun modelo
Masc./Fem.

fashion show noun desfile Masc.
de modas.

fast adjective **1** rápido/rápida; **a
fast car** un coche rápido; **2 my
watch is fast** mi reloj adelanta;
you're ten minutes fast vas diez
minutos adelantado.

fast adverb **1** rápido; **she swims
very fast** nada muy rápido; **2 to be
fast asleep** estar [2]
profundamente dormido.

fast food noun comida Fem.
rápida.

fat noun grasa Fem.

fat adjective gordo/gorda; **a fat
man** un hombre gordo; **to get fat**
engordar [17].

fatal adjective (accident) fatal.

father noun padre Masc.; **my
father's office** la oficina de mi
padre.

Father Christmas noun Papá
Masc. Noel.

father-in-law noun suegro Masc.

father's day noun día Masc. del
padre.

fault noun **1** (responsibility) culpa
Fem.; **it's Steve's fault** es culpa de
Steve; **it's not my fault** no es culpa
mía; **2** (in tennis) falta Fem.

favour noun **1** (a kindness) favor
Masc.; **to do somebody a favour**
hacerle [7] un favor a alguien; **can
you do me a favour?** ¿me haces un
favor?; **to ask a favour of
somebody** pedirle [57] un favor a
alguien; **2 to be in favour of
something** estar [2] a favor de algo.

favourite adjective favorito/
favorita; **my favourite band** mi
grupo favorito.

fax noun fax Masc.; **a fax machine**
un fax.

fear noun miedo Masc.

fear verb temer [18].

feather noun pluma Fem.

feature noun **1** (of your face) rasgo Masc.; **to have delicate features** tener [9] rasgos delicados; **2** (of a machine, product, etc.) característica Fem.

February noun febrero Masc.; **in February** en febrero.

fed up adjective **I'm fed up** estoy harto/harta (informal); **I'm fed up with working every day** estoy harta de trabajar todos los días.

feed verb dar [4] de comer a; **have you fed the dog?** ¿has dado de comer al perro?

feel verb **1** sentirse [14]; **I feel tired** me siento cansada; **I don't feel well** no me siento bien; **2** sentir [14]; **I didn't feel a thing** no sentí nada; **3** to feel afraid tener [9] miedo; **to feel cold** tener [9] frío; **to feel thirsty** tener [9] sed; **4** I feel like some chocolate me apetece un poco de chocolate; **do you feel like a walk?** ¿te apetece dar un paseo?; **I don't feel like it** no me apetece; **5** to feel like doing tener [9] ganas de hacer; **I feel like going to the cinema** tengo ganas de ir al cine; **6** (touch) tocar [31].

feeling noun **1** (in your mind) sentimiento Masc.; **a feeling of embarrassment** un sentimiento de vergüenza; **to show your feelings** de mostrar los sentimientos; **to hurt somebody's feelings** herir [14] los sentimientos de alguien; **2** (in your body) sensación Fem.; **a dizzy feeling** una sensación de mareo; **3** (impression) impresión Fem.; **I have the feeling James doesn't like me** tengo la impresión de que no le caigo bien a James.

felt-tip (pen) noun rotulador Masc.

female noun (animal) hembra Fem.

female adjective **1** femenino/ femenina (person, population); **2** hembra (animal, insect).

feminine adjective femenino/ femenina.

feminist noun, adjective feminista Masc./Fem.

fence noun valla Fem.

fern noun helecho Masc.

ferry noun ferry Masc.

fetch verb ir [8] a por; **Tom's fetching the children** Tom ha ido a por los niños; **fetch me the other knife!** ¡vete a por el otro cuchillo!

fever noun fiebre Fem.

few adjective, pronoun **1** pocos/ pocas; **few people think that ...** pocos piensan que ...; **2 a few** (followed by a noun) algunos/ algunas; **a few weeks earlier** algunas semanas antes; **in a few minutes** dentro de algunos minutos; **3 a few** (by itself) unos cuantos/unas cuantas; **have you any tomatoes?** **we want a few for the salad** ¿tienes tomates? queremos unos cuantos para la ensalada; **a few more books** unos cuantos libros más; **4 quite a few** bastantes; **there were quite a few questions** hubo bastantes preguntas.

fewer adjective menos; **there are fewer tourists this year** hay

a b c d e f g h i j k l m n o p q r s t u v w x y z

menos turistas este año; **fewer than six** menos de seis.

fiancé noun prometido Masc.

fiancée noun prometida Fem.

fiction noun ficción Fem.

field noun campo Masc.; **a field of wheat** un campo de trigo; **a football field** un campo de fútbol.

fifteen number quince Masc.; **Lara's fifteen** Lara tiene quince años.

fifth noun **1** (fraction) **a fifth** una quinta parte; **2 the fifth of January** el cinco de enero.

fifth adjective quinto/quinta; **on the fifth floor** en la quinta planta.

fifties plural noun **the fifties** los años cincuenta; **in the fifties** en los años cincuenta.

fifty number cincuenta Masc.; **she's fifty** tiene cincuenta años; **fifty-five** cincuenta y cinco.

fig noun higo Masc.

fight noun **1** (a scuffle or in boxing) pelea Fem.; **2** (in war or against illness or poverty) lucha Fem.

fight verb **1** (in war or against poverty or a disease) luchar [17]; **2** (to quarrel) pelear [17]; **they're always fighting** siempre se están peleando.

figure noun **1** (number) cifra Fem.; **a four-figure number** un número de cuatro cifras; **2** (body shape) figura Fem.; **3** (a person) personaje Masc.; **a public figure** un personaje público.

file noun **1** (for records of a person or case) archivo Masc.; **2** (in computer system) fichero Masc.;

3 (ring binder) archivador Masc.; **4** (cardboard folder for documents) carpeta Fem.; **5 a nail file** una lima.

file verb **1** archivar [17] (documents); **2 to file your nails** limarse [17] las uñas.

fill verb llenar [17]; **she filled my glass** me llenó el vaso.

● **to fill in** rellenar [17] (a form).

filling noun **1** (of pie) relleno Masc.; **2** (in tooth) empaste Masc.

film noun **1** (in a cinema) película Fem.; **shall we go and see a film?** ¿vamos a ver una película?; **the new film about Picasso** la nueva película sobre Picasso; **2** (for a camera) carrete Masc. de fotos; **a 24-exposure colour film** un carrete de color de veinticuatro fotos.

film star noun estrella Fem. de cine.

filthy adjective asqueroso/ asquerosa (informal).

final noun (in sport) final Fem.

final adjective **1** (definite) final; **the final result** el resultado final; **2** (last) último/última; **the final instalment** el último plazo.

finally adverb finalmente.

find verb encontrar [24]; **did you find your passport?** ¿has encontrado tu pasaporte?; **I can't find my keys** no puedo encontrar mis llaves.

● **to find out** **1** (to enquire) informarse [17]; **I don't know, I'll find out** no lo sé, me informaré; **2 to find something out** descubrir [46] algo (the facts or an answer);

when Lucy found out the truth cuando Lucy se enteró de la verdad.

fine noun multa Fem.

fine adjective **1** bien; 'how are you?' – 'fine, thanks' ¿cómo estás? – 'bien, gracias'; **ten o'clock?** yes, that's fine ¿a las diez? sí, está bien; **Friday will be fine** el viernes está bien; **2** (very good) muy bueno/buena; **she's a fine athlete** es muy buena atleta; **3** (weather or a day;) bueno/buena; **if it's fine** si hace buen tiempo; **4** (not coarse or thick) fino/fina; **in fine wool** de lana fina.

finely adjective (chopped or grated) muy fino/fina.

finger noun dedo Masc.; ★ **I'll keep my fingers crossed for you** te deseo suerte.

fingernail noun uña Fem.

finish noun **1** (end) final Masc.; **2** (in a race) llegada Fem.

finish verb **1** terminar [17]; **wait, I haven't finished** espera, no he terminado; **when does school finish?** ¿cuándo termina el colegio?; **have you finished the book?** ¿has terminado el libro?; **2 to finish doing** terminar [17] de hacer; **have you finished telephoning?** ¿has terminado de llamar por teléfono?.

● **to finish with** terminar [17] con; **have you finished with the computer?** ¿has terminado con el ordenador?.

finishing line noun meta Fem.

Finland noun Finlandia Fem.

Finn noun Finlandés Masc., Finlandesa Fem.

Finnish noun (the language) finlandés Masc.

Finnish adjective finlandés/finlandesa.

fire noun **1** (in a grate) fuego Masc.; **to light the fire** encender [36] el fuego; **2** (accidental) incendio Masc.; **3 to catch fire** prenderse [18] fuego; **to be on fire** estar [2] ardiendo.

fire verb (to shoot) disparar [17]; **to fire at somebody** disparar a alguien.

fire alarm noun alarma Fem. contra incendios.

fire brigade noun cuerpo Masc. de bomberos.

fire engine noun coche Masc. de bomberos.

fire escape noun escalera Fem. de incendios.

fire extinguisher noun extintor Masc.

firefighter noun bombero Masc./Fem.

fireplace noun chimenea Fem.

fire station noun estación Fem. de bomberos.

fireworks plural noun fuegos Masc. plural artificiales.

firm noun (business) empresa Fem.

firm adjective firme.

first noun **the first of May** el primero de mayo.

first pronoun, adjective, adverb **1** primero/primera; **Susan's the first** Susan es la primera; **the first of May** el primero de Mayo; **for the**

a b c d e f g h i j k l m n o p q r s t u v w x y z

a

b

c

d

e

f

g

h

i

j

k

l

m

n

o

p

q

r

s

t

u

v

w

x

y

z

first time por primera vez; **Christy got here first** Christy llegó aquí la primera; **Ben came first in the 200 metres** Ben llegó el primero en los doscientos metros; **2** (*to begin with*) primero; **first, I'm going to make some tea** primero voy a hacer té; **first of all** en primer lugar; **3 at first** al principio; **at first he didn't want to** al principio no quería.

first aid *noun* primeros auxilios *Masc. plural.*

first aid kit *noun* botiquín *Masc.* de primeros auxilios.

first class *adjective, adverb* de primera (*a ticket, carriage, or hotel*); **a first-class compartment** un compartimento de primera; **he always travels first class** siempre viaja en primera.

first floor *noun* primera planta *Fem.*; **on the first floor** en la primera planta.

firstly *adverb* en primer lugar.

first name *noun* nombre *Masc.* de pila.

fir tree *noun* abeto *Masc.*

fish *noun* **1** (*as a meal*) pescado *Masc.*; **do you like fish?** ¿te gusta el pescado?; **2** (*in the sea*) pez *Masc.* (*plural* peces).

fish *verb* pescar [31]; **Dad was fishing for trout** papá estaba pescando truchas.

fish and chips *noun* pescado *Masc.* con patatas fritas.

fisherman *noun* pescador *Masc.*

fishing *noun* pesca *Fem.*; **fishing is my favourite sport** la pesca es mi

deporte favorito; **I love fishing** me encanta pescar; **to go fishing** ir a pescar.

fishing rod *noun* caña *Fem.* de pescar.

fishing tackle *noun* aparejos *Masc. plural* de pesca.

fist *noun* puño *Masc.*

fit *noun* ataque *Masc.*; **an epileptic fit** un ataque epiléptico; **I had a fit** me dio un ataque; **your dad'll have a fit when he sees your hair!** ¡a tu padre le va a dar un ataque cuando te vea el pelo!

fit *adjective* (*healthy*) en forma; **I feel really fit** me siento muy en forma; **to keep fit** mantenerse [9] en forma.

fit *verb* **1** (*a garment or shoes*) estar [2] bien (*a person*); **this skirt doesn't fit me** esta falda no me está bien; **does it fit you okay?** ¿te está bien?; **2** (*go into*) entrar [17] en; **will my cases all fit in the car?** ¿entrarán todas mis maletas en el coche?; **3** (*install*) poner [11].

fitness *noun* estado *Masc.*, físico; **fitness training** entrenamiento *Masc.*

fitted carpet *noun* moqueta *Fem.*

five *number* cinco *Masc.*; **Oskar's five** Oskar tiene cinco años; **it's five o'clock** son las cinco.

fix *verb* **1** (*repair*) arreglar [17]; **Mum's fixed the computer** mamá ha arreglado el ordenador; **2** (*to decide on*) fijar [17]; **to fix a date** fijar [17] una fecha; **at a fixed price** a un precio fijo; **3** preparar [17] (*a meal*).

fizzy *adjective* con gas; **fizzy water** agua con gas.

flag *noun* bandera *Fem.*

flame *noun* llama *Fem.*

flan *noun* **1** (*savoury*) quiche *Masc.*; **an onion flan** un quiche de cebolla; **2** (*sweet*) tarta *Fem.*

flap *verb* (*a flag or sail*) agitarse [17].

flash *noun* **1 a flash of lightning** un relámpago; **2** (*of light*) destello *Masc.*; **3 to do something in a flash** hacer [7] algo a la velocidad del rayo; **4** (*on a camera*) flash *Masc.*

flash *verb* **1** (*a light*) destellar [17]; **2 to flash by or past** pasar [17] como un rayo; **3 to flash your headlights** hacer [7] señas con los faros del coche.

flask *n* **1** (*insulated bottle*) termo *Masc.*; **2** (*container*) frasco *Masc.*

flat *noun* piso *Masc.*; **a third-floor flat** un piso en la tercera planta.

flat *adjective* **1** plano/plana; **flat shoes** zapatos planos; **a flat surface** una superficie plana; **2** (*landscape*) llano/llana; **3 a flat tyre** una rueda pinchada.

flatmate *noun* compañero *Masc.*, compañera *Fem.* de piso.

flavour *noun* sabor *Masc.*; **the sauce had no flavour** la salsa no tenía sabor; **what flavour of ice cream would you like?** ¿de qué sabor quieres el helado?

flavour *verb* sazonar [17]; **vanilla-flavoured** con sabor a vainilla.

flea *noun* pulga *Fem.*

fleet *n* **1** (*of ships*) flota *Fem.*; **2** (*of vehicles*) parque *Masc.* móvil.

flight *noun* **1** vuelo *Masc.*; **a charter flight** un vuelo chárter; **the flight from Moscow is delayed** el vuelo procedente de Moscú lleva retraso; **2 a flight of stairs** un tramo de escalera; **four flights of stairs** cuatro tramos de escalera.

flight attendant *noun* auxiliar *Masc./Fem.* de vuelo.

fling *verb* lanzar [22].

flipper *noun* (*for a swimmer*) aleta *Fem.*

flirt *verb* flirtear [17].

float *verb* flotar [17].

flood *noun* **1** (*of water*) inundación *Fem.*; **the floods in the south** las inundaciones del sur; **2** (*of letters or complaints*) avalancha *Fem.*; **3 to be in floods of tears** estar [2] llorando a mares (*literally: to be weeping oceans*).

flood *verb* inundar [17].

floodlight *noun* foco *Masc.*

floor *noun* **1** suelo *Masc.*; **on the floor** en el suelo; **to sweep the floor** barrer [18]; **2** (*a storey*) planta *Fem.*; **on the second floor** en la segunda planta.

floppy disk *noun* disquete *Masc.*

florist *noun* florista *Masc./Fem.*

florist's *noun* floristería *Fem.*

flour *noun* harina *Fem.*

flower *noun* flor *Fem.*; **a bunch of flowers** un ramo de flores.

flower *verb* florecer [35].

flu *noun* gripe *Fem.*; **to have flu** tener [9] la gripe.

a b c d e f g h i j k l m n o p q r s t u v w x y z

a

fluent *adjective* she speaks fluent Italian habla italiano con fluidez.

b

fluently *adverb* con fluidez.

c

fluid *noun* fluido *Masc.*

d

flush *verb* 1 (*to go red*) enrojecer [35]; 2 to flush the lavatory tirar [17] de la cadena.

e

flute *noun* flauta *Fem.*; to play the flute tocar [30] la flauta.

f

fly *noun* mosca *Fem.*

g

fly *verb* 1 (*a bird, an insect, or a plane*) volar [24]; 2 (*in a plane*) ir [8] en avión; we flew to Edinburgh fuimos en avión a Edimburgo; we flew from Gatwick salimos desde Gatwick; 3 hacer [7] volar (*a kite*); 4 (*to pass quickly*) (*time*)pasar [17] volando.

h

i

j

k

foam *noun* 1 (*foam rubber*) goma *Fem.* espuma; a foam mattress un colchón de goma espuma; 2 (*on a drink*) espuma *Fem.*

l

m

n

focus *noun* to be in focus estar [2] enfocado; to be out of focus estar [2] desenfocado.

o

focus *verb* enfocar [31] (*a camera*).

p

fog *noun* niebla *Fem.*

q

foggy *adjective* it was foggy había niebla; a foggy day un día de niebla.

r

s

foil *noun* (*kitchen foil*) papel *Masc.* de aluminio.

t

fold *noun* doblez *Masc.*

u

fold *verb* doblar [17]; to fold something up doblar algo.

v

folder *noun* carpeta *Fem.*

w

follow *verb* seguir [64]; follow me! ¡sígueme!; followed by a dinner seguido de una cena; do you follow me? ¿me sigues?

x

y

z

following *adjective* siguiente; the following year el año siguiente.

fond *adjective* 1 to be fond of somebody tenerle [9] cariño a alguien; I'm very fond of him le tengo mucho cariño; 2 I'm fond of dogs me gustan los perros.

food *noun* comida *Fem.*; to buy food comprar [17] comida; I like Italian food me gusta la comida italiana.

food poisoning *n* intoxicación *Fem.* alimenticia.

fool *noun* idiota *Masc./Fem.*

foot *noun* 1 pie *Masc.*; he stepped on my foot me pisó el pie; Lucy came on foot Lucy vino a pie; at the foot of the stairs al pie de las escaleras; 2 (*of animal*) pata *Fem.*

football *noun* 1 (*the game*) fútbol *Masc.*; to play football jugar [27] al fútbol; 2 (*ball*) balón *Masc.* de fútbol.

footballer *noun* futbolista *Masc./Fem.*

footpath *noun* sendero *Masc.*

for *preposition* 1 para; a present for my mother un regalo para mi madre; petrol for the car gasolina para el coche; sausages for lunch salchichas para comer; it's for cleaning es para limpiar; what's it for? ¿para qué es?; 2 (*in time expressions in the past or future, 'for' is not usually translated*) I studied Spanish for four years estudié español cuatro años; I'll be away for four days estaré fuera cuatro días; I've been waiting here for an hour llevo esperando aquí una hora; **my brother's been living in London for three years** mi hermano lleva tres años viviendo en Londres; **3** (*cost or amount*) por; **I sold my bike for fifty pounds** vendí mi bicicleta por cincuenta libras; **4 what's the Spanish for 'bee'?** ¿cómo se dice 'bee' en español?.

forbid *verb* prohibir [58]; **to forbid somebody to do something** prohibir [58] a alguien hacer algo; **I forbid you to go out** te prohíbo salir.

forbidden *adjective* prohibido/ prohibida.

force *noun* fuerza *Fem.*

force *verb* forzar [26]; **to force somebody to do something** forzar a alguien a hacer.

forecast *noun* (*weather forecast*) pronóstico *Masc.*

forehead *noun* frente *Fem.*

foreign *adjective* extranjero/ extranjera; **in a foreign country** en un país extranjero.

foreigner *noun* extranjero *Masc.*, extranjera *Fem.*

forest *noun* bosque *Masc.*

forever *adverb* **1** para siempre; **I'd like to stay here forever** me gustaría quedarme aquí para siempre; **2** (*non-stop*) siempre; **he's forever asking questions** siempre está preguntando.

forgery *noun* falsificación *Fem.*

forget *verb* olvidarse [17]; **I forget his name** se me ha olvidado su nombre; **we've forgotten the bread!** ¡se nos ha olvidado el pan!;

to forget to do olvidarse [17] de hacer; **I forgot to phone** se me olvidó llamar por teléfono; **to forget about something** olvidarse [17] de algo.

forgetful *adjective* olvidadizo/ olvidadiza.

forgive *verb* perdonar [17]; **I forgave him** le perdoné; **to forgive somebody for doing** perdonar [17] a alguien que (*followed by subjunctive*); **I forgave her for losing my ring** la perdoné por perderme el anillo.

fork *noun* tenedor *Masc.*

form *noun* **1** formulario *Masc.*; **to fill in a form** rellenar [17] un formulario; **2** (*shape or kind*) forma *Fem.*; **in the form of** bajo forma de; **3 to be on form** estar [2] en forma; **4** (*school class*) clase *Fem.*; **5** (*school year*) curso *Masc.*

form *verb* formar [17].

formal *adjective* formal (*invitation, event, complaint, etc*).

former *adjective* antiguo/antigua (*goes before the noun*); **a former pupil** un antiguo alumno.

formula *noun* fórmula *Fem.*

fortnight *noun* quince días *Masc. plural*; **we're going to Spain for a fortnight** vamos quince días a España.

fortress *noun* fortaleza *Fem.*

fortune *noun* fortuna *Fem.*; **to make a fortune** hacer [7] una fortuna.

fortunate *adjective* afortunado/ afortunada.

a b c d e f g h i j k l m n o p q r s t u v w x y z

a

fortunately *adverb* afortunadamente.

b

forty *number* cuarenta *Masc.*; **he's forty** tiene cuarenta años; **forty-five** cuarenta y cinco.

c

forward *noun* (*in sport*) delantero *Masc./Fem.*

d

e

forward *adverb* **a seat further forward** un asiento de más adelante; **to move forward** ir [8] hacia adelante.

f

g

foster child *noun* hijo *Masc.* acogido, hija *Masc.* acogida.

h

i

foster family *noun* familia *Fem.* de acogida.

j

foul *noun* (*in sport*) falta *Fem.*

k

foul *adjective* asqueroso/asquerosa (*smell or taste*); **the weather's foul** el tiempo es horroroso.

l

fountain *noun* fuente *Fem.*

m

fountain pen *noun* pluma *Fem.*

n

four *number* cuatro *Masc.*; **Simon's four** Simon tiene cuatro años; **it's four o'clock** son las cuatro.

o

p

fourteen *number* catorce *Masc.*; **Susie's fourteen** Susie tiene catorce años.

q

r

fourth *noun* **1** (*fraction*) **a fourth** un cuarto; **2 the fourth of July** el cuatro de julio.

s

fourth *adjective* cuarto/cuarta; **on the fourth floor** en la cuarta planta.

t

u

fox *noun* zorro *Masc.*

v

fracture *noun* fractura *Fem.*

w

fragile *adjective* frágil.

x

frame *noun* (*of picture or photograph*) marco *Masc.*

y

z

France *noun* Francia *Fem.*

frantic *adjective* **1** (*desperate*) desesperado/desesperada (*efforts or a search*); **2** (*very upset*) **Mum was frantic with worry** mamá estaba muerta de preocupación.

freckle *noun* peca *Fem.*

free *adjective* **1** (*when you don't pay*) gratis; **the bus is free** el autobús es gratis; **a free ticket** un billete gratis; **2** (*not occupied*) libre; **are you free on Thursday?** ¿estás libre el jueves?; **3 sugar-free** sin azúcar; **lead-free** sin plomo.

free *verb* **1** (*a person*) poner [11] en libertad; **2** (*an animal*) soltar [24].

free kick *noun* tiro *Masc.* libre.

freedom *noun* libertad *Fem.*

free gift *noun* regalo *Masc.*

freeze *verb* **1** (*in a freezer*) congelar [17]; **frozen peas** guisantes congelados; **2** (*in cold weather*) helarse [29] (*person or ground*).

freezer *noun* congelador *Masc.*

freezing *noun* **three degrees below freezing** tres grados bajo cero.

freezing *adjective* **I'm freezing** ¡estoy helado! (*informal*); **it's freezing outside!** ¡fuera hace un frío que pela! (*informal*).

French *noun* **1** (*the language*) francés *Masc.*; **2** (*the people*) **the French** los franceses.

French *adjective* francés/francesa.

French beans *plural noun* judías *Fem. plural* verdes.

French fries *plural noun* patatas *Fem. plural* fritas.

Frenchman *noun* francés *Masc.*

French stick *noun* baguette *Fem.*

French window *noun* cristalera *Fem.*

Frenchwoman *noun* francesa *Fem.*

frequently *noun* frecuentemente, a menudo.

fresh *adjective* fresco/fresca; **fresh eggs** huevos frescos; **I'm going out for some fresh air** voy fuera a tomar un poco el aire.

Friday *noun* viernes *Masc.* (*plural* viernes); **last Friday** el pasado viernes; **on Friday** el viernes; **I'll phone you on Friday evening** te llamaré el viernes por la tarde; **on Fridays** los viernes; **closed on Fridays** cerrado los viernes; **every Friday** cada viernes; **Good Friday** Viernes Santo.

fridge *noun* nevera *Fem.*; **put it in the fridge** ponlo en la nevera.

friend *noun* amigo *Masc.*, amiga *Fem.*; **a friend of mine** un amigo mío/una amiga mía; **to make friends** hacer [7] amigos; **he made friends with Danny** se hizo amigo de Danny.

friendly *adjective* **1** (*a person*) simpático/simpática; **2** (*a letter or gesture*) amable.

friendship *noun* amistad *Fem.*

fries *plural noun* patatas *Fem. plural* fritas.

fright *noun* susto *Masc.*; **to get a fright** asustarse [17]; **to give**

somebody a fright asustar [17] a alguien; **you gave me a fright!** ¡me has asustado!

frighten *verb* asustar [17].

frightened *adjective* **to be frightened** estar [2] asustado/asustada; **I'm frightened of asking her** me da miedo preguntarle; **Martin's frightened of snakes** a Martin le dan miedo las serpientes.

frightening *adjective* espantoso/espantosa.

fringe *noun* (*of hair*) flequillo *Masc.*.

frog *noun* rana *Fem.*

from *preposition* **1** de; **a letter from Tom** una carta de Tom; **100 metres from the cinema** a cien metros del cine; **he comes from Dublin** es de Dublín; **from seven o'clock onwards** de las siete en adelante; **2 from ... to ...** de ... a ...; **from Monday to Friday** de lunes a viernes; **the train from London to Liverpool** el tren de Londres a Liverpool; **from here to the wall** de aquí a la pared; **3** (*starting from*) desde; **tickets from ten pounds** entradas desde diez libras; **from today** desde hoy; **4 two years from now** dentro de dos años; **from then on** a partir de entonces.

front *noun* **1** (*of a car, train, envelope, or queue*) parte *Fem.* de delante; **sitting in the front** sentado en la parte de delante; **the address is on the front** las señas están en la parte de delante; **from the front** por delante; **2** (*of a building*) fachada *Fem.*; **3** (*of a*

a
garment) delantera Masc.; **4 the front of the class** el frente de la clase; **5 in front of** delante de; **in front of the TV** delante de la televisión; **in front of me** delante de mí.

b

c

d
front adjective **1** delantero/delantera; **the front seat** (of a car) el asiento delantero; **2 in the front row** en la fila de delante.

e

f

g
front door noun puerta Fem. de la calle.

h
frontier noun frontera Fem.

i
frost noun helada Fem.

frosty adjective **1 it was frosty this morning** había helada esta mañana; **2** cubierto/cubierta de escarcha (windscreen, grass, etc).

j

k

l
frown verb fruncir [66] el ceño.

m
frozen adjective (in a freezer) congelado/congelada; **a frozen pizza** una pizza congelada.

n
fruit noun fruta Fem.; **fruit juice** zumo Masc. de fruta.

o

p
fruit salad noun macedonia Fem. de frutas.

q
frustrating adjective frustrante.

r
fry verb freír [53]; **we fried the fish** freímos el pescado; **a fried egg** un huevo frito.

s

t
frying pan noun sartén Fem.

u
fuel noun (for a vehicle or plane) combustible Masc.

v

w
full adjective **1** lleno/llena; **this glass is full** este vaso está lleno; **the train was full of tourists** el tren estaba lleno de turistas; **I'm full** estoy lleno; **2** completo/completa (a hotel or flight); **3** (top) **at full speed** a toda velocidad; **at**

x

y

z

full volume a todo volumen; **4** (complete) todo/toda; **the full story** toda la historia; **5 to write your name out in full** escribir [52] su nombre completo.

full stop noun punto Masc.

full-time adjective a tiempo completo Masc.; **a full-time job** un trabajo a tiempo completo.

full time noun final Masc. de partido.

fully adverb completamente.

fun noun **to have fun** divertirse [14]; **have fun!** ¡que te diviertas!; **we had fun catching the ponies** nos divertimos atrapando a los poneys; **skiing is fun** esquiar es divertido; **I do it for fun** lo hago para divertirme; **to make fun of somebody** reírse [61] de alguien.

funds noun fondos Masc. plural.

funeral noun **1** (ceremony) funeral Masc.; **2** (burial) entierro Masc.

funfair noun feria Fem.

funny adjective **1** (when you laugh) gracioso/graciosa; **how funny you are!** ¡qué gracioso eres!; **a funny story** una historia graciosa; **2** (strange) raro; **that's funny, I'm sure I paid** qué raro, estoy seguro de que pagué; **a funny noise** un ruido raro.

fur noun **1** (on an animal) pelaje Masc.; **2** (for a coat) piel Fem.; **a fur coat** un abrigo de piel.

furious adjective furioso/furiosa; **she was furious with Steve** estaba furiosa con Steve.

furniture noun muebles Masc. plural; **to buy some furniture** comprar muebles; **a piece of furniture** un mueble.

further adverb further than the station más allá de la estación; **ten kilometres further on** diez kilómetros más adelante; **further forward** más adelante; **further back** más atrás; **further in** más adentro.

fuse noun fusible Masc.

fuss noun escándalo Masc.; **to make a fuss** montar [17] un escándalo; **to make a fuss about the bill** montar [17] un escándalo a causa de la factura.

fussy adjective **1** (about how things are done) quisquilloso/ quisquillosa; **to be fussy about something** ser [1] muy quisquilloso/quisquillosa para algo; **2** (about food) maniático/ maniática. **to be fussy about food** ser [1] muy maniático/maniática para la comida.

future noun futuro Masc.; **in the future** en el futuro; **in future** en el futuro; **in future, ask me first** en el futuro, pregúntame antes.

Gg

gadget noun aparato Masc.

gain verb ganar [17]; **in order to gain time** para ganar tiempo; **to gain weight** ganar peso.

gale noun vendaval Masc.

Galicia noun Galicia Fem.

Galician noun **1** (the language) gallego Masc.; **2** (person) gallego Masc., gallega Fem.

Galician adjective gallego/ gallega.

galaxy noun galaxia Fem.

gallery noun **an art gallery** (public) un museo de pintura (private) una galería de arte.

gambling noun juego Masc.

game noun **1** juego Masc.; **a board game** un juego de mesa; (to be good at games) **Jack's very good at games** Jack es muy buen deportista; **2 a game of** una partida de; **a game of cards** una partida de cartas; **to play cards** jugar [27] a las cartas; **3** partido Masc.; **a game of football** un partido de fútbol.

gang noun **1** panda Fem. (of friends); **all the gang were there** toda la panda estaba allí; **2** banda Fem. (of criminals).

gangster noun gángster Masc./ Fem.

gap noun **1** (hole) hueco Masc.; **2** (in time) intervalo Masc.; **a two-year gap** un intervalo de dos años; **3 an age gap** una diferencia de edad.

gap year noun año Masc. libre antes de entrar a la universidad.

garage noun garaje Masc.

garden noun jardín Masc.

gardener noun jardinero Masc., jardinera Fem.; **he's a gardener** es jardinero.

gardening noun jardinería Fem.

garlic noun ajo Masc.

a b c d e f g h i j k l m n o p q r s t u v w x y z

garment noun prenda Fem.

gas noun gas Masc.

gas cooker noun cocina Fem. de gas.

gas fire noun estufa Fem. de gas.

gas meter noun contador Masc. de gas.

gate noun 1 (garden) verja Fem.; 2 (field) portillo Masc.; 3 (at the airport) puerta Fem. (de embarque).

gather verb 1 (people) juntarse [17]; **a crowd gathered** se juntó una multitud; 2 recoger [3] (fruit, vegetables, flowers); 3 **as far as I can gather** según tengo entendido.

gay adjective gay (homosexual).

GCSEs noun plural (You can explain GCSEs briefly as follows: Son exámenes que se realizan alrededor de los 16 años y abarcan hasta 12 asignaturas. Se califican desde A-star (nota máxima), a N (sin calificar). Muchos alumnos estudian para los A levels después de hacer los GCSEs) SEE **A levels**.

gear noun 1 (in a car) marcha Fem.; **to change gear** cambiar [17] de marcha; **in third gear** en tercera; 2 (equipment) equipo Masc.; **camping gear** equipo de acampada; 3 **fishing gear** aparejos Masc. plural de pesca; 4 (things) cosas Fem. plural; **I've left all my gear at Gary's** he dejado todas mis cosas en casa de Gary.

gear lever noun palanca Fem. de cambio.

gel noun gel Masc.; **hair gel** gel para el pelo.

Gemini noun Géminis Masc. plural; **Steph's Gemini** Steph es Géminis.

gender noun (of a word) género Masc.; **what is the gender of 'casa'?** ¿de qué género es 'casa'?

general adjective general; **in general** en general.

general noun general Masc.; **General Jackson** el general Jackson.

general election noun elecciones Fem. plural generales.

general knowledge noun cultura Fem. general.

generally adverb generalmente.

generation noun generación Fem.

generous adjective generoso/generosa.

genetics noun genética Fem.

genius noun genio Masc.; **Lisa, you're a genius!** Lisa, ¡eres un genio!

gentle adjective 1 (person, voice or nature) dulce; 2 (breeze, murmur, heat) suave.

gentleman noun caballero Masc.; **ladies and gentlemen** señoras y caballeros.

gently adverb 1 (talk) dulcemente; 2 (touch) suavemente; 3 (handle) con cuidado.

gents noun servicios Masc. plural de caballeros; (sign) Caballeros; **where's the gents?** ¿dónde están los servicios de caballeros?

genuine adjective 1 (real) auténtico/auténtica; **a genuine diamond** un diamante auténtico;

2 sincero/sincera (*person*); **she's very genuine** es muy sincera.

geography *noun* geografía *Fem.*

geology *noun* geología *Fem.*

geometry *noun* geometría *Fem.*

germ *noun* germen *Masc.*

German *noun* **1** alemán *Masc.*, alemana *Fem.*; **2** (*language*) alemán *Masc.*

German *adjective* alemán/alemana.

Germany *noun* Alemania *Fem.*

get *verb* **1** (*to obtain*) **I got fifteen for my maths exam** saqué un quince en el examen de matemáticas; **where did you get that jacket?** ¿de dónde has sacado esa chaqueta?; **2** (*as a present*) **I got a bike for my birthday** me regalaron una bicicleta por mi cumpleaños; **3** (*a parcel or letter*) recibir [19]; **I got your letter yesterday** recibí tu carta ayer; **4** (*a job*) conseguir [64]; **Fred's got a job** Fred ha conseguido un trabajo; **5** (*fetch*) ir [8] a buscar; **go and get some bread** vete a buscar pan; **I'll get your bag for you** voy a buscar tu bolso; **6** (*to buy*) comprar [17]; **I got a nice shirt in the sales** compré una camisa muy bonita en las rebajas; **7 to have got** tener [9]; **he's got lots of money** tiene mucho dinero; **she's got long hair** tiene el pelo largo; **8 to have got to do** tener [9] que hacer; **I've got to phone before midday** tengo que llamar antes del mediodía; **9 to get to** llegar [28] a; **when we got to London** cuando llegamos a Londres; **to get here/there** llegar

[28]; **we got here this morning** llegamos esta mañana; **what time did they get there?** ¿a qué hora llegaron?; **10** (*become*) **to get tired** cansarse [17]; **she was getting worried** se estaba preocupando; **it's getting late** se está haciendo tarde; **I'm getting hungry** me está entrando hambre; **11 to get your hair cut** cortarse [17] el pelo.

● **to get back** volver [45]; **Mum gets back at six** mamá vuelve a las seis.

● **to get something back: we got the money back** nos devolvieron el dinero; **did you get your books back?** ¿te devolvieron los libros?.

● **to get into something** entrar [17] (*a vehicle*); **he got into the car** entró en el coche.

● **to get off something** bajarse [17] de; **I got off the train at Banbury** me bajé del tren en Banbury.

● **to get on: how's Amanda getting on?** ¿cómo le va a Amanda?

● **to get on something** subir [19] a (*a vehicle*); **she got on the train at Reading** subió al tren en Reading.

● **to get on with somebody** llevarse [17] bien con alguien; **she doesn't get on with her brother** no se lleva bien con su hermano.

● **to get out of something** salir [63] de algo (*vehicle*); **Laura got out of the car** Laura salió del coche.

● **to get something out** sacar [31] algo; **Robert got his guitar out** Robert sacó la guitarra.

● **to get together** verse [16]; **we must get together soon** tenemos que vernos pronto.

● **to get up** levantarse [17]; **I get up at seven** me levanto a la siete.

ghost noun fantasma Masc.

giddy adjective mareado/mareada; **I'm feeling giddy** me siento mareado/mareada.

gift noun **1** regalo Masc.; **a Christmas gift** un regalo de Navidad; **2 to have a gift for something** estar [2] dotado/dotada para; **Jo has a real gift for languages** Jo está realmente dotada para los idiomas.

gig noun concierto Masc.

gigabyte noun gigabyte Masc.; **a fifty gigabyte hard disk** un disco duro de cincuenta gigabytes.

gin noun ginebra Fem.

ginger noun jengibre Masc.

giraffe noun jirafa Fem.

gipsy noun gitano Masc., gitana Fem.

girl noun **1** niña Fem.; **three boys and four girls** tres niños y cuatro niñas; **a little girl** una niña pequeña; **when I was a little girl** cuando yo era pequeña; **2** (a teenager or young woman) chica Fem.; **an eighteen-year-old girl** una chica de dieciocho años.

girlfriend noun **1** (in relationship) novia Fem.; **Darren's girlfriend** la novia de Darren; **2** (female friend) amiga Fem.; **Lizzie and her girlfriends have gone to the cinema** Lizzie y sus amigas han ido al cine.

give verb dar [4]; **to give something to somebody** darle [4]

algo a alguien; **I'll give you my address** te daré mis señas; **give me the key** dame la llave; **I gave Sandy the books** le di los libros a Sandy; **Yasmin's dad gave her the money** el padre de Yasmin le dio el dinero.

● **to give something away** regalar [17] algo; **she's given away all her books** ha regalado todos sus libros.

● **to give something back to somebody** devolverle [45] algo a alguien; **I gave her back the keys** le devolví las llaves.

● **to give in** ceder [18]; **she gave in in the end** al final cedió.

● **to give up** rendirse [57]; **I give up!** ¡me rindo!

● **to give up doing** dejar [17] de hacer; **she's given up smoking** ha dejado de fumar.

glacier noun glaciar Masc.

glad adjective **to be glad to** alegrarse [17]; **I'm glad to hear he's better** me alegra saber que está mejor; **I'm glad to be back** me alegro de haber vuelto.

glamorous adjective **1** (life, job) con mucho glamour; **2** (woman) elegante.

glass noun **1** (for drinking) vaso Masc.; **a glass of water** un vaso de agua; **2** (material) cristal Masc.; **a glass table** una mesa de cristal.

glasses plural noun gafas Fem. plural; **to wear glasses** llevar [17] gafas.

global adjective global.

global warming noun calentamiento Masc. global.

globe noun globo Masc. terráqueo.

gloomy adjective **1** (expression) lúgubre; **2** (weather) gris.

glory noun gloria Fem.

glove noun guante Masc.; **a pair of gloves** un par de guantes.

glue noun pegamento Masc.

go noun **1** (in a game) whose go is it? ¿a quién le toca?; it's my go me toca a mí; **2** to have a go at doing intentar [17] hacer; I'll have a go at mending it for you intentaré arreglártelo.

go verb **1** ir [8]; we're going to London tomorrow mañana vamos a Londres; Mark's gone to the dentist's Mark ha ido al dentista; to go for a walk ir [8] a dar un paseo; to go shopping ir [8] de compras; **2** (with another verb) to go to do ir [8] a hacer; I'm going to make some tea voy a hacer té; he was going to phone me él iba a llamarme; **3** (leave) irse [8]; Pauline's already gone Pauline ya se ha ido; we're going on holiday tomorrow nos vamos de vacaciones mañana; **4** (a train or plane) salir [63]; the train goes at seven el tren sale a las siete; **5** (time) pasar [17]; the time goes quickly el tiempo pasa rápido; **6** (an event) ir [8]; did the party go well? ¿qué tal fue la fiesta?; **7** (a pain) pasarse [17]; my headache's gone se me ha pasado el dolor de cabeza.

● to go away irse [8]; go away! ¡vete!

● to go back volver [45]; I'm going back to Madrid in March vuelvo a Madrid en marzo; I'm not going back there again! ¡no voy a volver nunca!; I went back home volví a casa.

● to go down **1** bajar [17]; she's gone down to the kitchen ha bajado a la cocina; to go down the stairs bajar las escaleras; prices have gone down los precios han bajado; **2** (tyre, balloon, airbed) desinflarse [17].

● to go in entrar [17]; he went in and shut the door entró y cerró la puerta.

● to go into entrar [17]; Fran went into the kitchen Fran entró en la cocina; this file won't go into my bag esta carpeta no entra en mi bolsa.

● to go off **1** (bomb) estallar [17]; **2** (alarm clock) sonar [24]; my alarm clock went off at six mi despertador sonó a las seis; **3** (fire or burglar alarm) disparase [17]; the fire alarm went off la alarma contra incendios se disparó.

● to go on **1** pasar [17]; what's going on? ¿qué pasa?; **2** to go on doing seguir [64] haciendo; she went on talking siguió hablando; **3** to go on about something hablar [17] de algo; he's always going on about his dog siempre está hablando de su perro.

● to go out **1** salir [63]; I'm going out tonight voy a salir esta noche; she went out of the kitchen salió de la cocina; **2** to be going out with somebody salir [63] con alguien; she's going out with my brother está saliendo con mi

a b c d e f g h i j k l m n o p q r s t u v w x y z

hermano; **3** (*light, fire*) apagarse [28]; **the light went out** la luz se apagó.

● **to go past something** pasar [17] por algo; **we went past your house** pasamos por tu casa.

● **to go round: to go round to somebody's house** ir [8] a casa de alguien; **I went round to Fred's last night** anoche fui a casa de Fred.

● **to go round something 1** recorrer [18] (*building, park, garden*); **2** visitar [17] (*museum, monument*).

● **to go through** pasar [17] por; **the train went through York** el tren pasó por York; **you can go through my office** puedes pasar por mi oficina.

● **to go up** subir [19]; **she's gone up to her room** ha subido a su habitación; **to go up the stairs** subir las escaleras; **the price of petrol has gone up** el precio de la gasolina ha subido.

goal *noun* gol *Masc.*; **to score a goal** marcar un gol; **to win by three goals to two** ganar [17] por tres goles a dos.

goalkeeper *noun* portero *Masc.*, portera *Fem.*

goat *noun* cabra *Fem.*; **goat's cheese** queso *Masc.* de cabra.

god *noun* dios *Masc.*

God *noun* Dios *Masc.*; **to believe in God** creer en Dios.

godchild *noun* ahijado *Masc.*, ahijada *Fem.*

goddaughter *noun* ahijada *Fem.*

goddess *noun* diosa *Fem.*

godfather *noun* padrino *Masc.*

godmother *noun* madrina *Fem.*

godparent *noun* padrino *Masc.*, madrina *Fem.*; **my godparents** mis padrinos.

godson *noun* ahijado *Masc.*

goggles *plural noun* **swimming goggles** gafas *Fem. plural* de natación; **skiing goggles** gafas *Fem. plural* de esquí.

go-karting *noun* karting *Masc.*; **to go-karting** hacer karting.

gold *noun* oro *Masc.*; **a gold bracelet** una pulsera de oro.

goldfish *noun* pececito *Masc.* (rojo).

golf *noun* golf *Masc.*; **to play golf** jugar [31] al golf.

golf club *noun* **1** (*place*) club *Masc.* de golf; **2** (*iron*) palo *Masc.* de golf.

golf course *noun* campo *Masc.* de golf.

golfer *noun* golfista *Masc./Fem.*

good **to do somebody good** irle [15] bien a alguien; **it will do you good** te irá bien.

good *adjective* **1** bueno/buena (*'bueno' becomes 'buen' before a masculine singular noun*) **she's a good teacher** es una buena profesora; **a good deal** un buen negocio; **be good!** ¡sé bueno!; **to feel good** sentirse [14] bien; **2 to be good for you** ser [1] bueno para la salud; **tomatoes are good for you** los tomates son muy buenos para la salud; **3 she's good at art** se la da bien el arte; **I'm good at cooking** se me da bien cocinar; **4** (*kind*) amable; **she's been very**

good to me ha sido muy amable conmigo; **5** bien; **it smelled good** olía bien; **it tastes good** sabe bien; **his Spanish is very good** habla español muy bien; **good!** (*well done*) ¡muy bien!; **6 for good** para siempre; **I've stopped smoking for good** he dejado de fumar para siempre.

good afternoon *exclamation* buenas tardes.

goodbye *exclamation* adiós.

good evening *exclamation* **1** (*up to eight or nine*) buenas tardes; **2** (*from nine onwards*) buenas noches.

Good Friday *noun* Viernes *Masc.* Santo.

good-looking *adjective* guapo/guapa; **Maya's boyfriend's really good-looking** el novio de Maya es muy guapo.

good morning *exclamation* buenos días.

goodness *exclamation* ¡Dios mío!; **for goodness sake!** ¡por Dios!

goodnight *exclamation* buenas noches.

goods *plural noun* artículos *Masc. plural.*

goods train *noun* tren *Masc.* de mercancías.

goose *noun* ganso *Masc.*

goose pimples *noun* carne *Fem.* de gallina.

gorgeous *adjective* precioso/preciosa; **a gorgeous dress** un vestido precioso; **it's a gorgeous day** un día precioso.

gorilla *noun* gorila *Masc.*

gosh *exclamation* ¡Dios mío!

gossip *noun* **1** (*person*) cotilla *Masc./Fem.*; **2** (*news*) cotilleo *Masc.*; **what's the latest gossip?** ¿qué hay de nuevo?

gossip *verb* cotillear [17].

government *noun* gobierno *Masc.*

grab *verb* **1** agarrar [17]; **she grabbed my arm** me agarró el brazo; **2 to grab something from somebody** arrebatarle [17] algo a alguien; **he grabbed the book from me** me arrebató el libro.

graceful *adjective* elegante.

grade *noun* (*mark*) notas *Fem. plural*; **to get good grades** sacar [31] buenas notas.

gradual *adjective* gradual.

gradually *adverb* poco a poco; **the weather got gradually better** el tiempo mejoró poco a poco.

graffiti *plural noun* grafitti *Masc. plural.*

grain *noun* grano *Masc.*

grammar *noun* gramática *Fem.*

grammar school *noun* colegio *Masc.*

grammatical *adjective* gramatical; **a grammatical error** un error gramatical.

gramme *noun* gramo *Masc.*

gran *noun* abuelita *Fem.*

grandchildren *plural noun* nietos *Masc. plural.*

granddad *noun* abuelito (*informal*) *Masc.*

granddaughter *noun* nieta *Fem.*

grandfather *noun* abuelo *Masc.*

a b c d e f g h i j k l m n o p q r s t u v w x y z

grandma noun abuelita (*informal*) Fem.

grandmother noun abuela Fem.

grandpa noun abuelito (*informal*) Masc.

grandparents plural noun abuelos Masc. plural.

grandson noun nieto Masc. plural.

granny noun abuelita (*informal*) Fem.

grape noun a grape una uva; **to buy some grapes** comprar uvas; **a bunch of grapes** un racimo de uvas.

grapefruit noun pomelo Masc.

graph noun gráfico Masc.

graphic designer noun diseñador Masc. gráfico, diseñadora Fem. gráfica.

graphics noun gráficos Masc. plural.

grass noun 1 hierba Fem.; **he was sitting on the grass** estaba sentado en la hierba; 2 (*lawn*) césped Masc.; **to cut the grass** cortar [17] el césped.

grasshopper noun saltamontes Masc. (*plural* saltamontes).

grate verb rallar [17]; **grated cheese** queso rallado.

grateful adjective agradecido/ agradecida.

grater noun rallador Masc.

grave noun tumba Fem.

gravel noun grava Fem.

graveyard noun cementerio Masc.

gravity noun gravedad Fem.

gravy noun salsa Fem. del asado.

grease noun grasa Fem.

greasy adjective 1 (*hands or surface*) grasiento/grasienta; 2 (*hair, skin or food*) graso/grasa; **to have greasy skin** tener [9] la piel grasa; **I hate greasy food** no soporto la comida grasa.

great adjective 1 gran (*plural* grandes); **a great poet** un gran poeta; **a great opportunity** una gran oportunidad; **great expectations** grandes esperanzas; 2 (*terrific*) estupendo/estupenda; **it was a great party!** ¡fue una fiesta estupenda!; **great!** ¡estupendo!; 3 **a great deal of** un montón de; **a great many** muchos/muchas; **there are a great many things still to be done** aún quedan muchas cosas por hacer.

Great Britain noun Gran Bretaña Fem.

Greece noun Grecia Fem.

greedy adjective (*with food*) glotón/glotona.

Greek noun 1 (*person*) griego Masc., griega Fem.; 2 (*language*) griego Masc.

Greek adjective griego/griega.

green noun 1 (*colour*) verde Masc.; **a pale green** un verde pálido; 2 **greens** (*vegetables*) verduras Fem. plural; 3 **the Greens** (*ecologists*) los verdes (*informal*).

green adjective 1 verde; **a green door** una puerta verde; 2 ecologista; **the Green Party** el partido ecologista.

greengrocer noun verdulero Masc., verdulera Fem.; **the greengrocer's** la verdulería.

greenhouse noun invernadero Masc.

greenhouse effect noun efecto Masc. invernadero.

greetings plural noun **Season's Greetings** Feliz Navidad.

greetings card noun tarjeta Fem. de felicitación.

grey adjective 1 gris; **a grey skirt** una falda gris; 2 (hair) canoso/canosa; **to have grey hair** tener el pelo canoso.

greyhound noun galgo Masc.

grid noun 1 (grating) parrilla Fem.; 2 (network) red Fem.

grief noun dolor Masc.

grill noun (of a cooker) grill Masc.

grill verb **to grill something** hacer [7] algo al grill; **I grilled the sausages** hice las salchichas al grill.

grin noun sonrisa Fem.

grin verb sonreír [61].

grip verb agarrar [17].

grit noun (for roads) arenilla Fem.

groan noun 1 (of pain) gemido Masc.; 2 (of disgust, boredom) gruñido Masc.

groan verb 1 (in pain) gemir [57]; 2 (in disgust, boredom) refunfuñar [17].

grocer noun tendero Masc., tendera Fem.; **my dad's a grocer** mi padre es tendero.

groceries plural noun cosas Fem. plural de comer; **to buy some groceries** comprar [17] cosas de comer.

grocer's noun tienda Fem. de comestibles.

groom noun (bridegroom) novio Masc.

gross adjective 1 **a gross injustice** una flagrante injustica; 2 **a gross error** un grave error; 3 (disgusting) repugnante; **the food was gross!** ¡la comida era repugnante!

ground noun 1 suelo Masc.; **to sit on the ground** sentarse [29] en el suelo; **to throw something on the ground** tirar [17] algo al suelo; 2 (for sport) campo Masc.; **a football ground** un campo de fútbol.

ground adjective molido/molida; **ground coffee** café Masc. molido.

ground floor noun planta Fem. baja; **they live on the ground floor** viven en la planta baja.

group noun grupo Masc.

grow verb 1 (plant, hair or person) crecer [35]; **your hair's grown!** te ha crecido el pelo; **my little sister's grown a lot this year** mi hermana pequeña ha crecido mucho este año; 2 cultivar [17] (fruit, vegetables); **our neighbour grows strawberries** nuestro vecino cultiva fresas; 3 **to grow a beard** dejarse [17] barba; 4 **to grow old** envejecer [35].

● **to grow up** crecer [35]; **the children are growing up** los niños están creciendo; **she grew up in Scotland** creció en Escocia.

growl verb gruñir [65].

grown-up noun adulto Masc., adulta Fem.

growth noun crecimiento Masc.

grudge noun to bear a grudge against somebody guardarle [17] rencor a alguien; she bears me a grudge me guarda rencor.

gruesome adjective horrible.

grumble verb refunfuñar [17]; she's always grumbling siempre está refunfuñando; to grumble about something refunfuñar por algo.

guarantee noun garantía Fem.; a year's guarantee una garantía de un año.

guarantee verb garantizar [22].

guard noun 1 a prison guard un guardia de prisiones; 2 (on a train) jefe Masc. de tren, jefa Fem. de tren; 3 a security guard un guardia de seguridad.

guard verb vigilar [17].

guard dog noun perro Masc. guardián.

guardian noun tutor Masc., tutora Fem.

Guatemalan noun guatemalteco Masc., guatemalteca Fem.

Guatemalan adjective guatemalteco/guatemalteca.

guess noun have a guess! ¡adivina!; it's a good guess lo has adivinado.

guess verb 1 adivinar [17]; guess who I saw last night! ¡adivina a quién vi anoche!; you'll never guess! ¡no lo vas a adivinar nunca!; guess what! ¿sabes qué?; 2 (suppose) suponer [11]; I guess so supongo que sí.

guest noun 1 invitado Masc., invitada Fem.; we've got guests coming tonight tenemos invitados

esta noche; 2 (in a hotel) cliente Masc./Fem.; 3 a paying guest un huésped de pago.

guide noun 1 (book, girl guide) guía Fem.; 2 (person) guía Masc./Fem.

guidebook noun guía Fem.

guide dog noun perro Masc. lazarillo.

guideline noun pauta Fem.

guilty adjective culpable; to feel guilty sentirse [14] culpable.

guinea pig noun (pet) cobaya Fem., (in an experiment) conejillo Masc. de indias.

guitar noun guitarra Fem.; to play the guitar tocar [31] la guitarra; on the guitar a la guitarra.

guitarist noun guitarrista Masc./Fem.

gum noun 1 (in mouth) encía Fem.; 2 (chewing gum) chicle Masc.

gun noun 1 pistola Fem.; 2 (rifle) fusil Masc.

guy noun tipo Masc. (informal); he's a nice guy es un tipo muy majo; a guy from Newcastle un tipo de Newcastle.

guy rope noun viento Masc. de una tienda de campaña.

gym noun 1 (gymnasium) gimnasio Masc.; to go to the gym ir [8] al gimnasio; 2 (gymnastics) gimnasia Fem.

gymnasium noun gimnasio Masc.

gymnast noun gimnasta Masc./Fem.

gymnastics noun gimnasia Fem.

gym shoe noun zapatilla Fem. de gimnasia.

Hh

habit noun costumbre Fem.; **to have a habit of doing** tener [9] la costumbre de hacer; **it's a bad habit** es una mala costumbre.

hail noun granizo Masc.

hailstone noun granizo Masc.

hailstorm noun granizada Fem.

hair noun 1 pelo Masc.; **to have short hair** tener [9] el pelo corto; **to brush your hair** cepillarse [17] el pelo; **to wash your hair** lavarse [17] el pelo; **to have your hair cut** cortarse [17] el pelo; **she's had her hair cut** se ha cortado el pelo; 2 **a hair** (from the head) un pelo (from the body) un vello.

hairbrush noun cepillo Masc. del pelo.

haircut noun 1 corte Masc. de pelo; **I like your new haircut** me gusta tu nuevo corte de pelo; 2 **to have a haircut** cortarse [17] el pelo.

hairdresser noun peluquero Masc., peluquera Fem.; **she's a hairdresser** es peluquera; **at the hairdresser's** en la peluquería.

hair drier noun secador Masc. de pelo.

hair gel noun gel Masc. para el cabello.

hairslide noun pasador Masc.

hairspray noun laca Fem. del pelo.

hairstyle noun peinado Masc.

hairy adjective peludo/peluda.

Haiti noun Haití Masc.

Haitian noun haitiano Masc., haitiana Fem.

Haitian adjective haitiano/haitiana.

half noun, pronoun 1 mitad Fem.; **half of** la mitad de; **I gave him half of the money** le di la mitad del dinero; 2 **to cut something in half** cortar algo por la mitad; 3 (as a fraction) medio; **three and a half** tres y medio; **she's five and a half** tiene seis años y medio; 4 (in time) media; **half an hour** media hora; **an hour and a half** una hora y media; **it's half past three** son las tres y media; 5 **half** a medio/media; **half a litre** medio litro; **half an apple** media manzana; 6 **half the people** la mitad de la gente; **half the time he's not here** la mitad del tiempo no está aquí.

half hour noun media hora Fem.; **every half hour** cada media hora.

half price adjective, adverb a mitad de precio; **half-price CDs** compactos a mitad de precio; **I bought it half price** lo compré a mitad de precio.

half-time noun descanso Masc.; **at half-time** en el descanso.

halfway adverb a mitad de camino; **halfway between Madrid and Barcelona** a mitad de camino

a
b
c
d
e
f
g
h
i
j
k
l
m
n
o
p
q
r
s
t
u
v
w
x
y
z

entre Madrid y Barcelona; **2 to be halfway through** ir [8] por la mitad de; **I'm halfway through my homework** voy por la mitad de los deberes.

hall noun **1** (*in a house*) entrada *Fem.*; **2** (*public*) salón *Masc.*; **the village hall** el salón de actos del pueblo; **3 a concert hall** una sala de conciertos.

ham noun **1** (*cooked*) jamón *Masc.* de York; **2** (*cured*) jamón *Masc.* serrano.

hamburger noun hamburguesa *Fem.*

hammer noun martillo *Masc.*

hammock noun hamaca *Fem.*

hamster noun hámster *Masc.*

hand noun **1** mano *Fem.*; **to have something in your hand** tener [9] algo en la mano; **to be holding hands** (*two people*) ir [8] cogidos de la mano; **they were holding hands** iban cogidos de la mano; **2 to give somebody a hand** echar [17] una mano a alguien; **can you give me a hand to move the table?** ¿puedes echarme una mano para mover la mesa?; **do you need a hand?** ¿necesitas que te echen una mano?; **3 on the other hand** ... por otro lado ...; **4** (*of a watch or clock*) manecilla *Fem.*; **the hour hand** la manecilla de las horas.

hand verb **to hand something to somebody** pasarle [17] algo a alguien; **I handed him the keys** le pasé las llaves.

handbag noun bolso *Masc.*

handbrake noun freno *Masc.* de mano.

handcuffs plural noun esposas *Fem. plural.*

handful noun **a handful of** un puñado de.

handkerchief noun pañuelo *Masc.*

handicapped adjective disminuido/disminuida.

handle noun **1** (*of a door*) picaporte *Masc.*; **2** (*of a drawer*) tirador *Masc.*; **3** (*on a cup or basket*) asa *Fem.*; **4** (*of a knife, tool, or pan*) mango *Masc.*

handle verb **1** encargarse [28] de; **Gina handles the accounts** Gina se encarga de la contabilidad; **2 she's good at handling people** se le da muy bien tratar con la gente.

handlebars plural noun manillar *Masc.*

hand luggage noun equipaje *Masc.* de mano.

handsome adjective guapo; **he's a very handsome guy** es un tipo muy guapo.

handwriting noun letra *Fem.*

handy adjective **1** práctico/práctica; **this little knife's very handy** este cuchillito es muy práctico; **2** a mano; **I always keep a notebook handy** siempre guardo un cuaderno a mano.

hang verb colgar [23]; **we hung the mirror on the wall** colgamos el espejo en la pared; **there was a mirror hanging on the wall** había un espejo colgado en la pared.

- **to hang on** esperar [17]; **hang on a second!** ¡espera un poco!
- **to hang up** (*on the phone*) colgar [23]; **she hung up on me** me colgó.
- **to hang something up** colgar [23] algo; **you can hang your coat up in the hall** puedes colgar el abrigo en la entrada.

hangover *noun* resaca *Fem.*; **to have a hangover** tener [9] resaca.

happen *verb* **1** pasar [17]; **what's happening?** ¿qué pasa?; **what happened to him?** ¿qué le pasó?; **it happened in June** pasó en junio; **2 what's happened to the can-opener?** ¿dónde se ha metido el abridor?; **3 if you happen to see Jill** si ves a Jill.

happily *adverb* **1** alegremente; **she smiled happily** sonrió alegremente; **2** (*willingly*) con mucho gusto; **I'll happily do it for you** lo haré por ti con mucho gusto.

happiness *noun* felicidad *Fem.*

happy *adjective* feliz; **a happy child** un niño feliz; **happy birthday!** ¡feliz cumpleaños!

harbour *noun* puerto *Masc.*

hard *adjective* **1** duro/dura; **2** (*difficult*) difícil; **a hard question** una pregunta difícil; **it's hard to know ...** es difícil saber ....

hard *adverb* mucho; **to study hard** estudiar [17] mucho; **to try hard** esforzarse [26] mucho; **to work hard** trabajar [17] duro.

hard-boiled egg *noun* huevo *Masc.* duro.

hard disk *noun* (*in a computer*) disco *Masc.* duro.

hardly *adverb* **1** apenas; **I can hardly hear him** apenas puedo oírle; **2 hardly any** casi nada; **there's hardly any milk** casi no hay nada de leche; **3 hardly ever** casi nunca; **I hardly ever see them** casi nunca los veo; **4 there was hardly anybody** no había casi nadie.

hard up *adjective* **to be hard up** estar [2] mal de dinero (*informal*).

harm *noun* **it won't do you any harm** no te va a pasar nada.

harm *verb* **to harm somebody** hacerle [7] daño a alguien; **a cup of coffee won't harm you** una taza de café no te va a hacer daño.

harvest *noun* cosecha *Fem.*; **to get the harvest in** hacer [7] la cosecha.

hat *noun* sombrero *Masc.*

hate *verb* odiar [17]; **I hate geography** odio la geografía.

hatred *noun* odio *Masc.*

haunted *adjective* embrujado/embrujada.

have *verb* **1** tener [9]; **Anna has three brothers** Anna tiene tres hermanos; **how many sisters do you have?** ¿cuántas hermanas tienes?; **2 to have got** tener [9]; **we've got a dog** tenemos un perro; **what have you got in your hand?** ¿qué tienes en la mano?; **3** (*to form past tenses, verbs in Spanish take 'haber'*) **I've finished** he terminado; **have you seen the film?** ¿has visto la película; **Rosie hasn't arrived yet** Rosie aún no ha llegado; **he had left** se había ido (*in* *question tags "have" is not translated)* **you've done this before, haven't you?** tú has hecho esto antes, ¿no?; **4 to have to do** tener [9] que hacer; **I have to phone my mum** tengo que llamar a mi madre; **5** tomar [17] *(food or drink)*; **we had a coffee** tomamos un café; **what will you have?** ¿qué vais a tomar?; **I'll have an omelette** voy a tomar una tortilla; **6 to have a shower** ducharse [17]; **to have a bath** bañarse [17]; **7 to have lunch** comer [18]; **to have dinner** *(in the evening)* cenar [17]; **8 to have a party** dar [4] una fiesta; **9** *(for illnesses)* tener [9]; **he has cancer** tiene cáncer; **I had flu** tuve la gripe; **10** *(for aches)* **she has stomachache** le duele el estómago; **I had a terrible headache** me dolía mucho la cabeza; **11 I'm going to have my hair cut** voy a cortarme el pelo; **she's had her TV repaired** ha arreglado la tele.

hawk *noun* halcón *Masc.*

hay *noun* heno *Masc.*

hay fever *noun* fiebre *Fem.* del heno.

hazelnut *noun* avellana *Fem.*

he *pronoun* 1 *('he', like other subject pronouns, is generally not translated in Spanish; the form of the verb tells you whether the subject of the verb is 'he/she/it, you, they', etc., so 'he' is only translated for emphasis)* **he lives in Newcastle** vive en Newcastle; **he's a student** es estudiante; **he's a very good teacher** es muy buen

profesor; **here he is!** ¡aquí está!; **2** *(for emphasis)* él; **he did it** lo hizo él.

head *noun* **1** cabeza *Fem.*; **he had a cap on his head** tenía un sombrero en la cabeza; **at the head of the queue** a la cabeza de la cola; **2** *(of school)* director *Masc.*, directora *Fem.*; **3** *(when tossing a coin)* **'heads or tails?' – 'heads'** '¿cara o cruz?' – 'cara'.

● **to head for something** dirigirse [49] a; **Liz headed for the door** Liz se dirigió a la puerta.

headache *noun* **I've got a headache** me duele la cabeza.

headlight *noun* faro *Masc.*

headline *noun* titular *Masc.*; **to hit the headlines** aparecer [35] en los titulares.

headmaster *noun* director *Masc.*

headmistress *noun* directora *Fem.*

headphones *plural noun* auriculares *Masc. plural.*

headquarters *n (plural)* **1** *(of organization)* sede *Fem.*; **2** *(military)* cuartel *Masc.* general.

headteacher *noun* director *Masc.*, directora *Fem.*

health *noun* salud *Fem.*

health centre *noun* centro *Masc.* médico.

healthy *adjective* **1** *(person)* **to be healthy** estar [2] sano; **2 a healthy diet** una dieta sana.

heap *noun* montón *Masc.*; **I've got heaps of things to do** tengo montones de cosas que hacer.

a b c d e f g h i j k l m n o p q r s t u v w x y z

hear verb oír [56]; **I can't hear you** no te oigo; **I can't hear anything** no oigo nada; **I hear you've bought a dog** he oído que te has comprado un perro.

● **to hear about something** enterarse [17] de algo; **have you heard about the concert?** ¿te has enterado de lo del concierto?

● **to hear from somebody: have you heard from Amanda?** ¿sabes algo de Amanda?; **I haven't heard from them** no sé nada de ellos.

hearing aid noun audífono Masc.

heart noun **1** corazón Masc.; **2** (in cards) **hearts** corazones Masc. plural; **the jack of hearts** la jota de corazones; ★ **to learn something by heart** aprender [18] algo de memoria.

heart attack noun ataque Masc. al corazón.

heat noun calor Masc.

heat verb **1** calentarse [29]; **the soup's heating** la sopa se está calentando; **2 to heat something** calentar [29] algo; **I'll go and heat the soup** voy a calentar la sopa.

heater noun estufa Fem.

heating noun calefacción Fem.

heaven noun cielo Masc.

heavy adjective **1** pesado/pesada; **a heavy bag** una bolsa pesada; **to be heavy** pesar [17] mucho; **my rucksack's really heavy** mi mochila pesa mucho; **2** (busy) ocupado/ocupada; **I've got a heavy day tomorrow** mañana tengo un día muy ocupado; **3 heavy rain** lluvia fuerte.

hectic adjective **a hectic day** un día muy ajetreado.

hedge noun seto Masc.

hedgehog noun erizo Masc.

heel noun **1** (of foot) talón Masc.; **2** (of shoe) tacón Masc.

height noun **1** (of a person) estatura Fem.; **2** (of a building) altura Fem.; **3** (of a mountain) altitud Fem.

helicopter noun helicóptero Masc.

hell noun infierno Masc.; **it's hell here!** ¡esto es un infierno!

hello exclamation **1** (greeting) hola; **2** (on the telephone) ¿dígame?

helmet noun casco Masc.

help noun ayuda Fem.; **do you need any help?** ¿necesitas ayuda?

help verb **1** ayudar [17]; **to help somebody to do** ayudar [17] a alguien a hacer; **can you help me move the table?** ¿me ayudas a mover la mesa?; **2 to help yourself to something** servirse [57] algo; **help yourselves to vegetables** serviros verdura; **help yourself!** ¡sírvete!; **3 help!** ¡socorro!

helping noun porción Fem.; **would you like a second helping?** ¿quieres repetir?.

hem noun dobladillo Masc.

hen noun gallina Fem.

her pronoun **1** la; **I know her** la conozco; **I saw her last week** la vi la semana pasada (with an infinitive or when telling someone to do something, 'la' joins onto the verb) **I can hear her** puedo oírla; **listen to her!** ¡escúchala!; (but *when telling someone NOT to do something, comes before the verb)* don't push her! ¡no la empujes!; **2** *(to her)* le; **I gave her my address** le di mis señas *('le' becomes 'se' before pronouns 'lo' or 'la')* **I lent it to her** se lo dejé; **3** *(after a preposition, in comparisons, or after the verb 'to be')* ella; **with her** con ella; **without her** sin ella; **he's older than her** él es mayor que ella; **it was her** era ella.

her *adjective* **1** *(before a singular noun)* su; **her brother** su hermano; **her house** su casa; **2** *(before a plural noun)* sus; **her children** sus niños; **3** *(with parts of the body)* el, la, los, las; **she had a glass in her hand** tenía un vaso en la mano; **she's washing her hands** se está lavando las manos.

herb *noun* hierba *Fem.*

herd *n* **1** *(of cattle)* manada *Fem.*; **2** *(of goats)* rebaño *Masc.*

here *adverb* **1** aquí; **not far from here** no lejos de aquí; **and here they are!** ¡aquí están!; **Tom isn't here at the moment** Tom no está aquí en este momento; **2** *(giving something)* **here it is** toma; **here's my address** toma mis señas; **here you are** toma.

hero *noun* héroe *Masc.*

heroin *noun* heroína *Fem.*

heroine *noun* heroína *Fem.*

hers *pronoun* **1** *(referring to a singular noun)* el suyo/la suya; **I took my hat and she took hers** yo cogí mi sombrero y ella cogió el

suyo; **I phoned my mum and Donna phoned hers** llamé a mi madre y Donna llamó a la suya; **2** *(referring to a plural noun)* los suyos/las suyas; **I've invited my parents and Karen's invited hers** yo he invitado a mis padres y Karen a los suyos; **I showed her my photos and she showed me hers** yo le enseñé mis fotos y ella me enseñó las suyas.

herself *pronoun* **1** *(as reflexive)* se; **she's hurt herself** se ha hecho daño; **she washed herself** se lavó; **2** *(for emphasis)* ella misma; **she said it herself** lo dijo ella misma; **3** **she did it by herself** lo hizo ella sola.

hesitate *verb* dudar [17]; **to hesitate to do** dudar en hacer.

heterosexual *noun* heterosexual *Masc./Fem.*

hi *exclamation* hola.

hiccups *plural noun* **to have the hiccups** tener [9] hipo.

hidden *adjective* escondido/escondida.

hide *verb* **1** *(person)* esconderse [18]; **she hid behind the door** se escondió detrás de la puerta; **2** **to hide something** esconder [18] algo; **who's hidden the chocolate?** ¿quién ha escondido el chocolate?

hide-and-seek *noun* **to play hide-and-seek** jugar [27] al escondite.

hi-fi *noun* equipo *Masc.* de alta fidelidad.

high *adjective* **1** alto/alta; **on a high shelf** en una estantería alta;

the wall is very high la pared es muy alta; **how high is the wall?** ¿qué altura tiene la pared?; **the wall is two metres high** la pared tiene dos metros de altura; **2** (*number, price, temperature*) alto/alta; **food prices are very high** el precio de la comida es muy alto; **3 at high speed** a alta velocidad; **4 high winds** vientos fuertes.

Highers, Advanced Highers *noun plural* selectividad *Fem.* (*Students take 'la selectividad' at the same age as Advanced Highers in Scotland.*)*You can explain Highers and Advanced Highers briefly as follows: Son exámenes que se hacen en todas cinco asignaturas, en el penúltimo año de la educación secundaria. Algunos alumnos también se presentan al Advanced Highers en el último años que pueden abarcar hasta tres asignaturas que ya se hayan estudiado para el nivel de los Highers* SEE **selectividad**.

high-heeled *adjective* de tacón alto; **high-heeled shoes** zapatos de tacón alto.

high jump *noun* salto *Masc.* de altura.

hijacking *noun* secuestro *Masc.*

hiking *noun* senderismo *Masc.*

hilarious *adjective* divertidísimo/divertidísima.

hill *noun* **1** (*low*) colina *Fem.* (*higher*) montaña *Fem.*; **2** (*sloping street or road*) **to go up the hill** subir la cuesta.

him *pronoun* **1** lo; **I know him** lo conozco; **I saw him last week** lo vi la semana pasada (*with an infinitive or when telling someone to do something, 'lo' joins onto the verb*) **I can't hear him** no puedo oírlo; **listen to him!** ¡escúchalo!; (*but when telling someone NOT to do something, 'lo' comes before the verb*) **don't push him!** ¡no lo empujes!; **2** (*to him*) le; **I gave him my address** le di mis señas (*'le' becomes 'se' before pronouns 'lo' or 'la'*) **I lent it to him** se lo dejé; **3** (*after a preposition, in comparisons, or after the verb 'to be'*) él; **with him** con él; **without him** sin él; **she's older than him** ella es mayor que él; **it was him** era él.

himself *pronoun* **1** (*as a reflexive*) se; **he's hurt himself** se hizo daño; **2** (*for emphasis*) él mismo; **he said it himself** lo dijo él mismo; **he did it by himself** lo hizo él solo.

hip *noun* cadera *Fem.*

hire *noun* alquiler *Masc.*; **car hire** alquiler de coches; **for hire** se alquila.

hire *verb* alquilar [17]; **we're going to hire a car** vamos a alquilar un coche.

his *adjective* **1** (*before a singular noun*) su; **his brother** su hermano; **his house** su casa; **2** (*before a plural noun*) sus; **his children** sus niños; **3** (*with parts of the body*) el, la, los, las; **he had a glass in his hand** tenía un vaso en la mano; **he's washing his hands** se está lavando las manos.

a
b
c
d
e
f
g
h
i
j
k
l
m
n
o
p
q
r
s
t
u
v
w
x
y
z

a b c d e f g h i j k l m n o p q r s t u v w x y z

his pronoun **1** (referring to a singular noun) el suyo/la suya; **I took my hat and he took his** yo cogí mi sombrero y él cogió el suyo; **I phoned my mum and Danny phoned his** llamé a mi madre y Danny llamó a la suya; **2** (referring to a plural noun) los suyos/las suyas; **I've invited my parents and Steve's invited his** he invitado a mis padres y Steve a los suyos; **I showed him my photos and he showed me his** yo le enseñé mis fotos y él me enseño las suyas.

historic adjective histórico/histórica.

history noun historia Fem.

hit noun (song) éxito Masc.; **their latest hit** su último éxito; **the film is a huge hit** la película es un gran éxito.

hit verb **1** golpear [17]; **to hit the ball** golpear la pelota; **2 to hit your head on something** darse [4] un golpe en la cabeza con algo; **3** chocar [31] con; **the car hit a tree** el coche chocó con el árbol; **4 she was hit by a car** la atropelló un coche.

hitch noun problema Masc.; **there's been a slight hitch** ha habido un pequeño problema.

hitch verb **to hitch a lift** hacer [7] dedo (informal).

hitchhike verb hacer [7] dedo (informal); **we hitchhiked to Valencia** hicimos dedo hasta Valencia.

hitchhiker noun autoestopista Masc./Fem.

hitchhiking noun autostop Masc.

HIV-negative adjective seronegativo/seronegativa.

HIV-positive adjective seropositivo/seropositiva.

hobby noun pasatiempo Masc.

hockey noun hockey Masc.; **to play hockey** jugar al hockey.

hockey stick noun palo Masc. de hockey.

hold verb **1** sostener [9]; **to hold something in your hand** sostener algo en la mano; **can you hold the torch?** ¿puedes sostener la linterna?; **2** (contain) contener [9]; **a jug which holds a litre** una jarra que contiene un litro; **3 to hold a meeting** celebrar [17] una reunión; **4 can you hold the line, please** no se retire, por favor; **5 hold on!** (wait) ¡un momento!, (on telephone) ¡no cuelgue!

● **to hold somebody up** (delay) entretener [9] a alguien; **I don't want to hold you up** no quiero entretenerte; **I was held up at the dentist's** me entretuve en el dentista.

● **to hold something up** (raise) levantar [17]; **he held up his glass** levantó su vaso.

hold-up noun **1** (delay) retraso Masc.; **2** (traffic jam) atasco Masc.; **3** (robbery) atraco Masc.

hole noun agujero Masc.

holiday noun **1** vacaciones Fem. plural; **where are you going for your holiday?** ¿dónde vas de vacaciones?; **have a good holiday!** ¡que pases unas buenas vacaciones!; **to be away on**

holiday estarde vacaciones; **to go on holiday** irse de vacaciones; **the school holidays** las vacaciones escolares; **2 a public holiday** un día de fiesta; **Monday's a holiday** el lunes es fiesta.

Holland noun Holanda Fem.

hollow adjective hueco/hueca.

holly noun acebo Masc.

holy adjective santo/santa.

home noun casa Fem.; **I was at home** estaba en casa; **to stay at home** quedarse [17] en casa; **make yourself at home** ponte cómodo.

home adverb a casa; **Susie's gone home** Susie se ha ido a casa; **I'll call in and see you on my way home** te iré a visitar de camino a mi casa; **to get home** llegar [28] a casa; **we got home at midnight** llegamos a casa a media noche.

homeless adjective sin hogar; **the homeless** la gente sin hogar.

homemade adjective casero/ casera; **homemade cakes** pasteles caseros.

home match noun **to play a home match** jugar [27] en casa.

homeopathic adjective homeopático/homeopática.

homesick adjective **to be homesick** tener [9] morriña.

homework noun deberes Masc. plural; **I did my homework** hice mis deberes; **my Spanish homework** mis deberes de español.

homosexual noun, adjective homosexual.

Honduran noun hondureño Masc., hondureña Fem.

Honduran adjective hondureño/ hondureña.

Honduras noun Honduras Fem.

honest adjective **1** honrado/ honrada; **2 to be honest** ... para serte sincero ...

honestly adverb sinceramente.

honesty noun honradez Fem.

honey noun miel Fem.

honeymoon noun luna Fem. de miel.

honour noun honor Masc.

hood noun capucha Fem.

hook noun **1** (in clothes) corchete Masc.; **2** (for fishing) anzuelo Masc.; **3** (for hanging pictures or clothes) gancho Masc.; **4 to take the phone of the hook** descolgar [23] el teléfono.

hooligan noun gamberro Masc., gamberra Fem.

hooray exclamation ¡hurra!

hoover verb pasar [17] la aspiradora por; **I hoovered my bedroom** pasé la aspiradora por mi habitación.

Hoover™ noun aspirador Masc., aspiradora Fem.

hope noun esperanza Fem.; **to give up hope** perder [36] la esperanza.

hope verb esperar [17]; **hoping to see you on Friday** esperando verte el domingo; **here's hoping!** ¡esperemos!; **I hope so** espero que sí; **I hope not** espero que no; **we hope you'll be able to come** esperamos que puedas venir (*'espero que' is followed by the subjunctive*).

a
b
c
d
e
f
g
h
i
j
k
l
m
n
o
p
q
r
s
t
u
v
w
x
y
z

hopeless adjective **to be hopeless at something** ser [1] un negado para algo (informal); **I'm hopeless at geography** soy un negado para la geografía.

horizon noun horizonte Masc.

horn noun **1** (of an animal) cuerno Masc.; **2** (of a car) bocina Fem.; **to sound your horn** tocar [31] la bocina; **3** (musical instrument) trompa Fem.; **to play the horn** tocar [31] trompa.

horoscope noun horóscopo Masc.

horrible adjective **1** horrible; **the weather was horrible** el tiempo era horrible; **she's really horrible!** ¡es realmente horrible!; **2 he was really horrible to me** me trató muy mal.

horrific adjective horroroso/horrorosa; **a horrific accident** un accidente horroroso.

horror noun horror Masc.

horror film noun película Fem. de terror.

horse noun caballo Masc.

horse racing noun carreras Fem. plural de caballos.

hose noun manguera Fem.

hospital noun hospital Masc.; **to be in hospital** estar [2] en el hospital; **to be taken into hospital** ser [1] hospitalizado.

hospitality noun hospitalidad Fem.

host noun anfitrión Masc., anfitriona Fem.; **my host family is very nice** la familia que me hospeda es muy amable.

hostage noun rehén Masc.

hostel noun youth hostel albergue Masc. juvenil.

hostess noun azafata Fem.; **an air hostess** una azafata de vuelo.

hot adjective **1** caliente; **a hot drink** una bebida caliente; **be careful, the plates are hot!** ¡cuidado! los platos están calientes; **2** (a person) **to be hot** tener [9] calor; **I'm hot** tengo calor; **I'm very hot** tengo mucho calor; **I'm too hot** tengo demasiado calor; **3** (the weather or temperature in a room) **it's hot** hace calor; **it's hot today** hace calor hoy; **it's very hot in the kitchen** hace mucho calor en la cocina; **4 a hot climate** un clima cálido; **5** (food: spicy) picante; **this curry's too hot for me** este curry es demasiado picante para mí.

hot dog noun perrito Masc. caliente.

hotel noun hotel Masc.

hour noun hora Fem.; **two hours later** dos horas más tarde; **we waited for two hours** esperamos dos horas; **two hours ago** hace dos horas; **to be paid by the hour** cobrar [17] por hora; **I earn six pounds an hour** gano seis libras por hora; **every hour** cada hora; **half an hour** media hora; **a quarter of an hour** un cuarto de hora; **an hour and a half** una hora y media.

hourly adjective there is an **hourly bus** hay un bus que sale cada hora.

hourly adverb the trains leave **hourly** los trenes salen cada hora.

house noun casa Fem.; **I'm at Judy's house** estoy en casa de Judy; **I'm going to Judy's house tonight** voy a casa de Judy esta noche; **I phoned from Judy's house** llamé desde casa de Judy.

housework noun tareas Fem. plural de la casa; **to do the housework** hacer [7] las tareas de la casa.

hovercraft noun aerodeslizador Masc.

how adverb **1** cómo; **how did you do it?** ¿cómo lo hiciste?; **how are you?** ¿cómo estás?; **I know how to do it** sé cómo hacerlo; **2 how was the party?** ¿qué tal fue la fiesta?; **3 how much?** ¿cuánto?; **how much money do you have?** ¿cuánto dinero tienes?; **how much is it?** ¿cuánto cuesta?; **4 how many?** ¿cuántos?; **how many brothers do you have?** ¿cuántos hermanos tienes?; **5 how old are you?** ¿cuántos años tienes?; **how heavy is it?** ¿cuánto pesa?; **how far is it?** ¿a qué distancia está?; **how far is it to Bilbao?** ¿a qué distancia está Bilbao?; **7 how long will it take?** ¿cuánto tardará?; **how long have you known her?** ¿cuánto tiempo hace que la conoces?; **8** (in exclamations) qué; **how nice!** ¡qué bonito!

however adverb sin embargo.

hug noun **to give somebody a hug** darle [4] un abrazo a alguien; **she gave me a hug** me dio un abrazo.

huge adjective enorme.

hum verb tararear [17] (a person).

human adjective humano/humana.

human being noun ser Masc. humano.

humour noun humor Masc.; **to have a sense of humour** tener [9] sentido del humor.

hundred number **1** cien; **a hundred** cien; **about a hundred** unos/unas cien; **about a hundred people** unas cien personas; **2** (for numbers 101 to 199) ciento; **one hundred and six** ciento seis; **3** (for numbers 200 to 999) two hundred doscientos/doscientas; **two hundred and ten** doscientos diez; **six hundred** seiscientos/seiscientas.

Hungary noun Hungría Fem.

hunger noun hambre Fem. (even though 'hambre' is feminine, it takes 'el' and 'un').

hungry adjective **to be hungry** tener [9] hambre; **I'm hungry** tengo hambre.

hunt verb cazar [22] (animals).

● **hunt for** (search for) buscar.

hurricane noun huracán Masc.

hurry noun **to be in a hurry** tener [9] prisa; **I'm in a hurry** tengo prisa.

hurry verb darse [4] prisa; **I must hurry** debo darme prisa; **we hurried home** nos dimos prisa para llegar a casa; **hurry up!** ¡date prisa!

hurt verb **1 to hurt somebody** hacer [7] daño a alguien; **you're hurting me!** me estás haciendo

a b c d e f g h i j k l m n o p q r s t u v w x y z

daño; **that hurts!** ¡eso hace daño!;
2 my back hurts me duele la
espalda; **my legs hurt** me duelen
las piernas; **3 to hurt yourself**
hacerse [7] daño; **did you hurt
yourself?** ¿te has hecho daño?; **4 to
hurt your hand** hacerse [7] daño en
la mano; **I hurt my arm** me hice
daño en el brazo.

husband noun marido Masc.

hymn noun himno Masc.

hypermarket noun
hipermercado Masc.

hyphen noun guión Masc.

hypnotize verb hipnotizar [25].

Ii

I pronoun **1** (like other subject
pronouns, 'I' is generally not
translated; in Spanish the form of
the verb tells you whether the
subject of the verb is 'I, we, they',
etc., so 'I' is only translated for
emphasis) **I am Scottish** soy
escocés; **I have two sisters** tengo
dos hermanas; **2** (for emphasis) yo;
I did it lo hice yo; **I went but
Robert didn't** yo fui pero Robert
no; **Tony and I** Tony y yo.

Iberia noun Iberia Fem.

Iberian adjective ibérico/ibérica.

ice noun hielo Masc.

iceberg noun iceberg Masc.

ice cream noun helado Masc.; **a
chocolate ice cream** un helado de
chocolate.

ice-cube noun cubito Masc. de
hielo.

ice hockey noun hockey Masc.
sobre hielo.

ice rink noun pista Fem. de hielo.

ice-skating noun patinaje Masc.
sobre hielo; **to go ice-skating** ir [8]
a patinar sobre hielo.

icing noun azúcar Masc. glaseado.

icon noun icono Masc.

icy adjective **1** cubierto/cubierta de
hielo (a road); **2** (very cold) helado/
helada; **an icy wind** un viento
helado.

idea noun idea Fem.; **what a good
idea!** ¡qué buena idea!; **I've no idea**
no tengo ni idea.

ideal adjective ideal.

identical adjective idéntico/
idéntica; **identical twins** gemelos
(male, or male and female),
gemelas (female only).

identity card noun carné Fem. de
identidad.

idiot noun idiota Masc./Fem.

idiotic adjective idiota.

i.e. (in writing) i.e. (in speech) esto
es.

if conjunction **1** si; **if Sue's there** si
Sue está allí; **if it rains** si llueve; **if
not** si no (when talking about
something that might or might not
happen, 'si' is followed by the
subjunctive) **if I won the lottery** si
ganase la lotería; **2 if only** ... ojalá
...; **if only you'd told me** ojalá me lo
hubieses dicho; **3 even if** incluso
si; **even if it snows** incluso si
nieva; **4 if I were you** ... yo que tú
...; **if I were you, I'd forget it** yo que
tú me olvidaría del asunto.

ignore verb 1 ignorar [17] (a person); 2 no hacer [7] caso de (what somebody says); **just ignore it** no hagas caso.

ill adjective enfermo/enferma; **to fall ill, to be taken ill** enfermar [17]; **to feel ill** sentirse [14] mal.

illegal adjective ilegal.

illness noun enfermedad Fem.

illustrated adjective ilustrado/ ilustrada.

illustration noun ilustración Fem.

imagination noun imaginación Fem.; **to show imagination** demostrar [24] imaginación.

imaginative adjective imaginativo/imaginativa.

imagine verb imaginar [17]; **imagine that you're very rich** imagina que eres muy rico; **you can't imagine how hard it was!** ¡no puedes imaginarte lo difícil que fue!

imitate verb imitar [17].

imitation noun imitación Fem.

immediate adjective inmediato/ inmediata.

immediately adverb inmediatamente; **I rang them immediately** los llamé inmediatamente; **immediately before** justo antes; **immediately after** justo después.

immigrant noun inmigrante Masc./Fem.

immigration noun inmigración Fem.

impact noun impacto Masc.

impatience noun impaciencia Fem.

impatient adjective 1 impaciente; **2 to get impatient with somebody** impacientarse [17] con alguien.

impatiently adverb con impaciencia.

imperfect noun (of a verb) imperfecto Masc.; **in the imperfect** en imperfecto.

import noun importación Fem.

import verb importar [17].

importance noun importancia Fem.

important adjective importante.

impossible adjective imposible; **it's impossible to find a telephone** es imposible encontrar un teléfono.

impressed adjective impresionado/impresionada.

impression noun impresión Fem.; **to make a good impression on somebody** causar [17] una buena impresión a alguien; **I got the impression he was hiding something** me dio la impresión de que estaba ocultando algo.

improve verb mejorar [17]; **to improve something** mejorar [17] algo; **the weather is improving** el tiempo está mejorando.

improvement noun 1 (a change for the better) mejora Fem.; **2** (gradual progress) progreso Masc. (in schoolwork, for example).

in preposition, adverb 1 en; **in Spain** en España; **in Spanish** en español; **in Barcelona** en Barcelona; **in my**

a b c d e f g h i j k l m n o p q r s t u v w x y z

a pocket en mi bolsillo; **in the**
b **newspaper** en el periódico; **in my**
class en mi clase; **I was in the**
c **bath** estaba en el baño; **a house in**
the country una casa en el campo;
d **in school** en el colegio; **in town** en
e la ciudad; **in the photo** en la foto;
2 in pencil a lápiz; **in twos** de dos
f en dos; **3** (*wearing*) de; **the girl in**
g **the pink shirt** la chica de la falda
rosa; **he was in a suit** llevaba un
h traje; **dressed in white** vestida de
i blanco; **4** (*with month, season, or*
year) en mayo; **in 1998** en mil
j novecientos noventa y ocho; **in**
k **winter** en invierno; **5** (*with parts of*
the day) **in the morning** por la
l mañana; **in the night** por la noche;
m **at eight in the morning** a las ocho
de la mañana; **6 I'll phone you in**
n **ten minutes** te llamaré dentro de
o diez minutos; **she did it in five**
minutes lo hizo en cinco minutos;
p **7** (*after superlative*) de; **the tallest**
q **boy in the class** el chico más alto
de la clase; **the biggest city in the**
r **world** la ciudad más grande del
s mundo; **8 in time** con el tiempo;
9 in the sun al sol; **in the rain** bajo
t la lluvia; **10 to come in** entrar [17];
u **to go in** entrar [17]; **we went into**
the cinema entramos en el cine; **to**
v **run in** entrar [17] corriendo; **11 to**
w **be in** (*at home, around*) estar [2];
Mick's not in at the moment Mick
x no está en este momento.

y **include** *verb* incluir [54]; **dinner is**
z **included in the price** la cena está
incluida en el precio; **service**
included servicio incluido.

including *preposition* incluido; **50**
pounds including VAT cincuenta
libras IVA incluido; **everyone,**
including children todo el mundo
incluidos los niños; **including**
Sundays incluidos los domingos;
not including Sundays sin incluir
los domingos.

income *noun* ingresos *Masc.*
plural.

income tax *noun* impuesto *Masc.*
sobre la renta.

inconvenient *adjective* **1** poco
conveniente (*a place or an*
arrangement); **2** inoportuno/
inoportuna (*a time*).

increase *noun* aumento *Masc.* (*in*
price, for example).

increase *verb* aumentar [17]; **the**
price has increased by ten
pounds el precio ha aumentado
diez libras.

incredible *adjective* increíble.

incredibly *adverb* (*very*)
increíblemente; **the film's**
incredibly boring la película es
increíblemente aburrida.

indeed *adverb* **1** (*to emphasize*)
she's very pleased **indeed** está
contentísima; **I'm very hungry**
indeed tengo muchísima hambre;
thank you very much **indeed**
muchísimas gracias; **2** (*certainly*)
'can you hear his radio?' –
'indeed I can!' ¿oyes su radio?' –
'ya lo creo'; **'do you like it?' – 'I do**
indeed!' ¿te gusta? – 'sí,
muchísimo'.

indefinite article noun (in grammar) artículo Masc. indefinido.

independence noun independencia Fem.

independent adjective 1 (a country or person) independiente; 2 **an independent school** una escuela privada.

index noun índice Masc.

index finger noun dedo Masc. índice.

India noun India Fem.

Indian noun (of India) indio Masc., india Fem.

Indian adjective (of India) indio/india.

indigestion noun indigestión Fem.; **to have indigestion** tener [9] indigestión.

indirect adjective indirecto/indirecta.

individual noun individuo Masc.

individual adjective 1 individual (a serving or a contribution, for example); 2 **individual tuition** clases Fem. plural particulares.

indoor adjective **an indoor swimming pool** una piscina cubierta; **an indoor plant** una planta de interior.

indoors adverb dentro; **it's cooler indoors** hace más fresco dentro; **to go indoors** entrar [17]; **to stay indoors** quedarse [17] dentro.

industrial adjective industrial.

industrial estate noun zona Fem. industrial.

industry noun industria Fem.; **the advertising industry** la industria de la publicidad.

inevitable adjective inevitable.

inevitably adverb inevitablemente.

inexperienced adjective inexperto/inexperta.

infected adjective infectado/infectada.

infection noun infección Fem.; **an eye infection** una infección de ojos; **a throat infection** anginas Fem. plural.

infectious adjective infeccioso/infecciosa.

infinitive noun infinitivo Masc.; **in the infinitive** en infinitivo.

inflation noun inflación Fem.

influence noun influencia Fem.; **to be a good influence on somebody** ser [1] una buena influencia para alguien.

inform verb informar [17]; **to inform somebody that** informar a alguien de que; **they informed us that there was a problem** nos informaron de que había un problema; **to inform somebody of something** informar a alguien de algo.

informal adjective 1 informal (a meal or event, for example); 2 (language) familiar; **an informal expression** una expresión familiar.

information noun información Fem.; **I need some information about flights to Madrid** necesito información sobre vuelos a

a b c d e f g h i j k l m n o p q r s t u v w x y z

Madrid; **a piece of information** un dato.

information desk noun
mostrador Masc. de información.

information office noun oficina Fem. de información.

information technology, IT noun informática Fem.

infuriating adjective exasperante.

ingredient noun ingrediente Masc.

initials plural noun iniciales Fem. plural; **put your initials here** pon tus iniciales aquí.

injection noun inyección Fem.; **to give somebody an injection** ponerle [11] una inyección a alguien.

injure verb herir [14].

injured adjective herido/herida.

injury noun herida Fem.

ink noun tinta Fem.

in-laws plural noun suegros Masc. plural.

innocent adjective inocente.

insane adjective loco/loca.

inscription noun inscripción Fem.

insect noun insecto Masc.; **an insect bite** una picadura de insecto.

insert verb insertar [17].

inside noun interior Masc.; **the inside of the oven** el interior del horno.

inside preposition dentro de; **inside the cinema** dentro del cine.

inside adverb dentro; **she's inside, I think** creo que está dentro; **to go inside** entrar [17].

inside out adjective, adverb del revés; **your jumper's inside out** llevas el jersey del revés.

insist verb 1 insistir [19]; **if you insist** si insistes; **to insist on doing** insistir en hacer; **he insisted on paying** insistió en pagar; 2 **to insist that** insistir en que; **Ruth insisted I was wrong** Ruth insistió en que yo estaba equivocada.

inspection noun inspección Fem.

inspector noun inspector Masc., inspectora Fem.

inspiration noun inspiración Fem.

install verb instalar [17].

instalment noun 1 (of a TV or radio serial) episodio Masc.; 2 (payment) plazo Masc.; **to pay by instalments** pagar [28] a plazos.

instance noun **for instance** por ejemplo.

instant noun instante Masc.; **come here this instant!** ¡ven aquí ahora mismo!

instant adjective 1 instantáneo/ instantánea (coffee or soup); 2 (immediate) inmediato/ inmediata (an effect or a success, for example).

instead adverb 1 **Ted couldn't go, so I went instead** Ted no pudo ir, así que fui yo en su lugar; **we didn't go to the concert, we went to Lucy's instead** no fuimos al concierto, fuimos a casa de Lucy; 2 **instead of** en vez de; **instead of pudding I had cheese** en vez de dulce tomé queso; **instead of**

playing tennis we went swimming en vez de jugar al tenis nos fuimos a nadar.

instinct noun instinto Masc.

instruct verb **to instruct somebody to do** ordenar [17] a alguien que haga ('que' is followed by the subjunctive); **the teacher instructed us to stay together** la profesora nos ordenó que nos quedásemos juntos.

instructions plural noun instrucciones Fem. plural; **follow the instructions on the packet** siga las instrucciones del paquete; **'instructions for use'** 'modo de empleo'.

instructor noun **1** monitor Masc., monitora Fem.; **my skiing instructor** mi monitor de esquí; **2** profesor Masc., profesora Fem.; **my driving instructor** mi profesor de conducir.

instrument noun instrumento Masc.; **to play an instrument** tocar [31] un instrumento.

insulin noun insulina Fem.

insult noun insulto Masc.

insult verb insultar [17].

insurance noun seguro Masc.; **travel insurance** seguro de viaje; **fire insurance** seguro contra incendios; **do you have medical insurance?** ¿tienes seguro médico?

intelligence noun inteligencia Fem.

intelligent adjective inteligente.

intend verb **1** querer [12]; **as I intended** como yo quería; **2 to intend to do** tener [9] pensado

hacer; **we intend to spend the night in Rome** tenemos pensado pasar la noche en Roma.

intensive adjective intensivo/intensiva; **an intensive course** un curso intensivo; **in intensive care** en cuidados intensivos.

intention noun intención Fem.; **I have no intention of paying** no tengo ninguna intención de pagar.

interest noun **1** (hobby) afición Fem.; **what are your interests?** ¿qué aficiones tienes?; **2** (keenness) interés Masc.; **she showed interest** mostró interés.

interest verb interesar [17]; **that doesn't interest me** eso no me interesa.

interested adjective **Sean's very interested in cooking** a Sean le interesa mucho la cocina.

interesting adjective interesante.

interfere verb **1 to interfere with something** (to fiddle with it) tocar [31] algo; **don't interfere with my computer!** ¡no toques mi ordenador!; **2 to interfere in** entrometerse [18] en (someone else's affairs).

interior adjective interior.

interior designer noun interiorista Masc./Fem.

international adjective internacional.

Internet noun Internet Fem.; **on the Internet** en Internet ('Internet' is never used with an article).

Internet cafe noun cibercafé Masc.; **where is there an Internet cafe?** ¿dónde hay un cibercafé?

a b c d e f g h i j k l m n o p q r s t u v w x y z

a   **interpreter** noun intérprete Masc./Fem.

b   **interrupt** verb interrumpir [19].

c   **interruption** noun interrupción Fem.

d

e   **interval** noun intermedio Masc. (in a play or concert).

f   **interview** noun entrevista Fem.; **a job interview** una entrevista de trabajo; **a TV interview** una entrevista en la tele.

g

h

i   **interview** verb entrevistar [17] (on TV, radio).

j

k   **interviewer** noun entrevistador Masc., entrevistadora Fem.

l   **into** preposition **1** dentro; **I put the cat into his basket** puse al gato dentro de su cesta; **2 to go into** entrar, entrar [17] a; **he's gone into the bank** ha entrado al banco; **3 to get into** entrar [17] en (car); **we all got into the car** entramos todos en el coche; **4 to go into town** ir [8] a la ciudad; **Mum's gone into town** mamá se ha ido a la ciudad; **to get into bed** meterse [18] a la cama; **5 to translate into Spanish** traducir [60] al español; **to change pounds into euros** cambiar [17] libras a euros.

m

n

o

p

q

r

s

t

u   **introduce** verb presentar [17]; **she introduced me to her brother** me presentó a su hermano; **can I introduce you to my mother?** ¿te puedo presentar a mi madre?

v

w

x   **introduction** noun (in a book) introducción Fem.

y

z   **invade** verb invadir [19].

invalid noun inválido Masc., inválida Fem.

invasion noun invasión Fem.

invent verb inventar [17].

invention noun invento Masc.

inverted commas plural noun comillas Fem. plural; **in inverted commas** entre comillas.

investigation noun investigación Fem.; **an investigation into the fire** una investigación sobre el fuego.

invisible adjective invisible.

invitation noun invitación Fem.; **an invitation to dinner** una invitación a cenar.

invite verb invitar [17]; **Kirsty invited me to lunch** Kirsty me invitó a comer; **he's invited me out on Tuesday** me ha invitado a salir el martes.

invoice noun factura Fem.

involve verb **1** suponer [11]; **it involves a lot of work** supone mucho trabajo; **2** (consist in) **what does the job involve?** ¿en qué consiste el trabajo?; **3 to be involved in** tomar [17] parte en; **I am involved in the new project** estoy tomando parte en el nuevo proyecto.

Iran noun Iran Masc.

Iraq noun Irak Masc.

Ireland noun Irlanda Fem.; **the Republic of Ireland** la República Irlandesa.

iris noun lirio Masc.

Irish noun 1 (*the language*)
irlandés Masc.; 2 (*the people*) the
Irish los irlandeses.
Irish adjective irlandés/irlandesa.

Irishman noun irlandés.

Irish Sea noun mar Masc. de
Irlanda.

Irishwoman noun irlandesa Fem.

iron noun 1 (*for clothes*) plancha
Fem.; 2 (*the metal*) hierro Masc.
iron verb planchar [17].

ironing noun to do the ironing
planchar [17].

ironing board noun tabla Fem. de
planchar.

irregular adjective irregular.

irresponsible adjective
irresponsable.

irritating adjective irritante.

Islam noun Islam Masc.

Islamic adjective islámico/
islámica.

island noun isla Fem.

isolated adjective aislado/aislada.

Israel noun Israel Masc.

Israeli noun israelí Masc./Fem.
Israeli adjective israelí.

issue noun 1 (*something you
discuss*) tema Masc.; a political
issue un tema político; 2 (*of a
magazine*) número Masc.
issue verb distribuir [54].

it pronoun 1 ('*it*' *like other subject
pronouns is generally not
translated; in Spanish the form of
the verb tells you whether the
subject of the verb is 'he/she/it, we,
they', etc*) 'where is my bag?' – 'it's
in the kitchen' '¿dónde está mi
bolso?' – 'está en la cocina'; **read**

this book, it's great lee este libro,
es genial; '**how old is your car?**' –
'**it's five years old**' '¿cuántos años
tiene tu coche?' - 'cinco'; 2 (*as the
object of the verb*) lo/la; **where's
my book? I've lost it** ¿dónde está
mi libro? lo he perdido; **give me
the suitcase, I'll carry it** dame la
maleta, yo la llevo (*with a verb in
the infinitive or when telling
somebody to do something, 'lo' or
'la' join onto the verb*) **I've finished
the letter, I only have to sign it** he
terminado la carta, sólo me queda
firmarla; **it's your money, take it**
es tu dinero, cógelo (*but when
telling somebody NOT to do
something, 'lo' or 'la' goes before the
verb*) **it's an expensive vase, don't
break it** es un jarrón caro, no lo
rompas; 3 **who is it?** ¿quién es?;
it's me soy yo; **what is it?** ¿qué es?;
4 **yes, it's true** sí, es verdad; **it
doesn't matter** no importa; 5 **it's
raining** está lloviendo; **it's a nice
day** hace buen día; **it's very cold
here** hace mucho frío aquí; **it's two
o'clock** son las dos; 6 (*after a
preposition*) **I don't want to talk
about it** no quiero hablar de ello;
the box goes behind it la caja va
detrás.

IT noun (*short for information
technology*) informática Fem.

Italian noun 1 (*the language*)
italiano Masc.; 2 (*person*) italiano
Masc., italiana Fem.

Italian adjective 1 italiano/
italiana; **Italian food** la comida
italiana; 2 de italiano (*a teacher or*

a *a lesson;* **my Italian class** mi clase de italiano.

b **italics** noun cursiva *Fem.;* **in italics** en cursiva.

c **Italy** noun Italia *Fem.*

d **itch** verb **1** (*a garment*) picar [31]; **this sweater itches** este jersey pica; **2** (*a part of the body*) **my back is itching** me pica la espalda; **I'm itching all over** me pica todo el cuerpo.

f

g

h **item** noun artículo *Masc.*

i **its** adjective **1** (*before a singular noun*) su; **its ear** su oreja; **2** (*before a plural noun*) sus; **its toys** sus juguetes.

j

k **itself** pronoun **1** (*as a reflexive*) se; **the cat is washing itself** el gato se está lavando; **2** (*by itself*) solo/sola; **he left the dog by itself** dejó al perro solo.

l

m

n **ivory** noun marfil *Masc.*

o **ivy** noun hiedra *Fem.*

p

q

r

Jj

s **jack** noun **1** (*in cards*) jota *Fem.;* **the jack of clubs** la jota de tréboles; **2** (*for a car*) gato *Masc.*

t

u **jacket** noun **1** chaqueta *Fem.;* **2** (*casual*) americana *Fem.*

v **jagged** adjective dentado/dentada.

w **jail** noun cárcel *Fem.*

jail verb meter [18] en la cárcel.

x **jam** noun **1** (*that you eat*) mermelada *Fem.;* **raspberry jam** mermelada de frambuesa; **2 a traffic jam** un atasco (de tráfico).

y

z

Jamaica noun Jamaica *Fem.*

Jamaican noun jamaicano *Masc.,* jamaicana *Fem.*

Jamaican adjective jamaicano/ jamaicana.

January noun enero *Masc.*

Japan noun Japón *Masc.*

Japanese noun **1** (*the language*) japonés *Masc.;* **2** (*person*) japonés *Masc.,* japonesa *Fem.;* **the Japanese** los japoneses.

Japanese adjective japonés/ japonesa.

jar noun bote *Masc.;* **a jar of jam** un bote de mermelada.

jazz noun jazz *Masc.*

jealous adjective celoso/celosa.

jealousy noun celos *Masc. plural.*

jeans noun vaqueros *Masc. plural;* **my jeans** mis vaqueros; **a pair of jeans** unos vaqueros.

jelly noun **1** (*clear jam*) jalea *Fem.;* **2** (*dessert*) gelatina *Fem.*

jellyfish noun medusa *Fem.*

jersey noun **1** (*sweater*) jersey *Masc.;* **2** (*for football*) camiseta *Fem.*

Jesus noun Jesús *Masc.;* **Jesus Christ** Jesucristo.

Jew noun judío *Masc.,* judía *Fem.*

jewel noun joya *Fem.*

jeweller noun joyero *Masc.,* joyera *Fem.*

jeweller's noun joyería *Fem.*

jewellery noun joyas *Fem. plural.*

Jewish adjective judío/judía.

jigsaw noun rompecabezas *Masc.* puzzle *Masc.*

job noun 1 (paid work) trabajo Masc.; **a job as a secretary** un trabajo de secretaria; **he's got a job** tiene un trabajo; **out of a job** sin trabajo; **what's your job?** ¿en qué trabajas?; 2 (a task) tarea Fem.; **it's not an easy job** no es una tarea fácil; **she made a good job of it** lo hizo muy bien.

jobless adjective en paro.

jog verb **to go jogging** hacer [7] footing.

join verb 1 (become a member of) hacerse [7] socio de; **I've joined the judo club** me he hecho socio del club de judo; 2 (to meet up with) **you go ahead, I'll join you later** id vosotros, yo voy más tarde; **we are going for a meal, do you want to join us?** vamos a salir a comer, ¿quieres venirte con nosotros?; 3 **to join two things together** unir [19] dos cosas; 4 **to join a queue** ponerse [11] a la cola.

● **to join in** 1 participar [17]; **Ruth never joins in** Ruth nunca participa; 2 **to join in something** tomar [17] parte en algo; **won't you join in the game?** ¿no quieres tomar parte en el juego?

joiner noun carpintero Masc., carpintera Fem.

joint noun 1 (of meat) corte Masc.; **a joint of beef** un corte de carne; 2 (in your body) articulación Fem.; 3 **the joint winner of the Nobel Prize** uno de los ganadores del Premio Nobel.

joke noun 1 (a funny story) chiste Masc.; **to tell a joke** contar [24] un chiste; 2 (directed against somebody) broma Fem.; **to play a joke on somebody** gastarle [17] una broma a alguien.

joke verb bromear [17]; **you must be joking!** ¡estás bromeando!

joker noun (in cards) comodín Masc.

journalism noun periodismo Masc.

journalist noun periodista Masc./Fem.; **Sean's a journalist** Sean es periodista.

journey noun viaje Masc.; **our journey to Turkey** nuestro viaje a Turquía; **a bus journey** un viaje en autobús.

joy noun alegría Fem.

joystick noun (for computer games) mando Masc.

Judaism noun judaismo Masc.

judge noun juez Masc., jueza Fem.

judge verb juzgar [28].

judgement noun 1 (sense) juicio Masc.; 2 (judge's decision) sentencia Fem.

judo noun judo Masc.; **he does judo** hace judo.

jug noun jarra Fem. (big) jarrita Fem. (small).

juggle verb hacer [17] malabarismos.

juice noun zumo Masc.; **two orange juices, please** dos zumos de naranja, por favor.

juicy adjective jugoso/jugosa.

jukebox noun máquina Fem. de discos.

July noun julio Masc.

a b c d e f g h i j k l m n o p q r s t u v w x y z

a

jumble sale *noun* mercadillo Masc. de beneficencia.

b

jumbo jet *noun* jumbo Masc.

jump *noun* salto Masc.; **a parachute jump** un salto en paracaídas.

c

d

jump *verb* saltar [17].

e

jumper *noun* jersey Masc.

f

junction *noun* **1** (*of roads*) cruce Masc.; **2** (*on railway*) empalme Masc..

g

h

June *noun* junio Masc.

jungle *noun* selva Fem.

i

j

junior *adjective* **a junior school** una escuela primaria; **the juniors** los alumnos de primaria.

k

l

junk *noun* **1** (*rubbish*) basura Fem.; **2** (*discarded things*) trastos Masc. plural viejos.

m

n

junk food *noun* comida Fem. basura.

o

jury *noun* jurado Masc.

p

just *adverb* **1** justo; **just on time** justo a tiempo; **just after the church** justo después de misa; **it's just what I need** es justo lo que necesito; **2 to have just done** acabar [17] de hacer; **Tom has just arrived** Tom acaba de llegar; **Helen had just called** Helen acaba de llamar; **3 I'm just finishing the ironing** estoy terminando de planchar; **4** (*only*) sólo; **just for fun** sólo por pasarlo bien; **he's just a child** es sólo un niño; **there's just me and Justine** sólo estamos Justine y yo; **5 just as** igual; **it's just as good as the other** es igual de bueno que el otro; **it's just as**

q

r

s

t

u

v

w

x

y

z

possible es igualmente posible; **6 just coming!** ¡ahora mismo voy!

justice *noun* justicia Fem.

Kk

kangaroo *noun* canguro Masc.

karate *noun* kárate Masc.

kebab *noun* brocheta Fem.

keen *adjective* **1** (*enthusiastic*) **you don't look too keen** no pareces muy entusiasmado; **they were keen on the idea** estaban interesados en la idea; **he's not keen on fish** no le gusta el pescado; **2** (*committed*) **he's a keen photographer** le encanta la fotografía.

keep *verb* **1** quedarse [17] con; **I kept the letter** me quedé con la carta; **keep the change** quédese con el cambio; **2 to keep something for someone** guardar [17] algo a alguien; **will you keep my seat?** ¿me guardas el sitio?; **to keep a secret** guardar [17] un secreto; **3 to keep somebody waiting** hacer [7] esperar a alguien; **4** (*to store*) guardar; **I keep my bike in the garage** guardo mi bici en el garaje; **where do you keep the saucepans?** ¿dónde guardas las cacerolas?; **5 to keep on doing** seguir [64] haciendo; **she kept on talking** siguió hablando; **keep straight on** siga todo recto; **6 to keep on doing** (*time after time*) no

parar de hacer; **he keeps on ringing me up** no para [17] de llamarme; **7 keep calm!** ¡no te pongas nervioso!; **keep still!** ¡estate quieto!; **keep out of the sun** no te pongas al sol; **8 to keep a promise** mantener [9] una promesa.

kerb *noun* bordillo *Masc.* de la acera.

ketchup *noun* ketchup *Masc.*

kettle *noun* hervidora *Fem.*; **to put the kettle on** enchufar la hervidora (*electric*).

key *noun* **1** (*for a lock*) llave *Fem.*; **a bunch of keys** un manojo de llaves; **2** (*on a piano or typewriter*) tecla *Fem.*

keyboard *noun* (*for a piano or a computer*) teclado *Masc.*

keyhole *noun* ojo *Masc.* de la cerradura.

kick *noun* (*from a person or a horse*) patada *Fem.*; **to give somebody a kick** darle [4] una patada a alguien; ★ **to get a kick out of doing** disfrutar [17] haciendo.

kick *verb* **to kick somebody** darle [4] una patada a alguien; **to kick the ball** darle [4] una patada al balón.

● **to kick off** empezar [25].

kick-off *noun* saque *Masc.* inicial.

kid *noun* niño *Masc.*, niña *Fem.* (*child*); **Dad's looking after the kids** papá está cuidando de los niños.

kidnap *verb* secuestrar [17].

kidnapper *noun* secuestrador *Masc.*, secuestradora *Fem.*

kidney *noun* riñón *Masc.*

kill *verb* matar [17]; **she was killed in an accident** se mató en un accidente.

killer *noun* (*murderer*) asesino *Masc.*, asesina *Fem.*

kilo *noun* kilo *Masc.*; **a kilo of sugar** un kilo de azúcar; **five euros a kilo** cinco euros el kilo.

kilogramme *noun* kilogramo *Masc.*

kilometre *noun* kilómetro *Masc.*

kilt *noun* falda *Fem.* escocesa.

kind *noun* tipo *Masc.*; **it's a kind of fruit** es un tipo de fruta; **all kinds of people** todo tipo de personas.

kind *adjective* amable; **Marion was very kind to me** Marion fue muy amable conmigo.

kindness *noun* amabilidad *Fem.*

king *noun* rey *Masc.*; **King Juan Carlos** el rey Juan Carlos; **the king of hearts** el rey de corazones.

kingdom *noun* reino *Masc.*; **the United Kingdom** el Reino Unido.

kiosk *noun* **1** (*for newspapers or snacks*) quiosco *Masc.*; **2** (*for a phone*) cabina *Fem.*

kiss *noun* beso *Masc.*; **to give somebody a kiss** darle [4] un beso a alguien.

kiss *verb* besar [17]; **kiss me!** ¡bésame!; **to kiss somebody goodbye** darle [4] un beso de despedida a alguien; **we kissed each other** nos besamos.

kit *noun* **1** (*of tools*) **a tool kit** una caja de herramientas; **a first-aid**

a b c d e f g h i j k l m n o p q r s t u v w x y z

kit un botiquín; **2** (*clothes*) equipo Masc.; **where's my gym kit?** ¿dónde está mi equipo de gimnasia?; **3** (*for making a model, a piece of furniture, etc*) kit Masc.

kitchen noun cocina Fem.; **the kitchen table** la mesa de la cocina.

kitchen roll noun papel Masc. de cocina.

kite noun (*toy*) cometa Fem.; **to fly a kite** hacer [7] volar una cometa.

kitten noun gatito Masc., gatita Fem.

kiwi fruit noun kiwi Masc.

knack noun tranquilito Mac.

knee noun rodilla Fem.; **to be on your knees** estar [2] de rodillas.

kneel verb (*to kneel down*) arrodillarse [17] (*to be on your knees*) estar [2] de rodillas.

knickers plural noun bragas Fem. plural.

knife noun cuchillo Masc.

knight noun (*in chess*) caballo Masc.

knit verb hacer [7] punto.

knitting noun punto Masc.

knocker noun aldaba Fem.

knob noun pomo Masc. (*on a door*); tirador Masc. (*on a drawer*).

knock noun golpe Masc.; **a knock on the head** un golpe en la cabeza; **a knock at the door** un golpe en la puerta.

knock verb **1** (*to bang*) darse [4] un golpe; **I knocked my arm on the table** me di un golpe en el brazo con la mesa; **2 to knock at the door** llamar [17] a la puerta.

● **to knock down 1** (*in a traffic* *accident*) atropellar [17] (*a person*); **2** (*to demolish*) derribar [17] (*an old building*).

● **to knock out 1** (*to make unconscious*) dejar [17] sin sentido; **2** (*in sport, to eliminate*) eliminar [17].

knot noun nudo Masc.; **to tie a knot in something** hacer [7] un nudo a algo.

know verb **1** (*facts*) saber [13]; **do you know where Tim is?** ¿sabes dónde está Tim?; **I know they've moved house** sé que se han cambiado de casa; **he knows it by heart** se lo sabe de memoria; **yes, I know** sí, ya lo sé; **you never know!** ¡nunca se sabe!; **2** (*be personally acquainted with*) conocer [35] (*a person, place, book, or music, for example*); **do you know that song?** ¿conoces esa canción?; **all the people I know** toda la gente que conozco; **I don't know his mother** no conozco a su madre; **3 to know how to do** saber [13] hacer; **Steve knows how to make paella** Steve sabe hacer paella; **4 to know about** estar [2] al corriente de (*the latest news*); **5 to know about** saber [13] de (*a subject, machines*); **Lindy knows about computers** Lindy sabe de ordenadores.

knowledge noun conocimientos Masc. plural; **scientific knowledge** conocimientos científicos.

knuckle noun nudillo Masc.

koala noun koala Masc.

Koran noun Corán Masc.

kosher adjective kosher.

LI

lab *noun* laboratorio *Masc.*

label *noun* etiqueta *Fem.*

laboratory *noun* laboratorio *Masc.*

Labour *noun* los laboristas *Masc. plural*; **to vote for Labour** votar [17] por los laboristas; **the Labour Party** el partido laborista.

lace *noun* 1 (*for a shoe*) cordón *Masc.*; **to do up your laces** atarse los cordones; 2 (*fabric*) encaje *Masc.*

lad *noun* chaval *Masc.* (*informal*).

ladder *noun* 1 (*for climbing*) escalera *Fem.*; 2 (*in your tights*) carrera *Fem.*

ladies *noun* (*lavatory*) servicio *Masc.* de señoras; (*sign*) **'Ladies'** 'Señoras'.

lady *noun* señora *Fem.*; **ladies and gentlemen** señoras y señores.

lager *noun* cerveza *Fem.* rubia.

laid-back *adjective* relajado/relajada.

lake *noun* lago *Masc.*

lamb *noun* cordero *Masc.*; **a leg of lamb** una pierna de cordero.

lamp *noun* lámpara *Fem.*

lamp-post *noun* farola *Fem.*

lampshade *noun* pantalla *Fem.*

land *noun* tierra *Fem.*; 2 (*property*) **a piece of land** un terreno; **he has land** tiene tierras.

land *verb* 1 (*plane, passenger*) aterrizar [22]; 2 (*leave a ship*) desembarcar [31].

landing *noun* 1 (*on the stairs*) descansillo *Masc.*; 2 (*of a plane*) aterrizaje *Masc.*; 3 (*from a boat*) desembarco *Masc.*

landlady *noun* 1 (*of rented house*) casera *Fem.*; 2 (*of pub*) dueña *Fem.*

landlord *noun* 1 (*of rented house*) casero *Masc.*; 2 (*of pub*) dueño *Masc.*

lane *noun* 1 (*in the country*) camino *Masc.*; 2 (*of a motorway or road*) carril *Masc.*; **bus lane** carril de autobuses.

language *noun* 1 (*Spanish, Italian, etc.*) idioma *Masc.*; **a foreign language** un idioma extranjero; 2 (*way of speaking*) lenguaje *Masc.*; **scientific language** lenguaje científico; 3 **bad language** palabrotas *Fem. plural*; **to use bad language** decir [5] palabrotas.

language lab *noun* laboratorio *Masc.* de idiomas.

language school *noun* academia *Fem.* de idiomas.

lap *noun* 1 (*your knees*) rodillas *Fem. plural*; **on my lap** en mis rodilla; 2 (*in races*) vuelta *Fem.*

laptop *noun* ordenador *Masc.* portátil.

laser *noun* láser *Masc.*; **a laser beam** un rayo láser; **a laser printer** una impresora láser.

last *adjective* 1 último/última; **the last time** la última vez; **the last thing** I did lo último que hice; 2 **last week** la semana pasada; **last night** (*in the evening*) ayer por la tarde; (*in the night*) anoche.

a
b
c
d
e
f
g
h
i
j
k
l
m
n
o
p
q
r
s
t
u
v
w
x
y
z

last adverb **1** (in final position) (to arrive or leave); **Rob arrived last** Rob llegó el último; **I came last in the race** llegué en último lugar en la carrera; **2** (most recently) **I last saw him in May** la última vez que lo vi fue en mayo; **3 at last!** ¡por fin!

last verb durar [17]; **the play lasted two hours** la obra duró dos horas.

late adjective, adverb **1** tarde; **we're late** llegamos tarde; **they arrived late** llegaron tarde; **to be late for something** llegar [28] tarde a algo; **we were late for the film** llegamos tarde a la película; **2 to be late** (a bus or train) llegar [28] con retraso; **the train was an hour late** el tren llegó con una hora de retraso; **3** (late in the day) tarde; **we got up late** nos levantamos tarde; **it's getting late** se está haciendo tarde; **late last night** ayer por la noche ya tarde; **too late!** ¡demasiado tarde!

later adverb más tarde; **I'll explain to you later** te lo explicaré más tarde; **later that same day** ese mismo día más tarde; **no later than Thursday** no más tarde del jueves; **see you later!** ¡hasta luego!

latest adjective último/última; **the latest news** las últimas noticias.

latest noun **at the latest** a más tardar; **the latest in audio equipment** lo último en equipo de audio.

Latin noun latín Masc.

Latin America noun América Fem. Latina.

Latin American adjective latinoamericano/latinoamericana.

laugh noun risa Fem.; **to do something for a laugh** hacer [7] algo por divertirse.

laugh verb **1** reírse [61]; **everybody laughed** todo el mundo se rió; **2 to laugh at** reírse [61] de; **I tried to explain but they laughed at me** intenté explicarlo pero se rieron de mí.

laughter noun risas Fem. plural.

launch noun **1** (of product, spacecraft) lanzamiento Masc.; **1** (of ship) botadura Fem.

launch verb **1** (product, spacecraft) lanzar [22]; **1** (ship) botar [17].

launderette noun lavandería Fem.

laundry noun lavandería Fem.

lavatory noun servicio Masc., aseo Masc.

lavender noun lavanda Fem.

law noun **1** ley Fem.; **it's against the law** es ilegal; **2** (subject of study) derecho Masc.

lawn noun césped Masc.

lawnmower noun cortacésped Masc.

lawyer noun abogado Masc., abogada Fem.

lay verb poner [11]; **she laid the card on the table** puso la tarjeta en la mesa; **to lay the table** poner la mesa.

lay-by noun área Fem. de reposo (even though 'área' is a feminine, it takes 'el' and 'un' in the singular); **a lay-by** un área de reposo.

layer noun capa Fem.

laziness noun pereza Fem.

lazy adjective perezoso/perezosa.

lead noun 1 (when you are ahead) **to be in the lead** llevar [17] la delantera; **Sam's in the lead** Sam lleva la delantera; **we have a lead of three points** llevamos una ventaja de tres puntos; 2 (electric) cable Masc.; 3 (for a dog) correa Fem.; **on a lead** con correa.

lead adjective (a role or a singer) principal.

lead verb 1 llevar [17]; **the path leads to the sea** el sendero lleva al mar; 2 **to lead the way** ir [8] delante; 3 (in a competition) llevar [17] la delantera; 4 **this will lead to problems** esto traerá problemas; **to lead to an accident** causar [17] un accidente.

leader noun 1 (of a gang) cabecilla Masc./Fem.; 2 (of a political party) líder Masc./Fem.; 3 (in a competition) primero Masc., primera Fem.

lead-free petrol noun gasolina Fem. sin plomo.

lead singer noun cantante Masc./ Fem. principal.

leaf noun hoja Fem.

leaflet noun folleto Masc.

league noun (in sport) liga Fem.

lean adjective (meat) magro/ magra.

lean verb 1 **to lean on something** apoyarse [17] en algo; 2 (prop) apoyar [17]; **lean the ladder**

against the tree apoya la escalera en el árbol; 3 (a person) echarse [17]; **lean forward a bit** échate para delante un poco; 4 **to lean out of the window** asomarse [17] por la ventana.

leap year noun año Masc. bisiesto.

learn verb aprender [18]; **to learn Russian** aprender ruso; **to learn to drive** aprender a conducir.

learner driver noun she's a learner driver está aprendiendo a conducir.

least adverb, adjective

least pronoun 1 menos; **the least expensive** el hotel menos caro; **the least expensive glasses** las gafas menos caras; **Tony has the least money** Tony es el que menos dinero tiene; **I like the blue shirt least** la camisa azul es la que menos me gusta; 2 (slightest) más mínimo/más mínima; **I haven't the least idea** no tengo ni la más mínima idea; **he didn't show the least interest** no mostró el más mínimo interés; 3 **at least** (at a minimum) por lo menos; **there must be at least twenty people** debe haber por lo menos veinte personas; 4 **at least** (at any rate) al menos; **at least, that's what I think** al menos eso creo.

leather noun cuero Masc.; **a leather jacket** una chaqueta de cuero.

leave verb 1 (go away) irse [8]; **they're leaving tomorrow** se van mañana; **we left at six** se fueron a las seis; 2 (go away from) irse [8] de; **I left the office at five** me fui de

a b c d e f g h i j k l m n o p q r s t u v w x y z

la oficina a las cinco; **3** (*go out of*) salir [63] de; **she left the cinema at ten** salió del cine a las diez; **4** (*abandon*) dejar [17] a (*family or partner*); **he left his wife** dejó a su mujer; **5** (*deposit*) dejar [17]; **you can leave your coats in the hall** podéis dejar los abrigos en la entrada; **6** (*forget*) dejarse [17]; **he left his umbrella on the train** se dejó el paraguas en el tren; **7 to leave school** dejar [17] los estudios; **Guy left school at sixteen** Guy dejó los estudios a los dieciséis años; **8 be left** quedar [17]; **there are two cakes left** quedan dos pasteles; **we have ten minutes left** nos quedan diez minutos; **I don't have any money left** no me queda dinero.

lecture noun **1** (*at university*) clase Fem.; **2** (*public*) conferencia Fem.

lecturer noun profesor Masc., profesora Fem.

ledge noun **1** (*of window*) repisa Fem.; **2** (*on cliff*) saliente Masc.

leek noun puerro Masc.

left noun izquierda Fem.; **to drive on the left** conducir [60] por la izquierda; **turn left at the church** tuerce a la izquierda en la iglesia; **on my left** a mi izquierda.

left adjective izquierdo/izquierda; **his left foot** su pie izquierdo.

left-click noun clic Masc. con el botón izquierdo.

left-click verb hacer [7], clic con el botón izquierdo; **left-click the icon** haz clic en el icono con el botón izquierdo.

left-hand noun **the left-hand side** la parte izquierda.

left-handed adjective zurdo/zurda.

left luggage office noun consigna Fem.

leftovers plural noun sobras Fem. plural.

leg noun **1** (*of a person*) pierna Fem.; **my left leg** mi pierna izquierda; **to break your leg** romperse [40] una pierna; **2** (*of a table, chair, or animal*) pata Fem.; **3** (*in cooking*) **a leg of chicken** un muslo de pollo; **a leg of lamb** una pierna de cordero; ★ **to pull somebody's leg** tomarle [17] el pelo a alguien (*literally: to take somebody's hair*).

legal adjective legal.

legend noun **1** (*story*) leyenda Fem.; **2** (*star, personality*) leyenda Fem.

leggings plural noun leggings Masc. plural.

leisure noun tiempo Masc. libre; **in my leisure time** en mi tiempo libre.

leisure centre noun polideportivo Masc.

lemon noun limón Masc.; **a lemon yoghurt** un yogur de limón.

lemonade noun **1** (*made with lemons*) limonada Fem.; **2** (*fizzy drink*) gaseosa Fem.

lemon juice noun zumo Masc. de limón.

lend verb dejar [17]; **to lend something to somebody** dejarle algo a alguien; **I lent Judy my bike**

le dejé mi bici a Judy; **will you lend it to me?** ¿me lo dejas?

length noun **1** (of fabric, board, etc.) largo Masc.; **2** (of film, play) duración Fem.; **3** (of book, list) extensión Fem.

lens noun **1** (in a camera) lente Fem.; **2** (in spectacles) cristal Masc.; **3 contact lenses** lentillas Fem. plural.

Lent noun Cuaresma Fem.

lentil noun lenteja Fem.

Leo noun Leo Masc.; **I'm Leo** soy Leo.

leotard noun malla Fem.

lesbian noun lesbiana Fem.

less pronoun, adjective

less adverb **1** menos; **Richard eats less** Richard come menos; **less time** menos tiempo; **less interesting** menos interesante; **less quickly than us** menos rápido que nosotros; **2 less than** menos de; **less than a kilo** menos de un kilo; **less than three hours** menos de tres horas; **3 less than** (in comparisons) menos que; **you spend less than me** gastas menos que yo.

lesson noun clase Fem.; **the history lesson** la clase de historia; **a driving lesson** una clase de conducir; **to take tennis lessons** tomar [17] clases de tenis.

let[1] verb **1** (allow) dejar [17]; **will you let me go alone?** ¿me dejas ir sola?; **the police let us through** la policía nos dejó pasar; **let me help you** déjame que te ayude; **she lets me borrow her bike** me deja que

coja su bici prestada; **let me see** (show me) déjame ver; **2** (as a suggestion or a command) **let's go!** ¡vámonos!; **let's not talk about it** no hablemos de ello; **let's see, if Tuesday is the third ...** vamos a ver, si el martes es el tres ...; **let's eat out** vamos a comer fuera.

● **to let off 1** tirar [17] (fireworks); **2** hacer [7] estallar (a bomb); **3** (to excuse from) perdonar [17] (homework or task); **I'll let you off doing the dishes** te perdono que no laves los platos.

let[2] verb (to rent out) alquilar [17]; **'flat to let'** 'se alquila apartamento'.

lethal adjective mortal.

letter noun **1** carta Fem.; **a letter for you from Delia** una carta de Delia para ti; **2** (of alphabet) letra Fem.; **M is the letter after L** M es la letra que viene depués de L.

letterbox noun buzón Masc.

lettuce noun lechuga Fem.

leukaemia noun leucemia Fem.

level noun nivel Masc.; **at street level** a nivel de la calle.

level adjective **1** plano/plana (a shelf or floor); **2** llano/llana (ground).

level crossing noun paso Masc. a nivel.

lever noun palanca Fem.

liar noun mentiroso Masc., mentirosa Fem.

liberal adjective liberal; **the Liberal Democrats** los demócratas liberales.

liberty noun libertad Fem.

a
b
c
d
e
f
g
h
i
j
k
l
m
n
o
p
q
r
s
t
u
v
w
x
y
z

a

Libra noun Libra Fem.; **Sean's Libra** Sean es Libra.

b

librarian noun bibliotecario Masc.; bibliotecaria Fem.; **Mark's a librarian** Mark es bibliotecario.

c

d

library noun biblioteca Fem.; **the public library** la biblioteca pública.

e

f

licence noun 1 (for driving or fishing) permiso Masc.; **a driving licence** un permiso de conducir; 2 (for a TV) licencia Fem.

g

h

lick verb lamer [18].

i

lid noun tapa Fem.; **she took the lid off** quitó la tapa.

j

k

lie noun mentira Fem.; **to tell lies** decir [5] mentiras.

lie verb 1 (to be stretched out) estar [2] tumbado; **Jimmy was lying on the bed** Jimmy estaba tumbado en la cama; 2 **to lie down** tumbarse [17] (for a little while); **come and lie down in the sun** ven y a tumbarte al sol; 3 (object) estar [2]; **my coat lay on the bed** mi abrigo estaba sobre la cama; 4 (not to tell the truth) mentir [14].

l

m

n

o

p

q

lieutenant noun teniente Masc./Fem.

r

s

life noun vida Fem.; **all her life** toda su vida; **full of life** lleno/llena de vida; **that's life!** ¡así es la vida!

t

u

lifebelt noun salvavidas Masc. (does not change in the plural).

v

lifeboat noun bote Masc. salvavidas.

w

x

lifeguard noun socorrista Masc./Fem.; **is there a lifeguard at the pool?** ¿hay un socorrista en la piscina?

y

z

life jacket noun chaleco Masc. salvavidas.

life-style noun estilo Masc. de vida.

lift noun 1 ascensor Masc.; **let's take the lift** vamos a coger el ascensor; 2 (a ride) **to give somebody a lift to the station** llevar [17] a alguien a la estación; **Tom gave me a lift home** Tom me llevó a casa; **can you give me a lift?** ¿me puedes llevar?

lift verb levantar [17].

light noun 1 (electric) luz Fem.; **can you turn the light on?** ¿puedes encender la luz?; **to turn off the light** apagar la luz; **are your lights on?** (on a car) ¿tienes las luces encendidas?; 2 (streetlight) farola Fem.; 3 (on a machine) piloto Masc.; 4 **traffic lights** semáforo Masc.; **the lights were green** el semáforo estaba en verde; 5 **have you got a light?** ¿tienes fuego?

light adjective 1 (in colour) claro/clara; **light blue eyes** ojos azul claro; 2 (not night) **it gets light at six** se hace de día a las seis; 3 (not heavy) ligero/ligera; **a light sweater** un jersey fino.

light verb encender [36] (the oven, the fire, a match, or a cigarette); **we lit a fire** encendimos un fuego.

light bulb noun bombilla Fem.

lighter noun encendedor Masc.

lightning noun relámpago Masc.; **a flash of lightning** un relámpago; **the tree was struck by lightning** cayó un rayo en el árbol.

light switch noun interruptor Masc. de la luz.

like[1] *preposition, conjunction*
1 como; **like me** como yo; **like this** como esto; **like a duck** como un pato; **like I said** como dije (yo); **what's it like?** ¿cómo es?; **what was the weather like?** ¿qué tiempo hizo?; **2 to look like** parecerse [35] a; **Cindy looks like her father** Cindy se parece a su padre.

like[2] *verb* **1 I like fish** me gusta el pescado; **I don't like dogs** no me gustan los perros; **Mum likes travelling** a mamá le gusta viajar; **she likes my brother** le gusta mi hermano; **I like Picasso best** el que más me gusta es Picasso; **2 I would like** quiero; **would you like a coffee?** ¿quieres un café?; **what would you like to eat?** ¿qué quieres comer?; **yes, if you like** sí, si tú quieres.

likely *adjective* probable; **it's not very likely** no es muy probable; **she's likely to phone** es probable que llame.

lime *noun* lima *Fem.* (*fruit*).

limit *noun* límite *Masc.*; **the speed limit** el límite de velocidad.

line *noun* **1** línea *Fem.*; **a straight line** una línea recta; **to draw a line** trazar [22] una línea; **2 a railway line** (*from one place to another*) una línea de ferrocarril; **on the railway line** (*the track*) en la vía férrea; **3** (*queue*) cola *Fem.*; **to stand in line** hacer [7] cola; **4** (*telephone*) línea *Fem.*; **the line's bad** no se oye bien; **hold the line, please** no cuelgue, por favor.

linen *noun* lino *Masc.*; **a linen jacket** una chaqueta de lino.

link *noun* conexión *Fem.*; **what's the link between the two?** ¿qué conexión hay entre los dos?

link *verb* conectar [17] (*two places*); **the terminals are linked by a shuttle service** las terminales están conectadas por un servicio de enlace.

lion *noun* león *Masc.*

lip *noun* labio *Masc.*

lip-read *verb* leer [37] los labios.

lipstick *noun* lápiz *Masc.* de labios.

liquid *noun* líquido *Masc.*

liquid *adjective* líquido/líquida.

liquidizer *noun* licuadora *Fem.*

list *noun* lista *Fem.*

listen *verb* escuchar [17]; **I wasn't listening** no estaba escuchando; **to listen to** escuchar [17]; **listen to the music** escucha la música; **you're not listening to me** no me estás escuchando.

literature *noun* literatura *Fem.*

litre *noun* litro *Masc.*; **a litre of milk** un litro de leche.

litter *noun* (*rubbish*) basura *Fem.*

litter bin *noun* papelera *Fem.*

little *adjective, pronoun* **1** (*small*) pequeño/pequeña; **a little boy** un niño pequeño; **a little break** una pequeña pausa; **2** (*not much*) poco/poca; **we have very little time** tenemos muy poco tiempo; **3 a little** un poco; **we have a little money** tenemos un poco de dinero; **just a little, please** sólo un poco, por favor; **it's a little late** es un poco tarde; **a little more** un poco

a
b
c
d
e
f
g
h
i
j
k
l
m
n
o
p
q
r
s
t
u
v
w
x
y
z

más; **a little less** un poco menos; ★ **little by little** poco a poco.

live[1] *verb* vivir [19]; **Susan lives in York** Susan vive en York; **they live at number 57** viven en el número cincuenta y siete; **they live together** viven juntos.

live[2] *adjective* **1** en directo (*a broadcast*); **a live concert** un concierto en directo; **2** (*alive*) vivo/ viva.

liver *noun* hígado *Masc.*

living *noun* **to earn a living** ganarse [17] la vida.

living room *noun* salón *Masc.*

load *noun* **1** (*on a lorry*) cargamento *Masc.*; **2 a bus-load of tourists** un autobús lleno de turistas; **3 loads of** un montón de (*informal*); **loads of people** un montón de gente; **they've got loads of money** tienen un montón de dinero.

load *verb* cargar [28].

loaf *noun* **a loaf of bread** un pan; **a loaf of wholemeal bread** un pan integral.

loan *noun* préstamo *Masc.*

loan *verb* prestar [17].

lobster *noun* langosta *Fem.*

local *noun* **1** (*a pub*) **our local** el bar de nuestro barrio; **2 the locals** (*people*) la gente del lugar.

local *adjective* **the local library** la biblioteca del barrio; **the local newspaper** el periódico local.

locally *adverb* en la zona.

lock *noun* **1** (*with a key*) cerradura *Fem.*; **2** (*on a canal*) esclusa *Fem.*

lock *verb* **to lock the door** cerrar [29] la puerta con llave; **the door**

was locked la puerta estaba cerrada con llave.

locker *noun* armario *Masc.*

locker room *noun* vestuario *Masc.*

lodger *noun* inquilino *Masc.*, inquilina *Fem.*

loft *noun* desván *Masc.*

log *noun* tronco *Masc.*

logical *adjective* lógico/lógica.

lollipop *noun* piruleta *Fem.*

London *noun* Londres *Masc.*; **to London** a Londres; **the London streets** las calles de Londres.

Londoner *noun* londinense *Masc./ Fem.*

loneliness *noun* soledad *Fem.*

lonely *adjective* **1** solitario/ solitaria; **she has a lonely life** tiene una vida solitaria; **2 to feel lonely** sentirse solo.

long *adjective, adverb* **1** largo/ larga; **a long film** una película larga; **a long illness** una enfermedad larga; **it's five metres long** mide cinco metros de largo; **how long is the corridor?** ¿cuánto mide el pasillo de largo?; **how long is the play?** ¿cuánto dura la obra?; **it's been a long day** ha sido un día muy largo; **2 a long time** mucho tiempo; **he stayed for a long time** se quedó mucho tiempo; **it's an hour long** dura una hora; **I've been here for a long time** he pasado mucho tiempo aquí; **a long time ago** hace mucho tiempo; **this won't take long** esto no llevará mucho tiempo; **I won't be long** no tardaré mucho; **3 how long?** ¿cuánto tiempo?; **how long have you been here?** ¿cuánto tiempo llevas aquí?; **4 a long way** muy lejos; **we're a long way from the cinema** estamos muy lejos del cine; **5 all night long** toda la noche.

long *verb* **to long to do** anhelar [17] hacer; **I'm longing to see you** anhelo verte.

longer *adverb* **no longer** ya no; **he doesn't work here any longer** ya no trabaja aquí; **I no longer know** ya no lo sé; **they no longer live here** ya no viven aquí.

long jump *noun* salto *Masc.* de longitud.

longlife milk *noun* leche *Fem.* uperizada.

loo *noun* váter *Masc.* (*informal*).

look *noun* **1** (*a glance*) mirada *Fem.*; **to have a look at something** mirar [17] algo; **2 to have a look round the town** visitar [17] la ciudad; **to have a look round the shops** ver [16] tiendas; **3 to have a look for** buscar [31] (*something you've lost*).

look *verb* **1** mirar [17]; **I wasn't looking** no estaba mirando; **to look out of the window** mirar por la ventana; **2 to look at** mirar [17]; **Andy was looking at the photos** Andy estaba mirando las fotos; **3** (*to seem*) parecer [35]; **Melanie looked pleased** Melanie parecía contenta; **you look well** tienes buen aspecto; **he looks ill** tiene mal aspecto; **the salad looks delicious** la ensalada tiene un aspecto delicioso; **4 to look like** parecerse [35] a ; **Sally looks like**

her aunt Sally se parece a su tía; **they look like each other** se parecen; **it looks like rain** parece que va a llover; **5 what does the house look like?** ¿cómo es la casa?

● **to look after** cuidar [17]; **Dad's looking after the baby** papá está cuidando del niño; **I'll look after your luggage** yo te cuido el equipaje.

● **to look for** buscar [31]; **I'm looking for the keys** estoy buscando las llaves.

● **to look forward to something: I'm looking forward to the holidays** estoy deseando que lleguen las vacaciones; **she's looking forward to the trip** está deseando ir de viaje.

● **to look out** (*to be careful*) tener [9] cuidado; **look out, it's hot!** ¡cuidado, está caliente!

● **to look something up** buscar [17] algo (*in a dictionary or directory*); **you can look it up in the dictionary** puedes buscarlo en el diccionario.

loose *adjective* **1** (*a screw or knot*) flojo/floja; **2** (*a garment*) amplio/amplia; **3 loose change** cambio *Masc.*; ★ **I'm at a loose end** no sé qué hacer.

lorry *noun* camión *Masc.*

lorry driver *noun* camionero *Masc.*, camionera *Fem.*

lose *verb* **1** perder [36]; **we lost** perdimos; **we lost the match** perdimos el partido; **Sam's lost his watch** Sam ha perdido su reloj; **2 to get lost** perderse [36]; **we got**

a b c d e f g h i j k l m n o p q r s t u v w x y z

loss 472 ENGLISH-SPANISH

lost in the woods nos perdimos en el bosque.

loss *noun* pérdida *Fem.*

lost *adjective* perdido/perdida; **I'm lost** me he perdido; **are you lost?** ¿te has perdido?

lost property *noun* objetos *Masc. plural* perdidos.

lot *noun* **1 a lot** mucho; **Jason eats a lot** Jason come mucho; **I spent a lot** gasté mucho; **your house is a lot bigger than ours** tu casa es mucho más grande que la nuestra; **2 a lot of** mucho/mucha (*plural* muchos/muchas); **a lot of coffee** mucho café; **lots of people** mucha gente; **a lot of books** muchos libros; **'what are you doing tonight?' – 'not a lot'** ¿qué haces esta noche?' – 'no mucho'.

lottery *noun* lotería *Fem.*; **to win the lottery** ganar [17] la lotería.

loud *adjective* **1** fuerte; **a loud banging** unos golpes fuertes; **a loud shout** un grito fuerte; **the radio is very loud** la radio está muy fuerte; **2 in a loud voice** en voz alta; **to say something out loud** decir algo en voz alta.

loudspeaker *noun* altavoz *Masc.*

lounge *noun* **1** (*in a house or hotel*) salón *Masc.*; **2** (*in an airport*) **the departure lounge** la sala de embarque.

love *noun* **1** amor *Masc.*; **to be in love with somebody** estar [2] enamorado de alguien; **she's in love with Jake** está enamorada de Jake; **2 Gina sends her love** Gina manda recuerdos; **3 with love**

from Charlie con cariño de Charlie; **lots of love, Ann** con mucho cariño: Ann; **4** (*in tennis*) cero *Masc.*

love *verb* **1** querer [12] (*a person*) **I love you** te quiero; **2 she loves London** le encanta Londres; **I'd love to come** me encantaría venir; **I love dancing** me encanta bailar; **Wayne loves seafood** a Wayne le encanta el marisco.

lovely *adjective* **1** (*to look at*) precioso/preciosa; **a lovely house** una casa preciosa; **2 it's a lovely day** hace un día muy bueno; **we had lovely weather** tuvimos un tiempo muy bueno; **3 I had a lovely time at their house** lo pasé muy bien en su casa; **4 it's lovely to see you!** ¡qué alegría verte!; **5** (*food, meal*) riquísimo/riquísima.

lover *noun* amante *Masc./Fem.*

low *adjective* bajo/baja; **a low table** una mesa baja; **at a low price** a un precio bajo; **in a low voice** en voz baja.

lower *adjective* (*not as high*) inferior.

loyalty *noun* lealtad *Fem.*; **a loyalty card** una tarjeta de fidelidad.

luck *noun* suerte *Fem.*; **good luck!** ¡buena suerte!; **bad luck!** ¡qué mala suerte!; **with a bit of luck** con un poco de suerte.

luckily *adverb* afortunadamente; **luckily for them** afortunadamente para ellos.

lucky adjective **1** to be lucky (a person) tener [9] suerte; **we were lucky** tuvimos suerte; **2** to be lucky (bringing luck) traer [42] suerte; **it's supposed to be lucky** se supone que trae suerte; **my lucky number** mi número de la suerte.

luggage noun equipaje Masc.

lump noun **1** bulto Masc. (on the body); **2** terrón Masc. (of sugar); **3** trozo Masc. (of cheese).

lunch noun comida Fem.; **to have lunch** comer [18]; **we had lunch in Oxford** comimos en Oxford.

lunch break noun descanso Masc. para comer.

lunch hour, lunch time noun hora Fem. de comer.

Luxembourg noun Luxemburgo Masc.

luxurious adjective lujoso/lujosa.

luxury noun lujo Masc.; **a luxury hotel** un hotel de lujo.

lyrics plural noun letra Fem.

Mm

macaroni noun macarrones Masc. plural.

machine noun máquina Fem.

machinery noun maquinaria Fem.

mad adjective **1** loco/loca; **she's completely mad!** ¡está completamente loca!; **2** (angry) enfadado/enfadada; **to be mad**

with somebody estar enfadado/ enfadada con alguien; **my mum will be mad!** ¡mamá se pondrá hecha una furia! (informal); **3** she's mad about horses le encantan los caballos.

madam noun señora Fem.

madness noun locura Fem.

magazine noun revista Fem.

maggot noun gusano Masc.

magic noun magia Fem.

magic adjective **1** mágico/mágica; **a magic wand** una varita mágica; **2** (great) fantástico/fantástica.

magician noun mago Masc., maga Fem.

magnet noun imán Masc.

magnifying glass noun lupa Fem.

maid noun criada Fem.; **is there a maid service?** ¿ha asistenta?.

maiden name noun nombre Masc. de soltera.

mail noun correo Masc.; **e-mail** (electronic mail) correo Masc. electrónico.

mail order noun to buy something by mail order comprar [17] algo por correo; **a mail order catalogue** un catálogo de venta por correo.

main adjective principal; **the main entrance** la entrada principal.

main course noun plato Masc. principal, segundo plato Masc.

mainly adverb principalmente.

main road noun carretera Fem. principal.

a
b
c
d
e
f
g
h
i
j
k
l
m
n
o
p
q
r
s
t
u
v
w
x
y
z

major *adjective* muy importante; **a major problem** un problema muy importante.

major *noun* comandante *Masc./Fem.*

Majorca *noun* Mallorca *Fem.*

majority *noun* mayoría *Fem.*

make *noun* marca *Fem.*; **what make is your bike?** ¿de qué marca es tu bici?

make *verb* **1** hacer [7]; **I made an omelette** hice una tortilla; **she made her bed** hizo su cama; **he made me wait** me hizo esperar; **she makes me laugh** me hace reír; **to make a phone call** hacer una llamada de teléfono; **I have to make a few phone calls** tengo que hacer varias llamadas de teléfono; **2** fabricar [31]; **they make computers** fabrican ordenadores; **'made in Spain'** 'fabricado en España'; **3** that makes me hungry eso me da hambre; **it made me sleepy** me dio sueño; **4** (*sad, happy*) **to make somebody sad** poner [11] triste a alguien; **it made me sad** me puso triste; **to make somebody happy** hacer [7] feliz a alguien; **it made him really annoyed** le dio mucha rabia; **it makes me so angry** me da tanta rabia; **5** ganar [17] (*money*); **he makes forty pounds a day** gana cuarenta libras al día; **to make a living** ganarse [17] la vida; **6** (*force*) **to make somebody do ...** obligar [28] a alguien a hacer ...; **she made him give the money back** le obligó a devolver el dinero; **7 to make a meal** preparar [17] una comida; **8** (*add up to*) sumar [17]; **two and three make five** dos y tres suman cinco; **9 I can't make it tonight** no puedo venir esta noche.

● **to make something up**
1 inventarse [17] algo; **she made up an excuse** se inventó una excusa; **2 to make it up** (*after a quarrel*) hacer [7] las paces; **they've made it up now** han hecho las paces ahora.

make-up *noun* maquillaje *Masc.*; **to put on your make-up** ponerse [11] el maquillaje; **Jo's putting on her make-up** Jo se está poniendo el maquillaje; **I don't wear make-up** yo no uso maquillaje.

male *adjective* **1** (*animal*) macho; **a male rat** una rata macho; **2** (*of a man*) masculino/masculina; **a male voice** una voz masculina; **3** (*sex : on a form*) varón.

male chauvinist *noun* machista *Masc.*

mall *noun* centro *Masc.* comercial.

mammal *noun* mamífero *Masc.*

man *noun* hombre *Masc.*; **modern man is taller than his ancestors** el hombre moderno es más alto que sus antepasados.

manage *verb* **1** dirigir [49] (*business, team*); **she manages a travel agency** ella dirige una agencia de viajes; **2** (*cope*) arreglárselas [17]; **I can manage** puedo arreglármelas; **3 to manage to do** conseguir [64] hacer; **I didn't manage to get in touch with her** no conseguí ponerme en contacto con ella.

management noun **1** dirección Fem.; **the management of the company** la dirección de la empresa; **2** (*management staff*) directivos Masc. plural.

manager noun **1** (*of a company or a bank*) director Masc., directora Fem.; **2** (*of a shop or restaurant*) encargado Masc., encargada Fem.; **3** (*in sport and entertainment*) manager Masc./Fem.

manageress noun encargada Fem.

managing director noun consejero Masc. delegado, consejera Fem. delegada.

mango noun mango Masc.

maniac noun loco Masc., loca Fem.; **she drives like a maniac** conduce como una loca.

mankind noun humanidad Fem.

manner noun **1 in a manner of speaking** por así decirlo; **2 to have good manners** tener [9] buena educación; **it's bad manners to talk like that** no es de es buena educación hablar así.

mansion noun mansión Fem.

mantelpiece noun repisa Fem. de la chimenea.

manual noun manual Masc.

manufacture verb fabricar [31].

manufacturer noun fabricante Masc.

many adjective, pronoun **1** muchos/muchas; **does she have many friends?** ¿tiene muchos amigos?; **there aren't many onions left** no quedan muchas

cebollas; **not many** no muchos/ muchas; **many of them forgot** muchos de ellos se olvidaron; **many people** mucha gente; **2 very many** muchos/muchas; **there aren't very many glasses** no hay muchos vasos; **3 so many** tantos/ tantas; **I have so many things to do!** ¡tengo tantas cosas que hacer!; **I've never eaten so many cakes** nunca he comido tantos pasteles; **4 as many as** todos los que/todas las que; **you can take as many as you like** puedes llevarte todos los que quieras; **5 too many** demasiados/demasiadas; **I've got too many things to do** tengo demasiadas cosas que hacer; **that's far too many!** ¡ésos son demasiados!; **there were too many people** había demasiada gente; **6 how many?** ¿cuántos?/ ¿cuántas?; **how many are there?** ¿cuántos hay?; **how many sisters have you got?** ¿cuántas hermanas tienes?; **how many are there left?** ¿cuántos quedan?; **7 as many as** tantos/tantas como; **there aren't as many as before** no hay tantos como antes; **she got as many points as I did** consiguió tantos puntos como yo.

map noun **1** mapa Masc.; **a road map** un mapa de carreteras; **2** (*of a town*) plano Masc.

marathon noun maratón Masc./ Fem.

marble noun **1** mármol Masc.; **a marble fireplace** una chimenea de mármol; **2** canica Fem.; **to play marbles** jugar [27] a las canicas.

a
b
c
d
e
f
g
h
i
j
k
l
m
n
o
p
q
r
s
t
u
v
w
x
y
z

March noun marzo Masc.

march noun (demonstration) manifestación Fem.

march verb (demonstrators) manifestarse [29].

mare noun yegua Fem.

margarine noun margarina Fem.

margin noun margen Masc.

marijuana noun marihuana Fem.

mark noun 1 (at school) nota Fem.; I got a good mark for my Spanish homework he sacado una buena nota en los deberes de español; what mark did you get for Spanish? ¿que nota sacaste en español?; 2 (stain) mancha Fem.

mark verb (correct) corregir [48].

market noun mercado Masc.

marketing noun marketing Masc.

marmalade noun mermelada Fem. de naranja.

marriage noun matrimonio Masc. (relationship).

married adjective casado/casada; to be married estar [2] casado/casada; he's married está casado; they've been married for twenty years llevan casados veinte años; a married couple un matrimonio.

marry verb 1 to marry somebody casarse [17] con alguien; she married a Spaniard se casó con un español; 2 to get married casarse [17]; they got married in July se casaron en julio.

marvellous adjective maravilloso/maravillosa; the weather's marvellous el tiempo es maravilloso; how marvellous! ¡qué maravilla!

marzipan noun mazapán Masc.

mascara noun rímel Masc.

masculine noun (in Spanish and other grammars) masculino Masc.; in the masculine en masculino.

mash verb triturar [17] (vegetables).

mashed potatoes noun puré Masc. de patatas.

mask noun máscara Fem.

mass noun 1 a mass of un montón de; 2 masses of un montón de; they've got masses of money tienen un montón de dinero; there's masses left over queda un montón; 3 (religious) misa Fem.; to go to mass ir [8] a misa.

massacre noun matanza Fem.

massage noun masaje Masc.

massive adjective enorme.

mat noun 1 (doormat) felpudo Masc.; 2 (bathmat) alfombrilla Fem.; 3 (for hot dish) salvamanteles Masc. (does not change in the plural).

match noun 1 cerilla Fem.; a box of matches una caja de cerillas; 2 (sports) partido Masc.; a football match un partido de fútbol; to watch the match ver [16] el partido; to win the match ganar [17] el partido; to lose the match perder [36] el partido.

match verb hacer [7] juego con; the jacket matches the skirt la chaqueta hace juego con la falda.

mate noun amigo Masc., amiga Fem.; I'm going out with my mates tonight voy a salir esta noche con mis amigos.

material noun 1 (fabric) tela Fem.;
2 (information) material Masc.;
teaching materials material
educativo; 3 (substance) materia
Fem.; **raw materials** materias
primas.

mathematics noun matemáticas
Fem. plural.

maths noun matemáticas Fem.
plural; **I like maths** me gustan las
matemáticas; **Anna's good at
maths** a Anna se le dan bien las
matemáticas.

matter noun **what's the matter?**
¿qué pasa?

matter verb 1 importar [17]; **the
things that matter** lo que importa;
it matters a lot to me me importa
mucho; **2 it doesn't matter** no
importa; **it doesn't matter if it
rains** no importa que llueva; **3 it
doesn't matter** (whether one thing
or another) da lo mismo; **you can
write it in Spanish or French, it
doesn't matter** puedes escribirlo
en español o en francés, da lo
mismo.

mattress noun colchón Masc.

maximum noun máximo Masc.

maximum adjective máximo/
máxima.

May noun mayo Masc.

may verb 1 **she may be ill** puede
que esté enferma; **we may go to
Spain** puede que vayamos a
España; 2 (asking permission) **may
I close the door?** ¿puedo cerrar la
puerta?

maybe adverb quizás; **maybe not**
quizás no; **maybe he's forgotten**
quizás se ha olvidado; **maybe**

they've got lost quizás se han
perdido.

mayonnaise noun mayonesa
Fem.

mayor noun alcalde Masc.,
alcaldesa Fem.

mayoress noun alcaldesa Fem.

me pronoun 1 me; **she knows me**
me conoce; **she gave me the
documents** me dio los
documentos; 2 (with an infinitive
or when telling someone to do
something, 'me' joins onto the verb)
can you help me, please? ¿puedes
ayudarme por favor?; **listen to me!**
¡escúchame!; **wait for me!**
¡espérame!; (but when telling
someone NOT to do something, 'me'
comes before the verb) **don't push
me!** ¡no me empujes!; 3 (after a
preposition) mí; **behind me** detrás
de mí; **they left without me** se
fueron sin mí; **with me** conmigo; **I
took her with me** la traje conmigo;
4 (in comparisons or after the verb
'to be') yo; **she's older than me** es
mayor que yo; **it's me** soy yo; **me
too!** ¡yo también!; 5 **excuse me!**
¡perdona!

meadow noun prado Masc.

meal noun comida Fem.; **they have
three meals a day** hacen tres
comidas al día.

mean verb 1 querer [12] decir;
what do you mean? ¿qué quieres
decir?; **what does that mean?**
¿qué quiere decir eso?; **that's not
what I meant** eso no es lo que
quería decir; 2 (imply) suponer
[11]; **that means that I'll have to
do it again** eso supone que voy a

a
b
c
d
e
f
g
h
i
j
k
l
m
n
o
p
q
r
s
t
u
v
w
x
y
z

a
b
c
d
e
f
g
h
i
j
k
l
m
n
o
p
q
r
s
t
u
v
w
x
y
z

tener que hacerlo otra vez; **3 to mean to do** tener [9] la intención de; **I meant to phone my mother** tenía la intención de llamar a mi madre; **4 she was meant to be here at six** se supone que ella tenía que estar aquí a las seis; **this is meant to be easy** se supone que esto es fácil.

mean *adjective* **1** *(with money)* tacaño/tacaña; **2** *(nasty)* **she's really mean to her brother** trata muy mal a su hermano; **what a mean thing to do!** ¡qué maldad!

meaning *noun* significado *Masc.*

means *noun* **1** medio *Masc.*; **a means of transport** un medio de transporte; **by means of** por medio de; **2 a means of doing** una forma de hacer; **we have no means of contacting him** no tenemos forma de contactar con él; **3 by all means** por supuesto.

meantime *adverb* **for the meantime** por ahora; **in the meantime** mientras tanto.

meanwhile *adverb* mientras tanto; **meanwhile she was waiting at the station** mientras tanto ella estaba esperando en la estación.

measles *noun* sarampión *Masc.*

measure *verb* medir [57].

measurements *plural noun* **1** *(of a room or an object)* medidas *Fem. plural*; **the measurements of the room** las medidas de la habitación; **2** *(of a person)* medida *Fem.*; **my waist measurement** mi medida de cintura.

meat *noun* carne *Fem.*

Mecca *noun* La Meca *Fem.*

mechanic *noun* mecánico *Masc.*, mecánica *Fem.*; **he's a mechanic** es mecánico.

medal *noun* medalla *Fem.*; **the gold medal** la medalla de oro.

media *noun* **the media** los medios de comunicación.

medical *noun* revisión *Fem.* médica; **to have a medical** someterse [18] a una revisión médica.

medical *adjective* médico/médica; **on medical grounds** por razones de salud.

medicine *noun* **1** medicamento *Masc.*; **2** *(science)* medicina *Fem.*; **she's studying medicine** está estudiando medicina; **alternative medicine** medicina alternativa.

medieval *adjective* medieval.

Mediterranean *noun* **the Mediterranean** el Mediterráneo.

medium *adjective* mediano/mediana.

medium-sized *adjective* de tamaño mediano.

meet *verb* **1** *(by chance)* encontrarse [24] con; **I met Rosie outside the baker's** me encontré con Rosie en la puerta de la panadería; **2** *(by appointment)* haber [6] quedado (con); **we're meeting at six** hemos quedado a las seis; **I'm meeting him at the museum** he quedado con él en el museo; **shall we meet after work?** ¿quedamos después del trabajo?; **3** *(get to know)* conocer [35] a; **I met**

a Spanish girl last week conocí a una chica española la semana pasada; **have you met Oskar?** ¿conoces a Oskar?; **4 Tom, meet Ann** Tom, te presento a Ann; **pleased to meet you!** ¡encantado/ encantada!; **5** (off a train, bus, plane) recoger [3]; **my dad's meeting me at the station** mi padre va a ir a recogerme a la estación.

meeting noun reunión Fem.; **there's a meeting a ten o'clock** hay una reunión a las diez; **she's in a meeting** está en una reunión.

megabyte noun megabyte Masc.

melon noun melón Masc.

melt verb **1** (snow, butter, ice cream) derretirse [57]; **it melts in your mouth** se derrite en la boca; **2 to melt something** derretir [57] algo; **melt the butter in a saucepan** derretir la mantequilla en una sartén.

member noun **1** (of party or committee) miembro Masc./Fem.; **she's a member of the Labour Party** es miembro del partido laborista; **2** (of club) socio Masc., socia Fem.

Member of Parliament noun diputado Masc., diputada Fem.

memorial noun monumento Masc.; **a war memorial** un monumento a los caídos.

memorize verb **to memorize something** aprender [18] algo de memoria.

memory noun **1** (of a person or computer) memoria Fem.; **you have**

a good memory! ¡tienes buena memoria!; **I have a bad memory** tengo mala memoria; **2** (of the past) recuerdo Masc.; **I have good memories of my stay in Spain** tengo buenos recuerdos de mi estancia en España.

mend verb arreglar [17].

mental adjective mental; **a mental illness** una enfermedad mental; **a mental hospital** un hospital psiquiátrico.

mention verb mencionar [17].

menu noun **1** (in restaurant) carta Fem., menú Masc.; **what's on on the menu?** ¿qué hay en la carta?; **have you got a set menu?** ¿tienen un menú del día?; **2** (in computer program) menú Masc.

merge verb **1** (documents) fusionar [17]; **2** (roads) confluir [54].

meringue noun merengue Masc.

merit noun mérito Masc.

merry adjective **1** alegre; **Merry Christmas** Feliz Navidad; **2** (from drinking) achispado/achispada (informal).

merry-go-round noun tiovivo Masc.

mess noun desorden Masc.; **my papers are in a mess** mis papeles están desordenados; **don't make a mess!** ¡no desordenes nada!; **what a mess!** ¡qué desastre! (informal).

● **to mess about** hacer [7] el tonto; **stop messing about!** ¡deja de hacer el tonto!.

● **to mess about with something** jugar [27] con algo; **it's**

a

dangerous to mess about with matches es peligroso jugar con cerillas.

b

c

● **to mess something up** desordenar [17] algo; **you've messed up all my papers** ¡me has desordenado todos mis papeles!.

d

message noun mensaje Masc.; **a telephone message** un recado.

e

f

messenger noun mensajero Masc., mensajera Fem.

g

h

messy adjective **1 it's a messy job** es un trabajo sucio; **2 he's a messy eater** se ensucia mucho comiendo; **her writing's really messy** escribe sin poner cuidado.

i

j

k

metal noun metal Masc.

l

meter noun **1** (electricity, gas, taxi) contador Masc.; **to read the meter** leer [37] el contador; **2 a parking meter** un parquímetro.

m

n

method noun método Masc.

o

Methodist noun metodista Masc./ Fem.; **I'm a Methodist** soy metodista.

p

q

metre noun metro Masc.

r

metric adjective métrico/métrica.

s

Mexico noun Méjico Masc.

Mexican noun mexicano Masc., mexicana Fem.

t

u

Mexican adjective mexicano/ mexicana.

v

w

microchip noun microchip Masc.

x

microphone noun micrófono Masc.

y

z

microscope noun microscopio Masc.

microwave oven noun microondas Masc. (does not change in the plural).

midday noun mediodía Masc.; **at midday** al mediodía.

middle noun **1** medio Masc.; **in the middle of the room** en medio de la habitación; **2 in the middle of the night** en mitad de la noche; **in the middle of the day** alrededor del mediodía; **in the middle of the year** a mediados de año; **3 to be in the middle of doing** estar [2] haciendo; **when she phoned I was in the middle of washing my hair** cuando llamó estaba lavándome el pelo.

middle-aged adjective de mediana edad; **a middle-aged woman** una mujer de mediana edad.

middle-class adjective de clase media; **a middle-class family** una familia de clase media.

Middle-East noun Oriente Masc. Medio.

middle finger noun dedo Masc. corazón.

midge noun mosquito Masc. pequeño.

midnight noun medianoche Fem.; **at midnight** a medianoche.

Midsummer's Day noun la noche de San Juan.

midwife noun comadrona Fem.

might verb **I might invite Jo** puede que invite a Jo; **Amanda might know** puede que Amanda lo sepa; **he might have forgotten** puede que se haya olvidado; **'are you**

a
b
c
d
e
f
g
h
i
j
k
l
m
n
o
p
q
r
s
t
u
v
w
x
y
z

going to phone him?' – 'I might'
'¿vas a llamarlo?' – 'quizás'.

migraine noun jaqueca Fem.

mike noun micro Masc. (informal).

mild adjective **1** suave (soap or cheese); **2** templado/templada (climate); **it's quite mild today** hoy no hace frío.

mile noun **1** milla Fem. (in Spain distances are measured in kilometres; to convert miles roughly to kilometres, multiply by 8 and divide by 5) **the village is ten miles from Oxford** el pueblo está a dieciseis kilómetros de Oxford; **2 it's miles better!** ¡es mil veces mejor! (informal).

mileage noun distancia Fem. en millas; **what's the mileage on your car?** ¿cuántas millas ha hecho tu coche?

milk noun leche Fem.; **full-cream milk** leche entera; **skimmed milk** leche desnatada; **semi-skimmed milk** leche semidesnatada.

milk verb ordeñar [17].

milk chocolate noun chocolate Masc. con leche.

milkman noun lechero Masc.

milkshake noun batido Masc.

millennium noun milenio Masc.

millimetre noun milímetro Masc.

million noun millón Masc.; **a million people** un millón de personas; **two million people** dos millones de personas.

millionaire noun millonario Masc., millonaria Fem.

mince noun carne Fem. picada.

mind noun **1** mente Fem.; **a logical mind** una mente lógica; **2 it crossed my mind that ...** se me pasó por la cabeza que ...; **3 to change your mind** cambiar [17] de opinión; **I've changed my mind** he cambiado de opinión; **4 to make up your mind** decidirse [19]; **I can't make up my mind** no puedo decidirme.

mind verb **1** cuidar [17]; **can you mind my bag for me?** ¿me cuidas el bolso?; **could you mind the baby for ten minutes?** ¿puedes cuidar del niño diez minutos?; **2 do you mind if ...?** ¿te importa que ...?; **do you mind if I close the door?** ¿te importa que cierre la puerta?; **I don't mind** no me importa; **never mind!** ¡no importa!; **3 I don't mind the heat** no me molesta el calor; **4 mind the step!** ¡cuidado con el escalón!.

mine[1] noun mina Fem.; **a coal mine** una mina de carbón.

mine[2] pronoun **1** (referring to a singular noun) el mío/la mía; **she took her hat and I took mine** ella cogió su sombrero y yo cogí el mío; **Tessa phoned her mum and I phoned mine** Tessa llamó a su madre y yo llamé a la mía; **2** (referring to a plural noun) los míos/las mías; **Karen's invited her parents and I've invited mine** Karen ha invitado a sus padres y yo a los míos; **she showed me her photos and I showed her mine** ella me enseñó sus fotos y yo le enseñé las mías.

a

miner noun minero Masc., minera Fem.

b

mineral water noun agua Fem. mineral.

c

minibus noun microbús Masc.

d

minimum noun mínimo Masc.

minimum adjective mínimo/mínima; **the minimum age** la edad mínima.

e

f

miniskirt noun minifalda Fem.

g

minister noun 1 (in government) ministro Masc., ministra Fem.; 2 (of a church) pastor Masc., pastora Fem..

h

i

minor adjective menor.

j

minority noun minoría Fem.

k

mint noun 1 (herb) menta Fem.; 2 (sweet) caramelo Masc. de menta.

l

m

minus preposition 1 menos; **seven minus three is four** siete menos tres es cuatro; 2 **it was minus ten this morning** esta mañana hacía diez grados bajo cero.

n

o

p

minute noun minuto Masc.; **it's five minutes' walk from here** está a cinco minutos andando de aquí; **I'll be ready in two minutes** en dos minutos estoy lista; **just a minute!** ¡un momento!

q

r

s

t

miracle noun milagro Masc.

u

mirror noun 1 espejo Masc.; **I looked at myself in the mirror** me miré al espejo; 2 (rearview mirror in a car) retrovisor Masc.

v

w

misbehave verb portarse [17] mal.

x

y

mischief noun **to get up to mischief** hacer [7] travesuras.

z

mischievous adjective travieso/traviesa.

miser noun avaro/avara.

miserable adjective 1 triste; **he was miserable without her** estaba triste sin ella; **I feel really miserable today** hoy tengo el ánimo por los suelos; 2 **it's miserable weather** un tiempo deprimente; 3 **she gets paid a miserable wage** le pagan un sueldo miserable.

misery noun miseria Fem.; **he was in misery** estaba muy triste.

miss verb 1 perder [36]; **she missed her train** perdió el tren; **I missed the film** me perdí la película; **to miss an opportunity** perder una oportunidad; 2 **the ball missed the goal** la pelota no entró en la portería; **you missed!** ¡fallaste!; 3 faltar [17] a; **he's missed several classes** ha faltado a varias clases; 4 **I miss you** te echo de menos; **she's missing her sister** echa de menos a su hermana; **I miss Madrid** echo de menos Madrid.

Miss noun señorita Fem. (usually abbreviated to 'Srta'); **Miss Jones** la señorita Jones.

missile noun misil Masc.

missing adjective 1 **the missing piece** la pieza que falta; **the missing documents** los documentos que faltan; **the missing link** el eslabón perdido; 2 faltar [17]; **there's a plate missing** falta un plato; **there are three forks missing** faltan tres tenedores; **is there anybody missing?** ¿falta alguien?; **3 to go missing** desaparecer [35]; **several things have gone missing lately** han desaparecido varias cosas últimamente; **three people have gone missing** han desaparecido tres personas.

mist *noun* neblina *Fem.*

mistake *noun* **1** error *Masc.*; **by mistake** por error; **it was my mistake** fue un error mío; **2** falta *Fem.*; **a spelling mistake** una falta de ortografía; **you've made lots of mistakes** has cometido muchas faltas; **3 to make a mistake** (*be mistaken*) cometer [18] un error; **sorry, I made a mistake** perdona, he cometido un error.

mistake *verb* confundir [19]; **I mistook you for your brother** te confundí con tu hermano.

mistaken *adjective* **to be mistaken** estar [2] equivocado/ equivocada; **you're mistaken** estás equivocado.

mistletoe *noun* muérdago *Masc.*

misunderstand *verb* entender [36] mal; **I misunderstood** lo entendí mal.

misunderstanding *noun* malentendido *Masc.*; **there's been a misunderstanding** hay un malentendido.

mix *noun* **1** mezcla *Fem.*; **a good mix of people** una buena mezcla de gente; **2 a cake mix** un preparado para hacer un pastel.

mix *verb* **1** mezclar [17]; **mix all the ingredients together** mezclar todos los ingredientes; **2 to mix**

with tratarse [17] con; **she mixes with lots of interesting people** se trata con mucha gente interesante.

● **to mix up 1** desordenar [17]; **you've mixed up all my papers** has desordenado todos mis papeles; **2** (*confuse*) confundir [19] (*confuse*) **I get him mixed up with his brother** lo confundo con su hermano; **you've got it all mixed up!** ¡te has confundido!.

mixed *adjective* variado/variada; **a mixed programme** un programa variado.

mixed salad *noun* ensalada *Fem.* mixta.

mixer *noun* batidora *Fem.*

mixture *noun* mezcla *Fem.*; **it's a mixture of jazz and rock** es una mezcla de jazz y rock.

moan *verb* (*complain*) quejarse [17]; **stop moaning!** ¡deja de quejarte!

mobile home *noun* caravana *Fem.* fija.

mobile phone *noun* teléfono *Masc.* móvil, móvil *Masc.*

mock *noun* (*mock exam*) examen *Masc.* de práctica.

mock *verb* burlarse [17] de; **stop mocking me!** ¡deja de burlarte de mí!

model *noun* **1** (*type*) modelo *Masc.*; **the latest model** el último modelo; **2** (*fashion model*) modelo *Masc./ Fem.*; **she's a model** es modelo; **3** (*of a plane, car, etc.*) maqueta *Fem.*; **he makes models** construye maquetas; **a model of**

a b c d e f g h i j k l m n o p q r s t u v w x y z

Westminster Abbey una maqueta de la abadía de Westminster.

model aeroplane noun aeromodelo Masc.

model railway noun ferrocarril Masc. de juguete.

modem noun módem Masc.

moderate adjective moderado/moderada.

modern adjective moderno/moderna.

modern languages noun lenguas Fem. plural modernas.

modernize verb modernizar [22].

moisturizer noun 1 (lotion) loción Fem. hidratante; 2 (cream) crema Fem. hidratante.

mole noun 1 (animal) topo Masc.; 2 (on skin) lunar Masc.

moment noun momento Masc.; **he'll be here in a moment** llegará en cualquier momento; **at any moment** en cualquier momento; **at the moment** en este momento; **at the right moment** en el momento preciso; **for the moment** de momento.

monarchy noun monarquía Fem.

Monday noun lunes Masc. (does not change in the plural); **on Monday** el lunes; **I'm going out on Monday** voy a salir el lunes; **see you on Monday!** ¡te veo el lunes!; **on Mondays** los lunes; **the museum is closed on Mondays** el museo cierra los lunes; **every Monday** todos los lunes; **last Monday** el lunes pasado; **next Monday** el próximo lunes.

money noun dinero Masc.; **I don't have enough money** no tengo suficiente dinero; **to make money** hacer [7] dinero; **they gave me my money back** (in a shop) me devolvieron el dinero.

money box noun hucha Fem.

mongrel noun chucho Masc. (informal).

monitor noun (on computer) monitor Masc.

monkey noun 1 mono Masc.; 2 **you little monkey!** ¡diablillo! (informal).

monster noun monstruo Masc.

month noun mes Masc.; **in the month of May** en el mes de mayo; **this month** este mes; **next month** el próximo mes; **we're leaving next month** nos vamos el próximo mes; **last month** el mes pasado; **every month** todos los meses; **in two months' time** dentro de dos meses; **at the end of the month** a final de mes.

monthly adjective mensual; **a monthly payment** una mensualidad.

monument noun monumento Masc.

mood noun humor Masc.; **to be in a good mood** estar [2] de buen humor; **to be in a bad mood** estar [2] de mal humor; **I'm not in the mood** no estoy de humor.

moody adjective temperamental.

moon noun luna Fem.; **by the light of the moon** a la luz de la luna; ★ **to be over the moon** estar loco/

loca de contento (*literally: to be mad with happiness*).

moonlight *noun* luz *Fem.* de la luna; **by moonlight** a la luz de la luna.

moped *noun* ciclomotor *Masc.*

moral *noun* moraleja *Fem.*; **the moral of the story** la moraleja de la historia.

moral *adjective* moral.

morals *plural noun* moralidad *Fem.*

more *adverb, adjective*

more *pronoun* **1** más; **more interesting** más interesante; **more easily** más fácilmente; **a little more milk** un poco más de leche; **a few more glasses** unos cuantos vasos más; **would you like some more cake?** ¿quieres más pastel?; **we need three more** necesitamos tres más; **2 more ... than** más ... que; **the book's more interesting than the film** el libro es más interesante que la película; **he eats more than me** come más que yo; **3 more and more** cada vez más; **books are getting more and more expensive** los libros están cada vez más caros; **it takes more and more time** lleva cada vez más tiempo; **4 more or less** más o menos; **it's more or less finished** está más o menos terminado; **5 any more** más; **I don't want any more** no quiero más; **I don't like it any more** ya no me gusta.

morning *noun* mañana *Fem.*; **this morning** esta mañana; **tomorrow morning** mañana por la mañana; **yesterday morning** ayer por la mañana; **in the morning** por la mañana; **she doesn't work in the morning** no trabaja por las mañanas; **on Friday mornings** los viernes por la mañana; **at six o'clock in the morning** a las seis de la mañana; **I spent the whole morning doing the washing-up** me pasé toda la mañana lavando los platos.

Morocco *noun* Marruecos *Masc.*

mortgage *noun* hipoteca *Fem.*

Moscow *noun* Moscú *Masc.*

Moslem *noun* musulmán *Masc.*, musulmana *Fem.*

mosque *noun* mezquita *Fem.*

mosquito *noun* mosquito *Masc.*; **a mosquito bite** una picadura de mosquito.

most *adjective, adverb, pronoun* **1** (*followed by a plural noun*) la mayoría de; **most children like chocolate** a la mayoría de los niños les gusta el chocolate; **most of my friends** la mayoría de mis amigos; **2** (*followed by a singular noun*) casi todo; **they've eaten most of the chocolate** se han comido casi todo el chocolate; **3 most of the time** la mayor parte del tiempo; **most of it is clear** la mayor parte está claro; **4 the most** (*followed by adjective*) más; **the most interesting film** la película más interesante; **the most exciting story** la historia más emocionante; **the most boring books** los libros más aburridos; **5 the most** (*followed by noun*); **I've got the most time** soy el que más

a b c d e f g h i j k l m n o p q r s t u v w x y z

tiempo tiene; **6** (*after a verb*) **what I hate most is the noise** lo que más odio es el ruido.

mother *noun* madre *Fem.*; **my mother** mi madre; **Kate's mother** la madre de Kate.

mother-in-law *noun* suegra *Fem.*

Mother's Day *noun* día *Masc.* de la Madre (*in Spain, the first Sunday in May*).

motivated *adjective* motivado/motivada.

motivation *noun* motivo *Masc.*

motor *noun* motor *Masc.*

motorbike *noun* motocicleta *Fem.*

motorboat *noun* motora *Fem.*

motorcyclist *noun* motociclista *Masc./Fem.*

motorist *noun* automovilista *Masc./Fem.*

motor racing *noun* carreras *Fem. plural* de coches.

motorway *noun* autopista *Fem.*

mouldy *adjective* mohoso/mohosa.

mountain *noun* montaña *Fem.*; **in the mountains** en las montañas.

mountain bike *noun* bicicleta *Fem.* de montaña.

mountaineer *noun* montañero *Masc.*, montañera *Fem.*

mountaineering *noun* montañismo *Masc.*; **to go mountaineering** hacer [7] montañismo.

mountainous *adjective* montañoso/montañosa.

mouse *noun* ratón *Masc.* (*both the animal and for a computer*).

mousse *noun* mousse *Fem.*; **chocolate mousse** mousse de chocolate.

moustache *noun* bigote *Masc.*

mouth *noun* boca *Fem.*

mouthful *noun* bocado *Masc.* (*of food*) trago *Masc.* (*of drink*).

mouth organ *noun* armónica *Fem.*; **to play the mouth organ** tocar [31] la armónica.

move *noun* **1** (*to a different house*) mudanza *Fem.*; **2** (*in a game*) **your move!** ¡tu turno!

move *verb* **1** moverse [38]; **she didn't move** no se movió; **2 move up a bit** córrete un poco; **3** (*an object*) cambiar [17] de sitio; **you've moved the picture** has cambiado el cuadro de sitio; **can you move your bag, please?** ¿puedes correr tu bolsa, por favor?; **4** mover [38] (*an object or part of the body*); **she moved her hand** movió la mano; **5** (*car, traffic*) avanzar [22]; **the traffic was moving slowly** el tráfico avanzaba lentamente; **6 to move forward** avanzar [22]; **he moved forward a step** avanzó un paso; **7** (*move house*) mudarse [17]; **we're moving on Tuesday** nos mudamos el martes; **they've moved house** se han mudado de casa; **they've moved to Spain** se han ido a vivir en España; **8** (*emotionally*) conmover [38]; **it really moved me** me conmovió de verdad; **to be moved** estar [2] conmovido/conmovida.

● **to move in** mudarse [17]; **when are you moving in?** ¿cuándo se mudan.

● **to move out** mudarse [17]; **I'm moving out at the end of the month** me mudo a finales del mes.

movie *noun* película *Fem.*; **to go to the movies** ir [8] al cine.

moving *adjective* **1** en marcha; **a moving vehicle** un vehículo en marcha; **2** (*emotionally*) conmovedor/conmovedora; **it's a very moving film** es una película muy conmovedora.

MP *noun* diputado *Masc.*, diputada *Fem.*; **she's an MP** es diputada.

Mr *noun* Señor (*usually abbreviated to 'Sr.'*); **Mr Angus Brown** el Sr. Angus Brown.

Mrs *noun* Señora (*usually abbreviated to 'Sra.'*); **Mrs Mary Hendry** la Sra. Mary Hendry.

Ms *noun* Señora (*usually abbreviated to 'Sra.'; note that there is no direct equivalent for 'Ms' in Spanish, but 'Señora' may be used whether a woman is married or not*).

much *adverb, pronoun, adjective* **1** mucho; **she doesn't eat much** no come mucho; **we don't go out much** no salimos mucho; **much more** mucho más; **much shorter** mucho más bajo; **2** (*followed by a noun*) mucho/mucha; **we don't have much time** no tenemos mucho tiempo; **there isn't much butter left** no queda mucha

mantequilla; **3 very much** mucho; **I don't watch television very much** no veo mucho la tele; **thank you very much** muchas gracias; **4 very much** (*followed by a noun*) mucho/mucha; **there isn't very much milk** no queda mucha leche; **5 not much** (*referring to a verb*) no mucho; **'do you go out?' – 'not much'** ¿sales? – 'no mucho'; **6 not much** (*referring to a noun*) no mucho/no mucha; **did you add salt?' – 'yes, but not much'** ¿has puesto sal?' – 'sí, pero no mucha'; **7 so much** tanto; **we liked it so much!** ¡nos gustó tanto!; **I have so much to do!** ¡tengo tanto que hacer!; **you shouldn't have given me so much** no deberías haberme dado tanto; **8 as much as** tanto como; **you can take as much as you like** puedes coger tanto como quieras; **9 too much** demasiado; **that's far too much!** ¡eso es demasiado!; **10 too much** (*followed by noun*) demasiado/demasiada; **too much ink** demasiada tinta; **11 how much?** ¿cuánto?; **how much is it?** ¿cuánto cuesta?; **how much do you want?** ¿cuánto quieres?; **12 how much?** (*followed by a noun*) ¿cuánto?/¿cuánta?; **how much milk do you want?** ¿cuánta leche quieres?

mud *noun* barro *Masc.*

muddle *noun* desorden *Masc.*; **to be in a muddle** estar [2] todo desordenado.

muddy *adjective* lleno de barro/llena de barro; **your boots are all muddy** tus botas están llenas de

a
b
c
d
e
f
g
h
i
j
k
l
m
n
o
p
q
r
s
t
u
v
w
x
y
z

barro; **a muddy road** una carretera llena de barro.

mug noun taza Fem. alta; **a mug of coffee** una taza alta de café.

mug verb **to mug somebody** atracar [31] a alguien; **my brother was mugged in the park** atracaron a mi hermano en el parque.

mugging noun atraco Masc.

multiplication noun multiplicación Fem.

multiply verb multiplicar [31]; **to multiply six by four** multiplicar seis por cuatro.

mum, mummy noun 1 madre Fem.; **Tom's mum** la madre de Tom; **I'll ask my mum** preguntaré a mi madre; 2 (within the family or as a name) mamá Fem.; **Mum's not back yet** mamá no ha vuelto todavía.

mumps noun paperas Fem. plural.

murder noun asesinato Masc.

murder verb asesinar [17].

murderer noun asesino Masc., asesina Fem.

muscle noun músculo Masc.

museum noun museo Masc.; **to go to the museum** ir [8] al museo.

mushroom noun champiñón Masc.

music noun música Fem.; **pop music** música pop; **classical music** música clásica.

musical noun musical Masc.

musical adjective 1 **a musical instrument** un instrumento musical; 2 **they're a very musical**

family toda la familia tiene dotes para la música.

musician noun músico Masc., música Fem.

Muslim noun musulmán Masc., musulmana Fem.

mussel noun mejillón Masc.

must verb 1 (expressing obligation) tener [9] que; (stronger) deber [18]; **you must be there at eight** tienes que estar allí a las ocho, debes estar allí a las ocho; 2 (expressing probability) deber [18]; **you must be tired** debes estar cansado; **it must be five o'clock** deben ser las cinco en punto; **he must have forgotten** debe haberse olvidado.

mustard noun mostaza Fem.

my adjective 1 (before a singular noun) mi; **my book** mi libro; **my sister** mi hermana; 2 (before a plural noun) mis; **my children** mis hijos; 3 (with parts of the body) el/la/los/las; **I had a glass in my hand** tenía un vaso en la mano; **I'm washing my hands** me estoy lavando las manos.

myself pronoun 1 (as a reflexive) me; **I've hurt myself** me he hecho daño; 2 **I said it myself** lo dije yo mismo; 3 (for emphasis) yo; **by myself** yo solo/yo sola; **I did it by myself** lo hice yo solo/yo sola.

mysterious adjective misterioso/misteriosa.

mystery noun 1 misterio Masc.; 2 (book) novela Fem. de misterio.

Nn

nail noun **1** (on finger or toe) uña Fem.; **to bite your nails** morderse [38] las uñas; **2** (metal) clavo Masc.

nailbrush noun cepillo Masc. de uñas.

nailfile noun lima Fem. de uñas.

nail scissors noun tijeras Fem. plural de uñas.

nail varnish noun esmalte Masc. de uñas.

nail varnish remover noun quitaesmalte Masc.

name noun **1** nombre Masc.; **I've forgotten her name** se me ha olvidado su nombre; **what's your name?** ¿cómo te llamas?; **my name's Lily** me llamo Lily; **2** (of a book or film) título Masc.

nanny noun niñera Fem.

napkin noun servilleta Fem.

nappy noun pañal Masc.

narrow adjective estrecho/estrecha; **a narrow street** una calle estrecha.

nasty adjective **1** (mean) cruel; **they were nasty to him** fueron crueles con él; **that was a nasty thing to do** eso fue una crueldad; **2** (unpleasant) desagradable; **that's a nasty job** ese es un trabajo desagradable; **3** (bad) repugnante; **a nasty smell** un olor repugnante.

nation noun nación Fem.

national adjective nacional.

national anthem noun himno Masc. nacional.

nationality noun nacionalidad Fem.

national park noun parque Masc. nacional.

Nativity scene noun belén Masc.

natural adjective natural.

naturally adverb naturalmente.

nature noun naturaleza Fem.

nature reserve noun reserva Fem. natural.

naughty adjective malo/mala.

nausea noun náuseas Fem. plural.

navel noun ombligo Masc.

navigate verb navegar [28].

navy noun marina Fem.; **my uncle's in the navy** mi tío está en la marina.

navy-blue adjective azul marino; **navy-blue gloves** guantes azul marino.

near adjective cercano/cercana; **the nearest shop** la tienda más cercana.

near adverb, preposition **1** cerca; **they live quite near** viven bastante cerca; **to come nearer** acercarse [31]; **2 near (to)** cerca de; **near the station** cerca de la estación.

nearby adverb cerca; **there's a park nearby** hay un parque cerca.

nearly adverb casi; **nearly empty** casi vacío; **we're nearly there** ya casi hemos llegado.

neat adjective **1** (well-organized) ordenado/ordenada; **a neat desk** un pupitre ordenado; **2** arreglado/arreglada (your clothes, or the way you look); **she always looks very neat** siempre va muy arreglada;

a
b
c
d
e
f
g
h
i
j
k
l
m
n
o
p
q
r
s
t
u
v
w
x
y
z

3 muy cuidado/muy cuidada (*a garden*).

necessarily *adverb* **not necessarily** no necesariamente.

necessary *adjective* necesario/ necesaria; **if necessary** si es necesario.

neck *noun* cuello Masc. (*of a person or garment*).

necklace *noun* collar Masc.

nectarine *noun* nectarina Fem.

need *noun* necesidad Fem.; **there's no need, I've done it already** no hay necesidad, ya lo he hecho; **there's no need to wait** no hay necesidad de esperar.

need *verb* **1** necesitar [17]; **we need bread** necesitamos pan; **they need help** necesitan ayuda; **everything you need** todo lo que necesites; **2** (*to have to*) tener [9] que; **I need to drop in at the bank** tengo que pasarme por el banco; **she'll need to check** tendrá que comprobarlo; **3 you needn't decide today** no hace falta que decidas hoy; **you needn't wait** no hace falta que esperes.

needle *noun* aguja Fem.

negative *noun* (*of a photo*) negativo Masc.

neglected *adjective* descuidado/ descuidada.

neighbour *noun* vecino Masc., vecina Fem.; **we're going round to the neighbours'** vamos a casa de los vecinos.

neighbourhood *noun* barrio Masc.; **a nice neighbourhood** un barrio agradable.

neither *conjunction* **1 neither ... nor** ni ... ni; **I have neither the time nor the money** no tengo ni tiempo ni dinero; **2 neither do I** yo tampoco; **'I didn't go'** – **'neither did I'** 'no fui' – 'yo tampoco'; **3** (*with 'gustar'*) **'I don't like fish'** – **'neither do I'** 'no me gusta el pescado' – 'ni a mí tampoco'; **'I didn't like the film'** – **'neither did Kirsty'** 'no me gustó la película' – 'ni a Kirsty tampoco'; **'which do you like?'** – **'neither'** ¿cuál te gusta?' – 'ninguno'.

nephew *noun* sobrino Masc.

nerve *noun* **1** (*in the body*) nervio Masc.; **2 to lose one's nerve** perder [36] el valor; **3 you've got a nerve!** ¡vaya cara que tienes! (*informal*); ★ **he gets on my nerves** me pone los nervios de punta (*informal*).

nervous *adjective* nervioso/ nerviosa; **to feel nervous** (*before a performance or an exam*) estar nervioso.

nervous breakdown *noun* crisis Fem. nerviosa.

nest *noun* nido Masc.

net *noun* red Fem.

Netherlands *noun* **the Netherlands** los Países Bajos.

nettle *noun* ortiga Fem.

network *noun* red Fem.

neutral *noun* (*in a gearbox*) punto Masc. muerto; **to be in neutral** estar [2] en punto muerto.

neutral *adjective* **1** (*impartial*) neutral; **2** (*colour*) neutro.

never *adjective* **1** nunca; **Ben never smokes** Ben no fuma nunca;

I've never seen the film no he visto nunca la película; **'have you ever been to Spain?' – 'no, never'** ¿has estado alguna vez en España? – 'no, nunca'; **2 never again!** ¡nunca jamás!; **3 never mind** no importa.

nevertheless *adverb* sin embargo.

new *adjective* nuevo/nueva; **have you seen their new house?** ¿has visto su casa nueva?; **Debbie's new boyfriend** el nuevo novio de Debbie; **it's a new car** es un coche nuevo.

news *plural noun* **1** (*everyday gossip*) noticia *Fem.*; **a piece of good news** una buena noticia; **have you heard the news?** ¿te has enterado de la noticia?; **any news?** ¿hay alguna noticia?; **2** (*on TV or radio*) noticias *Fem. plural*; **the midday news** las noticias del mediodía.

newsagent *noun* vendedor *Masc.* de periódicos vendedora *Fem.* de periódicos; **at the newsagent's** en la tienda de periódicos.

newspaper *noun* periódico *Masc.*

newsreader *noun* presentador *Masc.*, presentadora *Fem.*

New Year *noun* Año *Masc.* Nuevo; **Happy New Year!** ¡Feliz Año Nuevo!

New Year's Day *noun* día *Masc.* de Año Nuevo.

New Year's Eve *noun* Nochevieja *Fem.*

New Zealand *noun* Nueva Zelanda *Fem.*

New Zealander *noun* neozelandés *Masc.*, neozelandesa *Fem.*

next *adjective* **1** próximo/próxima; **the next train is at ten** el próximo tren sale a las diez; **next week** la próxima semana; **next Thursday** el próximo jueves; **next year** el próximo año; **the next time I see you** la próxima vez que te vea; **2** (*following*) siguiente; **the next day** el día siguiente; **at the next stop** en la siguiente parada; **3** (*next-door*) **in the next room** en la habitación de al lado.

next *adverb* **1** (*afterwards*) luego; **what did he say next?** ¿qué dijo luego?; **2** (*now*) ahora; **what shall we do next?** ¿qué hacemos ahora?; **3 next to** al lado de; **the girl next to Pat** la chica que está al lado de Pat; **it's next to the baker's** está al lado de la panadería.

next door *adverb* al lado; **they live next door** viven al lado; **the girl next door** la chica de al lado.

Nicaraguan *noun* nicaragüense *Masc./Fem.*

Nicaraguan *adjective* nicaragüense.

nice *adjective* **1** (*pleasant*) agradable; **we had a very nice evening** pasamos una tarde muy agradable; **Brighton's a very nice town** Brighton es una ciudad muy agradable; **have a nice time!** ¡que lo pases bien!; **2** (*attractive to look at*) bonito/bonita (*an object or place*); **that's a nice dress** ese vestido es bonito; **3** (*attractive to look at*) guapo/guapa (*a person*);

a b c d e f g h i j k l m n o p q r s t u v w x y z

you look nice in that dress estás muy guapa con ese vestido; **4** (*kind, friendly*) majo/maja (*informal*); **she's really nice** es muy maja (*informal*); **5 to be nice to somebody** ser [1] bueno/buena con alguien; **she's been very nice to me** ha sido muy buena conmigo; **6** (*tasting good*) rico/rica; **the food was really nice** la comida estaba muy rica; **7** (*weather*) bueno/buena; **it's a nice day** hace buen día; **we had nice weather** tuvimos buen tiempo.

nick *verb* (*steal*) mangar [28] (*informal*).

nickname *noun* apodo *Masc.*

niece *noun* sobrina *Fem.*

night *noun* noche *Fem.*; **what are you doing tonight?** ¿qué haces esta noche?; **see you tonight!** ¡hasta esta noche!; **I saw Greg last night** anoche vi a Greg; **it's cold at night** hace frío por la noche; **to stay the night with somebody** pasar [17] la noche con alguien.

night club *noun* club *Masc.* nocturno.

nightie *noun* camisón *Masc.*

nightmare *noun* pesadilla *Fem.*; **to have a nightmare** tener [9] una pesadilla.

night-time *noun* noche *Fem.*

nil *noun* cero *Masc.*; **they won four-nil** ganaron cuatro a cero.

nine *number* nueve *Masc.*; **Jake's nine** Jake tiene nueve años; **it's nine o'clock** son las nueve.

nineteen *number* diecinueve *Masc.*; **Jonny's nineteen** Jonny tiene diecinueve años.

nineties *plural noun* **the nineties** los años noventa; **in the nineties** en los años noventa.

ninety *number* noventa *Masc.*; **he's ninety** tiene noventa años; **ninety-five** noventa y cinco.

ninth *noun* **1** (*fraction*) **a ninth** una novena parte; **2 the ninth of June** el nueve de junio.

ninth *adjective* noveno/novena; **on the ninth floor** en la novena planta.

nitrogen *noun* nitrógeno *Masc.*

no *adverb* no; **I said no** he dicho que no; **no thank you** no, gracias.

no *adjective* **1 we've got no bread** no tenemos pan; **no problem!** ¡sin problema!; **2** (*on a notice*) **'no smoking'** 'prohibido fumar'; **'no parking'** 'prohibido aparcar'.

nobody *pronoun* nadie; **'who's there?' – 'nobody'** '¿quién está ahí?' – 'nadie'; **there's nobody in the kitchen** no hay nadie en la cocina; **nobody knows me** nadie me conoce; **nobody answered** no contestó nadie.

nod *verb* (*to say yes*) asentir [14] con la cabeza; **he nodded** asintió con la cabeza.

noise *noun* ruido *Masc.*; **to make a noise** hacer [7] ruido.

noisy *adjective* ruidoso/ruidosa.

none *pronoun* **1** (*not one*) ninguno/ninguna; **'how many students failed the exam?' – 'none'** '¿cuántos estudiantes suspendieron?' – 'ninguno'; **none of the girls knows him** ninguna de las chicas lo conoce; **2 there's none left** no queda nada; **there are none left** no queda ninguno/ninguna.

nonsense *noun* tonterías *Fem. plural*; **to talk nonsense** decir [5] tonterías; **nonsense! she's at least thirty** ¡tonterías! tiene por lo menos treinta años.

non-smoker *noun* no fumador *Masc.*, no fumadora *Fem.*

non-stop *adjective* directo/directa (*a train or flight*).

non-stop *adverb* **she talks non-stop** habla sin parar.

noodles *plural noun* fideos *Masc. plural.*

noon *noun* mediodía *Masc.*; **at (twelve) noon** a mediodía.

no-one *pronoun* nadie; **'who's there?' – 'no-one'** '¿quién está ahí?' – 'nadie'; **there's no-one in the kitchen** no hay nadie en la cocina; **no-one knows me** nadie me conoce; **no-one answered** nadie contestó.

nor *conjunction* **1** neither ... nor ni ... ni; **I have neither the time nor the money** no tengo ni tiempo ni dinero; **2 nor do I** yo tampoco; **'I didn't go' – 'nor did I'** 'no fui' – 'yo tampoco'; **3** (*with 'gustar'*) **'I don't like fish' – 'nor do I'** 'no me gusta el pescado' – 'ni a mí tampoco'; **"I didn't like the film' – 'nor did Kirsty'** 'no me gustó la película' – 'ni a Kirsty tampoco'.

normal *adjective* normal.

normally *adverb* normalmente.

north *noun* norte *Masc.*; **in the north** en el norte.

north *adjective, adverb* norte (*never changes*); **the north side** la parte norte; **a north wind** un viento del norte; **north of Madrid** al norte de Madrid.

North America *noun* Norteamérica *Fem.*

North American *noun* norteamericano *Masc.*, norteamericana *Fem.*

North American *adjective* norteamericano/norteamericana.

northeast *noun* noreste *Masc.*

northeast *adjective* **in northeast England** en el noreste de Inglaterra.

Northern Ireland *noun* Irlanda *Fem.* del Norte.

North Pole *noun* Polo *Masc.* Norte.

North Sea *noun* **the North Sea** el mar del Norte.

northwest *noun* noroeste *Masc.*

northwest *adjective* **in northwest England** en el noroeste de Inglaterra.

Norway *noun* Noruega *Fem.*

Norwegian *noun* **1** (*person*) noruego *Masc.*, noruega *Fem.*; **2** (*language*) noruego *Masc.*

Norwegian *adjective* noruego/noruega.

nose *noun* nariz *Fem.*; **to blow your nose** sonarse [24] la nariz.

nosebleed *noun* **to have a nosebleed** tener [9] una hemorragia nasal.

nostril *noun* fosa *Fem.* nasal.

a
b
c
d
e
f
g
h
i
j
k
l
m
n
o
p
q
r
s
t
u
v
w
x
y
z

not adverb 1 no; **not on Saturdays** los sábados no; **not all alone!** ¡completamente solo no!; **it's not bad** no está mal; **not at all** (in no way) en absoluto (after somebody says 'thank you') de nada; **not yet** todavía no; **of course not!** ¡por supuesto que no!; 2 (when used with a verb) no; **it's not my car** no es mi coche; **I don't know** no sé; **Sam didn't phone** Sam no llamó; **we decided not to wait** decidimos no esperar; 3 **I hope not** espero que no.

note noun 1 (a short letter) nota Fem.; **she left me a note** me dejó una nota; 2 **to take notes** tomar [17] apuntes; 3 (a banknote) billete Masc.; **a ten-pound note** un billete de diez libras; 4 (in music) nota Fem.

notebook noun cuaderno Masc.

notepad noun bloc Masc.

nothing pronoun 1 nada; **'what did you say?' – 'nothing'** ¿qué has dicho?' – 'nada'; **nothing new** nada nuevo; **nothing special** nada especial; 2 (when used with a verb) no ... nada; **she knows nothing** no sabe nada; **but there was nothing there** pero no había nada allí; **I saw nothing** no vi nada; **there's nothing happening** no está pasando nada; **there's nothing new** no hay nada nuevo; 3 **they do nothing but fight** no hacen más que pelearse.

notice noun 1 (a sign) letrero Masc.; 2 **don't take any notice of her!** ¡no le hagas caso!; 3 **to do**

something at short notice hacer [7] algo con poca antelación.

notice verb notar [17]; **I didn't notice anything** no noté nada.

notice board noun tablón Masc. de anuncios.

nought noun cero Masc.

noun noun nombre Masc.

novel noun novela Fem.

novelist noun novelista Masc./Fem.

November noun noviembre Masc.

now adverb 1 ahora; **where is he now?** ¿dónde está? **they live in the country now** ahora viven en el campo; 2 **he's busy just now** está ocupado en este momento; **I saw her just now in the corridor** acabo de verla en el pasillo; 3 **do it right now!** ¡hazlo ahora mismo!; 4 **now and then** de vez en cuando; **from now on** de ahora en adelante.

nowadays adverb hoy en día; **nowadays they are quite common** hoy en día son bastante comunes.

nowhere adverb 1 ninguna parte; **nowhere in Spain** en ninguna parte de España; **'where did she go after work?' – 'nowhere'** ¿dónde fue después del trabajo?' – 'a ninguna parte'; 2 **there's nowhere to park** no hay sitio donde aparcar.

nuclear adjective nuclear; **a nuclear power station** una central nuclear.

nuisance noun 1 (a person) pesado/pesada; **he's a real nuisance** es un verdadero pesado; 2 **it's a nuisance** es un fastidio.

numb *adjective* entumecido/entumecida; **my fingers are numb with cold** tengo los dedos entumecidos del frío.

number *noun* número *Masc.*; **I live at number thirty-one** vivo en el número treinta y uno; **my new phone number** mi nuevo número de teléfono; **a large number of visitors** un gran número de visitantes; **the third number is a 7** el tercer número es un siete.

number plate *noun* matrícula *Fem.*

nun *noun* monja *Fem.*

nurse *noun* enfermero *Masc.*, enfermera *Fem.*; **Janet's a nurse** Janet es enfermera.

nursery *noun* **1** (*for children*) guardería *Fem.*; **2** (*for plants*) vivero *Masc.*

nursery school *noun* jardín *Masc.* de infancia.

nursing *noun* enfermería *Fem.*

nut *noun* **1** (*walnut*) nuez *Fem.*; **2** (*almond*) almendra *Fem.*; **3** (*peanut*) cacahuete *Masc.*; **4** (*for a bolt*) tuerca *Fem.*

nylon *noun* nylon *Masc.*

Oo

oak *noun* roble *Masc.*

oar *noun* remo *Masc.*

oasis *noun* oasis *Masc.*

obedient *adjective* obediente.

obey *verb* obedecer [35] (*a person*); **to obey the rules** respetar [17] las reglas.

object *noun* objeto *Masc.*

object *verb* oponerse [11]; **if you don't object** si no te opones.

objection *noun* objeción *Fem.*

oboe *noun* oboe *Masc.*; **to play the oboe** tocar [31] el oboe.

obsessed *adjective* obsesionado/obsesionada; **she's obsessed with her diet** está obsesionada con su dieta.

obsession *noun* obsesión *Fem.*; **he has an obsession with cleanliness** tiene obsesión con la limpieza.

obvious *adjective* obvio/obvia.

obviously *adverb* evidentemente; **the house is obviously empty** evidentemente la casa está vacía; **'do you want to come too?' – 'obviously, but it's a bit difficult'** '¿tú quieres venir también?' – 'evidentemente, pero es un poco difícil'.

occasion *noun* ocasión *Fem.*; **a special occasion** una ocasión especial.

occasional *adjective* **he sends us the occasional letter** de vez en cuando nos manda una carta.

occasionally *adverb* de vez en cuando.

occupation *noun* ocupación *Fem.*

occupied *adjective* ocupado/ocupada.

occur *verb* ocurrir [19]; **the accident occurred on Monday** el accidente ocurrió el lunes; **it never**

a
b
c
d
e
f
g
h
i
j
k
l
m
n
o
p
q
r
s
t
u
v
w
x
y
z

a occurred to me nunca se me había ocurrido.

b **ocean** noun océano Masc.

c **o'clock** adverb at ten o'clock a las diez; it's three o'clock son las tres; exactly five o'clock exactamente las cinco en punto.

d

e **October** noun octubre Masc.

f **odd** adjective **1** (strange) raro/rara; that's odd, I'm sure I heard the phone qué raro, estoy seguro de que he oído el teléfono; **2** (number) impar; three is an odd number el tres es un número impar.

g

h

i

j **odds and ends** plural noun cachivaches Masc. plural.

k **of** preposition **1** (note that 'de+el' becomes 'del'); a kilo of tomatoes un kilo de tomates; the end of my work el final de mi trabajo; the beginning of the concert el principio del concierto; the name of the flower el nombre de la flor; the sixth of June el seis de junio; a cup of tea una taza de té; **2** Ray has four horses but he's selling three of them Ray tiene cuatro caballos, pero va a vender tres; we ate a lot of it comimos mucho; a lot of them muchos/muchas; some of them algunos/algunas; **3** two of us dos de nosotros; there are two of us somos dos; a friend of mine un amigo mío; **4** a bracelet made of silver una pulsera de plata.

l

m

n

o

p

q

r

s

t

u

v

w **off** adverb, adjective

x **off** preposition **1** (switched off) apagado/apagada; is the telly off? ¿está apagada la tele?; to turn off the lights apagar [28] la luz; **2** (tap,

y

z

water, gas) cerrado/cerrada; to turn off the tap cerrar [29] el grifo; **3** to be off (to leave) irse [8]; I'm off me voy; **4** a day off un día libre; Caro took three days off work Caro se tomó tres días libres en el trabajo; Maya's off school today Maya no ha venido al colegio hoy; **5** he's off sick no ha venido al trabajo porque está enfermo; **6** (cancelled) suspendido/suspendida; the match is off el partido se ha suspendido; **7** to be off (meat or fish) estar malo/mala; the milk's off la leche está cortada.

offence noun **1** (crime) delito Masc.; **2** to take offence ofenderse [18]; he takes offence easily se ofende fácilmente.

offer noun **1** oferta Fem.; a job offer una oferta de trabajo; **2** 'on (special) offer' 'de oferta (especial)'.

offer verb **1** ofrecer [35] (a present, a reward, or a job) he offered her a chair le ofreció una silla; **2** to offer to do ofrecerse [35] a hacer; Mike offered to drive me to the station Mike se ofreció a llevarme a la estación.

office noun oficina Fem.; he's still at the office aún está en la oficina.

office block noun bloque Masc. de oficinas.

officer noun oficial Masc./Fem.

official adjective oficial; the official version la versión oficial.

off-licence noun tienda Fem. de vinos y licores.

offside adverb fuera de juego.

often *adverb* 1 a menudo; **he's often late** a menudo llega tarde; **I'd like to see Eric more often** me gustaría ver a Eric más a menudo; **do you go often?** ¿vas a menudo?; **2 how often?** ¿con qué frecuencia?; **how often do you see Rosie?** ¿con qué frecuencia ves a Rosie?

oil *noun* aceite *Masc.*; **olive oil** aceite de oliva; **suntan oil** aceite bronceador.

oil painting *noun* óleo *Masc.* (*picture*).

ointment *noun* pomada *Fem.*

okay *adjective* 1 (*showing agreement*) vale; **okay, tomorrow at ten** vale, mañana a las diez; **2** (*asking or giving permission*) **is it okay to use the phone?** ¿puedo usar el teléfono?; **is it okay with you if I don't come till Friday?** ¿te va bien si no vengo hasta el viernes?; **it's okay if you don't want to do it** no pasa nada si no quieres hacerlo; **3** (*person*) majo/ maja (*informal*); **Daisy's okay** Daisy es maja; **4** (*nothing special*) **the film was okay** la película no estuvo mal; **5** (*not ill*) **are you okay?** ¿estás bien?; **I've been ill but I'm okay now** he estado enferma, pero ahora estoy bien.

old *adjective* 1 (*not young, not new*) viejo/vieja; **an old man** un hombre viejo; **an old lady** una señora vieja; **bring some old clothes** trae ropa vieja; **an old friend of mine** un viejo amigo mío; **old people** los ancianos; **2** (*previous*) antiguo/ antigua; **our old car was a Rover** su antiguo coche era un Rover; **their old address** su antigua dirección; **3** (*talking about age*) **how old are you?** ¿cuántos años tienes?; **James is ten years old** James tiene diez años; **a three-year-old child** un niño de tres años; **4 my older sister** mi hermana mayor; **she's older than me** es mayor que yo; **he's a year older than me** es un año mayor que yo.

old age *noun* vejez *Fem.*

old age pensioner *noun* pensionista *Masc./Fem.*

old-fashioned *noun* 1 (*clothes, music, style*) pasado de moda/ pasada de moda; **2** (*a person*) anticuado/anticuada; **my parents are so old-fashioned** mis padres son tan anticuados.

olive *noun* aceituna *Fem.*

olive oil *noun* aceite *Fem.* de oliva.

Olympic Games, Olympics *plural noun* Juegos *Masc.* plural Olímpicos.

ombudsman *noun* **the ombudsman** el defensor/la defensora del pueblo *Masc./Fem.*

omelette *noun* tortilla *Fem.*; **a cheese omelette** una tortilla de queso.

omit *verb* omitir [19].

on *preposition* 1 en; **on the desk** en el escritorio; **on the road** en la carretera; **on the beach** en la playa; **2** (*in expressions of time*) **on March 21st** el 21 de marzo; **he's arriving on Tuesday** llega el martes; **it's shut on Saturdays**

a b c d e f g h i j k l m n o p q r s t u v w x y z

a
cierra los sábados; **on rainy days** los días de lluvia; **3** (for buses, trains, etc.) **she arrived on the bus** llegó en autobús; **I met Jackie on the bus** me encontré con Jackie en el autobús; **I slept on the plane** dormí en el avión; **let's go on our bikes!** ¡vayamos en las bicis!; **4 on TV** en la tele; **on the radio** en la radio; **on video** en vídeo; **5 on holiday** de vacacciones; **on strike** de huelga.

on adjective **1** (TV, light, oven, radio) **to be on** estar [2] encendido/encendida; **all the lights were on** todas las luces estaban encendidas; **is the radio on?** ¿está encendida la radio?; **I've put the oven on** he encendido el horno; **2** (machine) estar en marcha; **the dishwasher's on** el lavaplatos está en marcha; **3** (happening) **what's on TV?** ¿qué ponen en la tele?; **what's on this week at the cinema?** ¿qué ponen en el cine esta semana?

once adverb **1** una vez; **I've tried once already** ya lo he intentado una vez; **try once more** inténtalo una vez más; **once a day** una vez al día; **more than once** más de una vez; **once upon a time** érase una vez; **2 at once** (immediately) inmediatamente; **the doctor came at once** vino el médico inmediatamente; **3 at once** (at the same time) a la vez; **I can't do two things at once** no puedo hacer dos cosas a la vez.

one number **1** uno/una; **one apple** una manzana; (note that 'uno' becomes 'un' before a masculine singular noun) **one son** un hijo; **2 it's one o'clock** es la una.

one pronoun **1** uno/una; **if you want a pen I've got one** si quieres un boli yo tengo uno; **one of us** uno de nosotros; **one of my friends** uno de mis amigos; **you never know** uno nunca sabe; **2 this one** éste/ésta; **I like that jumper, but this one's cheaper** me gusta ese jersey, pero éste es más barato; **do you want this red tie or this one?** ¿quieres esta corbata roja o ésta otra?; **3 that one** ése/ésa; **'which video?' – 'that one'** '¿qué vídeo?' – 'ése'; **4 which one?** ¿cuál?; **'my foot's hurting' – 'which one?'** 'me duele el pie' – '¿cuál?'; **5 another one** otro/otra; **I've already had a coffee, but I'll have another one** ya he tomado un café pero voy a tomar otro; **I liked the shirt so much that I bought another one** me gustó tanto la camisa que compré otra.

one's adjective **to pay for one's car** pagar su coche; **to wash one's hands** lavarse las manos.

oneself pronoun **1** (as a reflexive) se; **to wash oneself** lavarse; **to hurt oneself** hacerse daño; **2** (for emphasis) uno mismo/una misma; **one has to do everything oneself** lo tiene que hacer todo uno mismo.

one-way street noun calle Fem. de sentido único.

onion noun cebolla Fem.

only adjective único/única; **the only free seat** el único sitio libre; **the only thing to do** lo único que se puede hacer; **I am an only child** soy hijo único.

only adverb **1** (with a verb) sólo; **they've only got two bedrooms** sólo tienen dos habitaciones; **Anne's only free on Fridays** Anne sólo tiene libres los viernes; **there are only three left** sólo quedan tres; **'how long did they stay?' – 'only two days'** '¿cuánto tiempo se quedaron?' – 'sólo dos días'; **2** (but) pero; **I'd walk, only it's raining** iría andando, pero está lloviendo; **3** I've only just seen it acabo de verlo.

onto preposition sobre.

open noun **in the open** al aire libre.

open adjective **1** (not shut) abierto/abierta; **the door's open** la puerta está abierta; **the baker's isn't open** la panadería no está abierta; **2 in the open air** al aire libre.

open verb **1** abrir [46]; **can you open the door for me?** ¿me puedes abrir la puerta?; **Sam opened his eyes** Sam abrió los ojos; **the banks open at nine** los bancos abren a las nueve; **2** (by itself) abrirse [46]; **the door opened slowly** la puerta se abrió lentamente.

open-air adjective al aire libre; **an open-air swimming pool** una piscina al aire libre.

opener noun abridor Masc.

opening noun **1** (space) abertura Fem.; **2** (opportunity) oportunidad Fem.

opera noun ópera Fem.

operate verb **1** (a machine) manejar [17]; **2** (on a patient, organ) operar [17]; **will they have to operate** ¿tendrán que operarlo?

operation noun operación Fem.; **she's had an operation** le han operado.

opinion noun opinión Fem.; **in my opinion** en mi opinión.

opinion poll noun encuesta Fem. de opinión.

opponent noun oponente Masc./Fem.

opportunity noun oportunidad Fem.; **to have the opportunity of doing** tener [9] la oportunidad de hacer; **I took the opportunity to visit the museum** aproveché la oportunidad para visitar el museo.

opposed adjective **to be opposed to something** oponerse [11] a algo; **they are opposed to any change in the rules** se oponen a cualquier cambio de las reglas.

opposite noun **the opposite** lo contrario; **no, quite the opposite** no, todo lo contrario.

opposite adjective **1** opuesto/opuesta (a direction, side, or view, for example); **she went off in the opposite direction** se fue en la dirección opuesta; **2** (facing) de enfrente; **in the house opposite** en la casa de enfrente.

opposite adverb enfrente; **they live opposite** viven enfrente.

opposite preposition enfrente de; **opposite the station** enfrente de la estación.

opposition noun oposición Fem.

a
b
c
d
e
f
g
h
i
j
k
l
m
n
o
p
q
r
s
t
u
v
w
x
y
z

a **optician** noun oculista Masc./Fem.

optimistic adjective optimista.

b **or** conjunction **1** o (note that 'o' becomes 'u' before a word starting with 'o-' or 'ho-'); **English or Spanish?** ¿inglés o español?; **yesterday or today?** ¿ayer u hoy?; **2** (in negatives) **I don't have a cat or a dog** no tengo ni un gato ni un perro; **not in June or July** ni en junio ni en julio; **3** (or else) si no; **phone Mum, or she'll worry** llama a mamá, si no se va a preocupar.

oral noun (an exam) oral Masc.; **the Spanish oral** el oral de español.

orange noun (the fruit) naranja Fem.; **an orange juice** un zumo de naranja.

orange adjective naranja (never changes); **my orange socks** mis calcetines naranja.

orchard noun huerto Fem.

orchestra noun orquesta Fem.

order noun **1** (arrangement) orden Masc.; **in the right order** ordenado/ordenada; **the books are in the right order** los libros estan ordenados; **in the wrong order** desordenado/desordenada; **in alphabetical order** en orden alfabético; **2** (command) orden Fem.; **that's an order** es una orden; **3** (in a restaurant or café) **can I take your orders?** ¿les tomo la nota?; **4** **'out of order'** 'no funciona'; **5** **in order to do** para hacer; **we hurried in order to be on time** nos dimos prisa para llegar a tiempo.

order verb **1** (in a restaurant or a shop) pedir [57]; **we ordered**

steaks pedimos filetes; **2** llamar [17] a (a taxi).

ordinary adjective normal.

organ noun (the instrument) órgano Masc.; **to play the organ** tocar [31] el órgano.

organic adjective biológico/biológica (food).

organization noun organización Fem.

organize verb organizar [22].

original adjective original; **the original version was better** la versión original era mejor; **it's a really original novel** es una novela realmente original.

originally adverb al principio; **originally we wanted to take the car** al principio queríamos llevar el coche.

Orkneys plural noun **the Orkneys** las Órcadas Fem. plural.

ornament noun adorno Masc.

orphan noun huérfano Masc., huérfana Fem.

other adjective **1** (before a singular noun) otro/otra; **the other day** el otro día; **we took the other road** cogimos la otra carretera; **the other one** el otro/la otra; **I don't like this book, give me the other one** no me gusta este libro, dame el otro; **2** **the others** los otros/las otras; **where are the others?** ¿dónde están los otros?; **the other two cars** los otros dos coches; **3** **every other week** una semana sí y otra no; **4** **somebody or other** alguien; **something or other** algo;

somewhere or other en algún sitio.

otherwise *adverb* (*in other ways*) aparte de eso; **the flat's a bit small but otherwise it's lovely** el piso es pequeño, pero aparte de eso es precioso.

otherwise *conjunction* (*or else*) si no; **I'll phone home, otherwise they'll worry** voy a llamar a casa, si no van a preocuparse.

ought *verb* deber [18] ('*ought*' *is translated by the conditional tense of* '*deber*'); **I ought to go now** debería irme ahora; **they ought to know the address** deberían saber las señas; **you oughtn't to have any problems** no deberías tener ningún problema.

our *adjective* **1** (*before a singular noun*) nuestro/nuestra; **our house** nuestra casa; **2** (*before a plural noun*) nuestros/nuestras; **our parents** nuestros padres; **our address** nuestras señas; **3** (*with parts of the body*) el/la/los/las; **we'll go and wash our hands** vamos a lavarnos las manos.

ours *pronoun* **1** (*referring to a singular noun*) el nuestro/la nuestra; **their garden's bigger than ours** su jardín es más grande que el nuestro; **their house is smaller than ours** su casa es más pequeña que la nuestra; **2** (*referring to a plural noun*) los nuestros/las nuestras; **they've invited their friends and we've invited ours** han invitado a sus amigos y nosotros a los nuestros; **they showed us their photos and**

we showed them ours ellos nos enseñaron sus fotos y nosotros les enseñamos las nuestras.

ourselves *pronoun* **1** (*as a reflexive*) nos; **we introduced ourselves** nos presentamos; **2** (*for emphasis*) nosotros solos/nosotras solas; **in the end we did it ourselves** al final lo hicimos nosotros solos.

out *adverb* **1** (*outside*) fuera; **it's cold out there** hace frío ahí fuera; **out in the rain** bajo la lluvia; **they're out in the garden** están en el jardín; **2 to go out** salir [63]; **he went out of the room** salió de la habitación; **are you going out this evening?** ¿vas a salir esta noche?; **Alison's going out with Danny at the moment** Alison está saliendo ahora con Danny; **he's asked me out** me ha pedido que salga con él; **3 to be out** (*absent*) no estar [2]; **my mum's out** mi madre no está; **when they were out** cuando ellos no estaban; **4** (*light, fire*) apagado/apagada; **are all the lights out?** ¿están todas las luces apagadas?; **the fire was out** el fuego estaba apagado; **5** he threw it out of the window lo tiró por la ventana; **to drink out of a glass** beber [18] de un vaso; **she took the photo out of her bag** sacó la foto del bolso.

outing *noun* excursión *Fem.*; **to go on an outing** ir [8] de excursión.

outline *noun* (*of an object*) contorno *Masc.*

out-of-date *adjective* **1** (*no longer valid*) caducado/caducada; **my passport's out of date** mi

a
b
c
d
e
f
g
h
i
j
k
l
m
n
o
p
q
r
s
t
u
v
w
x
y
z

pasaporte está caducado; **2** (*old-fashioned*) pasado/pasada de moda; **they played out-of-date music** tocaron música pasada de moda.

outside *noun* parte Fem. de fuera; **it's blue on the outside** la parte de fuera es azul.

outside *adjective* exterior.

outside *adverb* fuera; **it's cold outside** hace frío fuera.

outside *preposition* fuera de; **I'll meet you outside the cinema** te veo fuera del cine.

outskirts *noun* afueras Fem. *plural*; **on the outskirts of York** en las afueras de York.

outstanding *adjective* excepcional.

oven *noun* horno Masc.; **I've put it in the oven** lo he puesto en el horno.

over *preposition, adverb* **1** (*above*) encima de; **there's a mirror over the sideboard** hay un espejo encima del aparador; **2** (*involving movement*) por encima de; **she jumped over the fence** saltó por encima de la valla; **he threw the ball over the wall** tiró la pelota por encima del muro; **3 over here** aquí; **the drinks are over here** las bebidas están aquí; **4 over there** allí; **she's over there talking to Julian** está allí, hablando con Julián; **5** (*more than*) más de; **it will cost over a hundred pounds** costará más de cien libras; **he's over sixty** tiene más de sesenta años; **6** (*during*) durante; **over the weekend** durante el fin de semana; **over Christmas** durante las Navidades; **7** (*finished*) **when the meeting's over** cuando la reunión haya acabado; **it's all over now** ahora todo ha acabado; **8 over the phone** por teléfono; **9 to ask someone over** invitar [17] a alguien; **can you come over on Saturday?** ¿puedes venir el sábado?; **10 all over the place** por todas partes; **all over the house** por toda la casa.

overcast *adjective* nublado/nublada.

overcrowded *adjective* abarrotado/abarrotada.

overdose *noun* sobredosis Fem.

overdraft *noun* descubierto Masc.

overflow *verb* **1** (*water*) derramarse [17]; **2** (*river*) desbordarse [17].

overseas *adverb* en el extranjero; **Dave works overseas** Dave trabaja en el extranjero.

overtake *verb* adelantar [17] (*another car*).

overtime *noun* horas Fem. *plural* extras; **to work overtime** trabajar [17] horas extras.

owe *verb* deber [18]; **I owe Rick ten pounds** le debo diez libras a Rick.

owing *adjective* **1** (*to pay*) a pagar; **there's five pounds owing** quedan cinco libras a pagar; **2 owing to** debido a; **owing to the snow** debido a la nieve.

owl *noun* búho Masc.

own *adjective* **1** propio/propia (*goes before the noun*); **my own computer** mi propio ordenador; **I've got my own room** tengo mi propia habitación; **2 on your own** solo/sola; **Annie did it on her own** Annie lo hizo sola.

own *verb* tener [9].

owner *noun* dueño *Masc.*, dueña *Fem.*

oxygen *noun* oxígeno *Masc.*

oyster *noun* ostra *Fem.*

ozone layer *noun* capa *Fem.* de ozono.

Pp

Pacific *noun* **the Pacific Ocean** el océano *Masc.* Pacífico.

pack *noun* **1** paquete *Masc.*; **2 a pack of cards** baraja *Fem.*.

pack *verb* **1** hacer [7] las maletas; **2 I'll pack my case tonight** voy a hacer la maleta esta noche.

package *noun* paquete *Masc.*

package holiday, package tour *noun* viaje *Masc.* organizado.

packed lunch *noun* comida *Fem.* preparada desde casa.

packet *noun* **1** paquete *Masc.*; **a packet of biscuits** un paquete de galletas; **2** (*bag*) bolsa *Fem.*; **a packet of crisps** una bolsa de patatas.

packing *noun* **to do your packing** hacer [7] las maletas.

pad *noun* (*of paper*) bloc *Masc.*

padlock *noun* cercado *Masc.*

page *noun* página *Fem.*; **on page seven** en la página siete.

pain *noun* dolor *Masc.*; **to be in pain** tener [9] dolor; **I've got a pain in my leg** me duele la pierna; ★ **Eric's a real pain (in the neck)** Eric es un verdadero pesado.

painkiller *noun* analgésico *Masc.*

paint *noun* pintura *Fem.*; **'wet paint'** 'recién pintado'.

paint *verb* pintar [17]; **to paint something pink** pintar algo de rosa.

paintbrush *noun* **1** (*for painting pictures*) pincel *Masc.*; **2** (*for decorating*) brocha *Fem.*

painter *noun* pintor *Masc.*, pintora *Fem.*

painting *noun* (*picture*) cuadro *Masc.*; **a painting by Monet** un cuadro de Monet.

pair *noun* **1** par *Masc.*; **a pair of socks** un par de calcetines; **a pair of shoes** un par de zapatos; **a pair of jeans** unos vaqueros; **a pair of trousers** unos pantalones; **a pair of knickers** unas bragas; **a pair of scissors** unas tijeras; **2** (*of people*) pareja *Fem.*; **to work in pairs** trabajar [1] en parejas.

Pakistan *noun* Pakistán *Masc.*

Pakistani *noun* pakistaní *Masc./Fem.*

Pakistani *adjective* pakistaní.

palace *noun* palacio *Masc.*

pale *adjective* pálido/pálida; **pale green** verde pálido (*never changes*); **pale green curtains** cortinas verde pálido; **to turn pale** palidecer [35].

a
b
c
d
e
f
g
h
i
j
k
l
m
n
o
p
q
r
s
t
u
v
w
x
y
z

palm noun **1** (*of your hand*) palma Fem.; **2** (*a palm tree*) palmera Fem.

pan noun **1** (*saucepan*) cacerola Fem.; **a pan of water** una cacerola de agua; **2** (*frying-pan*) sartén Fem.

pancake noun crepe Masc.

panel noun **1** (*on radio or TV*) (*for a discussion*) panel Masc. (*for a quiz show*) equipo Masc.; **2** (*for a wall or a bath, for example*) panel Masc.

panel game noun concurso Masc. por equipos.

panic noun pánico Masc.

panic verb dejarse [17] llevar por el pánico; **don't panic!** ¡no pierdas la calma!

panties plural noun bragas Fem. plural.

pantomime noun pantomima Fem.

pants plural noun calzoncillos Masc. plural.

paper noun **1** papel Masc.; **a sheet of paper** una hoja de papel; **2 a paper hanky** un pañuelo de papel; **3** (*newspaper*) periódico Masc.; **it was in the paper** salió en el periódico.

paperback noun libro Masc. en rústica.

paperclip noun clip Masc.

paper towel noun toalla Fem. de papel.

parachute noun paracaídas Masc. (*does not change in the plural*).

parade noun desfile Masc.

paradise noun paraíso Masc.

paragraph noun párrafo Masc.; **'new paragraph'** 'punto y aparte'.

Paraguayan noun paraguayo Masc., paraguaya Fem.

Paraguayan adjective paraguayo/paraguaya.

parallel adjective paralelo/paralela.

Paralympics plural noun the **Paralympic Games** los Juegos Paralímpicos.

paralysed adjective paralizado/paralizada.

parcel noun paquete Masc.

pardon noun **I beg your pardon** (*to someone you know*) perdón (*to show respect*) perdone; **pardon?** (*to someone you know*) ¿cómo dices? (*to show respect*) ¿cómo dice?

parents noun **my parents** mis padres; **a parents' evening** una reunión de padres.

park noun **1** parque Masc.; **a theme park** un parque temático; **2 a car park** un aparcamiento.

park verb aparcar [31]; **you can park outside the house** puedes aparcar fuera de la casa; **2 to park a car** aparcar [31] un coche; **where did you park the car?** ¿dónde has aparcado el coche?

parking noun aparcamiento Masc.; **'no parking'** 'no aparcar'.

parking meter noun parquímetro Masc.

parking space noun sitio Masc. para aparcar.

parking ticket noun multa Fem.

parliament noun parlamento Masc.

parrot noun loro Masc.

parsley noun perejil Masc.

part noun 1 parte Fem.; **part of the garden** parte del jardín; **the last part of the concert** la última parte del concierto; **that's part of your job** eso es parte de tu trabajo; 2 **to take part in something** participar [17] en algo; 3 (in a play) papel Masc.

particular adjective particular; **nothing in particular** nada en particular.

particularly adverb especialmente; **not particularly interesting** no especialmente interesante.

partly adverb en parte.

partner noun 1 (in a game) pareja Fem.; 2 (the person you live with) compañero Masc., compañera Fem.; 3 (in business) socio Masc., socia Fem.

partridge noun perdiz Fem.

part-time adjective, adverb a tiempo parcial; **part-time work** trabajo a tiempo parcial; **to work part-time** trabajar [17] a tiempo parcial.

party noun 1 fiesta Fem.; **a Christmas party** una fiesta de Navidad; **to have a birthday party** celebrar [17] una fiesta de cumpleaños; **we've been invited to a party at the Smiths' house** estamos invitados a una fiesta en casa de los Smith; 2 (group) grupo Masc.; **a party of schoolchildren** un grupo de colegiales; **a rescue party** un equipo de rescate; 3 (in politics) partido Masc.; **the Labour party** el partido laborista.

pass noun 1 (to let you in) pase Masc.; 2 **a bus pass** un abono de autobús; 3 (a mountain pass) paso Masc.; 4 (in an exam) aprobado Masc.; **to get a pass in history** sacar [31] un aprobado en historia.

pass verb 1 (go past) pasar [17] por (a place or building); **we passed your house** pasamos por tu casa; 2 (to overtake) adelantar [17] (a car); 3 (give) pasar [17]; **could you pass me the paper please?** ¿me pasas el papel, por favor?; 4 (time) pasar [17]; **the time passed slowly** el tiempo pasaba lentamente; 5 (in an exam) aprobar [24]; **did you pass?** ¿aprobaste?; **to pass an exam** aprobar un examen.

passenger noun pasajero Masc., pasajera Fem.

passion noun pasión Fem.

passionate adjective apasionado/apasionada.

passive noun voz Fem. pasiva.

passive adjective pasivo/pasiva.

Passover noun Pascua Fem. judía.

passport noun pasaporte Masc.; **an EU passport** un pasaporte de la Comunidad Europea.

password noun contraseña Fem.

past noun pasado Masc.; **in the past** en el pasado.

past adjective 1 (recent) último/última (goes before the noun); **in the past few weeks** en las últimas semanas; 2 (over) **winter is past** ya ha pasado el invierno.

past preposition, adverb 1 **to walk or drive past something** pasar [17] por delante de algo; **we went past the school** pasamos por delante

a b c d e f g h i j k l m n o p q r s t u v w x y z

del colegio; **Ray went past in his new car** Ray pasó en su coche nuevo; **2** (*the other side of*) pasado/pasada; **it's just past the post office** está justo pasada la oficina de correos; **3** (*talking about time*) **ten past six** las seis y diez; **half past four** las cuatro y media; **a quarter past two** las dos y cuarto.

pasta *noun* pasta *Fem.*; **I don't like pasta** no me gusta la pasta.

pasteurized *adjective* pasteurizado/pasteurizada.

pastry *noun* masa *Fem.*

patch *noun* **1** (*of colour*) mancha *Fem.*; **2** (*for repairs*) parche *Masc.*

path *noun* camino *Masc.* (*very narrow*) sendero *Masc.*

patience *noun* **1** paciencia *Fem.*; **2** (*card game*) solitario *Masc.*

patient *noun* paciente *Masc./Fem.*.

patient *adjective* paciente.

patiently *adverb* pacientemente.

patio *noun* patio *Masc.*

patrol *noun* patrulla *Fem.*

patrol car *noun* coche *Masc.* patrulla.

pattern *noun* **1** (*on wallpaper or fabric*) diseño *Masc.*; **2** (*dressmaking*) patrón *Masc.*; **3** (*knitting*) modelo *Masc.*

pavement *noun* acera *Fem.*; **on the pavement** en la acera.

paw *noun* pata *Fem.*

pawn *noun* peón *Masc.*

pay *noun* sueldo *Masc.*

pay *verb* **1** pagar [28]; **I'm paying** yo pago; **to pay cash** pagar al contado; **2** to pay for something pagar [28] algo; **Tony paid for the**

drinks Tony pagó las bebidas; **it's all paid for** está todo pagado; **3 to pay by credit card** pagar [28] con tarjeta de crédito; **to pay by cheque** pagar [28] con cheque; **4 to pay somebody back** (*money*) devolverle [45] dinero a alguien; **5 to pay attention** prestar [17] atención; **6 to pay a visit to somebody** hacer [7] una visita a alguien.

payment *noun* pago *Masc.*

pay phone *noun* teléfono *Masc.* público.

PC *noun* (*computer*) PC *Masc.*

pea *noun* guisante *Masc.*

peace *noun* paz *Fem.*

peaceful *adjective* tranquilo/tranquila (*day, scene*).

peach *noun* melocotón *Masc.*

peacock *noun* pavo *Masc.* real.

peak *noun* (*of a mountain*) pico *Masc.*

peak period (*for holidays*) temporada *Fem.* alta.

peak rate *noun* (*for phoning*) tarifa *Fem.* máxima.

peak time *noun* (*for traffic*) hora *Fem.* punta.

peanut *noun* cacahuete *Masc.*

peanut butter *noun* mantequilla *Fem.* de cacahuete.

pear *noun* pera *Fem.*

pearl *noun* perla *Fem.*

peasant *noun* campesino *Masc.*, campesina *Fem.*

pebble *noun* guijarro *Masc.*

pedal *noun* pedal *Masc.*

pedal *verb* pedalear [17].

pedestrian *noun* peatón *Masc.*, peatona *Fem.*

pedestrian crossing *noun* paso *Masc.* peatonal.

pedestrian precinct *noun* zona *Fem.* peatonal.

pee *noun* **to have a pee** hacer [7] pis (*informal*).

peel *noun* **1** (*of an apple*) piel *Fem.*; **2** (*of an orange*) cáscara *Fem.*

peel *verb* pelar [17] (*fruit, vegetables*).

peg *noun* **1** (*hook*) gancho *Masc.*; **2 a clothes peg** una pinza de la ropa; **3 a tent peg** una piqueta.

pen *noun* **1** bolígrafo *Masc.*, boli *Masc.* (*informal*); **2** (*fountain pen*) pluma *Fem.*; **3 a felt pen** un rotulador.

penalty *noun* **1** (*a fine*) multa *Fem.*; **2** (*in football or rugby*) penalty *Masc.*

penalty area *noun* área *Fem.* de castigo (*even though 'area' is feminine it takes 'el' and 'un'*).

pence *plural noun* peniques *Masc.* plural.

pencil *noun* lápiz *Masc.*; **to write in pencil** escribir [52] a lápiz.

pencil case *noun* estuche *Masc.* para lápices.

pencil sharpener *noun* sacapuntas *Masc.* (*does not change in the plural*).

pendant *noun* colgante *Masc.*

penfriend *noun* amigo *Masc.* por correspondencia, amiga *Fem.* por correspondencia; **my Spanish pen-friend is called Cristina** mi amiga, por correspondencia española se llama Cristina.

penis *noun* pene *Masc.*

penknife *noun* navaja *Fem.*

penny *noun* penique *Masc.*

pension *noun* pensión *Fem.*

pensioner *noun* pensionista *Masc./Fem.*

people *plural noun* **1** gente *Fem.* (*singular*); **people round here** la gente de por aquí; **nice people** gente simpática; **people say he's very rich** la gente dice que es muy rico; **2** (*when you're counting them*) persona *Fem.*; **ten people** diez personas; **several people** varias personas; **how many people have you asked?** ¿a cuántas personas has preguntado?

pepper *noun* **1** (*spice*) pimienta *Fem.*; **2** (*pepper*) pimiento *Masc.*; **a green pepper** un pimiento verde.

peppermill *noun* pimentero *Masc.*

peppermint *noun* menta *Fem.*; **peppermint tea** infusión *Fem.* de menta.

per *preposition* por; **ten pounds per person** diez libras por persona.

per cent *adverb* por ciento; **sixty per cent of the students** el sesenta por ciento de los estudiantes.

percentage *noun* porcentaje *Masc.*

percussion *noun* percusión *Fem.*; **to play percussion** tocar [31] la percusión.

a b c d e f g h i j k l m n o p q r s t u v w x y z

perfect *adjective* **1** perfecto/perfecta; **she speaks perfect English** habla un inglés perfecto; **2** (*ideal*) ideal; **the perfect place for a picnic** el sitio ideal para un picnic.

perfectly *adverb* perfectamente.

perform *verb* **1** interpretar [17] (*a piece of music or a role*); **2** representar [17] (*a play*); **3** cantar [17] (*a song*).

performance *noun* **1** (*playing or acting*) interpretación *Fem.*; **a wonderful performance of Macbeth** una maravillosa interpretación de Macbeth; **2** (*show*) espectáculo *Masc.*; **the performance starts at eight** el espectáculo empieza a las ocho; **3** (*the results of a team or company*) actuación *Fem.*

performer *noun* artista *Masc./Fem.*

perfume *noun* perfume *Masc.*

perhaps *adverb* quizás; **perhaps it's in the drawer?** ¿a lo mejor está el cajón?; **perhaps he's missed the train** quizás ha perdido el tren.

period *noun* **1** periodo *Masc.*; **a two-year period** un periodo de dos años; **2** (*in school*) clase *Fem.*; **a forty-five-minute period** una clase de cuarenta y cinco minutos; **3** (*menstruation*) periodo *Masc.*; **to have your period** tener [9] el periodo.

perm *noun* permanente *Fem.*

permanent *adjective* permanente.

permanently *adverb* permanentemente.

permission *noun* permiso *Masc.*; **to get permission to do** conseguir [64] permiso para hacer.

permit *noun* permiso *Masc.*

permit *verb* permitir [19]; **to permit somebody to do** permitir [19] a alguien hacer; **smoking is not permitted** está prohibido fumar; **weather permitting** si el tiempo lo permite.

person *noun* persona *Fem.*; **there's room for one more person** hay sitio para una persona más; **in person** en persona.

personal *adjective* personal.

personality *noun* personalidad *Fem.*

personally *adverb* personalmente; **personally, I'm against it** personalmente, estoy en contra.

personal stereo *noun* walkman™ *Masc.*

perspiration *noun* sudor *Masc.*

persuade *verb* convencer [44]; **to persuade somebody to do** convencer a alguien para que haga (*note that 'para que' is followed by the subjunctive*); **we persuaded Tim to wait a bit** convencimos a Tim para que esperara un poco.

peseta *noun* peseta *Fem.* (*former Spanish currency replaced by the euro; 500 pesetas = 3.00 euros*).

pessimistic *adjective* pesimista.

pest *noun* **1** (*greenfly for example*) plaga *Fem.*; **2** (*annoying person*) pesado *Masc.*, pesada *Fem.*

pester *verb* fastidiar [17].

pet noun **1** animal Masc. de compañía; **do you have a pet?** ¿tienes un animal de compañía?; **a pet dog** un perro de compañía; **2** (favourite person) favorito Masc., favorita Fem.; **Julie is teacher's pet** Julie es la favorita de la maestra.

petal noun pétalo Masc.

pet name noun apodo Masc. cariñoso.

petrol noun gasolina Fem.; **to fill up with petrol** llenar [17] de gasolina; **to run out of petrol** quedarse [17] sin gasolina.

petrol station noun gasolinera Fem.

petticoat noun enagua Fem.

pharmacist noun farmacéutico Masc., farmacéutica Fem.

pharmacy noun farmacia Fem.

pheasant noun faisán Masc.

philosophy noun filosofía Fem.

phone noun teléfono Masc.; **she's on the phone** está hablando por teléfono; **I was on the phone to Sophie** estaba hablando por teléfono con Sophie; **you can book by phone** puedes reservar por teléfono.

phone verb **1** llamar [17] por teléfono; **while I was phoning** mientras llamaba por teléfono; **2 to phone somebody** llamar [17] a alguien; **I'll phone you tonight** te llamaré esta noche.

phone book noun guía Fem. telefónica.

phone box noun cabina Fem. telefónica.

phone call noun llamada Fem. telefónica; **phone calls are free** las llamadas telefónicas son gratis; **to make a phone call** hacer [7] una llamada (telefónica).

phone card noun tarjeta Fem. telefónica.

phone number noun número Masc. de teléfono.

photo noun foto Fem.; **to take a photo** hacer [7] una foto; **to take a photo of somebody** hacerle [7] una foto a alguien; **I took a photo of their house** hice una foto de su casa.

photocopier noun fotocopiadora Fem.

photocopy noun fotocopia Fem.

photocopy verb fotocopiar [17].

photograph noun fotografía Fem.; **to take a photograph** hacer [7] una fotografía; **to take a photograph of somebody** hacerle [7] una fotografía a alguien.

photograph verb fotografiar [32].

photographer noun fotógrafo Masc., fotógrafa Fem.

photography noun fotografía Fem.

phrase noun frase Fem.

phrase-book noun manual Masc. de conversación.

physicist noun físico Masc., física Fem.

physics noun física Fem.

physiotherapist noun fisioterapeuta Masc./Fem.

physiotherapy noun fisioterapia Fem.

pianist noun pianista Masc./Fem.

a

piano noun piano Masc.; **to play
the piano** tocar [31] el piano; **Steve
played it on the piano** Steve lo
tocó al piano; **a piano lesson** una
clase de piano.

b

c

d

pick noun **take your pick!** ¡escoge!

e

pick verb **1** (to choose) escoge [3];
pick a card escoger una carta;
2 (for a team) seleccionar [17]; **I've
been picked for Saturday** me han
seleccionado para el sábado;
3 recoger [3] (fruit); **4** coger [3]
(flowers).

f

g

h

i

● **to pick up 1** (lift) coger [3]; **he
picked up the papers and went
out** cogió los papeles y salió; **to
pick up the phone** coger el
teléfono; **2** (from the floor) recoger
[3]; **pick up that piece of paper**
recoge ese papel; **3** (collect
together) recoger [3]; **I'll pick up
the toys** voy a recoger los juguetes;
4 (to collect) recoger [3]; **I'll pick
you up at six** te recogeré a las seis;
I'll pick up the keys tomorrow
recogeré las llaves mañana;
5 (learn) aprender [18]; **you'll soon
pick it up** lo aprenderás pronto.

j

k

l

m

n

o

p

picnic noun picnic Masc.; **to have a
picnic** hacer [7] un picnic.

q

pickpocket noun carterista
Masc./Fem.

r

s

t

picture noun **1** (a painting)
cuadro Masc.; **a picture by Picasso**
un cuadro de Picasso; **he painted a
picture of a horse** pintó un
caballo; **2** (a drawing) dibujo Masc.;
draw me a picture of your house
hazme un dibujo de tu casa; **3** (in a
book) ilustración Fem.; **a book
with lots of pictures** un libro con

u

v

w

x

y

z

muchas ilustraciones; **4 the
pictures** el cine; **to go to the
pictures** ir [8] al cine.

pie noun **1** (sweet) pastel Masc.; **an
apple pie** un pastel de manzana;
2 (savoury) empanada Fem.; **a
meat pie** una empanada de carne.

piece noun **1** (a bit) trozo Masc.; **a
big piece of cheese** un trozo
grande de queso; **2** (that you fit
together) pieza Fem.; **the pieces of
a jigsaw** las piezas de un
rompecabezas; **to take something
to pieces** desmontar [17] algo; **3 a
piece of furniture** un mueble; **four
pieces of luggage** cuatro maletas;
a piece of information un dato;
that's a piece of luck! ¡qué
suerte!; **4** (coin) moneda Fem.; **a
10p piece** una moneda de diez
peniques.

pierced adjective **to have pierced
ears** tener [9] agujeros en las
orejas.

pig noun cerdo Masc., cerda Fem.

pigeon noun paloma Fem.

piggy bank noun hucha Fem.

pigsty noun pocilga Fem.; **your
room is a pigsty** tu habitación está
hecha una pocilga.

pigtail noun trenza Fem.

pile noun **1** (a neat stack) pila Fem.;
a pile of plates una pila de platos;
2 (a heap) montón Masc.; **a pile of
dirty shirts** un montón de camisas
sucias.

● **to pile something up** (neatly)
apilar [17] algo, (in a heap)
amontonar [17] algo.

pilgrimage noun peregrinación Fem.; **to go on a pilgrimage** irse [8] de peregrinación.

pill noun pastilla Fem.; **the pill** (contraceptive) la píldora.

pillow noun almohada Fem.

pillow case noun almohadón Masc.

pilot noun piloto Masc./Fem.

pimple noun grano Masc.

pin noun 1 (for sewing) alfiler Masc.; 2 **a three-pin plug** un enchufe de tres clavijas.

● **to pin up** 1 prender [18] con alfileres (a hem); 2 poner [11] (a notice).

PIN noun (personal identification number) PIN Masc.

pinball noun flipper Masc.; **to play pinball** jugar [27] al flipper; **a pinball machine** un flipper.

pinch noun (of salt, for example) pellizco Masc.

pinch verb 1 (steal) mangar [28] (informal); **somebody's pinched my bike** alguien me ha robado la bici; 2 **to pinch somebody** pellizcar [31] a alguien.

pine noun pino Masc.; **a pine table** una mesa de pino.

pineapple noun piña Fem.

pine cone noun piña Fem.

ping-pong noun ping-pong Masc.; **to play ping-pong** jugar [27] al ping-pong.

pink adjective rosa (never changes); **my pink dress** mi vestido rosa; **pink socks** calcetines rosa.

pint noun pinta Fem.

pip noun pepita Fem.

pipe noun 1 (for gas or water) tubería Fem.; 2 (to smoke) pipa Fem.; **he smokes a pipe** fuma en pipa.

Pisces noun Piscis Masc.; **Amanda's Pisces** Amanda es Piscis.

pistachio noun pistacho Masc.

pit noun foso Masc.

pitch noun campo Masc.; **a football pitch** un campo de fútbol.

pitch verb **to pitch a tent** montar [17] una tienda.

pity noun 1 lástima Fem.; **what a pity!** ¡qué lástima!; **it would be a pity to miss the beginning** sería una lástima perderse el principio; 2 (for a person) piedad Fem.

pity verb **to pity somebody** compadecer [35] a alguien.

pizza noun pizza Fem.

place noun 1 sitio Masc.; **in a warm place** en un sitio caliente; **Rome is a wonderful place** Roma es un lugar maravilloso; **all over the place** por todos sitios; **a place for the car** un sitio para el coche; **will you keep my place?** ¿me guardas el sitio?; **to change places** cambiarse [17] de sitio; 2 (in a race) lugar Masc.; **in first place** en primer lugar; 3 **at your place** en tu casa; **we'll go round to Zafir's place** iremos a casa de Zafir; 4 **to take place** tener [9] lugar; **the competition will take place at four** la competición tendrá lugar a las cuatro; 5 **if I was in your place** ... si yo estuviese en tu lugar ....

a
b
c
d
e
f
g
h
i
j
k
l
m
n
o
p
q
r
s
t
u
v
w
x
y
z

a

place verb poner [11]; **he placed his cup on the table** puso su taza en la mesa.

b

plain adjective **1** sencillo/sencilla; **plain cooking** la cocina sencilla; **2** (unflavoured) natural; **a plain yoghurt** yogur natural; **3** **plain chocolate** chocolate sin leche; **4** (not patterned) liso/lisa; **plain curtains** cortinas lisas.

c

d

e

f

plait noun trenza Fem.

g

plan noun **1** plan Masc.; **what are your plans for this summer?** ¿qué planes tienes para este verano?; **to go according to plan** salir [63] según el plan; **everything went according to plan** todo salió según el plan; **2** (a map) plano Masc.

h

i

j

k

plan verb **1** planear [17]; **Ricky's planning a trip to Italy** Ricky está planeando un viaje a Italia; **to plan to do** planear [17] hacer; **we're planning to leave at eight** planeamos salir a las ocho; **2** (organize) organizar [22]; **I'm planning my day** estoy organizándome el día; **3** (to design) diseñar [17] (a house or garden) **a well-planned kitchen** una cocina bien diseñada.

l

m

n

o

p

q

r

plane noun avión Masc.; **we went by plane** fuimos en avión.

s

planet noun planeta Masc.

t

plant noun planta Fem.; **a house plant** una planta de interior.

u

plant verb plantar [17].

v

w

plaster noun **1** (sticking plaster) tirita™ Fem.; **2** (for walls) yeso Masc.; **3 to have your leg in**

x

y

z

plaster tener [9] una pierna escayolada.

plastic noun plástico Masc.; **a plastic bag** una bolsa de plástico.

plate noun plato Masc.

platform noun **1** (in a station) andén Masc.; **the train arriving at platform six** el tren que llega al andén número seis; **2** (for lecturing or performing) estrado Masc.

play noun obra Fem.; **a play by Shakespeare** una obra de Shakespeare; **our school is putting on a play** nuestro colegio está preparando una obra.

play verb **1** jugar [27]; **the children were playing with a ball** los niños estaban jugando con una pelota; **to play tennis** jugar al tenis; **they were playing cards** estaban jugando a las cartas; **2** (music or an instrument) tocar [31]; **Helen plays the violin** Helen toca el violín; **they play all kinds of music** tocan todo tipo de música; **3** poner [11] (a tape, CD, or record) **play me your new CD** ponme tu nuevo compacto; **4** who's playing Hamlet? ¿quién hace el papel de Hamlet?

player noun **1** (in sport) jugador Masc., jugadora Fem.; **a football player** un jugador de fútbol; **2** (musician) músico Masc., música Fem.

playground noun patio Masc. de recreo.

playing card noun naipe Masc.

playing field noun campo Masc. de juego.

playroom noun cuarto Masc. de los juguetes.

pleasant adjective agradable.

please adverb por favor; **two coffees, please** dos cafés, por favor; **could you turn the TV off, please?** ¿puedes apagar la tele, por favor?

pleased adjective contento/contenta; **I'm very pleased** estoy muy contento (in the past tense 'ponerse' is used in place of 'estar'); **I was really pleased!** ¡me puse muy contento!; **she was pleased with her present** se puso muy contenta con su regalo; **pleased to meet you!** ¡encantado de conocerte!

pleasure noun placer Masc.

plenty pronoun 1 (lots) mucho/mucha; **there's plenty of bread** hay mucho pan; **he's got plenty of experience** tiene mucha experiencia; 2 (with a plural noun) muchos/muchas; **there are plenty of cases** hay muchos casos; **she's got plenty of ideas** tiene muchas ideas; **there were plenty of them** había muchos; 3 (quite enough) más que suficiente; **we've got plenty of time for a coffee** tenemos tiempo más que suficiente para tomar un café; **thank you, that's plenty!** gracias, esto es más que suficiente.

pliers plural noun alicates Masc. plural.

plug noun 1 (electrical) enchufe Masc.; 2 (in a bath or sink) tapón Masc.; **to pull out the plug** quitar [17] el tapón.

● **to plug something in** enchufar [17] algo.

plum noun ciruela Fem.; **a plum tart** una tarta de ciruelas.

plumber noun fontanero Masc., fontanera Fem.; **he's a plumber** es fontanero.

plump adjective regordete/regordeta.

plural noun plural Masc.; **in the plural** en plural.

plus preposition más; **three children plus the baby** tres niños más el bebé.

p.m. adverb (Spanish people usually use 'de la tarde', for times up to approximately 8 p.m. and 'de la noche' for times approximately after 8 p.m.) **at two p.m.** a las dos de la tarde; **at nine p.m.** a las nueve de la noche.

poached egg noun huevo Masc. escalfado.

pocket noun bolsillo Masc.

pocket money noun 1 (for children) paga Fem.; 2 (for minor purchases) dinero Masc. para gastos personales.

poem noun poema Masc.

poet noun poeta Masc./Fem.

poetry noun poesía Fem.

point noun 1 (tip) punta Fem.; **the point of a nail** la punta de un clavo; 2 (in time) momento Masc.; **at that point the police arrived** en ese momento llegó la policía; **3 to get the point** entender [36]; **I don't get the point** no lo entiendo; **4 what's the point of waiting?** ¿qué sentido tiene esperar?;

a
b
c
d
e
f
g
h
i
j
k
l
m
n
o
p
q
r
s
t
u
v
w
x
y
z

there's no point phoning, he's out no tiene sentido llamar, ha salido; **that's not the point** no se trata de eso; **5 that's a good point!** ¡es verdad!; **6 from my point of view** desde mi punto de vista; **7 her strong point** su punto fuerte; **8** (*in scoring*) punto *Masc.*; **fifteen points to eleven** quince puntos a once; **9** (*in decimals*) (*in Spanish, a comma is used for the decimal point, so 6.4 = 6,4, said*) 6 point 4 seis coma cuatro.

point *verb* **1** señalar [17]; **a notice pointing to the station** un cartel señalando hacia la estación; **James pointed out the cathedral** James señaló la catedral; **he pointed at one of the children** señaló a uno de los niños; **2 I'd like to point out that I'm paying** quisiera dejar claro que pago yo.

poison *noun* veneno *Masc.*

poison *verb* envenenar [17].

poisonous *adjective* venenoso/venenosa.

poker *noun* **1** (*for fire*) atizador *Masc.*; **2** (*card game*) póker *Masc.*

Poland *noun* Polonia *Fem.*

polar bear *noun* oso *Masc.* polar.

pole *noun* **1** (*for a tent*) mástil *Masc.*; **2 the North Pole** el Polo Norte.

Pole *noun* (*a Polish person*) polaco *Masc.*, polaca *Fem.*

police *noun* **the police** la policía; **the police are coming** ya viene la policía (*note that a singular verb is used with 'la policía'*).

police *verb* patrullar [17] (*the streets*).

police car *noun* coche *Masc.* de policía.

policeman *noun* policía *Masc.*

police station *noun* comisaría *Fem.*

policewoman *noun* mujer *Fem.* policía.

policy *noun* **1** (*plan of action*) política *Fem.*; **2** (*document*) póliza *Fem.*

polish *noun* **1** (*for furniture*) cera *Fem.*; **2** (*for shoes*) betún *Masc.*

polish *verb* sacar [31] brillo a (*shoes or furniture*).

Polish *noun* **1** (*language*) polaco *Masc.*; **2** (*people*) **the Polish** los polacos (*plural*).

Polish *adjective* polaco/polaca.

polite *adjective* educado/educada; **to be polite to somebody** ser [1] educado/educada con alguien.

political *adjective* político/política.

politician *noun* político *Masc.*, política *Fem.*

politics *noun* política *Fem.*

polluted *adjective* contaminado/contaminada.

pollution *noun* contaminación *Fem.*

polo-necked *adjective* de cuello alto; **a polo-necked jumper** un jersey de cuello alto.

polythene bag *noun* bolsa *Fem.* de plástico.

pond *noun* **1** (*natural*) laguna *Fem.*; **2** (*man-made*) estanque *Masc.*

pony *noun* poni *Masc.*

ponytail *noun* cola *Fem.* de caballo.

poodle noun caniche Masc.

pool noun 1 (swimming pool) piscina Fem.; 2 (in the country) alberca Fem.; 3 (puddle) charco Masc.; 4 (game) billar Masc. americano; **to have a game of pool** jugar [27] al billar americano; **5 the football pools** las quinielas; **to do the pools** hacer [7] las quinielas.

poor adjective 1 pobre; **a poor area** un zona pobre; **a poor family** una familia pobre; **poor Tanya's failed her exam** la pobre Tanya suspendió el examen; 2 (bad) malo/mala; **this is poor quality** esto es de mala calidad; **the weather was pretty poor** el tiempo fue bastante malo.

pop noun pop Masc.; **a pop concert** un concierto de pop; **a pop star** una estrella del pop; **a pop song** una canción de pop.

● **to pop into** entrar [17] un momento en; **I'll just pop into the bank** voy a entrar un momento en el banco.

popcorn noun palomitas Fem. plural de maíz.

pope noun papa Masc.

poppy noun amapola Fem.

popular adjective popular.

population noun población Fem.

porch noun porche Masc.

pork noun cerdo Masc.; **a pork chop** una chuleta de cerdo.

porridge noun gachas Fem. plural.

port noun 1 (for ships) puerto Masc.; 2 (wine) oporto Masc.

portable computer noun (ordenador) portátil Masc.

porter noun 1 (at a station or airport) mozo Masc. de las maletas; 2 (in a hotel) portero Masc.

portion noun (of food) ración Fem.

portrait noun retrato Masc.

Portugal noun Portugal Masc.

Portuguese noun 1 (language) portugués Masc.; 2 (a person) portugués Masc., portuguesa Fem.

Portuguese adjective portugués/portuguesa.

posh adjective elegante; **a posh house** una casa elegante.

position noun posición Fem.

positive adjective 1 (sure) seguro/segura; **I'm positive he's left** estoy seguro de que se ha ido; 2 (enthusiastic) positivo/positiva; **her reaction was very positive** su reacción fue muy positiva; **try to be more positive** intenta tener una actitud más positiva.

possessions plural noun pertenencias Fem. plural; **all my possessions are in the flat** todas mis pertenencias están en el piso.

possibility noun posibilidad Fem.

possible adjective posible; **it's possible** es posible; **if possible** si es posible; **as quickly as possible** tan rápidamente como sea posible.

possibly adverb 1 (maybe) posiblemente; **'will you be at home at midday?' – 'possibly'** ¿estarás en casa a mediodía? – 'posiblemente'; 2 (for emphasis) **how can you possibly believe that?** pero, ¿cómo puedes creerte

a
b
c
d
e
f
g
h
i
j
k
l
m
n
o
p
q
r
s
t
u
v
w
x
y
z

eso?; **I can't possibly arrive before Thursday** no puedo llegar antes del jueves de ninguna manera.

post noun 1 correo Masc.; **to send something by post** mandar [17] algo por correo; 2 (letters) **is there any post for me?** ¿hay alguna carta para mí?; 3 (a pole) poste Masc.; 4 (a job) puesto Masc.

post verb **to post a letter** echar [17] una carta al correo; **to post something to somebody** mandarle [17] algo a alguien.

postbox noun buzón Masc.

postcard noun postal Fem.

postcode noun código Masc. postal.

poster noun 1 (for decoration) póster Masc.; **I've bought an Oasis poster** he comprado un póster de Oasis; 2 (advertising) cartel Masc.; **I saw a poster for the concert** vi un cartel del concierto.

postman noun cartero Masc.; **has the postman been?** ¿ha venido el cartero?

post office noun oficina Fem. de correos.

postpone verb **to postpone something** posponer [11] algo.

postwoman noun cartera Fem.

pot noun 1 (jar) tarro Masc.; **a pot of honey** un tarro de miel; 2 (teapot) tetera Fem.; **I'll make a pot of tea** voy a hacer té; 3 **the pots and pans** los cacharros; ★ **to take pot luck** probar [24] suerte.

potato noun patata Fem.; **fried potatoes** patatas fritas; **mashed potatoes** puré de patatas.

potato crisps plural noun patatas Fem. plural fritas de bolsa.

pottery noun cerámica Fem.

pound noun 1 (money) libra Fem.; **fourteen pounds** catorce libras; **how much is that in pounds?** ¿cuánto es eso en libras?; 2 (in weight) libra Fem.; **a pound of apples** una libra de manzanas.

pour verb 1 echar [17] (liquid); **he poured the milk into the pan** echó la leche en la cacerola; 2 servir [57] (a drink); **to pour the tea** servir el té; **I poured him a drink** le serví una bebida; ★ **it's pouring down** (with rain) está lloviendo a cántaros (literally: it's raining jugfuls).

poverty noun pobreza Fem.

powder noun polvo Masc.

power noun 1 (electricity) corriente Fem. eléctrica; 2 (energy) energía Fem.; **nuclear power** energía nuclear; 3 (over other people) poder Masc.; **to be in power** estar en el poder.

power cut noun apagón Masc.

powerful adjective poderoso/ poderosa.

power point noun enchufe Masc.

power station noun central Fem. eléctrica.

practical adjective práctico/ práctica.

practical joke noun broma Fem. pesada.

practice noun 1 (for sport) entrenamiento Masc.; **hockey practice** entrenamiento de hockey; **2** (for an instrument) **to do your piano practice** hacer [7] los ejercicios de piano; **3 to be out of practice** (for a sport) estar desentrenado/desentrenada; **4 in practice** en la práctica.

practise verb 1 practicar [31] (music, language, etc); **a week in Granada to practise my Spanish** una semana en Granada para practicar mi español; **2** (in a sport) entrenar [17]; **the team practises on Wednesdays** el equipo entrena los miércoles.

praise verb **to praise somebody for something** elogiar [17] a alguien por algo.

pram noun cochecito Masc. de bebé.

prawn noun gamba Fem.

pray verb rezar [22].

prayer noun oración Fem.

precious adjective precioso/ preciosa.

precise adjective preciso/precisa.

prefer verb preferir [14]; **I prefer coffee to tea** prefiero el café al té; **he'd prefer not to see them** preferiría no verlos.

pregnant adjective embarazada.

pregnancy noun embarazo Masc.

prejudice noun prejuicio Masc.; **a prejudice** un prejuicio; **to fight against racial prejudice** luchar [17] contra los prejuicios raciales.

prejudiced adjective **to be prejudiced** tener [9] prejuicios.

premiere noun estreno Masc. (of a play or film).

prep noun deberes Masc. plural; **my English prep** mis deberes de inglés.

preparation noun 1 preparación Fem.; **2 the preparations for** los preparativos para.

prepare verb 1 **to prepare for something** prepararse para algo; **2** preparar [17]; **to prepare somebody for** preparar [17] a alguien para (a surprise or shock); **to be prepared for the worst** estar [2] preparado para lo peor.

prepared adjective dispuesto/ dispuesta; **I'm prepared to pay half** estoy dispuesta a pagar la mitad.

preposition noun preposición Fem.

prescribe verb recetar [17].

prescription noun receta Fem.; **on prescription** con receta.

present noun 1 (a gift) regalo Masc.; **to give somebody a present** regalarle [17] algo a alguien; **2** (the time now) presente Masc.; **in the present (tense)** en presente; **that's all for the present** eso es todo por ahora.

present adjective 1 (attending) presente; **is Tracy present?** ¿está Tracy presente?; **to be present at** asistir [19] a; **fifty people were present at the funeral** cincuenta personas asistieron al funeral; **2** (existing now) actual; **the present situation** la situación

a

actual; **3 at the present time** en este momento.

b

present *verb* **1** entregar [28] (*a prize*); **2** (*introduce*) presentar [17].

c

presenter *noun* (*on TV*) presentador *Masc.*, presentadora *Fem.*

d

e

president *noun* presidente *Masc.*, presidenta *Fem.*

f

press *noun* **the press** la prensa.

g

press *verb* **1** (*to push*) empujar [17]; **press here to open** para abrir, empuje aquí; **2** apretar [29] (*a button or doorbell*); **she pressed the button** apretó el botón.

h

i

j

press conference *noun* conferencia *Fem.* de prensa.

k

l

pressure *noun* presión *Fem.*

m

pressure gauge *noun* manómetro *Masc.*

n

pressure group *noun* grupo *Masc.* de presión.

o

p

pretend *verb* **to pretend to do** fingir [49] hacer; **he's pretending not to hear** está fingiendo no oír.

q

pretty *adjective* bonito/bonita; **a pretty dress** un vestido bonito.

r

pretty *adverb* bastante; **it was pretty embarrassing** fue bastante vergonzoso.

s

t

prevent *verb* **1** evitar [17] (*a war or disaster*); **2 to prevent somebody from doing** impedir [57] a alguien hacer; **there's nothing to prevent you from leaving** no hay nada que te impida irte.

u

v

w

x

previous *adjective* anterior.

y

previously *adverb* antes.

z

---

price *noun* precio *Masc.*; **the price per kilo** el precio por kilo; **CDs have gone up in price** los compactos han subido de precio.

price list *noun* lista *Fem.* de precios.

price ticket *noun* etiqueta *Fem.* del precio.

pride *noun* orgullo *Masc.*

priest *noun* sacerdote *Masc.*

primary school *noun* escuela *Fem.* primaria.

prime minister *noun* primer ministro *Masc.*, primera ministra *Fem.*

prince *noun* príncipe *Masc.*; **Prince Charles** el príncipe Carlos.

princess *noun* princesa *Fem.*; **Princess Anne** la Princesa Ana.

principal *noun* (*of a college*) rector *Masc.*, rectora *Fem.*

principal *adjective* (*main*) principal.

print *noun* **1** (*letters*) letra *Fem.*; **in small print** en letra pequeña; **2** (*a photo*) copia *Fem.*; **a colour print** una copia a color.

printer *noun* (*machine*) impresora *Fem.*

print-out *noun* copia *Fem.* en papel.

prison *noun* cárcel *Fem.*; **in prison** en la cárcel.

prisoner *noun* preso *Masc.*, presa *Fem.*

private *adjective* **1** privado/privada; **a private school** una escuela privada; **'private property'** 'propiedad privada'; **2** particular (*lesson*); **to have private lessons** tener [9] clases particulares.

prize *noun* premio *Masc.*; **to win a prize** ganar [17] un premio.

prize-giving *noun* entrega *Fem.* de premios.

prizewinner *noun* ganador *Masc.*, ganadora *Fem.*

probable *adjective* probable.

probably *adverb* probablemente.

problem *noun* problema *Masc.*; **it's a serious problem** es un problema grave; **no problem!** ¡no hay problema!

procession *noun* **1** (*at religious festival*) procesión *Fem.*; **2** (*parade*) desfile *Masc.*

produce *noun* (*food*) productos *Masc. plural.*

produce *verb* **1** producir [60]; **it produces a lot of heat** produce mucho calor; **2** (*show*) presentar [17]; **I produced my passport** presenté mi pasaporte.

producer *noun* (*of a film or programme*) productor *Masc.*, productora *Fem.*

product *noun* producto *Masc.*

production *noun* **1** (*of a film*) producción *Fem.*; **2** (*of a play or opera*) puesta *Fem.* en escena; **a new production of Hamlet** una nueva puesta en escena de Hamlet; **3** (*by a factory*) producción *Fem.*

profession *noun* profesión *Fem.*

professional *noun* profesional *Masc./Fem.*; **he's a professional** es un profesional.

professional *adjective* profesional; **she's a professional singer** es cantante profesional.

professor *noun* catedrático *Masc.*, catedrática *Fem.*

profit *noun* beneficios *Masc. plural.*

profitable *adjective* rentable.

program *noun* **a computer program** un programa de ordenador.

programme *noun* programa *Masc.*

programmer *noun* programador *Masc.*, programadora *Fem.*

progress *noun* **1** progreso *Masc.*; **to make progress** (*in your work*) hacer [7] progresos; **2 to be in progress** estar [2] en curso.

project *noun* **1** (*at school*) trabajo *Masc.*; **2** (*a plan*) proyecto *Masc.*; **a project to build a bridge** un proyecto para construir un puente.

projector *noun* proyector *Masc.*

promise *noun* promesa *Fem.*; **to make a promise** hacer [7] una promesa; **to break a promise** romper [40] una promesa; **it's a promise!** ¡lo prometo!

promise *verb* **to promise to do** prometer [18] hacer; **I've promised to be home by ten** he prometido estar en casa a las diez.

promote *verb* ascender [36]; **she's been promoted** la han ascendido.

promotion *noun* ascenso *Masc.*

prompt *adjective* pronto/pronta; **a prompt reply** una pronta respuesta.

pronoun *noun* pronombre *Masc.*

a b c d e f g h i j k l m n o p q r s t u v w x y z

a

b **pronounce** verb pronunciar [17]; **it's hard to pronounce** es difícil de pronunciar.

c **pronunciation** noun pronunciación Fem.

d **proof** noun pruebas Fem. plural; **they've got proof** tienen pruebas; **there's no proof that** ... no hay pruebas de que ....

e

f

g **propaganda** noun propaganda Fem.

propeller noun hélice Fem.

h **proper** adjective 1 (real, genuine) de verdad; **a proper doctor** un médico titulado; **I need a proper meal** necesito una comida de verdad; 2 (correct) adecuado/ adecuada; **the proper tool** la herramienta adecuada; 3 **in its proper place** en su sitio.

i

j

k

l

m **properly** adverb bien; **hold it properly** sujétalo bien; **is it properly wrapped?** ¿está bien envuelto?

n

o **property** noun (your belongings) propiedad Fem.; **'private property'** 'propiedad privada'.

p **propose** verb 1 (suggest) proponer [11]; 2 (marriage) **he proposed to her** le pidió que se casara con él.

q **prostitute** noun prostituta Fem.

r **protect** verb proteger [3].

protection noun protección Fem.

s **protein** noun proteína Fem.

t **protest** noun protesta Fem.; **in spite of their protests** a pesar de sus protestas.

u

v **protest** verb 1 (to grumble) protestar [17]; **he protested, but** ...

w

x

y

z

él protestó, pero ...; 2 (demonstrate) manifestarse [29].

Protestant noun, adjective protestante Masc./Fem.

protester noun manifestante Masc./Fem.

protest march noun manifestación Fem.

proud adjective orgulloso/ orgullosa.

prove verb probar [24].

proverb noun refrán Masc.

provide verb proveer [37].

provided conjunction siempre que; **provided you do it now** siempre que tú lo hagas (note that 'que' is followed by the subjunctive).

province noun provincia Fem.

prune noun ciruela Fem. pasa.

PS abbreviation (in letter) PD.

psychiatrist noun psiquiatra Masc./Fem.; **he's a psychiatrist** es psiquiatra.

psychological adjective psicológico/psicológica.

psychologist noun psicólogo Masc., psicóloga Fem.; **she's a psychologist** es psicóloga.

psychology noun psicología Fem.

PTO abbreviation sigue al dorso.

pub noun bar Masc.

public noun **the public** el público; **in public** en público.

public adjective 1 público/pública; 2 **the public library** la biblioteca pública.

public address system noun sistema Masc. de megafonía.

public holiday noun día Masc. de fiesta; **the first of January is a public holiday** el uno de enero es fiesta.

publicity noun publicidad Fem.

public school noun colegio Masc. privado.

public transport noun transporte Masc. público.

publish verb publicar [31].

publisher noun 1 (person) editor Masc., editora Fem.; 2 (company) editorial Fem.

pudding noun (dessert) postre Masc.; **for pudding we've got strawberries** de postre tenemos fresas.

puddle noun charco Masc.

Puerto Rican noun puertorriqueño Masc., puertorriqueña Fem.

Puerto Rican adjective puertorriqueño/puertorriqueña.

puff pastry noun hojaldre Masc.

pull verb tirar [17]; **pull hard!** ¡tira fuerte!; **to pull a rope** tirar de una cuerda; ★ **you're pulling my leg!** ¡me estás tomando el pelo! (literally: you are taking my hair).

● **to pull down** bajar [17] (a blind).

● **to pull in** (at the roadside) parar [17].

● **to pull something out** sacar [31] algo; **he pulled a letter out of his pocket** sacó una carta del bolsillo.

pullover noun jersey Masc.

pulse noun pulso Masc.; **the doctor took my pulse** el médico me tomó el pulso.

pump noun 1 bomba Fem.; **a bicycle pump** una bomba de bicicleta; 2 **a petrol pump** un surtidor de gasolina.

pump verb bombear [17]; **they were pumping the water out of the cellar** estaban bombeando el agua del sótano.

● **to pump up** inflar [17] (a tyre).

punch noun 1 (in boxing) puñetazo Masc.; 2 (drink) ponche Masc.

punch verb 1 **to punch somebody** darle [4] un puñetazo a alguien; **he punched me** me dio un puñetazo; 2 picar [31] (a ticket).

punctual adjective puntual.

punctuation noun puntuación Fem.

punctuation mark noun signo Masc. de puntuación.

puncture noun pinchazo Masc.; **we had a puncture on the way** tuvimos un pinchazo en el camino.

punish verb castigar [28].

punishment noun castigo Masc.

pupil noun alumno Masc., alumna Fem.

puppet noun títere Masc.

puppy noun cachorro Masc. (female) cachorra Fem.; **a labrador puppy** un cachorro de labrador.

pure adjective puro/pura.

purple adjective morado/morada.

purpose noun 1 propósito Masc.; **what was the purpose of her call?** ¿qué propósito tenía su llamada?; 2 **on purpose** a propósito; **she did it on purpose** lo hizo a propósito.

a
b
c
d
e
f
g
h
i
j
k
l
m
n
o
p
q
r
s
t
u
v
w
x
y
z

purr *verb* ronronear [17].

purse *noun* monedero *Masc.*

push *noun* empujón *Masc.*; **to give something a push** dar [4] un empujón a alguien.

push *verb* 1 empujar [17]; **he pushed me** me empujó; 2 (*to press*) apretar [29] (*a bell or button*); **to push somebody to do** presionar [17] a alguien para que haga (*note that 'que' is followed by the subjunctive*) **his teacher is pushing him to sit the exam** su profesor le está presionando para que se presente al examen.

● **to push something away** apartar [17] algo; **she pushed her plate away** apartó su plato.

pushchair *noun* sillita *Fem.* de niño.

put *verb* 1 poner [11]; **you can put the cream in the fridge** puedes poner la nata en la nevera; **where did you put my bag?** ¿dónde has puesto mi bolso?; **put your suitcase here** pon tu maleta aquí; **put your address here** pon tus señas aquí; 2 (*put inside*) meter [18]; **I put it in the drawer** lo metí en el cajón.

● **to put away** guardar [17]; **I'll put the shopping away** voy a guardar la compra.

● **to put back** 1 volver [45] a poner; **I put it back in the drawer** lo volví a poner en el cajón; 2 (*postpone*) aplazar [22]; **the meeting has been put back until Thursday** han aplazado la reunión hasta el jueves.

● **to put down** poner [11]; **she put**

the vase down on the table puso el jarrón en la mesa.

● **to put off** 1 (*postpone*) aplazar [22]; **he's put off my lesson till Thursday** ha aplazado mi clase hasta el jueves; 2 **it put me off Chinese food!** ¡hizo que se me quitaran las ganas de tomar comida china!; 3 **to be put off** (*doing something*) desanimarse [17]; **don't be put off!** ¡no te desanimes!

● **to put on** 1 ponerse [11] (*clothing, make-up*); **I'll just put my shoes on** voy a ponerme los zapatos; 2 poner [11] (*TV, radio*); **shall we put on the telly?** ¿ponemos la tele?; **he's put on Oasis** ha puesto a Oasis; 3 (*switch on*) encender [36] (*a light or heating*); **could you put the lamp on?** ¿puedes encender la lámpara?; 4 montar [17] (*a play*); **we're putting on a Spanish play** estamos montando una obra española.

● **to put out** 1 (*put outside*) sacar [31]; **have you put the rubbish out?** ¿has sacado la basura?; 2 apagar [28] (*a fire, light, or cigarette*); **I've put the lights out** he apagado las luces; 3 **to put out your hand** extender [36] la mano.

● **to put through** pasar [17] con; **I'll put you through to the manager** le paso con el gerente.

● **to put up** 1 levantar [17] (*your hand*); **I put up my hand** levanté la mano; 2 poner [11] (*picture*); **I've put up some photos in my room** he puesto algunas fotos en mi habitacion; 3 colgar [23] (*a notice*);

4 subir [19] (*the price*); **they've put up the price of the tickets** han subido el precio de las entradas; **5** (*for the night*) **can you put me up on Friday?** ¿puedo quedarme a dormir en tu casa el viernes?

● **to put up with something** aguantar [17] algo; **I don't know how she puts up with it** no sé cómo lo aguanta.

puzzle *noun* (*jigsaw*) rompecabezas *Masc.*, puzzle *Masc.*

puzzled *adjective* confuso/ confusa.

pyjamas *plural noun* pijama *Masc.*; **a pair of pyjamas** un pijama; **where are my pyjamas?** ¿dónde está mi pijama?

pylon *noun* torre *Fem.* de alta tensión.

Pyrenees *noun* **the Pyrenees** los Pirineos.

Qq

quail *noun* codorniz *Fem.*

qualification *noun* **1** título *Masc.* (*certificate, exam, degree*); **2 qualifications** titulación *Fem.*; **vocational qualifications** titulación profesional.

qualified *adjective* **1** cualificado/ cualificada; **she's a qualified ski instructor** es una monitora de esquí cualificada; **2** (*having a degree or a diploma*) titulado/ titulada; **a qualified architect** un arquitecto titulado.

qualify *verb* **1** (*to be eligible*) tener [9] derecho a; **we don't qualify for a reduction** no tenemos derecho a una reducción; **2** (*in sport*) clasificarse [31].

quality *noun* calidad *Fem.*; **good quality vegetables** verduras de buena calidad.

quantity *noun* cantidad *Fem.*

quarantine *noun* cuarentena *Fem.*

quarrel *noun* pelea *Fem.*; **to have a quarrel** tener [9] una pelea.

quarrel *verb* pelearse [17]; **they're always quarrelling** siempre se están peleando.

quarry *noun* cantera *Fem.*

quarter *noun* **1** cuarta parte *Fem.*; **a quarter of the class** una cuarta parte de la clase; **three quarters of the class** tres cuartas partes de la clase; **2** (*telling the time*) cuarto *Masc.*; **a quarter past ten** las diez y cuarto; **a quarter to ten** las diez menos cuarto; **a quarter of an hour** un cuarto de hora; **three quarters of an hour** tres cuartos de hora; **an hour and a quarter** una hora y cuarto.

quarter finals *plural noun* cuartos *Masc. plural* de final.

quartet *noun* cuarteto *Masc.*; **a jazz quartet** un cuarteto de jazz.

quay *noun* muelle *Masc.*

queen *noun* reina *Fem.*; **Queen Elizabeth** la reina Isabel; **the Queen Mother** la reina madre.

query *noun* duda *Fem.*; **are there any queries?** ¿hay alguna duda?

a
b
c
d
e
f
g
h
i
j
k
l
m
n
o
p
q
r
s
t
u
v
w
x
y
z

question noun 1 pregunta Fem.; to ask a question hacer [7] una pregunta; I asked her a question le hice una pregunta; 2 it's a question of time es una cuestión de tiempo; it's out of the question! ¡es completamente imposible!

question verb interrogar [28].

question mark noun signo Masc. de interrogación.

questionnaire noun cuestionario Masc.; to fill in a questionnaire rellenar [17] un cuestionario.

queue noun 1 (of people) cola Fem.; to stand in a queue estar [2] en la cola; 2 (of cars) fila Fem.

queue verb hacer [7] cola; we were queueing for check-in estábamos haciendo cola para facturar.

quick adjective 1 rápido/rápida; a quick lunch una comida rápida; it's quicker on the motorway es más rápido por la autopista; to have a quick look at something echarle [17] un vistazo rápido a algo; 2 quick! there's the bus! ¡de prisa, que viene el autobús!; be quick! ¡date prisa!

quickly adverb rápidamente; I'll just quickly phone my mother voy a llamar rápidamente a mi madre.

quiet adjective 1 (silent) silencioso/silenciosa; the children are very quiet los niños están muy silenciosos; 2 to keep quiet no hablar [17]; please keep quiet por favor, no hablen; 3 (gentle) suave; some quiet music

una música suave; in a quiet voice en voz baja; 4 (peaceful) tranquilo/tranquila; a quiet street una calle tranquila; a quiet day at home un día tranquilo en casa.

quietly adverb 1 (to move) sin hacer ruido; he got up quietly se levantó sin hacer ruido; 2 (speak) en voz baja; 3 (read or play) en silencio.

quilt noun edredón Masc.

quite adverb 1 bastante; it's quite cold outside hace bastante frío fuera; that's quite a good idea es una idea bastante buena; he sings quite well canta bastante bien; quite often bastante a menudo; 2 not quite no ... todavía; the meat's not quite cooked la carne no está hecha todavía; 3 quite a lot of bastante; quite a lot of money bastante dinero; quite a lot of friends here tengo bastantes amigos aquí.

quiz noun concurso Masc.

quotation noun (from a book) cita Fem.

quotation marks plural noun comillas Fem. plural; in quotation marks entre comillas.

quote noun 1 (from a book) cita Fem.; 2 (estimate) presupuesto Masc.; 3 in quotes entre comillas.

quote verb citar [17].

Rr

rabbi noun rabino Masc., rabina Fem.

rabbit noun conejo Masc.

race noun 1 (a sports event) carrera Fem.; **a cycle race** una carrera de bicicletas; **to have a race** echar [17] una carrera; **2** (an ethnic group) raza Fem.

racer noun (bike) bicicleta Fem. de carreras.

racetrack noun 1 (for horses) pista Fem. de carreras; **2** (for cars) circuito Masc.; **3** (for cycles) velódromo Masc.

racing noun carreras Fem. plural.

racing car noun coche Masc. de carreras.

racing driver noun piloto Masc./ Fem. de carreras.

racial adjective racial; **racial discrimination** discriminación racial.

racism noun racismo Masc.

racist noun, racista Masc./Fem..
racist adjective racista.

racket noun 1 (for tennis) raqueta Fem.; **2** (noise) jaleo Masc.; **what a racket!** ¡qué jaleo!.

radar noun radar Masc.

radiator noun radiador Masc.

radio noun radio Fem.; **to listen to the radio** escuchar [17] la radio; **to hear something on the radio** oír [56] algo en la radio.

radio station noun emisora Fem. de radio.

radish noun rabanito Masc.

radius noun radio Masc.

raffle noun rifa Fem.

raft noun balsa Fem.

rag noun trapo Masc.

rage noun furia Fem.; **she's in a rage** está furiosa; ★ **it's all the rage** hace furor (informal).

rail noun 1 (the railway) **to go by rail** ir [8] en tren; **2** (on a balcony or bridge) baranda Fem.; **3** (on stairs) pasamanos Masc.; **4** (for a train) raíl Masc.

rail strike noun huelga Fem. de trenes.

railings noun verja Fem.

railway noun 1 (the system) ferrocarril Masc.; **the railways** el ferrocarril; **2 a railway line** una línea de ferrocarril (from one place to another); **3 on the railway line** en la vía férrea (the rails).

railway carriage noun vagón Masc. de tren.

railway station noun estación Fem. de tren; **opposite the railway station** enfrente de la estación de tren.

rain noun lluvia Fem.; **in the rain** bajo la lluvia.

rain verb llover [38]; **it's raining** está lloviendo; **it's going to rain** va a llover.

rainbow noun arco Masc. iris.

raincoat noun impermeable Masc.

rainfall noun precipitaciones Fem. plural.

rainy adjective lluvioso/lluviosa.

a b c d e f g h i j k l m n o p q r s t u v w x y z

raise *verb* **1** (*lift up*) levantar [17]; **she raised her head** levantó la cabeza; **2** (*increase*) subir [19] (*a price or a salary*); **3 to raise money for something** recaudar [17] dinero para algo; **4 to raise the alarm** dar [4] la alarma; **5 to raise somebody's spirits** animar [17] a alguien.

raisin *noun* pasa *Fem*.

rally *noun* **1** (*a meeting*) concentración *Fem*.; **2** (*for sport*) rally *Masc*.; **3** (*in tennis*) peloteo *Masc*.

rambler *noun* excursionista *Masc./Fem*.

rambling *noun* **to go rambling** ir [8] de excursión.

ramp *noun* (*for a wheelchair, for example*) rampa *Fem*.

range *noun* **1** (*a choice*) gama *Fem*.; **in a wide range of colours** en una amplia gama de colores; **2** (*of mountains*) cordillera *Fem*.

rap *noun* rap *Masc*. (*music*).

rape *noun* violación *Fem*.

rape *verb* violar [17].

rare *adjective* **1** (*a choice*) poco común; **a rare bird** un pájaro poco común; **2** poco hecho (*a steak*); **medium-rare** un filete poco hecho.

raspberry *noun* frambuesa *Fem*.; **raspberry jam** mermelada de frambuesa; **a raspberry tart** una tarta de frambuesas.

rat *noun* rata *Fem*.

rate *noun* **1** (*a charge*) tarifa *Fem*.; **what are the rates for children?** ¿cuáles son las tarifas para niños?;

reduced rates tarifas reducidas; **2 at any rate** en todo caso.

rather *adverb* **1** bastante; **I'm rather busy** estoy bastante ocupado; **2 rather a lot** bastante; **I've got rather a lot of work** tengo bastante trabajo; **3 rather a lot of** (*with a plural noun*) bastantes; **there are rather a lot of mistakes** hay bastantes errores; **4 rather than** en vez de; **in summer rather than winter** en verano más que en invierno; **5 I'd rather wait** preferiría esperar; **they'd rather come on Thursday** preferirían venir el jueves.

raw *adjective* crudo/cruda.

ray *noun* rayo *Masc*.

razor *noun* máquina *Fem*. de afeitar (*safety*).

razor blade *noun* cuchilla *Fem*.

RE *noun* religión *Fem*.

reach *noun* alcance *Masc*.; **out of my reach** fuera de mi alcance; **within reach** (*of your hand*) al alcance; **within easy reach of the sea** cerca del mar.

reach *verb* llegar [28]; **when you reach the church** cuando llegues a la iglesia; **to reach the final** llegar [28] a la final.

read *verb* leer [37]; **what are you reading at the moment?** ¿qué estás leyendo en este momento?; **I'm reading a detective novel** estoy leyendo una novela policiaca; **he read out the list** leyó la lista.

reading *noun* lectura *Fem*.; **I don't much like reading** no me gusta mucho la lectura; **some easy reading for the beach** lectura fácil para la playa.

ready *adjective* **1** preparado/ preparada; **supper's not ready yet** la cena aún no está preparada; **2** (*person*) listo/lista; **are you ready to leave?** ¿estás listo para salir?; **3 to get ready** (*meal or things*) preparar [17]; **I'll get your room ready** voy a preparar tu habitación; **4 to get ready** (*a person*) prepararse [17]; **I'm getting ready to go out** me estoy preparando para salir; **I was getting ready for bed** estaba preparándome para irme a la cama.

real *adjective* verdadero/ verdadera; **is that his real name?** ¿es ése su verdadero nombre?; **her real father is dead** su verdadero padre está muerto; **he's a real bore** es un verdadero pesado; **it's a real diamond** es un diamante de verdad.

realize *verb* darse [4] cuenta; **I hadn't realized** no me había dado cuenta; **to realize (that)** ... darse cuenta de que ...; **I didn't realize (that) he was French** no me di cuenta de que era francés; **do you realize what time it is?** ¿te das cuenta de la hora que es?

really *adverb* **1** (*truly*) de verdad; **is it really midnight?** ¿de verdad son las doce de la noche?; **really?** ¿de verdad?; **not really** la verdad es que no; **2 I really don't know** realmente no lo sé; **3** (*extremely*) (*Spanish uses the superlative of the adjective to*

express this sense) **the film was really good** la película fue buenísima.

reason *noun* razón *Fem.*; **the reason for the delay** la razón del retraso; **the reason why I phoned** la razón por la que llamé.

reasonable *adjective* razonable.

rebel *noun* rebelde *Masc./Fem.*

rebellion *noun* rebelión *Fem.*

receipt *noun* recibo *Masc.*

receive *verb* recibir [19].

receiver *noun* auricular *Masc.*; **to pick up the receiver** descolgar [23] el teléfono.

recent *adjective* reciente; **a recent change** un cambio reciente.

recently *adverb* recientemente.

reception *noun* **1** recepción *Fem.*; **he's waiting at reception** está esperando en recepción; **a big wedding reception** un gran banqueté de bodas; **2 to get a good reception** tener [9] buena acogida.

receptionist *noun* recepcionista *Masc./Fem.*

recipe *noun* receta *Fem.*; **can I have the recipe for your salad?** ¿me puedes dar tu receta de la ensalada?

reckon *verb* creer [37]; **I reckon it's a good idea** creo que es una buena idea.

recognize *verb* reconocer [35].

recommend *verb* recomendar [29]; **can you recommend a dentist?** ¿puedes recomendarme un dentista?; **I recommend the**

a
b
c
d
e
f
g
h
i
j
k
l
m
n
o
p
q
r
s
t
u
v
w
x
y
z

fish soup recomiendo la sopa de pescado.

recommendation *noun* recomendación *Fem.*

record *noun* 1 récord *Masc.*; **it's a world record** es un récord mundial; **record sales** récord de ventas; **the hottest summer on record** el verano más caluroso del que se tienen datos; 2 **to keep a record of something** llevar [17] un registro de algo; 3 (*music*) disco *Masc.*; **a Miles Davis record** un disco de Miles Davis; 4 (*office files*) archivo *Masc.*; **I'll just check your records** voy a mirar tu ficha; 5 (*of attendance*) registro *Masc.*

record *verb* (*on tape or CD*) grabar [17]; **they're recording a new album** están grabando un nuevo álbum.

recorder *noun* 1 flauta *Fem.* dulce; **to play the recorder** tocar [31] la flauta dulce; 2 **a cassette recorder** un cassette; **a video recorder** una cámara de vídeo.

recording *noun* grabación *Fem.*

record player *noun* tocadiscos *Masc.* (*does not change in the plural*).

recover *verb* recuperarse [17]; **she's recovered now** ya se ha recuperado.

recovery *noun* (*from an illness*) recuperación *Fem.*

recovery vehicle *noun* grúa *Fem.*

rectangle *noun* rectángulo *Masc.*

rectangular *adjective* rectangular.

recycle *verb* reciclar [17].

red *adjective* 1 rojo/roja; **a red shirt** una camisa roja; **a bright red car** un coche rojo vivo; 2 **to go red** ponerse [11] colorado; 3 (*hair*) **to have red hair** ser [1] pelirrojo.

Red Cross *noun* **the Red Cross** la Cruz Roja.

redcurrant *noun* grosella *Fem.*; **redcurrant jelly** jalea de grosellas.

reduce *verb* reducir [60]; **they've reduced the price** han reducido el precio.

reduction *noun* rebaja *Fem.* (*in price*).

redundant *adjective* **he was made redundant** lo despidieron por reducción de plantilla.

refer to *verb* referirse [14] a; **she's referring to you** se refiere a ti.

referee *noun* (*in sport*) árbitro *Masc./Fem.*

reference *noun* referencia *Fem.* (*for a job*); **she gave me a good reference** me dio una buena referencia.

referendum *noun* referendum *Masc.*

refill *noun* 1 (*for pen*) recambio *Masc.*; 2 (*for lighter*) carga *Fem.*

reflect *verb* reflejar [17].

reflection *noun* 1 (*in a mirror*) reflejo *Masc.*; 2 (*thought*) reflexión *Fem.*; **on reflection** pensándolo bien.

reflexive *adjective* **a reflexive verb** un verbo reflexivo.

refreshing *adjective* refrescante.

refreshment noun refresco Masc.

refrigerator noun nevera Fem.

refuge noun refugio Masc.; **a mountain refuge** un refugio (de montaña); **to take refuge in** refugiarse [17] en.

refugee noun refugiado Masc., refugiada Fem.

refund noun reembolso Masc.

refund verb reembolsar [17].

refuse noun (rubbish) desperdicios Masc. plural.

refuse verb negarse [30]; **I refused** me negué; **he refuses to help** se niega a ayudar.

regards plural noun recuerdos Masc. plural; **'regards to your parents'** 'recuerdos a tus padres'; **Nat sends his regards** Nat manda recuerdos.

reggae noun reggae Masc.

region noun región Fem.

regional adjective regional.

register noun (in school) lista Fem.

register verb inscribirse [52].

registered letter noun carta Fem. certificada.

registration number noun número Masc. de matrícula (of a vehicle).

regret verb **to regret something** arrepentirse [14] de algo.

regular adjective 1 regular visits visitas frecuentes; 2 habitual (customer).

regularly adverb regularmente.

regulation noun norma Fem.

rehearsal noun ensayo Masc.

rehearse verb ensayar [17].

reign noun reinado Masc.

rein noun rienda Fem.

reject verb rechazar [22].

related adjective 1 relacionado/relacionada (subject or ideas); 2 **we're not related** no somos parientes.

relation noun pariente Masc./Fem.; **my relations** mis parientes.

relationship noun relación Fem.; **we have a good relationship** tenemos una buena relación.

relative noun pariente Masc./Fem.; **all my relatives** todos mis parientes.

relax verb relajarse [17]; **I'm going to relax and watch telly tonight** esta noche voy a relajarme y ver la tele.

relaxation noun esparcimiento Masc.; **tennis is her relaxation** el tenis es su esparcimiento.

relaxed adjective relajado/relajada.

relaxing adjective relajante.

relay race noun carrera Fem. de relevos.

release noun 1 estreno Masc.; **this week's new releases** los estrenos de esta semana; 2 (of a prisoner or hostage) puesta Fem. en libertad.

release verb 1 sacar [31] (a record or a video); 2 estrenar [17] (a film); 3 poner [11] en libertad (a person).

reliable adjective 1 responsable (person); 2 fidedigno/fidedigna (information).

a b c d e f g h i j k l m n o p q r s t u v w x y z

relief noun alivio Masc.; **what a relief!** ¡qué alivio!

relieved adjective aliviado/aliviada; **I was relieved to hear you'd arrived** fue un alivio oír que habías llegado.

religion noun religión Fem.

religious adjective religioso/religiosa; **Jane's not religious** Jane no es religiosa.

reluctant adjective reacio/reacia; **he's reluctant to go** se muestra reacio a ir.

rely verb **to rely on somebody** contar [24] con alguien; **I'm relying on you for Saturday** cuento contigo el para sábado.

remain verb permanecer [35].

remark noun comentario Masc.; **to make remarks about** hacer [7] comentarios sobre.

remember verb **1** acordarse [24]; **I don't remember** no me acuerdo; **2 to remember something** acordarse de algo; **I can't remember the number** no me acuerdo del número; **3 to remember to do** acordarse de hacer; **remember to shut the door!** ¡acuérdate de cerrar la puerta!; **I remembered to bring the CDs** me acordé de traer los compactos.

remind verb **1** recordar [24]; **to remind somebody to do** recordarle a alguien que haga (note that 'que' is followed by the subjunctive) **remind your mother to pick me up** recuérdale a tu madre que me recoja; **2 it reminds**

me **of Paris** me recuerda a París; **he reminds me of Frank** me recuerda a Frank; **oh, that reminds me ...** ¡ah!, por cierto ....

remove verb quitar [17]; **he removed his jacket** se quitó la chaqueta; **the chairs had all been removed** habían quitado todas las sillas.

renew verb renovar [24] (a passport or licence).

rent noun alquiler Masc.

rent verb alquilar [17]; **Simon's rented a flat** Simon ha alquilado un piso.

repair noun reparación Fem.

repair verb arreglar [17]; **to get something repaired** arreglar [17] algo; **we've had the television repaired** hemos arreglado la televisión.

repay verb devolver [45]; **he repaid me the money he owed me** me devolvió el dinero que me debía.

repeat noun repetición Fem. (of a programme).

repeat verb repetir [57].

replacement noun **1** (person) sustituto Masc., sustituta Fem.; **2** (thing) **when can you find me a replacement?** ¿para cuándo me puedes encontrar otro?

reply noun contestación Fem.; **I didn't get a reply to my letter** no recibí contestación a mi carta; **there's no reply** no contestan (on the telephone).

reply verb contestar [17]; **I still haven't replied to the letter** aún no he contestado a la carta.

report noun 1 (of an event) informe Masc.; 2 (school report) boletín Masc. de notas.

report verb 1 informar [17] sobre (a problem or accident); 2 denunciar [17] (a crime); **we've reported the theft** hemos denunciado el robo; 3 presentarse [17]; **I had to report to reception** tuve que presentarme en recepción.

reporter noun periodista Masc./Fem.

representative noun representante Masc./Fem.

reproach noun reproche Masc.

reproach verb reprochar [17].

republic noun república Fem.

reputation noun 1 reputación Fem.; **a good reputation** una buena reputación; 2 **to have a reputation for something** tener [9] fama de algo; **she has a reputation for honesty** tiene fama de honesta.

request noun petición Fem.; **on request** a solicitud.

request verb pedir [57].

rescue noun 1 rescate Masc.; 2 **to come to somebody's rescue** acudir [19] en auxilio de alguien.

rescue verb rescatar [17]; **they rescued the dog** rescataron al perro.

rescue party noun equipo Masc. de rescate.

rescue worker noun socorrista Masc./Fem.

research noun investigación Fem.; **for research into Aids** para la investigación sobre el sida; **to do research** investigar [28].

research verb to research into investigar [28] sobre; **a well-researched programme** un programa bien documentado.

resemble verb parecerse [35] a; **she looks like her aunt** se parece a su tía.

reservation noun (a booking) reserva Fem.; **to make a reservation** hacer [7] una reserva.

reserve noun 1 reserva Fem.; **we have some in reserve** tener [9] algo de reserva; 2 **a nature reserve** una reserva natural; 3 (for a match) reserva Masc./Fem.

reserve verb reservar [17]; **this table is reserved** la mesa está reservada.

resident noun residente Masc./Fem.

residential adjective residencial; **a residential area** un área residencial.

resign verb dimitir [19].

resignation noun (from a post) dimisión Fem.

resist verb resistir [19] (an offer or temptation); **I can't resist!** ¡no puedo resistirlo!

resit verb to resit an exam volver [45] a presentarse a un examen.

resort noun 1 (for holidays) **a holiday resort** un centro turístico; **a ski resort** una estación de esquí; **a seaside resort** un centro turístico costero; 2 **as a last resort** como último recurso.

respect noun respeto Masc.

respect verb respetar [17].

respectable adjective respetable.

respectful adjective respetuoso/respetuosa.

responsibility noun responsabilidad Fem.

responsible adjective responsable; **he's responsible for the delay** él es el responsable del retraso; **I'm responsible for booking the rooms** soy responsable de reservar las habitaciones; **he's not very responsible** no es muy responsable.

rest noun 1 (the rest) el resto; **the rest of the day** el resto del día; **the rest of the bread** el resto del pan; 2 (the others) los otros; **the rest have gone home** los otros se han ido a casa; 3 descanso Masc.; **ten days' complete rest** diez días de completo descanso; **to have a rest** descansar [17]; 4 (a short break) **to stop for a rest** parar [17] para descansar.

rest verb (have a rest) descansar [17].

restaurant noun restaurante Masc.

restore verb restaurar [17].

result noun 1 resultado Masc.; **the exam results** los resultados del examen; 2 **as a result** como consecuencia de ello; **as a result we missed the ferry** como consecuencia de ello perdimos el ferry.

retire verb (from work) jubilarse [17]; **she retires in June** se jubila en junio; **for retired people** para los jubilados.

retirement noun jubilación Fem.

return noun 1 vuelta Fem.; **the return journey** el viaje de vuelta; **by return of post** a vuelta de correo; 2 **in return** a cambio; **in return for his help** a cambio de su ayuda; ★ **many happy returns!** ¡muchas felicidades!

return verb 1 (come back or get home) volver [45]; **he returned ten minutes later** volvió diez minutos más tarde; **to return from holiday** volver de vacaciones; **I'll ask her to phone as soon as she returns** le diré que la llame en cuanto vuelva; 2 (to give back) devolver [45]; **Gemma's never returned the video** Gemma no devolvió nunca el vídeo.

return fare noun precio Masc. del billete de ida y vuelta.

return ticket noun billete Masc. de ida y vuelta.

reunion noun reunión Fem.; **a class reunion** una reunión de ex compañeros de clase.

revenge noun venganza Fem.; **to get one's revenge on someone** vengarse [28] de alguien.

reverse noun 1 (of coin) anverso Masc.; 2 (gear) marcha Fem. atrás; 3 (of page) dorso Masc.; 4 (opposite) **the reverse is true** es al contrario.

reverse verb 1 (in a car) dar [4] marcha atrás; 2 **to reverse the charges** llamar [17] a cobro revertido.

review noun (of a book, play, or film) crítica Fem.

review verb escribir [52] la crítica de; **the film was well reviewed** la película recibió buenas críticas.

revise verb repasar [17]; **Tessa's busy revising for her exams** Tessa está muy ocupada repasando para los exámenes.

revision noun repaso Masc.

revolting adjective asqueroso/asquerosa; **the sausages are revolting** las salchichas están asquerosas.

revolution noun revolución Fem.; **the Fench Revolution** la Revolución Francesa.

reward noun recompensa Fem.; **a £100 reward** una recompensa de cien libras.

reward verb recompensar [17].

rewarding adjective gratificante.

rhubarb noun ruibarbo Masc.

rhyme noun rima Fem.

rhythm noun ritmo Masc.

rib noun costilla Fem.

ribbon noun cinta Fem.

rice noun arroz Masc.; **chicken and rice** pollo y arroz; **rice pudding** arroz con leche.

rich adjective rico/rica; **we're not very rich** no somos muy ricos; **the rich and the poor** los ricos y los pobres.

rid adjective **to get rid of something** deshacerse [7] de algo; **we got rid of the car** nos deshicimos del coche.

riddle noun adivinanza Fem.

ride noun **to go for a ride (on a bike)** ir [8] a montar en bicicleta;

to go for a ride (on a horse) ir [8] a montar a caballo.

ride verb **1 to learn to ride a bike** aprender [18] a montar en bicicleta; **can you ride a bike?** ¿sabes montar en bicicleta?; **2 to learn to ride (a horse)** aprender [18] a montar a caballo; **I've never ridden a horse** nunca he montado a caballo.

rider noun **1** (of horse) jinete Masc., amazona Fem.; **2** (of bicycle) ciclista Masc./Fem.; **3** (of motorbike) motorista Masc./Fem.

ridiculous adjective ridículo/ridícula.

riding noun equitación Fem.; **to go riding** hacer [7] equitación.

riding school noun escuela Fem. de equitación.

rifle noun rifle Masc.

right noun **1** (not left) derecha Fem.; **on the right** a la derecha; **on my right** a mi derecha; **2** (to do something) derecho Masc.; **the right to strike** el derecho a hacer huelga; **you have no right to say that** no tienes derecho a decir eso.

right adjective **1** (not left) derecho/derecha; **my right hand** mi mano derecha; **2** (correct) correcto/correcta; **the right answer** la respuesta correcta; **the right telephone number** el teléfono correcto; **is this the right address?** ¿son éstas las señas?; **3 to be right** (a person) tener [9] razón; **you see, I was right** ¿ves? tenía yo razón; **4 you were right to stay at home** hiciste bien en quedarte en casa; **he was right not**

a
b
c
d
e
f
g
h
i
j
k
l
m
n
o
p
q
r
s
t
u
v
w
x
y
z

a

to say anything hizo bien en no decir nada; **5 it's not right to talk like that** no está bien hablar así.

b

right *adverb* **1** (*direction*) derecha; **turn right at the lights** gira a la derecha en el semáforo; **2** (*correctly*) bien; **you're not doing it right** no lo estás haciendo bien; **3** (*completely*) **right at the bottom** al fondo del todo; **right now** ahora mismo; **right at the beginning** justo al principio; **right in the middle** justo en medio; **4** (*okay*) vale; **right, let's go** vale, vamos.

c

d

e

f

g

right click *noun* clic *Masc.* con el botón derecho del ratón.

h

right-hand *adjective* **on the right-hand side** a mano derecha.

i

right-handed *adjective* diestro/diestra.

j

ring *noun* **1** (*on the phone*) **to give somebody a ring** llamar [17] a alguien; **2** (*for your finger*) anillo *Masc.*; **3** (*circle*) círculo *Masc.*; **4 there was a ring at the door** llamaron a la puerta.

k

l

m

n

ring *verb* **1** (*a bell or phone*) sonar [24]; **the phone rang** sonó el teléfono; **2** (*to phone*) llamar [17]; **I'll ring you tomorrow** te llamaré mañana; **could you ring for a taxi?** ¿podrías llamar un taxi?.

o

p

q

r

● **to ring back** volver [45] a llamar; **I'll ring you back later** te volveré a llamar más tarde.

s

● **to ring off** colgar [23].

t

rinse *verb* enjuagar [28].

u

ripe *adjective* maduro/madura; **are the tomatoes ripe?** ¿están maduros los tomates?

v

w

x

y

z

rip-off *noun* **it's a rip-off!** ¡es una estafa!

rise *noun* **1** subida *Fem.*; **a rise in price** una subida de precio; **2 a pay rise** un aumento de sueldo.

rise *verb* **1** (*the sun*) salir [63]; **when the sun rose** cuando salió el sol; **2** (*prices*) subir [19].

risk *noun* riesgo *Masc.*; **to take risks** arriesgarse [28].

risk *verb* arriesgar [28] (*your life or reputation*); **she risked her life** arriesgó su vida.

rival *noun* rival *Masc./Fem.*

river *noun* río *Masc.*

road *noun* **1** carretera *Fem.*; **the road to London** la carretera de Londres; **2** (*in a town*) calle *Fem.*; **on the other side of the road** al otro lado de la calle; **3 across the road** enfrente; **they live across the road from us** viven enfrente de nosotros.

road accident *noun* accidente *Masc.* de carretera.

road map *noun* mapa *Masc.* de carreteras.

roadside *noun* **by the roadside** al borde de la carretera.

road sign *noun* señal *Fem.* de tráfico.

roadworks *plural noun* obras *Fem. plural.*

roast *noun* asado *Masc.*

roast *adjective* asado/asada; **roast potatoes** patatas asadas; **roast beef** rosbif *Masc.*

rob *verb* **1** robar [17] (*a person*); **2** atracar [31] (*a bank*).

robber noun bank robber atracador/atracadora Masc./Fem..

robbery noun atraco Masc.; **a bank robbery** un atraco a un banco.

rock noun 1 (a big stone) roca Fem.; **she was sitting on a rock** estaba sentada en una roca; 2 (the material) piedra Fem.; 3 (music) rock Masc.; **a rock band** un grupo de rock; **to dance rock and roll** bailar [17] rock and roll.

rock climbing noun escalada Fem. en roca; **to go rock climbing** hacer [7] escalada.

rock star noun estrella Fem. de rock.

rocket noun cohete Masc.

rocking horse noun caballito Masc. de balancín.

rocky adjective rocoso/rocosa.

rod noun **a fishing rod** una caña de pescar.

role noun papel Masc.; **to play the role of** interpretar [17] el papel de.

roll noun 1 rollo Masc.; **a roll of fabric** un rollo de tela; **a toilet roll** un rollo de papel higiénico; **2 a bread roll** un panecillo.

● **to roll something up** (a carpet) enrollar [17] algo; **he rolled up his sleeves** se remangó las mangas.

rollerblades™ plural noun patines Masc. plural en línea.

rollercoaster noun montaña Fem. rusa (literally: Russian mountain).

roller skates plural noun patines Masc. plural.

Roman Catholic noun católico Masc., católica Fem.

Roman Catholic adjective católico/católica.

romantic adjective romántico/ romántica.

roof noun tejado Masc.

roof rack noun baca Fem.

rook noun 1 (in chess) torre Fem.; 2 (bird) grajo Masc.

room noun 1 habitación Fem.; **she's in the other room** está en la otra habitación; **it's the biggest room in the house** es la habitación más grande de la casa; **a three-room flat** un piso de tres habitaciones; 2 (a bedroom) habitación Masc.; **Lola's in her room** Lola está en su habitación; 3 (space) sitio Masc.; **enough room for two** sitio suficiente para dos; **very little room** muy poco sitio.

root noun raíz Fem.

rope noun cuerda Fem.

rose noun rosa Fem.

rosebush noun rosal Masc.

rot verb pudrirse [59].

rota noun lista Fem. de turnos.

rotten adjective podrido/podrida.

rough adjective 1 (scratchy) áspero/áspera; 2 (vague) aproximado/aproximada; **a rough idea** una idea aproximada; 3 (stormy) **a rough sea** un mar agitado; 4 (difficult) **to have a rough time** pasarlo [17] mal; **5 to sleep rough** dormir [51] a la intemperie.

roughly adjective (approximately) aproximadamente; **roughly ten per cent** aproximadamente el diez

a
b
c
d
e
f
g
h
i
j
k
l
m
n
o
p
q
r
s
t
u
v
w
x
y
z

por ciento; **it takes roughly three hours** lleva aproximadamente tres horas.

round noun **1** (in a tournament) vuelta Fem.; **2** (of cards) partida Fem.; **3 a round of drinks** una ronda de bebidas; **it's my round** esta ronda la pago yo.

round adjective redondo/redonda; **a round table** una mesa redonda.

round preposition **1** alrededor de; **round the city** alrededor de la ciudad; **round my arm** alrededor de mi brazo; **they were sitting round the table** estaban sentados alrededor de la mesa; **2 to go round the shops** ir de tiendas; **to go round a museum** visitar un museo; **it's just round the corner** está a la vuelta de la esquina.

round adverb **1 to go round to somebody's house** ir a casa de alguien; **we invited Sally round for lunch** invitamos a Sally a comer; **2 all the year round** todo el año.

roundabout noun **1** (for traffic) rotonda Fem.; **2** (in a fairground) tiovivo Masc.

route noun **1** (that you plan) ruta Fem.; **the best route is via Leeds** la mejor ruta es pasando por Leeds; **2 a bus route** el recorrido de un autobús.

row[1] noun **1** fila Fem. (of seats); **in the front row** en la primera fila; **in the back row** en la última fila; **2** hilera Fem.; **a row of huts** un hilera de cabañas; **3 four times in a row** cuatro veces seguidas.

row[2] verb (in a boat) remar [17]; **it's your turn to row** te toca remar; **we rowed across the lake** cruzamos el lago remando.

row[3] noun **1** (a quarrel) pelea Fem.; **to have a row** pelearse [17]; **they've had a row** se han peleado; **I had a row with my parents** me peleé con mis padres; **2** (noise) ruido Masc.; **they are making a terrible row!** ¡están haciendo un ruido terrible!

rowing noun remo Masc.; **to go rowing** practicar [31] el remo.

rowing boat noun bote Masc. de remos.

royal adjective real; **the royal family** la familia real.

rub verb frotar [17]; **to rub your eyes** frotarse los ojos.

• **to rub something out** borrar [17] algo.

rubber noun **1** (an eraser) goma Fem. de borrar; **2** (material) goma Fem.; **rubber soles** suelas de goma.

rubber band noun goma Fem. elástica.

rubbish noun **1** (for the bin) basura Fem.; **2** (nonsense) estupideces Fem. plural; **you're talking rubbish!** ¡estás diciendo estupideces!

rubbish adjective **the film was rubbish** la película fue una porquería; **they're a rubbish band** es una porquería de grupo.

rubbish bin noun cubo Masc. de la basura.

rucksack noun mochila Fem.

rude *adjective* **1** maleducado/maleducada (*a person*); **2** that's rude eso es de mala educación; **3** a rude joke una broma grosera; a rude word una palabrota.

rug *noun* **1** alfombra *Fem.*; **2** (*a blanket*) manta *Fem.* de viaje.

rugby *noun* rugby *Masc.*; to play rugby jugar [27] al rugby; a rugby match un partido de rugby.

ruin *noun* ruina *Fem.*; in ruins en ruinas.

ruin *verb* **1** estropear [17]; you'll ruin your jacket vas a estropear tu chaqueta; **2** fastidiar [17] (*informal*) (*day, holiday*); it ruined my holiday me fastidió las vacaciones.

rule *noun* **1** regla *Fem.*; the rules of the game las reglas del juego; **2** the school rules el reglamento del colegio; **3** as a rule como norma.

ruler *noun* regla *Fem.*; I've lost my ruler he perdido mi regla.

rumour *noun* rumor *Masc.*

run *noun* **1** to go for a run ir [8] a correr; **2** (*in cricket*) carrera *Fem.*; **3** in the long run a la larga.

run *verb* **1** correr [18]; I ran ten kilometres corrí diez kilómetros; he ran across the pitch cruzó el campo corriendo; Kitty ran for the bus Kitty corrió para coger el autobús; **2** (*organize*) organizar [22]; who's running this concert? ¿quién organiza el concierto?; **3** dirigir [49] (*a business*); he ran the firm for forty years dirigió la compañía durante cuarenta años; **4** (*a train or bus*) circular [17]; the buses don't run on Sundays los autobuses no circulan los domingos; **5** (*to operate*) hacer [7] funcionar; to run a bath preparar [17] un baño.

● to run away huir [54].

● to run into chocar [31] con; the car ran into a tree el coche chocó con un árbol.

● to run out of something I'm running out of money se me está acabando el dinero.

● to run somebody over atropellar [17] a alguien; you'll get run over! ¡te van a atropellar!.

runner-up *noun* segundo *Masc.*, segunda *Fem.*

running *noun* running is good exercise correr es un buen ejercicio.

runway *noun* pista *Fem.*

rush *noun* (*a hurry*) to be in a rush tener [9] prisa; sorry, I'm in a rush perdona, tengo prisa.

rush *verb* **1** (*hurry*) darse [4] prisa; I must rush! ¡tengo que darme prisa!; **2** (*run*) she rushed into the street salió corriendo a la calle; I rushed into the room entré corriendo en la habitación; **3** Louise was rushed to hospital llevaron a Louise corriendo al hospital.

rush hour *noun* hora *Fem.* punta; in the rush hour a la hora punta.

Russia *noun* Rusia *Fem.*

Russian *noun* **1** (*a person*) ruso *Masc.*, rusa *Fem.*; **2** (*the language*) ruso *Masc.*

Russian *adjective* ruso/rusa.

rye *noun* centeno *Masc.*

a b c d e f g h i j k l m n o p q r s t u v w x y z

a
b
c
d
e
f
g
h
i
j
k
l
m
n
o
p
q
r
s
t
u
v
w
x
y
z

Ss

Sabbath noun 1 (*Jewish*) sábado Masc.; 2 (*Christian*) domingo Masc.

sack noun 1 saco Masc.; 2 he got the sack le despidieron.

sack verb to sack somebody despedir [57] a alguien.

sacred adjective sagrado/sagrada.

sacrifice noun sacrificio Masc.

sad adjective triste.

saddle noun silla Fem. de montar.

saddlebag noun alforja Fem. (on bike).

safe adjective 1 (*out of danger*) seguro/segura; to feel safe sentirse [14] seguro/segura; 2 (*not dangerous*) seguro/segura; the path is safe el camino es seguro; it's not safe no es seguro; 3 (*unharmed*) to be safe estar [2] sano y salvo.

safety noun seguridad Fem.

safety belt noun cinturón Masc. de seguridad.

safety pin noun imperdible Masc.

Sagittarius noun Sagitario Masc.; Kylie's Sagittarius Kylie es Sagitario.

sail noun vela Fem.

sailing noun vela Fem.; to go sailing ir [8] a hacer vela; she does a lot of sailing practica mucho la vela.

sailing boat noun bote Masc. de vela.

sailor noun marinero Masc.

saint noun santo Masc., santa Fem.

sake noun 1 for your mother's sake por tu madre; 2 for heaven's sake! ¡por el amor de Dios!

salad noun ensalada Fem.; a tomato salad una ensalada de tomate.

salad dressing noun aliño Masc. para la ensalada.

salary noun sueldo Masc.

sale noun 1 (*selling*) venta Fem.; the sale of the house la venta de la casa; 'for sale' 'se vende'; 2 the sales las rebajas; I bought it in the sales lo compré en las rebajas.

sales assistant noun dependiente Masc., dependienta Fem.

salesman noun representante Masc.; he's a salesman es representante.

saleswoman noun representante Fem.

saliva noun saliva Fem.

salmon noun salmón Masc.

salt noun sal Fem.

salty adjective salado/salada.

Salvadorean noun salvadoreño Masc., salvadoreña Fem.

Salvadorean adjective salvadoreño/salvadoreña.

Salvation Army noun Ejército Masc. de Salvación.

same adjective 1 mismo/misma; she said the same thing ella dijo lo mismo; her birthday's the same day as mine es el mismo día que el mío; at the same time al mismo tiempo; their car's the same as ours su coche es el mismo que el nuestro; 2 (*with* *a plural noun)* mismos/mismas; **they were wearing the same shoes** llevaban los mismos zapatos; **3 to look the same** parecer [35] iguales; **they all look the same to me** a mí todos me parecen iguales.

same *pronoun* the same lo mismo; **it's not the same** no es lo mismo; **it's always the same** siempre pasa lo mismo.

sample *noun* muestra *Fem.*; **a free sample** una muestra gratuita.

sand *noun* arena *Fem.*

sandal *noun* sandalia *Fem.*; **a pair of sandals** un par de sandalias.

sand castle *noun* castillo *Masc.* de arena.

sandpaper *noun* papel *Masc.* de lija.

sandwich *noun* sándwich *Masc.*; **a ham sandwich** un sándwich de jamón.

sanitary towel *noun* compresa *Fem.*

Santa Claus *noun* Papá *Masc.* Noel.

sarcasm *noun* sarcasmo *Masc.*

sarcastic *adjective* sarcástico/ sarcástica.

sardine *noun* sardina *Fem.*

SARS *noun* síndrome *Masc.* respiratorio agudo severo.

satchel *noun* cartera *Fem.*

satellite *noun* satélite *Masc.*

satellite dish *noun* antena *Fem.* parabólica.

satellite television *noun* televisión *Fem.* por vía satélite.

satisfactory *adjective* satisfactorio/satisfactoria.

satisfied *adjective* satisfecho/ satisfecha.

satisfy *verb* satisfacer [7].

satisfying *adjective* **1** *(pleasing)* satisfactorio/satisfactoria; **2 a satisfying meal** una comida que llena.

Saturday *noun* sábado *Masc.*; **on Saturday** el sábado; **I'm going out on Saturday** voy a salir el sábado; **see you on Saturday!** ¡te veo el sábado!; **on Saturdays** los sábados; **the museum is closed on Saturdays** el museo cierra los sábados; **every Saturday** todos los sábados; **last Saturday** el sábado pasado; **next Saturday** el próximo sábado; **to have a Saturday job** trabajar [17] los sábados.

sauce *noun* salsa *Fem.*

saucepan *noun* cazo *Masc.*

saucer *noun* platillo *Masc.*

sausage *noun* **1** salchicha *Fem.*; **2** *(salami)* salchichón *Masc.*

savage *noun* salvaje *Masc./Fem.*

save *verb* **1** *(rescue)* salvar [17]; **to save somebody's life** salvarle la vida a alguien; **the doctors saved his life** los médicos le salvaron la vida; **2** ahorrar [17] *(money or energy)*; **I've saved £60** he ahorrado sesenta libras; **try to save electricity** intenta ahorrar electricidad; **3** *(put aside)* guardar [17] *(food)*; **save the cake for later** guarda el pastel para luego; **4** *(avoid spending)* no gastar [17]; **I walk to school to save money**

a
b
c
d
e
f
g
h
i
j
k
l
m
n
o
p
q
r
s
t
u
v
w
x
y
z

voy andando al colegio para no gastar dinero; **5 to save time** ahorrar [17] tiempo; **we'll take a taxi to save time** cogeremos un taxi para ahorrar tiempo; **6** (*on a computer*) guardar [17].

● **to save up** ahorrar [17]; **I'm saving up to go to Spain** estoy ahorrando para ir a España.

savings *plural noun* ahorros *Masc. plural*; **I've spent all my savings** me he gastado todos los ahorros.

savoury *adjective* salado/salada; **I prefer savoury things to sweet things** prefiero lo salado a lo dulce.

saw *noun* sierra *Fem.*

saxophone *noun* saxofón *Masc.*; **to play the saxophone** tocar [31] el saxofón.

say *verb* **1** decir [5]; **what did you say?** ¿qué has dicho?; **she says she's tired** dice que está cansada; **he said to wait here** dijo que esperásemos aquí; **as they say** como se suele decir; **that goes without saying** eso no hace falta ni decirlo; **2 to say something again** repetir [57] algo.

saying *noun* refrán *Masc.*; **as the saying goes** como dice el refrán.

scab *noun* costra *Fem.*

scale *noun* **1** (*size*) escala *Fem.*; **on a large scale** en gran escala; **the scale of the disaster** la escala del desastre; **2** (*in music*) escala *Fem.*; **3** (*of a fish*) escama *Fem.*

scales *noun* **1** balanza *Fem.*; **kitchen scales** una balanza de cocina; **2 bathroom scales** una báscula de baño.

scalp *noun* cuero *Masc.* cabelludo.

scandal *noun* **1** escándalo *Masc.*; **2** (*gossip*) chismorreo *Masc.*

Scandinavia *noun* Escandinavia *Fem.*

Scandinavian *adjective* escandinavo/escandinava.

scanner *noun* escáner *Masc.*

scar *noun* cicatriz *Fem.*

scarce *adjective* escaso/escasa.

scarcely *adverb* apenas; **I could scarcely see it** apenas lo veía.

scare *noun* **1** susto *Masc.*; **to give somebody a scare** darle [4] un susto a alguien; **2 a bomb scare** una amenaza de bomba.

scare *verb* **to scare somebody** asustar [17] a alguien; **you scared me!** ¡me has asustado!

scarecrow *noun* espantapájaros *Masc.* (*does not change in the plural*).

scared *adjective* **to be scared** estar [2] asustado/asustada; **I'm scared!** estoy asustado; **to be scared of** tenerle [9] miedo a; **he's scared of dogs** le tiene miedo a los perros.

scarf *noun* **1** (*long, warm*) bufanda *Fem.*; **2** (*silky*) foulard *Masc.*

scary *adjective* de miedo (*book or film*).

scene *noun* **1** (*of an incident or a crime*) escena *Fem.*; **the scene of the crime** la escena del crimen; **2** (*world*) mundo *Masc.*; **the music scene** el mundo de la música; **3 scenes of violence** escenas violentas; **4 to make a scene** montar [17] un número (*informal*).

scenery noun 1 (landscape) paisaje Masc.; 2 (theatrical) decorado Masc.

schedule noun programa Masc.

scheduled flight noun vuelo Masc. regular.

scheme noun plan Masc.

scholarship noun beca Fem.

school noun colegio Masc.; **to go to school** ir [8] al colegio; **she's still at school** todavía va al colegio.

schoolbook noun libro Masc. de texto.

schoolboy noun colegial Masc.

schoolchildren plural noun colegiales Masc. plural.

schoolfriend noun amigo Masc., amiga Fem. del colegio.

schoolgirl noun colegiala Fem.

science noun ciencia Fem.; **I like science** me gustan las ciencias; **the science teacher** el profesor de ciencias.

science fiction noun ciencia Fem. ficción.

scientific adjective científico/ científica.

scientist noun científico Masc., científica Fem.

scissors plural noun tijeras Fem. plural; **a pair of scissors** unas tijeras.

scoop noun 1 (of ice-cream) bola Fem.; **how many scoops would you like?** ¿cuántas bolas quieres?; 2 (in newspaper) primicia Fem.

score noun (in game) resultado Masc.; **the score was three two** el resultado fue tres a dos; **what's the score?** ¿a cómo van?

score verb 1 (goal) marcar [31]; **Lenny scored a goal** Lenny marcó un gol; 2 (points) **I scored three points** conseguí tres puntos; 3 (keep score) llevar [17] la puntuación; 4 (in test or card game) puntuación Fem.

Scorpio noun Escorpio Masc.; **Jess is Scorpio** Jess es Escorpio.

Scot noun escocés Masc., escocesa Fem.; **the Scots** los escoceses.

Scotland noun Escocia Fem.; **in Scotland** en Escocia; **Pauline's from Scotland** Pauline es de Escocia.

Scots adjective escocés/escocesa; **a Scots accent** un acento escocés.

Scotsman noun escocés Masc.

Scotswoman noun escocesa Fem.

Scottish adjective escocés/ escocesa; **a Scottish accent** un acento escocés.

scout noun explorador Masc., exploradora Fem.

scrambled eggs noun huevos Masc. plural revueltos.

scrap noun **a scrap of paper** un trocito de papel.

scrape verb rayar [17].

scratch noun 1 (on your skin) arañazo Masc.; 2 (on a surface) rayón Masc.; ★ **to start from scratch** empezar [25] de cero.

scratch verb (scratch yourself) rascarse [31]; **to scratch your head** rascarse [31] la cabeza.

scream noun grito Masc.

scream verb gritar [17].

a
b
c
d
e
f
g
h
i
j
k
l
m
n
o
p
q
r
s
t
u
v
w
x
y
z

screen noun pantalla Fem.; **on the screen** en la pantalla.

screw noun tornillo Masc.

screw verb atornillar [17].

screwdriver noun destornillador Masc.

scribble verb garabatear [17].

scrub verb 1 fregar [30] (a saucepan); 2 **to scrub your nails** cepillarse [17] las uñas.

scuba diving noun submarinismo Masc.

sculpture noun escultura Fem.

sculptor noun escultor Masc., escultora Fem.; **Frazer's a sculptor** Frazer es escultor.

sea noun mar Masc.

seafood noun marisco Masc.

seagull noun gaviota Fem.

seal noun (animal) foca Fem.

seal verb cerrar [29] (envelope).

seaman noun marinero Masc.

search noun 1 búsqueda Fem.

search verb 1 (to look for) buscar [31]; **I've searched my desk but I can't find the letter** he buscado en mi escritorio pero no encuentro la carta; **to search for something** buscar [31] algo; **I've been searching everywhere for the scissors** he buscado las tijeras por todas partes; 2 (a building, a person) registrar [17]; **the police searched the house** la policía registró la casa.

seashell noun concha Fem. de mar.

seasick adjective **to be seasick** estar [2] mareado/mareada; **to get seasick** marearse [17].

seaside noun costa Fem.; **at the seaside** en la costa.

season noun temporada Fem.; **the rugby season** la temporada de rugby; **strawberries are not in season at the moment** ahora no es temporada de fresas; **off-season prices** billetes de fuera de temporada.

season ticket noun abono Masc. de temporada.

seat noun 1 asiento Masc.; **the front seat** (in a car) el asiento delantero; **the back seat** el asiento trasero; **take a seat** toma asiento; 2 (in a cinema, theatre, etc.) localidad Fem.; **to book a seat** reservar [17] una localidad; 3 **can you keep my seat?** ¿puedes guardarme el sitio?

seatbelt noun cinturón Masc. de seguridad.

second noun 1 (time unit) segundo Masc.; **can you wait a second?** ¿puedes esperar un segundo?; 2 **the second of July** el dos de julio.

second adjective segundo/ segunda; **for the second time** por segunda vez; **on the second floor** en la segunda planta.

second class adjective de segunda clase (a ticket, hotel); **a second class team** un equipo de segunda clase.

secondary school noun colegio Masc. de enseñanza secundaria.

secondhand adjective, adverb de segunda mano; **a secondhand bike** una bicicleta de segunda mano; **I bought it secondhand** lo compré de segunda mano.

secondly *adverb* en segundo lugar.

secret *noun* secreto *Masc.*; **to keep a secret** guardar [17] un secreto; **in secret** en secreto.

secret *adjective* secreto/secreta; **a secret plan** un plan secreto.

secretarial college *noun* escuela *Fem.* de secretariado.

secretary *noun* secretario *Masc.*, secretaria *Fem.*; **she's a secretary** es secretaria; **the secretary's office** la secretaría.

secretly *adverb* en secreto.

sect *noun* secta *Fem.*

section *noun* sección *Fem.*

security *noun* seguridad *Fem.*

security guard *noun* guarda *Masc.* jurado; guarda *Fem.* jurada; **he's a security guard** es guarda jurado.

see *verb* **1** ver [16]; **I saw Lindy yesterday** vi a Lindy ayer; **have you seen the film?** ¿has visto la película?; **I haven't seen her for ages** hace años que no la veo; **I'll see what I can do** veré lo que puedo hacer; **let's see** a ver; **2 to be able to see** ver [16]; **I can't see anything** no veo nada; **3 see you!** ¡hasta luego!; **see you on Saturday!** ¡hasta el sábado!; **see you soon!** ¡hasta pronto!; **see you tomorrow!** ¡hasta mañana!; **4 to see somebody home** acompañar [17] a alguien a casa.

● **to see to something** ocuparse [17] de algo; **Jo's seeing to the**

drinks Jo se está ocupando de las bebidas.

seed *noun* semilla *Fem.*; **to plant seeds** plantar [17] semillas.

seem *verb* parecer [35]; **it seems odd to me** me parece raro; **it seems she's left** parece que se ha ido; **he seems a bit shy** parece un poco tímido; **the museum seems to be closed** parece que el museo está cerrado.

seesaw *noun* balancín *Masc.*

select *verb* seleccionar [17].

selection *noun* selección *Fem.*

self-confidence *noun* confianza *Fem.* en si mismo; **I don't have much self-confidence** no tengo mucha confianza en mí misma.

self-confident *adjective* seguro/segura de si mismo/misma.

self-conscious *adjective* cohibido/cohibida.

self-employed *noun* autónomo *Masc.*, autónoma *Fem.*; **the self-employed** los autónomos.

self-employed *adjective* autónomo/autónoma; **to be self-employed** ser [1] autónomo.

selfish *adjective* egoísta.

self-service *adjective* **a self-service restaurant** un autoservicio.

sell *verb* vender [18]; **to sell something to somebody** venderle algo a alguien; **I sold him my bike** le vendí mi bici; **the house has been sold** la casa se ha vendido; **the concert's sold out** se han agotado las localidades para el concierto.

a b c d e f g h i j k l m n o p q r s t u v w x y z

sell-by date noun fecha Fem. límite de venta.

seller noun vendedor Masc., vendedora Fem.

Sellotape™ noun celo™ Masc.

semi noun casa Fem. adosada; **we live in a semi** vivimos en una casa adosada.

semicircle noun semicírculo Masc.

semicolon noun punto Masc. y coma.

semi-detached house noun casa Fem. adosada.

semi-final noun semifinal Fem.

semi-skimmed milk noun leche Fem. semidesnatada.

send verb mandar [17]; **to send something to somebody** mandarle algo a alguien; **I sent her a present for her birthday** le mandé un regalo por su cumpleaños.

● **to send somebody back** hacer [7] volver a alguien.

● **to send something back** devolver [45] algo.

senior citizen noun persona Fem. de la tercera edad.

sensation noun 1 (feeling) sensibilidad Fem.; **she had no sensation in her fingers** no tenía sensibilidad en los dedos; 2 (impact) sensación Fem.; **she caused a sensation** causó sensación.

sensational adjective sensacional.

sense noun 1 sentido Masc.; **common sense** sentido común; **it doesn't make sense** no tiene sentido; **it makes sense** tiene sentido; **to have a sense of humour** tener [9] sentido del humor; **she has no sense of humour** no tiene sentido del humor; 2 **the sense of smell** el olfato; **the sense of touch** el tacto.

sensible adjective sensato/sensata; **she's very sensible** es muy sensata; **it's a sensible decision** es una decisión sensata.

sensitive adjective sensible; **for sensitive skin** para pieles sensibles.

sentence noun 1 frase Fem.; **write a sentence in Spanish** escribe una frase en español; 2 (by judge) sentencia Fem.

sentence verb condenar [17].

sentimental adjective sentimental.

separate adjective 1 aparte; **in a separate pile** en un montón aparte; **on a separate sheet of paper** en una hoja de papel aparte; 2 (different) distinto/distinta; **that's a separate problem** ese es un problema distinto; 3 (individual) separado/separada; **they have separate rooms** tienen habitaciones separadas.

separate verb 1 separar [17]; 2 (a couple) separarse [17].

separately adverb por separado.

separation noun separación Fem.

September noun septiembre Masc.

...ación Fem.

...ón

...em.; a
...s una serie de

... adjective 1 serio/seria; a
...ous discussion una discusión
...ria; are you serious? ¿lo dices
en serio?; 2 grave (illness, injury,
mistake, problem); we have a
serious problem tenemos un
problema grave.

seriously adverb 1 en serio;
seriously, I have to go now en
serio, tengo que irme; seriously?
¿en serio?; 2 to take somebody
seriously tomarse [17] en serio a
alguien; 3 gravemente (ill,
injured).

servant noun criado Masc., criada
Fem.

serve noun (in tennis) saque Masc.;
it's my serve me toca sacar.

serve verb 1 servir [57]; can you
serve the vegetables, please?
¿puedes servir la verdura, por
favor?; 2 are you being served?
¿le atienden?; 3 (in tennis) sacar
[31]; ★ it serves him right lo tiene
bien merecido.

service noun 1 (in a restaurant,
from a company, etc.) servicio
Masc.; the service is very slow el
servicio es muy lento; service is
included el servicio está incluido;
2 the emergency services los
servicios de emergencia;
3 (church) oficio Masc. religioso;
4 (of a car or machine) revisión
Fem.

service verb hacerle [7] una
revisión a (a car or a machine).

service charge noun servicio
Masc.; what's the service charge?
¿cuánto se cobra por el servicio?

service station noun estación
Fem. de servicio.

serviette noun servilleta Fem.

session noun sesión Fem.

set noun 1 (for playing a game)
juego Masc.; a chess set un juego
de ajedrez; 2 (of keys, tools, etc.)
juego Masc.; 3 a train set un tren
de juguete; 4 (in tennis) set Masc.

set adjective at a set time a una
hora determinada; a set menu un
menú del día; a set price un
precio fijo.

set verb 1 fijar [17] (date, time);
2 establecer [35] (record); 3 to set
the table poner [11] la mesa; to set
the alarm clock poner [11] el
despertador; I've set my alarm for
seven he puesto el despertador
para las siete; 4 to set a watch
poner [11] el reloj en hora; 5 (the
sun) ponerse [11].

● to set off salir [63]; we're
setting off at ten salimos a las
diez; they set off for Barcelona
yesterday salieron ayer para
Barcelona.

● to set off something 1 tirar
[17] (firework); 2 hacer [7] sonar
(alarm).

● to set out salir [63]; they set out
for Seville yesterday salieron
ayer para Sevilla.

settee noun sofá Masc.

settle verb 1 (a bill) pagar [28];
2 (a problem) solucionar [17].

a

seven number siete Masc.; **Khalil's seven** Khalil tiene siete años; **it's seven o'clock** son las siete.

b

c

seventeen number diecisiete Masc.; **Jason's seventeen** Jason tiene diecisiete años.

d

seventh noun 1 (fraction) **a seventh** una séptima parte; **2 the seventh of July** el siete de julio.

e

f

seventh adjective séptimo/ séptima; **on the seventh floor** en la séptima planta.

g

h

i

seventies plural noun **the seventies** los años setenta; **in the seventies** en los años setenta.

j

k

seventy number setenta Masc.; **he's seventy** tiene setenta años; **seventy-five** setenta y cinco.

l

m

several adjective, pronoun varios/ varias; **I've seen her several times** la he visto varias veces; **I've read several of her novels** he leído varias novelas suyas; **he took several** cogió varios.

n

o

severe adjective 1 (person) severo/ severa; **2** (weather) malo/mala; **3** (injury) grave.

p

q

Seville noun Sevilla Fem.

r

s

sew verb coser [18].

t

sewer noun alcantarilla Fem.

sewing noun costura Fem.; **I like sewing** me gusta la costura.

u

sewing machine noun máquina Fem. de coser.

v

w

sex noun 1 (gender) sexo Masc.; **2** (intercourse) relaciones Fem. plural sexuales; **to have sex with someone** tener [9] relaciones sexuales con alguien.

x

y

z

sex education noun educa... Fem. sexual.

sexism noun sexismo Masc.

sexist adjective sexista; **sexist remarks** comentarios sexistas.

sexual adjective sexual.

sexual harassment noun acoso Masc. sexual.

sexuality noun sexualidad Fem.

sexy adjective sexy.

shabby adjective gastado/gastada.

shade noun 1 (of a colour) tono Masc.; **a pretty shade of green** un bonito tono verde; **2 in the shade** en la sombra.

shadow noun sombra Fem.

shake verb 1 (tremble) temblar [29]; **my hands are shaking** me tiemblan las manos; **2 to shake something** agitar [17] algo; **3 to shake hands with somebody** estrecharle [17] la mano a alguien; **she shook hands with me** me dio la mano; **we shook hands** nos estrechamos la mano; **4 to shake your head** (meaning no) negar [30] con la cabeza.

shall verb **shall I come with you?** ¿voy contigo?; **shall we stop now?** ¿paramos ya?

shallow adjective poco profundo/ poco profunda; **the water's very shallow here** el agua es muy poco profunda aquí.

shallow end noun (of a swimming pool) **the shallow end** la parte poco profunda de la piscina.

shambles noun caos *Masc.*; **it was a total shambles!** ¡fue un caos total!

shame noun **1** vergüenza *Fem.*; **shame on you!** ¡debería darte vergüenza!; **2 what a shame!** ¡qué pena!; **it's a shame she can't come** ¡qué pena que no pueda venir! (*note that 'que' is followed by the subjunctive*)

shampoo noun champú *Masc.*; **I bought some shampoo** compré champú.

shamrock noun trébol *Masc.*

shandy noun clara *Fem.*; **a shandy** una clara.

shape noun forma *Fem.*; **to be in good shape** estar [2] en buena forma.

share noun **1** parte *Fem.*; **your share of the money** tu parte del dinero; **2** (*in a company*) acción *Fem.*

share verb compartir [19]; **I'm sharing a room with Emma** comparto una habitación con Emma.

● **to share out** repartir [19].

sharp adjective **1** (*knife*) afilado/afilada; **this knife isn't very sharp** este cuchillo no está muy afilado; **2 a sharp pencil** un lápiz con mucha punta; **3 a sharp bend** una curva cerrada; **4** (*clever*) agudo/aguda.

sharpen verb **1** sacarle [31] punta a (*a pencil*); **2** afilar [17] (*a knife*).

sharpener noun sacapuntas *Masc.* plural.

shave verb **1** (*have a shave*) afeitarse [17]; **he's shaving** se está afeitando; **2 to shave your legs** afeitarse [17] las piernas; **to shave off your beard** afeitarse [17] la barba.

shaving cream noun crema *Fem.* de afeitar.

shaving foam noun espuma *Fem.* de afeitar.

she pronoun **1** (*'she' like other subject pronouns is generally not translated; in Spanish the form of the verb tells you whether the subject of the verb is he/she/it, you', they', etc., so 'she' is only translated for emphasis*) **she's in her room** está en su cuarto; **she's a student** es estudiante; **she's a very good teacher** es muy buena profesora; **here she is!** ¡aquí está!; **2** (*for emphasis*) ella; **she did it** lo hizo ella.

shed noun **1** cabaña *Fem.*; **2** (*in garden*) cobertizo *Masc.*

sheep noun oveja *Fem.*

sheepdog noun perro *Masc.* pastor.

sheet noun **1** (*for a bed*) sábana *Fem.*; **2 a sheet of paper** una hoja de papel; **a blank sheet** una hoja en blanco; **3** (*of glass or metal*) plancha *Fem.*; ★ **to be as white as a sheet** estar [2] blanco como el papel.

shelf noun **1** (*in the home*) estante *Masc.*; **a set of shelves** una estantería *Fem.*; **2** (*in a shop or a fridge*) balda *Fem.*

a
b
c
d
e
f
g
h
i
j
k
l
m
n
o
p
q
r
s
t
u
v
w
x
y
z

a

shell noun 1 (of an egg or a nut) cáscara Fem.; 2 (seashell) concha Fem.; 3 (explosive) proyectil Masc.

b

shellfish noun marisco Masc.

c

shelter noun 1 refugio Masc.; **to take shelter from the rain** refugiarse [17] de la lluvia; **in the shelter of** al abrigo de; 2 **a bus shelter** una marquesina.

d

e

f

sherry noun jerez Masc.

g

Shetland Islands noun islas Fem. plural Shetland.

h

shield noun escudo Masc.

i

shift noun turno Masc.; **the night shift** el turno de noche; **to be on night shift** hacer [7] el turno de noche.

j

k

shift verb **to shift something** mover [38] algo.

l

m

shin noun espinilla Fem.

n

shine verb brillar [17].

shiny adjective brillante.

o

ship noun 1 barco Masc.; **a passenger ship** un barco de pasajeros; 2 **a sailing ship** un velero.

p

q

shirt noun camisa Fem.

r

shiver verb temblar [29].

s

shock noun 1 shock Masc.; **it was a shock** fue un shock; **it gave me a shock** me llevé un shock; **in a state of shock** en estado de shock; 2 **an electric shock** una descarga eléctrica; **I got an electric shock** me dio una descarga eléctrica.

t

u

shock verb horrorizar [22].

v

shocked adjective horrorizado/ horrorizada.

w

x

shocking adjective espantoso/ espantosa.

y

z

shoe noun zapato Masc.; **a pair of shoes** un par de zapatos.

shoelace noun cordón Masc. de zapato.

shoe polish noun betún Masc.

shoe shop noun zapatería Fem.

shoot verb 1 (fire) disparar [17]; **to shoot at somebody** disparar a alguien; **she shot him in the leg** le disparó en la pierna; **he was shot in the arm** le dispararon en el brazo; 2 (kill) matar [17] a tiros; **he was shot by terrorists** los terroristas lo mataron a tiros; 3 (execute) fusilar [17]; 4 (in football, hockey) lanzar [22]; 5 **to shoot a film** rodar [24] una película.

shooting noun tiro Masc. al blanco.

shop noun tienda Fem.; **a record shop** una tienda de discos; **a shoe shop** una zapatería; **to go round the shops** ir [8] de tiendas.

shop assistant noun dependiente Masc., dependienta Fem.; **Brad's a shop assistant** Brad trabaja de dependiente.

shopkeeper noun tendero Masc., tendera Fem.

shoplifter noun ladrón Masc., ladrona Fem.

shoplifting noun hurto Masc. en las tiendas.

shopping noun compras Fem. plural; **can you put the shopping away?** ¿puedes guardar las compras?; **I've got a lot of shopping to do** tengo muchas cosas que comprar; **to go**

shopping ir [8] a hacer la compra; (*for fun, to buy clothes or presents*) ir [8] de compras.

shopping centre noun centro Masc. comercial.

shop window noun escaparate Masc.

shore noun orilla Fem. del mar.

short adjective **1** corto/corta; **a short dress** un vestido corto; **she has short hair** tiene el pelo corto; **2** (*person*) bajo/baja (*in height*); **he's quite short** es bastante bajo; **3 a short break** un descanso corto; **a short visit** una visita corta; **to go for a short walk** ir [8] a dar un pequeño paseo; **it's a short walk from the station** es un pequeño paseo desde la estación; **4 a short time ago** hace poco tiempo; **5 to be short of** no tener mucho; **we're a bit short of money at the moment** no tenemos mucho dinero en este momento; **we're getting short of time** se nos está acabando el tiempo.

shortage noun escasez Fem.

shortbread noun galleta Fem. de mantequilla.

shortcrust pastry noun pasta Fem. quebrada.

short cut noun atajo Masc.; **we took a short cut** tomamos un atajo.

shorten verb acortar [17].

shortly adverb dentro de poco.

shorts plural noun shorts Masc. plural; **a pair of shorts** unos shorts; **my red shorts** mis shorts rojos.

short-sighted adjective miope; **I'm short-sighted** soy miope.

shotgun noun escopeta Fem.

should verb **1** deber [18] ('should' is translated by the conditional tense of 'deber'); **you should ask Simon** deberías preguntárselo a Simon; **the potatoes should be cooked now** las patatas deberían estar hechas ya; **2** ('should have' is translated by the past conditional tense of 'deber') **you should have told me** deberías habérmelo dicho; **I shouldn't have stayed** no deberías haberte quedado; **3** ('should' meaning 'would' is translated by the conditional tense of the appropriate verb) **I should forget it if I were you** yo en tu lugar me olvidaría del asunto; **4 I should think** yo diría; **I should think he's forgotten** yo diría que se ha olvidado.

shoulder noun hombro Masc.

shoulder bag noun bolso Masc.

shout noun grito Masc.

shout verb gritar [17]; **stop shouting!** ¡deja de gritar!; **they shouted at us to come back** nos gritaron que volviésemos.

shovel noun pala Fem.

show noun **1** (*on stage*) espectáculo Masc.; **we went to see a show** fuimos a ver un espectáculo; **2** (*on TV*) programa Masc.; **he has a TV show** tiene un programa en la tele; **3** (*exhibition*) salón Masc.; **the motor show** el salón del automóvil.

show verb **1** enseñar [17]; **to show something to somebody** enseñar

a b c d e f g h i j k l m n o p q r s t u v w x y z

a alguien algo; **I'll show you my photos** te enseñaré mis fotos; **to show somebody how to do** enseñar algo a alguien cómo hacer; **he showed me how to make pancakes** me enseñó cómo hacer crepes; **2 it shows!** ¡ya se ve!

● **to show off** presumir [19]; **stop showing off!** ¡déjate de hacer fanfarronadas!

shower noun **1** (in a bathroom) ducha Fem.; **to have a shower** ducharse [17]; **2** (of rain) chaparrón Masc.

show-off noun fanfarrón Masc., fanfarrona Fem.

shriek verb gritar [17].

shrimp noun camarón Masc.

shrine noun santuario Masc.

shrink verb encoger [3].

Shrove Tuesday noun martes Masc. de Carnaval.

shrug verb **to shrug your shoulders** encogerse [3] de hombros.

shuffle verb **to shuffle the cards** barajar [17] las cartas.

shut adjective cerrado/cerrada; **the shops are shut** las tiendas están cerradas.

shut verb cerrar [29]; **can you shut the door please?** ¿puedes cerrar la puerta por favor?; **the shops shut at six** las tiendas cierran a las seis.

● **to shut up** (be quiet) callarse [17]; **shut up!** ¡cállate!.

shuttlecock noun volante Masc.

shy adjective tímido/tímida.

shyness noun timidez Fem.

Sicily noun Sicilia Fem.

sick adjective **1** (ill) enfermo/ enferma; **2 to be sick** (vomit) devolver [45]; **I was sick several times** devolví varias veces; **to feel sick** tener [9] ganas de devolver; **3 a sick joke** una broma de mal gusto; **4 to be sick of something** estar [2] harto/harta de algo; **I'm sick of staying at home every night** estoy harto de quedarme en casa todas las noches.

sickness noun enfermedad Fem.

side noun **1** lado Masc.; **on the other side of the street** al otro lado de la calle; **on the wrong side** en el lado equivocado; **I'm on your side** (I agree with you) estoy de tu lado; **2** (edge) borde Masc.; **at the side of the road** al borde de la carretera; **by the side of the pool** al borde de la piscina; **by the side of the river** a la orilla del río; **3** (team) equipo Masc.; **she plays on our side** juega en nuestro equipo; **4 to take sides** tomar [17] partido; **5 side by side** unió al lado del otro.

sideboard noun aparador Masc.

siege noun sitio Masc.

sieve noun tamiz Masc.

sigh noun suspiro Masc.

sigh verb suspirar [17].

sight noun **1** espectáculo Masc.; **it was a marvellous sight** era un espectáculo maravilloso; **2 at the sight of** a la vista de; **at first sight** a primera vista; **3** (eyesight) vista Fem.; **to have poor sight** tener [9] mala vista; **to know somebody by sight** conocer [35] a alguien de vista; **I'd lost sight of them** los había perdido de vista; **4 to see the sights** visitar [17] los lugares de interés.

sightseeing noun **to do some sightseeing** visitar [17] los lugares de interés.

sign noun **1** (notice) letrero Masc.; **there's a sign on the door** hay un letrero en la puerta; **2** (trace, indication) señal Fem.; **3** (of the Zodiac) signo Masc.; **what sign are you?** ¿de qué signo eres?

sign verb **1** firmar [17]; **to sign a cheque** firmar un cheque; **2** (using sign language) comunicarse [31] por señas.

● **to sign on** (as unemployed) inscribirse [17] al paro.

signal noun señal Fem.

signature noun firma Fem.

significance noun importancia Fem.

significant adjective importante.

sign language noun lenguaje Masc. de gestos.

signpost noun señal Fem.

silence noun silencio Masc.

silent adjective silencioso/silenciosa.

silk noun seda Fem.

silk adjective de seda; **a silk shirt** una blusa de seda.

silky adjective sedoso/sedosa.

silly adjective tonto/tonta; **it was a really silly thing to do** hacer eso fue una verdadera tontería.

silver noun plata Fem.

silver adjective de plata; **a silver spoon** una cuchara de plata.

similar adjective parecido/parecida.

similarity noun parecido Masc.

simple adjective sencillo/sencilla.

simplify verb simplificar [31].

simply adverb sencillamente.

sin noun pecado Masc.

since preposition, adverb

since conjunction **1** desde (notice that Spanish uses the present tense where English uses 'have done' or 'have been doing') **I've been in Madrid since Saturday** llevo en Madrid desde el sábado; **I've been learning Spanish since last year** estoy aprendiendo español desde el año pasado; **2** desde que (the same thing happens with times here as above) **since I have known her** desde que la conozco; **since I've been learning Spanish** desde que estoy aprendiendo español; **3 I haven't seen her since** no la he visto desde entonces; **I haven't seen her since Monday** no la he visto desde el lunes; **since when?** ¿desde cuándo?; **4** (because) como; **since it was raining, the match was cancelled** como estaba lloviendo, cancelaron el partido.

sincere adjective sincero/sincera.

sincerely adverb **Yours sincerely** Atentamente.

sing verb cantar [17].

singer noun cantante Masc./Fem.

singing noun **1** canto Masc.; **a singing lesson** una lección de

a
b
c
d
e
f
g
h
i
j
k
l
m
n
o
p
q
r
s
t
u
v
w
x
y
z

canto; **2** I like singing me gusta cantar.

single noun (*ticket*) billete Masc. de ida; **a single to Barcelona** un billete de ida para Barcelona.

single adjective **1** (*not married*) soltero/soltera; **2 a single room** una habitación individual; **a single bed** una cama individual; **3 not a single** ... ni un solo/ni una sola ...; **I haven't had a single reply** no he tenido ni una sola respuesta; **4 every single day** todos los días; **every single morning** todas las mañanas.

single parent noun **she's a single parent** es madre soltera; **a single-parent family** una familia monoparental.

singular noun singular Masc.; **in the singular** en singular.

sink noun **1** (*in kitchen*) fregadero Masc.; **2** (*in bathroom*) lavabo Masc.

sink verb hundirse [19].

sir noun señor Masc.; **yes, sir** sí, señor.

sister noun hermana Fem.; **my sister's ten** mi hermana tiene diez años.

sister-in-law noun cuñada Fem.

sit verb **1** sentarse [29]; **you can sit on the sofa** puedes sentarte en el sofá; **I can sit on the floor** me puedo sentar en el suelo; **2 to be sitting** estar [2] sentado; **Leila was sitting on the sofa** Leila estaba sentada en el sofá; **3 to sit an exam** presentarse [17] a un examen; **she's sitting her driving test on Thursday** se presenta al examen de conducir el jueves.

● **to sit down** sentarse [29]; **he sat down on a chair** se sentó en una silla; **do sit down** siéntate.

site noun **1 a building site** una obra; **2 a camping site** un camping.

sitting room noun salón Masc.

situation noun situación Fem.

six number seis Masc.; **Tom's six** Tom tiene seis años; **it's six o'clock** son las seis.

sixteen number dieciséis Masc.; **Hannah's sixteen** Hannah tiene dieciséis años.

sixth noun **1** (*fraction*) **a sixth** una sexta parte; **2 the sixth of July** el seis de julio.

sixth adjective sexto/sexta; **on the sixth floor** en el sexto piso.

sixties plural noun **the sixties** los años sesenta; **in the sixties** en los años sesenta.

sixty number sesenta Masc.; **she's sixty** tiene sesenta años; **sixty-five** sesenta y cinco.

size noun **1** tamaño Masc.; **it depends on the size of the house** depende del tamaño de la casa; **2** (*precise measurements*) medidas Fem. plural; **what size is the window?** ¿qué medidas tiene la ventana?; **3** (*in clothes*) talla Fem.; **what size do you take?** ¿qué talla usas?; **4** (*of shoes*) número Masc.; **I take a size thirty-eight** calzo el número treinta y ocho.

skate noun **1 an ice skate** un patín de hielo; **2 a roller skate** un patín de ruedas.

skate verb **1** (*ice-skate*) hacer [7] patinaje sobre hielo; **2** (*roller-skate*) hacer [7] patinaje sobre ruedas.

skateboard noun monopatín Masc.

skateboarding noun **to go skateboarding** patinar [17] con el monopatín.

skater noun patinador Masc., patinadora Fem.

skating noun **1** (*ice*) patinaje Masc. sobre hielo; **to go skating** ir [8] a patinar sobre hielo; **2** roller-skating patinaje Masc. sobre ruedas; **to go roller-skating** ir [8] a patinar sobre ruedas.

skating rink noun pista Fem. de patinaje.

sketch noun **1** (*drawing*) boceto Masc.; **2** (*comedy routine*) sketch Masc.

ski noun esquí Masc.
ski verb esquiar [32].

ski boot noun bota Fem. de esquí.

skid verb derrapar [17]; **the car skidded** el coche derrapó.

skier noun esquiador Masc., esquiadora Fem.

skiing noun esquí Masc.; **to go skiing** ir [8] a esquiar.

skilful noun habilidoso/habilidosa.

skill noun habilidad Fem.

ski lift noun telesquí Masc.

skill noun habilidad Fem.; **it's not one of my skills** no es una de mis habilidades.

skimmed milk noun leche Fem. desnatada.

skin noun piel Fem.

skinhead noun cabeza Masc. rapada, cabeza Fem. rapada.

skinny adjective flaco/flaca.

skip noun (*for rubbish*) contenedor Masc.

skip verb **1** saltarse [17] (*a meal, part of a book*); **I skipped a few chapters** me salté algunos capítulos; **2 to skip a lesson** hacer [7] pellas de una clase (*informal*).

ski pants noun pantalones Masc. plural de esquí.

skipping rope noun comba Fem.

ski suit noun traje Masc. de esquí.

skirt noun falda Fem.; **a long skirt** una falda larga; **a straight skirt** una falda de tubo; **a mini-skirt** una minifalda.

sky noun cielo Masc.

skyscraper noun rascacielos Masc. (*does not change in the plural*).

slam verb cerrar [29] de un portazo; **she slammed the door** cerró la puerta de un portazo.

slang noun argot Masc.

slap noun **1** (*on the face*) bofetada Fem.; **2** (*on the leg, bottom*) azote Masc.

slap verb **to slap somebody** (*on the face*) dar [4] una bofetada a alguien (*on the leg or bottom*) dar [4] un azote a alguien.

slate noun pizarra Fem.

slave noun esclavo Masc., esclava Fem.

a b c d e f g h i j k l m n o p q r s t u v w x y z

sledge noun trineo Masc.

sledging noun to go sledging ir [8] en trineo.

sleep noun sueño Masc.; **six hours' sleep** seis horas de sueño; **I had a good sleep** dormí bien; **to go to sleep** dormirse [51].

sleep verb dormir [51]; **she's sleeping** está durmiendo.

sleeping bag noun saco Masc. de dormir.

sleeping pill noun somnífero Masc.

sleepy adjective **to be sleepy** tener [9] sueño; **I feel sleepy** tengo sueño; **I was getting sleepy** me estaba entrando sueño.

sleeve noun manga Fem.; **a long-sleeved jumper** un jersey de manga larga; **a short-sleeved shirt** una camisa de manga corta; **to roll up your sleeves** arremangarse [28].

slice noun **1** (of bread, cheese) rebanada Fem.; **2** (of meat) loncha Fem.; **a slice of ham** una loncha de jamón; **3** (of cake) trozo Masc.; **4** (a round slice: of lemon, tomato, etc.) rodaja Fem.

slice verb **to slice something** cortar [17] algo en rebanadas (or 'lonchas', 'trozos', etc, depending on what you are slicing: see noun translations above).

slide noun **1** (photo) diapositiva Fem.; **2** (hairslide) pasador Masc.; **3** (for sliding down) tobogán Masc.

slight adjective ligero/ligera; **there's a slight problem** hay un pequeño problema.

slightly adverb ligeramente.

slim adjective delgado/delgada.

slim verb adelgazar [22]; **I'm slimming** estoy adelgazando.

slip noun **1** (mistake) error Masc.; **2** (petticoat) combinación Fem.

slip verb **1** (slide) resbalarse [17]; **2 the jar slipped out of my hands** el frasco se me resbaló de las manos; **3 it slipped my mind** se me olvidó completamente.

slipper noun zapatilla Fem.

slippery adjective resbaladizo/resbaladiza.

slope noun cuesta Fem.

slow adjective **1** lento/lenta; **the service is a bit slow** el servicio es un poco lento; **2 my watch is slow** mi reloj está atrasado.

● **to slow down** reducir [60] la velocidad (a car).

slowly adverb despacio; **he got up slowly** se levantó despacio; **can you speak more slowly, please?** ¿puedes hablar más despacio, por favor?

slum noun barrio Masc. bajo.

smack noun **1** (on the face) bofetada Fem.; **2** (on the leg or bottom) azote Masc.

smack verb **to smack somebody** (on the face) dar [4] una bofetada a alguien; (on the leg or bottom) dar [4] un azote a alguien.

small adjective pequeño/pequeña; **a small dog** un perro pequeño.

smart adjective **1** (well-dressed, posh) elegante; **a smart restaurant** un restaurante elegante; **2** (clever) inteligente.

smash verb romper [40]; **they smashed the window** rompieron la ventana.

smashing adjective fantástico/ fantástica.

smell noun olor Masc.; **a nasty smell** un mal olor; **there's a smell of burning** huele a quemado.

smell verb 1 oler [39]; **I can't smell anything** no huelo nada; **I can smell lavender** huele a lavanda; **2** (smell bad) oler [39] mal; **the drains smell** las alcantarillas huelen mal.

smelly adjective apestoso/ apestosa.

smile noun sonrisa Fem.

smile verb sonreír [61].

smoke noun humo Masc.

smoke verb fumar [17]; **she doesn't smoke** no fuma; **he smokes a pipe** fuma en pipa.

smoked adjective ahumado/ ahumada; **smoked salmon** salmón ahumado.

smoker noun fumador Masc., fumadora Fem.

smoking noun 'no smoking' 'prohibido fumar'; **to give up smoking** dejar [17] de fumar.

smooth adjective 1 (stone or surface) liso/lisa; **a smooth surface** una superficie lisa; **2** (skin) suave.

SMS noun SMS Masc.; **an SMS message** un mensaje SMS.

smuggle verb **to smuggle something** pasar [17] algo de contrabando.

smuggler noun 1 contrabandista Masc./Fem.; **2 a drugs smuggler** un/una traficante de drogas.

smuggling noun 1 contrabando Masc.; **2 drugs smuggling** tráfico Masc. de drogas; **arms smuggling** tráfico Masc. de armas.

snack noun tentempié Masc.

snack bar noun cafetería Fem., bocatería Fem.

snail noun caracol Masc.

snake noun serpiente Fem.

snap verb 1 (break) romperse [40]; **2 to snap your fingers** chasquear [17] los dedos.

snatch verb 1 arrebatar [17]; **to snatch something from somebody** arrebatar algo a alguien; **he snatched my book** me arrebató el libro; **2** (steal) robar [17]; **she had her bag snatched** le robaron el bolso.

sneak verb **to sneak in** entrar [17] a escondidas; **to sneak out** salir [63] a escondidas; **he sneaked up on me** se acercó a mí sin que yo me diese cuenta.

sneeze noun estornudo Masc.

sneeze verb estornudar [17].

sniff verb olisquear [17].

snob noun esnob Masc./Fem.

snobbery noun esnobismo Masc.

snooker noun snooker Masc.; **to play snooker** jugar [27] al snooker.

snore verb roncar [31].

snow noun nieve Fem.

snow verb nevar [29]; **it's snowing** está nevando; **it's going to snow** va a nevar.

snowball noun bola Fem. de nieve.

snow drift noun montón Masc. de nieve.

snowman noun muñeco Masc. de nieve.

snowy adjective it was very snowy hubo mucha nieve.

so conjunction, adverb **1** tan; he's so lazy es tan vago; the coffee's so hot I can't drink it este café está tan caliente que no puedo beberlo; **2** not so no tan; our house is like yours, but not so big nuestra casa es parecida a la tuya pero no tan grande; **3** so much (after a verb) tanto; I hate it so much! ¡lo odio tanto!; **4** so much (before a noun) tanto/tanta; I have so much work to do tengo tanto trabajo que hacer; **5** so many (before a noun) tantos/tantas; we've got so many problems tenemos tantos problemas; **6** (therefore) así que; he got up late so he missed his train se levantó tarde así que perdió el tren; **7** (starting a sentence: there is no direct translation) so what's your name? ¿y cómo te llamas?; so what shall we do? ¿y entonces qué hacemos?; so what? ¿y qué?; **8** so do I, so did I yo también; 'I live in Leeds' – 'so do I' 'vivo en Leeds' – 'yo también'; so am I, so was I yo también; so do we, so did we nosotros también; 'I have a headache' – 'so do I' 'me duele la cabeza' – 'a mí también'; 'I like Miró' – 'so do I' 'me gusta Miró' – 'a mí tambien'; **9** I think so creo que sí; I hope so espero que sí.

soap noun **1** jabón Masc.; a cake of soap una pastilla de jabón; **2** (soap opera: on TV) telenovela Fem.

soap powder noun jabón Masc. en polvo.

sober adjective to be sober estar [2] sobrio/sobria.

soccer noun fútbol Masc.; to play soccer jugar [27] al fútbol.

social adjective social.

socialism noun socialismo Masc.

socialist noun, socialista Masc./Fem.

socialist adjective socialista.

social security noun **1** asistencia Fem. social; to be on social security recibir [19] asistencia social; **2** the social security (the system) la seguridad social.

social worker noun asistente Masc./Fem. social; she's a social worker es asistente social.

society noun sociedad Fem.

sociology noun sociología Fem.

sock noun calcetín Masc.; a pair of socks un par de calcetines.

sofa noun sofá Masc.

sofa bed noun sofá-cama Masc.

soft adjective suave; ★ to have a soft spot for somebody tener [9] debilidad por alguien.

soft drink noun refresco Masc.

software noun software Masc.

soft toy noun muñeco Masc. de peluche.

soil noun tierra Fem.

solar energy noun energía Fem. solar.

son-in-law

soldier *noun* soldado *Masc./Fem.*

solicitor *noun* abogado *Masc.*, abogada *Fem.*; **she's a solicitor** es abogada.

solid *adjective* **1** macizo/maciza; **a table made of solid pine** una mesa de pino macizo; **a solid gold ring** un anillo de oro macizo; **solid silver** plata maciza; **2** (*not flimsy*) sólido/sólida; **a solid structure** una estructura sólida.

solo *noun* solo *Masc.*; **a guitar solo** un solo de guitarra.

solo *adjective, adverb* en solitario; **a solo album** un álbum en solitario; **to play solo** tocar [31] en solitario.

soloist *noun* solista *Masc./Fem.*

some *adjective, adverb* **1** (*with a singular noun*) un poco de; **would you like some butter?** ¿quieres un poco de mantequilla?; **may I have some salad?** ¿puedo tomar un poco de ensalada?; **can you lend me some money?** ¿puedes prestarme un poco de dinero?; **2** (*with a plural noun*) unos/unas; **I've bought some apples** he comprado unas manzanas; **we picked some flowers** cogimos unas flores; **3** (*referring to something that has already been mentioned, 'some' is not translated*) **'would you like butter?' – 'thanks, I've got some'** '¿quieres mantequilla?' – 'gracias ya tengo'; **he's eaten some of it** ya ha comido un poco; **4** (*certain*) algunos/algunas; **some people think he's wrong** algunas

personas piensan que él no tiene razón; **5 some day** algún día.

somebody, someone *pronoun* alguien; **there's somebody in the garden** hay alguien en el jardín.

somehow *adverb* **1** de alguna forma; **I've got to finish this essay somehow** tengo que terminar esta composición de alguna forma; **2 I somehow think they won't come** no sé por qué, pero creo que no van a venir.

somersault *noun* voltereta *Fem.*

something *pronoun* algo; **I've got something to tell you** tengo algo que decirte; **something pretty** algo bonito; **something interesting** algo interesante; **there's something wrong** algo va mal; **their house is really something!** ¡su casa es increíble!; **a guy called Colin something or other** un tipo llamado Colin, o algo así.

sometime *adverb* un día de estos; **give me a ring sometime** llámame un día de estos; **I'll ring you sometime next week** te llamaré un día de la semana que viene.

sometimes *adverb* a veces; **I sometimes take the train** a veces cojo el tren.

somewhere *adverb* en algún sitio; **I've put my bag down somewhere** he puesto mi bolso en algún sitio; **I've met you somewhere before** te he conocido antes en algún sitio.

son *noun* hijo *Masc.*

song *noun* canción *Fem.*

son-in-law *noun* yerno *Masc.*

a
b
c
d
e
f
g
h
i
j
k
l
m
n
o
p
q
r
s
t
u
v
w
x
y
z

soon *adverb* **1** pronto; **it will soon be the holidays** pronto llegarán las vacaciones; **see you soon!** ¡hasta pronto!; **it's too soon** es demasiado pronto; **2 as soon as** tan pronto como; **as soon as she arrives** tan pronto como llegue; **as soon as possible** tan pronto como sea posible.

sooner *adverb* **1** antes; **we should have started sooner** deberíamos haber empezado antes; **2 I'd sooner wait** prefiero esperar; ★ **sooner or later** tarde o temprano.

soprano *noun* soprano *Masc./Fem.*

sore *noun* llaga *Fem.*

sore *adjective* **he has a sore leg** le duele la pierna; **my arm's sore** me duele el brazo; ★ **it's a sore point** es un tema delicado.

sorry *adjective* **1 I'm really sorry** lo siento mucho; **I'm sorry I forgot your birthday** siento haberme olvidado de tu cumpleaños; **2 sorry to disturb you** perdona que te moleste; **3 sorry!** ¡perdón!; **4 sorry?** ¿cómo?; **5 to feel sorry for somebody** compadecer [35] a alguien; **6 to say you're sorry** pedir [57] perdón.

sort *noun* tipo *Masc.*; **what sort of music do you like?** ¿qué tipo de música te gusta?; **all sorts of** todo tipo de; **for all sorts of reasons** por todo tipo de razones.

● **to sort something out
1** ordenar [17] algo (*room, desk, papers, possessions*); **I must sort out my room tonight** tengo que ordenar mi habitación esta noche;

2 solucionar [17] (*problem, arrangement*); **Liz is sorting it out** Liz se está ocupando de ello.

soul *noun* alma *Fem.* (*even though 'alma' is feminine, it takes 'el' and 'un' in the singular*) **the soul** el alma; **2** (*music*) soul *Masc.*

sound *noun* **1** (*noise*) ruido *Masc.*; **the sound of voices** el ruido de voces; **2** (*volume*) volumen *Masc.*; **to turn down the sound** bajar el volumen.

sound *verb* **it sounds easy** parece fácil; **it sounds as if she's happy** parece que está contenta.

sound asleep *adjective* profundamente dormido/dormida.

sound effect *noun* efecto *Masc.* sonoro.

soundtrack *noun* banda *Fem.* sonora.

soup *noun* **1** (*clear*) consomé *Masc.*; **2** (*thick*) sopa *Fem.*; **3** (*pureed*) crema *Fem.*; **mushroom soup** crema de champiñones.

soup plate *noun* plato *Masc.* de sopa.

soup spoon *noun* cuchara *Fem.* de sopera.

sour *adjective* **1** (*taste*) agrio/agria; **2 the milk's gone sour** la leche se ha cortado.

south *noun* sur *Masc.*; **in the south** en el sur.

south *adjective, adverb* sur (*never changes*); **the south side** la parte sur; **a south wind** un viento del sur; **south of Paris** al sur de París.

South Africa *noun* Sudáfrica *Fem.*

South America *noun* Sudamérica *Fem.*

South American *noun* suramericano *Masc.*, suramericana *Fem.*

South American *adjective* suramericano/suramericana.

southeast *noun* sureste *Masc.*

southeast *adjective* sureste (*never changes*); **in southeast England** en el sureste de Inglaterra.

South Pole *noun* Polo *Masc.* Sur.

southwest *noun* suroeste *Masc.*

southwest *adjective* suroeste (*never changes*); **in southwest England** en el suroeste de Inglaterra.

souvenir *noun* recuerdo *Masc.*

soya *noun* soja *Fem.*

space *noun* **1** (*room*) sitio *Masc.*; **is there enough space?** ¿hay sitio suficiente?; **there's enough space for two** hay sitio suficiente para dos; **2** (*gap*) espacio *Masc.*; **leave a space** deja un espacio; **3** (*outer space*) espacio *Masc.*; **in space** en el espacio.

spacecraft *noun* nave *Fem.* espacial.

spade *noun* **1** pala *Fem.*; **2** (*in cards*) pica *Fem.*; **the queen of spades** la reina de picas.

spaghetti *noun* espaguetis *Masc. plural.*

Spain *noun* España *Fem.*

Spaniard *noun* español *Masc.*, española *Fem.*

spaniel *noun* spaniel *Masc.*

Spanish *noun* **1** (*language*) español *Masc.*; **to speak Spanish** hablar [17] español; **say it in Spanish** dilo en español; **I'm learning Spanish** estoy aprendiendo español; **2 the Spanish** (*people*) los españoles *Masc. plural.*

Spanish *adjective* **1** español/ española; **Pedro's Spanish** Pedro es español; **2** de español (*a teacher or lesson*); **the Spanish class** la clase de español.

spanner *noun* llave *Fem.* inglesa.

spare *adjective* **1** (*part, battery*) de repuesto; **a spare battery** una batería de repuesto; **2** (*extra*) de más; **we have a spare ticket** tenemos una entrada de más.

spare *verb* **I can't spare the time** no tengo tiempo para eso; **can you spare a moment?** ¿tienes un momento libre?; **I don't have any money to spare** no me sobra el dinero.

spare room *noun* habitación *Fem.* de invitados.

spare time *noun* tiempo *Masc.* libre; **in my spare time** en mi tiempo libre.

spare wheel *noun* rueda *Fem.* de repuesto.

sparrow *noun* gorrión *Masc.*

speak *verb* **1** hablar [17]; **do you speak Spanish?** ¿hablas español?; **spoken Spanish** el español hablado; **'Spanish spoken here'** 'aquí se habla español'; **2 to speak to somebody** hablar [17] con alguien; **she's speaking to Mike**

a
b
c
d
e
f
g
h
i
j
k
l
m
n
o
p
q
r
s
t
u
v
w
x
y
z

a

b

c

d

e

f

g

h

i

j

k

l

m

n

o

p

q

r

s

t

u

v

w

x

y

z

está hablando con Mike; **I've never spoken to her** nunca he hablado con ella; **I'll speak to him about it** hablaré sobre ello con él; **3 who's speaking?** (on the phone) ¿quién es?; **Mike speaking** soy Mike.

speaker noun **1** (on a music system) altavoz Masc.; **2** (at a public lecture) conferenciante Masc./Fem.; **3** (of a language) **a Spanish speaker** un hablante de español; **an English speaker** un hablante de inglés.

spear noun lanza Fem.

special adjective especial.

specialist noun especialista Masc./Fem.

specialize verb **to specialize in** especializarse [22] en.

specially adverb especialmente; **not specially** no especialmente; **the poems have been specially chosen for small children** los poemas han sido escogidos especialmente para niños pequeños; **I came specially in order to see you** vine especialmente para verte.

spectacles noun gafas Fem. plural.

spectacular adjective espectacular.

spectator noun espectador Masc., espectadora Fem.

speech noun discurso Masc.; **to make a speech** dar [4] un discurso.

speechless adjective **1** sin habla; **I was speechless** me quedé sin

habla; **2 to be speechless with rage** quedarse [17] mudo de cólera.

speed noun velocidad Fem.; **what speed was he doing?** ¿a qué velocidad iba?; **a twelve-speed bike** una bici de doce marchas.

● **to speed up** acelerar [17].

speeding noun **he was fined for speeding** le multaron por exceso de velocidad.

speed limit noun límite Masc. de velocidad.

spell noun **1** (of time) periodo Masc.; **2** (talking about weather) **a cold spell** una ola de frío; **sunny spells** intervalos de sol.

spell verb **1** (in writing) escribir [52]; **how do you spell it?** ¿cómo se escribe?; **how do you spell your surname?** ¿cómo se escribe tu apellido?; **2** (out loud) deletrear [17]; **shall I spell it for you?** ¿se lo deletreo?

spelling noun ortografía Fem.; **a spelling mistake** una falta de ortografía.

spelling checker noun corrector Masc. ortográfico.

spend verb **1** gastar [17] (money); **I've spent all my money** me he gastado todo el dinero; **2** pasar [17] (time); **we spent three days in Barcelona** pasamos tres días en Barcelona; **she spends her time writing letters** pasa el tiempo escribiendo cartas.

spice noun especia Fem.

spicy adjective picante; **I don't like spicy food** no me gustan los platos picantes.

sports bag

spider noun araña Fem.

spill verb derramar [17]; **I've spilled my wine on the carpet** he derramado vino en la alfombra.

spinach noun espinacas Fem. plural; **do you like spinach?** ¿te gustan las espinacas?

spire noun aguja Fem.

spirit noun 1 (energy) brío Masc.; 2 **to get into the spirit of the occasion** entrar [17] en el ambiente.

spirits noun 1 (alcohol) bebidas Fem. plural alcohólicas; 2 **to be in good spirits** estar [2] de buen humor.

spit verb escupir [19]; **to spit something out** escupir algo.

spite noun 1 **in spite of** a pesar de; **we decided to go in spite of the rain** decidimos ir a pesar de la lluvia; 2 (nastiness) maldad Fem.; **to do something out of spite** hacer [7] algo por maldad.

spiteful adjective 1 (person) malo/mala; 2 (comment) malicioso/maliciosa.

splash noun 1 (noise) **we heard a splash** oímos el ruido de algo que caía al agua; 2 **a splash of colour** un toque de color.

splash verb salpicar [31].

splendid adjective espléndido/espléndida.

splinter noun astilla Fem.

split verb 1 (with an axe or a knife) partir [19]; **to split a piece of wood** partir un trozo de madera; 2 (come apart) rajarse [17]; **the lining has split** el forro se ha

rajado; 3 (divide up) dividirse [19]; **they split the money between them** se dividieron el dinero entre ellos.

● **to split up** 1 (a married couple or group) separarse [17]; 2 **she's split up with her boyfriend** ha roto con su novio.

spoil verb 1 arruinar [17]; **it completely spoiled the evening** arruinó la tarde completamente; **to spoil the surprise** arruinar la sorpresa; 2 malcriar [32] (a child).

spoiled adjective malcriado/malcriada; **a spoiled child** un niño malcriado.

spoilsport noun aguafiestas Masc./Fem. (does not change in the plural).

spokesperson noun portavoz Masc./Fem.

sponge noun esponja Fem.

sponge cake noun bizcocho Masc.

sponsor noun patrocinador Masc., patrocinadora Fem.

sponsor verb patrocinar [17].

spooky adjective espeluznante.

spoon noun cuchara Fem.; **a soup spoon** una cuchara sopera; **a teaspoon** una cucharilla.

spoonful noun (large) cucharada Fem.; (small) cucharadita Fem.

sport noun deporte Masc.; **to be good at sport** tener [9] facilidad para los deportes; **my favourite sport** mi deporte favorito.

sports bag noun bolsa Fem. de deportes.

a
b
c
d
e
f
g
h
i
j
k
l
m
n
o
p
q
r
s
t
u
v
w
x
y
z

a **sports car** noun coche Masc.
deportivo.

b **sports centre** noun
polideportivo Masc.

c **sports club** noun club Masc.
deportivo.

d **sportsman** noun deportista Masc.

e **sportswear** noun ropa Fem. de
deporte.

f **sportswoman** noun deportista
Fem.

g **spot** noun 1 (in fabric) lunar Masc.;
a red tie with black spots una
corbata roja con lunares negros;
2 (on your skin) grano Masc.; **I've
got spots** tengo granos; **to be
covered in spots** estar [2] cubierto
de granos; 3 (stain) mancha Fem.;
4 (place) sitio Masc.; **a beautiful
spot** un sitio precioso; 5 (spotlight)
foco Masc.; (in the home) luz Fem.
direccional.

spot verb 1 divisar [17] (a person or
object); **I spotted her in the crowd**
la divisé entre la multitud;
2 encontrar [24] (an error).

spotlight noun 1 foco Masc.; 2 (in
the home) luz Fem. direccional.

spotty adjective (pimply) lleno de
granos/llena de granos.

sprain noun esguince Masc.

sprain verb **to sprain your ankle**
hacerse [7] un esguince en el
tobillo.

spray noun (spray can) espray
Masc.

spread verb 1 (news or a disease)
propagarse [28]; 2 extender [36]
(butter, jam, cement, glue, etc).

spring noun 1 (the season)
primavera Fem.; **in the spring** en
primavera; **spring flowers** flores
de primavera; 2 (made of metal)
muelle Masc.; 3 (providing water)
manantial Masc.

springtime noun primavera Fem.;
in springtime en primavera.

spring water noun agua Fem. de
manantial.

sprint noun esprint Masc.

sprint verb correr [18] a toda
velocidad.

sprout noun (Brussels sprout) col
Fem. de Bruselas.

spy noun espía Masc./Fem.

spy verb **to spy on somebody**
espiar [32] a alguien.

spying noun espionaje Masc.

square noun 1 (shape) cuadrado
Masc.; 2 (in a town or village) plaza
Fem.; **the village square** la plaza
del pueblo; ★ **to go back to square
one** volver [45] a empezar de cero.

square adjective cuadrado/
cuadrada; **a square box** una caja
cuadrada; **three square metres**
tres metros cuadrados; **the room
is four metres square** la
habitación tiene cuatro metros
cuadrados.

squash noun 1 (drink) **lemon
squash** limonada Fem.; **orange
squash** naranjada Fem.; 2 (sport)
squash Masc.; **to play squash** jugar
[27] al squash.

squeak verb 1 (door, hinge)
chirriar [32]; 2 (person, animal)
chillar [17].

squeeze verb **1** apretar [29] (*somebody's arm, hand or a toothpaste tube*); **2** exprimir [19] (*a lemon or an orange*).

squid noun calamar Masc.

squirrel noun ardilla Fem.

stab verb apuñalar [17].

stable noun cuadra Fem.

stable adjective estable.

stack noun **1** (*pile*) montón Masc.; **2 stacks** of montones de; **she's got stacks of CDs** tiene montones de compactos.

stadium noun estadio Masc.

staff noun **1** (*of a company*) personal Masc.; **2** (*in a school*) profesorado Masc.

stage noun **1** (*for a performance*) escenario Masc.; **on stage** en el escenario; **2** (*phase*) etapa Fem.; **the earlier stages of the project** las primeras etapas del proyecto; **3 at this stage it's hard to know** a estas alturas es difícil saberlo.

stain noun mancha Fem.

stain verb manchar [17].

stainless steel noun acero Masc. inoxidable; **a stainless steel sink** un fregadero de acero inoxidable.

stair noun **1** (*step*) escalón Masc.; **2 stairs** escaleras Fem. plural; **I met her on the stairs** me la encontré en las escaleras.

staircase noun escaleras Fem. plural.

stale adjective (*bread*) correoso/correosa.

stalemate noun (*in chess*) tablas Fem. plural.

stall noun **1** (*at a market or fair*) puesto Masc.; **2 the stalls** (*in a theatre*) patio Masc. de butacas.

stamp noun sello Masc.

stamp verb **1** poner [11] sello(s) a (*a letter*); **2 to stamp your foot** dar [4] una patada en el suelo.

stamp album noun álbum Masc. de sellos.

stamp collection noun colección Fem. de sellos.

stand verb **1** estar [2] de pie; **several people were standing** varias personas estaban de pie; **2** (*when you say somebody is standing somewhere, 'standing' is not usually translated*) **we were standing outside the cinema** estábamos delante del cine; **I'm standing here waiting for you** estoy aquí esperándote; **3 to stand on something** pisar [17] algo; **4** (*bear*) soportar [17]; **I can't stand her** no la soporto; **I can't stand waiting** no soporto esperar.

● **to stand for something** (*be short for*) significar [31]; **what does 'plc' stand for?** ¿qué significa 'plc'?.

● **stand up** levantarse [17]; **everybody stood up** todo el mundo se levantó.

standard noun nivel Masc.; **the standard of living** el nivel de vida.

standard adjective estándar; **the standard price** el precio estándar.

Standard grades noun plural (*You can explain Standard grades as follows: Son exámenes que se realizan alrededor de los 16 años y pueden abarcar hasta 7*

a
b
c
d
e
f
g
h
i
j
k
l
m
n
o
p
q
r
s
t
u
v
w
x
y
z

asignaturas. *Se califican desde 1 (nota máxima) hasta 7 (por haber terminado el curso). Muchos alumnos continúan estudiando para los Highers y Advanced Highers después de hacer los Standard grades.)* SEE **Highers.**

stands noun *(in a stadium)* tribuna *Fem.*

staple noun grapa *Fem.*

staple verb grapar [17]; **to staple the pages together** grapar las hojas.

stapler noun grapadora *Fem.*

star noun *(in the sky or rock star, etc)* estrella *Fem.*; **he's a film star** es una estrella de cine.

star verb **to star in a film** protagonizar [22] una película.

stare verb mirar [17] fijamente; **he was staring at me** me estaba mirando fijamente; **what are you staring at?** ¿qué miras?

star sign noun signo *Masc.* del zodíaco; **what star sign are you?** ¿de qué signo eres?

start noun **1** principio *Masc.*; **at the start** al principio; **at the start of the book** al principio del libro; **from the start** desde el principio; **we knew from the start that it was dangerous** sabíamos desde el principio que era peligroso; **2 to make a start on something** empezar [25] algo; **I've made a start on my homework** he empezado mis deberes; **3** *(of a race)* salida *Fem.*

start verb **1** empezar [25]; **the film starts at eight** la película empieza a las ocho; **I've started the book**

he empezado el libro; **2 to start doing** empezar [25] a hacer; **I've started learning Spanish** he empezado a aprender español; **3 to start a business** montar [17] un negocio; **4 to start a car** arrancar [31] un coche; **she started the car** arrancó el coche; **the car wouldn't start** el coche no arrancaba.

starter noun *(in a meal)* entrante *Masc.*; **what would you like as a starter?** ¿qué quieres de entrante?

starve verb morirse [55] de hambre; **I'm starving!** ¡me muero de hambre!

state noun **1** estado *Masc.*; **the house is in a very bad state** la casa está en muy mal estado; **2** *(administrative)* estado *Masc.*; **the state** el estado; **3 the States** (los) Estados Unidos; **they live in the States** viven en Estados Unidos.

state verb **1** declarar [17] *(intention, opinion)*; **2** indicar [31] *(address, income, occupation, reason, etc)*.

statement noun declaración *Fem.*

station noun **1** estación *Fem.*; **the railway station** la estación de trenes; **the bus station** la estación de autobuses; **2 the police station** la comisaría; **3 a radio station** una emisora de radio; **a TV station** un canal de televisión.

stationary adjective estacionario/estacionaria.

stationer's noun papelería *Fem.*

stationery noun artículos *Masc. plural* de papelería.

statistics *noun* **1** (*subject*) estadística *Fem.*; **2 the statistics** (*figures*) las estadísticas.

statue *noun* estatua *Fem.*

status *noun* estatus *Masc.*

stay *noun* estancia *Fem.*; **our stay in Paris** nuestra estancia en París; **enjoy your stay!** ¡que disfruten de su estancia!

stay *verb* **1** quedarse [17]; **I'll stay here** me quedaré aquí; **how long are you staying?** ¿cuánto tiempo te quedas?; **2** (*with time*) **we're going to stay in Berlin for three days** vamos a pasar tres días en Berlín; **3** (*at somebody's house*) **to stay with somebody** quedarse [17] con alguien; **I'm going to stay with my sister this weekend** me voy a quedar con mi hermana este fin de semana; **4** (*be temporarily lodged*) hospedarse [17]; **where are you staying?** ¿dónde te hospedas?

● **to stay in** no salir [63]; **I'm staying in tonight** esta noche no salgo.

steady *adjective* **1** estable; **a steady job** un trabajo estable; **2** constante; **a steady increase** un incremento constante; **3** (*hand, voice*) firme; **4 to hold something steady** sostener [9] algo firmemente.

steak *noun* filete *Masc.*; **steak and chips** filete con patatas fritas.

steal *verb* robar [17].

steam *noun* vapor *Masc.*

steam engine *noun* locomotora *Fem.* de vapor.

steam iron *noun* plancha *Fem.* a vapor.

steel *noun* acero *Masc.*

steep *adjective* empinado/empinada; **a steep slope** una cuesta empinada.

steeple *noun* **1** (*spire*) aguja *Fem.*; **2** (*bell tower*) campanario *Masc.*

steering wheel *noun* volante *Masc.*

step *noun* **1** paso *Masc.*; **to take a step forwards** dar [4] un paso hacia adelante; **2** (*stair*) escalón *Masc.*; **'mind the step'** 'cuidado con el escalón'.

● **to step back** retroceder [18].

● **to step forward** avanzar [22].

● **to step into** entrar [17] en (*a lift*).

stepbrother *noun* hermanastro *Masc.*

stepdaughter *noun* hijastra *Fem.*

stepfather *noun* padrastro *Masc.*

stepladder *noun* escalera *Fem.* de mano.

stepmother *noun* madrastra *Fem.*

stepsister *noun* hermanastra *Fem.*

stepson *noun* hijastro *Masc.*

stereo *noun* estéreo *Masc.*

sterling *noun* libra *Fem.* esterlina; **in sterling** en libras esterlinas.

stew *noun* estofado *Masc.*

steward *noun* camarero *Masc.*

stewardess *noun* camarera *Fem.*

stick *noun* **1** palo *Masc.*; **2 a walking stick** un bastón; **3 a hockey stick** un palo de hockey.

a b c d e f g h i j k l m n o p q r s t u v w x y z

a

stick *verb* **1** *(with glue)* pegar [28];
2 *(put)* poner [11]; **stick them on
my desk** ponlos en mi mesa.

b

sticker *noun* pegatina *Fem.*

c

sticky *adjective* **1** pegajoso/
pegajosa; **my hands are sticky**
tengo las manos pegajosas;
2 adhesivo/adhesiva; **sticky paper**
papel *Masc.* adhesivo.

d

e

f

sticky tape *noun* cinta *Fem.*
adhesiva.

g

stiff *adjective* **to feel stiff** estar [2]
entumecido; **to have stiff legs**
tener [9] las piernas entumecidas;
to have a stiff neck tener [9]
torticolis; ★ **to be bored stiff** estar
más aburrido que una ostra
(*literally: to be more bored than an
oyster*); ★ **to be scared stiff** estar
muerto de miedo (*literally: to be
dead from fear*).

h

i

j

k

l

m

still *adjective* **1** quieto/quieta; **sit
still!** ¡siéntate quieto!; **keep still!**
¡estate quieto!; **2 still mineral
water** agua *Fem.* mineral sin gas.

n

o

still *adverb* **1** todavía, aún; **do you
still live in London?** ¿vives todavía
en Londres?, ¿vives aún en
Londres?; **I've still not finished**
todavía no he terminado, aún no
he terminado; **he's still working**
está trabajando todavía; **there's
still a lot of beer left** todavía
queda mucha cerveza; **2 better
still** todavía mejor, aún mejor.

p

q

r

s

t

u

sting *noun* aguijón *Masc.*; **a wasp
sting** un aguijón de avispa.

v

w

sting *verb* picar [31]; **I was stung
by a bee** me picó una abeja.

x

y

stink *noun* peste *Fem.*; **what a
stink!** ¡qué peste!

z

stink *verb* apestar [17]; **it stinks of
cigarette smoke in here** aquí
apesta a tabaco.

stir *verb* remover [38].

stitch *noun* **1** *(in sewing)* puntada
Fem.; **2** *(in knitting)* punto *Masc.*;
3 *(surgical)* punto *Masc.* de sutura.

stock *noun* **1** *(in a shop)* estock
Masc.; **to have something in stock**
tener [9] algo en estock; **2** *(supply)*
reserva *Fem.*; **I always have a
stock of pencils** siempre tengo
una reserva de lápices; **3** *(for
cooking)* caldo *Masc.*; **chicken
stock** caldo de pollo.

stock *verb* *(in a shop)* vender [18];
they don't stock dictionaries no
venden diccionarios.

stock cube *noun* pastilla *Fem.* de
caldo.

stock exchange *noun* bolsa
Fem. de valores.

stocking *noun* media *Fem.* (de
liguero).

stomach *noun* estómago *Masc.*

stomachache *noun* dolor *Masc.*
de estómago; **to have
stomachache** tener [9] dolor de
estómago.

stone *noun* **1** piedra *Fem.*; **a stone
wall** una pared de piedra; **to throw
a stone** tirar [17] una piedra; **2** *(in
fruit)* hueso *Masc.*

stool *noun* taburete *Masc.*

stop *noun* parada *Fem.*; **the bus
stop** la parada del autobús.

stop *verb* **1** *(person or vehicle)*
parar [17]; **he stopped in front of
the shop** paró enfrente de la
tienda; **does the train stop in**

Cordoba? ¿para el tren en Córdoba?; **the music stopped** la música paró; **2** (engine or machine) pararse [17]; **3 to stop something/ somebody** parar [17] algo/a alguien; **she stopped me in the street** me paró en la calle; **4 to stop doing** dejar [17] de hacer; **he's stopped smoking** ha dejado de fumar; **she never stops asking questions** nunca deja de hacer preguntas; **5 to stop somebody doing** impedir [57] a alguien hacer; **there's nothing to stop you going on your own** nada te impide ir solo.

stopwatch noun cronómetro Masc.

store noun (shop) tienda Fem.

store verb **1** guardar [17]; **2** (on a computer) almacenar [17].

storey noun piso Masc.; **a three-storey house** una casa de tres pisos.

stork noun cigüeña Fem.

storm noun tormenta Fem.; **a snowstorm** una tormenta de nieve; **a rainstorm** una tormenta de lluvia.

stormy adjective de tormenta.

story noun **1** historia Fem.; **to tell a story** contar [24] una historia; **2** (tale) cuento Masc.

stove noun (cooker) cocina Fem.

straight adjective **1** recto/recta; **a straight line** una línea recta; **2 to have straight hair** tener [9] el pelo liso; **3** (not crooked) derecho/derecha; **the candle's not straight** la vela no está derecha.

straight adverb **1** (in direction) recto; **go straight ahead** sigue todo recto; **2** (in time) directamente; **he went straight to the doctor's** fue directamente al médico; **3 straight away** en seguida.

strain verb **1** colar [17] (vegetables, rice); **2** hacerse [7] un esguince en (a muscle).

strain noun tensión Fem.

strange adjective extraño/extraña; **a strange situation** una situación extraña.

stranger noun desconocido Masc., desconocida Fem.

strangle verb estrangular [17].

strap noun **1** (on camera or watch) correa Fem.; **a watchstrap** una correa de reloj; **2** (on case or bag) asa Fem.; **3** (on a garment) tirante Masc.; **4** (on a shoe) tira Fem.

straw noun paja Fem. (both the material and for drinking with); **a straw hat** un sombrero de paja.

strawberry noun fresa Fem.; **strawberry jam** mermelada de fresa.

stream noun (small river) arroyo Masc.

street noun calle Fem.; **I met Simon in the street** me encontré con Simon en la calle.

streetlamp noun farol Masc.

street map noun plano Masc. de la ciudad.

streetwise adjective avispado/avispada.

a b c d e f g h i j k l m n o p q r s t u v w x y z

a **strength** noun fuerza Fem.

stress noun 1 tensión Fem.; 2 (in a word) acento Fem.

b **stress** verb (emphasize) recalcar [31]; **to stress the importance of something** recalcar la importancia de algo.

c

d **stretch** verb (garment or shoes) dar [4] de sí; **this jumper has stretched** este jersey ha dado de sí.

e

f **strict** adjective estricto/estricta.

g **strike** noun huelga Fem.; **to go on strike** ponerse [11] en huelga; **to be on strike** estar [2] en huelga.

h

strike verb 1 (hit) golpear [17] (a person); 2 (clock) dar [4]; **the clock struck six** el reloj dio las seis; 3 (go on strike) ponerse [11] en huelga.

i

j

k **striker** noun 1 (in football) delantero Masc., delantera Fem.; 2 (person on strike) huelguista Masc./Fem.

l

m **string** noun 1 (for tying) cordel Masc.; 2 (for a musical instrument) cuerda Fem.

n

o **strip** noun tira Fem.

p **strip** verb (undress) desnudarse [17].

q **strip cartoon** noun tira Fem. cómica.

r **stripe** noun raya Fem.

s **striped** adjective de rayas.

t **stroke** noun 1 (in swimming) brazada Fem.; 2 (medical) derrame Masc. cerebral; **to have a stroke** sufrir [19] un derrame cerebral; ★ **a stroke of luck** un golpe de suerte.

u

v

w

x **stroke** verb acariciar [17].

y

z

strong adjective 1 (person, drink, smell, taste, or feeling) fuerte; 2 (material) resistente; 3 (accent) marcado.

struggle noun 1 lucha Fem.; **the struggle for independence** la lucha por la independencia; **a power struggle** una lucha por el poder; 2 **it's been a struggle** ha sido muy difícil.

struggle verb 1 (to obtain something) luchar [17]; **they have struggled to survive** han luchado para sobrevivir; 2 (physically, in order to escape or get something) forcejear [17]; 3 (have difficulty in doing) **I'm struggling to finish my homework** me está costando terminar mis deberes.

stubborn adjective terco/terca.

stuck adjective (jammed) atascado/atascada; **the drawer's stuck** el cajón está atascado.

stud noun 1 (on a belt or jacket) tachuela Fem.; 2 (on a boot) taco Masc.; 3 (earring) pendiente Masc. de bolita.

student noun estudiante Masc./Fem.

studio noun estudio Masc.

studio flat noun estudio Masc.

study verb estudiar [17]; **he's busy studying for his exams** está muy ocupado estudiando para los exámenes; **she's studying medicine** estudia medicina.

stuff noun 1 (things) cosas Fem. plural; **we can put all that stuff in the attic** podemos poner todas estas cosas en el ático; **you can leave your stuff at my house**

puedes dejar tus cosas en mi casa; **2** (*substance*) cosa *Fem*.

stuff *verb* **1** (*shove*) meter [18]; **she stuffed some things into a suitcase** metió algunas cosas en una maleta; **2** rellenar [17] (*chicken, turkey, vegetables*); **stuffed aubergines** berenjenas rellenas.

stuffing *noun* (*for cooking*) relleno *Masc*.

stuffy *adjective* (*amazed*) viciado/viciada; **it's very stuffy in here** aquí dentro falta aire.

stunned *adjective* (*amazed*) atónito/atónita.

stunning *adjective* sensacional.

stunt *noun* (*in a film*) escena *Fem*. peligrosa.

stupid *adjective* estúpido/ estúpida; **a stupid man** un hombre estúpido; **that was really stupid** eso fue una verdadera estupidez; **to do something stupid** hacer [7] una estupidez.

stutter *noun* **to have a stutter** tartamudear [17].

stutter *verb* tartamudear [17].

style *noun* **1** estilo *Masc*.; **a style of living** un estilo de vida; **he has his own style** tiene su propio estilo; **2** (*fashion*) moda *Fem*.; **it's the latest style** es la última moda.

subject *noun* **1** tema *Masc*.; **the subject of my talk** el tema de mi charla; **2** (*at school*) asignatura *Fem*.; **my favourite subject is biology** mi asignatura favorita es la biología.

submarine *noun* submarino *Masc*.

subscription *noun* suscripción *Fem*.; **to take out a subscription to** suscribirse [52] a.

subsidy *noun* subvención *Fem*.

substance *noun* sustancia *Fem*.

substitute *noun* (*person*) sustituto *Masc*., sustituta *Fem*.

substitute *verb* sustituir [54].

subtitled *adjective* (*film*) subtitulado/subtitulada.

subtitles *plural noun* subtítulos *Masc. plural*.

subtract *verb* restar [17].

suburb *noun* barrio *Masc*. residencial de las afueras; **a suburb of Edinburgh** un barrio residencial de las afueras de Edimburgo; **in the suburbs of London** en los barrios residenciales de las afueras de Londres.

subway *noun* (*underpass*) paso *Masc*. subterráneo.

succeed *verb* **1** lograr [17]; **to succeed in doing** lograr hacer; **we've succeeded in contacting her** hemos logrado contactar con ella; **2** (*be successful*) tener [9] éxito; **to succeed in business** tener éxito en los negocios.

success *noun* éxito *Masc*.; **a great success** un gran éxito.

successful *adjective* **1** de éxito; **he's a successful writer** es un escritor de éxito; **2** to **be successful in doing** lograr [17] hacer.

a b c d e f g h i j k l m n o p q r s t u v w x y z

successfully adverb
satisfactoriamente.

such adjective, adverb **1** tan;
they're such nice people! ¡son
gente tan agradable!; **I've had
such a busy day!** ¡he tenido un día
tan ocupado!; **it's such a long way**
está tan lejos; **it's such a pity** es
una verdadera lástima; **2 such a
lot of** tantos/tantas; **I've got such
a lot of things to tell you!** ¡tengo
tantas cosas que contarte!; **3 such
as** como; **in big cities such as
Glasgow** en ciudades grandes
como Glasgow; **4 there's no such
thing** eso no existe.

sudden adjective repentino/
repentina; ★ **all of a sudden** de
repente.

suddenly adverb de repente; **he
suddenly started to laugh** de
repente empezó a reír; **suddenly
the light went out** de repente se
apagó la luz; **to die suddenly**
morir [55] de repente.

suede noun ante Masc.; **a suede
jacket** una chaqueta de ante.

suffer verb sufrir [19].

sugar noun azúcar Masc. or Fem.;
would you like sugar? ¿quieres
azúcar?; **brown sugar** azúcar
morena.

suggest verb sugerir [14]; **he
suggested I should speak to you
about it** sugirió que hablase
contigo acerca de ello.

suggestion noun sugerencia
Fem.; **to make a suggestion** hacer
[7] una sugerencia.

suicide noun suicidio Masc.; **to
commit suicide** suicidarse [17].

suit noun **1** (man's) traje Masc.;
2 (woman's) traje Masc. de
chaqueta.

suitable adjective **1** adecuado/
adecuada; **a suitable hotel** un
hotel adecuado; **to be suitable for**
ser [1] adecuado para; **2** (clothing)
apropiado/apropiada; **I don't have
any suitable shoes** no tengo
zapatos apropiados.

suitcase noun maleta Fem.

sulk verb enfurruñarse [17].

sum noun **1** cantidad Fem.; **a sum
of money** una cantidad de dinero;
a large sum una cantidad grande;
2 (calculation) suma Fem.

● **to sum up** resumir [19].

summarize verb resumir [19].

summary noun resumen Masc.

summer noun verano Masc.; **in
summer** en verano; **summer
clothes** ropa Fem. de verano; **the
summer holidays** las vacaciones
de verano.

summertime noun verano Masc.;
in summertime en verano.

summit noun cumbre Fem.

sun noun sol Masc.; **in the sun** en el
sol.

sunbathe verb tomar [17] el sol.

sunblock noun filtro Masc. solar.

sunburn noun quemadura Fem.
solar.

sunburned adjective **1** (tanned)
moreno/morena; **2 to get
sunburned** (burned) quemarse
[17].

Sunday noun domingo Masc.; **on Sunday** el domingo; **I'm going out on Sunday** voy a salir el domingo; **see you on Sunday!** ¡hasta el domingo!; **on Sundays** los domingos; **the museum is closed on Sundays** el museo cierra los domingos; **every Sunday** todos los domingos; **last Sunday** el domingo pasado; **next Sunday** el próximo domingo.

sunflower noun girasol Masc.; **sunflower oil** aceite Masc. de girasol.

sunglasses plural noun gafas Fem. plural de sol.

sunlight noun luz Fem. del sol.

sunny adjective **1** it's a sunny day hace sol; **it's going to be sunny** va a hacer sol; **2** (place) soleado/soleada; **in a sunny corner of the garden** una esquina soleada del jardín.

sunrise noun salida Fem. del sol; **at sunrise** al amanecer.

sunroof noun techo Masc. solar.

sunset noun puesta Fem. de sol; **at sunset** al atardecer.

sunshine noun sol Masc.

sunstroke noun insolación Fem.; **to get sunstroke** coger [3] una insolación.

suntan noun bronceado Masc.; **to get a suntan** broncearse [17].

suntan lotion noun loción Fem. bronceadora.

suntan oil noun aceite Masc. bronceador.

super adjective genial; **we had a super time!** ¡lo pasamos genial!

supermarket noun supermercado Masc.

supernatural adjective supernatural.

superstitious adjective supersticioso/supersticiosa.

supervise verb supervisar [17].

supervisor noun supervisor Masc., supervisora Fem.

supper noun cena Fem.; **I had supper at Sandy's** cené en casa de Sandy.

supplement noun suplemento Masc.

supplies plural noun (of food) provisiones Fem. plural.

supply noun **1** (stock) reservas Fem. plural; **2 to be in short supply** escasear [17].

supply verb suministrar [17]; **the school supplies the paper** el colegio suministra el papel; **to supply somebody with something** suministrar algo a alguien.

supply teacher noun profesor Masc. suplente, profesora Fem. suplente.

support noun apoyo Masc.; **he has a lot of support** tiene mucho apoyo.

support verb **1** (back up) apoyar [17]; **her teachers have really supported her** sus profesoras la han apoyado mucho; **2** ser [1] hincha de (a team); **Graeme supports Liverpool** Graeme es hincha del Liverpool;

a
b
c
d
e
f
g
h
i
j
k
l
m
n
o
p
q
r

3 (*financially*) **to support a family**
mantener [9] una familia.

supporter *noun* hincha *Masc./
Fem.*; **an Arsenal supporter** un
hincha del Arsenal.

suppose *verb* suponer [11]; **I
suppose she's forgotten** supongo
que se ha olvidado.

supposed *adjective* **to be
supposed to do** tener [9] que;
**you're supposed to wear a
helmet** tienes que usar casco; **he
was supposed to be here at six**
tenía que estar aquí a las seis.

sure *adjective* **1** seguro/segura;
are you sure? ¿estás seguro?; **are
you sure you've had enough to
eat?** ¿seguro que has comido
suficiente?; **are you sure you saw
her?** ¿estás seguro de que la viste?;
2 **sure!** ¡claro!; **'can you shut the
door?' – 'sure!'** ¿puedes cerrar la
puerta?' – '¡por supuesto!'

surely *adverb* **surely she couldn't
have forgotten!** ¡no es posible que
se haya olvidado! (*note that 'que' is
followed by the subjunctive*).

surf *noun* rompiente *Masc.*

surf *verb* **1** (*in the sea*) hacer [7]
surfing; **2** (*on the Net*) navegar [28].

surface *noun* superficie *Fem.*

surfboard *noun* tabla *Fem.* de surf.

surfer *noun* **1** (*in the sea*) surfista
Masc./Fem.; **2** (*on the Net*)
internauta *Masc./Fem.*

surfing *noun* surfing *Masc.*; **to go
surfing** hacer [7] surfing.

surgeon *noun* cirujano *Masc.*,
cirujana *Fem.*; **she's a surgeon** es
cirujana.

surgery *noun* **1** (*treatment*)
cirugía *Fem.*; **laser surgery** cirugía
láser; **to have surgery** operarse
[17]; **2** (*doctor's*) consultorio *Masc.*;
the dentist's surgery la consulta
del dentista.

surname *noun* apellido *Masc.*

surprise *noun* sorpresa *Fem.*;
what a surprise! ¡qué sorpresa!

surprised *adjective* sorprendido/
sorprendida; **I was surprised to
see her** me sorprendió verla.

surprising *adjective*
sorprendente.

surrender *noun* rendición *Fem.*

surrender *verb* **1** (*to give up*)
rendirse [57]; **2** entregar [28] (*a
castle, town*).

surround *verb* **1** rodear [17]; **2 to
be surrounded by** estar [2]
rodeado de; **she's surrounded by
friends** está rodeada de amigos.

survive *verb* sobrevivir [19].

survivor *noun* superviviente
Masc./Fem.

suspect *noun* sospechoso *Masc.*,
sospechosa *Fem.*

suspect *adjective* sospechoso/
sospechosa.

suspect *verb* sospechar [17].

suspend *verb* **1** (*hang*) suspender
[18]; **2 to be suspended** (*from
school*) ser [1] expulsado.

suspense *noun* suspense *Masc.*

suspicious *adjective* sospechoso/
sospechosa; **to be suspicious of**
sospechar [17] de; **a suspicious**

t
u
v
w
x
y
z

parcel un paquete sospechoso; **a suspicious-looking individual** un individuo de apariencia sospechosa.

swallow noun (*bird*) golondrina *Fem.*

swallow verb tragar [28].

swamp noun pantano *Masc.*

swan noun cisne *Masc.*

swap verb **1** cambiar [17]; **do you want to swap?** ¿quieres que cambiemos?; **he's swapped his bike for a computer** ha cambiado su bici por un ordenador; **2 to swap seats with somebody** cambiarse [17] de sitio con alguien.

swear verb (*use bad language*) decir [5] palabrotas; **he swears a lot** dice muchas palabrotas.

swearword noun palabrota *Fem.*

sweat noun sudor *Masc.*

sweat verb sudar [17].

sweater noun suéter *Masc.*

sweatshirt noun sudadera *Fem.*

Swede noun sueco *Masc.*, sueca *Fem.*

Sweden noun Suecia *Fem.*

Swedish noun (*language*) sueco *Masc.*

Swedish adjective sueco/sueca.

sweep verb barrer [18].

sweet noun **1** caramelo *Masc.*; **I bought her some sweets** le he comprado unos caramelos; **2** (*dessert*) postre *Masc.*

sweet adjective **1** (*food or smile*) dulce; **I try not to eat sweet things** intento no comer cosas dulces; **2** (*kind*) encantador/encantadora; **she's a really sweet person** es

realmente encantadora; **it was really sweet of him** ha sido un detalle encantador; **3** (*cute*) rico/rica; **he looks really sweet in that hat!** ¡está muy rico con ese sombrero!

sweetcorn noun maíz *Masc.* tierno.

swelling noun hinchazón *Fem.*

swerve verb virar [17] bruscamente; **the car swerved to avoid the dog** el coche viró bruscamente para esquivar al perro.

swim noun **to go for a swim** ir [8] a nadar.

swim verb nadar [17]; **can he swim?** ¿sabe nadar?; **to swim across something** cruzar [22] algo a nado.

swimmer noun nadador *Masc.*, nadadora *Fem.*; **she's a strong swimmer** es muy buena nadadora.

swimming noun natación *Fem.*; **to go swimming** ir [8] a nadar.

swimming cap noun gorro *Masc.* de baño.

swimming pool noun piscina *Fem.*

swimming trunks noun bañador *Masc.*

swimsuit noun traje *Masc.* de baño.

swindle noun estafa *Fem.*; **what a swindle!** ¡qué estafa!

swing noun columpio *Masc.*

a
b
c
d
e
f
g
h
i
j
k
l
m
n
o
p
q
r
s
t
u
v
w
x
y
z

Tt

Swiss noun (person) suizo Masc., suiza Fem.; **the Swiss** los suizos.

Swiss adjective suizo/suiza.

switch noun interruptor Masc.

switch verb (change) cambiar [17]; **to switch places** cambiar de sitio.

● **to switch something off** apagar [28] algo.

● **to switch something on** encender [36] algo.

Switzerland noun Suiza Fem.

swollen adjective hinchado/hinchada.

swop verb SEE swap.

sword noun espada Fem.

swordfish noun pez Masc. espada.

syllabus noun programa Masc.; **to be on the syllabus** estar [2] en el programa.

sympathetic adjective comprensivo/comprensiva.

sympathize verb **to sympathize with somebody** compadecer [35] a alguien; **I sympathize with her** la compadezco.

sympathy noun compasión Fem.

symphony noun sinfonía Fem.

symphony orchestra noun orquesta Fem. sinfónica.

symptom noun síntoma Masc.

synagogue noun sinagoga Fem.

synthesizer noun sintetizador Masc.

synthetic adjective sintético/sintética.

syringe noun jeringa Fem.

system noun sistema Masc.

table noun mesa Fem.; **on the table** en la mesa; **to set the table** poner [11] la mesa; **to clear the table** quitar [17] la mesa.

tablecloth noun mantel Masc.

table football noun futbolín Masc.

table mat noun salvamanteles Masc. (doesn't change in the plural).

tablespoon noun cuchara Fem. de servir; (in recipes) **a tablespoon of flour** una cucharada grande de harina.

tablet noun pastilla Fem.

table tennis noun ping-pong Masc.; **to play table tennis** jugar [27] al ping-pong.

tackle noun **1** (in football) entrada Fem.; **2** (in rugby) placaje Masc.

tackle verb **1** (in football or hockey) entrarle [17] a; **2** abordar [17] (a job or problem).

tact noun tacto Masc.

tactful adjective diplomático/diplomática; **that wasn't very tactful** eso no ha sido muy diplomático.

tactic noun táctica Fem.

tadpole noun renacuajo Masc.

tail noun **1** (of dog, cat) rabo Masc.; **2** (of horse, fish, bird) cola Fem.; **3** '**heads or tails**?' – '**tails**' ¿cara o cruz?' – 'cruz'.

tailor noun sastre Masc.

take verb 1 coger [3]; **he took a chocolate** cogió un bombón; **take my hand** cógeme la mano; **I took the bus** cogí el autobús; **who's taken my keys?** ¿quién ha cogido mis llaves?; **to take a holiday** cogerse [3] unas vacaciones; 2 *(person or car)* llevar [17]; **I'm taking Jake to the doctor's** voy a llevar a Jake al médico; **I must take the car to the garage** debo llevar el coche al garaje *(carry away)* llevar [17]; **I'll take my camera with me** me llevaré la cámara; 4 **to take something up(stairs)** subir [19] algo; **could you take these towels up?** ¿puedes subir estas toallas?; 5 **to take something down(stairs)** bajar [17] algo; **Cheryl's taken the cups down** Cheryl ha bajado las tazas; 6 *(time: for a task or job)* llevar [17]; **it takes two hours** lleva dos horas; 7 *(food or medicine)* tomar [17]; **do you take sugar?** ¿tomas azúcar?; 8 aceptar [17] *(a credit card or a cheque)* **do you take cheques?** ¿aceptan cheques?; 9 hacer [7] *(an exam)*; **she's taking her driving test tomorrow** va a hacer el examen de conducir mañana; 10 **what size do you take?** ¿qué talla usas?

● **to take something apart** desmontar [17] algo.

● **to take something back** devolver [45] algo.

● **to take off 1** *(a plane)* despegar [28]; 2 quitarse [17] *(clothes or shoes)*; **he took off his shirt** se quitó la camisa; 3 rebajar [17] *(money)*; **he took five pounds off the price** rebajó cinco libras del precio.

● **to take out 1** *(from a bag or pocket)* sacar [31]; **Eric took out his wallet** Eric sacó su cartera; 2 **he's taking me out to lunch** me ha invitado a comer fuera; **she took me out to the theatre** me invitó a ir al teatro.

takeaway noun 1 *(a meal)* comida Fem. para llevar; **an Indian takeaway** comida india para llevar; 2 *(where you buy it)* restaurante Masc. que hace comida para llevar.

tale noun historia Fem.

talent noun talento Masc.; **to have a talent for something** estar [2] dotado/dotada para algo.

talented adjective **he's really talented** tiene mucho talento.

talk noun 1 *(a chat)* conversación Fem.; **after our talk** después de nuestra conversación; **I had a talk with Rob about it** hablé con Rob acerca de ello; 2 *(lecture)* charla Fem.; **she's giving a talk on Hungary** va a dar una charla sobre Hungría.

talk verb hablar [17]; **I was talking to Jeevan about football** estuve hablando con Jeevan sobre fútbol; **what's he talking about?** ¿de qué está hablando?; **we'll talk about it later** hablaremos de ello más tarde.

talkative adjective hablador/ habladora; **he's not very talkative!** ¡no es muy hablador!

a b c d e f g h i j k l m n o p q r s t u v w x y z

tall adjective alto/alta; **she's very tall** es muy alta; **I'm 1.7 metres tall** mido un metro setenta; **how tall is she?** ¿cuánto mide?; **the tallest buildings in the city** los edificios más altos de la ciudad.

tambourine noun pandereta Fem.

tame adjective domesticado/ domesticada (an animal).

tampon noun tampón Masc.

tan noun bronceado Masc.; **to get a tan** broncearse [17].

tan verb broncearse [17]; **I tan easily** me bronceo fácilmente.

tangerine noun mandarina Fem.

tank noun **1** (for petrol or water) depósito Masc.; **2 a fish tank** una pecera; **3** (military) tanque Masc.

tanker noun **1** (ship) petrolero Masc.; **2** (on road) camión Masc. cisterna.

tanned adjective bronceado/ bronceada.

tap noun **1** grifo Masc.; **to turn on the tap** abrir [46] el grifo; **to turn off the tap** cerrar [29] el grifo; **the hot tap** el grifo del agua caliente; **2** (a pat) golpecito Masc.

tap verb dar [4] golpecitos.

tap-dancing noun claqué Masc.; **to do tap-dancing** hacer [7] claqué.

tape noun **1** cinta Fem.; **my tape of the Stones** mi cinta de los Stones; **I've got it on tape** lo tengo en cinta; **2 sticky tape** cinta Fem. adhesiva.

tape verb grabar [17]; **I want to tape the film** quiero grabar la película.

tape measure noun cinta Fem. métrica.

tar noun alquitrán Masc.

target noun objetivo Masc.

tart noun tarta Fem.; **a raspberry tart** una tarta de frambuesas.

tartan adjective escocés/escocesa; **a tartan skirt** una falda escocesa.

task noun tarea Fem.

taste noun **1** (flavour) sabor Masc.; **the taste of onions** el sabor a cebolla; **2** (judgement) gusto Masc.; **she has good taste** tiene buen gusto; **in bad taste** de mal gusto.

taste verb **1** saber [13]; **the soup tastes horrible** la sopa sabe fatal; **to taste of** saber a; **it tastes of strawberries** sabe a fresas; **2 do you want to taste?** ¿quieres probarlo?

tasty adjective sabroso/sabrosa.

tattoo noun tatuaje Masc.; **he's got a tattoo on his arm** tiene un tatuaje en el brazo.

Taurus noun Tauro Masc.; **Jo's Taurus** Jo es Tauro.

tax noun impuesto Masc.

taxi noun taxi Masc.; **by taxi** en taxi; **to take a taxi** coger [3] un taxi.

taxi driver noun taxista Masc./ Fem.

taxi rank noun parada Fem. de taxis.

TB noun tuberculosis Fem.

tea noun **1** té Masc.; **a cup of tea** una taza de té; **to have tea** tomar [17] té; **a herbal tea** una infusión; **2** (evening meal) cena Fem.

teabag noun bolsita Fem. de té.

teach verb **1** enseñar [17]; **she's teaching me Italian** me está enseñando italiano; **that'll teach you!** ¡así aprenderás!; **2** (working as a teacher) dar [4] clases de; **her mum teaches maths** su madre da clases de matemáticas; **3** to teach yourself something aprender [18] algo por su cuenta; **Anne taught herself Italian** Anne ha aprendido italiano por su cuenta.

teacher noun **1** (in a secondary school) profesor Masc., profesora Fem.; **my mother's a teacher** mi madre es profesora; **our biology teacher** nuestra profesora de biología; **2** (in primary school) maestro Masc., maestra Fem.; **she's a primary school teacher** es maestra.

teaching noun enseñanza Fem.

team noun equipo Masc.; **a football team** un equipo de fútbol; **our team won** nuestro equipo ganó.

teapot noun tetera Fem.

tear[1] noun (a rip) roto Masc.; **I've got a tear in my jeans** tengo un roto en los vaqueros.

tear verb **1** romper [40]; **you've torn your shirt** te has roto la camisa; **she tore up my letter** rompió mi carta; **2** romperse [40]; **be careful, it tears easily** cuidado, se rompe fácilmente.

● **to tear off 1** (carefully) recortar [17]; **2** (violently) arrancar [31].

● **to tear open 1** (carefully) abrir [46]; **2** (violently) rasgar [28].

tear[2] noun (when you cry) lágrima Fem.; **to be in tears** estar [2]

llorando; **to burst into tears** ponerse [11] a llorar.

teaspoon noun cucharita Fem.; (in recipes) **a teaspoonful of** ... una cucharadita de ....

teatime noun hora Fem. merendar.

tea towel noun paño Masc. de cocina.

technical adjective técnico/técnica.

technical college noun escuela Fem. politécnica.

technician noun técnico Masc., técnica Fem.

technological adjective tecnológico/tecnológica.

technology noun tecnología Fem.; **information technology** informática Fem.

teddy bear noun osito Masc. de peluche.

teenage adjective **1** adolescente; **they have a teenage son** tienen un hijo adolescente; **2** (films, magazines, etc.) para adolescentes; **a teenage magazine** una revista para adolescentes.

teenager noun adolescente Masc./Fem.; **a group of teenagers** un grupo de adolescentes.

teens plural noun adolescencia Fem.; **he's in his teens** es un adolescente.

tee-shirt noun camiseta Fem.

telegraph pole noun poste Masc. telegráfico.

telephone noun teléfono Masc.; **on the telephone** al teléfono.

a **telephone** verb llamar [17] por teléfono; **I'll telephone the bank** llamaré al banco por teléfono.

b **telephone box** noun cabina Fem. telefónica.

c **telephone call** noun llamada Fem. de teléfono.

d **telephone card** noun carta Fem. telefónica.

e **telephone directory** noun guía Fem. telefónica.

f **telephone number** noun número Masc. de teléfono.

g **television** noun televisión Fem.; **she was watching television** estaba viendo la televisión; **I saw it on television** lo vi en televisión.

h **television programme** noun programa Masc. de televisión.

i **tell** verb **1 to tell somebody something** decirle [5] algo a alguien; **that's what she told me** eso es lo que ella me dijo; **I told him it was silly** le dije que era una tontería; **have you told Sara?** ¿se lo has dicho a Sara?; **I didn't tell anyone** no se lo dije a nadie; **2 to tell somebody to do** decirle [5] a alguien que haga (note that 'que' is followed by the subjunctive) **he told me to do it myself** me dijo que lo hiciese solo; **she told me not to wait** me dijo que no esperase; **3** (explain) decir [5]; **can you tell me how to do it?** ¿puedes decirme cómo hacerlo?; **4** (a story) contar [24] (a story); **tell me about your holiday** cuéntame qué tal tus vacaciones; **5** (to see) notar [17]; **to tell the difference** notar la diferencia; **you**

can tell ... se nota ...; **you can tell it's old** se nota que es viejo; **you can tell she's cross** se nota que está enfadada; **I can't tell them apart** no puedo distinguirlos.

telly noun tele Fem. (informal); **to watch telly** ver [16] la tele; **I saw her on telly** la vi en la tele.

temper noun **to be in a temper** estar [2] de mal humor; **to lose your temper** perder [36] los estribos.

temperature noun
1 temperatura Fem.; **the oven temperature** la temperatura del horno; **2 to have a temperature** tener [9] fiebre Fem.

temporary adjective temporal.

temptation noun tentación Fem.

tempted adjective tentado/tentada; **I'm really tempted to go** estoy realmente tentado de ir.

tempting adjective tentador/tentadora.

ten number diez Masc.; **Harry's ten** Harry tiene diez años; **it's ten o'clock** son las diez.

tend verb **to tend to do** tender [36] a hacer; **he tends to talk a lot** tiende a hablar mucho.

tendency noun tendencia Fem.

tennis noun tenis Masc.; **to play tennis** jugar [27] al tenis.

tennis ball noun pelota Fem. de tenis.

tennis court noun cancha Fem. de tenis.

tennis player noun jugador/jugadora Masc./Fem. de tenis.

tennis racket noun raqueta Fem. de tenis.

tenor noun tenor Masc.

tenpin bowling noun bolos Masc. plural [27] a los bolos; **to go tenpin bowling** jugar [27] a los bolos.

tense noun **the present tense** el presente; **in the future tense** en futuro.

tense adjective tenso/tensa.

tent noun tienda Fem.

tenth noun 1 (fraction) **a tenth** una décima parte; **2 the tenth of April** el diez de abril.

tenth adjective décimo/décima; **on the tenth floor** en la décima planta.

term noun 1 (in school) trimestre Masc.; **2 to be on good terms with somebody** llevarse [17] bien con alguien.

terminal noun terminal Fem.; **terminal two** la terminal dos; **a computer terminal** una terminal de ordenador.

terrace noun 1 (of a house or hotel) terraza Fem.; **2 the terraces** (at a stadium) las gradas.

terrible adjective espantoso/ espantosa; **the weather was terrible** el tiempo fue espantoso.

terribly adverb 1 (very) muy; **not terribly clean** no muy limpio que digamos; **2** (badly) fatal; **I played terribly** jugué fatal.

terrific adjective 1 increíble; **at a terrific speed** a una velocidad increíble; **a terrific amount** una cantidad increíble; **2 terrific!** ¡fenomenal!

terrified adjective aterrorizado/ aterrorizada.

terrify verb aterrar [17].

territory noun territorio Masc.

terrorism noun terrorismo Masc.

terrorist noun terrorista Masc./ Fem.

test noun 1 (in school) examen Masc.; **we've got a maths test tomorrow** tenemos un examen de matemáticas mañana; **2** (of your skills or patience) prueba Fem.; **3** (medical) análisis Masc.; **a blood test** un análisis de sangre; **4 a driving test** un examen de conducir; **she's sitting her driving test on Friday** va a hacer el exámen de conducir mañana; **he passed his driving test** ha aprobado el examen de conducir.

test verb 1 (in school) examinarse [17]; **2 to test something out** probar [24] algo.

text noun texto Masc.

text verb mandar [17] un mensaje de texto a; **I'll text you tomorrow** te mandaré un mensaje (de texto) mañana.

textbook noun libro Masc. de texto.

text message noun mensaje Masc. de texto.

Thames noun **the Thames** el Támesis.

than preposition, conjunction 1 que; **their new album's better than the last one** su nuevo álbum es mejor que el último; **they have more money than we do** tienen más dinero que nosotros; **2** (for

a
b
c
d
e
f
g
h
i
j
k
l
m
n
o
p
q
r
s
t
u
v
w
x
y
z

a   *quantities*) de; **more than forty** más de cuarenta; **more than thirty years** más de treinta años.

b   **thank** *verb* dar [4] las gracias a.

c   **thanks** *plural noun* **1** gracias *Fem. plural*; **no thanks** no gracias; **thanks a lot** muchas gracias;

d   **thanks for your letter** gracias por tu carta; **2 thanks to** gracias a; **it

e   was thanks to Micky** fue gracias a Micky.

f

g   **thank you** *exclamation* gracias; **thank you very much for the

h   cheque** muchas gracias por el cheque; **no thank you** no, gracias;

i   **a thank-you letter** un carta de agradecimiento.

j

k   **that** *adjective* **1** (*before a masculine noun*) ese; **that dog** ese perro; **that

l   blue car** ese coche azul; **2** (*before a feminine noun*) esa; **that woman**

m   esa mujer; **3 that one** (*referring to a masculine noun*) ese, ése;

n   (*referring to a feminine noun*) esa, ésa; **'which cake would you like?'**

o   **– 'that one, please'** ¿qué pastel quieres?' – 'ese, por favor'; **I like all

p   the skirts but I'm going to buy that one** me gustan todas las

q   faldas pero voy a comprar esa.

r   **that** *pronoun* **1** (*referring to a masculine noun*) ese, ése; (*referring

s   to a masculine noun*) esa, ésa; **that's not his car** ese no es su

t   coche; **that's my bedroom** esa es mi habitación; **2** eso; **that's not

u   what you told me** eso no es lo que tú me dijiste; **that's not true** eso no

v

w

x

y

z

es cierto; **did you see that?** ¿has visto eso?; **what's that?** ¿qué es eso?; **who's that?** ¿quién es?; **where's that?** ¿dónde está?; **3** que; **the book that's on the table** el libro que está en la mesa; **the girl that I saw** la chica que yo vi; **4** (*when the verb is followed by a preposition*) (*referring to a masculine noun*) el que; (*referring to a feminine noun*) la que; **the drawer that I put it in** el cajón en el que lo metí.

that *conjunction* que; **I knew that he was wrong** sabía que no tenía razón.

thaw *noun* deshielo *Masc.*

the *definite article* **1** (*before a masculine noun*) el; **the cat** el gato; **the tree** el árbol (*when 'el' follows 'de', they join to become 'del'*); **the branches of the tree** las ramas del árbol; (*when 'el' follows 'a' they join to become 'al'*) **we went to the park** fuimos al parque; **2** (*before a feminine noun*) la; **the table** la mesa; **the orange** la naranja; **3** (*before masculine plural nouns*) los; **the plates** los platos; **4** (*before feminine plural nouns*) las; **the windows** las ventanas.

theatre *noun* teatro *Masc.*; **to go to the theatre** ir [8] al teatro.

theft *noun* robo *Masc.*

their *adjective* **1** (*before a singular noun*) su; **their flat** su piso; **their mother** su madre; **2** (*before a plural noun*) sus; **their presents** sus regalos; **3** (*with parts of the body*) el, la, los, las; **they had tatoos on their arms** tenían tatuajes en los brazos; **they're washing their hands** se están lavando las manos.

theirs *pronoun* **1** (*when referring to a singular noun*) el suyo/la suya; **our garden's smaller than theirs** nuestro jardín es más pequeño que el suyo; **our house is bigger than theirs** nuestra casa es más grande que la suya; **2** (*when referring to a plural noun*) los suyos/las suyas; **our shoes were newer than theirs** nuestros zapatos eran más nuevos que los suyos; **our photos were better that theirs** nuestras fotos eran mejores que las suyas.

them *pronoun* **1** los/las; **she's got two brothers, but I don't know them** tiene dos hermanos, pero no los conozco; **remember Ann and Lisa? I saw them last week** ¿te acuerdas de Ann y Lisa? las vi la semana pasada; **2** (*with an infinitive or when telling somebody to do something 'los'/'las' join onto the verb*) **I don't want to see them** no quiero verlos; **listen to them!** ¡escúchalos!; (*but when telling someone NOT to do something, 'los' or 'las' comes before the verb*) **don't push them!** ¡no los empujes!; **3** (*to them*) **I gave them my address** les di mis señas (*'les' becomes 'se' before pronouns 'lo' or 'la'*) **I lent it to them** se lo dejé; (*when giving an order 'se' joins the verb*) **give it back to them** ¡devuélveselo!; **4** (*after a preposition, in comparisons, or after the verb 'to be'*) ellos/ellas; **I'll go with them** iré con ellos/ellas; **without them**

sin ellos/sin ellas; **she's older than them** es mayor que ellos; **it's them!** ¡son ellos!/¡son ellas!

theme park *noun* parque *Masc.* temático.

themselves *pronoun* **1** (*as a reflexive*) se; **they've helped themselves** se sirvieron; **2** (*for emphasis*) ellos mismos/ellas mismas; **the boys can do it themselves** los chicos pueden hacerlo ellos mismos; **the girls will tell you themselves** las chicas te lo dirán ellas mismas; **3 by themselves** ellos solos/ellas solas.

then *adverb* **1** (*next*) luego; **have a shower and then make your bed** dúchate y luego haz la cama; **I went to the post office and then the bank** fui a Correos y luego al banco; **2** (*at that time*) entonces; **we were living in York then** vivíamos en York; **3** (*in that case*) entonces; **then why worry?** entonces ¿para qué preocuparse?; **that's all right then** entonces vale; **4 by then** para entonces; **by then it was too late** para entonces era demasiado tarde.

theory *noun* teoría *Fem.*; **in theory** en teoría.

there *adverb* **1** ahí; (*further away*) allí; **put it there** ponlo ahí; (*further away*) ponlo allí; **stand there** ponte ahí; **they're living in York then** están ahí dentro; **look up there!** ¡mira ahí arriba!; **2 over there** ahí; (*further away*) allí; **she's over there talking to Mark** está ahí hablando con Mark; (*further away*) está allí hablando con Mark; **3 down there**

ahí abajo; (further away) allí abajo; **up there** ahí arriba; (further away) allí arriba; **4** (when there stands for something already mentioned, it is usually not translated) **I've seen photos of Oxford but I've never been there** he visto fotos de Oxford, pero nunca he estado; **yes, I'm going there on Tuesday** sí, voy a ir el martes; **5 there is/there are** hay; **there's a cat in the garden** hay un gato en el jardín; **there was no bread** no había pan; **yes, there's enough** sí, hay suficiente; **there are plenty of seats** hay muchos asientos; **6 there they are!** ¡ahí están!; **there she is!** ¡ahí está!; **there's the bus coming!** ¡ahí viene el autobús!

thermometer noun termómetro Masc.

these adjective **1** (with a masculine noun) estos; **these envelopes** estos sobres; **2** (with a feminine noun) estas; **these postcards** estas postales.

they pronoun **1** (like other subject pronouns 'they' is generally not translated; in Spanish the form of the verb tells you whether the subject of the verb is 'we, you, they', etc., so 'they' is only translated for emphasis) **'where are the knives?'** **- 'they're in the drawer'** '¿dónde están los cuchillos?' - 'están en el cajón'; **I bought some apples but they're not very nice** compré unas manzanas pero no están muy buenas; **2** (for emphasis) ellos/ ellas; **they did it** lo hicieron ellos.

thick adjective **1** grueso/gruesa; **a thick layer of butter** una capa gruesa de mantequilla; **2** denso/ densa (fog, fumes).

thickness noun **1** (of wall, paper) espesor Masc.; **2** (of fog) densidad Fem.

thief noun ladrón Masc., ladrona Fem.

thigh noun muslo Masc.

thin adjective **1** delgado/delgada (a person); **to get thin** adelgazar [22]; **2** fino/fina (a slice); **3** (too thin, skinny) flaco/flaca; **she's very thin** está muy flaca.

thing noun **1** (an object) cosa Fem.; **shops full of pretty things** tiendas llenas de cosas preciosas; **she told me some surprising things** me dijo algunas cosas sorprendentes; **2** (a whatsit) chisme Masc. (informal); **you can use that thing to open it** puedes usar ese chisme para abrirlo; **3 things** (belongings) cosas Fem. plural; **you can put your things in my room** puedes poner tus cosas en mi habitación; **4 the best thing to do is ...** lo mejor es ...; **the thing is, I've lost her address** la cuestión es que he perdido sus señas; **5 how are things with you?** ¿qué tal te van las cosas?

think verb **1** pensar [29]; **I'm thinking about you** estoy pensando en ti; **Tony thinks it's silly** Tony piensa que es una tontería; **what do you think of my new jacket?** ¿qué piensas de mi chaqueta nueva?; **what do you think of that?** ¿qué piensas de eso?; **he thought for a moment** pensó un momento; **she's thinking of studying medicine** está pensando estudiar medicina; **2** (*believe*) creer [37]; **do you think they'll come?** ¿crees que vendrán?; **no, I don't think so** no, creo que no; **I don't think he's already left** creo que ya se ha ido; **3** (*imagine*) imaginar [17]; **I never thought it would be like this!** ¡nunca imaginé que sería así!; **just think!** ¡imagínate! **we'll soon be in Spain!** ¡pronto estaremos en España!

third *noun* **1** (*fraction*) a third un tercio; **2 the third of March** el tres de marzo.

third *adjective* tercero/tercera; **on the third floor** en la tercera planta.

thirdly *adverb* en tercer lugar.

Third World *noun* the Third World el Tercer Mundo.

thirst *noun* sed *Fem.*

thirsty *adjective* **to be thirsty** tener [9] sed; **I'm thirsty** tengo sed; **we were all thirsty** todos teníamos sed.

thirteen *number* trece *Masc.*; **Ahmed's thirteen** Ahmed tiene trece años.

thirty *number* treinta *Masc.*; **she's thirty** tiene treinta años; **thirty-five** treinta y cinco.

this *adjective* **1** este (*before a masculine noun*); esta (*before a feminine noun*); **this paintbrush** este pincel; **this tree** este árbol; **this cup** esta taza; **this morning** esta mañana; **2 this one** (*referring to a masculine noun*) este, éste;

(*referring to a feminine noun*) esta, ésta; **if you need a pen you can use this one** si necesitas un boli puedes usar este; **if you want a lamp you can borrow this one** si quieres una lámpara puedes coger esta.

this *pronoun* **1** (*referring to a masculine noun*) este, éste; **this is my car** este es mi coche; **2** (*referring to a feminine noun*) esta, ésta; **this is the best photo** esta es la mejor foto; **3** esto; **can you hold this for a moment?** ¿puedes sostener esto un momento?; **what's this?** ¿qué es esto?; **4 this is Tracy speaking** (*on the phone*) soy Tracy; **5** (*in introductions*) **this is my sister Carla** te presento a mi hermana Carla.

thistle *noun* cardo *Masc.*

thorough *adjective* **1** (*search*) a fondo; **2** (*person*) concienzudo/ concienzuda.

those *adjective* (*before a masculine noun*) esos; (*before a feminine noun*) esas; **those books** esos libros; **those cups** esas tazas.

those *pronoun* (*referring to a masculine noun*) esos, ésos; (*referring to a feminine noun*) esas, ésas; **if you want some knives you can take those** si quieres cuchillos puedes coger esos; **if you want some cups you can take those** si quieres tazas puedes coger esas.

though *conjunction* **1** aunque; **though it's cold** aunque hace calor; **though he's older than she**

a b c d e f g h i j k l m n o p q r s t u v w x y z

is aunque es mayor que ella; **2 it was a good idea, though** aun así era una buena idea.

thought noun pensamiento Masc.

thoughtful adjective
1 (considerate) amable; **it was really thoughtful of you** fue muy amable de tu parte; **2** (deep in thought) pensativo/pensativa.

thoughtless adjective desconsiderado/desconsiderada.

thousand number **1** mil Masc.; **a thousand** mil; **a thousand euros** mil euros; **three thousand** tres mil; **2 thousands of** miles de; **there were thousands of tourists in Barcelona** había miles de turistas en Barcelona.

thread noun hilo Masc.

thread verb enhebrar [17] (a needle).

threat noun amenaza Fem.

threaten verb amenazar [22]; **to threaten to do** amenazar con hacer.

three number tres Masc.; **Lily's three** Lily tiene tres años.

three-quarters noun tres cuartos Masc. plural.

thrilled adjective encantado/encantada; **I was thrilled to hear from you** me encantó tener noticias tuyas.

thriller noun **1** (book) novela Fem. de suspense; **2** (film) película Fem. de suspense.

thrilling adjective emocionante.

throat noun garganta Fem.; **to have a sore throat** tener [9] dolor de garganta.

through preposition **1** (across) a través de; **a path through the forest** un camino a través del bosque; **to go through something** atravesar [29] algo; **we went through the park** atravesamos el parque; **2** (by way of) por; **the train went through Leeds** el tren fue por Leeds; **through the window** por la ventana; **3 to go through customs** pasar [17] la aduana.

through adjective directo/directa (a train or flight).

throughout preposition **throughout the match** durante todo el partido; **throughout the world** por todo mundo.

throw verb tirar [17]; **I threw the letter into the bin** tiré la carta a la basura; **he threw the book on the floor** tiró el libro al suelo; **throw me the ball!** ¡tírame la pelota!; **we were throwing snowballs** estábamos tirando bolas de nieve.

● **to throw something away** tirar [17] algo; **I've thrown away the old newspapers** he tirado los periódicos viejos.

● **to throw somebody out** echar [17] a alguien.

● **to throw something out** tirar [17] algo (rubbish).

● **to throw up** devolver [45].

thumb noun pulgar Masc.

thunder noun truenos Masc. plural; **a peal of thunder** un trueno.

thunderstorm noun tormenta Fem. eléctrica.

Thursday noun jueves Masc.; **on Thursday** el jueves; **I'm going out**

585

on Thursday voy a salir el jueves; see you on Thursday! ¡hasta el jueves!; on Thursdays los jueves; the museum is closed on Thursdays el museo cierra los jueves; every Thursday todos los jueves; last Thursday el jueves pasado; next Thursday el próximo jueves.

tick verb **1** (clocks) hacer [7] tictac; **2** (on paper) marcar [31].

ticket noun **1** entrada Fem. (for an exhibition, a theatre or cinema) two tickets for the concert dos entradas para el concierto; **2** (for a plane, a train, a bus or the underground) billete Masc.; a bus ticket un billete de autobús; **3** (for left luggage) ticket Masc.; **4** a parking ticket una multa.

ticket inspector noun revisor Masc., revisora Fem.

ticket office noun **1** (at a station) mostrador Masc. de venta de billetes; **2** (at a cinema) taquilla Fem.

tickle verb hacer [7] cosquillas.

tide noun marea Fem.; at high tide cuando la marea está alta; the tide is out la marea está baja.

tidy adjective **1** ordenado/ ordenada (a room); **2** bien escrito/ bien escrita (homework); **3** bien arreglado/bien arreglada (a person).

tidy verb ordenar [17].

tie noun **1** corbata Fem.; a red tie una corbata roja; **2** (in a match) empate Masc.

tie verb **1** atar [17]; **to tie your shoelaces** atarse los zapatos; **2** to

tie a knot in something hacer [7] un nudo a algo; **3** (in a match) we tied two all empatamos a dos.

tiger noun tigre Masc.

tight adjective **1** to be tight apretar [29]; the skirt's a bit tight la falda aprieta un poco; these shoes are too tight estos zapatos aprietan mucho; **2** (close-fitting) ceñido/ ceñida; she was wearing a tight dress llevaba un vestido ceñido.

tighten verb apretar [29].

tightly adverb fuerte; hold it tightly agárralo fuerte.

tights plural noun medias Fem. plural; a pair of purple tights un par de medias moradas.

tile noun **1** (on a floor or wall) azulejo Masc.; **2** (on a roof) teja Fem.

till[1] preposition hasta; they're here till Sunday están aquí hasta el domingo; till then hasta entonces; till now hasta ahora; she won't be back till ten no volverá hasta las diez.

till[2] noun caja Fem.; pay at the till pase a pagar por caja.

time noun **1** (on the clock) hora Fem.; what time is it? ¿qué hora es?; it's time for lunch es hora de comer; ten o'clock Spanish time las diez hora española; on time a la hora; **2** (an amount of time) tiempo Masc.; we've got lots of time tenemos mucho tiempo; there's not much time left no queda mucho tiempo; he talked for a long time habló durante mucho tiempo; she hasn't called me for a long time hace mucho que no me

a b c d e f g h i j k l m n o p q r s t u v w x y z

a llama; **3** (*moment*) momento *Masc.*; **is this a good time to phone?** ¿es buen momento para llamar?; **at any time** en cualquier momento; **4 from time to time** de vez en cuando; **at times** a veces; **for the time being** por ahora; **5** (*in a series*) vez *Fem.* (*plural* veces); **six times** seis veces; **the first time** la primera vez; **the first time I saw you** la primera vez que te vi; **three times a year** tres veces al año; **6** (*multiplying*) **three times two is six** tres por dos son seis; **7 to have a good time** pasárselo [17] bien; **we had a really good time** nos lo pasamos muy bien; **have a good time!** ¡pásatelo bien!

time off *noun* **1** (*free time*) tiempo *Masc.* libre; **2** (*leave*) días *Masc. plural* libres.

timetable *noun* horario *Masc.*; **the bus timetable** el horario de los autobuses.

tin *noun* lata *Fem.*; **a tin of tomatoes** una lata de tomates.

tin foil *noun* papel *Masc.* aluminio.

tinned *adjective* en lata; **tinned peas** guisantes en lata.

tin opener *noun* abrelatas *Masc.* (*does not change in the plural*).

tiny *adjective* diminuto/diminuta.

tip *noun* **1** (*the end*) punta *Fem.*; **the tip of my finger** la punta de mi dedo; **2** (*money*) propina *Fem.*; **3** (*a useful hint*) consejo *Masc.*

tip *verb* **1** (*to give money to*) darle [4] una propina a; **we tipped the waiter** le dimos una propina al camarero; **2** tirar [17] (*liquid*).

tiptoe *noun* **on tiptoe** de puntillas.

tired *adjective* **1** cansado/cansada; **I'm tired** estoy cansado; **you look tired** pareces cansado; **2 to be tired of** estar [2] harto de/harta de; **he's tired of London** está harto de Londres; **she says she's tired of watching TV** dice que está harta de ver la tele.

tiring *adjective* cansado/cansada.

tissue *noun* (*a paper hanky*) pañuelo *Masc.* de papel; **do you have a tissue?** ¿tienes un pañuelo de papel?

title *noun* título *Masc.*

to *preposition* **1** (*to a place*) a; **to London** a Londres; **to Spain** a España; **she's gone to the office** se ha ido a la oficina; **to Paul's house** a casa de Paul; **from Monday to Friday** de lunes a viernes; (*when 'el' follows 'a' they join to become 'al'*) **I'm going to school** voy al colegio; **I'm going to the dentist's tomorrow** voy al dentista mañana; **2** (*to a person*) a; **give the book to Leila** dale el libro a Leila; **who did you give it to?** ¿a quién se lo diste?; **to talk to somebody** hablar [17] con alguien; **he didn't talk to me** no habló conmigo; **I was nice to them** fui amable con ellos; **3 we're ready to go** estamos listos para irnos; **it's easy to do** es fácil de hacer; **I have nothing to do** no tengo nada que hacer; **I have a lot of homework to do** tengo muchos deberes que hacer; **4** (*talking about the time*) **it's ten to nine** son las nueve menos diez; **it's twenty to** son menos veinte; **5** (*in order to*) para; **he gave me some money to buy a sandwich** me dio dinero para comprar un sandwich.

toast *noun* **1** pan *Masc.* tostado; **a piece of toast** una tostada; **two slices of toast** dos tostadas; **2** (*to your health*) brindis *Masc.*; **to drink a toast to the future** brindar [17] por el futuro.

toaster *noun* tostador *Masc.*

tobacco *noun* tabaco *Masc.*

tobacconist's *noun* estanco *Masc.*

today *adverb, noun* hoy; **today's her birthday** hoy es su cumpleaños.

toe *noun* dedo *Masc.* del pie; **my big toe** mi dedo gordo del pie.

toenail *noun* uña *Fem.* de un dedo del pie.

toffee *noun* toffee *Masc.*

together *adverb* juntos/juntas; **Kate and Lindy arrived together** Kate y Lindy llegaron juntas; **they all left together** se fueron todos juntos.

toilet *noun* **1** (*in a house*) baño *Masc.*; **she's gone to the toilet** ha ido al baño; **2** (*in a public place*) servicio *Masc.*; **where's the toilet?** ¿dónde está el servicio?; **3 toilets** (*in a public place*) servicios *Masc. plural*; **where are the toilets?** ¿dónde están los servicios.

toilet paper *noun* papel *Masc.* higiénico.

toilet roll *noun* rollo *Masc.* de papel higiénico.

token *noun* **1** (*for a machine or game*) ficha *Fem.*; **2** (*as a present*) cheque *Masc.* regalo; **a record token** un cheque regalo para un disco.

toll *noun* **1** (*on motorway*) peaje *Masc.*; **2** (*number*) número *Masc.*; **the death toll is 25** el número de víctimas mortales asciende a 25.

tomato *noun* tomate *Masc.*; **a tomato salad** una ensalada de tomate; **tomato sauce** salsa *Fem.* de tomate.

tomorrow *adverb* mañana; **I'll do it tomorrow** lo haré mañana; **tomorrow afternoon** mañana por la tarde; **tomorrow morning** mañana por la mañana; **tomorrow night** mañana por la noche; **the day after tomorrow** pasado mañana.

ton *noun* tonelada *Fem.*; **she gets tons of letters** recibe montones de cartas.

tongue *noun* lengua *Fem.*; **to stick your tongue out** sacar [31] la lengua; ★ **it's on the tip of my tongue** lo tengo en la punta de la lengua.

tonic *noun* tónica *Fem.*; **a gin and tonic** un gin tonic.

tonight *adverb* esta noche; **I'm going out with my mates tonight** esta noche voy a salir con mis amigos.

tonsillitis *noun* anginas *Fem. plural.*

too *adverb* **1** demasiado; **it's too expensive** es demasiado caro; **the tickets are too expensive** los

a b c d e f g h i j k l m n o p q r s t u v w x y z

billetes son demasiado caros; **too often** demasiado a menudo; **2 too much** (*before a masculine noun*) demasiado; (*before a feminine noun*) demasiada; **it takes too much time** lleva demasiado tiempo; **I watch too much TV** veo demasiada televisión; **3 too much** (*before verb*) demasiado; **he eats too much** come demasiado; **4 too many** (*before a masculine noun*) demasiados; (*before a feminine noun*) demasiadas; **there are too many accidents** hay demasiados accidentes; **5** (*as well*) también; **Karen's coming too** Karen también viene; **me too!** ¡yo también!; **6** (*very*) muy; **I'm not too convinced** no estoy muy convencida.

tool *noun* herramienta *Fem.*

tool kit *noun* juego *Masc.* de herramientas.

tooth *noun* **1** diente *Masc.*; **to brush your teeth** cepillarse [17] los dientes; **2** (*back tooth*) muela *Fem.*

toothache *noun* dolor *Masc.* de muelas; **to have toothache** tener [9] dolor de muelas.

toothbrush *noun* cepillo *Masc.* de dientes.

toothpaste *noun* pasta *Fem.* de dientes.

top *noun* **1** alto *Masc.* (*of a ladder, or stairs*); **at the top of the stairs** en lo alto de las escaleras; **2** (*of a page, container or box*) parte *Fem.* superior; **the top of the box is red** la parte superior de la caja es roja; **3 on top of** (*a table, wardrobe, etc*) encima de; **it's on top of the**

chest-of-drawers está encima de la cómoda; **4** (*of a mountain*) cima *Fem.*; **5** (*a lid, cap*) (*of a bottle*) tapón *Masc.* (*of a pan or jar*) tapa *Fem.* (*of a pen*) capuchón *Masc.*; **6 to be at the top of the list** encabezar [22] una lista.

top *adjective* **1** (*a step or floor*) último/última; **it's on the top floor** está en el último piso; **2 de arriba** (*a bunk, drawer or shelf*); **3 in the top left-hand corner** en la esquina superior izquierda; **★ and on top of all that** y para colmo; **★ it was a bit over the top** fue un poco excesivo.

topic *noun* tema *Masc.*

topping *noun* guarnición *Fem.*; **which topping do you want?** ¿qué guarnición quieres?

torch *noun* linterna *Fem.*

torn *adjective* roto/rota.

tornado *noun* tornado *Masc.*

tortoise *noun* tortuga *Fem.*

torture *noun* tortura *Fem.*

torture *verb* torturar [17].

Tory *noun* conservador *Masc.*, conservadora *Fem.*

total *noun* total *Masc.*

total *adjective* total.

totally *adverb* totalmente.

touch *noun* **1** (*contact*) **to get in touch with somebody** contactar [17] con alguien; **to stay in touch with somebody** mantenerse [9] en contacto con alguien; **we've lost touch** hemos perdido el contacto; **2** (*a little bit*) poco *Masc.*; **a touch of vanilla** un poco de vainilla; **it was a touch embarrassing** fue un poco embarazoso.

touch verb **1** tocar [31]; **2** (*emotionally*) conmover [38].

tough adjective **1** duro/dura; **the meat's a bit tough** la carne está un poco dura; **a tough guy** un tipo duro; **you need to be tough to survive** tienes que ser duro para sobrevivir; **2** (*severe*) severo/severa; **3** (*fabric*) resistente; **4** (*question, problem or job*) difícil; **things are a bit tough at the moment** las cosas están un poco difíciles en este momento; **5 tough luck!** ¡mala suerte!

tour noun **1** visita Fem.; **we did the tour of the castle** hicimos la visita al castillo; **a tour of the city** una visita a la ciudad; **2 a package tour** un viaje organizado; **2** (*by a band or theatre group*) gira Fem.; **to go on tour** ir [8] de gira.

tourism noun turismo Masc.

tourist noun turista Masc./Fem.

tourist information office noun oficina Fem. de información y turismo.

towards adverb hacia; **she went off towards the lake** se fue hacia el lago.

towel noun toalla Fem.

tower noun torre Fem.; **the Eiffel Tower** la torre Eiffel.

tower block noun bloque Masc. de apartamentos.

town noun ciudad Fem.; **to go into town** ir [8] a la ciudad; (*to the centre*) ir [8] al centro.

town centre noun centro Masc. de la ciudad.

town hall noun ayuntamiento Masc.

toxic adjective tóxico/tóxica.

toy noun juguete Masc.

trace noun rastro Masc.; **there is no trace of it** no hay rastro de ello.

trace verb **1** (*on paper*) calcar [31]; **2** (*a missing person*) localizar [22].

tracing paper noun papel Masc. de calco.

track noun **1** (*for sport*) pista Fem.; **a track event** una prueba de atletismo; **a racing track** (*for cars*) un circuito; **2** (*a path*) sendero Masc.; **3** (*song*) tema Masc.; **this is my favourite track** es mi tema favorito.

track suit noun chándal Masc.

tractor noun tractor Masc.

trade noun (*a profession*) oficio Masc.

trade mark noun marca Fem. comercial; **a registered trade mark** una marca registrada.

trade union noun sindicato Masc.

tradition noun tradición Fem.

traditional adjective tradicional.

traffic noun tráfico Masc.

traffic jam noun embotellamiento Masc.

traffic lights plural noun semáforo Masc.

traffic warden noun guardia Masc./Fem. municipal.

tragedy noun tragedia Fem.

tragic adjective trágico/trágica.

trail noun (*a path*) sendero Masc.; **a nature trail** un sendero ecológico.

trailer noun remolque Masc.

a

train noun tren Masc.; **he's coming by train** viene en tren; **I met her off the train** fui a recogerla en la estación; **the train for York** el tren para York.

b

c

train verb **1** estudiar [17] (a student); **2** to **train to be something** estudiar para algo; **he's training to be a nurse** está estudiando para ser enfermero; **3** (in sport) entrenar [17]; **the team trains on Saturdays** el equipo entrena los sábados.

d

e

f

g

h

train ticket noun billete Masc. de tren.

i

train timetable noun horario Masc. de trenes.

j

k

trainer noun **1** (of an athlete or a horse) entrenador Masc., entrenadora Fem.; **2** (shoe) zapatilla Fem. de deporte; **my new trainers** mis zapatillas de deporte nuevas.

l

m

n

training noun **1** (for a career) formación Fem.; **2** (for sport) entrenamiento Masc.

o

p

tram noun tranvía Masc.

q

trampoline noun cama Fem. elástica.

r

s

t **transfer** noun **1** (of money) transferencia Fem.; **2** (to new post) traslado Masc.; **3** (sticker) calcomanía Fem.

u

v

translate verb traducir [60]; to **translate something into Spanish** traducir algo al español.

w

x

translation noun traducción Fem.

y

translator noun traductor Masc., traductora Fem.; **I'd like to be a**

z

translator me gustaría ser traductora.

transparent adjective transparente.

transplant noun trasplante Masc.

transport noun transporte Masc.; **air transport** transporte aéreo; **public transport** transporte público.

trap noun trampa Fem.

travel noun viajes Masc. plural; **foreign travel** viajes al extranjero; **a travel brochure** un folleto de viajes.

travel verb viajar [17].

travel agency noun agencia Fem. de viajes.

travel agent noun agente Masc. de viajes.

traveller noun **1** viajero Masc., viajera Fem.; **2** (gypsy) gitano Masc., gitana Fem.

traveller's cheque noun cheque Masc. de viaje.

travelling noun **I like travelling** me gusta viajar.

travel-sick noun to **be/get travel-sick** marearse [17] en los viajes.

tray noun bandeja Fem.

tread verb to **tread on something** pisar [17] algo.

treasure noun tesoro Masc.

treat noun **1** capricho Masc.; to **give yourself a treat** darse [4] un capricho; **it's a little treat** es un caprichito; **2** I **took them to the circus as a treat** les llevé al circo como algo especial.

treat verb **1** tratar [17]; **he treats his dog well** trata bien a su perro;

the doctor who treated you el médico que te trató; **2 to treat somebody to something** invitar [17] a alguien a algo; **I'll treat you to a drink** te invito a una copa; **3 I treated myself to a new dress** me compré un vestido para darme un capricho.

treatment noun tratamiento Masc. (medical).

treaty noun tratado Masc.

tree noun árbol Masc.

tree trunk noun tronco Masc.

tremendous adjective tremendo/tremenda; **a tremendous victory/defeat** una tremenda victoria/derrota.

trend noun **1** (a fashion) moda Fem.; **2** (a tendency) tendencia Fem.

trendy adjective de moda.

trial noun juicio Masc. (legal).

triangle noun triángulo Masc.

trick noun **1** (card or conjuring trick, knack) truco Masc.; **a card trick** un truco con las cartas; **it doesn't work, there must be a trick to it** no funciona, debe tener truco; **2** (a joke) broma Fem.; **to play a trick on somebody** gastarle [17] una broma a alguien.

trick verb engañar [17]; **he tricked me!** me engañó!

tricky adjective delicado/delicada; **it's a tricky situation** es una situación delicada.

tricycle noun triciclo Masc.

tribe noun tribu Fem.

tribute noun homenaje Masc.

Trinidad noun Trinidad Fem.

Trinidadian noun trinitense Masc./Fem.

Trinidadian adjective trinitense.

trip noun viaje Masc.; **a trip to Florida** un viaje a Florida; **he's on a business trip** está en viaje de negocios; **a day trip to France** un viaje de un día a Francia.

trip verb (to stumble) tropezar [25]; **Nicky tripped over a stone** Nicky tropezó con una piedra.

triple verb triplicar [31]; **the price has tripled** el precio se ha triplicado.

trolley noun carro Masc.

trombone noun trombón Masc.; **to play the trombone** tocar [31] el trombón.

trophy noun trofeo Masc.

trouble noun **1** problemas Masc. plural; **we had trouble with the car** tuvimos problemas con el coche; **Steve's in trouble** Steve tiene problemas; **to get into trouble** meterse [18] en problemas; **2 what's the trouble?** ¿cuál es el problema?; **3** (difficulty) **I had trouble finding a seat** me costó encontrar un sitio; **it's not worth the trouble** no vale la pena; **the trouble is, I've forgotten the number** el problema es que he olvidado el número; **it's no trouble!** ¡no es ningún problema!

trousers plural noun pantalones Masc. plural; **a new pair of trousers** unos pantalones nuevos, un nuevo par de pantalones.

trout noun trucha Fem.

truant noun estudiante Masc./Fem. que falta a clase sin autorización;

a
b
c
d
e
f
g
h
i
j
k
l
m
n
o
p
q
r
s
t
u
v
w
x
y
z

she's playing truant está haciendo novillos.

truck noun camión Masc.

true adjective a true story una historia verídica; to be true ser [1] verdad; is that true? ¿es eso verdad?; it's true she's absent-minded es verdad que es despistada.

truly adverb de veras.

trump noun triunfo Masc.; **spades are trumps** las picas son triunfo.

trumpet noun trompeta Fem.; to play the trumpet tocar [31] la trompeta.

trunk noun **1** (of a tree) tronco Masc.; **2** (of an elephant) trompa Fem.; **3** (a suitcase) baúl Masc.

trunks plural noun **swimming trunks** bañador Masc.

trust noun confianza Fem.

trust verb confiar [32]; I trust her confío en ella.

truth noun verdad Fem.; to tell the truth, I'd completely forgotten si quieres que te diga la verdad, me he olvidado completamente.

try noun intento Masc.; **I'm my first try** es mi primer intento; to have a try intentar [17]; you should give it a try deberías intentarlo.

try verb **1** intentar [17]; to try to do something intentar hacer; **I'm trying to open the door** estoy intentando abrir la puerta; **2** (taste) probar [24]; try this sauce prueba esta salsa; to try hard to do esforzarse [26] por hacer.

• to try something on probarse [26] algo (a garment).

T-shirt noun camiseta Fem.

tub noun **1** (food container) tarrina Fem.; **2** (bath) bañera Fem.

tube noun **1** tubo Masc.; **2 the tube** (London underground) (informal) el metro.

tuberculosis noun tuberculosis Fem.

Tuesday noun martes Masc.; **on Tuesday** el martes; **I'm going out on Tuesday** voy a salir el martes; **see you on Tuesday!** ¡hasta el martes!; **on Tuesdays** los martes; **the museum is closed on Tuesdays** el museo cierra los martes; **every Tuesday** todos los martes; **last Tuesday** el martes pasado; **next Tuesday** el próximo martes.

tuition noun clases Fem. plural; **piano tuition** clases de piano; **private tuition** clases particulares.

tulip noun tulipán Masc.

tumble-drier noun secadora Fem.

tummy noun barriga Fem.

tuna noun atún Masc.

tune noun melodía Fem.

tunnel noun túnel Masc.; **the Channel Tunnel** el Eurotúnel.

turban noun turbante Masc.

turkey noun pavo Masc.

Turkey noun Turquía Fem.

Turkish noun turco Masc. (language).

Turkish adjective turco/turca.

turn noun **1** (in a game) turno Masc.; **it's your turn** es tu turno; **whose turn is it?** ¿a quién le toca?; **it's Jane's turn to play** es el turno de Jane; **to take turns driving** turnarse [17] para conducir; **2** (*in a road*) curva Fem.

turn verb **1** girar [17]; **turn your chair round** gira la silla; **turn left at the next set of lights** gira a la izquierda en el próximo semáforo; **2** dar [4] la vuelta a (*a page or mattress*); **3** (*become*) ponerse [11]; **she turned red** se puso roja.

● **to turn back** volverse [45]; **we turned back** nos volvimos.

● **to turn off 1** (*from a road*) girar [17]; **2** (*switch off*) apagar [28] (*a light, an oven, a TV, or radio*), cerrar [29] (*gas, electricity or a tap*).

● **to turn on** encender [36] (*a light, an oven, a TV, or radio*), abrir [46] (*a tap*).

● **to turn out: 1 to turn out well/badly** salir [63] bien/mal; **it all turned out well in the end** todo salió bien al final; **the holiday turned out badly** las vacaciones salieron mal; **2 it turned out that I was wrong** resultó que estaba equivocado.

● **to turn over 1** (*roll over*) darse [4] la vuelta; **2** dar [4] la vuelta a (*a page*).

● **to turn up 1** (*to arrive*) presentarse [17]; **they turned up an hour late** se presentaron con una hora de retraso; **2** abrir [46] más (*the gas*); **3** subir [19] (*the heating or volume*); **can you turn up the volume?** ¿puedes subir el volumen?

turning noun bocacalle Fem.; **take the first turning on the right/left** toma la primera bocacalle a la derecha/izquierda.

turnip noun nabo Masc.

turquoise adjective turquesa.

turtle noun tortuga Fem.

TV noun tele Fem.; **I saw her on TV** la vi en la tele.

tweezers noun pinzas Fem. plural.

twelfth noun **the twelfth of May** el doce de mayo.

twelfth adjective doceavo/doceava; **on the twelfth floor** en la planta duodécima.

twelve number doce Masc.; **Tara's twelve** Tara tiene doce años; **it's twelve o'clock** (*midday*) son las doce de la mañana, (*midnight*) son las doce de la noche.

twenty number veinte; **Marie's twenty** Marie tiene veinte años; **twenty-one** veintiuno; **twenty-five** veinticinco.

twice adverb **1** dos veces; **I've asked him twice** le he preguntado dos veces; **2 twice as much** el doble.

twig noun ramita Fem.

twilight noun anochecer Masc.

twin noun gemelo Masc., gemela Fem.; **Helen and Tim are twins** Helen y Tim son gemelos; **her twin sister** su hermana gemela.

twin verb girar [17] (*knob or cap of bottle*).

twin Oxford is twinned with León Oxford está hermanado con León.

twist verb girar [17] (*knob or cap of bottle*).

two number dos Masc.; **Ben's two** Ben tiene dos años; **two by two** dos por dos.

a b c d e f g h i j k l m n o p q r s t u v w x y z

a
b
c
d
e
f
g
h
i
j
k
l
m
n
o
p
q
r
s
t
u
v
w
x
y
z

type noun tipo Masc.; **what type of computer is it?** ¿qué tipo de ordenador es?

type verb (on a typewriter) escribir [52] a máquina; **I'm learning to type** estoy aprendiendo a escribir a máquina; **I was busy typing some letters** estaba ocupada escribiendo unas cartas a máquina.

typewriter noun máquina Fem. de escribir.

typical adjective típico/típica.

typing noun mecanografía Fem.; **her typing is awful** escribe muy mal a máquina.

tyre noun neumático Masc.

Uu

UFO noun ovni Masc.

ugly adjective feo/fea.

UK noun Reino Masc. Unido.

Ulster noun el Ulster.

ulcer noun úlcera Fem.

umbrella noun paraguas Masc. (does not change in the plural).

umpire noun árbitro Masc., árbitra Fem.

UN noun ONU Fem. (short for 'Organización de las Naciones Unidas').

unable adjective **to be unable to do** no poder [10] hacer; **he's unable to come** no puede venir.

unavoidable adjective inevitable.

unbearable adjective insoportable.

unbelievable adjective increíble.

uncertain adjective incierto/incierta, no seguro/no segura; **I'm uncertain whether they are coming** no estoy seguro/segura si vienen o no.

uncle noun tío Masc.; **my Uncle Tom** mi tío Tom.

uncomfortable adjective incómodo/incómoda.

unconscious adjective (out cold) sin sentido; **Tessa's still unconscious** Tessa está todavía sin sentido.

under preposition **1** (underneath) debajo de; **under the bed** debajo de la cama; **perhaps it's under there** quizás está ahí debajo; **to go under something** pasar por debajo de algo; **2** (less than) menos de; **under £20** menos de veinte libras; **3 children under five** niños menores de cinco años.

under-age noun **to be under-age** ser [1] menor de edad.

underground noun (a railway) metro Masc.; **shall we go by underground?** ¿vamos en metro?

underground adjective subterráneo/subterránea; **an underground carpark** un parking subterráneo.

underline verb subrayar [17].

underneath preposition debajo de; **it's underneath these papers** está debajo de esos papeles.

underneath adverb debajo; **look underneath** mira debajo.

underpants *plural noun* calzoncillos *Masc. plural*; **my underpants** mis calzoncillos; **a pair of underpants** unos calzoncillos.

underpass *noun* 1 (*pedestrian*) paso *Masc.* subterráneo; 2 (*for traffic*) paso *Masc.* inferior.

understand *verb* entender [36]; **I don't understand** no entiendo; **I couldn't understand what he was saying** no entendí lo que estaba diciendo.

understandable *adjective* comprensible; **that's understandable** eso es comprensible.

underwear *noun* ropa *Fem.* interior.

undo *verb* 1 desabrochar [17] (*a button or a garment*); 2 desatar [17] (*shoelaces*); 3 deshacer [7] (*a parcel or knot*).

undone *adjective* **to come undone** desabrocharse [17] (*a button*) desatarse [17] (*shoelaces*).

undress *verb* **to get undressed** desvestirse [57]; **I got undressed** me desvestí.

unemployed *noun* **the unemployed** los parados.

unemployed *adjective* parado/parada; **she's unemployed** está parada.

unemployment *noun* paro *Masc.*

uneven *adjective* irregular.

unexpected *adjective* inesperado/inesperada.

unexpectedly *adverb* (*to happen, arrive*) de improviso.

unfair *adjective* injusto/injusta; **it's unfair to young people** es injusto para la gente joven.

unfasten *verb* desabrochar [17].

unfold *verb* desdoblar [17].

unforgettable *adjective* inolvidable.

unfortunate *adjective* desgraciado/desgraciada.

unfortunately *adverb* desgraciadamente.

unfriendly *adjective* antipático/antipática.

ungrateful *adjective* desagradecido/desagradecida.

unhappy *adjective* 1 infeliz; **an unhappy childhood** una infancia infeliz; 2 (*discontented*) **to be unhappy** no estar [2] contento/contenta.

unhurt *adjective* ileso/ilesa.

uniform *noun* uniforme *Masc.*; **in school uniform** con el uniforme del colegio.

uninhabited *adjective* desierto/desierta.

union *noun* (*a trade union*) sindicato *Masc.*

Union Jack *noun* **the Union Jack** la bandera del Reino Unido.

unique *adjective* único/única.

unit *noun* 1 (*for measuring, for example*) unidad *Fem.*; 2 (*in a kitchen*) módulo *Masc.*; 3 (*a hospital department*) servicio *Masc.*

United Kingdom *noun* Reino *Masc.* Unido.

United Nations *noun* Naciones *Fem. plural* Unidas.

a b c d e f g h i j k l m n o p q r s t u v w x y z

United States (of America)
plural noun Estados Masc. plural
Unidos (de América).

universe *noun* universo Masc.

university *noun* universidad
Fem.; **to go to university** ir [8] a la
universidad.

unjust *adjective* injusto/injusta.

unkind *adjective* poco amable.

unknown *adjective* desconocido/
desconocida.

unleaded petrol *noun* gasolina
Fem. sin plomo.

unless *conjunction* a no ser que
(*followed by subjunctive*); **unless
he does it** a no ser que él lo haga;
unless you tell her a no ser que tú
se lo digas.

unlikely *adjective* poco probable;
it's unlikely es poco probable.

unload *verb* descargar [28].

unlock *verb* **to unlock a door**
abrir [46] una puerta; **the car's
unlocked** el coche está abierto; **the
door was unlocked** la puerta no
estaba cerrada con llave.

unlucky *adjective* **1** (*a person*) **to
be unlucky** no tener [9] suerte; **I
was unlucky, it was shut** no tuve
suerte, estaba cerrado; **2 thirteen
is an unlucky number** el trece trae
mala suerte.

unmarried *adjective* soltero/
soltera.

unnatural *adjective* poco natural.

unnecessary *adjective* no
necesario; **it's unnecessary to
book** no es necesario reservar.

unpack *verb* **I unpacked my
rucksack** saqué las cosas de mi
mochila; **I'll just unpack and then
come down** voy a deshacer las
maletas y bajo.

unpaid *adjective* **1** sin pagar (*a
bill*); **2** no remunerado (*work*).

unpleasant *adjective*
desagradable.

unpopular *adjective* poco popular.

unrealistic *adjective* poco
realista.

unreasonable *adjective* poco
razonable; **he's being really
unreasonable** no está siendo nada
razonable.

unreliable *adjective* **1** poco
fidedigno (*information*); **2 this
computer is unreliable** no te
puedes fiar de este ordenador; **3**
informal (*person*); **he's
unreliable** es informal.

unroll *verb* desenrollar [17].

unsafe *adjective* peligroso/
peligrosa (*wiring, for instance*).

unscrew *verb* destornillar [17].

unsuccessful *adjective* **to be
unsuccessful** fracasar [17]; **I tried,
but I was unsuccessful** lo intenté
pero fracasé; **an unsuccessful
attempt** un intento fallido.

untidy *adjective* desordenado/
desordenada; **the house is always
untidy** la casa siempre está
desordenada.

untie *verb* desatar [17].

until *preposition* **1** hasta; **until
Monday** hasta el lunes; **until the
tenth** hasta el diez; **until now** hasta

ahora; **until then** hasta entonces; **2 not until** no hasta; **not until September** no hasta septiembre; **it won't be finished until Friday** no estará terminado hasta el viernes.

unusual *adjective* poco corriente; **an unusual beetle** un escarabajo poco corriente; **storms are unusual in June** las tormentas son poco corrientes en junio.

unwilling *adjective* **to be unwilling to do** no estar [2] dispuesto a hacer; **he's unwilling to wait** no está dispuesto a esperar.

unwrap *verb* desenvolver [45].

up *preposition, adverb* **1** (*higher up*) arriba; **hands up!** ¡manos arriba!; **up here** aquí arriba; **up there** ahí arriba; **it's just up the road** está en esta calle un poco más arriba; **up on the roof** en el tejado; **up in Glasgow** en Glasgow; **2 to go up** subir [19] (*stairs or road*); **we went up the street** subimos la calle; **I ran up the street** subí la calle corriendo; **I'll go up to Glasgow this weekend** iré a Glasgow este fin de semana; **3** (*out of bed*) **to be up** estar [2] levantado; **Liz isn't up yet** Liz aún no está levantada; **to get up** levantarse [17]; **we got up at six** nos levantamos a las seis; I was up late last night me acosté tarde anoche; she was up all night no se acostó en toda la noche; **4** (*wrong*) **what's up?** ¿qué pasa?; **what's up with him?** ¿qué le pasa?; **5 up to** hasta; **up to here** hasta aquí; **up to fifty people** hasta cincuenta personas; **she came up to me** se acercó a mí; **6 what's she**

up to? ¿qué está haciendo?; **it's up to you (to decide)** tú tienes que decidir; ★ **time's up!** ¡se acabó el tiempo!

uphill *adverb* cuesta arriba.

upright *adjective* derecho/ derecha; **put it upright** ponlo derecho; **to stand upright** estar [2] derecho.

upset *noun* **a stomach upset** un dolor de estómago.

upset *adjective* disgustado/ disgustada; **he's upset** está disgustado.

upset *verb* **to upset somebody** disgustar [17] a alguien.

upside down *adjective* boca abajo.

upstairs *adverb* arriba; **Mum's upstairs** mamá está arriba; **to go upstairs** subir [19].

up-to-date *adjective* **1** (*in fashion*) moderno/moderna; **2** (*information*) actualizado/ actualizada.

urgent *adjective* urgente.

urgently *adverb* urgentemente; **she wants to see you urgently** quiere verte urgentemente.

us *pronoun* **1** nos; **she knows us** nos conoce; **they saw us** nos vieron; **he gave us a cheque** nos dio un cheque (*when there are two pronouns, 'nos' comes first*) **they lent it to us** nos lo dejaron; **2** (*with an infinitive or when telling someone to do something, 'nos' joins onto the verb*) **can you help us, please?** ¿puedes ayudarnos por favor?, ¿nos puedes ayudar, por

a b c d e f g h i j k l m n o p q r s t u v w x y z

a
b
c
d
e
f
g
h
i
j
k
l
m
n
o
p
q
r
s
u
v
w
x
y
z

favor?; **listen to us!** ¡escúchanos!; **wait for us!** ¡espéranos!; (but when telling someone NOT to do something, 'nos' comes before the verb) **don't push us!** ¡no nos empujes!; **3** (after a preposition, in comparisons, or after the verb 'to be') nosotros/nosotras; **behind us** detrás de nosotros/nosotras; **they left without us** se fueron sin nosotros/nosotras; **with us** con nosotros/nosotras; **she's older than us** es mayor que nosotros/nosotras; **it's us!** ¡somos nosotros/nosotras!

US, USA noun EE.UU Masc. (short for Estados Unidos).

use noun **1** uso Masc.; **instructions for use** instrucciones de uso; **2 it's no use** no sirve de nada; **it's no use phoning** no sirve de nada llamar.

use verb usar [17]; **we use the dictionary** usamos el diccionario; **to use something to do** usar [17] algo para hacer; **I used a knife to open the parcel** usé un cuchillo para abrir el paquete.

● **to use up 1** consumir [19] todo (food); **2** gastar [17] todo (money or petrol).

used adjective **1 to be used to something** estar [2] acostumbrado/acostumbrada a algo; **I'm not used to cats** no estoy acostumbrado a los gatos; **I'm not used to it** no estoy acostumbrado; **I'm not used to eating in restaurants** no estoy acostumbrado a comer en restaurantes; **2 to get used to**

acostumbrarse [17] a; **I've got used to living here** me he acostumbrado a vivir aquí; **you'll get used to it!** ¡ya te acostumbrarás!

used verb **they used to live in the country** vivían en el campo; **she used to smoke** antes fumaba.

useful adjective útil.

useless adjective **1** inútil (person); **you're completely useless!** ¡eres un completo inútil!; **2 this knife is useless** este cuchillo no sirve para nada.

user noun usuario Masc., usuaria Fem.

user-friendly adjective fácil de usar.

usual adjective, adverb **1** (time, place, problem) de siempre; **it's the usual problem** es el problema de siempre; **2** (method) habitual; **3 as usual** como siempre; **4 it's colder than usual** hace más frío de lo normal.

usually adverb normalmente; **I usually leave at eight** normalmente salgo a las ocho.

utensil noun utensilio Masc.

Vv

vacancy noun **1** (in a hotel) **'vacancies'** 'habitaciones libres'; **'no vacancies'** 'completo'; **2 a job vacancy** una oferta de trabajo.

vacant adjective libre (room or seat).

599 **version**

vaccinate *verb* vacunar [17].

vaccination *noun* vacuna *Fem.*

vacuum *noun* vacío *Masc.*

vacuum *verb* pasar [17] la aspiradora; **I'm going to vacuum my room** voy a pasar la aspiradora por mi habitación.

vacuum cleaner *noun* aspiradora *Fem.*

vagina *noun* vagina *Fem.*

vague *adjective* poco preciso/poco precisa.

vaguely *adverb* vagamente.

vain *adjective* vano/vana (*attempt*); **in vain** en vano.

valentine card *noun* tarjeta *Fem.* que se envía el día de los enamorados.

Valentine's Day *noun* día *Masc.* de San Valentín.

valid *adjective* válido/válida.

valley *noun* valle *Masc.*

valuable *adjective* valioso/valiosa; **to be valuable** ser [1] valioso/valiosa; **that watch is very valuable** este reloj es muy valioso; **he gave us some valuable information** nos dio información muy valiosa.

value *noun* valor *Masc.*

value *verb* valorar [17] (*somebody's help, opinion, or friendship*).

van *noun* furgoneta *Fem.*

vandal *noun* gamberro *Masc.*, gamberra *Fem.*

vandalism *noun* gamberrismo *Masc.*

vandalize *verb* destrozar [22].

vanilla *noun* vainilla *Fem.*; **a vanilla ice cream** un helado de vainilla.

vanish *verb* desaparecer [35].

variety *noun* variedad *Fem.*

various *adjective* varios/varias (*always goes before the noun*); **there are various ways of doing it** hay varias formas de hacerlo.

vary *verb* variar [32]; **it varies a lot** varia mucho.

vase *noun* jarrón *Masc.*

VAT *noun* IVA *Masc.*

VCR *noun* cámara *Fem.* de vídeo.

VDU *noun* monitor *Masc.*

veal *noun* ternera *Fem.*

vegetable *noun* verdura *Fem.*

vegetarian *noun* vegetariano *Masc.*, vegetariana *Fem.*

vegetarian *adjective* vegetariano/vegetariana; **he's vegetarian** es vegetariano.

vehicle *noun* vehículo *Masc.*

vein *noun* vena *Fem.*

velvet *noun* terciopelo *Masc.*

vending machine *noun* máquina *Fem.* expendedora.

ventilation *noun* ventilación *Fem.*

verb *noun* verbo *Masc.*

verdict *noun* veredicto *Masc.*

verge *noun* 1 (*the roadside*) arcén *Masc.*; 2 **to be on the verge of doing** estar [2] a punto de hacer; **I was on the verge of leaving** estaba a punto de irme.

version *noun* versión *Fem.*

a b c d e f g h i j k l m n o p q r s t u v w x y z

versus *preposition* contra; **Arsenal versus Chelsea** Arsenal contra Chelsea.

vertical *adjective* vertical.

vertigo *noun* vértigo *Masc.*

very *adverb* **1** muy; **it's very difficult** es muy difícil; **very well** muy bien; **2 very much** mucho; **I like it very much** me gusta mucho.

very *adjective* **1 the very person I need!** ¡justo la persona que necesito!; **the very thing he was looking for** justo lo que estaba buscando; **2 in the very middle** justo en medio; **at the very end** justo al final; **at the very front** justo delante.

vest *noun* camiseta *Fem.*

vet *noun* veterinario *Masc.*, veterinaria *Fem.*; **she's a vet** es veterinaria.

via *preposition* **to go via** ir [8] por; **we're going via Dover** vamos por Dover; **we'll go via the bank** pasaremos por el banco.

vicar *noun* párroco *Masc.*

vicious *adjective* **1** fiero/fiera (*a dog*); **2** feroz (*an attack*).

victim *noun* víctima *Fem.*

victory *noun* victoria *Fem.*

video *noun* **1** (*film*) vídeo *Masc.*; **to watch a video** ver [16] un vídeo; **I've got it on video** lo tengo en vídeo; **2** (*cassette*) cinta *Fem.* de vídeo; **I bought a video** he comprado una cinta de vídeo; **3** (*video recorder*) vídeo *Masc.*

video *verb* grabar [17]; **I'll video it for you** yo te lo grabo.

video cassette *noun* cinta *Fem.* de vídeo.

video game *noun* videojuego *Masc.*

video recorder *noun* vídeo *Masc.*

video shop *noun* tienda *Fem.* de vídeos.

view *noun* **1** vista *Fem.*; **a room with a view of the lake** una habitación con vista al lago; **2** (*opinion*) opinión *Fem.*; **in my view** en mi opinión; **a point of view** una opinión.

viewer *noun* (*of TV*) televidente *Masc./Fem.*

viewpoint *noun* punto *Masc.* de vista.

vile *adjective* horrible.

villa *noun* chalet *Masc.*

village *noun* pueblo *Masc.*

villager *noun* habitante *Masc./Fem.* de un pueblo.

vine *noun* vid *Fem.*

vinegar *noun* vinagre *Masc.*

vineyard *noun* viñedo *Masc.*

violence *noun* violencia *Fem.*

violent *adjective* violento/violenta.

violin *noun* violín *Masc.*; **to play the violin** tocar [31] el violín.

violinist *noun* violinista *Masc./Fem.*

virgin *noun* virgen *Fem.*

Virgo *noun* Virgo *Masc.*; **Robert's Virgo** Robert es virgo.

virtual reality *noun* realidad *Fem.* virtual.

virus noun virus Masc.; **anti-virus software** software anti virus.

visa noun visado Masc.

visible adjective visible.

visit noun visita Fem.

visit verb visitar [17]; **we visited Auntie Pat at Christmas** visitamos a la tía Pat en Navidad.

visitor noun 1 visita Fem.; **we've got visitors tonight** hoy tenemos visita; 2 (a tourist) visitante Masc./Fem.

visual adjective visual.

vital adjective muy importante; **it's vital to book** es muy importante reservar.

vitamin noun vitamina Fem.

vivid adjective 1 (colour or imagination) vivo/viva; **to have a vivid imagination** tener una imaginación muy viva; 2 (memory or dream) vívido/vívida.

vocabulary noun vocabulario Masc.

vocational adjective vocacional.

vodka noun vodka Masc.

voice noun voz Fem.

volcano noun volcán Masc.

volleyball noun vóleibol Masc.; **to play volleyball** jugar [27] al vóleibol.

volume noun volumen Masc.; **could you turn down the volume?** ¿puedes bajar el volumen?

voluntary adjective 1 (not compulsory) voluntario/voluntaria; 2 **to do voluntary work** trabajar [17] de voluntario.

volunteer noun voluntario Masc., voluntaria Fem.

vomit verb vomitar [17].

vote noun voto Masc.

vote verb votar [17]; **she always votes for the Greens** siempre vota a los verdes.

voucher noun vale Masc.

vowel noun vocal Fem.

voyage noun viaje Masc.

vulgar adjective grosero/grosera (person or speech).

Ww

waffle noun (to eat) gofre Masc.

wage(s) (plural) noun sueldo Masc.

wagon noun vagón Masc.

waist noun cintura Fem.

waistcoat noun chaleco Masc.

waist measurement noun medida Fem. de cintura.

wait noun espera Fem.; **an hour's wait** una espera de una hora.

wait verb 1 esperar [17]; **they're waiting in the car** están esperando en el coche; **she kept me waiting** me tuvo esperando; 2 **to wait for** esperar algo; **wait for me!** ¡espérame!; **wait for the signal** espera la señal; 3 **I can't wait to open it!** ¡estoy deseando abrirlo!

waiter noun camarero Masc.

waiting list noun lista Fem. de espera.

waiting room noun sala Fem. de espera.

waitress noun camarera Fem.

wake verb 1 despertar [29] (somebody else); **Jess woke me at six** Jess me despertó a las seis; **2** despertarse [29]; **I woke (up) at six** me desperté a las seis; **wake up!** ¡despiértate!

Wales noun País Masc. de Gales.

walk noun paseo Masc.; **to go for a walk** ir [8] a dar un paseo; **we went for a walk in the woods** fuimos a dar un paseo por el bosque; **we'll go for a little walk round the village** daremos un paseo por el pueblo; **to take the dog for a walk** sacar [31] a pasear al perro; **it's about five minutes' walk from here** está a unos cinco minutos de aquí a pie.

walk verb 1 andar [21]; **I like walking on sand** me gusta andar sobre la arena; **2** (on foot rather than by car or bus) ir [8] andando; **it's not far, we can walk** no está lejos, podemos ir andando.

● **to walk around** dar [4] una vuelta por; **we walked around the old town** dimos una vuelta por la parte vieja de la ciudad.

● **to walk with somebody** acompañar a alguien; **I'll walk to the bus stop with you** te acompaño hasta la parada del autobús.

walking noun (hiking) hacer [7] senderismo; **we're going walking in Scotland** vamos a hacer senderismo en Escocia.

walking distance noun **it's within walking distance of the sea** se puede ir andando hasta la playa.

walking stick noun bastón Masc.

walkman™ noun walkman™ Masc.

wall noun **1** (of a house) pared Fem.; **2** (of a city) muralla Fem.; **the Great Wall of China** la Gran Muralla de China.

wallet noun cartera Fem.

wallpaper noun papel Masc. pintado.

walnut noun nuez Fem.

wander verb **to wander around town** pasear [17] por la ciudad; **to wander off** alejarse [17].

want noun **all our wants** todo lo que necesitamos.

want verb querer [12]; **do you want some coffee?** ¿quieres café?; **what do you want to do?** ¿qué quieres hacer?; **I don't want to bother him** no quiero molestarlo; **I want them to help me** quiero que me ayuden (note that 'querer que' is followed by the subjunctive).

war noun guerra Fem.

ward noun sala Fem. (in a hospital).

wardrobe noun **1** (piece of furniture) armario Masc.; **2** (clothes) vestuario Masc.

warehouse noun almacén Masc.

warm adjective **1** (water) templado/templada (not very hot); **2** (breeze) cálido/cálida; **3** (hot) caliente; **a warm drink** una bebida caliente; **I'll keep your dinner warm** te tendré la comida caliente;

a
b
c
d
e
f
g
h
i
j
k
l
m
n
o
p
q
r
s
t
u
v
w
x
y
z

a warm bath un baño caliente; **4 it's warm today** hoy hace calorcito; **I'm warm** tengo calor; **are you warm enough?** ¿tienes frío?; **5** *(friendly)* caluroso/ calurosa; **a warm welcome** una bienvenida calurosa; **a warm person** una persona cariñosa.
warm *verb* calentar [29]; **to warm the plates** calentar los platos.

● **to warm up 1** *(the weather)* **it's warming up** está empezando a hacer más calor; **2** *(an athlete)* entrar [17] en calor; **3** *(to heat up)* calentar [29] *(food)*; **I'll warm up some soup for you** te calentaré un poco de sopa.

warmth *noun* calor *Masc.*

warn *verb* advertir [14]; **I warn you, it's expensive** te lo advierto, es caro; **to warn somebody to do** advertir a alguien que haga *(note that 'que' is followed by the subjunctive)*; **he warned me to lock the car** me advirtió que cerrase el coche.

warning *noun* advertencia *Fem.*

wart *noun* verruga *Fem.*

wash *noun* **to give something a wash** lavar [17] algo; **to have a wash** lavarse.

wash *verb* lavar [17]; **I've washed your jeans** he lavado tus vaqueros; **to wash your hands** lavarse las manos; **I washed my hands** me he lavado las manos; **to wash your hair** lavarse la cabeza; **I have to wash my hair** tengo que lavarme la cabeza; **to get washed** lavarse; **to wash the dishes** lavar los platos.

● **to wash up** lavar los platos.

washbasin *noun* lavabo *Masc.*

washing *noun* **1** *(dirty)* ropa *Fem.* sucia; **2** *(clean)* ropa *Fem.* limpia.

washing machine *noun* lavadora *Fem.*

washing powder *noun* detergente *Masc.*

washing-up *noun* platos *Fem.* sucios; **to do the washing-up** lavar [17] los platos.

washing-up liquid *noun* lavavajillas *Masc. (does not change in the plural).*

wasp *noun* avispa *Fem.*

waste *noun* **1** *(of food, money, paper)* desperdicio *Masc.*; **2** *(of time)* **it's a waste of time** es una pérdida de tiempo.

waste *verb* **1** desperdiciar [17] *(food, money, paper)*; **2** perder [36] *(time)*; **you're wasting your time** estás perdiendo el tiempo.

waste-bin *noun* papelera *Fem.*

wastepaper-basket *noun* papelera *Fem.*

watch *noun* reloj *Masc.*; **my watch is fast** mi reloj está adelantado; **my watch is slow** mi reloj está atrasado.

watch *verb* **1** *(to look at)* mirar [17]; **I was watching TV** estaba viendo la televisión; **2 to watch a film** ver [16] una película; **3** *(keep a check on)* **watch the time** estate atento al reloj; **could you watch the baby for a while?** ¿puedes cuidar al niño un rato?; **4** *(suspect)* vigilar [17]; **5** *(to be careful)* **watch you don't spill it** ten cuidado de no

a
b
c
d
e
f
g
h
i
j
k
l
m
n
o
p
q
r
s
t
u
v
x
y
z

a tirarlo; **watch out for nettles**
    cuidado con las ortigas; **watch**
b **out!** ¡cuidado!

c **water** noun agua Fem. (even
    though 'agua' is feminine, it takes
    'el' in the singular)

d **water** verb regar [30]; **to water the**
    plants regar las plantas.
e
    watercolours plural noun
f   acuarelas Fem. plural.

g **waterfall** noun cascada Fem.

h **watering can** noun regadera
    Fem.
i
    water melon noun sandía Fem.
j
    waterproof adjective
k impermeable.

l **water-skiing** noun esquí Masc.
    acuático; **to go water-skiing** hacer
m [7] esquí acuático.

n **water sports** plural noun
    deportes Masc. náuticos.
o
    wave noun 1 (in the sea) ola Fem.;
p 2 (with your hand) (to say hello)
    saludo Masc.; (to say goodbye) adiós
q Masc.; **she gave him a wave from**
    the bus le saludó con la mano
r desde el autobús; (to say goodbye)
    le dijo adiós con la mano desde el
s autobús.

t **wave** verb 1 (with your hand) (to
    say hello) saludar [17]; (to say
u goodbye) decir [5] adiós; 2 (flap)
    agitar [17] (your ticket or the
v newspaper, for example).

w **wax** noun cera Fem.

x **way** noun 1 (a route or road)
    camino Masc.; **the way to town** el
y camino a la ciudad; **we asked the**
    way to the station preguntamos el
z camino a la estación; **on the way**

back en el camino de vuelta; **on**
the way en camino; **'way in'**
'entrada'; **'way out'** 'salida';
2 (direction) dirección Fem.; **which**
way did he go? ¿en qué dirección
se fue?; **come this way** ven por
aquí; **to be in the way** estorbar
[17]; 3 **put it the right way up**
ponlo bien; **the wrong way up**
boca abajo; **your jumper is the**
wrong way round tu jersey está al
revés; 4 (distance) **it's a long way**
está muy lejos; **Terry went all the**
way to York Terry fue hasta York;
5 (manner) manera Fem.; **a way of**
talking una manera de hablar; **he**
does it his way lo hace a su
manera; **I did it the wrong way** lo
hice mal; **that's not the way to do**
it no se hace así; **either way, she's**
wrong sea como sea, está
equivocada; **do it this way** hazlo de
esta manera; 6 **no way!** ¡ni hablar!;
7 **by the way** por cierto.

way in noun entrada Fem.

way out noun salida Fem.

we pronoun 1 ('we' like other
subject pronouns is generally not
translated; in Spanish the form of
the verb tells you whether the
subject of the verb is 'we', you',
they', etc., so 'we' is only translated
for emphasis) **we live in Carlisle**
vivimos en Carlisle; **we're going**
to the cinema tonight vamos a ir
al cine esta noche; 2 (for emphasis)
nosotros/nosotras; **we did it** lo
hicimos nosotros.

weak adjective 1 (feeble) débil; **her**
voice was weak su voz era débil;

2 poco cargado/poco cargada (*coffee or tea*).

wealth noun riqueza *Fem.*

wealthy adjective rico/rica.

weapon noun arma *Fem.*

wear noun children's wear ropa *Fem.* de niños; **sports wear** ropa de deporte.

wear verb llevar [17]; **Tamsin's wearing her trainers** Tamsin lleva sus zapatillas de deporte; **he was wearing black trousers** llevaba pantalones negros; **she often wears red** a menudo viste de rojo; **to wear make-up** llevar maquillaje.

weather noun tiempo *Masc.*; **what's the weather like?** ¿qué tiempo hace?; **in fine weather** cuando hace buen tiempo; **the weather was cold** hacía frío; **the weather here is terrible** aquí hace un tiempo horrible.

weather forecast noun pronóstico *Masc.* del tiempo; **the weather forecast says it will rain** el pronóstico del tiempo dice que va a llover.

web noun **1** (*spider's*) telaraña *Fem.*; **2** (*Internet*) **the Web** la Web.

web site noun sitio *Masc.* web.

wedding noun boda *Fem.*

Wednesday noun miércoles *Masc.* (*does not change in the plural*); **on Wednesday** el miércoles; **I'm going out on Wednesday** voy a salir el miércoles; **see you on Wednesday!** ¡hasta el miércoles!; **on Wednesdays** los miércoles; **the museum is closed on Wednesdays** el museo cierra los miércoles; **every Wednesday** cada miércoles; **last Wednesday** el miércoles pasado; **next Wednesday** el próximo miércoles.

weed noun mala hierba *Fem.*

week noun semana *Fem.*; **last week** la semana pasada; **next week** la próxima semana; **this week** esta semana; **for weeks** durante semanas; **a week today** una semana a partir de hoy.

weekday noun **on weekdays** entre semana.

weekend noun fin *Masc.* de semana; **last weekend** el fin de semana pasado; **next weekend** el próximo fin de semana; **they're coming for the weekend** vienen a pasar el fin de semana; **I'll do it at the weekend** lo haré durante el fin de semana; **have a nice weekend!** ¡que pases un buen fin de semana!

weekly adverb semanalmente, cada semana; **I see her weekly** la veo cada semana.

weekly adjective semanal; **a weekly magazine** una revista semanal.

weigh verb pesar [17]; **to weigh something** pesar algo; **how much do you weigh?** ¿cuánto pesas?; **I weigh 50 kilos** peso cincuenta kilos; **to weigh yourself** pesarse [17].

weight noun peso *Masc.*; **to put on weight** engordar [17]; **to lose weight** adelgazar [17].

weird adjective extraño/extraña.

welcome noun bienvenida *Fem.*; **they gave us a warm welcome**

a

nos dieron una calurosa bienvenida.

welcome *adjective* **1** bienvenido/ bienvenida; **you're welcome any time** siempre eres bienvenido; **welcome to Oxford!** ¡bienvenido a Oxford!; **2 'thank you!' – 'you're welcome!'** 'gracias'– 'de nada'.

welcome *verb* dar [4] la bienvenida a.

well[1] *noun* (*for water*) pozo *Masc.*

well[2] *adverb* **1** bien; **to feel well** sentirse [14] bien; **I'm very well, thank you** estoy muy bien, gracias; **2** bien; **Terry played well** Terry jugó bien; **the operation went well** la operación salió bien; **well done!** ¡bien hecho!; **3 as well** también; **Kevin's coming as well** Kevin también viene; **4 as well as** además de; **5 well then, what's the problem?** entonces, ¿cuál es el problema?; **6 very well then, you can go** muy bien, entonces ya puedes irte.

well-behaved *adjective* **a well behaved child** un niño que se porta bien; **be well-behaved** pórtate bien.

well-done *adjective* muy hecho/ muy hecha (*a steak*).

wellington (boot) *noun* catiusca *Fem.*

well-known *adjective* conocido/ bien conocida.

well-off *adjective* acomodado/ acomodada.

Welsh *noun* **1 the Welsh** (*people*) los galeses; **2** (*language*) galés *Masc.*

Welsh *adjective* galés/galesa.

Welshman *noun* galés *Masc.*

Welshwoman *noun* galesa *Fem.*

west *noun* oeste *Masc.*; **in the west** al oeste.

west *adjective, adverb* (*does not change*) **the west side** la parte oeste; **a west wind** un viento del oeste; **west of Paris** al oeste de París.

western *noun* (*a film*) película *Fem.* de vaqueros.

West Indian *noun* afroantillano *Masc.*, afroantillana *Fem.*

West Indian *adjective* afroantillano/afroantillana.

West Indies *plural noun* Antillas *Fem.*; **in the West Indies** en las Antillas.

wet *adjective* **1** (*damp*) húmedo/ húmeda; **the grass is wet** la hierba está húmeda; **to get wet** mojarse [17]; **we got wet** nos mojamos; **2 a wet day** un día lluvioso.

whale *noun* ballena *Fem.*

what *pronoun, adjective* **1** qué (*in questions*); **what did you say?** ¿qué has dicho?; **what's she doing?** ¿qué está haciendo?; **what did you buy?** ¿qué has comprado?; **what is it?** ¿qué es?; **what's the matter?** ¿qué pasa?; **what's happening?** ¿qué está pasando?; **2 what's your address?** ¿cuál es su dirección?; **what country is it in?** ¿en qué país está?; **what colour is it?** ¿de qué color es?; **what make is it?** ¿de qué marca es?; **3 what's her name?** ¿cómo se llama?; **what?** ¿cómo?; **what's it like?** ¿cómo es?; **4 what for?** ¿para qué?; **what's it for?** ¿para qué sirve?; **what did you buy**

b c d e f g h i j k l m n o p q r s t u v w x y z

it for? ¿para qué lo has comprado?; **5** lo que; **tell me what you bought** dime lo que has comprado; **she told me what had happened** me dijo lo que había pasado; **what I want is a car** lo que quiero es un coche.

wheat *noun* trigo *Masc.*

wheel *noun* rueda *Fem.*; **the spare wheel** la rueda de repuesto; **the steering wheel** el volante.

wheelbarrow *noun* carretilla *Fem.*

wheelchair *noun* silla *Fem.* de ruedas.

when *adverb* cuándo; **when's she arriving?** ¿cuándo llega?; **when's your birthday?** ¿cuándo es tu cumpleaños?; **ask when the next train is leaving** pregunta cuándo sale el próximo tren.

when *conjunction* cuando; **it was raining when I went out** estaba lloviendo cuando salí.

whenever *adverb* **1** (*any time*) cuando; **come whenever you like** ven cuando quieras; **2** (*each time*) siempre que; **whenever we go out, we lock the door** siempre que salimos, cerramos la puerta con llave.

where *adverb* dónde; **where are the plates?** ¿dónde están los platos?; **where do you live?** ¿dónde vives?; **where are you going?** ¿dónde vas?; **I don't know where they live** no sé dónde viven.

where *pronoun* donde; **the place where I live** el lugar dónde vivo.

where *conjunction* donde; **this is where I left it** ahí es donde lo dejé.

whether *conjunction* si; **I don't know whether he's back or not** no sé si ha vuelto o no.

which *adjective* qué; **which CD did you buy?** ¿qué compacto compraste?; **which drawer did you put it in?** ¿en qué cajón lo metiste?; **which one cuál; 'I saw your brother' – 'which one?'** 'ví a tu hermano' –'¿a cuál?'.

which *pronoun* **1** (*in questions*) which of these jackets is yours? ¿cuál de estas chaquetas es la tuya?; **2** (*relative pronoun*) que; **the lamp which is on the table** la lámpara que está en la mesa; **the book which you chose** el libro que escogiste; **the film which I told you about** el libro del que te hablé.

while *noun* **for a while** (*long time*) durante un tiempo; (*short time*) durante un rato; **she worked here for a while** trabajó allí durante un tiempo; **I read for a while** leí durante un rato; **after a while** (*long time*) después de un tiempo; (*short time*) después de un rato.

while *conjunction* mientras; **you can make some tea while I'm finishing my homework** puedes hacer un té mientras termino los deberes.

whip *noun* (*for a horse*) látigo *Masc.*

whip *verb* montar [17] (*cream*); **whipped cream** nata *Fem.* montada.

whirlpool *noun* remolino *Masc.*

whiskers *plural noun* bigotes *Masc. plural.*

whisky *noun* whisky *Masc.*

a
b
c
d
e
f
g
h
i
j
k
l
m
n
o
p
q
r
s
t
u
v
w
x
y
z

a

whisper noun susurro Masc.; **to speak in a whisper** hablar [17] en susurros.

whisper verb susurrar [17].

b

whistle noun 1 (sound) silbido Masc.; 2 (instrument) silbato Masc.

c

whistle verb silbar [17].

d

white noun 1 (colour) blanco Masc.; 2 **an egg white** una clara de huevo.

e

white adjective blanco/blanca; **a white shirt** una camisa blanca.

f

g

white coffee noun café Masc. con leche.

h

Whitsun noun Pentecostés Masc.

i

who pronoun 1 (in questions) quién; **who wants some sweets?** ¿quién quiere caramelos?;

j

k

2 (relative pronoun as subject of the verb) que; **my friend who lives in Madrid** el amigo mío que vive en Madrid; 3 (as object of the verb: referring to one person) el que/la que; **the girl who I gave it to** la chica a la que se lo di; 4 (as object of the verb: referring to more than one person) los que/las que; **the friends who we invited** los amigos a los que hemos invitado.

l

m

n

o

p

q

r

whole noun the whole of the class toda la clase; **on the whole** en general.

s

t

whole adjective todo/toda; **the whole family** toda la familia; **the whole morning** toda la mañana; **the whole time** todo el tiempo; **the whole world** todo el mundo.

u

v

w

wholemeal adjective integral; **wholemeal bread** pan integral.

x

whom pronoun 1 (in questions) quién; **whom did you see?** ¿a

y

z

quién viste?; 2 (as relative pronoun) que; **the person whom I saw** la persona que vi; 3 (after a preposition: referring to one person) el que/la que; **the person to whom I wrote** la persona a la que escribí; 4 (after a preposition: referring to more than one person) los que/las que; **the people to whom I wrote** las personas a las que escribí.

whose pronoun, adjective 1 de quién; **whose is this jacket?** ¿de quién es esta chaqueta?; **whose shoes are these?** ¿de quién son estos zapatos?; **whose is it?** ¿de quién es?; 2 **I know whose it is** sé de quién es; 3 (as relative: before a singular noun) cuyo/cuya (agree with the noun that follows); **the man whose car has been stolen** el hombre cuyo coche había sido robado; 3 (as relative: before a plural noun) cuyos/cuyas (agree with the noun that follows); **the people whose names are on the list** las personas cuyos nombres están en la lista; **a friend whose children I give lessons to** un amigo a cuyos hijos doy clase.

why adverb por qué; **why did she phone?** ¿por qué llamó?; **nobody knows why he did it** nadie sabe por qué lo hizo.

wicked adjective 1 (bad) malvado/malvada; 2 (brilliant) genial.

wide adjective 1 ancho/ancha; **the Thames is very wide here** el Támesis es muy ancho por aquí; **a piece of paper 20 cm wide** un trozo de papel de veinte centímetros de ancho; **how wide is**

it? ¿cuánto mide de ancho?; **2 a wide range** una amplia gama.
wide *adverb* **the door was wide open** la puerta estaba abierta de par en par.

wide awake *adjective* completamente despierto/despierta.

widen *verb* ensanchar [17].

widow *noun* viuda *Fem.*

widower *noun* viudo *Masc.*

width *noun* ancho *Masc.*

wife *noun* mujer *Fem.*

wig *noun* peluca *Fem.*

wild *adjective* **1** (*an animal*) salvaje, (*plant*) silvestre; **2** (*idea*) disparatado/disparatada; **3** (*party*) desenfrenado/desenfrenada; **4** (*person*) loco/loca; **5 to be wild about something** estar [2] loco por algo.

wildlife *noun* **a programme on wildlife in Africa** un programa sobre la flora y la fauna de África.

wildlife park *noun* reserva *Fem.* natural.

will *verb* **1** (*if you are unsure of the future tense of a Spanish verb, you can check it in the dictionary's verb tables*) **I will/I'll see you soon** te veré pronto; **he'll be pleased to see you** estará contento de verte; **it won't rain** no lloverá; **there won't be a problem** no habrá problemas; **2 ir** [8] **a hacer** (*can be used for the immediate future*); **I'll phone them at once** voy a llamarlos ahora mismo; **3** (*in questions and requests*) **'will you write to me?'** – **'of course I will!'** ¿me escribirás?

– **'claro que sí'**; **will you have a drink?** ¿quieres beber algo?; **will you help me?** ¿me ayudas?; **4 he won't open the door** no quiere abrir la puerta; **the car won't start** el coche no arranca; **the drawer won't open** el cajón no abre.

willing *adjective* **to be willing to do** estar [2] dispuesto/dispuesta a hacer; **I'm willing to pay half** estoy dispuesto a pagar la mitad.

willingly *adverb* con gusto.

willow *noun* sauce *Masc.*; **a weeping willow** un sauce llorón.

win *noun* victoria *Fem.*; **our win over Everton** nuestra victoria sobre Everton.

win *verb* ganar [17]; **we won!** ¡hemos ganado!; **Rovers won by two goals** Rovers ganó por dos goles.

wind[1] *noun* viento *Masc.*; **the North wind** el viento del norte.

wind[2] *verb* **1** enrollar [17] (*a wire or a rope, for example*); **2 dar** [4] **cuerda a** (*a clock*).

wind farm *noun* parque *Masc.* aeólico.

wind instrument *noun* instrumento *Masc.* de viento.

window *noun* **1** (*in a building*) ventana *Fem.*; **to look out of the window** mirar [17] por la ventana; **2** (*in a car, bus, train*) ventanilla *Fem.*

windscreen *noun* parabrisas *Masc.* (*doesn't change in the plural*).

windscreen wipers *plural noun* limpiaparabrisas *Masc.*

a b c d e f g h i j k l m n o p q r s t u v **w** x y z

a

b **plural** (*doesn't change in the plural*).

windsurfing *noun* windsurf
c Masc.; **to go windsurfing** hacer [7] windsurf.

d **windy** *adjective* **1** con mucho viento (*a place*); **2** de viento (*a day*); **3 it's windy today** hoy hace viento.

e

f **wine** *noun* vino Masc.; **a glass of white wine** una copa de vino
g blanco.

wing *noun* **1** ala Fem. (*even though 'ala' is feminine, it takes 'el' and 'un' in the singular*); **the wing** el
i ala; **2** (*in sport*) alero Masc./Fem.

j **wink** *verb* **to wink at somebody** guiñar [17] el ojo a alguien.

k

l **winner** *noun* ganador Masc., ganadora Fem.

winning *adjective* ganador (*team for example*).

n **winnings** *plural noun* ganancias Fem. plural.

o

p **winter** *noun* invierno Masc.; **in winter** en invierno.

q **wipe** *verb* limpiar [17]; **I'll just wipe the table** voy a limpiar la
r mesa; **to wipe your nose** limpiarse [17] la nariz.

s
● **to wipe up** (*dishes*) secar [17].

t **wire** *noun* alambre Masc.; **an electric wire** un cable.

u

v **wire netting** *noun* red Fem. de alambre.

w **wise** *adjective* sabio/sabia.

x **wish** *noun* **1** deseo Masc.; **make a wish!** ¡piensa un deseo!; **2 best wishes on your birthday** nuestros
y mejores deseos en tu cumpleaños;
z

'best wishes, Ann' 'saludos de: Ann' (*in letters*).

wish *verb* **1 I wish he were here** ojalá estuviese aquí (*note that 'ojalá' is followed by the subjunctive*); **2 I wished him happy birthday** le deseé un feliz cumpleaños.

wit *noun* ingenio Masc.

witch *noun* bruja Fem.

with *preposition* **1** con; **with James** con James; **with me** conmigo; **with them** con ellos; **with pleasure** con gusto; **beat the eggs with a fork** bate los huevos con un tenedor; **he took his umbrella with him** se llevó el paraguas; **2** (*at the house of*) **we're staying the night with Frank** nos quedamos a dormir en casa de Frank; **3** (*in descriptions*) **a man with blue eyes** un hombre de ojos azules; **the boy with the broken arm** el chico con el brazo roto; **4** (*filled with*) **filled with water** lleno de agua; **covered with mud** cubierto de barro; **red with rage** rojo de ira.

without *preposition* sin; **without you** sin ti; **without sugar** sin azúcar; **without a sweater** sin un jersey; **without looking** sin mirar.

witness *noun* testigo Masc./Fem.

witty *adjective* ingenioso/ ingeniosa.

wizard *noun* brujo Masc.

wolf *noun* lobo Masc.

woman *noun* mujer Fem.; **a woman friend** una amiga.

wonder noun **1** maravilla Fem.; **2 it's no wonder you're tired** no es extraño que estés cansado.

wonder verb preguntarse [17]; **I wonder why** me pregunto por qué; **I wonder where Jack is** me pregunto dónde está Jack.

wonderful adjective maravilloso/ maravillosa.

wood noun madera Fem.; **the lamp is made of wood** la lámpara está hecha de madera.

wooden adjective de madera.

woodwork noun carpintería Fem.

wool noun lana Fem.

woollen adjective de lana.

word noun **1** palabra Fem.; **a long word** una palabra larga; **what's the French word for 'window'?** ¿cómo se dice 'ventana' en francés?; **in other words** en otras palabras; **to have a word with somebody** hablar [17] con alguien; **2** (promise) **to give somebody your word** prometer [18] algo a alguien; **he broke his word** rompió su promesa; **3 the words of a song** la letra de una canción.

word processing noun tratamiento Masc. de textos.

word processor noun procesador Masc. de textos.

work noun **1** trabajo Masc.; **Mum's at work** mamá está en el trabajo; **I've got some work to do** tengo trabajo que hacer; **he's out of work** está sin trabajo; **Ben's off work** (sick) Ben no ha ido a trabajar porque está enfermo; **2 to be hard work** ser [1] difícil; **it's**

hard work to understand it es difícil entenderlo.

work verb **1** trabajar [17]; **she works in an office** trabaja en una oficina; **Dad works at home** papá trabaja en la casa; **Ruth works in advertising** Ruth trabaja en publicidad; **he works nights** trabaja por las noches; **2** (to operate) hacer [7] funcionar; **can you work the video?** ¿sabes hacer funcionar el vídeo?; **3** (function) funcionar [17]; **the dishwasher's not working** el lavavajillas no funciona; **that worked really well!** ¡eso ha funcionado muy bien!

● **to work out 1** (understand) entender [36]; **I can't work out why** no entiendo por qué; **2** (exercise) hacer [7] ejercicio; **3** (to go well) (a plan) salir [63] bien; **4** (calculate) calcular [17]; **I'll work out how much it would cost** calcularé cuánto puede costar.

worked up adjective **to get worked up** ponerse [11] nervioso/ nerviosa.

worker noun **1** (in a factory) trabajador Masc., trabajadora Fem.; **2** (in an office or bank) empleado Masc., empleada Fem.

work experience noun prácticas Fem. plural de trabajo; **to do work experience** hacer [7] prácticas; **to be on work experience** estar [2] haciendo prácticas.

working-class adjective clase Fem. obrera; **a working-class background** un ambiente de clase obrera.

a
b
c
d
e
f
g
h
i
j
k
l
m
n
o
p
q
r
s
t
u
v
w
x
y
z

work of art noun obra Fem. de arte.

workshop noun taller Masc.

workstation noun (computer) terminal Fem. de trabajo.

world noun mundo Masc.; **the best in the world** lo mejor del mundo; **the Western world** el mundo occidental.

World Cup noun **the World Cup** el Mundial.

world war noun guerra Fem. mundial; **the Second World War** la segunda Guerra Mundial.

worm noun gusano Masc.

worn out adjective 1 (a person) agotado/agotada; 2 (clothes or shoes) muy gastado/muy gastada.

worried adjective preocupado/preocupada; **they're worried** están preocupados; **to be worried about** estar [2] preocupado/preocupada por; **we're worried about Susan** estamos preocupados por Susan.

worry noun preocupación Fem.

worry verb preocuparse [17]; **don't worry!** ¡no te preocupes!; **there's nothing to worry about** no hay razón para preocuparse.

worrying adjective preocupante.

worse adjective peor; **it was even worse than the last time** fue aún peor que la última vez; **to get worse** empeorar [17]; **the weather's getting worse** el tiempo está empeorando; **things are getting worse and worse** las cosas van cada vez peor.

worst adjective **the worst** el peor; **it was the worst day of my life** fue

el peor día de mi vida; **if the worst comes to the worst** en el peor de los casos.

worth adjective 1 **to be worth** valer [43]; **how much is it worth?** ¿cuánto vale?; 2 **to be worth doing** merecer [35] la pena hacer; **it's worth trying** merece la pena intentarlo; **it's not worth it** no merece la pena.

would verb 1 (if you are unsure of the conditional tense of a Spanish verb, you can check it in the dictionray's verb tables) **that would be a good idea** eso sería una buena idea; **if we asked her she would help us** si la preguntásemos, nos ayudaría; 2 (expressing wishes) **I'd like to go to the cinema** me gustaría ir al cine; **I would like an omelette** quisiera una tortilla (the subjunctive is used when ordering something); 3 **would you like ... ?** ¿quieres ... ?; **would you like something to eat?** ¿quieres comer algo?; 4 **would you mind ... ?** ¿te importaría ... ?; **would you mind closing the window?** ¿te importaría cerrar la ventana?; 5 **he wouldn't answer** no contestaba; **the car wouldn't start** el coche no arrancaba.

wound noun herida Fem.

wound verb herir [14].

wrap verb envolver [45]; **I'm going to wrap (up) my presents** voy a envolver mis regalos; **could you wrap it for me please?** ¿me lo envuelve, por favor?

wrapping paper noun papel Masc. de envolver.

wreck noun **I feel a wreck!** ¡estoy hecho/hecha polvo!

wreck verb **1** destrozar [22] (an object, a car); **2** arruinar [17] (plans, occasion); **it completely wrecked my evening!** ¡me arruinó la tarde!

wrestler noun luchador Masc., luchadora Fem.

wrestling noun lucha Fem.

wrinkle noun arruga Fem.

wrinkled adjective arrugado/ arrugada.

wrist noun muñeca Fem.

write verb **1** escribir [52] (a letter or a story); **I'll write her a letter** le escribiré una carta; **to write to somebody** escribirle a alguien; **I wrote to Jean yesterday** ayer le escribí a Jean; **2 to write somebody a cheque** extenderle [36] un cheque a alguien.

● **to write down** anotar [17]; **I wrote down her name** anoté su nombre.

writer noun escritor Masc., escritora Fem.

writing noun escritura Fem.

wrong adjective **1** (not correct) equivocado/equivocada; **the wrong answer** la respuesta equivocada; **I've brought the wrong file** he traído la carpeta equivocada; **it's the wrong address** no son las señas correctas; **2 to be wrong** (mistaken) equivocarse [31]; **I was wrong** me equivoqué; **I was wrong**

when I said it was finished me equivoqué cuando dije que estaba terminado; **3 what's wrong?** ¿qué pasa?; **what's wrong with her?** ¿qué le pasa?; **something's wrong** pasa algo; **4** (false) incorrecto/ incorrecta; **the information was wrong** la información era incorrecta.

Xx

xerox™ noun fotocopia Fem.

xerox™ verb fotocopiar [17].

X-ray noun radiografía Fem.; **I saw the X-rays** vi las radiografías.

X-ray verb hacer [7] una radiografía de; **they X-rayed her ankle** le hicieron una radiografía del tobillo.

Yy

yacht noun **1** (sailing boat) velero Masc.; **2** (large luxury boat) yate Masc.

yawn verb bostezar [22].

year noun año Masc.; **six years ago** hace seis años; **the whole year** todo el año; **they lived in Moscow for years** vivieron en Moscú durante años; **he's seventeen years old** tiene diecisiete años; **a two-year-old child** un niño de dos años.

yearly adverb anualmente, cada año.

yearly *adjective* anual; **a yearly event** un acontecimiento anual.

yell *verb* gritar [17].

yellow *adjective* amarillo/amarilla.

yes *adverb* **1** sí; **yes, I know** sí, ya lo sé; **'is Tom in his room?' – 'yes, he is'** ¿está Tom en su habitación? – 'sí'; **2** *(answering a negative)* que sí; **'you don't want to go, do you?' – ' yes I do!'** no quieres ir, ¿verdad? – 'que sí quiero'; **'you haven't finished, have you?' – 'yes, I have'** 'no has terminado, ¿verdad?' – 'que sí'.

yesterday *adverb* ayer; **I saw her yesterday** la vi ayer; **yesterday afternoon** ayer por la tarde; **yesterday morning** ayer por la mañana; **the day before yesterday** anteayer.

yet *adverb* **1** *(with a negative)* aún; **not yet** aún no; **it's not ready yet** no está listo aún; **2** *(in a question)* ya; **have you finished yet?** ¿has terminado ya?

yoga *noun* yoga *Fem.*

yoghurt *noun* yogur *Masc.*; **a banana yoghurt** un yogur de plátano.

yolk *noun* yema *Fem.*

you *pronoun* **1** *('you' like other subject pronouns is generally not translated; in Spanish the form of the verb tells you whether the subject of the verb is 'you', 'we, they', etc., so 'you' is only translated for emphasis)* **do you want to go to the cinema tonight?** *(talking to one person)* ¿quieres ir al cine esta noche?; *(talking to more than one person)* ¿quereis ir al cine esta noche?; **2** *(when emphasizing 'you')* *(talking to one person)* tú; *(talking to more than one person)* vosotros/vosotras; **you said it!** ¡tú lo dijiste!; **you all saw it** ¡todos vosotros lo vísteis!; **3** *(although 'tú', 'vosotros', and 'vosotras' are now commonly used in most situations, there are the formal translations of 'you', which you use in a job interview and other formal situations)* *(talking to one person)* usted; *(talking to more than one person)* ustedes; **are you our new teacher?** ¿es usted nuestro nuevo profesor?; **excuse me, are you Mr and Mrs Lawrence?** perdonen, ¿son ustedes los señores Lawrence?; **4** *(when used as the direct or indirect object of the verb)* *(talking to one person)* te; *(talking to more than one person)* os; **I'll lend you my bike** te presto mi bici; **I'll write to you both** os escribiré a los dos; **5** *(in formal situations)* *(talking to one person)* le; *(talking to more than one person)* les; **I shall send you the document** te mandaré el documento; **Dear Mr and Mrs Jones, I am sending you the information you requested** Estimados señor y señora Jones, les mando la información que solicitaron; *(when used with another pronoun, 'le' and 'les' become 'se')* **I shall send it to you on Monday** se lo mandaré el lunes; **6** *(in comparisons)* tú; *(more than one person)* vosotros/vosotras; **he's**

older than you es mayor que tú, es mayor que vosotros/vosotras; **7 for you** para ti (*more than one person*) para vosotros/vosotras; **I'll go with you** iré contigo; **8** (*in formal situations: after a preposition or in comparisons*) usted; (*talking to more than one person*) ustedes; **for you** para usted, para ustedes.

young *adjective* joven; **he's younger than me** es más joven que yo; **Tessa's two years younger than me** Tessa tiene dos años menos que yo; **young people** la gente joven.

your *adjective* **1** (*talking to one person*) (*with a singular noun*) tu, (*with a plural noun*) tus; **I like your skirt** me gusta tu falda; **you've forgotten your CDs!** ¡te has olvidado tus compactos!; **2** (*talking to more than one person*) (*with a singular noun*) vuestro/vuestra; (*with a plural noun*) vuestros/vuestras; **your Spanish test is on Friday** vuestro examen de español es el viernes; **your rucksacks are in the dining room** vuestras mochilas están en el comedor; **3** (*although 'tu', 'vuestro', 'vuestra' are now commonly used in most situations, there are formal translations of 'your' which you use in a job interview or other formal situation*) (*with a singular noun*) su; (*with a plural noun*) sus; **thank you for your hospitality** gracias por su hospitalidad; **4** (*with parts of the body or clothing*) (*with a singular noun*) el/la; (*with a plural noun*) los/las; **do you want to take your coat off?** ¿quieres quitarte el abrigo?; **wash your hands** lávate las manos.

yours *pronoun* **1** (*talking to one person*) (*referring to a singular noun*) el tuyo/la tuya, (*referring to a plural noun*) los tuyos/las tuyas; **my brother's computer is newer than yours** mi hermano es más joven que el tuyo; **these aren't my glasses – are they yours?** estas gafas no son mías – ¿son tuyas?; **yours are better** los tuyos/las tuyas son mejores; **a friend of yours** un amigo tuyo/una amiga tuya; **2** (*talking to more than one person*) (*referring to a singular noun*) el vuestro/la vuestra; (*referring to a plural noun*) los vuestros/las vuestras; **our house is smaller than yours** nuestra casa es más pequeña que la vuestra; **our car is smaller than yours** nuestro coche es más pequeño que el vuestro; **our children are older than yours** nuestros hijos son mayores que los vuestros; **a friend of yours** un amigo vuestro/una amiga vuestra; **3** (*as with 'you' and 'your' there are formal translations for formal situations*) (*referring to a singular noun*) el suyo/la suya; (*referring to a plural noun*) los suyos/las suyas (*note that here the translation is the same whether you are talking to one person or to more than one person*) **excuse me, is this book yours?** ¿perdone, es suyo este libro?; **excuse me, are these books yours?** ¿perdone, son suyos estos libros?

a
b
c
d
e
f
g
h
i
j
k
l
m
n
o
p
q
r
s
t
u
v
w
x
y
z

a

b

c

d

e

f

g

h

i

j

k

l

m

n

o

p

q

r

s

t

u

v

w

x

y

z

yourself *pronoun* **1** te; **you'll hurt yourself** te vas a hacer daño; **2** (*for emphasis*) tú mismo/tú misma; **did you do it yourself?** ¿lo hiciste tú mismo?/¿lo hiciste tú misma?; **by yourself** solo/sola; **3** (*like 'you' and 'your' there are formal translations for 'yourself' for formal situations*) se, (*for emphasis*) usted mismo/ usted misma; **as you yourself will understand** como usted mismo comprenderá.

yourselves *pronoun* **1** os; **when you have washed yourselves** cuando os hayáis lavado (*when used with a verb in the infinitive or in commands, 'os' is joined to the verb*) **help yourselves** servidos; **by yourselves** solos/solas; **2** (*for emphasis*) vosotros mismos/ vosotras mismas; **did you do it yourselves?** ¿lo hicisteis vosotros mismos?/¿lo hicisteis vosotras mismas?; **3** (*like 'you' and 'your' there are formal translations for 'yourself' for formal situations*) se (*when used with a verb in the infinitive or in commands, 'se' is joined to the verb*) **please, help yourselves** sírvanse, por favor; (*for emphasis*) ustedes mismos/ ustedes mismas; **did you do it yourselves?** ¿lo hicieron ustedes mismos?/¿lo hicieron ustedes mismas?

youth *noun* **1** (*stage of life*) juventud *Fem.*; **2** (*young people*) juventud *Fem.*; **today's youth** la juventud de hoy, los jóvenes de hoy; **3** (*young male*) joven *Masc.*

youth hostel *noun* albergue *Masc.* juvenil.

Yugoslavia *noun* Yugoslavia *Fem.*

Zz

zany *adjective* chiflado/chiflada (*informal*).

zebra *noun* cebra *Fem.*

zebra crossing *noun* paso *Masc.* de cebra.

zero *noun* cero *Masc.*

zigzag *verb* zigzaguear [17].

zip *noun* cremallera *Fem.*

zodiac *noun* zodiaco *Masc.*; **the signs of the zodiac** los signos del zodiaco.

zone *noun* zona *Fem.*

zoo *noun* zoo *Masc.*

zoom lens *noun* lente *Fem.* de zoom.

SPANISH LIFE AND CULTURE

At school

Voy al colegio a pie.	I walk to school.
Estoy en el primero de ESO.	I'm in year 8.
Hay 25 alumnos en mi curso.	There are 25 pupils in my class.
Los lunes, a las nueve, tengo matemáticas.	On Mondays, at 9 o'clock, I have maths.
Hago inglés y español.	I do English and Spanish.
Soy fuerte en/Voy bien en...	I'm good at...
Soy débil en...	I'm not very good at...
Estoy estudiando para el examen de...	I'm studying for the ... exam.
Tenemos muchos deberes.	We have a lot of homework.
Al mediodía, como en la cantina.	At midday, I have lunch in the canteen.

¡Pasa!	Come in! (to one pupil)
¡Entrad!	Come in! (to two or more pupils)
Sacad vuestros cuadernos.	Take out your exercise books.
Abrid vuestro libros a la página 23.	Open your books at page 23.
En silencio por favor.	Quietly, please.
Escuchad bien.	Listen carefully.
Escuchad y repetid.	Listen and repeat.
Trabaja con una pareja.	Work with a partner.
Leed el primer párrafo.	Read the first paragraph.
Escribid una descripción de...	Write a description of...
Buscad las palabras en un diccionario.	Look up the words in a dictionary.

Necesito...
I need...

un libro de texto.	a textbook.	una regla.	a ruler.
		una goma.	a rubber.
un cuaderno.	an exercise book.	un sacapuntas.	a pencil sharpener.
un lápiz.	a pencil.	unas tijeras.	scissors.
un bolígrafo.	a ballpoint pen.	una calculadora.	a calculator.
un rotulador.	a felt-tip pen.		

Mi asignatura preferida es...
My favourite subject is...

el alemán.	German.	*la geografía.*	geography.
la biología.	biology.	*la historia.*	history.
las ciencias.	science.	*la informática.*	ICT.
el diseño.	art.	*el inglés.*	English.
el español.	Spanish.	*las mates.*	maths.
la educación física.	PE.	*la música.*	music.
la física.	physics.	*la química.*	chemistry.
el francés.	French.	*la tecnología.*	technology.

Más tarde, quisiera...
Later on I'd like to...

ir a la universidad.	go to university.	*hacer un aprendizaje.*	do an apprenticeship.
estudiar.	study.	*encontrar un empleo.*	find a job.
hacer un diploma.	do a diploma.	*viajar al extranjero.*	go abroad.

Did you know...?

- that Spanish compulsory secondary school (*ESO*) is for young people between 12 and 16, while 16 to 18 year olds study for the Baccalaureate (*Bachillerato*).

- that pupils in state schools in Spain do not wear uniforms, but in many countries in Latin America pupils have to wear a uniform.

- that in Spain and most Latin American countries, parents have to pay for their children's school books and other learning materials.

- that the main school holidays in most Latin American countries are from Christmas to February?

At home

En mi familia, somos cinco.	There are five of us in my family.
Tengo un hermano/una hermana.	I have a brother/a sister.
un hermanastro/una hermanastra	a half-brother/a half-sister
un mellizo/una melliza	a twin brother/a twin sister
Soy hijo único.	I'm an only child *(boy speaking)*.
Soy hija única.	I'm an only child *(girl speaking)*.

Vivo en...	I live in...		
I live in...			
una casa.	a house.	en la segunda/ cuarta planta.	on the second/ fourth floor.
un apartamento.	a flat.	en la planta baja.	on the ground floor.

Hay...			
There is...			
una cocina.	a kitchen.	un WC.	a toilet.
una sala de estar.	a living room.	un estudio.	a study/an office.
un comedor.	a dining room.		
un dormitorio.	a bedroom.	un garaje.	a garage.
un cuarto de baño.	a bathroom.	un jardín.	a garden.

Mi pasatiempo preferido es...	
My favourite pastime is...	
salir con amigos.	going out with friends.
ir al centro (de la ciudad).	going into town.
ir de compras.	going shopping.
ir a un concierto.	going to concerts.
la lectura.	reading.
escuchar la música.	listening to music.
ver la tele.	watching TV.
jugar a la consola.	playing on a games console.
ir de fiestas/ir de discotecas.	going to parties/discos.
ir a montar en bici.	going cycling.

¿Qué programas hay en la tele?	What's on the telly ?

Mi programa/serie preferida es...
My favourite programme/series is...

un programa de	a sports	un concurso.	a game show.
deporte.	programme.	las noticias/el	the news.
un culebrón.	a soap.	noticiero.	

Tengo...
I've got...

un televisor (pantalla grande).	a (wide screen) TV.
una consola de juegos.	a games console.
una cámara digital.	a digital camera.
un iPod®.	an iPod®.
un (teléfono) móvil.	a mobile phone.

On the computer

el ordenador	computer
el sitio web, el web	website
el blog, la bitácora	blog
la webcam, la cámara	webcam

Con el ordenador...
On my computer I...

navego en Internet.	surf the Web.	busco algo en Internet.	look something up on the Internet.
mando mails a mis amigos.	email friends.	tuiteo.	tweet.
descargo música.	download music.	entro en redes sociales.	go on social network sites.
veo DVDs.	watch DVDs.	visito chats.	visit chatrooms.
hago los deberes.	do homework.		

Email

un correo electrónico, un email	an email
una dirección de correo electrónico	an email address
enviar un correo electrónico, un email	to send an email
recibir un correo electrónico, un email	to get an email
borrar un mensaje	to delete a message
correo basura	spam
responder	to reply
reenviar	to forward
hacer click (en)	to click (on)
copiar y pegar	to cut and paste
un archivo	a file

On the phone

¡Diga!	Hello!
¿Puedo hablar con?	Can I speak to...?
¿Quien llama?	Who's calling?
No cuelgas.	Hold on.
¿Puedo dejar un mensaje?	Can I leave a message?
Volveré a llamar más tarde.	I'll call back later.
un mensaje de texto, un SMS	a text
mandar un mensaje de texto	to send a text
mandar un mensaje de texto a alguien	to text someone

Did you know...?
• that in email addresses, @ is called *arroba* and dot is *punto*.

Food and eating out

¿Que desea?	What would you like?
Me gustaría tomar... I'd like...	
un zumo de naranja.	an orange juice.
¿Tiene usted helado de vainilla?	Have you got vanilla ice cream?

Para comenzar/como entrada deme... For a starter I'll have...	
una sopa de cebolla.	onion soup.
la crema de champiñones.	mushroom soup.
Como plato fuerte/principal deme... For my main course I'll have...	
el pollo asado	roast chicken
una hamburguesa	a burger
con... with...	
patatas fritas.	chips.
una ensalada de tomate.	tomato salad.
una ensalada de mixta.	mixed salad.
De postre me gustaría For dessert I'd like...	
el mousse de chocolate.	chocolate mousse.
la tarta de pera.	pear tart.
helado de fresa.	strawberry ice cream.
Para beber... To drink I'll have...	
agua mineral.	mineral water.
una Coca-Cola.	a Coke.
un zumo de fruta.	a fruit juice.

Tengo hambre.	I'm hungry.
Tengo sed.	I'm thirsty.
Tengo alergia.	I have an allergy.

Meals

el desayuno	breakfast
el almuerzo/la comida	lunch
la cena	dinner

Food and drink

agua	If you order bottled water in a restaurant in Spain, you will be asked if you want *agua con gas* (sparkling), or *agua sin gas* (still). A *gaseosa* is like bottled lemonade, whereas *limonada*, more common in Latin America, is made with fresh lemons and is not fizzy.
antojitos	In Mexico, *antojitos* (little snacks) are often served before a meal. This might be *guacamole* with *nachos* (tortilla chips), or it might be a variety of delicious small appetizers typical of the region.
bocadillo	This is the word in Spain for a sandwich made from French bread. In Mexico it is usually called a *torta*, and in other countries in Latin America a *sándwich*. In Spain a *sándwich* is always made from sliced bread (*pan de molde*).
café	Latin America produces some of the best quality coffee in the world, and it is drunk everywhere. In Colombia, a *tinto* is a small black coffee, and in Mexico *café de olla* is prepared on the stove, with spices and sugar. In Spain, *café con leche* is white coffee, usually half milk; *café cortado* is a black coffee with a dash of milk; and *café solo* is black coffee.
chorizo	A cured salami-shaped sausage, often eaten in Spain in *bocadillos*, as *tapas*, etc. They are always made with paprika, and may also contain chilli.

churrasco	This is steak and Argentina is famous for its beef. It is usually chargrilled, and often served with *chimichurri*, a hot sauce made with chilli, garlic, and vinegar.
dulce de coco or *cocada*	A popular sweet all over the Spanish Caribbean, made by boiling grated coconut with brown sugar and water.
empanadas	These small pies are a popular snack in most Spanish Caribbean countries. They are usually filled with meat, but other fillings such as shrimp or chicken can also be used.
enchiladas	These are wheat *tortillas* filled with meat or cheese and often served in Mexico in a spicy tomato sauce. *Tacos* are thinner *tortillas* made of maize and served with a variety of fillings.
frijoles or *frijoles*	These are beans, which are an essential part of most meals in many Spanish Caribbean and Latin American countries. Often served with rice.
guacamole	A salad made of mashed avocados, seasoned with diced onions, chilli, and sometimes tomatoes. In Mexico it is often eaten as a snack with *nachos*, or tortilla chips.
helados	Ice cream, flavours include *chocolate* (chocolate), *fresa* (strawberry), *pistacho* (pistachio), *vainilla* (vanilla), and many others.
horchata (de chufa)	A thick, creamy, chilled drink made in Spain, particularly around Valencia, from tiger nuts. Often sold in summer in open-air cafes.
jugos or *zumos (de fruta)*	The word *jugo* is more common in Latin America, and *zumo* in Spain. In Latin America many juices (*jugos*) are made from tropical fruits like mango, *guayaba* (guava), *papaya*, and *piña* (pineapple).
maíz	Maize, or corn, is very important in most Latin American countries, as it forms the basis of the diet. In Mexico and Central America it is usually eaten in the form of *tortillas*, but in other countries it is prepared in different ways.
pan	*Pan* is used to mean both 'bread' and 'loaf'. The most common kind is *una barra*. The narrower variety is called a *baguette* and rolls are *panecillos*. A British-style loaf is *un pan de molde*. A *panadería* (baker's) also sells *croissants*, *bollos* (buns), and *roscos* (a kind of doughnut).

patatas or papas	These are potatoes. The word *patatas* is used in Spain, except in the Canary Islands, and *papas* are everywhere in Latin America. Chips or French fries are *patatas/papas fritas*.
tamales	A popular Latin American dish found in many countries between Mexico and Peru, made from a corn-based dough stuffed with a spicy filling made of meat, together with carrots, onions, olives, or other ingredients. It is then cut into squares, wrapped in banana leaves and boiled.
tapas	Small snacks served in bars and cafes in Spain; the selection can be very varied.
tortilla	In Spain a *tortilla* is an omelette: a plain omelette is a *tortilla francesa*, and a potato omelette is a *tortilla española*. In Mexico and Central America, a *tortilla* is made of maize or wheat and is wrapped around fillings of various kinds.

Healthy living

Para mantenerse en forma, hay que...	To keep healthy, you have to...
levantarse temprano	get up early
acostarse temprano	go to bed early
hacer deporte	take exercise
ir a pie/caminar	walk
Es saludable/sano.	It's healthy.
No es saludable/sano.	It's unhealthy.
Hay que evitar...	You must avoid...
beber	drinking
fumar	smoking
todo los días	every day
una vez a la/por semana	once a week
de vez en cuando	now and then
nunca	never
siempre	always

Soy/Es...	I am/He/She is...
deportisa.	sporty.
Estoy/Está...	I am/He/She is...
lesionada/lesionado.	injured.
bien.	well.

Me gusta...	I like...

Me gustan...
I like... (+plural)

No me gusta...
I don't like...

No me gustan...
I don't like... (+plural)

la gaseosa.	fizzy drinks.	los dulces/	
el zumo de fruta.	fruit juice.	caramelos.	sweets.
el café.	coffee.	la verdura.	vegetables.
la leche.	milk.	la carne.	meat.
la fruta.	fruit.	el pescado.	fish.

Shopping

hacer las compras ...	to go shopping (for food) ...		
en la pastelería	at the cake shop	en la charcutería	at the delicatessen
en la panadería	at the baker's	en el mercado	at the market
en la carnicería	at the butcher's	en el supermercado	at the supermarket

Quisiera...	I'd like...		
un pan de molde.	a loaf of bread.	un kilo de	a kilo of
quattros panecillos.	four rolls.	manzanas.	apples.
¿Cuanto cuesta?	How much is it?		

On holiday

El verano pasado, fui a España.   Last summer, I went to Spain.
El próximo verano, voy a ir a Francia. Next summer, I'm going to France.

Fuimos...
We travelled...

en avión.	by plane.	*en autocar.*	by coach.
en coche.	by car.	*en bici.*	by bike.
en tren.	by train.		
en barco.	by ship.		

Did you know...?
- that in Spain you can buy stamps in a tobacconist's shop (*un estanco*)?

Did you know...?
- that football is the most popular sport throughout Latin America, except in some Caribbean countries like Cuba, the Dominican Republic, and Venezuela, where baseball is preferred?
- that basketball is very popular in Spain, second only to football?
- that FC Barcelona (nicknamed *Barça*) is one of Europe's biggest football clubs? *Barça's* home is the huge Camp Nou stadium.
- that *Real Madrid* is one of Europe's biggest football clubs and that they play at the huge Santiago Bernabéu stadium?
- that Spain's most important road cycle race is called the *Vuelta Ciclista a España*, and that cycling is very popular in Spain?

Places of interest in Spain

Alhambra
The famous fortified Moorish palace which dominates Granada.

Asturias
Northern Spain. A beautiful mountainous area where it is traditional to drink cider rather than wine, and where some people play the bagpipes.

Baleares or **las Islas Baleares**
Mediterranean islands of Mallorca, Menorca, Ibiza, and Formentera, popular holiday resorts.

Canarias or **las Islas Canarias**
A group of islands off the coast of West Africa including Tenerife, Gran Canaria, Lanzarote, and La Palma. They are popular holiday resorts.

Catalunya
The Catalan name for Catalonia, or *Cataluña* in Spanish. Barcelona is its capital and the majority of people speak Catalan as their first language.

Costa
The Spanish for 'coast'. Some of the famous tourist areas are *la Costa Brava* in the northeast, *la Costa Blanca* in the southeast, and *la Costa del Sol* on the southern coast.

Cuevas de Altamira
These caves in northern Spain are famous for their prehistoric paintings (18,000 BC), discovered in 1869.

Euzkadi
The Basque name for the Basque country, or *el País Vasco* in Spanish. A green, rainy area with the industrial city of Bilbao, famous for the Guggenheim Museum of modern art, and the resort of San Sebastián, known for the most elaborate *tapas* in Spain.

Galicia
The north-western part of Spain, famous for its wet climate, beautiful coast, excellent seafood, and Celtic culture. The language is *gallego*.

Museo del Prado
This museum in Madrid is one of the finest art galleries in the world.

Palacio de la Zarzuela
The official residence of the royal family in Madrid.

Puerta del Sol
A square in the old part of Madrid. Road distances from the capital are calculated from here.

las Ramblas
A tree-lined avenue in Barcelona famous for the variety of street stalls, entertainers, cafes, and strollers.

Sagrada Familia   This church in Barcelona is the unfinished masterpiece of the Catalan Art Nouveau architect, Gaudí.

> **Did you know...?**
> - that Spain's highest mountain is *Teide* (3710 m), on the island of Tenerife, and that the highest mainland mountain is *Mulhacén* (3482m), in the Sierra Nevada south of Granada?
> - that there are about 400 million speakers of Spanish, which makes it the third most spoken language in the world?
> - that as well as Spanish, Galician, Catalan, and Basque are important languages in Spain?

Places of interest in Latin America

The Amazon   This great river passes through Peru and Colombia before entering Brazil, forming by far the largest area of tropical rainforest left in the world. Many groups of Indian peoples still live a traditional lifestyle.

Iguazú falls   Spectacular and world-famous series of waterfalls on the Iguazú river, on the border between Argentina, Brazil, and Paraguay, set in a unique tropical forest full of birds and butterflies.

las Islas Galapagos   Small islands off the coast of Ecuador famous for their unique animals, including giant tortoises, iguanas, and many species of birds. Charles Darwin visited in the 19th century, and his study of the wildlife helped him to develop his theory of evolution.

Macchu Picchu   These ruins in the mountains of Peru, rediscovered in 1911, are one of the most beautiful and mysterious ancient sites in the world. The Inca people built the city near the top of a mountain in the early fifteenth century, and it contained palaces, baths, temples, and about 150 houses. There are many other Inca remains in Peru, and also in Ecuador and Bolivia.

ayan culture	In the south of Mexico (especially the Yucatán peninsula) and Guatemala, there are many relics of the Mayan civilization which existed before the Spanish conquest. These include palaces and great pyramids, often very well-preserved, like the ones at Chichén Itza and Tikal.
Salto del Angel	The highest waterfall in the world at 970m, the Salto del Angel (Angel Falls) is in the far south of Venezuela, close to the Amazon basin, and falls from a huge flat-topped mountain onto the plains far below.

Did you know...?

- that the highest mountain in South America, *Aconcagua*, is the highest in the world outside the Himalayas?
- that *Quechua*, the language of the Incas, is still spoken by 13 million people, and is an official language in Peru?
- that Mexico City has a population of over 20 million people and is the second largest city in the world?
- that the Amazon river system contains over 20% of all the world's fresh water?
- that the three countries in the world with the greatest biodiversity are all in Latin America—Brazil, Colombia, and Mexico?
- that most of the population of Paraguay speak *guaraní*, an Indian language, as well as Spanish?

Festivals and celebrations

Año Nuevo	New Year's Day. A public holiday throughout Spain and Latin America.
Carnaval	Carnival is celebrated the week before Lent. People often dress up in elaborate costumes, and there are usually processions.
Día de los Inocentes	28 December, the equivalent of April Fool's Day. People play tricks on each other called *inocentadas*, while saying the words *Mariposa Inocente*.

Día de los Muertos	Day of the Dead, 1 November. Known as *Día de Todos los Santos* outside Mexico, this is celebrated throughout Spain and Latin America, but is particularly important in Mexico, most famously in the city of Oaxaca.
Día del Trabajo	1 May, Labour Day is a public holiday in Spain and many countries in Latin America.
Inti Raymi or Fiesta del Sol	24 June, the Festival of the Sun, the most important feast of the Incas, is still celebrated in Peru.
Local holidays	Many cities and towns in Spain and Latin America celebrate local holidays, for example, 15 May in Madrid, and 24 September in Barcelona. These are usually associated with the patron saint of the city or town.
Navidades	Christmas Day is a holiday in Spain and Latin America, but is not as important as it is in Britain or the USA. In Spain the word *navidades* is used to refer to the period around Christmas when people are on holiday.
Nochebuena	Christmas Eve, and many people go to Midnight Mass, the *misa del gallo*. In most Spanish-speaking countries, this is also the night of a big family meal.
Nochevieja	New Year's Eve when people see the New Year in with parties, and in Spain twelve grapes are eaten (one for each month of the new year) at midnight. In Ecuador in South America, it is traditional to make figures, making fun of people who have been in the news in the previous year. These are then burnt.
Reyes (Fiesta de los Reyes Magos)	Feast of the Three Kings: 6th January. Traditionally Spaniards and Latin Americans exchange gifts on this day. Nowadays many people also give each other presents on Christmas Day.
Semana Santa	Holy Week, which precedes Easter, is a very important holiday in Spain and Latin America. Many cities and towns stage religious processions during *Semana Santa*, the most famous being in Seville in Spain.